Java™

UNLEASHED

201 West 103rd Street
Indianapolis, IN 46290

Copyright © 1996 by Sams.net Publishing

Trademarks

President, Sams Publishing	*Richard K. Swadley*
President, Sams.net Publishing	*George Bond*
Publishing Manager	*Mark Taber*
Managing Editor	*Cindy Morrow*
Marketing Manager	*John Pierce*

Acquisitions Editor
Beverly M. Eppink

Development Editor
Kelly Murdock

Software Development Specialist
Merle Newlon

Production Editor
Keith Davenport

Copy Editor
Rogers Cadenhead

Technical Reviewers
Billy Barron
Lay Wah Ooi

Editorial Coordinator
Bill Whitmer

Technical Edit Coordinator
Lynette Quinn

Formatter
Frank Sinclair

Editorial Assistants
Carol Ackerman
Andi Richter
Rhonda Tinch-Mize

Cover Designer
Tim Amrhein

Book Designer
Gary Adair

Production Team Supervisor
Brad Chinn

Production
Mary Ann Abramson, Stephen Adams, Carol Bowers, Michael Brumitt, Charlotte Clapp, Judy Everly, Jason Hand, Sonja Hart, Ayanna Lacey, Clint Lahnen, Paula Lowell, Steph Mineart, Laura Robbins, Bobbi Satterfield, Laura A. Smith, Mark Walchle, Todd Wente, Colleen Williams

Indexers
Ginny Bess, Tom Dinse

Contents

Part II Getting Started

Part IV The Java Class Libraries

Part VII Games, Multimedia, and VRML

Part IX JavaScript

Part X Appendixes and Glossary

        The Preprocessor 888
        Pointers 889
        Structures and Unions 889
        Functions 889
        Multiple Inheritance 890
        Strings 890
        The goto Statement 890
        Operator Overloading 891
        Automatic Coercions 891
        Variable Arguments 891
        Command-Line Arguments 891

E   Java Resources   893
        Sun's Java Sites 894
        Java Information Collection Sites 894
        Java Discussion Forums 895
        Notable Individual Java Webs 895
        Java Index Sites 896
        Object-Oriented Information 896
        Java Players and Licensees 897

F   VRML Resources   899
        General VRML Information 900
            VRML Repositories on the Web 900
            FAQ (Frequently-Asked Questions) Web Pages 900
            VRML Specification 900
        VRML Browsers 900
            Newsgroups 901
            E-Lists 901
        Software 902
        Authoring Tools 902
        Converters 903
        Java/VRML Companies 904
        Interesting VRML Web Sites 904
        Writings That Have Inspired VRML-ers 906

    Glossary   907

    Index   913

Acknowledgments

I would like to thank Beverly Eppink and Mark Taber for giving me the opportunity to contribute to this book, and for convincing me that chapters could be just like Geritol—one a day! I'd also like to thank everyone else at Sams.net, especially Kelly Murdock, who actually thinks I have a shred of writing ability. Thanks guys!

I'd like to thank my "lady friend," Mahsheed, who has tolerated my nocturnal lifestyle far longer than she deserves. I love you.

I would like to thank my parents, who from nearly 2,000 miles away were still able to provide plenty of support and encouragement. I love and miss you guys.

I'd also like to thank my friend Keith, who has nurtured my understanding of programming for many years now. Technically, I don't know what I would have done without you! Oh, I love you too.

I'd like to thank my friend Paul, for our late-night discussions, his impromptu music lectures, and for introducing me to Miles. And for a few flagrant fouls, too!

Finally, I would like to thank my informally adopted sisters, Masooda and Rasheda, who have turned me on to a whole new world of cooking and cheating at cards.

—*Michael Morrison*

I would like to thank my employer, BellSouth Wireless, for my network connection and for letting me have time to work on the book.

—*Mike Fletcher*

Dedications

To my friend Keith, who has always encouraged me to be the best nerd I can be, and who really wanted to be in a book dedication.—Michael Morrison

To Andy and Stef for their friendship and support. —David Gulbransen and Kenrick Rawlings

About the Authors

Michael Morrison wrote Part II, "Getting Started"; most of Part III, "The Java Language"; and Part IV, "The Java Class Library," which comprises Chapters 7 through 14, 17, 18, 20, and Appendix D. He also wrote the introduction that follows. He is the co-author of *Windows 95 Game Developer's Guide Using the Game SDK.* He holds a degree in electrical engineering, which he says is for the most part irrelevant in his current line of work. Michael is a co-owner and the creative force behind Red Herring, a Windows software entertainment company. When he's not unleashing Java on his friends and family, Michael enjoys dreaming about skateboard ramps he'll never get to skate. You can contact Michael on CompuServe at 74037,3444.

John December (`john@december.com`, `http://www.december.com`) wrote Part I, "Introducing Java," and contributed to Appendix E, "Java Resources." He is owner of December Communications, the publisher of *Computer-Mediated Communication Magazine,* and several widely used and frequently accessed World Wide Web-based reference publications about the Internet and the Web. An experienced Internet writer, teacher, software developer, and author, he holds an M.S. in computer science, an M.F.A. in creative writing, and is a Ph.D. candidate in communication and rhetoric at Rensselaer Polytechnic Institute. He is co-author of the books, *The World Wide Web Unleashed, HTML & CGI Unleashed,* and *Presenting Java*, all published in 1995 by Sams.net Publishing.

Paul Colton (`pc@livesoftware.com`) wrote Part IX on JavaScript comprising Chapters 41 through 44. He is the President and CEO of San Diego-based Live Software. Paul has written articles on client/server-based image processing and has developed numerous applications for the Internet and World Wide Web. Live Software's goal is to provide state-of-the-art Web solutions for corporations using advanced software and interactive content. Live Software is currently developing several Java and JavaScript-based applications. Live Software's Web site is located at `http://www.livesoftware.com/`.

Mike Fletcher (`fletch@ain.bls.com`) wrote most of Part XI, which covers network programming (Chapters 27 through 29 and 31). He graduated in 1994 from Georgia Institute of Technology. He's been working for BellSouth Wireless' AIN Services Group as system administrator since 1994. He once played tuba on stage with Jimmy Buffet. Interests include reading SF and juggling.

David Gulbransen (`dgulbran@indiana.edu`) and **Kenrick Rawlings** (`krawling@indiana.edu`) combined to produce most of Part V on applet programming, including Chapters 21 through 24. David is currently employed by the Indiana University School of Fine Art, where he specializes in helping integrate new technologies and the arts. In addition to his normal duties and outside consulting, he has contributed to *Tips and Tricks of the Internet Gurus* and *Electronic Publishing Unleashed.* He hopes someday computers will help him find more free time but isn't counting on it. Kenrick attended Indiana University and is currently employed by IU.

He has been programming in various languages for the last 10 years and hopes that with the advent of Java he'll never have to deal with pointers again.

Charles L. Perkins (`virtual@rendezvous.com`) wrote Chapters 15, 16, 38, 39, and Appendix B. He is the founder of Virtual Rendezvous (`http://rendezvous.com/java`), a company building a Java-based service that will foster socially focused, computer-mediated, real-time filtered interactions between people's personas in the virtual environments of the near future. In previous lives he has evangelized NeXTSTEP, Smalltalk, and UNIX, and has degrees in both physics and computer science.

Michael Afergan (`mikea@ai.mit.edu`) wrote Chapter 33, which covers multiuser programming. He began working with Java as early as the spring of 1995 through his research work at the MIT AI Labs. Since then, he has carefully studied its growth, developing practical applets for companies as an independent consultant. He has been programming for 10 years and has taught a class on computer science at MIT.

Tony Beveridge (`tonyb@akl.optimation.co.nz`) wrote Chapter 37, which covers Java documentation. He is a senior consultant with Optimation, a systems integration company based in Auckland, New Zealand. He has more than 10 years industry experience, primarily in software development. He specializes in object orientation, with principal language skills in C++, Smalltalk, Java, and Perl. His main interests are reusability, metrics, patterns, reflectivity, and frameworks. He is currently working on a server backend abstraction layer as part of Optimation's Internet group strategy.

Ben Bloch (`benb@intrsft.com`) wrote Chapter 33, which covers multimedia and Java. He is president of Intersoft Systems, Inc., an Internet software development company located in Connecticut. He was educated at Colgate and Harvard Universities, and he is now active in various trade organizations, including the Boston Computer Society and NSoft, the Northeast Software Association.

Suresh K. Jois (`sujo@netcom.com`) wrote Chapter 30, "Overview of Content and Protocol Handlers." He is an interactive media technologist with expertise in Java, VRML, software agents, graphics, and video. He has worked for Sun Microsystems, Silicon Graphics, and the Internet Shopping Network. At Sun he witnessed the birth of Java (then called Oak) and later, at ISN, developed the first Java-based commerce application, which was to conduct live auctions on the Internet. He is also deep into the creative and social aspects of interactive media, with interests in computer art, animation, music, and applications of networked virtual reality in the areas of rehabilitation and healthcare.

Richard Lesh (`rich@micros.umsl.edu`) wrote Chapter 19, which covers the utilities package. He is an instructor with the microcomputing program at the University of Missouri–St. Louis. He has developed a variety of applications for the Macintosh, PC, and various UNIX platforms. A number of software products that he has developed are in national distribution, including PLANMaker, a business plan building product, and a number of screen saver modules published by Now Software in Now Fun! and by Berkeley Systems in After Dark.

Gene Leybzon wrote Chapter 26, which details the building of an applet, "Phone Book and Telephone Dialer Applications." He is president of a consulting firm that specializes in Java and C++ software development. Originally, he was a system analyst and senior software developer at Washington University–St. Louis. He was the chief programmer for the Telephony Internet Browser project. He has written a number of shareware utilities including J-tools, a rich set of Java applets for HTML presentation designers. Currently he is working on design protocols for distribution of financial information over the Internet. Gene earned an M.S. in computer science and an M.S. in system science and mathematics, both from Washington University. He is an avid movie viewer, reads tons of science fiction, and enjoys spending time with his wife Olga and playing with his children, Alina and Daniel.

Tim Macinta wrote Chapter 32, which covers game programming with Java. He is currently working towards a degree in computer science and electrical engineering at the Massachusetts Institute of Technology. He has been working in Java nearly as long as it has been around. He has been developing Java programs for Dimension X, one of the leaders in Java development, since July 1995. His most notable work there thus far is the Dimension X Cafe (`http://www.dnx.com/chat/index.html`), which is an IRC client that can be seamlessly integrated into a Web page to provide a type of chat room for everyone looking at a particular Web page.

Tim Park (`Tim_F_Park@ccm.sc.intel.com`) wrote Chapter 36, which covers Java debugging. He is currently working on a 3D graphics library for Java at Intel Corporation in Santa Clara, California. A recent graduate of the Stanford Graduate School of Engineering, his professional interests include 3D graphics and distributed computing.

Adrian Scott (`scotta@rpi.edu`) wrote Chapter 34, which covers VRML and Java, as well as Appendix F, which contains VRML resources. He is founder and CEO of Aereal, Inc. (`http://www.aereal.com`), the first company to have a corporate VRML home world. He has helped Hewlett-Packard with its marketing on the Internet and advised one of the U.S. presidential campaigns on Internet campaigning. He is a former visiting professor in the department of management at Hong Kong Polytechnic University and V.P. of Marketing for a corporate accounting and finance software developer. He earned his Ph.D. in mathematics, with applications to DNA research, from Rensselaer Polytechnic Institute.

Chris Seguin wrote Chapter 25, which covers animation programming. He is an Eagle Scout. He completed a B.S. degree in computational mathematics at the University of Delaware in 1991. On June 25, 1994, he married his long-time sweetheart, Angela DiNunzio. Chris is currently working toward his Ph.D. at the University of Illinois in computer science in the area of artificial intelligence. For the past three years, he has been a teaching assistant for the introductory computer science class for majors. His research interests include using artificial neural networks for signal processing and developing teaching and collaboration tools on the World Wide Web in Java.

Dan Thomsen (thomsen@sctc.com) and **Tim Tiemens** (tiemens@sctc.com) wrote Chapter 40, which covers Java security issues. Dan is a Senior Research Scientist at Secure Computing Corporation. He has worked on the development of the high security DoD systems for the last eight years and has conducted extensive research into secure databases. He manages Secure Computing's Security Alert services, which monitors Internet threats and vulnerabilities. One of his duties in this position is to oversee the Sidewinder Firewall Challenge.

Prior to entering computer security, Dan was a UNIX system administrator. He has a B.A. in computer science and math from the University of Minnesota at Duluth, and an M.S. in computer science from the University of Minnesota at Minneapolis–St. Paul. He is a member of IEEE and IFIP working group 11.3 on database security.

Tim has been involved in security aspects of the World Wide Web and related technologies for over a year and also works for Secure Computing Corporation. He has eight years of experience in UNIX client/server application development and has an avid interest in programming languages and the creation of communication protocols. Tim has a B.S. in computer science from the University of Iowa and an M.S. in computer science from the Georgia Institute of Technology.

Introduction

Nothing short of the World Wide Web itself has captured the attention of the Internet community as much as Java. Java, the Web programming technology developed by Sun Microsystems, has the potential to forever alter the course of software development, especially in regard to the Internet. Java sports all the features necessary for extending the Web in ways previously impossible. Originally starting as part of an advanced consumer electronics project at Sun, Java was designed with issues such as portability and reliability in mind. These two issues, among others, are absolute essentials for applications that are to run on the Internet.

Java has stirred up such excitement primarily because of what all it makes possible on the Web. Inline sound and animation were first introduced in Web pages thanks to Java. Interactive Web pages, including games implemented in Java, were the next logical application of the Java technology. Because of Java, the entire concept of the Web and what it can do is being redefined.

In this book, you learn all about Java from the ground up. You learn what it is, what it can do, and how to use it. Many aspects of Java programming are covered, with lots of example source code to try out in your own Web pages. If you aren't interested in the programming details of Java, there's still lots of information here that you will find interesting. The impact of Java on various real-world issues is discussed, along with a look at what the future holds for Java and the Web in general.

In this book, you will learn about the following subjects related to Java and the Web:

- Java Fundamentals
- Programming with Java
- Java Applets
- Networking with Java
- JavaScript
- The Future of Java

Java Fundamentals

What exactly is Java and where did it come from? Sure, you've heard the hype and maybe skimmed over a few articles, but you want to really know why Java is such a big deal. Maybe you just want to improve on your set of buzzwords for your next computer club meeting.... Then again, maybe not!

Programming with Java

You understand what Java is all about in a general sense, and you want to jump in and start learning how to write Java programs. You want to find out why Java is often mentioned in the same breath with C++. And what's the big deal about the Java class libraries?

Java Applets

Java applets are currently the most popular usage of the Java programming language. You've heard of Java applets and you may have even seen a few in action, but you'd really like to know how to write your own. You're ready to add some real spice to your Web site!

Networking with Java

A programming language for the Internet wouldn't be complete without extensive support for networking. And in this area, Java definitely delivers. Maybe you're interested in writing your own chat program, or maybe you just want to learn how to load a URL from a Java applet. Either way, the Java networking support will not disappoint you.

JavaScript

Just when you thought Java could solve all your problems, along comes something called JavaScript. Why in the world would Sun team up with Netscape and create a whole new language based on Java? Maybe you don't feel like enough of a hard-core programmer to jump into full-blown Java development, or maybe you just need some simple enhancements to your Web site. Enter JavaScript.

The Future of Java

Java has a lot of potential with new support growing every day, but it is still in its infancy. What does the future hold for Java? You have an idea of what impact Java has on the Web as a baby, but what role will it play as a teenager or adult? Only time will tell....

—Michael Morrison

Conventions Used in This Book

This book uses the following conventions:

- New terms appear in *italic*.
- All code appears in `monospace`, as do filenames and directory names.
- Placeholders in code appear in *`italic monospace`*.
- When a line of code is too long to fit on only one line of this book, it is broken at a convenient place and continued to the next line. The continuation of the line is preceded by a code continuation character (➡).

Introducing Java

PART

I

Java Makes Executable Content Possible

1

by John December

By the mid 1990s, the World Wide Web had transformed the online world. Through a system of hypertext, users of the Web were able to select and view information from all over the world. However, while this system of hypertext gave users a high degree of selectivity over the information they chose to view, their level of interactivity with that information was low. Hypermedia had opened up many options for new kinds of sensory input a user might receive, including access to graphics, text, or even videos. However, the Web lacked true interactivity—real-time, dynamic, and visual interaction between the user and application.

Java brings this missing interactivity to the Web. With a Java-enabled Web browser, you can encounter animations and interactive applications. Java programmers can make customized media formats and information protocols that can be displayed in any Java-enabled browser. Java's features enrich the communication, information, and interaction on the Web by enabling users to distribute executable content—rather than just HTML pages and multimedia files—to users. This ability to distribute executable content is the power of Java.

With origins in Sun Microsystem's work to create a programming language to create software that can run on many different kinds of devices, Java evolved into a language for distributing executable content through the Web. Today, Java brings new interest to Web pages through applications that can all give the user immediate feedback and accept user input continuously through mouse or keyboard entries.

In this chapter, I first present a description and definition of Java and explore what Java brings to Web communication. Then I present a brief "armchair" tour of some examples of what Java can do. If you want to go directly to programming in Java, see the other parts of this book. Otherwise, read this chapter and the others in this part for a survey of the potential of Java and the basics of its technical organization. These chapters should prepare you for the more detailed look at existing Java programming in the rest of this book.

What Can Java Do?

Java animates pages on the Web and makes interactive and specialized applications possible. Figure 1.1 illustrates how the software used with the Web can support a variety of communication. With hypertext, the basis for information organization on the Web, you can select what information to view. Programmers can create some interactivity through gateway programs that use files of hypertext on the Web as interfaces. When you use a Web page with such a gateway program, you can access databases or receive a customized response based on a query.

Java adds to these communication possibilities by making it possible to distribute executable content. This gives Web information providers the opportunity to create a hypertext page that engages users in continuous, real-time, and complex interaction. This executable content is literally downloaded to the user's computer. Once downloaded, the executable content might run an animation, perform computation, or guide a user through more information at remote network sites.

FIGURE 1.1.
The Web's software supports selectivity, display, computation, and interactivity.

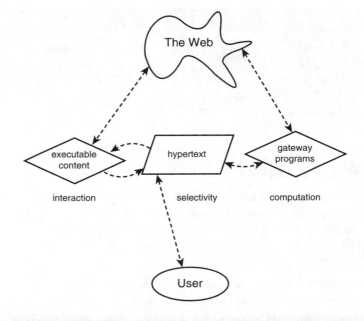

A METAPHOR FOR JAVA

One metaphor for hypertext is that it offers a visually static page of information (which can include text, graphics, sound, and video). The hypertext page can also have "depth" where it contains hyperlinks connecting to other documents or resources.

Java transforms this static page metaphor into a more dynamic one. The information on a Java page on the Web does not have to be visually static or limited to a pre-defined set of ways to interact with users. Users encountering Java programs can take part in a wider variety of interactive behavior, limited only by the imagination and skill of the Java programmer. Java thus transforms a hypertext page into a *stage*, complete with the chance for actors and players to appear and things to happen. And, instead of the user being in the audience, a user of a Java-enabled Web browser is actively a part of the activity on this stage, changing what transpires and reacting to it, and shaping the information content delivered on the Web.

Java thus brings Web pages alive through animation and a higher degree of interaction than what is possible through gateway programming alone.

What Is Java?

The name Java is a trademark of Sun Microsystems and refers to the programming language developed by Sun and released in public alpha and beta versions in 1995. Java is used to create executable content that can be distributed through networks. Used generically, the name Java refers to a set of software tools for creating and implementing executable content using the Java programming language.

In order for users to use Java content, they must have a key piece of Java software—the Java interpreter. To view Java content on the Web, a user's Web browser must be Java-enabled. In the alpha release of Java, available during the spring and summer of 1995, only the special browser called HotJava could interpret programs created by the Java language. HotJava was developed by Sun to showcase the capabilities of the Java programming language. Other brands of Web browsers have since been upgraded to be able to interpret Java programs, most notably, the Netscape Navigator Web browser.

A Java-enabled Web browser has the same capabilities as a non-Java Web browser, but additionally has the capability to interpret and display Java's executable content. A Web browser that is not Java-enabled does not recognize Java and thus can't display the Java executable content. Thus, Java-enabled browsers "see" the Web plus more—applications written using Java.

As described in the section on Java's origins (Java Origins and Direction), Java capability is expected to be integrated into future versions of other Web browsers and network tools.

You can download the Java Developer's Kit (JDK), which contains Java language development tools, from Sun Microsystems. Chapter 2 describes this software as well as Java's technical design in more detail.

What Is Executable Content?

Executable content is a general term that characterizes the important difference between the content that a Java-enabled Web browser downloads and the content a non–Java-enabled browser can download. Simply put: In a non-Java Web browser, the downloaded content is defined in terms of Multipurpose Internet Mail Extensions (MIME) specifications, which include a variety of multimedia document formats. This content, once downloaded by the user's browser, is *displayed* in the browser. The browser may employ a helper application (such as in displaying images, sound, and video). The overall pattern for the use of this content is user choice, browser download, and browser display.

A Java-enabled browser also follows this pattern, but adds another crucial step. First, the Java-enabled browser, following requests by the user, downloads content defined by MIME specifications and displays it. However, a Java-enabled browser recognizes a special hypertext tag called APPLET. When downloading a Web page containing an APPLET tag, the Java-enabled browser knows that a special kind of Java program called an *applet* is associated with that Web page. The browser then downloads another file of information, as named in an attribute of the APPLET tag, that describes the execution of that applet. This file of information is written in what are called *bytecodes*. The Java-enabled browser interprets these bytecodes and runs them as an executable program on the user's host. The resulting execution on the user's host then drives the animation, interaction, or further communication. This execution of content on the user's host is what sets Java content apart from the hypertext and other multimedia content of the Web.

The process of using executable content in a Java-enabled browser, for the user, is seamless. The downloading and start of the execution of content happens automatically. The user does not specifically have to request this content or start its execution. And, as will be explored more in the next chapter, this executable content is *platform-independent:* Java programmers need not create separate versions of the applets for different computer platforms, as long as the user has a Java interpreter (or Java-enabled browser) installed on his or her computer.

Thus, when surfing the Web with a Java-enabled browser, you might find not only all the hypertext content that the pre-Java age Web offered, but also animated, executable, and distributed content. Moreover, this executable content can include instructions for handling new forms of media and new information protocols.

How Java Changes the Web

Java profoundly changes the Web because it brings a richness of interactivity and information delivery not possible using previous Web software systems. Java makes it possible for programmers to create software that can be distributed across networks and run on many different kinds of computers. The resulting executable content shifts the site of activity from the Web server to the Web *client* (the Java-enabled browser).

Figure 1.2 illustrates the technical difference between Java's interactivity and hypertext selectivity and gateway programming. The figure illustrates how gateway programming allows for computation and response but not in realtime. Java's interactivity is much richer and is centered on the client rather than the server.

FIGURE 1.2.
Java interactivity is based on executable content downloaded to the user's computer.

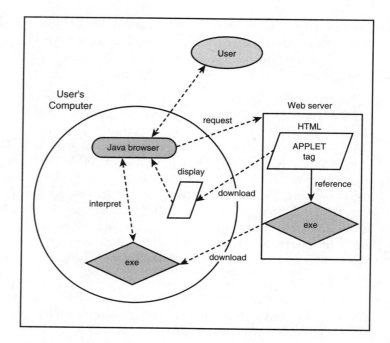

Java Origins and Direction

According to Michael O'Connell's feature article on the origins of Java in the July 7, 1995 issue of *SunWorld Online* (http://www.sun.com/sunworldonline/swol-07-1995/swol-07-java.html), the development of Java began at Sun Microsystems in California by a team which included Java creator James Gosling even as the World Wide Web was being developed in Switzerland in 1991. The goal of this early development team was to develop consumer electronic products that could be simple and bug-free. What was needed was a way to create platform-independent code and thus allow the software to run on any Central Processing Unit (CPU).

As a starting point for a computer language to implement this platform-independence, the development team focused first on C++. However, the team could not get C++ to do everything they wanted in order to create a system to support a distributed network of communicating heterogeneous devices. The team abandoned C++ and developed a language called Oak (later renamed Java). By the fall of 1992, the team had created a project named Star 7 (*7), which was a personal hand-held remote control.

The development team was incorporated as FirstPerson, Inc., but then lost a bid to develop a television set-top box for Time-Warner. By the middle of 1994, the growth in the Web's popularity drew the team's attention. They decided they could build an excellent browser using Java technology. With a goal of bringing their CPU-independent, real-time programming system to the Web, they built a Web browser.

The browser, called WebRunner, was written using Java and completed early in the fall of 1994. Executives at Sun Microsystems were impressed and saw the technology and commercial possibilities that could result from a new browser: tools, servers, and development environments.

On May 23, 1995, Sun Microsystems, Inc. formally announced Java and HotJava at SunWorld '95 in San Francisco. Throughout the summer of 1995, interest in Java grew rapidly. The first wave of developers downloaded and used the alpha release of Java and the HotJava browser and experimented with this new software. The alpha release of Java was the basis for the entries in the first Java contest, with prizes awarded in September 1995. In late September, the pre-beta release of Java was announced. The pre-beta release was Sun's move toward stabilizing the language so that programmers could begin investing their efforts into more significant applications.

By the end of 1995, Java had gained the attention of the major players in the online world. Sun licensed Java to Netscape Communications, Inc. for use in its very popular Netscape Navigator browser. In addition, other major computer software and network players announced products involving Java, including Borland, Mitsubishi Electronics, Dimension X, Adobe, Lotus, IBM, Macromedia, Natural Intelligence, Oracle, and Spyglass. Most dramatic was Microsoft's announcement on December 7, 1995 of their intent to license Java. Microsoft's announcement was particularly dramatic, because, during the summer and fall of 1995, Bill Gates, chairman and CEO of Microsoft, had downplayed Java's role, calling Java "just another language." However, Microsoft's year-end licensing announcement clearly showed that Microsoft considers Java part of an overall Internet strategy.

Java's Current Status and Timeline

A JAVA ONLINE BIBLIOGRAPHY

You can connect to a bibliography of online articles and key press releases tracing the history and current status of Java at `http://www.december.com/works/java/bib.html`.

Java was essentially not a player in the online world in the spring of 1995. However, by the end of that year, it had rocketed to a (perhaps over-hyped) prominence. Along the way, it passed through its alpha and beta stages and grabbed the attention of Web information providers.

At SunWorld in May 1995, Sun unveiled Java and HotJava to the world and Netscape announced that it would license Sun's Java programming language for its Netscape Navigator browser. By summer, Java and HotJava were in alpha stages of development. The Alphas were released for Sun Solaris 2.3, 2.4 and 2.5 SPARC-based and Microsoft Windows NT. Ports were underway for Microsoft Windows 95, and MacOS 7.5 and, in third-party projects, for other platforms and operating systems, including Windows 3.1, Amiga, NeXT, Silicon Graphics, and Linux.

By the end of 1995, in the wake of the splashy launch of Microsoft Windows 95, there was much debate about the possibility of a "Java terminal" or an "Internet PC" (IPC), a device which would provide an inexpensive view into the Internet. An IPC would have minimal hardware and software in it and be specifically dedicated to supporting a Java-enabled Web browser, which could be continuously upgraded. Potentially, such an IPC could be a cheap, efficient way to encounter Web information. Widespread use of such IPCs could overthrow years of "API lock" on personal computing communications based on the Microsoft Windows/Intel ("Wintel") standards.

For the most current information on Java's software releases for different platforms, see Sun Microsystem's Java site: `http://java.sun.com/` or other Java information sources at `http://www.december.com/works/java/info.html`.

Java Future Possibilities

Java technology is not necessarily limited only to the Web. Java technology can be deployed in embedded systems, such as handheld devices, telephones, and VCRs. Mitsubishi Electronics has been working to use Java technology in these devices.

The association of Netscape and Sun Microsystems that brought Java technology into Netscape browsers by late 1995 will be sure to have significance for Net software. With Netscape Navigator's widespread installed base, the use of Java in applications could rapidly increase. Therefore, other Web browser manufacturers might be compelled to also license Java in order to keep pace with the information environment on the Web.

The market for third-party object and tool libraries for Java is also a potential bonanza. Software layers on top of "raw" Java will enable developers to use more sophisticated tools to create applications and users to more easily build and incorporate Java applets in their Web pages. Chapter 2 describes how Java's nature as an object-oriented programming language makes it particularly amenable for creating reusable, extensible software components.

By integrating Java with Virtual Reality Modeling Language (VRML) (`http://www.vrml.org/`), developers can create virtual worlds that are not only three-dimensional but also animated and interactive. Dimension X (`http://www.dnx.com/`) has developed a Java-VRML mix called Iced Java which has the potential to take Web communication and interaction to an even richer level.

Illustrations of Java's Potential

Java is a new programming language, and programmers outside of Sun Microsystems have just begun to explore its potential. Since the public release of Java in its alpha and beta versions, however, many good examples of Java have already been developed. The rest of this chapter shows you examples of the kinds of functionality that Java can support, with an emphasis on the unique way Java enables the distribution of animated, executable content. Information on developing applications which can achieve this potential of Java is in later parts of this book.

ALPHA, BETA, JAVA

The initial, or alpha, release of Java is incompatible with later releases: the alpha bytecodes won't run in beta or later Java-enabled browsers; also, the alpha Java language used an HTML APP tag rather than the APPLET tag of the beta and later versions of Java. The development sections of this book focus on the beta version of Java which is upward compatible with later versions of Java.

Animation

Java's applications put animated figures on Web pages. Figure 1.3 shows a still image of Duke, the mascot of Java, who tumbles across a Web page displayed in the browser. Duke tumbles across the page, cycling through a set of graphic images that loop while the user has this page loaded.

FIGURE 1.3.

Tumbling Duke, mascot of Java. (Courtesy of Arthur van Hoff, Sun Microsystems)

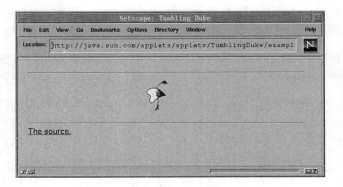

Animation isn't limited to cartoon figures, however. Pages can have animated logos or text that moves or shimmers across the screen. Java animations also need not just be a decorative pre-generated figure, but can be a graphic that is generated based on computation. Figure 1.4 shows a bar chart applet.

FIGURE 1.4.

A bar chart applet. (Courtesy of Sun Microsystems)

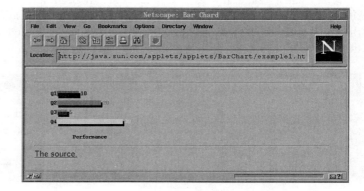

Interaction

While the animations shown can be static images that are drawn or generated, or animated images that can behave according to a preset algorithm (such as the tumbling Duke in Figure 1.3), animation can also be made interactive, where the user has some input on its appearance. Figure 1.5 shows a three-dimensional rendering of chemical models. Using the mouse, you can spin these models and view them from many angles. Unlike the source code for the graph applet shown in Figure 1.4, of course, the source code for the chemical modeling is more complicated. To the user, however, the chemical models seem three-dimensional, giving an insight into the nature of the atomic structure of these elements as no book could.

FIGURE 1.5.

Three-dimensional chemical models. (Courtesy of Sun Microsystems)

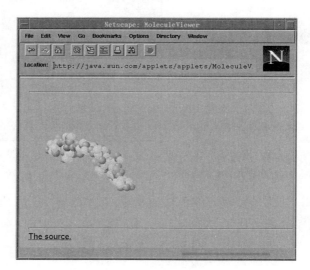

The chemical models in Figure 1.5 respond to user clicks of the mouse. Another variation on this animation involves providing the user with a way to interact with an interface to get feedback. The "impressionist" drawing canvas in Figure 1.6 is an excellent example of this. Paul Haeberli at Silicon graphics developed an "impressionist" Java applet at `http://reality.sgi.com/grafica/impression/imppaint.html`. He originally developed this technique for creating this kind of graphic in 1988 for a Silicon Graphics IRIS workstation. Later patented, this technique drives his Java applet. The result is that you can draw using various size brushes on a canvas and reveal one of several pictures.

FIGURE 1.6.

Interactive impressionist drawing. (Courtesy of Paul Haeberli at Silicon Graphics)

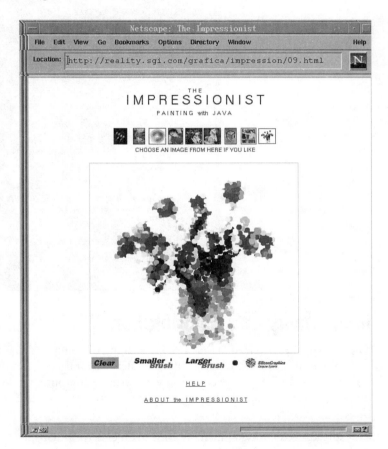

Another variation on interactivity is real-time interactivity. Figure 1.7 shows an interactive application that involves moving graphics that the user manipulates. This is the game of Tetris, in which you can try to line up the falling tile shapes to completely fill the rectangle. Using designated keys for playing, you interact with the interface to steer the falling shapes. This Tetris implementation demonstrates the possibilities for arcade-like games using Java technology.

FIGURE 1.7.
Tetris game. (Courtesy of Nathan Williams)

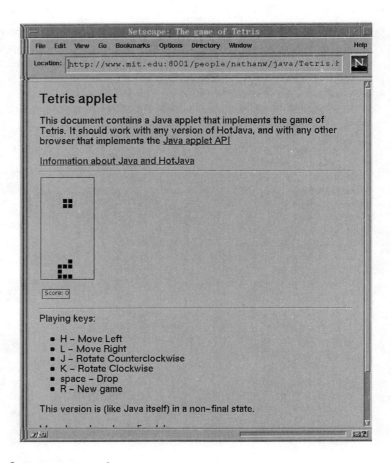

Interactivity and Computation

The Tetris game described in the previous section, for example, demonstrates how interactivity and animation can work together. Both applets customized their animated output based on user input, so both applets were actually performing computation. However, an example that shows this computational capability in more concrete terms is in Figure 1.8, a simple spreadsheet.

This spreadsheet works in much the same manner as the other applets, but emphasizes that the computational possibilities can enable users to have an environment in which to work instead of just a puzzle to solve. The spreadsheet shown enables you to change the contents of any of the 24 cells (A1 through D6) by replacing its label, value, or formula. (Not all cells are shown in the figure.) This is just like a real spreadsheet, which is more of an environment in which the user can work than a fixed game such as the crossword puzzle. This subtle difference is a profound one: using Java, a user can obtain an entire environment for open-ended interaction rather than a fixed set of options for interaction—opening up the Web page into a Web stage.

FIGURE 1.8.

A simple spreadsheet.
(Courtesy of Sami Shaio,
Sun Microsystems)

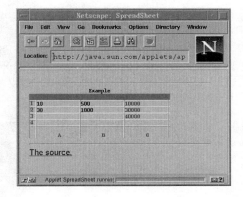

This ballistic simulator shown in Figure 1.9 (`http://jersey.uoregon.edu/vlab/Cannon2/`) en-ables you to explore how a canon operates. You can adjust the muzzle angle and velocity, gravi-tational field strength, wind speed, and the density of the projectile. The purpose of this applet is to help students understand the relation between muzzle velocity and gravitational potential and drag.

FIGURE 1.9.

A virtual canon. (Coding
by Sean Russell, Software
Manager, University of
Oregon; Graphic images by
Amy Hulse)

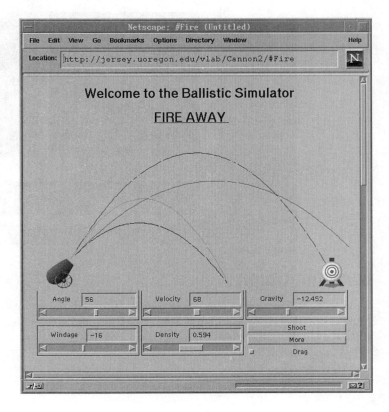

Just as the user can download a canon, so too can a user download a "kit" for doing almost anything. Patrick A. Worfolk of the Geometry Center, University of Minnesota) has created a simulation that users can use to discover the properties of Lorenz equations (`http://www.geom.umn.edu/~worfolk/apps/Lorenz/`). The user can see the results of the numerical integration (the equations in the bottom of Figure 1.10) as well as graphical representations of their numerical solution.

FIGURE 1.10.

Numerical Simulation of the Lorenz Equations. (Courtesy of The Geometry Center, University of Minnesota)

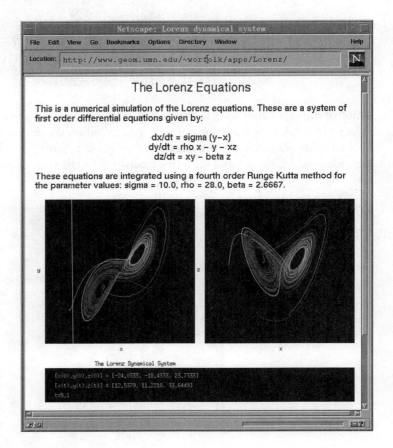

Communication

The preceding examples demonstrate many informational, animation, and computational applications of Java. Another application area is communication among people.

Paul Burchard has created a system for users to share "chats" over the Web using a Java applet (`http://www.cs.princeton.edu/~burchard/www/interactive/chat/express.html`).

Not only do users see each other's text, but they can follow each other on tours of the Web. Figure 1.11 shows this "chat touring" applet in action.

FIGURE 1.11.

A Java-based chat system. (Courtesy of Paul Burchard; Development of Chat Touring funded in part by the Woodrow Wilson National Fellowship Foundation, a nonprofit corporation whose mission is identifying issues in education at all levels, and administering programs which address them)

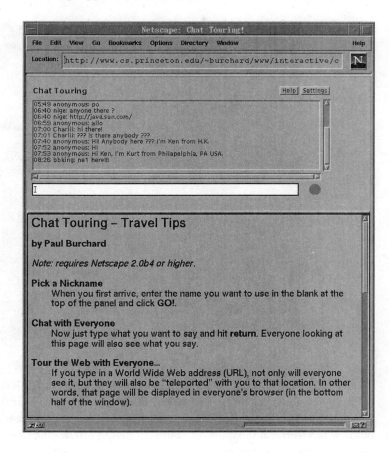

Of course, communication takes place all the time on nearly all Web pages through text or other media. But a Java-enabled browser can also display multimedia. Figure 1.12 illustrates a player piano applet—you see the keyboard play and hear the music at the same time.

FIGURE 1.12.

*A player piano roll.
(Courtesy of Mark Leather,
Silicon Graphics)*

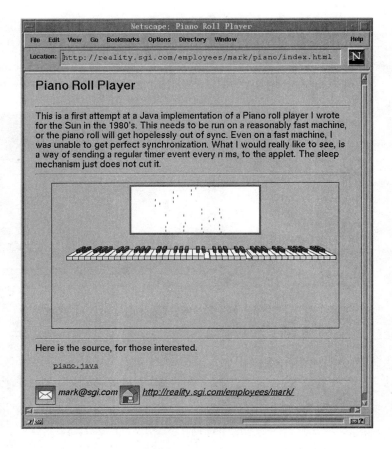

Java can also be used to support mass communication in new ways. The *Nando Times* is a Web-based news service that has been very innovative in news delivery on the Web. Using Java, this news agency now provides a tickertape of headlines across its front page. The text under the Nando banner in Figure 1.13 scrolls continuously to show the world, national, sports, and political top stories at the moment. The four pictures under the labels for these categories also change, giving a "slide show" that is very effective in displaying new information without requiring the user to select it for viewing. This transforms the Web into something people can watch to get new information.

FIGURE 1.13.

Headline feed on Nando Times. (Courtesy of Nando Times)

Similarly, Figure 1.14 shows how current information feeds can act as surveillance for specific activities. The figure shows an applet from The Sports Network (www.sportsnetwork.com). This provides you with a life sportswire pop-up window. You can follow NFL and NHL action live, as it happens. As the scores change, this display changes, so that the sports-minded can keep up with the current games and scores. Like the *Nando Times* news feed, this sports feed changes the Web into something to watch in addition to something to interact with.

Applications and Handlers

In addition to applets like the ones shown here, Java programmers can also create applications, or standalone programs, that don't require the Java-enabled browser to run. (The HotJava browser itself is such an application, written using Java.) Applications could thus conceivably be new browsers or interfaces that interact with other network or local resources.

FIGURE 1.14.

Java sports ticker. (Courtesy of The Sports Network)

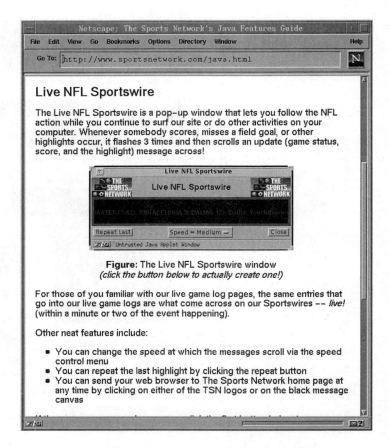

Another kind of software program available with Java is a *handler*. A protocol handler enables a Java programmer to specify how a Java browser should interpret a particular type of protocol. The HotJava browser knows how to interpret the Internet protocols such as HTTP, FTP, Gopher, and others because of the browser distribution code. But if new protocols are invented, a Java programmer can specify how they should be handled by creating a protocol handler.

Another type of handler is a content handler. This handler translates a particular specification for a file type based on Multipurpose Internet Mail Extensions (MIME). This content handler will specify how the HotJava browser should handle a particular type of file type. By creating a specification in a content handler, all Java-enabled browsers will be able to view this special format.

The handlers and applications that Java makes possible have the potential to dramatically extend what can be browsed on the Web. No longer will information developers have to be concerned about making sure their users have the proper software to view a particular type of file or handle a new kind of protocol. The protocol and content handlers, like the executable content Java makes possible as applets, can be distributed as needed to requesting Java-enabled browsers.

What Java Might Make Possible

The previous examples illustrate only some of the potential of Java. A few of these examples are "toy" demonstrations meant to show the possibilities of Java. What kind of communication might Java foster? The *Nando Times* example shows an innovative application for providing information in a way that lets you to sit back and observe rather than selecting hypertext links.

Java opens up a new degree of interactivity and customizability of interaction for the Web. Earlier Web development techniques of creating pages and linking them together will still be necessary in a Java-flavored Web. However, Java creates possibilities for richer kinds of content to be developed. The user can interact with and change the appearance of a Web page along with the state of a database using a Java-enabled browser. Thus, Java profoundly changes the texture of the Web in the following ways:

- Java creates places to stop on the paths of the Web: A well-done Java application on a single hypertext page can engage a user for a long time. Rather than just text, sound, images, or videos to observe, a Java page can offer a place to play, learn, or communicate and interact with others in a way that isn't necessarily based on going somewhere else on the Web through hyperlinks. If the hypertext links of the Web are like paths, the Java pages are like the towns, villages, and cities to stop on these paths and do something other than just observe or "surf."

- Java increases the dynamism and competitiveness of the Web: Just as new browser technology prompted Web developers to create still more applications and pages to exploit these features, so too does Java technology promise a new round of content development on the Web.

- Java enriches the interactivity of the Web: Java's interactivity is far richer, more immediate, and more transparent than the interactivity possible through gateway programming. Gateway programming still should have a role in Web applications, just as page design and multimedia presentation will still play a role. However, Java's interactivity brings new possibilities of what can happen on the Web. With Java, transactions on the Web can be more customized, with immediate and ongoing feedback to the user.

■ Java transforms the Web into a software delivery system: Java's essential design as a language to deliver executable content makes it possible for programmers to create software of any kind and deliver it to users of Java-enabled browsers. Rather than having to focus on the interface, the Java programmer focuses on the interaction desired and lets the built-in features of the graphics take care of the rest of the implementation. The result is that very simple programs like the drawing and spreadsheet applications can be created quickly and distributed worldwide.

The true potential of Java to transform the Web is still in its initial stages. New potential applications for commerce, information delivery, and user interaction still await the imagination and skill of future Java developers.

Summary

Java is a programming language designed to deliver executable content over networks. A user or programmer should know what kinds of interaction Java can make possible and what its true potential can be: enlivening the Web, enriching the display of information in the form of animation and interactive applications.

■ Java enriches the interactivity possible on the Web. Rather than making just informational content possible, Java can support interactive content in the form of software that can be downloaded and run on any computer host with the Java interpretation environment installed.

■ Java developed from ideas about platform-independent executable code. Sun Microsystems researchers have developed Java to be a powerful programming and information delivery system for use with the Web.

■ Java makes animation, interaction, computation, distributed applications, and new forms of communication possible. Through protocol and content handlers, Java has the potential to make new formats and new protocols available for use on the Web.

■ Java transforms the Web into a software delivery system where users have things to do rather than just places to go. Java may change the surfing behavior of Web users into playing and learning behavior in new interactive environments.

Java's Design Is
Flexible and Dynamic

2

by John
December

The Java programming language is uniquely suited for distributing executable content over networks. Java also offers a set of functions similar to many other programming languages. This chapter presents an overview of the technical design of Java. I begin with a minimal example of a "hello world" Java program. This should help you understand how Java and HTML connect. Using this information, you can then try out some of the Java programs shown in later parts of this book.

Java also has specialized characteristics. In the second part of this chapter, I discuss in more technical detail how Java supports executable, distributed applications.

A Hello to Java

The first part of understanding the technical details of Java is learning how Java interacts with the Web's hypertext. The example shown in this section demonstrates how a special tag of the hypertext markup language (HTML) associates a Java program called an applet to a page on the Web. Viewed through a Java-enabled Web browser, a page with a Java applet can come alive with animation or interaction.

Java's Connection to the Web

As a language for delivering information on the Web, Java connects to the Web's hypertext markup language (HTML) using a special tag called APPLET. Figure 2.1 summarizes this connection:

1. In response to a request from a user of a Web browser, a document on a Web server written in HTML is downloaded to the user's browser.

2. If the HTML document contains an APPLET tag and the user's Web browser is Java-enabled, the browser looks for the value of the Code attribute which identifies the Java bytecodes defining the applet.

3. The applet bytecodes are downloaded from the Web server (or possibly some other Web server or network site identified by attributes of the APPLET tag) and placed on the user's host computer.

4. The user's Java-enabled browser interprets these bytecodes and runs the applet in the user's browser. The applet commonly will provide a visual indication that it is operating and possibly accept input from some combination of the user's cursor position, mouse buttons, or keyboard. Once the applet is downloaded, it need not be downloaded again, even if the applet code defines repeated loops or other interaction. The user might use a downloaded applet several times over the course of an online session without any more network retrievals.

FIGURE 2.1.

Java's connection to the Web through the APPLET *tag.*

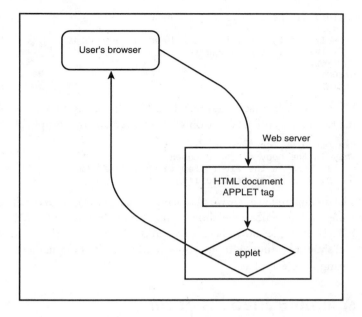

A technical understanding of Java also requires a familiarity with HTML. HTML is the markup language used to create the documents displayed in Web browsers. HTML is not a layout language for describing how a page of hypertext should look (although there are many features of HTML that can be used to manipulate a page's appearance). Rather, HTML tags the structure of a document and the meaning of text, so that a browser can display it in a scheme based on that browser's design and the user's preferences for the font size, style, and other features.

An HTML document consists of text and tags that mark the structure of the document. Tags in an HTML document are delimited by the brackets < and >. Some tags always appear in a pair, as a start and end tag. For example, you can identify the title of an HTML document by placing the tags <TITLE> and </TITLE> around the text of the document's title. Other tags don't require a corresponding ending tag. For example, you can identify a paragraph start using the <P> tag.

Some tags have *attributes*, which qualify the tag's meaning. For example, the APPLET tag has the attributes Code as well as Height and Width.

Here is a simple HTML document:

```
<HTML>
<HEAD>
   <TITLE>Example HTML Document</TITLE>
</HEAD>
<BODY>
   <P>
```

```
     This is the body of the document.
     <OL>
     <LI>This is the first item in an ordered list.
     <LI>This is the second item.
     </OL>
</BODY>
</HTML>
```

When a Web browser interprets these HTML tags and text, it displays the document without the brackets < and >. A text-only browser renders this simple HTML example as

```
Example HTML Document
This is the body of the document.
     1. This is the first item in an ordered list.
     2. This is the second item.
```

The document http://www.december.com/works/wdg/quickref.html contains HTML tags presented in a reference table, showing many more features of HTML that are available. The simple HTML example shown here is recognized by Sun's HotJava and other Java-enabled browsers and should be enough to get you started in understanding how HTML connects to Java and testing simple applets.

A Simple Java Program

The APPLET tag in an HTML document identifies the name of a Java program called an applet to be included in a Web page. The name of the applet is called its *class name*. This name is associated with the executable bytecodes that run the applet.

For example, the following HTML example demonstrates how you can include an applet in a Web document. If you want to test this, put the following lines in a file called HelloWorld.html:

```
<HTML>
<HEAD>
     <TITLE>HelloWorld</TITLE>
</HEAD>
<BODY>
  <P>"This is it!"
  <APPLET Code="HelloWorld.class" Width="600" Height="300">
  </APPLET>
</BODY>
</HTML>
```

Note that there is an open APPLET tag, <APPLET>, and a close APPLET tag, </APPLET>. The attributes shown here are Code, to identify the class file which contains the Java bytecodes and the Width and Height attributes, measured in pixels, to describe how much room should be reserved on the Web page for the applet.

THE APPLET TAG SYNTAX

Java uses an APPLET tag to place executable content in an HTML document.

General Format

```
<APPLET
    Codebase = "path to directory containing class files"
    Code = "name of class file"
    Width = "width of applet in pixels"
    Height = "height of applet in pixels">
    <PARAM Name="parameter name" Value="value of parameter">
    <PARAM Name="parameter name" Value="value of parameter">
</APPLET>
```

The parameter values are given to the applet for use in its computations.

Here is a sample use of the APPLET tag:

```
<APPLET
    Codebase  = "http://java.sun.com/applets/applets/TumblingDuke/"
    Code = "TumbleItem.class"
    Width = "400"
    Height = "95">
    <PARAM Name="maxwidth" Value = "100">
    <PARAM Name="nimgs" Value = "16">
    <PARAM Name="offset" Value = "-57">
    <PARAM Name="img" Value = "http://java.sun.com/applets/applets/TumblingDuke/
➥images/tumble">
</APPLET>
```

Of course, you need to create the Java source code for the applet named HelloWorld. You can find more details on programming in Java in Chapter 12, "Java Language Fundamentals." For now, here is a minimal Java applet as a simple demonstration:

```java
import java.awt.Graphics;
/**
 A first hello.
 */

public class HelloWorld extends java.applet.Applet {
    public void init() {
        resize(600, 300);
    }
    public void paint(Graphics context) {
        context.drawString("Hello, world!", 50, 100);
    }
}
```

THE HelloWorld JAVA SOURCE CODE

The source code for HelloWorld is on the CD-ROM that accompanies this book. I also provide the source code for the HelloWorld and other introductory Java applets at my book support Web page for *Presenting Java* at http://www.december.com/works/java.html.

You can place Java code in a file named HelloWorld.java. Next, you have to compile the Java source code using the Java compiler, javac. At the operating system prompt ($), enter:

```
$ javac HelloWorld.java
```

If there are no errors, the compiler will create a file named HelloWorld.class that contains the bytecodes for the HelloWorld applet.

So at this point, you have the following:

- A file called HelloWorld.html. This is the hypertext markup language (HTML) source file.
- A file called HelloWorld.java. This is the Java language source file.
- A file called HelloWorld.class. This is the Java bytecode file.

Figure 2.2 summarizes the Java source code and compilation relationships.

If you have a Java-enabled browser, you can test this applet. Use the browser to open the file HelloWorld.html. Alternatively, you can also use the applet viewer supplied with the Java Developer's Kit (JDK) to view applets without having to make an HTML page to reference them. Figure 2.3 shows what this example looks like in Netscape Navigator.

FIGURE 2.2.

Java source code and compilation relationships.

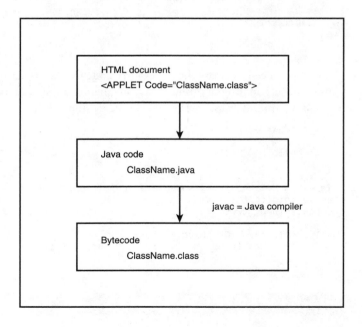

FIGURE 2.3.

Java browser display of the HelloWorld *applet.*

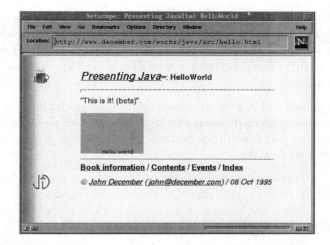

Java Technical Overview

The preceding example concretely demonstrates the connection of Java applets to the Web through the APPLET tag. But this is only a view of Java from a very beginning perspective. To help you understand Java's design and potential, this section provides a technical and conceptual overview of the language and its role in online communication.

Java is an object-oriented programming language that is used in conjunction with Java-enabled Web browsers. These browsers can interpret the bytecodes created by the Java language compiler. The technical design of Java is *architecture neutral*. The term *architecture* in this sense refers to computer hardware. For example, your computer's architecture could be an IBM personal computer with an Intel 386 chip. Programmers can create Java programs without having to worry about this underlying architecture of a user's computer. Instead, the HotJava browser is customized to the user's architecture. The HotJava browser interprets the bytecodes for the particular architecture of the user. This is a key characteristic of Java's technical design.

The Network Communication Support Ring Around Java

Java's technical characteristics also place it within the larger context of online communication. We can step back from the Java source and bytecode files and look at the "big picture" of how Java fits into cyberspace.

The operation of Java and Java-enabled browsers on the Web requires the interoperation of a variety of network systems. Of course, you don't have to understand the interoperation of all of these systems to use Java or a Java-enabled browser. But, stepping back a bit from the applet-scale view of Java, we can look at its place in a "support ring" of networks and applications.

The goal of Java is to bring executable content to the Web. When installed, a Java-enabled browser can provide an interface to animated and interactive applications. To view and interact with these applications, you must have a computer with a Java-enabled browser installed. If you want to download content from all over the Web, of course you also must have an Internet connection.

Beginning with the widest context for the operation of the Java technology, let's take a look at the systems necessary to support Java when delivering information globally (again, Java can be used on local networks not requiring the Internet, collapsing the set of support rings described here considerably):

1. Cyberspace is the mental model people have for communicating or interacting online or through computers. Cyberspace activity includes variety of information, communication, and interaction. Cyberspace can be thought of as consisting of non-networked and networked regions. The networked region in cyberspace includes activity on connected local, regional, and global computer networks. The non-networked region might be standalone personal computer applications like word processors or CD-ROMs that contain no network references.

2. The Internet computer network serves as a vehicle for data communication for many information dissemination protocols. Through gateways, many other networks in cyberspace can exchange data with the Internet. Because of this and also because of the large amount of information available on it, the Internet serves as a common ground for the networked region of cyberspace.

3. The Web is an application that relies on a client/server model for data communication for distributing hypermedia. While the Web can operate on local networks that have no connection to the Internet, the Web is popularly known for its collection of information that is available globally through the Internet.

4. A Web client, known as a browser, is a software program that interprets and displays information disseminated using a variety of Internet information protocols. A Web browser is a user's interface into the Web. A pre-Java Age (Mosaic class) browser usually operates in conjunction with a variety of helper applications to display multimedia. A Java-enabled browser can dynamically learn new protocols and media content types, so that it need not rely on these helper applications. However, a Netscape 2.0 browser, while Java-enabled, still makes use of helper applications, because the entire content of the Web isn't Java-ized.

5. HTML is used to create hypertext for the Web and marks the semantic structure of Web documents. HTML consists of tags and entities that identify the structure and meaning of text in documents. Documents contain references to other resources using a system of Uniform Resource Locators (URLs).

6. The HTML APPLET tag associates Java applications with HTML documents. This tag occurs in an HTML document and identifies a Java applet that will be placed in that document.

7. A Java programmer prepares a file of human-readable Java source code. This source code defines an applet, which is a class in the hierarchy of classes that make up the Java language.

8. A Java programmer compiles a Java source code and makes the resulting bytecodes available for use through a reference to them in an APPLET tag in an HTML document.

9. HotJava, or any other Java-enabled browser, downloads hypertext as well as the executable bytecodes of the applet. The browser interprets and displays the applet, allowing a user to view or interact with the applet.

Figure 2.4 summarizes the support rings for Java as it is used for worldwide distribution of information.

FIGURE 2.4.

The support ring of systems around Java.

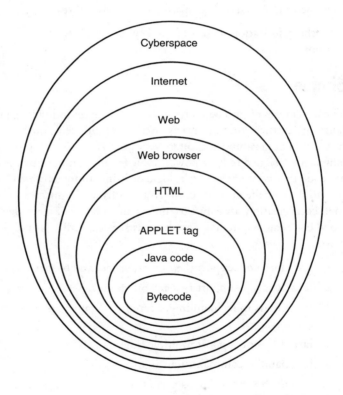

Again, you don't have to know how to set up the entire range of networks, software, and equipment in Java's "support ring." All you need is to install a Java-enabled browser on your Internet-accessible system. From your point of view as a user, your main focus is your browser, or the interior fourth ring, of Figure 2.4. A Java programmer, in contrast, inhabits the seventh ring, and tries to meld the user's experience of the Web's hypertext with the specialized content Java makes possible.

You can use Figure 2.4 to help place yourself in cyberspace as you fulfill different roles as an information user or producer.

Characteristics of Java as a Programming Language

While users may want to have some awareness of how Java fits into online communication, programmers need to understand more specific technical characteristics of Java. The description in this section introduces many terms programmers should learn.

According to the information provided by Sun Microsystems (http://java.sun.com/), Java is a

> " ...simple, object-oriented, distributed, interpreted, robust, secure, architecture neutral, portable, high-performance, multithreaded, and dynamic language."

This characterization identifies the key technical features of Java as shown in the following sections.

Simple

The developers of Java based it on the C++ programming language, but removed many of the language features that are rarely used or often used poorly. C++ is a language for object-oriented programming and offers very powerful features. However, as is the case with many languages designed to have power, some features often cause problems. Programmers can create code that contains errors in logic or is incomprehensible to other programmers trying to read it. Because the majority of the cost of software engineering is often code maintenance rather than code creation, this shift to understandable code rather than powerful but poorly understood code can help reduce software costs. Specifically, Java differs from C++ (and C) in these ways:

1. Java does not support the struct, union, and pointer data types.
2. Java does not support typedef or #define.
3. Java differs in its handling of certain operators and does not permit operator overloading.
4. Java does not support multiple inheritance.
5. Java handles command-line arguments differently than C or C++.
6. Java has a String class as part of the java.lang package. This differs from the null-terminated array of characters as used in C and C++.
7. Java has an automatic system for allocating and freeing memory (garbage collection), so it is unnecessary to use memory allocation and de-allocation functions as in C and C++.

Object-Oriented

Like C++, Java can support an object-oriented approach to writing software. Ideally, object-oriented design can permit the creation of software components that can be reused.

Object-oriented programming is based upon modeling the world in terms of software components called *objects*. An object consists of data and operations that can be performed on that data called *methods*. These methods can encapsulate, or protect, an object's data because programmers can create objects in which the methods are the only way to change the state of the data.

Another quality of object-orientation is *inheritance*. Objects can use characteristics of other objects without having to reproduce the functionality in those objects that supports those characteristics. Inheritance thus helps in software re-use, because programmers can create methods that do a specific job exactly once.

Another benefit of inheritance is software organization and understandability. By having objects organized according to classes, each object in a class inherits characteristics from parent objects. This makes the job of documenting, understanding, and benefiting from previous generations of software easier, because the functionality of the software has incrementally grown as more objects are created. Objects at the end of a long inheritance chain can be very specialized and powerful. Figure 2.5 summarizes the general qualities of data encapsulation, methods, and inheritance of an object-oriented language.

Technically, Java's object-oriented features are those of C++ with extensions from Objective C for dynamic method resolution.

Distributed

Unlike the languages C++ and C, Java is specifically designed to work within a networked environment. Java has a large library of classes for communicating using the Internet's TCP/IP protocol suite, including protocols such as HTTP and FTP. Java code can manipulate resources via URLs as easily as programmers are used to accessing a local file system using C or C++.

Interpreted

When the Java compiler translates a Java class source file to bytecodes, this bytecode class file can be run on any machine that runs a Java interpreter or Java-enabled browser. This allows the Java code to be written independently of the users' platforms. Interpretation also eliminates the compile and run cycle for the client because the bytecodes are not specific to a given machine but interpreted.

Robust

Robust software doesn't "break" easily because of programming bugs or logic errors in it. A programming language that encourages robust software often places more restrictions on the programmer when he or she is writing the source code. These restrictions include those on data types and the use of pointers. The C programming language is notoriously lax in its checking of compatible data types during compilation and runtime. C++ was designed to be more strongly typed than C; however, C++ retains some of C's approach toward typing. In Java, typing is more rigorous: a programmer cannot turn an arbitrary integer into a pointer by casting, for example. Also, Java does not support pointer arithmetic but has arrays instead. These simplifications eliminate some of the "tricks" that C programmers could use to access arbitrary areas of memory. In particular, Java does not allow the programmer to overwrite memory and corrupt other data through pointers. In contrast, a C programmer often can accidentally (or deliberately) overwrite or corrupt data.

Secure

Because Java works in networked environments, the issue of security is one that should be of concern to developers. Plans are in the works for Java to use public-key encryption techniques to authenticate data. In its present form, Java puts limits on pointers so that developers cannot forge access to memory where not permitted. These aspects of Java enable a more secure software environment. The last section of this chapter outlines the layers of Java's security in more detail.

Architecture Neutral

The Java compiler creates bytecodes that are sent to the requesting browser and interpreted on the browser's host machine, which has the Java interpreter or a Java-enabled browser installed.

Portable

The quality of being architecture neutral allows for a great deal of portability. However, another aspect of portability is how the hardware interprets arithmetic operations. In C and C++, source code may run slightly differently on different hardware platforms because of how these platforms implement arithmetic operations. In Java, this has been simplified. An integer type in Java, int, is a signed, two's complement 32-bit integer. A real number, float, is always a 32-bit floating-point number defined by the IEEE 754 standard. These consistencies make it possible to have the assurance that any result on one computer with Java can be replicated on another.

High-Performance

Although Java bytecodes are interpreted, the performance sometimes isn't as fast as direct compilation and execution on a particular hardware platform. Java compilation includes an option to translate the bytecodes into machine code for a particular hardware platform. This can give the same efficiency as a traditional compile and load process. According to Sun Microsystems testing, performance of this bytecode to machine code translation is "almost indistinguishable" from direct compilation from C or C++ programs.

Multithreaded

Java is a language that can be used to create applications in which several things happen at once. Based on a system of routines that allow for multiple "threads" of events based on C. A. R. Hoare's monitor and condition paradigm, Java presents the programmer with a way to support real-time, interactive behavior in programs.

Dynamic

Unlike C++ code, which often requires complete recompilation if a parent class is changed, Java uses a method of interfaces to relieve this dependency. The result is that Java programs can allow for new methods and instance variables in objects in a library without affecting their dependent client objects.

FIGURE 2.5.

Object-orientation in software.

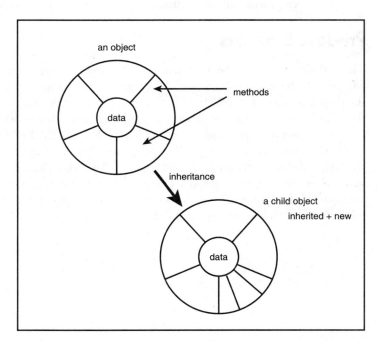

HotJava Is a New Kind of Web Browser

The HotJava browser that showcases Java marks the start of a new generation of smart browsers for the Web. Not constrained to a fixed set of functionality, the HotJava browser can adjust and learn new protocols and formats dynamically. Developers of Web information using Java need no longer be constrained to the text, graphics, and relatively low-quality multimedia of the fixed set available for Web browsers in the pre-Java age. Instead, the HotJava browser opens possibilities for new protocols and new media formats never before seen on the Web.

Through the past half-decade of development of the World Wide Web, new browser technologies have often altered the common view of what the Web and online communication could be. When the Mosaic browser was released in 1993, it rocketed the Web to the attention of the general public because of the graphical, seamless appearance it gave to the Web. Instead of a disparate set of tools to access a variety of information spaces, Mosaic dramatically and visually integrated Internet information. Its point-and-click operation changed ideas about what a Web browser could be, and its immediate successor, Netscape, has likewise grown in popularity and continued to push the bounds of what is presented on the Web.

HotJava, however, marks a new stage of technological evolution of browsers. HotJava breaks the model of Web browsers as only filters for displaying network information; rather, a Java-age browser acts more like an intelligent interpreter of executable content and a displayer for new protocol and media formats. The 2.0 release and above of Netscape Communications' Navigator browser is Java-enabled. Netscape justifiably characterizes their browser as a platform for development and applications rather than just a Web browser.

Pre-Java Browsers

The earliest browser of the Web was the line-mode browser from CERN. The subsequent Mosaic-class browsers (Mosaic and Netscape from 1993 to mid-1995) dramatically opened the graphical view of the Web. However, the Mosaic-type browsers acted as an information filter to Internet-based information. Encoded into these browsers was knowledge of the fundamental Internet protocols and media formats (such as HTTP, NNTP, Gopher, FTP, HTML, GIF). The browsers matched this knowledge with the protocols and media formats found on the Net, and then displayed the results. Figure 2.6 illustrates this operation as the browser finds material on the Net and interprets it according to its internal programming for protocols or common media formats. These browsers also used helper applications to display specialized media formats such as movies or sound.

FIGURE 2.6.

Pre-Java browsers acted as filters.

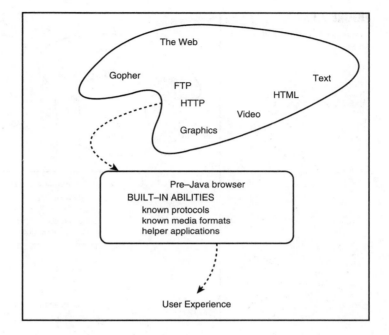

A pre-Java browser was very knowledgeable about the common protocols and media formats about the network (and therefore very "bulky"). Unfortunately, a pre-Java browser could not handle protocols for which it had not been programmed or media formats for which it did not have a helper application available. These are the technical shortcomings that a Java-age browser addresses.

Java-Age Browsers

A Java-age browser is lightweight because it actually has no *pre-defined protocols* or *media formats* programmed into its core functionality; instead the core functionality of a HotJava browser consists of the capability to learn how to interpret any protocol or media format. Of course, the HotJava browser is told about the most common protocols and formats as part of its distribution package. In addition, any new format or protocol that a Java programmer might devise, a HotJava browser can learn.

As Figure 2.7 shows, a Java-age browser is "lightweight," not coming with a monolithic store of knowledge of the Web, but with the most important capbility of all—the ability to learn.

FIGURE 2.7.

The Java-age browser can learn.

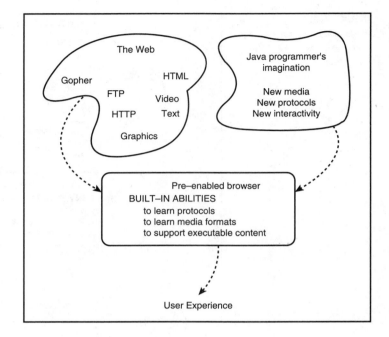

Java in Operation

Another way to put the Java language, a Java-enabled browser, and the larger context of online communications into perspective is to review the processes that occur when a user with a Java-enabled browser requests a page containing a Java applet. Figure 2.8 shows this process.

1. The user sends a request for an HTML document to the information provider's server.

2. The HTML document is returned to the user's browser. The document contains the APPLET tag, which identifies the applet.

3. The corresponding applet bytecode is transferred to the user's host. This bytecode had been previously created by the Java compiler using the Java source code file for that applet.

4. The Java-enabled browser on the user's host interprets the bytecodes and provides display.

5. The user may have further interaction with the applet but with no further downloading from the provider's Web server. This is because the bytecode contains all the information necessary to interpret the applet.

FIGURE 2.8.

Java operation within a Web page.

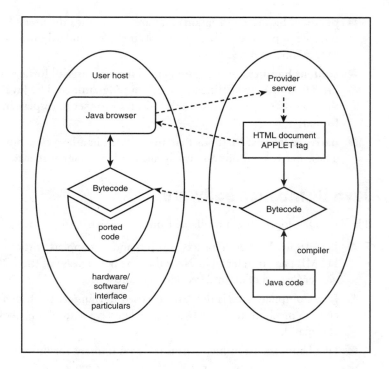

Java Software Components

Another aspect of the technical make-up of the Java environment is the software components that comprise its environment. See the Sun Microsystems Java site (http://java.sun.com/) for complete details on obtaining the Java Developer's Kit (JDK). Programmers need to learn the vocabulary of the pieces of the JDK as well as terms for what can be created with it.

Java Language Constructs

Java is the programming language used to develop executable, distributed applications for delivery to a Java-enabled browser or the Java Interpreter. A Java programmer can create the following:

- **applets:** Programs that are referenced in HTML pages through the APPLET tag and displayed in a Java-enabled browser. The simple "hello world" program shown at the start of this chapter is an applet.

- **applications:** Standalone programs written in Java and executed independently of a browser. This execution is done using the Java interpreter, java, included in the Java code distribution. The input and output of these applications need not be through the command line or text only. The HotJava browser itself is a Java application.

- **protocol handlers**: Programs that are loaded into the user's HotJava browser and interpret a protocol. These protocols include standard ones such as HTTP or programmer-defined protocols.

- **content handlers**: A program loaded into the user's HotJava browser, which interprets files of a type defined by the Java programmer. The Java programmer provides the necessary code for the user's HotJava browser to display/interpret this special format.

- **native methods**: Methods that are declared in a Java class but implemented in C. These native methods essentially allow a Java programmer to access C code from Java.

Java Distribution Software

The Java Development Kit available from Sun Microsystems includes the following pieces:

- Java Applet Viewer. This lets you run and test applets without having to create an HTML page to refer to it. Note that the beta release of the JDK included an applet viewer instead of an updated HotJava browser.

- Java Compiler. This is the software used to translate the human-readable Java source code to machine-readable bytecodes. The Java compiler is invoked using `javac` command.

- Java Language Runtime. This is the environment for interpreting Java applications.

- Java Debugger API and Prototype Debugger. This is a command-line debugger that uses this API.

The Java Application Programming Interface (API)

The Java Application Programming Interface (API) is a set of classes that are distributed with the JDK and which programmers can use in Java applications. The documentation of the API that is provided online is key reference material for Java programmers. The API consists of the packages in the Java language. The API documentation includes a list of

- All packages. These include:

  ```
  java.applet
  java.awt
  java.awt.image
  java.awt.peer
  java.io
  java.lang
  java.net
  java.util
  ```

- All classes in a package. At the package level, information available includes:

    Interfaces

    Classes

    Exceptions
- Documentation on each class. This includes:

    Variables

    Constructors

    Methods

The Java Virtual Machine Specification

A document available from the Sun Microsystems Java site (`http://java.sun.com/`) called "The Java Virtual Machine,' specifies how the Java language is designed to exchange executable content across networks. The aim of this specification is to describe Java as a non-proprietary, open language that may be implemented by many companies and sold as a package.

The Java Virtual Machine specification describes in abstract terms how Java operates. This leaves the details of implementation up to the programmers who creates Java interpreters and compilers. The Java Virtual Machine specification also concretely defines the specific interchange format for Java code. This is called "The Java Interchange Specification."

The other part of the Virtual Machine specification defines the abstractions that can be left to the implementor. These abstractions are not related to the interchange of Java code. These include, for example, management of runtime data areas, garbage collection algorithms, the implementation of the compiler and other Java environment software, and optimization algorithms on compiled Java code.

Java Security

Because a HotJava browser downloads code across the network and then executes it on the user's host, security is a major concern for Java-enabled browser users and Java programmers.

HotJava includes several layers of security, including the following:

- The Java language itself includes tight restrictions on memory access very different from the memory model used in the C language. These restrictions include removal of pointer arithmetic and removal of illegal cast operators.
- A bytecode verification routine in the Java interpreter verifies that bytecodes don't violate any language constructs (which might happen if an altered Java compiler were used). This verification routine checks to make sure the code doesn't forge pointers, access restricted memory, or access objects other than according to their definition.

This check also ensures that method calls include the correct number of arguments of the right type, and that there are no stack overflows.

- A verification of class name and access restrictions during loading.

- An interface security system that enforces security policies at many levels.

- At the file access level, if a bytecode attempts to access a file to which it has no permissions, a dialog box will pop up enabling the user to continue or stop the execution.

- At the network level, future releases will have facilities to use public-key encryption and other cryptographic techniques to verify the source of the code and its integrity after having passed through the network. This encryption technology will be the key to secure financial transactions across the network.

- At runtime, information about the origin of the bytecode can be used to decide what that code can do. The security mechanism can tell if a bytecode originated from inside a firewall or not. You can set a security policy that restricts code that you don't trust.

Summary

The Java programming language is uniquely designed to deliver executable content across networks. As a language, it flexibly offers features for programmers to create a variety of software. Java also assures interoperability among platforms as well as security:

- The Java programming language works in conjunction with a special kind of browser and bytecode interpreter. Java can exist within the context of World Wide Web communication and therefore "sits on top of" a set of applications on networks for data communications to support information retrieval.

- The Java language is object-oriented and specially designed to support distributed, executable applications.

- In operation, the Java language compiler creates bytecodes that are downloaded across the network to a user's computer. The user's computer runs these bytecodes.

- Components of Java software include the HotJava browser, the Java interpreter, the Java compiler, and tools for developing Java applications.

- Java's designs for security are tailored for distributing executable content on networks.

Java Transforms the World Wide Web

by John December

3

IN THIS CHAPTER

The World Wide Web has dramatically changed the online world and continues to grow in popularity. As a communication system, the Web can give information providers the ability to distribute and collect information globally and instantly. For users, the Web is a dynamic view into the works and ideas of millions of people and organizations worldwide. With origins in ideas about nonlinear thinking, the Web is an information integrator on the Internet and plays a major role in online cyberspace.

What Java brings to the Web is a new way of communicating. Instead of relying on the Web servers to provide information and functionality, Java's executable content makes Java-enabled Web browsers "smart."

This chapter briefly explores how Java transforms the World Wide Web. The Web supports a range of communication, information, and interaction using hypertext for organizing information. Multimedia used with hypertext, called *hypermedia*, can enrich the Web's information. Special programming techniques used with the Web's hypertext, such as gateway programming or languages such as Java or Virtual Reality Modeling Language, can expand the Web's possibilities for interactivity, information delivery, and communication.

To learn Java's power as it can be used for the global distribution of information, you should first understand what the Web is and the significance of Java's changes to it. If you are a seasoned Web user, you probably have already realized from the previous two chapters how Java extends the Web's potential; you might want to skip to Chapter 4 to begin looking at specifics. This chapter takes a close look at the Web and Java's part in it.

Overview of the Web

The World Wide Web was originally developed to meet the information needs of researchers in the high-energy physics community. Today, the World Wide Web offers a system for distributing hypermedia information locally or globally. Technically, the World Wide Web enables a seamless, global system of multimedia communication. This information is organized associatively and delivered according to user requests. This section briefly surveys the historical origins of the Web and how the confluence of ideas in network technology has reached fruition in the global Web of today. Java is just the latest installment of a series of innovations in hypertext and Web communication.

Ideas Leading to the Web

Vannevar Bush described a system for associatively linking information in his July 1945 article in *The Atlantic Monthly,* "As We May Think." (This article is available on the Web at `http:/ /www.isg.sfu.ca/~duchier/misc/vbush/`.)

The Origins of Hypertext

Bush called his system a *memex* (*mem*ory *ex*tension), and proposed it as a tool to help the human mind cope with information. Having observed that previous inventions had expanded human abilities for dealing with the physical world, Bush wanted his memex to expand human knowledge in a way that took advantage of the associative nature of human thought.

In 1965, Ted Nelson coined the term *hypertext* to describe text that closely followed Bush's model, in that Nelson's text was not constrained to be sequential. Hypertext, as Nelson described, links documents to form a web of relationships that draw on the possibilities for extending and augmenting the meaning of a "flat" piece of text with links to other texts. Hypertext is more than just footnotes that serve as commentary or further information about a text; rather, hypertext extends the structure of ideas by making "chunks of" ideas or information available for inclusion in many parts of multiple texts. Nelson also coined the term *hypermedia*, which is hypertext not constrained to be text. Hypermedia can include expressions of multimedia—pictures, graphics, sound, and movies.

The Origins of the Web

Vannevar Bush's and Ted Nelson's ideas about information systems showed up in another project in the late 1980s. In March 1989, Tim Berners-Lee, a researcher at the Conseil European pour la Recherche Nucleaire (CERN) European Laboratory for Particle Physics in Geneva, Switzerland, proposed a hypertext system to enable efficient information-sharing for members of the high-energy physics community. Berners-Lee had a background in text processing, real-time software, and communications, and had previously developed a hypertext system he called "Enquire" in 1980. Berners-Lee's 1989 proposal, called "HyperText and CERN," circulated for comment. The following were important components of the proposal:

- A user interface that would be consistent across all platforms and that would enable users to access information from many different computers
- A scheme for this interface to access a variety of document types and information protocols
- A provision for "universal access," which would enable any user on the network to access any information

By late 1990, an operating prototype of the World Wide Web ran on a NeXT computer, and a line-mode user interface (called "WWW") was completed. The essential pieces of the Web were in place, although not widely available for network use.

Throughout the early 1990s, interest in the Web grew and spread worldwide. In March 1991, the WWW interface was used on a local network, and by May of that year, it was made available on central CERN machines. On January 15, 1992, the WWW interface became publicly available from CERN, and the CERN team demonstrated the Web to researchers internationally throughout the rest of the year.

Mosaic: The First "Killer" App

In 1993, interest in the Web grew very rapidly. A young undergraduate who was then at the University of Illinois at Urbana-Champaign named Marc Andreessen worked on a project for the National Center for Supercomputing Applications (NCSA), and lead a team that developed a browser for the Web called *Mosaic*. The group released an alpha version of Mosaic for the X Window System in February 1993 that was among the first crop of graphical interfaces to the Web. Mosaic, with its fresh look and graphical interface presenting the Web using a point-and-click design, fueled great interest in the Web and online information. By the end of 1993, attendees at the Internet World conference and exposition in New York City were eager to learn about graphical interfaces to the Web. The *New York Times* hailed Mosaic as the Internet's "killer application."

In 1994, more commercial players got into the Web game. Companies announced commercial versions of Web browser software, including Spry, Inc. Marc Andreessen and colleagues left NCSA in March to form, with Jim Clark (former chairman of Silicon Graphics), a company that later became known as Netscape Communications Corporation (`http://home.netscape.com/`). By May 1994, interest in the Web was so intense that the first international conference on the World Wide Web, held in Geneva, overflowed with attendees. By June 1994, there were 1,500 known public Web servers.

By mid-1994, it was clear to the original developers of the Web at CERN that the stable development of the Web should fall under the guidance of an international organization. In July, the Massachusetts Institute of Technology (MIT) and CERN announced the formation of the World Wide Web Consortium, or W^3C.

The Web Today

Today, the W3C (`http://www.w3.org/hypertext/WWW/Consortium/`) guides the technical development and standards for the evolution of the Web. The W^3C is a consortium of universities and private industries, run by the Laboratory for Computer Science (LCS) at MIT collaborating with CERN (`http://www.cern.ch/`), and Institut National de Recherche en Informatique et en Automatique (INRIA), a French research institute in computer science (`http://www.inria.fr/`).

In 1995, the development of the Web was marked by rapid commercialization and technical change. Netscape Communication's *Mozilla* browser continued to include more extensions of the HyperText Markup Language (HTML), and issues of security for commercial cash transactions garnered much attention. By May 1995, there were more than 15,000 known public Web servers, a tenfold increase over the number from a year before. Many companies had joined the W3C by 1995, including among others, AT&T, Digital Equipment Corporation, Enterprise Integration Technologies, FTP Software, Hummingbird Communication, IBM, MCI, NCSA, Netscape Communications, Novell, Open Market, O'Reilly & Associates, Spyglass, and Sun Microsystems.

By mid-1995, the emergence of the Java and Virtual Reality Modeling Language (VRML) technologies placed the Web at the start of another cycle of rapid change and alteration. Java, in development for several years at Sun Microsystems, promises to make the Web far more interactive than ever before possible. (See Chapter 1, "Java Makes Executable Content Possible.") Virtual Reality Modeling Language, which can allow developers to model three-dimensional scenes for delivery through special Web browsers, may also dramatically change what the Web has to offer. For more information on VRML, see Chapter 34, "VRML and Java."

A Definition of the World Wide Web

Despite its rapid growth and technical developments, the Web in 1996 retains the essential functional components it had in its 1990 form. Its popularity as a view of the Internet, however, has muddied popular understanding of it, because the Web is sometimes viewed as equivalent to the Internet and browsers are sometimes thought of as equivalent to the Web rather than a view into it. However, the Web is a very distinct system from the Internet and its browsers. First, the Web is not a network, but an application system (a set of software programs). Second, the World Wide Web can be deployed and used on many different kinds of networks (not necessarily just Internet networks) and it can even be used on no network at all or on a local network unconnected to any other.

A METAPHOR FOR THE WEB

Imagine a library in which all the spines of the books have been removed and the gravity in the building has been turned off, allowing the pages to float freely. If people could connect one page to another using very light threads taped to the pages, this would be similar to the way the Web's hypertext is arranged. Pages free-float, so that users might encounter a work from any page within it, and reach other works by following the threads leading off a page.

Here is a more technical definition of the Web:

> The World Wide Web is a hypertext information and communication system popularly used on the Internet computer network with data communications operating according to a client/server model. Web clients (browsers) can access multiprotocol and hypermedia information.

Figure 3.1 summarizes the technical organization of the Web based on this definition.

FIGURE 3.1.
*The technical organization
of the Web.*

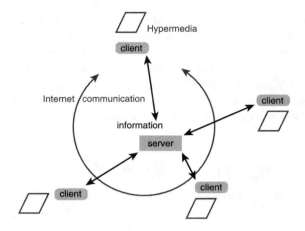

How Does Java Transform the Web?

Java changes the Web by bringing more "intelligence" to Web browsers. Although Java-enabled browsers have user interfaces that are much the same as many other Web browsers, their technical operation marks a significant shift in focus. Java's executable content requires Java-enabled browsers to be smart; that is, they must be able to interpret executable content.

Java Supports Client-Side Interactivity

A *client-server model* for networked computer systems involves three components: the client, the server, and the network. A *client* is a software application that most often runs on the end-user's computer host. A *server* is a software application that most often runs on the information provider's computer host. Client software can be customized to the user's hardware system and it acts as an interface from that system to information provided on the server. The user can initiate a request for information or action through the client software. This request travels over the network to the server. The server interprets the request and takes some desired action. This action might include a database lookup or a change in recorded database information. The results of the requested transaction (if any) are sent back to the client for display to the user. All client/server communication follows a set of rules, or protocols, which are defined for the client/server system. Figure 3.2 summarizes these relationships, showing the flow of a request from a client to a server and the passing back of information from a server to a client. A client might access many servers employing the protocols both the server and client understand.

The distributed form of "request" and "serve" activities of the client/server model allows for many efficiencies. Because the client software interacts with the server according to a predefined protocol, the client software can be customized for the user's particular computer host. (The server doesn't have to worry about the hardware particularities of the client software.) For example, a Web client (a browser) can be developed for Macintosh computers that can access any Web server. This same Web server might be accessed by a Web browser written for a UNIX workstation running the X Window system. This makes it easier to develop information, because there is a clear demarcation of duties between the client and the server. Separate versions of the information need not be developed for any particular hardware platform, because the customizations necessary are written into client software for each platform. An analogy to the client/server model is the television broadcast system. A customer can buy any kind of television set (client) to view broadcasts from any over-the-air broadcast tower (server). Whether the user has a wristband TV or a projection screen TV, the set receives information from the broadcast station in a standard format and displays it appropriate to the user's TV set. Separate TV programming need not be created for each kind of set, such as for color or black-and-white sets or different size sets. New television stations that are created will be able to send signals to all the currently in-use television sets.

FIGURE 3.2.

A client/server model for data communication.

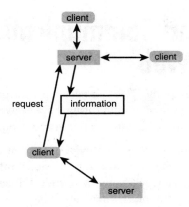

Java brings another dimension to the client/server model. Of course, Java does follow the basic model: A Java-enabled browser is a client that sends requests to Web servers for information. The Java-enabled browser interprets and displays the information sent from the server. This information includes both the hypertext as well as any bytecodes. These bytecodes are Java's new twist on this model. The Java clients execute the content distributed from the servers. These bytecodes, as described in Chapter 2, are also architecture-neutral, just like the other information sent from the Web server.

Java Can Eliminate the Need for Helper Applications

Helper applications include software that a (non-Java-enabled) Web browser invokes to display multimedia information to the user. For example, in order for the user to view movies, the Web browser must have movie display software installed and available. To display inline graphical images in an HTML document, the Web browser must be graphical—that is, employ a system such as X Window system, Macintosh Operating System, or Microsoft Windows as a graphical user interface.

Instead of relying on helper applications, programmers developing applets for Java-enabled browsers can create content handlers to handle media formats.

Java Adds to the Web's Communication Contexts and Potential

The Java language and its browsers are part of the larger context for communication on the Web. Whether you write and distribute applets or just observe them, you take part in communication activities and traditions that have been developing on the Web for many years. Because Java is still so new, it has not yet appeared in all Web communication contexts. You'll see more specific examples of Java used on the Web in later chapters of this book. This subsection briefly reviews the Web's context and potential and how Java can be a part of it.

Java and Communication Contexts on the Web

Communication on the Web can take many forms and take place in many contexts. Genres, or traditional ways for communicating, have evolved on the Web. These genres correspond, in many ways, to offline human communication contexts:

- **Interpersonal:** The Web provides a way for users to create a home page, which typically conveys personal or professional information. The practice of creating a home page emerged from the technical necessity of defining the "default" page that a Web browser displays when requesting information from a Web server when only the host name or a host and directory name is given. Home pages are thus traditionally the top-level page for a server, organization, or individual. When created by individuals, home pages often reveal detailed personal information about their authors and are often listed in directories of home pages. Also, individuals often follow the tradition of linking to colleagues' or friends' pages, creating *electronic tribes*. (Mathematically, these electronic tribes are defined by the cliques of home pages in the directed graph describing the Web.) When used interpersonally, personal home pages offer one-to-one communication, although the technical operation of all pages on the Web is one-to-many.

  Personal "applets" have not yet become prominent, but Java may enable individuals to create an executable "persona" with which other Web users can interact.

- **Group:** As described in the interpersonal definition, cliques of personal pages can define a particular Web tribe or group. Similarly, people can form associations on the Web that are independent of geography and focused on interest in a common topic. Subject-tree breakdowns of information on the Web often evolve from collaborative linking and the development of resource lists and original material describing a subject. (See the following section's discussion about locating subject-based information on the Web.) Similarly, groups of people associate on the Web based on common interests in communication.

■ **Organizational**: Many of the initial Web servers appearing on the Web belong to an organization, not individuals, so the home page for a server often identifies the institution or organization that owns the server. In this way, the genre of the Campus-Wide Information System (CWIS) evolved on Web servers of educational institutions. Similarly, commercial, governmental, and non-governmental organizations have followed the pattern established by CWISs to a large degree.

Many organizations now use Java in their Web pages to add interest and provide service to users. You will see examples of these pages in the next chapter.

■ **Mass**: Just as other media have been used for one-to-many dissemination of information (newspapers, radio, television), so too is the Web used for mass communication. Many commercial and non-commercial magazines and other publications are distributed through the Web. Moreover, as noted previously, all publicly available Web pages are potentially readable to anyone using the Web, and are thus potentially one-to-many communication.

Java is being used actively for mass communication, as shown in the example from the *Nando Times* in Chapter 1.

The key concept to understand is that the Web as a communication system can be flexibly used to communicate in a variety of ways. The classification of the communication (in the categories listed) depends on who is taking part in the communication. The exact classification of any expression on the Web can be blurred by the potentially global reach of any Web page. Thus, a personal home page may be used interpersonally, but it may be accessed far more times on the Web than a publication created and intended for mass consumption. Java's capability for delivering interactive content adds new possibilities to each of these categories.

Java and the Web's Potential

The Web is a flexible system for communication that can be used in many contexts, ranging from individual communication on home pages through group communication and mass communication. In addition to these contexts, the Web also serves the following functions:

■ **Information Delivery:** A Web browser provides the user with a "viewer" to look into FTP space, Gopherspace, or hypertext information on the Web. The structure of hypertext enables user selectivity because of the many ways a user can choose to follow links in hypertext. Java adds the potential for new protocol handlers and content handlers.

■ **Communication:** People can use Web hypertext to create forums for sharing information, discussion, and helping group members make contact with each other. Java's executable content introduces new forms of more interactive communication.

■ **Interaction:** Using gateway programming, a Web developer can build some degree of interactivity into an application, providing the user with a way to receive customized information based on queries. Gateway programs can also enable a user to change or add to an information structure. A higher degree of interactivity is possible using Java because of its executable content. (Chapter 1 surveys Java's unique contribution to the Web's interactivity.)

■ **Computation:** Using gateway programming, the Web can be used to provide an interface to other applications and programs for information processing. Based on user selections, a Web application can return a computed or customized result through a gateway program. Java programmers can create software for computation that can be distributed and executed.

Figure 3.3 shows the important distinction between selectivity and gateway programming interactivity. When the user accesses the Web server on the left, content is presented using hypertext. The links in the hypertext pages give the user a great deal of choice, or selectivity, for encountering information in the database. However, no information is customized to user inputs or computed based on user requests. Although this server offers the user great flexibility in information retrieval because of the hypertext design of its pages, this server is not interactive.

The key to the level of interactivity, as shown in the server on the right, is that the executable program accepts input from the user through a Web page. Based on these user inputs, this executable can compute a result and (possibly, also using information from the database) return this customized information result to the user. Moreover, the executable program also enables the user to (possibly) change the contents of the database, or make some other change in the database or files on the server. These changes might include altering the structure or contents of hypertext or the contents of other files. The construction of this executable program requires skills in gateway programming.

Java adds still another level of interactivity. Instead of the server computing a result, the Java-enabled browser is the mechanism for computation.

FIGURE 3.3.
Web selectivity and gateway interactivity.

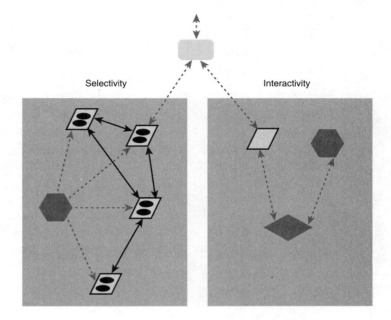

Summary

- The Web emerged from ideas about the associative, nonlinear organization of information. Java is another step in this evolution.

- The Web is a hypertext information and communication system popularly used on the Internet in a client/server model, offering hypermedia display capabilities through appropriate browsers, some of which require helper applications.

- Java-enabled browsers bring client-side interactivity and computation to the Web and can eliminate the need for helper applications.

- Communication on the Web can assume many forms and take place in many contexts, ranging from individual communication to group and mass communication. Java can potentially augment the Web's communication contexts and functions.

Java Animates Web Pages

4

by John December

The Java language and Java-enabled browsers allow a more visually dynamic Web than possible before. Instead of hypertext pages containing only still images with helper applications to display video, Java Web pages can include animated graphics, text, and any moving visual elements a Java programmer can dream up.

This chapter surveys several Java applets that implement animation. In some cases, the chapter also includes key portions of the source code to demonstrate how these applets are made. If you want to understand these code portions in more detail, you can read more about Java programming basics in later parts of this book. If not, you can skip over the programming sections for now and return to them later. If you'd like to try out the applets described here, you should be familiar with Java's connection with HTML as described in Chapter 2.

The purpose of this chapter is to familiarize you with the many types of animation possible using applets. If you are ready to place applets on your Web pages, this chapter will also be invaluable to you; it contains instructions for including some publicly available demonstration applets that you can customize and include on a hypertext page.

A TREASURE TROVE OF JAVA APPLETS

Visit the Gamelan web site at `http://www.gamelan.com/` to connect to a well-organized, frequently updated, and very comprehensive registry of Java applets, demonstrations, and documentation. This collection includes pointers to many of the demonstrations discussed in this book.

Applets in Motion

If you are a new user of a Java-enabled browser, you will immediately notice that some Java pages contain moving text, figures, and animations. These moving images are made possible by Java applets that implement Java's `Runnable` interface. These applets don't just display static text or graphics; they can execute their content continuously.

NervousText

One example of animated text is the `NervousText` applet. `NervousText` was originally developed by Daniel Wyszynski at the Center for Applied Large-Scale Computing. Wyszynski's `NervousText` applet displays `HotJava!` in jostling on-screen letters. David Leach modified this applet so that it can display any programmer-defined string. Figure 4.1 shows both Wyszynski's and David Leach's `NervousText` applets on a Web page.

FIGURE 4.1.

The NervousText *applet.*
*(Courtesy of Daniel
Wyszynski and David
Leach)*

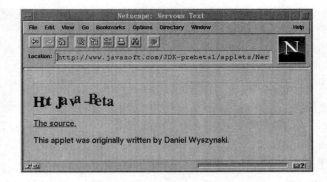

The NervousText applet is a good demonstration of how an applet can be included on any Web page, not just Web pages created by the applet's developer. You are not limited to using only applets that you write. You can modify and use other developer's applets from their sites, just as you link to hypertext pages at other sites. In fact, sharing applets across the Net is what Java's capability to distribute executable content is all about.

You use the APPLET tag in HTML to place a publicly available applet in a Web page. The Codebase attribute identifies the path (using a Uniform Resource Locator, or URL) to a Java class anywhere on a publicly available server on the Net. The Code attribute then specifies the applet's class name.

In general, the APPLET tag on an HTML page works like this:

```
<APPLET
   Codebase = "path (URL) of directory containing class files"
   Code     = "name of class file"
   Width    = "width of applet in pixels"
   Height   = "height of applet in pixels">
   <PARAM Name="parameter name" Value="value of parameter">
   <PARAM Name="parameter name" Value="value of parameter">
</APPLET>
```

In Figure 4.1, Leach's modification uses a parameter called msg to set the value of the message that the applet displays.

You can include a beta version of a NervousText applet in your page like this:

```
<APPLET
   Codebase="http://www.javasoft.com/JDK-prebeta1/applets/NervousText/"
   Code="NervousText.class" Width="200" Height="50">
<PARAM Name = "text" Value="HotJava-Beta">
</APPLET>
```

Note that the parameters use the PARAM tag in HTML, and that these parameter tags occur between the opening <APPLET> tag and closing </APPLET> tag. When the Java-enabled browser reads the PARAM attributes Name and Value, it passes these values to the applet.

USING JAVA APPLETS WITHOUT JAVA

You can put together a Web page that includes applets you didn't create or at any location using the APPLET element. You don't have to have a Java-enabled browser or the Java compiler to serve applets. You need only a reference to the class file of the applet. If you use applets that are at remote locations, you need to identify where on the Net the class file for the applet exists. To do so, use the Codebase attribute of the APPLET tag. Of course, users who do not have a Java-enabled browser cannot observe the applets.

If you use a remote applet in this way, consider downloading and serving a copy of the class file from your own site. Before taking this step, however, check with the information provider. And, of course, check out the applet's behavior—it is executable content and runs on the computer of anyone requesting to view it.

David Leach's modification of NervousText demonstrates the programming technique of passing values to the applet with parameters. In the Java applet code, David uses the getAttribute method to find out the value of the parameter msg passed from the HTML tags to the Java applet. Leach's class definition includes the data string userString; and the init() method includes this line:

```
userString = getAttribute("msg");
```

David uses this string in the paint() method to derive the characters that draw the applet. The trick of making the letters "nervous" is to vary their coordinates in the paint() method by using a random number generator for their X and Y coordinates:

```
x_coord = (int) (Math.random()*10+15*i);
y_coord = (int) (Math.random()*10+36);
```

TickerTape

Similar to the NervousText applet, another good demonstration of Java's animation capabilities is TickerTape. This applet was originally developed by Sven Heinicke at *HotWired* and later modified by David Leach and John Stone at the University of Missouri-Rolla. Many others have subsequently created variations on the TickerTape applet.

ARE JAVA USERS WASTING BANDWIDTH?

After a Java applet's bytecodes have been downloaded across the network, the user's host is the processor that interpets them. The information provider's host works only to distribute the bytecodes. Users of applets, therefore, might typically use far less bandwidth and far less time on the information provider's computer than might Web surfers.

Also, class files containing bytecodes aren't all that large. For example, the `TickerTape` applet (see Figure 4.2) is 3,186 bytes—easily smaller than many graphics files routinely downloaded from the *HotWired* server. Therefore, although users may see more action with applets, they are not *necessarily* using more bandwidth on the Web. Of course, leaving a browser on autopilot (such as in the Surf-o-Matic applet in Chapter 6) and walking away would cause a browser to use much bandwidth for downloading Web pages.

Information providers must be very careful about the size and processing power required by their applets; a CPU-intensive applet could bring the user's computer to its knees.

Figure 4.2 shows the display of the TickerTape applet. The text in the lines scrolls continuously to the left; with the bottom ticker line moving very rapidly.

FIGURE 4.2.

`TickerTape` *applet example. (Courtesy of Ashley Cheng)*

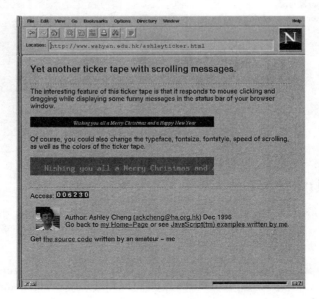

The `TickerTape` applet uses a key programming trick to cause the letters to move. The code changes the X position of the string by an amount equal to the speed attribute prior to repainting the string in each cycle. Here's the code to do this:

```
xpos -= speed;
```

This line of code subtracts the value of `speed` from the current horizontal position of the string. The line is a quick way of writing the equivalent `xpos = xpos - speed`.

You can include a beta version of a more elaborate kind of ticker tape on a Web page like this:

```
<APPLET
    Codebase = "http://www.digitalfocus.com/digitalfocus/faq/"
    Code = "reloadImage.class" Width="600" Height="70">
    <PARAM Name="rateOfMovement" Value="2">
    <PARAM Name="sleepInterval" Value="40">
    <PARAM Name="msgYLocation" Value="12">
    <PARAM Name="passedMsg"
           Value="Microsoft announces support for Java....Pigs were seen flying in
Wyoming.....Martians endorse Java....java to be used in ballot boxes during next
elections...">
    <PARAM Name="secondaryMsg"
           Value="This just in......Netscape stock fell 20% after Microsoft
announced i-net strategy....Next release of PowerBuilder to be java aware.....stay
tuned...">
</APPLET>
```

Figure 4.3 shows a ticker tape with controls in action.

FIGURE 4.3.

TickerTape *applet with controls. (Courtesy of Digital Focus)*

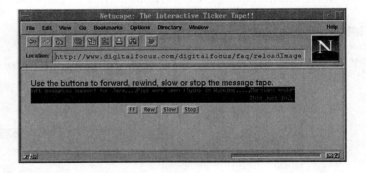

Fireworks

Another variation on animation is to have graphics—rather than words only—flash across a page. Erik Wistrand has created an applet that transforms a Web page into a fireworks show (see Figure 4.4).

Similar to the TickerTape applet, you can include the Fireworks applet on a Web page, and you can control aspects of its appearance. The fireworks parameters set the number of rockets, points, size of points, duration of rockets, and even the constant of gravity.

This example sets a series of 50 rockets on a page (shown in Figure 4.4). The COLOR parameter uses hexadecimal (base 16) notation to describe the red, green, and blue values of the background image color.

FIGURE 4.4.
Fireworks *applet example.*
(Courtesy of Erik Wistrand)

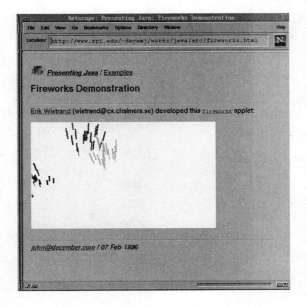

Animation

Not all animations involve moving text for aesthetic purposes. Other animations occur in instructional pages or as part of a user's interaction with a Web page.

Juggling

Chris Seguin has created a juggling instructional page (http://www.acm.uiuc.edu/webmonkeys/juggling/) that effectively uses animation to *show*—rather than *tell*—how to juggle. You see the juggling page in Figure 4.5. Viewed through a Java-enabled browser, the page shows the two model hands juggling one, two, and three balls. See Chapter 25, which was written by Chris, for more information on animation programming.

One of the programming keys in Chris's applet source code is his use of arrays to store the path of the balls. He uses the same ball graphic and repositions it along this path. This is unlike a cartoon in which individual frames would show a ball in its different positions on its path.

Java programmers use both the technique of using a path for a graphic and frames of graphics to animate graphics. In general, the graphic and path approach leads to less memory drain and more flexibility. Although for complicated or animated images (refer back to Duke in Figure 1.3 in the first chapter), the frame approach is desirable.

FIGURE 4.5.

*The Java juggling page.
(Courtesy of Chris Seguin)*

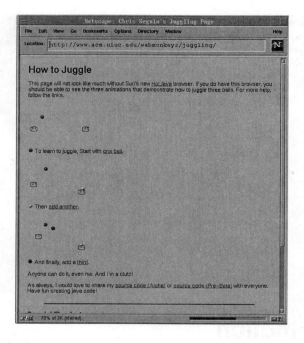

Drawing on Famous Pictures

Another variation in graphics on Web pages is to let you draw right on pictures on a page. Johan van der Hoeven has created the `Magic` applet, which has a fanciful appeal. You can use it to draw as if you were using a Magic Marker on famous pictures. Figure 4.6 shows markings on a world map and the Mona Lisa (this is an alpha applet).

WHO OWNS WHAT?

The drawing applet in this section demonstrates the blending of authorship and ownership that Java is opening on the Web. The author of the HTML page used an applet written by one person and an image created by another (and painted by still another—Leonardo da Vinci—long ago!) to create an environment for the user to alter the image. Who is the author of the resulting Web page and who finally owns the melded pieces? The talent of the Java programmer who made the applet? The Web page creator who put the pieces together? The browser manufacturer? The user who marks the image? The creator of the original image? da Vinci perhaps never would have imagined his painting would be transmitted around the world to be defaced with such glee. These questions raise just some of the legal and intellectual property issues involved in the use of Java and the Web.

FIGURE 4.6.

*Marking on the world and
the* Mona Lisa. *(Courtesy
of Johan van der Hoeven)*

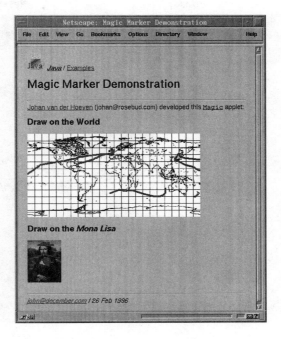

A Live Feedback Imagemap

Still another variation on Java graphics is to make images function just like HTML imagemaps;
when the user clicks on certain parts of the image, other resources are retrieved. Jim Graham at
Sun Microsystems has implemented an applet to demonstrate this capability. Shown in Figure
4.7, this applet demonstrates the equivalent functionality of an HTML imagemap, but with
the additional features of live feedback. When a user passes the cursor over a "hot" region of
the image, that region appears highlighted to indicate that clicking on it will retrieve another
resource or some media content.

FIGURE 4.7.
*Live feedback imagemap.
(Courtesy of Jim Graham,
Sun Microsystems)*

The Weather

While the images shown so far are interesting, a more useful example is in Figure 4.8, a live weather map. Created by Alan Steremberg and Christopher Schwerzler, with weather data provided by University of Michigan, this Java applet lets you look at current weather conditions. Figure 4.8 shows the infrared satellite image for the United States. Other options are available, as shown in the figure, for obtaining other weather information.

FIGURE 4.8.

Weather map. (Courtesy of Alan Steremberg and Christopher Schwerzler, with weather data provided by the University of Michigan)

Commercial Sites Using Java

The demonstrations in this chapter show many of Java's animation capabilities. But Java is more than a good show; it is also already at work on commercial Web sites. *The Nando Times* uses Java (refer back to Figure 1.13), as do George Coates Performance Works (refer back to Figure 1.10), ESPNET SportsZone (refer back to figure 1.14), Dimension X (`http://www.dimensionx.com/`), *HotWired* (`http://www.hotwired.com/`), and Sun Microsystems (`http://www.sun.com/`). Because Java brings so much visual interest to a Web page, it has great potential to draw attention, convey specialized information, and provide entertainment.

The Rolling Stones

The Rolling Stones is a rock band that made a big splash on the Internet Multicast Backbone (MBONE—`http://www.eit.com/techinfo/mbone/mbone.html`) when they used it to simulcast part of their November 18, 1994, Dallas Cotton Bowl concert. Today, the Stones Web site (`http://www.stones.com/`) is making a splash with Java.

The Stones site contains several interesting Java applets:

■ A Stones puzzle (`http://www.stones.com/javapuzzle.html`) in which you slide the squares to make the famous tongue logo.

- The Stones Java devil (`http://www.stones.com/new.html`), which animates the What's New page for the site.

- On the opening page of the Stones Voodoo Lounge (`http://www.stones.com/javaindex.html`), animated flags move back and forth across the screen. This page is shown in Figure 4.9.

FIGURE 4.9.

The Rolling Stones Voodoo Lounge with Java.
(Courtesy of Stephan Fitch and John Graham)

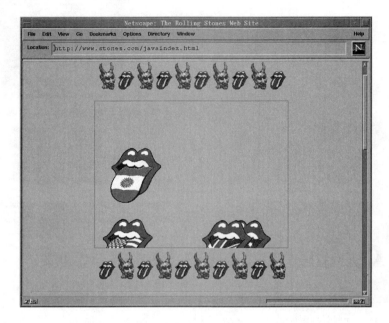

Accurate Information System Consultant

Other commercial providers are using Java to add interest to their pages through animation. Accurate Information Systems (`http://accurate.com.my/`) uses Java to greet users with a moving ticker tape and a bouncing ball (see Figure 4.10).

Of course, just as the BLINK tag and other graphics elements become overused to the point of excess on the Web, so might applets be used gratuitously. The potential for applets to add motion, interest, information, and real service to users of a Web is great, however, and we have yet to realize Java's full potential.

FIGURE 4.10.

Accurate Information System Consultant ticker tape greeting. (Courtesy of Accurate Information System Consultant)

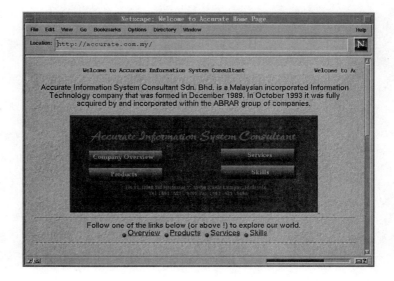

Summary

You can use Java applets to place animations on Web pages. A user can set the parameters of an existing applet using the PARAM tag and bring a customized applet to his or her own Web page. Developers can create new applets to provide this functionality and make them available for users.

- Text can shimmer using NervousText. Users can include this applet on their pages by using the APP element. By setting attributes of the applet, the user can control characteristics and behavior of the applet.
- Text can scroll, as shown in the TickerTape applet.
- Graphics can repeat a visual pattern, such as in the Fireworks applet.
- Moving applets can teach a lesson, as in the Juggling applet.
- The Magic applet enables users to alter graphics, allowing them to draw on an image.
- A Java applet can perform the equivalent function of an HTML imagemap. Java's advantage over traditional imagemaps is that Java imagemaps can give instant feedback regarding the user's cursor position. Feedback does not need to be delayed until after a mouse click.
- Many companies already use Java, including rock bands and computer companies, to provide interest on Web pages.

Java Makes Web Pages Interactive

5

*by John
December*

IN THIS CHAPTER

Java's capability to animate Web pages is just the surface of what you might first notice when experiencing the Web through a Java-enabled browser. Not only do items *move* on Java Web pages, but applets can also accept user input through mouse clicks or keyboard entries. Java enables people to create Web pages with embedded puzzles, chemical models, games, and even communication systems. (For some illustrations of these, refer to the figures in Chapter 1.)

This chapter surveys some Java applets that provide interactivity. These Java applets range from simple games to instructional modules. Because, as of this writing, Java is still in its infancy, this chapter shows just a glimpse of the rich interactivity Java may bring to the Web.

This chapter also points out key programming tricks used in each of these applets. You can learn the basics of Java programming in Part III of this book.

WHAT IS INTERACTIVITY?

The word *interactivity* has become a buzzword in media development. Products claim they have it, and developers promise to bring interactivity to various media (television, CD-ROMs, magazines, newspapers, games, and so on). Interactivity has been promised so much that it is nearly as hollow a term as *information superhighway*—meaning very little and lacking specific illustrations.

A dictionary definition touches on the main idea of mutual response and reciprocity:

in·ter·ac·tive adj 1. mutually or reciprocally active; 2. of, relating to, or being a two-way electronic communication system (as a telephone, cable television, or a computer) that involves a user's orders (as for information or merchandise) or responses (as to a poll). *(Definition from the online Webster's Dictionary.)*

In the broadest sense of the word, nearly everything could be considered interactive. Toasters and televisions, for example, respond based on a user's orders.

Richer levels of interactivity, however, involve more than response to the user's orders; the *level* and *quality* of these responses makes a big difference. The pre-Java Web provided a great deal of user *selectivity* through hypertext links, but its level of interactivity was fairly low. Gateway (Common Gateway Interface, or CGI) programming provides a higher degree of interactivity by making it possible to customize responses to users. Gateway programs are not continuously active, however, because they require the user to click an input button before the user's selections can be processed and a response can be sent.

Java raises the interactive quality of the Web by making possible immediate and continuous stimuli to the user. At the same time, a Java applet can continuously accept and process input from the user. Java can also respond to this direct input and respond with customized feedback. Thus, the Web has become richly interactive with the advent of the Java age.

Interactive Games

Games are a popular application for programmers to create. Games naturally fit into the give-and-take flow that Java applets make possible. Games fit well into the tireless, continuous looping possible in a Java program. The game applets described in this chapter are among the earliest Java applets, yet they display the interactivity Java can bring to Web pages.

Hang Duke

Patrick Chan at Sun Microsystems developed an applet called Hang Duke; the applet has been distributed with the Java browser as a demonstration. Figure 5.1 shows Duke, the mascot of Java. Notice that the user couldn't guess the word; consequently, Duke is in an advanced hanging stage.

FIGURE 5.1.

The Hang Duke game.
(Courtesy of Patrick Chan,
Sun Microsystems)

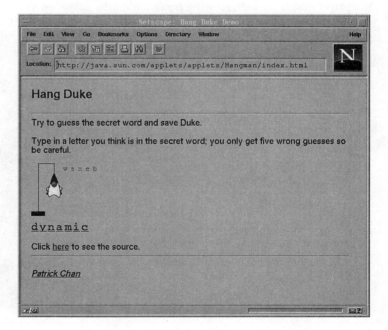

The applet accepts input from the keyboard and displays correct letters in the appropriate slots in the word; each incorrect letter appears near the top of the gallows, and for each wrong letter, another part of Duke's form is drawn.

The Hang Duke applet demonstrates how the simple metaphor of pencil-and-paper game translates easily to the Web with Java.

Hang Duke is a runnable applet. A key part of its source code accepts letters from the user through a method that detects key presses:

```
public void keyDown(int keyPressed)
```

The parameter `keyPressed` is an integer representing a character. This code can be changed to a character and placed in a string expression by casting, like this: `(char)keyPressed`.

3-D Tennis

Eiji Ito has created a simulation of tennis using a Java applet. By using your mouse to move your "racket" in a three-dimensional representation of a room, you can play tennis by blocking a ball. This applet is at `http://www.sfc.keio.ac.jp/~t93034ei/ja1.html`.

Figure 5.2 shows the tennis game in action. The bar at the right keeps track of the times that the player misses the ball, growing smaller until the game is over.

FIGURE 5.2.

3-D Tennis implemented in Java. (Courtesy of Eiji Ito)

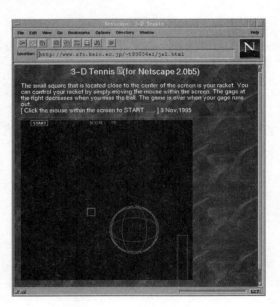

Educational Applications

The Java game applets described so far in this chapter are innovative in that they use Java technology to enable users to interact with Web pages. This interactivity can also be put to a more exciting use: education. Educators have been adopting the Web for several years now for course support webs, information about their schools, and even instructional modules. However, the Web's static text, its relatively low level of interactivity, and its limited capabilities for multimedia, have made it useful for information delivery but not as amenable to creating truly innovative, engaging applications. This section highlights some early Java applications that highlight its potential for education.

Fractal Figures

Fractals are geometric shapes whose individual parts resemble the whole shape. Fractals can be generated by starting from a basic shape, and then changing the shape based on patterns echoing the structure of the overall shape. Snowflakes are like fractals: their forms at the lowest level of detail reflect a crystalline pattern similar to the whole shape. Because fractals are so hard to explain in words, what a better candidate for a Java application?

Jim Graham at Sun Microsystems has created a Java applet that *shows* an algorithm that generates a fractal. (Check out `http://java.sun.com/applets/applets/fractal/index.html`.) Figures 5.3, 5.4, and 5.5 show this applet. The first panel displays a rendering of a snowflake curve. Starting from a simple peaked line (see Figure 5.3), more peaks are added on the line segments until the entire curve resembles the ragged, yet precisely intricate snowflake shape (progressing through Figure 5.4 and Figure 5.5).

Similarly, the last fractal shown in Figures 5.3 to 5.5 is called a *Hilbert curve*. Starting with a set of lines forming a *Y*, the algorithm adds detail until the entire fractal appears similar to a fine oriental rug—a pattern like a maze formed from a precise algorithm.

FIGURE 5.3.

Fractal lesson, initial state. (Courtesy of Jim Graham, Sun Microsystems)

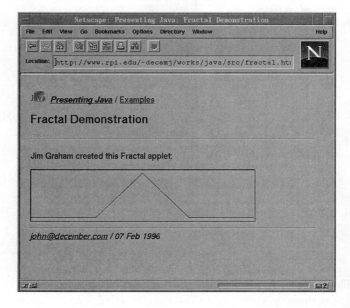

FIGURE 5.4.

Fractal lesson, middle state.
(Courtesy of Jim Graham,
Sun Microsystems)

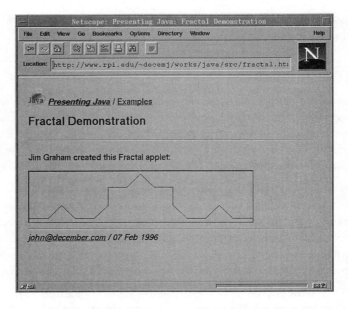

FIGURE 5.5.

Fractal lesson, final state.
(Courtesy of Jim Graham,
Sun Microsystems)

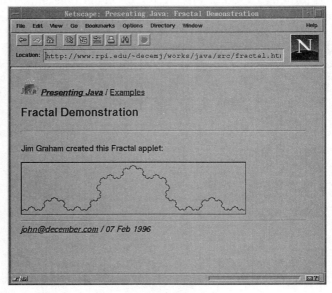

The progression of these fractals from their starting points to their ending points is key: an instructional module could show the stages frozen in images embedded in a Web page (much like the frozen illustrations in this book). However, the Java demonstration enables the user to restart the image, watch it over and over, and get a feel for the progression of the algorithm. The user sees the algorithm in action rather than just imagining how it works.

Word Match Game

The tireless capability of a Java applet to execute an algorithm over and over for the instruction of the user also shows up in the word-match game developed by Patrick Chan at Sun Microsystems (see Figure 5.6). This game is a demonstration of what could be more made even more elaborate. Users match pictures with words in foreign languages. To play this game, you first find a picture of an object you recognize. Then, click on the picture of that object, and then click on the corresponding word. The words can appear in many different languages, so playing the game builds your vocabulary. The applet draws lines from the picture to the word. Once you've completed matching all the words, you then click on the Score button and the applet reports the number of correct matches. The game also has a speaker icon available, so you can hear the pronunciation of the words in some of the languages.

FIGURE 5.6.

Word match game lesson.
(Courtesy of Patrick Chan, Sun Microsystems)

Many languages are available in this applet, as shown in the box to the left. Once you solve the puzzle, you can see it as solved in all the languages by clicking on the language name.

Just like the fractals demonstration, the word match game shows how interactive and multimedia content can give users a place to play on a Web page rather than just observe and select. Neither lesson is meant to be a comprehensive tutorial; instead, each is a demonstration of Java's possibilities. Even as they are, however, the applets are fairly instructive.

Fast Fourier Transform

The playground for users of Java pages can also include applets that perform complex computations and simulations. Through these applets, users can gain immediate feedback into processes. A good example of such a simulation is the Fast Fourier Transform (FFT) applet developed by Gopal Chand, David Nicol, and Calum Smeaton (`http://www.virtual-inn.co.uk/orbital/beta/fft/`). Fourier transforms are used in science and engineering to analyze data or signals. The FFT lessons (Figure 5.7), gives users a way to directly see the result of a Fourier Transform calculation. Given a set of input data points on a wave form, the FFT applet calculates and displays the resulting power spectrum.

FIGURE 5.7.

Fast Fourier Transform lesson. (Courtesy of Gopal Chand, David Nicol, and Calum Smeaton)

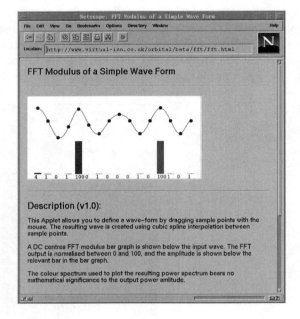

This FFT application, like the others shown in this chapter, reinforces concepts by providing direct experience to users. With sufficient programming work (the FFT application involved over 700 lines of Java code), a Java Web page can become a sophisticated scientific laboratory for learning. Given more time and experience, as well as more class libraries, educators using Java will be able to add new dimensions to their instructional materials delivered over the Web.

Voltage Circuit Simulator

Sean Russell, Software Manager of the University of Oregon has created a way for students to learn about electric circuits (`http://jersey.uoregon.edu/vlab/Voltage`). In this simulation, a student can explore the relationship among voltage, amperage, and resistance.

In the simulation, a battery outputs energy measured in volts, a wire conducts electrical energy with a given resistance measured in ohms, and a bulb operates with an energy requirement measured in amperes. A switch completes the circuit, connecting the energy from the batteries through the wire to the bulb.

The student chooses some combination of resistors and battery cells for the circuit. The goal is to discover how Ohm's law defines the mathematical relationship among voltage (V), amperage (I), and resistance (R).

If the student does not have enough resistance in the circuit, the bulb will receive too much energy and explode. If the resistance is too great, the bulb will not light. If the resistance and the power is just right, the bulb will light.

By experimenting with the applet, the student eventually can learn that V=IR is Ohm's law. Given that the bulb in Figure 5.8 is 3 amps (I) and the battery is 18 volts (V), then the student can solve for R, to get 6 ohms of resistance (R), and the bulb lights up.

An electrical circuit can be placed on a Web page like this example, showing a circuit with I=3 and V=36.

```
<APPLET Code="voltage"
        Codebase="http://jersey.uoregon.edu/vlab/Voltage/classes"
        Width="600" Height="150">
<PARAM Name="amperage" Value="3">
<PARAM Name="voltage"  Value="36">
</APPLET>
```

A lecturer can use this applet to create a set of circuits on the same page by including the applet with different settings for the parameters.

FIGURE 5.8.
Voltage circuit simulator. (Coding by Sean Russell, Software Manager, University of Oregon; Graphic images by Amy Hulse)

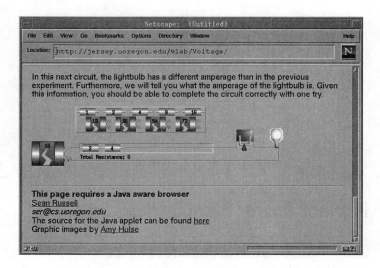

Complementary Metal-Oxide Semiconductor (CMOS) Demonstration

Norman Hendrich of the University of Hamburg in Germany's Department of Computer Science has created a set of applets which demonstrate the operation of transistors and electronic components at `http://tech-www.informatik.uni-hamburg.de/applets/cmos/cmosdemo.html`.

These applets demonstrate how CMOS (Complementary Metal-Oxide Semiconductor) transistors and basic gates work. The applets demonstrate the N-type and P-type transistors used in CMOS technology, the basic CMOS inverter, as well as NAND and NOR gates.

Figure 5.9 shows one applet in this collection. The user can click on the source and gate contacts of the transistors to toggle the voltage levels. The applet uses different colors to indicate voltage levels, and the output values on the drain contacts change in response to user input.

Similar to the phasor applet, the CMOS applet shows how students can have a virtual "lab bench" for exploration and study.

FIGURE 5.9.

*CMOS demonstration.
(Courtesy of Norman
Hendrich)*

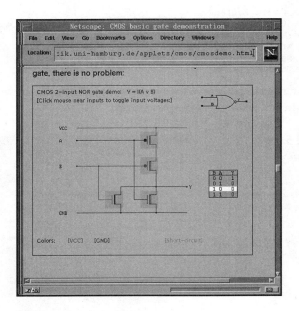

Nuclear Power Plant Demonstration

Henrik Eriksson of the Department of Computer and Information Science at Linköping University, Sweden has created a model of a nuclear power plant which is an intriguing simulation. This applet is at `http://www.ida.liu.se/~her/npp/demo.html`.

The applet simulates the "Kärnobyl" nuclear power plant's major components: the reactor, turbines, and the condenser. Pumps and valves in the applet allow the user to control flows and pressures.

The reactor heats the water to boiling, and the resulting steam drives the turbine. The condenser cools the steam. The pumps transport the water from the condenser back to the reactor tank.

The user can choose different simulation sequences to test their disaster management skills in the power plant, including scenarios involving a turbine failure or water pump failures.

The simulator calculates values based on the user's settings. Figure 5.10 shows the plant in a precarious situation.

According to developer Henrik Eriksson, the Kärnobyl plant was built to help students learn expert systems and rule-based programming. The applet uses a C-based interface to integrate the Java applet with a rule-based expert system of safety rules for operating a nuclear power plant. The result is an intelligent applet which helps students explore the complex relationships in operation.

FIGURE 5.10.

The Kärnobyl nuclear power plant. (Courtesy of Henrik Eriksson)

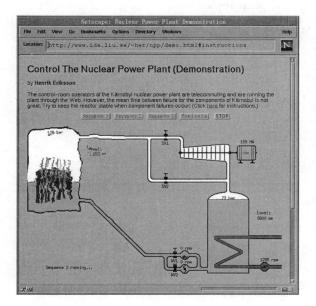

Summary

Java not only brings animation to Web pages, but it enables users to interact with those animations. Ranging from applets that implement Web-based versions of familiar games to new kinds of Java programs that help users learn, Java interactivity has much potential. Java is still in its infancy, and the key to developing more complex Java programs will be high-quality class libraries. These libraries should help Java programmers express the unique features of an applet without having to worry about coding all the details. The resulting applets, when well done and configurable through parameters, could be the instruments and simulations which help students learn a wide variety of lessons about language, science, and other fields of knowledge.

- A simple Hang Duke game demonstrates how user input through the keyboard can affect a graphical display.
- A 3-D tennis game adds the element of chance and a tactile visual metaphor to an applet.
- An applet demonstrating fractal algorithms can help users gain insight into how an algorithm progresses.
- A user can interact with an applet by matching a picture with foreign words in a word match game. With a speaker to deliver audio, the resulting applet is a model for a useful instructional tool.
- The examples of the Fast Fourier Transform, circuit simulator, CMOS, and nuclear power plant applets show how a Java Web page can become an adjunct to laboratory work. The applets can behave like scientific instruments or interpret and display input data so that students can focus on the meaning of scientific principles.

Java Distributes Content

6

by John December

Because Java is designed for distributing executable content, *all* Java applets, except those on the user's local host, are distributed across networks. However, Java's power as a language for expressing executable content involves more than the distribution of applets. Java also makes the following possible:

■ Protocol handlers that communicate to a Java-enabled browser how to handle a new method of processing information.

■ Content handlers that give a Java-enabled browser the capability to interpret new data formats.

■ Java language statements to access network resources. This enables Java programs to retrieve resources in a user's Java-enabled browser.

This chapter examines these capabilities in detail, showing examples and key Java statements that make these features possible. Later parts of this book will guide you through more details of Java programming. In particular, the `java.net` package is covered in Chapter 28, and protocol and content handlers are covered in Chapters 30 and 31.

The Significance of Network Distribution and Retrieval

Chapter 4 showed an applet (Magic) that allowed you to draw on images (refer to Figure 4.6). The network relationships involved in this simple applet are fairly significant. Figure 6.1 shows the connections among the content distribution, network retrieval, and display involved in this applet.

The figure shows the network retrieval taking place:

■ The Web server `www.rpi.edu` sends the hypertext file `marker.html` to the user's HotJava browser.

■ The `IMG` and `APPLET` elements in the file `marker.html` cause the HotJava browser to request an image from the Web server `www.paris.org` and an applet from `www.rosebud.com`.

■ The resulting image, applet, and hypertext page are assembled in the user's HotJava browser. The applet executes on the user's computer.

This network interaction involves three Web servers and the user's computer, besides the routers involved with the Internet network connections that relay the information from two continents. This intermingling of content demonstrates the integration Java can help accomplish. As a Web client, a Java-enabled browser is already an information integrator for many protocols. Combined with capabilities to distribute and retrieve content, Java adds another dimension to information retrieval and integration.

FIGURE 6.1.
Summary of information transfer in Magic applet demonstration.

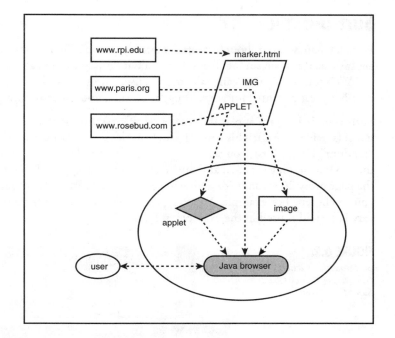

Handling New Protocols and Formats

The most significant feature of a Java-enabled browser is that it is not fixed. Instead of relying on a built-in set of code for handling information delivery protocols and a fixed set of helper applications to handle media formats, a Java-enabled browser is set up so that it can adjust to learn new protocols and media formats.

This capability significantly changes the Web:

- Developers no longer have to rely on just the fixed set of protocols.
- Java-enabled browsers can respond to new protocols. These protocols may support new applications or may be new kinds of protocols for information transfer.

Retrieving and Sharing Network Information

The protocol and content handlers can expand what a Java-enabled browser can interpret and display, opening the Web for delivery of diverse information. Java also has the capability to enrich how browsers retrieve information, giving Java programmers the chance to make applets to retrieve network information.

Surf-o-matic

Patrick Chan, writing about his Surf-o-matic demonstration program at `http://java.sun.com/applets/applets/autopilot/index.html`, calls it "almost as good as watching TV!" Surf-o-matic is a Web tour guide that can "take over" a user's browser and change the pages. This type of tour has great potential for advertising, education, and other applications.

Surf-o-matic is a Java applet that uses a set of classes to implement the Surf-o-matic Control Panel (see Figure 6.2). This control panel enables you to cruise the Web based on some lists of "random" URLs. First, you select which list or lists of URLs you want to surf. Then click on the Go button on the panel, and Surf-o-matic takes over your browser. Surf-o-matic switches the page every 20 seconds (or a time interval you can set) to a new page from the random lists you've chosen. For example, Yahoo's (`http://www.yahoo.com/`) random list of Web pages is very large and is used in the example in Figure 6.2.

FIGURE 6.2.

*Surf-o-matic in action.
(Courtesy of Patrick Chan,
Sun Microsystems)*

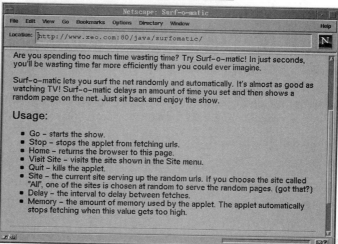

Figure 6.2 shows Surf-o-matic as it is retrieving a new page. Even in its present form, it is a useful standalone application. One use is as a kiosk application to demonstrate the content of the Web.

Surf-o-matic is based on Matthew Gray's Web Autopilot, which uses the Netscape browser's client-pull feature. However, a HotJava browser can use Java code to implement this same type of task; it then does not have to revert to a client-pull technique. Patrick Chan's demonstration in Surf-o-matic is a quick example showing this flexibility of Java for network information retrieval.

JavaScript

JavaScript (described in detail in part IX of this book) is another programming language that you can use in conjunction with Java to distribute executable content over the Web. JavaScript is different from Java. Rather than interpreting Java bytecodes in a separate file, JavaScript is written into an HTML document and is interpreted by a Netscape Web browser.

Many companies have endorsed JavaScript as an open standard for scripting. Using JavaScript, a programmer can detect and act upon many user navigation actions, such as button-clicking, mouse position, and so on. Figure 6.3 shows an example of JavaScript in action. This simple calculator operates using HTML forms elements. However, its processing isn't accomplished using Common Gateway Interface (CGI) programming. Instead, a JavaScript program gives the user the answer to the calculation. This shift changes the site of computation from the information provider's server to the user's client and host.

FIGURE 6.3.

JavaScript in action.
(Courtesy of Netscape
Communications)

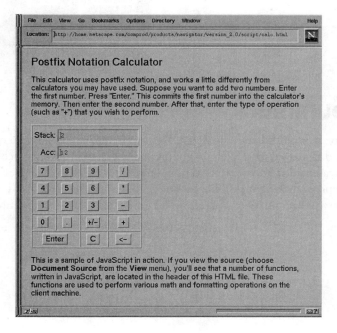

A Java Graffiti Board

Dan Guinan developed a Java Graffiti Chalkboard that demonstrates sharing information using a Java applet. This applet is located at `http://www.tisinc.com/beta/chalkboard.html`.

Through the applet, the user can manipulate tools such as chalk and an eraser to draw on the board; the resulting drawing is shared among users. Figure 6.4 shows a sample board.

Developer Dan Guinan explains that the Java Grafitti Chalkboard applet relies on a socket-based server to load and save chalkboard data. This server resides on the same machine as the Web server and communicates with the Java applet directly. The result is a "networked" applet that not only provides animation and interaction with the user but network communication as well.

FIGURE 6.4.

The Java Graffitti Board. (Copyright 1996, TESSERACT Information Solutions Inc., www.tisinc.com, *All Rights Reserved. Reprinted by permission. Courtesy of Dan Guinan)*

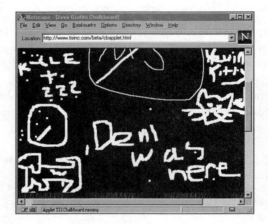

Summary

Java not only changes what can happen on a Web page, it also changes what can be retrieved and displayed on a Web page. Special handlers for new protocols and content extend what a Java-enabled browser can find and interpret. Java enables network information retrieval within applets, making it possible for an applet to "take over" a user's display and exhibit a series of network resources or provide a way for users to share information across a network.

PART

Getting Started

Putting Together Your Toolkit

7

by Michael Morrison

One of the most difficult aspects of learning and using Java is sorting out what the different applications of Java can do for you. There has and will continue to be much hype surrounding Java that can easily result in confusion as to what each new Java licensee brings to the table. Not only is Java quickly gaining acceptance as a programming standard, it is also spawning a new generation of development tools.

In this chapter, you learn about the various ways Java is being used in both new and existing products, including browsers and development tools. The goal is to provide you with a broad perspective on the Java development world so you can be more informed when deciding how to put together your own Java development toolkit. You will also learn about some of the most popular online resources for keeping up with the fast-moving animal known as Java.

Overview of Java Tools

The list of companies that have jumped up and pledged allegiance to Java is growing at a surprising rate. With the Java bandwagon steadily rolling along, it is somewhat difficult to see how and where Java fits into many of the products that promise Java support. This is especially true when it comes to Java development tools. The products and tools important to Java development can be broken down into three categories, which follow:

- Browsers
- Development Environments
- Programming Libraries

This chapter focuses on each of these categories and discusses the Java Developer's Kit and online sources of Java development information. Keep in mind that Java is still a growing technology, so many of the development tools are still in their infancy. Some haven't even reached the prototype stage, whereas a few others are ready for prime time. It's important for you to plan your Java development around what tools are available and what tools are on the horizon.

Browsers

The first category of Java applications to affect Java development is that of Web browsers. Without Java-compatible browsers, Java applets wouldn't be very useful. Java browsers practically serve as the operating system for Java programs. For this reason, Java is highly dependent on the availability and success of Java browsers. Fortunately, all the major players in the browser market have signed on to Java and promised to support it. Following is a list of major companies with Web browser products that have promised some support for Java either presently or in the near future:

Netscape

Sun

Microsoft

Spyglass

A quick overview of each of the major players and its connection to Java is presented in the following sections.

Netscape Navigator

The biggest player in the Web browser world, Netscape, is at the front of the Java support line. Netscape has already delivered a commercial browser with complete support for Java: Netscape Navigator 2.0. With the lion's share of the Web browser market prior to this release, Netscape Navigator alone will secure Java among Web users and developers alike.

Netscape has gone a step further than just supporting the Java language and run-time system. They also helped develop JavaScript, which is an object-based scripting language based on Java. The aim of JavaScript is to allow the rapid development of distributed client-server applications. However, the practical uses of JavaScript will no doubt expand as it gains acceptance. If you want to learn more about JavaScript, you're in luck; Part IX of this book, "JavaScript," is devoted entirely to JavaScript programming. If you want more information on Netscape Navigator itself, just sit tight because the next chapter is all about Netscape Navigator.

HotJava

The HotJava Web browser is Sun's contender in the browser market. Originally designed as an experiment in Java browser development, HotJava has become a powerful model for what the future holds for Web browsers. It isn't clear yet whether HotJava will end up being a serious competitor in the browser market, but there is no arguing its appeal to Java developers. Implemented entirely in Java itself, HotJava will no doubt be the most Java-compatible browser around. Regardless of whether HotJava catches on as a professional Web browser, it still serves as a very useful test bed for Java programmers.

Although it is still in an early alpha stage, HotJava already surpasses other browsers in terms of extensibility. HotJava is capable of dynamically handling and interacting with new object types and Internet protocols. This is the kind of extensibility that will be required of Web browsers in the already seriously muddied waters of the Internet. Sun has promised a commercial release of HotJava in the near future. For more details about HotJava, check out Chapter 9, "HotJava."

Microsoft Internet Explorer

You didn't seriously think Microsoft would sit idly by while Java soaked up so much press attention! Of course not. After some delay, Microsoft finally agreed to license the Java technology. It isn't clear yet exactly what technologies Microsoft plans to integrate Java into. It's safe to say that Microsoft's Internet Explorer Web browser will probably be the first Microsoft product to support Java. Considering the fact that Internet Explorer is tightly linked to Windows 95, it has the potential to gain a significant share of the Web browser market.

As of this writing, there is no tentative date for when a Java-compatible version of Internet Explorer will be available. Because Netscape has already beat them to the punch, you can probably expect Microsoft to get Internet Explorer up to speed with Java pretty rapidly.

Spyglass Mosaic

Spyglass Mosaic is another popular Web browser that has announced future support for Java. Like Microsoft, Spyglass has given no solid dates of when their Mosaic browser might be available with Java support. Again, with all of the different browsers battling head-to-head over supporting new technologies, you can probably expect a Java-compatible version of Mosaic very soon.

The Java Developer's Kit

The Java Developer's Kit (JDK) provides the core tools and information necessary for developing programs in Java. The JDK is the first thing you should take into consideration when putting together your own Java development toolkit. Although third-party add-ons and development environments promise to make Java development smoother and easier, the JDK provides all the essential tools and information necessary to write professional Java applets immediately. Also, the JDK is Sun's official development kit for Java, which means you can always count on it providing the most extensive Java support.

The JDK includes a Java runtime interpreter, a compiler, a debugger, lots of applet demos, and the complete Java API source code, along with a few other useful tools. For more information on the JDK, check out Chapter 10, "The Java Developer's Kit."

Development Environments

Currently, the most uncharted region of Java programming is that of development environments. In a time when developers have become spoiled with graphical drag-and-drop programming tools, everyone expects the same out of a Java development environment. Indeed, they are on their way, but Java is still very new.

Most of the big players in the programming-tool business have announced some type of development environment for Java. Some of this Java support will arrive in the form of add-ons for existing products, while others will be entirely new products. It's interesting to note that a few of the development environments are themselves being developed in Java, which means that they will be available for all of the platforms that support Java. All the Java development environments are covered in more detail in Chapter 11, "Other Tools and Environments."

Symantec Espresso

Symantec is the biggest PC-development tool player to have a Java development environment ready for testing. Symantec Espresso is an add-on for their Symantec C++ development system for Windows 95/NT that enables you to use the C++ facilities for Java development. Espresso features a project management system, a powerful editor, and browser tools. Symantec Espresso is already available and is a free add-on for users of Symantec C++.

Borland Latte

Borland, the developer of the popular Borland C++ and Delphi Windows development environments, was an early supporter of Java. Unlike Symantec, Borland has opted to develop an entirely new product for Java developers. Borland is developing their Java development environment, currently named Latte, completely in Java. This will enable them to break out of the PC market and sell Latte to Java developers on all Java-supported platforms.

Borland has stated that Latte will be highly derived from their successful Delphi product, which is a graphical development environment for Windows 95 that is based on object-oriented Pascal. An early version of the Latte Java debugger has been released, and holds a lot of promise coming from one of the strongest PC-development tool companies.

Microsoft Visual C++

Although there have been no formal announcements, it is very likely that Microsoft is busily working on their own Java development environment. Microsoft is committed to creating powerful development tools, and Java is no exception. In the meantime, the Visual C++ environment for Windows 95/NT is actually fairly well suited as-is for Java development. Chapter 11, "Other Tools and Environments," contains information on how to configure Visual C++ to work with Java.

JavaMaker

JavaMaker is a simple development environment—developed by Heechang Choi—that runs under Windows 95 and Windows NT. It doesn't have too many bells and whistles, but it does manage to put a front-end on the JDK. JavaMaker (currently still in beta) comes with a multiple document interface text editor and interfaces directly with the Java compiler and applet viewer. If you want to keep things simple, JavaMaker is a very useful application—even in its current prerelease state.

Natural Intelligence's Roaster

If you are a Macintosh user, you're probably thinking this discussion of development environments is skewed toward Windows. Not so! Natural Intelligence, the company that makes the popular Macintosh script editor Quick Code Pro, has released a Macintosh Java development environment. Natural Intelligence's Java Applet Development Kit, Roaster, provides an integrated development environment with a built-in class disassembler, debugger, and compiler. It is currently available for Power Macintosh, with a 68000 version expected soon.

Metrowerk's CodeWarrior

Lest you believe there is only one option for Macintosh Java programmers, Metrowerks has announced development of a Java environment based on their popular CodeWarrior C++ development environment. The Java environment, which is code-named Wired, is described by Metrowerks as a suite of Macintosh Java development tools. Metrowerks anticipates a first developer's release of their Java tools in the summer of 1996.

Silicon Graphic's Cosmo

Silicon Graphics has entered the Java foray in big way with its Cosmo development tools suite. The Cosmo technologies are aimed at providing more extensive multimedia and 3D graphics support to the Web. A core component of Cosmo is Cosmo Code, which is a Java development environment that promises to deliver a staggering array of features. Cosmo Code includes a runtime interpreter, compiler, graphical debugger, visual browser, and the Cosmo Motion and Cosmo MediaBase libraries. The core components of the Cosmo Code development kit are already available in beta form for Irix systems.

Programming Libraries

Because Java is object oriented, it is hard to overlook the potential for reusing Java objects. There is already a surprisingly large amount of Java classes available for free; most of which include source code. Additionally, a few commercial Java object libraries are appearing that show a lot of promise.

Even though the commercial Java tools market is still in an embryonic state, one company in particular looks poised to provide some very interesting and powerful class libraries: Dimension X. Dimension X currently has three Java class libraries nearing release: Ice, Liquid Reality, and JACK. Ice is a 3D graphics rendering package written in Java. Liquid Reality is a VRML toolkit, based on Ice, for creating and viewing 3D worlds on the Web. Finally, JACK (Java Animation Creation Kit) is a tool for creating Java animation applets through a simple drag-and-drop interface. For more information on VRML and Dimension X, see Chapter 34, "VRML and Java."

Online Resources

In the dynamic world of Java programming, nothing is perhaps more valuable than the Java Web sites. The various Java Web sites scattered around provide the latest breaking Java news and most recent releases of Java tools, not to mention a vast repository of educational material.

Sun's Java Site

The official Java site on the Web is maintained by Sun and contains all the latest Java information and tools produced by Sun. You'll definitely want to keep an eye on this site as it is the central location for obtaining Java updates. It also has a pretty extensive set of online documentation, including a really cool Java tutorial. The URL for the Sun Java site follows:

```
http://www.javasoft.com/
```

Figure 7.1 shows what Sun's Java Web site looks like.

FIGURE 7.1.

Sun's Java Web site.

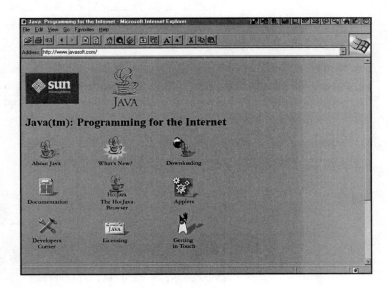

Gamelan

Look no further than Gamelan for the end-all Java resource directory! With the possible exception of the official Java Web site at Sun, Gamelan is by far the most useful and comprehensive source of Java information anywhere. It has Java conveniently divided up into different categories, with each leading to a wealth of information and sample applets. Check out Gamelan yourself and you'll see what I mean. Its URL follows:

```
http://www.gamelan.com/
```

Figure 7.2 shows what the Gamelan Web site looks like.

96

FIGURE 7.2.

The Gamelan Web site.

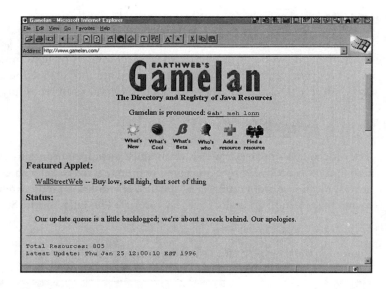

SunWorld Online

SunWorld Online is an online journal published by IDG Communications that often contains useful information that relates to Java. It has a regular column called "Java Developer" that usually tackles an interesting topic related to Java programming. SunWorld Online is located at the following URL:

```
http://www.sun.com/sunworldonline/
```

Figure 7.3 shows what an issue of SunWorld Online looks like.

FIGURE 7.3.

The SunWorld Online Web site.

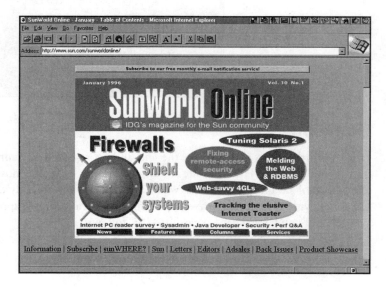

Digital Espresso

Digital Espresso is an online weekly summary of the traffic appearing in the various Java mailing lists and newsgroups. Digital Espresso is an excellent Java resource because it pulls information from a variety of sources into a single Web site. Following is the URL for Digital Espresso:

```
http://www.io.org/~mentor/phpl.cgi?J___Notes.html
```

Figure 7.4 shows what the Digital Espresso Web site looks like.

FIGURE 7.4.

The Digital Espresso Web site.

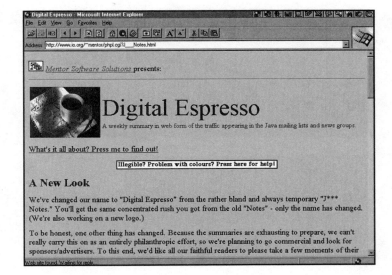

Summary

You learned in this chapter that putting together a Java toolkit isn't as easy as going out and buying a development environment. Because Java is such a new technology, many of the development options for developers have yet to mature into solid applications. At this stage, it's important to know what is available and what is being promised in the future.

You also learned about the different Java-compatible Web browsers and development environments that are in the works, along with a few that are available now. You then learned about the Java Developer's Kit and some class libraries that have the potential to raise the ante on Java development. Finally, some online resources for keeping up-to-date with Java were discussed.

Because Java-supported browsers are so important to Java developers, the next chapter focuses on what will possibly be the most established of the Java Web browsers: Netscape Navigator.

Netscape

8

*by Michael
Morrison*

IN THIS CHAPTER

Netscape is without a doubt the largest player in the Web browser business. It is insanely popular Netscape Navigator Web browser dwarfs all other browsers in terms of market share, with no signs of any significant losses in the near future. It is certainly going to see some fierce competition, but Netscape is staying on top of things and integrating the latest technology into Netscape Navigator.

Java currently is the most important of these new technologies. With the advent of Navigator 2.0, Netscape has provided complete support for the Java language. Additionally, Netscape has collaborated with Sun to create a scripting language based on Java called JavaScript. Together, these two technologies promise to keep Netscape firmly rooted as the king of the Web browser hill. For Web developers, this means that interactivity on the Web has finally come of age.

NOTE

As of this writing, the Macintosh and Windows 3.1 versions of Netscape Navigator still do not have support for Java. However, you can expect support to arrive for these platforms in the near future.

In this chapter, you learn about how Java and JavaScript impact Netscape's new product line, especially the Navigator Web browser. Netscape Navigator 2.0 provides very strong support for Java and JavaScript, as you'll see.

Netscape Products

Before getting into the Java-specific aspects of the latest release of Netscape Navigator, it's important to bring you up to date with this version of the popular Web browser, along with other Web-related products being offered by Netscape. First, Netscape has opted for two different versions of Navigator, standard and gold. Navigator 2.0 is the logical upgrade to the original Navigator Web browser. Navigator Gold 2.0 includes Navigator 2.0, along with a Web development environment, enabling users to edit HTML files graphically.

Additionally, Netscape is releasing Live Wire, which is a Web development environment that provides the tools necessary to create and manage Web sites. Live Wire includes Navigator Gold and the JavaScript scripting language. And if Live Wire isn't enough for you, Netscape also has Live Wire Pro, which adds to Live Wire the capability to browse, search, and update relational databases.

To summarize, Netscape is offering the following Java-supported products to the Web community:

Navigator 2.0

Navigator Gold 2.0

Live Wire

Live Wire Pro

Netscape's new Web tools will no doubt set the standard for others to follow. With its new features and wide support for new technologies, Navigator 2.0 should easily match the popularity of its predecessor. However, as impressive as the new Navigator browser appears to be, Netscape may ultimately gain more from the release of Navigator Gold and Live Wire. The early integration of Java into all of these products has set the stage to bring Java to the Web in full force.

Navigator 2.0

Navigator 2.0 is the first major upgrade to the immensely popular Netscape Navigator Web browser. This upgrade includes improved e-mail, newsgroup, FTP, and navigation capabilities, along with inline multimedia plug-ins. The inline multimedia plug-ins include support for Adobe Acrobat PDF documents and Macromedia Director presentations, among others. The Navigator plug-in supporting Macromedia Director presentations is called Shockwave. Additionally, a plug-in supporting Apple's QuickTime multimedia standard is expected soon. Navigator 2.0 is also the first browser to provide complete Java support. Figure 8.1 shows what Netscape Navigator 2.0 looks like.

FIGURE 8.1.

Netscape Navigator 2.0.

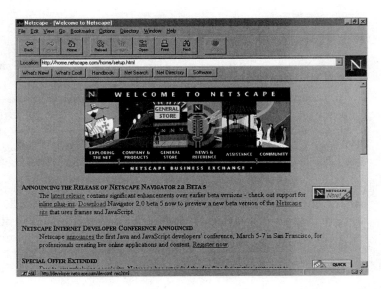

The new Navigator update also adds enhanced performance through client-side image maps, progressive JPEG images, and streaming audio and video. Its new security features include digital ID, secure courier for financial transactions, and secure e-mail and news. Navigator 2.0 also features advanced layout capabilities, including frames, which enable the display of multiple, independently scrollable panels on a single screen. Each of these panels can have a different Web address as its source.

Navigator Gold 2.0

Navigator Gold 2.0 is a tool built around Navigator 2.0 that enables Web developers to design and edit HTML documents graphically. The HTML editor is integrated into the Navigator environment, and effectively combines editing and viewing functions into one application. It will be interesting to see how Navigator Gold is perceived by the Web development community, as it is really the first attempt by a major Web player at providing a graphical HTML development system.

Live Wire and Live Wire Pro

Netscape's Live Wire goes a step beyond Navigator Gold by providing an environment that lets developers graphically build and manage applications and multimedia content for the Internet. Live Wire's graphical design approach is aimed at simplifying the management of complex Web document hyperlinks. Live Wire includes Navigator Gold and the JavaScript scripting language. Netscape is also offering Live Wire Pro, which adds database connectivity to Live Wire. With Live Wire Pro, users can interact with relational databases on the Web.

Netscape Support for Java

Netscape Navigator 2.0 is the first major Web browser to provide support for Java. Although this aspect of Navigator has generated a significant amount of press attention, it's important to realize that the bulk of Navigator's Java support takes place behind the scenes. Many Navigator users will likely see Web pages come to life and not fully realize that Java is the technology making it all happen. The point is that the Java support in Navigator affects the content of Web pages viewed in Navigator a great deal, but affects the Navigator interface and options very little.

Because the Java support in Navigator is a behind-the-scenes issue, it isn't always clear what parts of a Web page are using Java. If you saw a Java Web page and didn't know anything about Java, you might just think that Web page developers were pulling off neat tricks with CGI or some other scripting language. But you are well on your way to becoming a Java expert, so you know better; Java opens the door to doing things that are impossible with scripting languages like CGI.

Java programs appear in Navigator as applets that are embedded in Web pages. Java applets are referenced in HTML source code using a special APPLET tag. Navigator parses these tags and automatically launches an internal Java interpreter that executes the Java applets. By implementing a Java runtime interpreter, Navigator provides the layer of functionality that allows all Java applets to run. Beyond this, there isn't really anything particularly special about the way Navigator supports embedded Java applets. This simply means that the only significant component in Navigator necessary to support Java is the integrated Java runtime interpreter.

Other than seeing functionality in Web pages that you've never seen before, there's not much in Navigator to inform you that a Java applet is running. A few small things you might notice are the various messages that appear in the Navigator status bar when an applet is preparing to run. You may also notice a significant delay while Java applets are being transferred to your machine, especially those that use a lot of graphics and sound.

Another Java-specific feature of Navigator is located under the Options menu. The Show Java Console menu command causes Navigator to open a Java Output console window. The output window displays output generated by currently running Java applets. Figure 8.2 shows what the Navigator Java Output window looks like.

FIGURE 8.2.

The Netscape Navigator Java Output window.

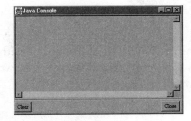

Configuring Java with Netscape

When you first install Netscape Navigator, Java support is automatically installed and enabled by default. Remember, the Java support in Navigator is built-in, so you don't have to do anything special to get it working. As a result, you can immediately start viewing and interacting with Java-enhanced Web sites.

The only real Java-specific option in Navigator is whether or not you want Java support enabled. Most of the time you will want to leave Java support enabled, so that you can enjoy the benefits of the Java technology. However, if you are experiencing problems with Java or with a particular Java Web site, you can disable Navigator Java support. To do this, select the Security Preferences command from the Navigator Options menu. The Disable Java checkbox is used to enable/disable Java support. Figure 8.3 shows the Navigator Security Preferences dialog box.

If Java is disabled, you will still be able to view Java-enhanced Web sites, you just won't be able to view or interact with the Java applets contained within them.

FIGURE 8.3.

The Netscape Navigator Security Preferences dialog box.

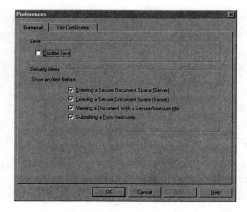

Java Applets

There are already many Java applets available for you to run and try out, ranging from games to educational instruction. Most of them come with source code, so you can use them as references for your own Java programs. Figure 8.4 shows a crossword puzzle Java applet running in Netscape Navigator.

FIGURE 8.4.

A crossword puzzle Java applet running in Netscape Navigator.

The different applications for Java are limitless. Figure 8.5 shows a very interesting application of Java: an instructional dance applet.

FIGURE 8.5.

An instructional dance Java applet running in Netscape Navigator.

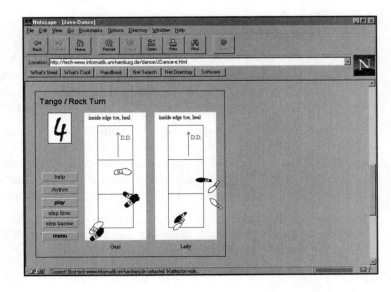

If you want to check out some of the Java applet demos, take a look at the Java Applet Demos Web page on Netscape's Web site, which is shown in Figure 8.6:

```
http://www.netscape.com/comprod/products/navigator/version_2.0/java_applets/
```

FIGURE 8.6.

Netscape's Java Applet Demos Web site.

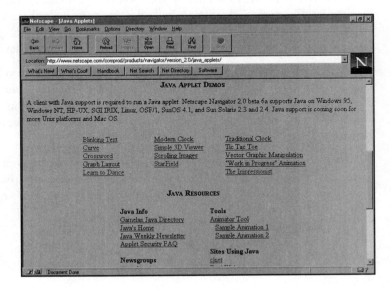

If you want to find out more about creating your own Java applets that can be integrated into Web pages, check out Part V of this book, "Applet Programming."

JavaScript

JavaScript is a scripting language described by Netscape as a lightweight version of Java. JavaScript promises to enable less technical Web users and developers the capability to create interactive content for the Web. You can think of JavaScript as a higher level complement to Java. Netscape Navigator supports JavaScript by providing an internal JavaScript interpreter.

JavaScript was designed with the goal of creating a simple and easy-to-use cross-platform scripting language that could connect objects and resources from both HTML and Java. While Java applets are primarily developed by programmers, JavaScript is intended to be used by HTML document authors to dynamically control the interaction and behavior of Web pages. JavaScript is unique in that is has been designed to be complementary to both HTML and Java.

If you can believe it, JavaScript is actually an even newer technology than Java. Because JavaScript was developed jointly by Sun and Netscape, it is almost guaranteed to be widely adopted by the Web community. However, it may still take some time before you see truly compelling applications of JavaScript. Part IX of this book, "JavaScript," is entirely devoted to understanding and using JavaScript.

Summary

The latest release of Netscape's line of Web products promises to further establish Netscape as the premier Web tool provider. A central technology present in these tools is Java, which brings interactivity to the Web. Netscape Navigator, along with already being the most popular Web browser available, is the first major Web browser to fully support Java.

In this chapter, you learned about the different tools available from Netscape and how Java relates to them. You also learned about JavaScript, and how it is positioned to provide a higher level option to HTML developers wishing to add interactivity without learning Java inside and out. Netscape's early support for both Java and JavaScript is a sure sign that these technologies are here to stay.

Now that you have an idea about how the most popular Web browser supports Java, you may be interested in learning about a new browser developed by the creators of Java, Sun Microsystems. The next chapter takes a close look at HotJava, Sun's new Web browser that is tightly integrated with Java.

HotJava

9

*by Michael
Morrison*

Java applets are only as useful as the Web browsers that support them. Although Netscape Navigator is certainly a strong contender for the Java support crown, Sun has its own browser that is specifically designed with Java in mind: HotJava. The HotJava Web browser builds on the techniques established by NCSA Mosaic and Netscape Navigator, while adding the capability to add new behaviors dynamically. The tight link to the Java language is what enables HotJava to have this dynamic behavior.

In this chapter, you learn all about HotJava, including its major features and how to install and use it. Although HotJava as a software product is still in the development stages, it is readily available and quite usable in its current alpha form. This chapter explores the primary features of HotJava and how they impact Web navigation and the Java language.

This Is HotJava

Before getting into the specifics of how to install and use HotJava, it's important to take a look at why HotJava is important. Actually, if you first want to literally take a look at HotJava, check out Figure 9.1.

FIGURE 9.1.

The HotJava Web browser.

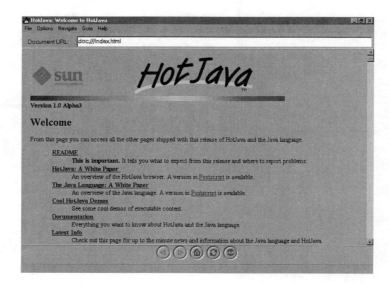

Figure 9.1 shows what HotJava looks like. You'll learn about how to use HotJava a little later in this chapter. For now, it's important to understand why HotJava is significant as a Web browser. There are a variety of technical innovations in HotJava that promise to make it more extensible than other Web browsers. These innovations stem largely from the fact that HotJava is designed around supporting the Java language.

The primary innovation that sets HotJava apart from other browsers is its extensibility. Where other browsers have most or all of their components hardwired to the executable browser application, HotJava opts for a more distributed approach. This means that by itself, HotJava doesn't really support any object types or Internet protocols. But its extensible design provides a very open path to add support without modifying the HotJava application itself. Furthermore, HotJava can be extended to provide new support automatically and on demand without the user even having to know.

Following is a list of the major features in HotJava:

- Dynamic Object Types
- Dynamic Protocols
- Network Security

Dynamic Object Types

Along with dynamic content within Web pages, HotJava also aims to be dynamic on a few other fronts. One of these fronts is the support for dynamic object types. An object type refers basically to a file format, such as the popular GIF (Graphics Interchange Format) graphics files. Although most Web browsers provide support for the most popular object types right now, who's to say what new object types will appear in the future? Obviously no one knows what object types will become popular in the future. For this reason, HotJava takes an open-ended approach to supporting object types. HotJava is capable of dynamically linking to Java code for handling a particular object type on the fly. Rather than Sun having to create a new version of HotJava each time a new object type appears on the scene, HotJava can instead locate an object handler and deal with it dynamically. Incidentally, object handlers are also known as content handlers. Figure 9.2 shows the difference between HotJava's dynamic connection to objects and a conventional Web browser's built-in support for objects.

Notice in the figure that both approaches provide similar support for object types that are currently popular. The difference arises when new types are introduced; HotJava transparently attaches to the handlers for new object types, whereas other browsers must implement handlers internally.

You may be wondering where the object handlers come from, and how HotJava knows about them to begin with. Typically, the vendor that creates an object will also create a handler routine for interpreting the object. As long as the handler is present on a server with the objects in question, HotJava can link to the code and automatically upgrade itself to support the new object type. While other Web browser developers are busily hacking in patches to support new object types, HotJava users will be automatically and transparently upgrading each time they encounter a new object type.

FIGURE 9.2.

*How HotJava and
conventional Web browsers
differ in their handling of
objects.*

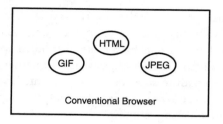

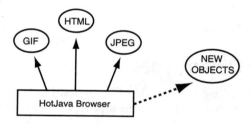

Dynamic Protocols

Similar to its dynamic support for new object types, HotJava also takes a dynamic approach to handling new Internet protocols. The most important components of the Internet are the protocols used for each medium of communication, such as HTTP or FTP. Think back to the days before the HTTP protocol and you'll realize what I mean! As with objects, there is no way to foresee what new Internet protocols will spring up in the future. The best way to handle this unknown is to anticipate a certain flux in protocol growth and write applications that can adapt to change. Sun did exactly this by designing HotJava so that it could dynamically link in support for new protocols.

You are probably familiar with Internet URLs, which define the location of Internet resources. An example URL follows:

```
http://www.javasoft.com/
```

This URL is for Sun's Java home page. As you can see, the protocol type for this URL is specified at the beginning of the URL name. In this case, the protocol type is specified as http, which stands for hypertext transfer protocol. Most Web browsers have built-in functionality to handle protocols such as HTTP. HotJava, on the other hand, looks externally to handle different protocols. When HotJava encounters a URL, it uses the protocol name to determine which protocol handler to use to find a document. Like a handler for an object, a protocol handler is a separate piece of code that defines how to interpret information from a particular protocol. Figure 9.3 shows the difference between how HotJava and conventional browsers manage protocols.

FIGURE 9.3.

How HotJava and conventional Web browsers differ in their handling of protocols.

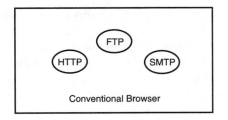

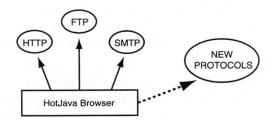

You may have noticed that Figure 9.3 looks very similar to Figure 9.2. Indeed, HotJava's support for new protocols parallels its support for new object types. The same approach of forcing outside handlers to provide the specific implementations for new objects works equally well when dealing with new protocols.

Network Security

When you start thinking about interactive content and what it means to the broad base of users it will affect, there is an unavoidable issue of security. To get an idea of how important the issue of security is, think back to how things were before the Web. Prior to the Web, online services, independent bulletin boards, and private networks served as the primary electronic communication mediums. Most of these mediums were and still are completely based on static content. Even so, the instances of viruses and other security-related problems have always been in relative abundance. In most of these cases, users would knowingly transfer a file to their computer that was assumed to be safe. The file would end up doing harm to their machine once it was transferred. Obviously, the users wouldn't have transferred the file if they had known about the virus beforehand. The point is that even with users having complete control over which files are transferred, viruses have still flourished.

Now consider the possibilities for security breaches with interactive content in the global Internet environment. Given that users are able to interact with Web pages in an interactive environment, the software must be able to respond dynamically. You've probably guessed that this creates a potentially dangerous situation. This brings us to the next key issue in the design of HotJava: security.

In HotJava, you can specify security options relating to what access you want to allow incoming executable content to have to your machine. You can specify whether and how much you want to allow applets to be able to read, write, or change files on your machine. You can set up security regions in HotJava by creating firewalls. A *firewall* is typically a set of computers within a certain domain name. Usually these computers are assumed to be safe, so they are listed as being located behind the firewall. You'll learn more about configuring firewalls later in this chapter.

Java and HotJava

The majority of the features implemented in HotJava stem from the fact that HotJava is designed around supporting Java. Before getting into more specifics regarding HotJava, it is important to clarify the relationship between Java and HotJava.

To recap prior chapters, Java is an object-oriented programming language derived in many ways from C++. Java enables you to write programs and applets that can be embedded in Web pages and executed interactively. HotJava is a Web browser written in Java that implements object and protocol handlers as external libraries. HotJava is akin to Netscape Navigator or NCSA Mosaic, with the primary difference being that it is written in the Java language and is far more extensible.

Java Versions

The Java language and HotJava browser are both very new technologies that are still in the developmental stages. The first released version of the Java language was known as the alpha release. A decent number of programs were written under the alpha release and are still around. However, Sun later released a beta version of Java with some major changes to the programming interface. This resulted in a rift between programs written using the alpha release of Java and programs written using the beta release. Add to this confusion the release of a final version of Java.

With the release of the beta version of Java, Sun declared the Java API frozen, meaning that none of the existing classes would be modified in the final release. However, this didn't restrict Sun from adding new classes and methods to Java; it just meant they couldn't change the old ones. This results in backward compatibility between the final and beta versions of Java; all beta programs should compile and run fine under the final release of Java.

The remaining problem then is what to do about the alpha programs still in existence? Most developers have already ported or begun porting their alpha programs to the beta, and now, final releases. All new Java development should be focused on the final release.

HotJava's Support for Java

But there's always a catch! The problem right now is that Sun has focused its efforts on polishing Java, and has kind of dropped the ball on bringing HotJava up to date. What this means is that the alpha release of HotJava, which is the latest, only supports alpha Java applets. You can't program to the final Java API and incorporate the applets into the current version of HotJava. Hopefully, by the time you read this Sun will be closer to releasing a beta or even final version of HotJava, but it's still too early to guess.

So, you may be wondering how to deal with this problem? Do you go ahead and write outdated alpha code so you can use HotJava, or do you blindly write final code and pray that a new version of HotJava that will run the final code will be released soon? The answer is neither. In light of this problem, Sun released an applet viewer program that supports the final release of Java. Additionally, Netscape Navigator 2.0 is supposed to fully support the Java final release. You'll learn more about the applet viewer in Chapter 10, "The Java Developer's Kit." You can use either of these applications as a test bed for final release Java applets.

You're probably wondering why bother discussing HotJava when it's currently not even useful for working with the final release of Java? The answer is that HotJava is an important technology, and all release delays aside, it will still be an important application for Web users and Java programmers in the future. Furthermore, because it is itself written in Java, it will be without a doubt the most Java-compatible browser around. In the meantime, you can still have a lot of fun with HotJava by running the many alpha Java programs that are available.

Setting Up HotJava

Installing and configuring HotJava is pretty straightforward. Before you begin installing HotJava, you may want to check and see if there is a newer release than the one you have. At the time of this writing, the latest release of HatJava was alpha release 3. This version will run alpha Java applets fine, but you may want to check directly with Sun to find out the latest version of HotJava available. Sun maintains a Web site devoted entirely to Java and HotJava. You actually saw the Java URL earlier in this chapter, but here it is again:

```
http://www.javasoft.com/
```

This is the same place where you can download the latest release of the Java Developer's Kit (JDK). You'll learn more about the JDK in Chapter 10. This is also the primary location for learning the latest news and support issues surrounding Java and HotJava. Figure 7.1 in Chapter 7 shows what the Java Web site at Sun looks like.

HotJava usually comes compressed in a self-extracting archive. To install HotJava, you simply execute the archive file from the directory where you want HotJava installed. For example, if you want to install HotJava on a Windows 95 machine, you would execute the self-extracting archive file from the C:\ root directory. The archive will automatically create a HotJava directory below C:\ and build a directory structure within it to contain the rest of the support files. All the related files are automatically copied to the correct locations in the HotJava directory structure.

> **NOTE**
>
> The current alpha release of HotJava only supports the Solaris and Windows 95/NT platforms. It is expected that a commercial release of HotJava will also support Macintosh and Windows 3.1, but at this point it is still speculation.

Once HotJava is installed, you are ready to run it. You run HotJava by executing the program HotJava.exe, which is located in the HotJava\bin directory. You can specify a URL as a parameter to HotJava. If specified, HotJava will open the document specified by this URL rather than the default URL document. Assuming you don't enter a URL when you start HotJava, you will be presented with the Welcome page shown in Figure 9.1 earlier. You'll definitely want to try out some of the links on this page later. If this is the first time you've run HotJava, you'll also be presented with the Security dialog box shown in Figure 9.4. Just click the Apply button for now and everything will be OK. You'll learn more about the security options in this dialog box a little later in this chapter.

FIGURE 9.4.

The HotJava Security dialog box.

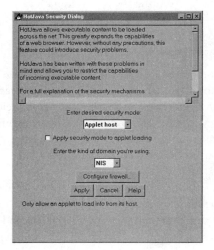

HotJava uses three system environment variables to determine various options for the browser. These environment variables follow:

- HOTJAVA_HOME
- WWW_HOME

- `HOTJAVA_READ_PATH`
- `HOTJAVA_WRITE_PATH`

The `HOTJAVA_HOME` variable specifies the path where HotJava looks for resources in order to run. `HOTJAVA_HOME` defaults to being set to the directory where HotJava was installed. The `WWW_HOME` variable specifies the default home page used in HotJava. This is the page HotJava attempts to load on startup. `WWW_HOME` defaults to being unset. If it is left unset, HotJava defaults to the URL `doc:///index.html`, which is the Welcome page.

The `HOTJAVA_READ_PATH` variable specifies a colon-separated list of files and directories to which Java applets have read access. The default setting for `HOTJAVA_READ_PATH` is `<hotjava-install-dir>:$HOME/public_html/`. You give read access to new files and directories by adding a colon and the file or directory onto the end of the list. For example, if you wanted to give the `Docs` directory read access, and it was located just off of the root directory, you would set `HOTJAVA_READ_PATH` to the following:

`<hotjava-install-dir>:$HOME/public_html/:$HOME/Docs/`

Similarly, `HOTJAVA_WRITE_PATH` specifies a list of files and directories that Java applets have write access to. Any files or directories not explicitly given read or write permission through these variables will be inaccessible to Java applets.

Using HotJava

Now that you have HotJava up and running, you're ready to learn some more about how to use it. The HotJava browser application is composed of five major parts, which follow:

- The menu bar
- The URL edit box
- The client area
- The toolbar
- The status bar

To see where these parts are located in HotJava, refer back to Figure 9.1, which shows the HotJava application window. The HotJava menu bar is located just below the caption bar for the application, and consists of a series of pull-down menus. You'll learn about the specific menu commands a little later in this chapter. The URL edit box is located just below the menu bar and is used to manually enter document URLs. You'll learn how to enter URLs in HotJava in the next section of this chapter.

The client area of HotJava is located just below the URL edit box and extends down to the toolbar near the bottom of the application window. The client area takes up most of HotJava's screen real estate, and is where documents are displayed. Because the client area is where documents are displayed, it is also the display area for Java applets.

The HotJava toolbar consists of five buttons and is located just below the client area. These buttons are used to navigate through Web pages. The Left and Right Arrow buttons are used to move forward and backward through documents that you have already viewed. The Home button takes you to the default home page for HotJava. If you recall, this page is specified by the WWW_HOME environment variable. The Reload button is used to reload the current document. And finally, the Stop button is used to stop the loading of a document.

The status bar is used to inform you of the status of operations. For example, while a document is being fetched, the status bar displays a message notifying you that it is fetching the document. The status bar also displays the names of links to documents when you drag the mouse over them.

Working with URLs

Document URLs are specified by entering them into the URL edit box near the top of the HotJava application window. To open a new URL document, simply type the name into the edit box and press Return. HotJava will immediately start fetching the document, which will be evident by the message displayed in the status bar.

To stop fetching a document, just click on the Stop button. The Stop button only stops the loading of HTML pages; it does not stop or even affect any running Java applets.

Menu Commands

The HotJava menu commands provide access to all the functionality in HotJava. These menu commands can be grouped into five categories, which correspond to the pull-down menu names shown in the menu bar. Following are the menu command categories:

- File
- Options
- Navigate
- Goto
- Help

File Commands

The File menu commands consist of commands related to managing URL documents. Some commands are listed under the File menu but remain unsupported in the alpha release of HotJava. The following File menu commands are supported under the alpha 3 release of HotJava:

- Open
- Reload

■ View Source
■ Quit

The Open command displays a dialog box where you can specify a document URL to open. This functionality is identical to typing a document URL in the URL edit box below the menu bar. The Reload command reloads the current document. Selecting the Reload command is exactly the same as clicking the Reload button on the toolbar. The View Source command opens up a window containing the HTML source code for the current Web page. Finally, the Quit command exits the HotJava application.

Options Commands

The Options menu commands are used to specify HotJava environment options. A few commands are listed under the Options menu but remain unsupported in the alpha release of HotJava. The following Options commands are supported under the alpha 3 release of HotJava:

■ Security
■ Properties
■ Flush Cache
■ Progress Monitor

The Security command opens a dialog box where you specify the level of security to be applied to incoming executable content. This is the same dialog shown in Figure 9.4 that is displayed the first time you run HotJava. The dialog box provides the following security modes to choose from: No access, Applet host, Firewall, or Unrestricted. The No access security mode specifies that HotJava cannot load any Java applets. This is the safest, but obviously most restricted security mode. The next safest mode is Applet host, which specifies that HotJava can only run Java applets residing on the local machine. Next comes the Firewall security mode, which specifies that HotJava can only run applets from behind the firewall. Finally, the Unrestricted mode allows HotJava to load any Java applets.

If you select the Firewall security mode, you'll need to configure the firewall. You do this by clicking the Configure Firewall button. When you click this button, the dialog box shown in Figure 9.5 appears.

The purpose of this dialog box is to enable you to specify which systems are located behind the firewall; that is, which systems are considered safe. You specify systems within the firewall by entering the domain or host name of the system, selecting whether it is a domain or host in the drop-down list, and then clicking the Add button. You can change or delete firewall entries by using the Change and Delete buttons. Once you are happy with the firewall settings, click Apply to accept them.

The Properties menu command opens a dialog box which lets you change general HotJava properties. The Properties dialog box is shown in Figure 9.6.

FIGURE 9.5.

The HotJava Configure Firewall dialog box.

FIGURE 9.6.

The HotJava Properties dialog box.

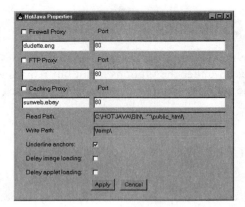

The first few properties in this dialog box enable you to specify different proxies and their associated ports. The Firewall Proxy refers to the host name and port number of a local firewall proxy server. The FTP Proxy is the host name and port number of an HTTP proxy to use for all FTP URLs. Finally, the Caching Proxy refers to the host name and port number of a caching server. If you don't want to use any of the proxies, just leave the check boxes next to each one unchecked.

The Properties dialog also enables you to view the read and write paths for HotJava. These are the same paths specified by the HOTJAVA_READ_PATH and HOTJAVA_WRITE_PATH environment variables. You cannot modify these variables from the Properties dialog box.

The Underline anchors property determines whether or not HTML anchors (links) are underlined when displayed. The Delay image loading and Delay applet loading properties determine how images and applets are loaded in HotJava. If you check these options, HotJava will only load images and applets when you click on them. This is sometimes useful when you have a slow connection. If you leave these options unchecked, HotJava will load all images and applets along with the rest of an HTML page.

The Flush Cache menu command flushes any images and audio that have been cached by HotJava. Typically HotJava will cache the most recently used images and audio to your hard drive in order to speed up loading time. You may want to use the Flush Cache command if you know a cached image or sound has changed and should be transferred again.

The Progress Monitor menu command brings up a window with a progress monitor for seeing how much of a document has been loaded. Figure 9.7 shows what the progress monitor looks like in action.

FIGURE 9.7.

The HotJava Progress
Monitor window.

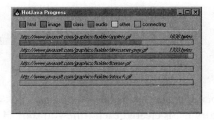

The progress monitor is considered an experimental tool, but is still interesting in its current form. You can watch and see the status of different objects as they are loaded.

Navigate Commands

The Navigate menu commands provide you with a means to navigate through documents. The commands listed under the Navigate pull-down menu that are supported under the alpha release of HotJava follow:

- Forward
- Back
- Home
- Show History
- Add Current to Hotlist
- Show Hotlist

The Forward command moves to the document viewed prior to selecting the Back command or button. This means that the Forward command can only be used after you have used the Back command. The Back command moves back to the last document viewed. The Home command displays the default HotJava home page, which is specified in the WWW_HOME environment variable. All three of these commands perform the exact same functionality as their equivalent buttons on the toolbar.

HotJava automatically maintains a history list of documents that have been viewed. The Show History command displays the history list and enables you to revisit a document in the list. Figure 9.8 shows what the HotJava History List window looks like.

FIGURE 9.8.

The HotJava History List window.

To open a document in the history list, simply click on the document and click the Visit button. The history list is cleared each time you start HotJava.

Along with the history list, HotJava also keeps up with a hotlist, which is a list of favorite documents. The Add Current to Hotlist command adds the currently viewed document to the hotlist. To see what documents are in the hotlist, use the Show Hotlist command. HotJava's hotlist is very similar in function to Netscape's bookmarks and Internet Explorer's favorite places. When you select Show Hotlist, you'll see the window shown in Figure 9.9.

FIGURE 9.9.

The HotJava Hotlist window.

You can visit a document in the hotlist by clicking on the document and clicking the Visit button. You can also delete documents from the list using the Delete button. There is one additional feature of the hotlist that you may be curious about: a check box labeled *In Goto Menu*. This check box enables you to choose documents in the hotlist that will also appear as menu selections under the Goto pull-down menu.

Goto Commands

The Goto menu consists of a single command and multiple document links. The Goto menu is used as a list of links to the most important documents in the hotlist. You can quickly open documents in the Goto menu by selecting the document entry in the menu. The only command supported under the Goto menu is Add Current, which adds the current document to the hotlist and the Goto menu itself.

Help Commands

The Help menu consists of a variety of links to useful HTML documents, along with one command. Each document link is pretty self-explanatory, so you can explore them on your own. The only command on the Help menu is the Search HotJava Documentation command. This command enables you to search the HotJava documentation for a particular topic. Figure 9.10 shows what the documentation search dialog box looks like.

FIGURE 9.10.

The HotJava documenta-tion search dialog box.

To search on a topic, just type the topic in the query edit box and click the Search button. Documents found matching the topic are listed in the list box. To go to one of the matching documents, just click on it in the list box.

Status Icons

HotJava provides visual status indicators when it is loading document information. These indicators, or icons, are displayed in place of the object they are loading until the object has been successfully loaded. The different status icons supported by HotJava follow:

- Raised gray box
- Yellow box
- Yellow box with arrow
- Orange box
- Red box
- Red box with arrow

The raised gray box means that an image or applet is still loading. The yellow box means that delayed image loading is in effect for an image. To load the image you must click on the icon. The yellow box with an arrow means that delayed image loading is in effect for an image and that the image is a link to another document. Clicking on the arrow opens the linked document, and clicking on any other part of the icon loads the image. The orange box is similar to the yellow box except it deals with Java applets rather than images; it specifies that delayed applet loading is in effect for an applet. To load the applet, just click on the icon.

Both red box icons mean that an error has occurred while attempting to load an image or applet. The difference between the two is that the icon with an arrow specifies that a document link has failed to load, rather than the image or applet itself.

Summary

In this chapter you learned all about the HotJava Web browser and how it relates to Java. It is not clear whether Sun intends for HotJava to be a serious competitor in the Web browser market. Nevertheless, it will be the browser to watch when it comes to providing complete Java support in the future. As a result of its support for Java, HotJava has the potential to be a technologically superior Web browser through its extensible support of dynamic content, objects, and Internet protocols.

The only downside to HotJava at this point is that it is still an unfinished product, and as a result has a versioning conflict with the latest version of Java. Nevertheless, it is only a matter of time before HotJava will be a crucial Internet technology, simply because of its tight link to the Java language.

Now that you have HotJava pretty well figured out, it's time to press on and learn more about Java itself. The next chapter covers the Java Developer's Kit, which is the standard toolkit for developing Java programs.

The Java Developer's Kit

10

by Michael Morrison

IN THIS CHAPTER

The Java Developer's Kit, or JDK, is a comprehensive set of tools, utilities, documentation, and sample code for developing Java programs. Without it, you wouldn't be able to do much with Java. This chapter focuses on the JDK and the tools and information supplied with it. Although some of the tools are discussed in more detail in later chapters, this chapter gives you a broad perspective on using the tools to develop Java programs using the JDK.

In this chapter you learn what tools are shipped in the JDK and how they are used in a typical Java development environment. With the information presented in this chapter, you will be well on your way to delving further into Java development; the Java Developer's Kit is the first step toward learning to program in Java.

Getting the Latest Version

Before you get started learning about the Java Developer's Kit, it's important to make sure that you have the latest version. As of this writing, the latest version of the JDK is the final release 1. This version will probably be around for a while, so you're probably OK. Just to be sure, you can check Sun's Java Web site to see what the latest version is. The URL for this site follows:

```
http://www.javasoft.com/
```

This Web site provides all the latest news and information regarding Java, including the latest release of the JDK. Keep in mind that Java is a new technology that is still in a state of rapid change. Be sure to keep an eye on the Java Web site for the latest information.

The JDK usually comes as a compressed self-extracting archive file. To install the JDK, simply execute the archive file from the directory where you want the JDK installed. The archive will automatically create a `java` directory within the directory you extract it from, and build a directory structure to contain the rest of the JDK support files. All the related files are then copied to the correct locations in the JDK directory structure automatically.

Overview

The Java Developer's Kit contains a variety of tools and Java development information. Following is a list of the main components of the JDK:

- The Runtime Interpreter
- The Compiler
- The Applet Viewer
- The Debugger
- The Class File Disassembler
- The Header and Stub File Generator
- The Documentation Generator

- Applet Demos
- API Source Code

The runtime interpreter is the core runtime module for the Java system. The compiler, applet viewer, debugger, class file disassembler, header and stub file generator, and documentation generator are the primary tools used by Java developers. The applet demos are interesting examples of Java applets, which all come with complete source code. And finally, if you are interested in looking under the hood of Java, the complete source code for the Java API (Application Programming Interface) classes is provided.

The Runtime Interpreter

The Java runtime interpreter (java) is a stand-alone version of the Java interpreter built into the HotJava browser. The runtime interpreter provides the support to run Java executable programs in compiled, bytecode format. The runtime interpreter acts as a command-line tool for running nongraphical Java programs; graphical programs require the display support of a browser. The syntax for using the runtime interpreter follows:

```
java Options Classname Arguments
```

The *Classname* argument specifies the name of the class you want to execute. If the class resides in a package, you must fully qualify the name. For example, if you want to run a class called Roids that is located in a package called ActionGames, you would execute it in the interpreter like this:

```
java ActionGames.Roids
```

When the Java interpreter executes a class, what it is really doing is executing the main method of the class. The interpreter exits when the main method and any threads created by it are finished executing. The main method accepts a list of arguments that can be used to control the program. The *Arguments* argument to the interpreter specifies the arguments passed into the main method. For example, if you have a Java class called TextFilter that performs some kind of filtering on a text file, you would likely pass the name of the file as an argument, like this:

```
java TextFilter SomeFile.txt
```

The *Options* argument specifies options related to how the runtime interpreter executes the Java program. Following is a list of the most important runtime interpreter options:

- -debug
- -checksource, -cs
- -classpath *Path*
- -verbose, -v
- -verbosegc

■ `-verify`

■ `-verifyremote`

■ `-noverify`

■ `-DPropertyName=NewValue`

The `-debug` option starts the interpreter in debugging mode, which enables you to use the Java debugger (`jdb`) in conjunction with the interpreter. The `-checksource` option causes the interpreter to compare the modification dates of the source and executable class files. If the source file is more recent, the class is automatically recompiled.

> **NOTE**
>
> The `-checksource` and `-verbose` options provide shorthand versions, `-cs` and `-v`. You can use these shorthand versions as a convenience to save typing.

The Java interpreter uses an environment variable, CLASSPATH, to determine where to look for user-defined classes. The CLASSPATH variable contains a semicolon-delimited list of system paths to user-defined Java classes. Actually, most of the Java tools use the CLASSPATH variable to know where to find user-defined classes. The `-classpath` option informs the runtime interpreter to override CLASSPATH with the path specified by *Path*.

The `-verbose` option causes the interpreter to print a message to standard output each time a Java class is loaded. Similarly, the `-verbosegc` option causes the interpreter to print a message each time a garbage collection is performed. A garbage collection is performed by the runtime system to clean up unneeded objects and to free memory.

The `-verify` option causes the interpreter to run the bytecode verifier on all code loaded into the runtime environment. The verifier's default function is to only verify code loaded into the system using a class loader. This default behavior can also be explicitly specified using the `-verifyremote` option. The `-noverify` option turns all code verification off.

The `-D` option enables you to redefined property values. *PropertyName* specifies the name of the property you want to change, and *NewValue* specifies the new value you want to assign to it.

The Compiler

The Java compiler (`javac`) is used to compile Java source code files into executable Java bytecode classes. In Java, source code files have the extension `.java`. The Java compiler takes files with this extension and generates executable class files with the `.class` extension. The compiler creates one class file for each class defined in a source file. This means that many times a single Java source code file will compile into multiple executable class files. When this happens, it means that the source file contains multiple class definitions.

The Java compiler is a command-line utility that works similarly to the Java runtime interpreter. The syntax for the Java compiler follows:

```
javac Options Filename
```

The `Filename` argument specifies the name of the source code file you want to compile. The `Options` argument specifies options related to how the compiler creates the executable Java classes. Following is a list of the compiler options:

- `-classpath Path`
- `-d Dir`
- `-g`
- `-nowarn`
- `-verbose`
- `-O`

The `-classpath` option tells the compiler to override the CLASSPATH environment variable with the path specified by `Path`. This causes the compiler to look for user-defined classes in the path specified by `Path`. The `-d` option determines the root directory where compiled classes are stored. This is important because many times classes are organized in a hierarchical directory structure. With the `-d` option, the directory structure will be created beneath the directory specified by `Dir`. An example of using the `-d` option follows:

```
javac -d ..\ Flower
```

In this example, the output file `Flower.class` would be stored in the parent directory of the current directory. If the file `Flower.java` contained classes that were part of a package hierarchy, the subdirectories and output classes would fan out below the parent directory.

The `-g` compiler option causes the compiler to generate debugging tables for the Java classes. Debugging tables are used by the Java debugger, and contain information such as local variables and line numbers. The default action of the compiler is to only generate line numbers.

The `-nowarn` option turns off compiler warnings. Warnings are printed to standard output during compilation to inform you of potential problems with the source code. It is sometimes useful to suppress warnings by using the `-nowarn` option. The `-verbose` option has somewhat of an opposite effect as `-nowarn`; it prints out extra information about the compilation process. You can use `-verbose` to see exactly what source files are being compiled.

The `-O` option causes the compiler to optimize the compiled code. In this case, optimization simply means that static, final, and private methods are compiled inline. When a method is compiled inline, it means that the entire body of the method is included in place of each call to the method. This speeds up execution because it eliminates the method call overhead. Optimized classes are usually larger in size, to accommodate the duplicate code. The `-O` optimization option also suppresses the default creation of line numbers by the compiler.

The Applet Viewer

The applet viewer is a tool that serves as a minimal test bed for final release Java applets. You can use the applet viewer to test your programs instead of having to wait for HotJava to support the final release of Java. Currently, the applet viewer is the most solid application to test final release Java programs, because the HotJava browser still only supports alpha release applets. You invoke the applet viewer from a command line, like this:

```
appletviewer Options URL
```

The *URL* argument specifies a document URL containing an HTML page with an embedded Java applet. The *Options* argument specifies how to run the Java applet. There is only one option supported by the applet viewer, -debug. The -debug option starts the applet viewer in the Java debugger, which enables you to debug the applet. To see the applet viewer in action, check out Figure 10.1.

FIGURE 10.1.

The MoleculeViewer *applet running in the Java applet viewer.*

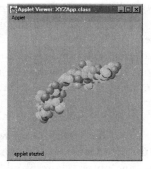

Figure 10.1 shows the MoleculeViewer demo applet that comes with the JDK running in the applet viewer. This program was launched in the applet viewer by changing to the directory containing the MoleculeViewer HTML file and executing the following statement at the command prompt:

```
appletviewer example1.html
```

example1.html is the HTML file containing the embedded Java applet. As you can see, there's nothing complicated about running Java applets using the applet viewer. The applet viewer is a useful tool for testing Java applets in a simple environment.

The Debugger

The Java debugger (jdb) is a command-line utility that enables you to debug Java applications. The Java debugger uses the Java Debugger API to provide debugging support within the Java runtime interpreter. The syntax for using the Java debugger follows:

`jdb Options`

The `Options` argument is used to specify different settings within a debugging session. Because the Java debugger is covered in detail in Chapter 36, "Java Debugging," you won't learn any more details about it in this chapter. If you are just dying to know more about Java debugging, feel free to jump ahead to Chapter 36 and get the whole scoop.

The Class File Disassembler

The Java class file disassembler (`javap`) is used to disassemble a class file. Its default output consists of the public data and methods for a class. The class file disassembler is useful in cases where you don't have the source code for a class, but you'd like to know a little more about how it is implemented. The syntax for the disassembler follows:

`javap Options ClassNames`

The `ClassNames` argument specifies the names of one or more classes to be disassembled. The `Options` argument specifies how the classes are to be disassembled. The disassembler supports the following options:

- `-c`
- `-p`
- `-h`
- `-classpath Path`
- `-verify`
- `-version`

The `-c` option tells the disassembler to output the actual bytecodes for each method. The `-p` option tells the disassembler to also include private variables and methods in its output. Without this option, the disassembler only outputs the public member variables and methods. The `-h` option specifies that information be created that can be used in C header files. This is useful when you are attempting to interface C code to a Java class that you don't have the source code for. You'll learn much more about interfacing Java to C code in Chapter 38, "Native Methods and Libraries."

The `-classpath` option specifies a list of directories to look for imported classes in. The path given by `Path` overrides the `CLASSPATH` environment variable. The `-verify` option tells the disassembler to run the verifier on the class and output debugging information. Finally, the `-version` option causes the disassembler to print its version number.

The Header and Stub File Generator

The Java header and stub file generator (`javah`) is used to generate C header and source files for implementing Java methods in C. The files generated can be used to access member variables of an object from C code. The header and stub file generator accomplishes this by generating a C structure whose layout matches that of the corresponding Java class. The syntax for using the header and stub file generator follows:

```
javah Options ClassName
```

The `ClassName` argument is the name of the class to generate C source files from. The `Options` argument specifies how the source files are to be generated. You'll learn how to use the Java header and stub file generator in Chapter 38. For that reason, you won't get into it in any more detail in this chapter.

The Documentation Generator

The Java documentation generator (`javadoc`) is a useful tool for generating API documentation directly from Java source code. The documentation generator parses through Java source files and generates HTML pages based on the declarations and comments. The syntax for using the documentation generator follows:

```
javadoc Options FileName
```

The `FileName` argument specifies either a package or a Java source code file. In the case of a package, the documentation generator will create documentation for all the classes contained in the package. The `Options` argument enables you to change the default behavior of `javadoc`.

Because the Java documentation generator is covered in detail in Chapter 37, "Java Documentation," you'll have to settle for this brief introduction for now. Or you could go ahead and jump to Chapter 37 to learn more.

Applet Demos

The JDK comes with a variety of interesting Java demo applets, all including complete source code. Following is a list of the demo Java applets that come with the JDK:

- `Animator`
- `ArcTest`
- `BarChart`
- `Blink`
- `BouncingHeads`
- `CardTest`
- `DitherTest`
- `DrawTest`
- `Fractal`

- GraphicsTest
- GraphLayout
- ImageMap
- ImageTest
- JumpingBox
- MoleculeViewer
- NervousText
- ScrollingImages
- SimpleGraph
- SpreadSheet
- TicTacToe
- TumblingDuke
- UnderConstruction
- WireFrame

Rather than go through the tedium of describing each of these applications, I'll leave most of them for you to explore and try out on your own. However, it's worth checking out a few of them here and discuss how they might impact the Web.

The first demo applet is the BarChart applet, which is shown in Figure 10.2.

FIGURE 10.2.

The BarChart *Java applet.*

The BarChart applet is a good example of how Java could be used to show statistical information on the Web graphically. The data represented by the bar graph could be linked to a live data source, such as a group of stock quotes. Then you could actually generate a live, to the minute, dynamically changing stock portfolio.

The GraphicsTest applet is a good example of how to use Java graphics. Java includes an extensive set of graphics features, including primitive shapes and more elaborate drawing routines. Figure 10.3 shows what the GraphicsTest applet looks like.

Keeping the focus on graphics, the SimpleGraph applet shows how Java can be used to plot a two-dimensional graph. There are plenty of scientific and educational applications for plotting. Using Java, data presented in a Web page could come to life with graphical plots. SimpleGraph is shown in Figure 10.4.

FIGURE 10.3.

The GraphicsTest *Java applet.*

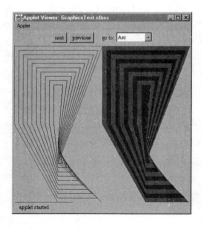

FIGURE 10.4.

The SimpleGraph *Java applet.*

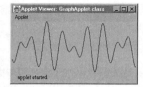

On the business front, there's nothing like a good spreadsheet. The SpreadSheet Java applet shows how to implement a simple spreadsheet in Java. I don't think I even need to say how many applications there are for interactive spreadsheets on the Web. Check out the SpreadSheet applet in Figure 10.5.

FIGURE 10.5.

The SpreadSheet *Java applet.*

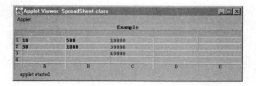

Once you've gotten a headache playing with the SpreadSheet applet, it's time to blow off a little steam with a game. The TicTacToe applet demonstrates a simple Java version of TicTacToe. This demo opens a new window of opportunity for having fun on the Web. Games will no doubt be an interesting application for Java, so keep your eyes peeled for new and interesting ways to waste time on the Web with Java games. The TicTacToe applet is shown in Figure 10.6.

FIGURE 10.6.

The TicTacToe *Java applet.*

The last applet you're going to look at is the UnderConstruction applet, which is a neat little applet that can be used to jazz up unfinished Web pages. This applet shows an animation of the Java mascot, Duke, with a jackhammer. It also has sound, so it's a true multimedia experience! Although this applet is strictly for fun, it nevertheless provides a cool alternative to the usual "under construction" messages that are often used in unfinished web pages. The UnderConstruction applet is shown in Figure 10.7.

FIGURE 10.7.

The UnderConstruction *Java applet.*

Although running these demo applets is neat, the real thing to keep in mind is that they all come with complete source code. This means that you can rip them apart and figure out how they work, and then use similar techniques in your own Java programs. The most powerful way to learn is by example, and the demo applets that come with the JDK are great examples of robust Java applets.

API Source Code

The final component of the Java Developer's Kit is the source code for the Java API. That's right, the JDK comes with the complete source code for all the classes that make up the Java API. Sun isn't concerned with keeping the internals of Java top secret. They followed the lead of the UNIX world and decided to make Java as available and readily understood as possible. Besides, the real value of Java is not the specific code that makes it work, it's the idea behind it.

The API source code is automatically installed to your hard drive when you decompress the JDK, but it remains in compressed form. The assumption here is that not everyone is concerned about how the internals of Java are implemented, so why waste the space. However, it is sometimes useful to be able to look under the hood and see how something works. And Java is no exception. So, the API source code comes compressed in a file called src.zip, which is located in the java directory that was created on your hard drive during installation of the JDK. All the classes that make up the Java API are included in this file.

Summary

The Java Developer's Kit provides a wealth of information, including the tools essential to Java programming. In this chapter you learned about the different components of the JDK, including tools, applet demos, and the Java API source code. Although you learn more about some of these tools throughout the rest of the book, it's important to understand what role each tool plays in the development of Java programs. A strong knowledge of the information contained in the Java Developer's Kit is necessary to become a successful Java developer.

However, you shouldn't stop with the Java Developer's Kit. There are many third-party tools available and in the works that supplement the JDK and enable you to put together a more complete Java programming toolkit. The next chapter highlights these tools and describes how they impact Java development now, and what they may mean for the future.

Other Tools and Environments

11

by Michael Morrison

136

Although the Java Developer's Kit provides the essential Java development tools required to program in Java, there are a variety of other tools and development environments that are poised to make Java programming much easier. Languages like C and C++ have a rich field of development environments and add-on libraries. Many of the same companies that created these C and C++ environments and add-ons are busily working on Java versions of their already popular tools. Some of these tools are even available now.

In addition to the wave of third-party Java development environments, there are also new Java class libraries that promise to add functionality never before seen on the Web. Using these libraries, you will be able to plug Java classes into your own programs and benefit from Java's code reuse capabilities. Because Java is truly a cross-platform language, these tools promise to bridge many gaps between different operating systems. What all of this means to you is that your trip through the world of Java development promises to be both dynamic and productive, not to mention fun.

Development Environments

The development tools provided with the Java Developer's Kit are all command-line tools, except for the applet viewer. Even though the applet viewer is invoked from a command line, it provides graphical output and is therefore a graphical tool. Most modern development environments include graphical editors, graphical debuggers, and visual class browsers. Java is too modern a language not to have a modern development interface to match, and Java programmers know this. Fortunately, the software tool developers know this, too. Most of the major players in the development tool business have already announced Java environments. A few companies even have tools in beta and ready for testing.

These third-party development environments span different operating systems and range from C/C++ environment add-ons to entirely new products. The goal here is to let you in on what development environments are out there and how they impact Java programming.

Symantec Espresso

Symantec is the first major PC tool developer to have a working Java development environment on the street. Symantec Espresso is a Java development environment in the form of an add-on to Symantec C++ for Windows 95 and Windows NT. Following is a list of the main features supported by Symantec Espresso:

- Graphical Programming Editor
- Visual Editors
- Project Manager
- Seamless Integration of the JDK Tools
- Code Generators

If you own Symantec C++, you can download Espresso for free. To download Espresso or get the latest news about it, check out Symantec's Java Web site:

`http://www.symantec.com/lit/dev/javaindex.html`

Graphical Programming Editor

The graphical programming editor in Espresso provides all the features expected in a modern programming editor. It supports full-color syntax and keyword highlighting, along with providing an integrated macro language for extending the editor. The editor also provides navigational features to jump to any Java declaration inside a Java program or the standard Java class libraries.

Visual Editors

Espresso includes a couple of visual editors for managing the many classes involved in Java programming. The Espresso Class Editor enables you to quickly create and navigate through your Java code. With the Class Editor, it is no longer necessary to work with individual Java source code files; you can work directly with Java class definitions and members. This class-centric approach frees you from the limitations of thinking of an application in terms of source files.

The Espresso Class Editor also enables you to quickly browse any part of an application; you simply enter the name of a class or class member, and the Class Editor locates the corresponding source code and loads it into the editor. You can also create and modify new classes from the Class Editor. Figure 11.1 shows what the Espresso Class Editor looks like in action.

FIGURE 11.1.

The Espresso Class Editor.

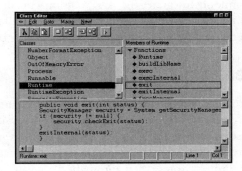

Espresso also includes a Hierarchy Editor for viewing and managing the logical relationships between classes. Figure 11.2 shows what the Hierarchy Editor looks like.

FIGURE 11.2.

The Espresso Hierarchy Editor.

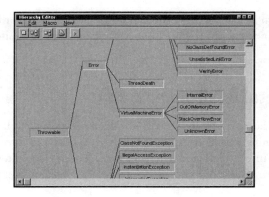

Project Manager

The Project Manager is a powerful component of Espresso that enables you to organize Java projects more effectively. The Project Manager supports projects within projects so you can keep up with nested libraries and project dependencies. Additionally, different project targets and options can be maintained through the Project Manager.

When you load or create a project in Espresso, the Project Manager launches a background source parser that automatically parses the Java source code and builds a bank of information about the project. This information is in turn used by the Class and Hierarchy Editors to provide browsing and editing support for all the Java classes in the project.

Seamless Integration of the JDK Tools

Espresso seamlessly integrates the JDK tools into the development environment with graphical support for the Java interpreter, compiler, and debugger. You can modify the command line arguments to these tools through graphical dialog box interfaces.

Code Generators

Espresso provides two code generation tools, which are sometimes referred to as "wizards." ProjectExpress is a code generation tool that automatically generates Java skeleton applications based on user preferences. ProjectExpress is useful in importing existing Java code into the Espresso environment. Using ProjectExpress, you specify the project type and then add the source files. ProjectExpress then automatically creates the project and loads the classes into Espresso.

AppExpress is another code generation tool that comes with Espresso. AppExpress provides an easy way to create new Java projects that are fully functional from the get go. AppExpress is especially useful for beginning programmers, who will greatly benefit from not having to provide the core functionality necessary to get a Java program up and running. The Java code created by AppExpress is perfectly suited for modification by the user, providing a time saving jumpstart on the development process.

Borland Latte

Borland, one of the largest development tool makers for the PC, has announced its contender in the Java market: Latte. Borland has stated that Latte will be heavily based on the graphical interface made popular in Delphi. Delphi is Borland's popular object-oriented Pascal development environment. Unlike Espresso, Latte is slated to be a completely new product. Another interesting twist is the fact that Latte is itself being written in Java.

The downside to Latte is that there are no alpha or beta versions available as of yet. Borland says that it will deliver the Latte technology in several stages, with the first commercial release scheduled sometime during the first half of 1996. Borland also says that the Latte technology will focus on the following areas:

- Visual Tools
- Component-Based Architecture
- High Performance Compilation
- Scalable, Distributable Database Access

For more information on Borland Latte, check out their Java Web site:

```
http://www.borland.com/Product/java/java.html
```

Microsoft Visual C++

Microsoft is the only big PC tool developer that has yet to officially announce a Java development environment in the works. Microsoft has agreed to license the Java technology for their Internet Explorer Web browser, so we can only assume that they are also gearing up to provide a development environment. Whether it will come as a twist on the Visual C++ or Visual Basic products, or as an entirely new product, no one knows.

Until Microsoft decides how they will enter the Java tools market, the most applicable tool they have for Java development is Visual C++ 4.0. Fortunately, Visual C++ 4.0 is extensible enough to enable you to integrate the Java JDK with it a little.

The first thing you can do to make Visual C++ more Java friendly is enable color syntax highlighting for Java source files. You can do this on a file by file basis by right-clicking on the editor window after you've opened the file. Select Properties from the popup menu and then select "C/C++" from the Languages dropdown list. If you want all Java source files to use C++ highlighting, you can add the java file extension to a key in the Windows Registry. To do this, run RegEdit and add java to the list of file extensions specified by the following key:

```
HKEY_CURRENT_USER->Software->Microsoft->Developer->Text Editor->Tabs/Language
➥Settings->C/C++
```

Keep in mind that using C++ highlighting with Java source files isn't perfect. Visual C++ will still only highlight C++ keywords. The main benefit is that comments will be highlighted.

A more useful modification to Visual C++ is setting it up to use the Java compiler (javac). The first step is to create a simple batch file that will launch the command-line compiler and display a message notifying you of the compile. You can call the file jcc.bat. Following is the source code for jcc.bat, which should be placed in your *java\bin* directory:

```
@echo off
echo Compiling %1...
\java\bin\javac %1
echo Compile complete.
```

The reason for creating a batch file rather than just calling javac directly from Visual C++ is that it enables you to include more information that will be displayed in the Visual C++ Output window.

To connect the batch file to Visual C++, select Customize from the Tools menu. Then select the Tools tab on the dialog box. You create a Java Compiler tool entry by first clicking the Add button and then filling out the information requested by the dialog box. First, type in the name of the tool, Java Compiler, and click OK. Then specify jcc.bat as the command in the Command edit box. You need to set the arguments to $(*FileName*)$(*FileExt*) in the Arguments edit box. Then set the initial directory to $(*FileDir*) in the Initial directory edit box. Finally, you need to specify that you want to redirect the output to the Output window, so check the appropriate check box. When you've done all this, you should see a dialog box similar to the one shown in Figure 11.3.

FIGURE 11.3.

Setting up the Java Compiler tool using the Visual C++ Customize dialog box.

You can now use the Java Compiler tool from the Tools menu to compile Java programs within Visual C++. The Java compiler output is even printed in the Output window of Visual C++! I'll bet you didn't know Visual C++ could do that.

In addition, you can also setup Visual C++ to run the Java applet viewer as a tool. Simply add appletviewer.exe as a tool just as you did for the compiler, but specify the HTML file you want to use in the Arguments edit box. In the Java demo applets, this HTML file is usually named `example1.html`. You can use this name to make things easier. The correct settings for the Applet Viewer Visual C++ tool are shown in Figure 11.4.

FIGURE 11.4.

Setting up the Java Applet Viewer using the Visual C++ Customize dialog box.

JavaMaker

The JavaMaker development environment for Windows 95 and Windows NT is a simple, yet useful programming environment for Java. It is the product of an individual effort by Heechang Choi, and basically serves as a front end for the Java compiler and applet viewer tools. Figure 11.5 shows what JavaMaker looks like.

FIGURE 11.5.

The JavaMaker development environment.

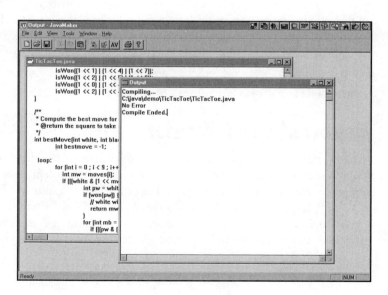

For more information on JavaMaker, or to download the latest version, check out the JavaMaker Web site:

```
http://net.info.samsung.co.kr/~hcchoi/javamaker.html
```

Natural Intelligence's Roaster

Natural Intelligence has announced that they have been working on a Macintosh Java development environment based on their popular Quick Code Pro script editor. The Applet Development Kit, also known as Roaster, should be entering a beta release stage at any time. Roaster is touted as having the following features:

- A complete integrated development environment
- A powerful programming editor
- A high-performance compiler
- A debugger
- A class disassembler
- A project manager
- Power Macintosh support

The Roaster development environment promises to include multiple clipboards for better organization of code snippets, as well as powerful macro capabilities. The Roaster programming editor will feature context-sensitive font and color highlighting, as well as bookmarks for keeping track of Java code. It will also feature powerful search and replace features, including regular expression matching and batch search capabilities. For more information about Roaster, check out Natural Intelligence's Roaster Web site:

```
http://www.natural.com/pages/products/roaster/
```

Metrowerks CodeWarrior

Metrowerks, the creators of the popular CodeWarrior C++ development environment for Macintosh, has also announced a Macintosh Java development environment. This new environment, codenamed *Wired,* is expected to be released as a suite of add-ons for a future release of CodeWarrior. Metrowerks has announced that Wired should be ready for release with CodeWarrior 9, which is scheduled to ship during the summer of 1996. For more information on Wired, take a look at the Metrowerks Web site:

```
http://www.metrowerks.com/
```

Silicon Graphics Cosmo

One of the most interesting Java development environments in the works is Cosmo Code by Silicon Graphics, which is a component of the larger Cosmo Web development system. Cosmo itself is aimed at providing more extensive multimedia and 3D graphics support for the Web. It is the primary development component of Cosmo, and is actually a Java development environment with a lot of promise. Cosmo Code is currently available for Irix systems, and contains the following core components:

- Visual Builder
- Graphical Source Debugger
- Visual Source Browser

To find out the latest information about Cosmo Code, or to download a copy to try out, refer to the Cosmo Web site:

```
http://www.sgi.com/Products/cosmo/
```

Visual Builder

The Cosmo Visual Builder is an extensible, interactive software development tool that enables you to create Java applets using drag-and-drop. Similar to Silicon Graphics RapidApp product for C++, the Visual Builder enables developers to quickly construct Java programs that use both the Cosmo and Java libraries. The extensibility of the Visual Builder provides a clear path to using new Java components as they become available.

Graphical Source Debugger

Cosmo Code includes its own graphical Java source debugger, which supports the following features:

- Graphical display of Java source while debugging
- Source-level traps
- Call stack display
- Data inspection and expression evaluation
- Memory functions and explicit garbage collection
- Thread controls
- Exception handling support

Figure 11.6 shows what the Cosmo Code graphical source debugger looks like.

FIGURE 11.6.

The Cosmo Code graphical source debugger.

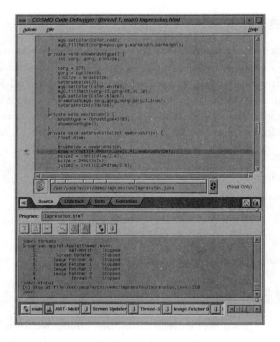

Visual Source Browser

The Cosmo Code visual source browser is a tool that provides the user with a visual perspective on their Java classes, including graphical class hierarchies. Figure 11.7 shows the Cosmo Code visual source browser in action.

FIGURE 11.7.

The Cosmo Code visual source browser.

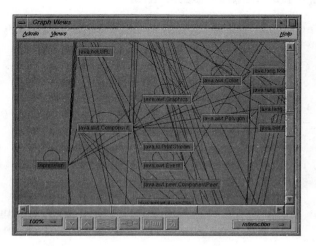

Programming Libraries

Beyond the Java development environments, third-party class libraries make up the other major market for Java tool vendors. Java provides a level of code compatibility and reuse previously unseen in the software world. A tool vendor is capable of creating a single class library in Java that spans all platforms. This opportunity has enormous appeal to tool developers, so expect to see an influx of Java class libraries in the very near future.

In the present, there are a decent amount of freeware type classes to pick and choose from, along with a few commercial class libraries that will be available any day. As far as getting the freely distributed, or noncommercial classes, check out the Gamelan Web site:

`http://www.gamelan.com/`

Gamelan provides a staggering array of Java classes, written primarily by individuals, that span many areas of Java programming. The majority of these classes come with complete source code, so they are useful both as tools and as educational resources.

As far as commercial class libraries go, there aren't too many options at the moment. One company that appears to be ahead of the pack is Dimension X, who has a couple of Java class libraries nearing completion: Ice and Liquid Reality. You can get the latest information on these libraries from Dimension X's Java Web site:

`http://www.dnx.com/dnx/java.html`

Ice

Dimension X's Ice class library is a high-performance 3D rendering package for Java. Ice is composed of two parts: a C library that implements low-level graphics primitives, and a set of Java classes that provide wrappers around the C library. Ice is designed with speed as a primary goal, along with the support of special-purpose 3D graphics hardware. With this in mind, the aim is for Ice to be used to generate interactive 3D graphics on the fly. Ice implements the following features:

- Z-buffered polygons, lines, and points
- Gouraud shading
- Texture mapping
- Support for up to eight light sources
- Rich set of light and material properties
- Fog and depth cueing
- Support for 8-, 16-, 24-, and 32-bit frame buffers

- 8-bit dithering
- Alpha blending
- Motion-blur and anti-aliasing

Liquid Reality

Liquid Reality is the first set of classes to be built on top of the Ice class library. It is composed of a set of Java classes for building dynamic VRML worlds, and uses Ice to handle rendering the worlds. Liquid Reality really just provides one extension to VRML: when the VRML parser encounters a node type that it doesn't understand, it queries the HTTP server that served the VRML file and requests a Java class describing the unknown node. Liquid Reality effectively provides VRML with the same kind of extensibility that HotJava provides to HTML documents.

Summary

As you've learned in this chapter, the Java development scene is in a state of rapid growth. The wide variety of third-party tools available now and on the horizon will certainly change the face of Java programming. Armed with the knowledge of what tools are available and what they can do, you should now have more insight into planning your own Java development.

Additionally, you should realize that the tools mentioned in this chapter are really only the first wave of third-party Java development products. As Java becomes more established, more tool vendors will see the light and take the steps necessary to enter the Java tools marketplace. This is good news for Java users and developers, as competition among tool vendors will result in better development tools and more affordable prices. Just in case it hasn't occurred to you yet, this is only the beginning!

Now that you know the whole scoop surrounding the different Java development tools, you're probably ready to learn about the Java language itself. I mean, it's fun to talk about the technology, but ultimately the Java language is the nuts and bolts that drive everything. The next part of the book, "The Java Language," covers all the juicy details of the Java language.

PART

IN THIS PART

The Java Language

Java Language Fundamentals

12

by Michael Morrison

IN THIS CHAPTER

Java is an object-oriented language. This means that the language is based on the concept of an object. Although a knowledge of object-oriented programming is necessary to put Java to practical use, it isn't required to understand the fundamentals of the Java language. This chapter focuses on the language and leaves the object-oriented details of Java for Chapter 14, "Classes, Packages, and Interfaces."

If you already have some experience with another object-oriented language such as C++ or Smalltalk, much of Java will be familiar territory. In fact, Java almost can be considered a new, revamped C++. Because Java is so highly derived from C++, many of the similarities and differences between Java and C++ will be highlighted throughout the next few chapters. Additionally, Appendix D provides a more thorough look at the differences between Java and C++.

This chapter covers the essentials of the Java language, including a few sample programs to help you hit the ground running.

Hello, World!

The best way to learn a programming language is to jump right in and see how a real program works. In keeping with a traditional introductory programming example, your first program will be a Java version of the classic "Hello, World!" program. Listing 12.1 contains the source code for the `HelloWorld` class, which also is located on the CD-ROM in the file `HelloWorld.java`.

> **NOTE**
>
> You may be thinking that you've already said hello to the world with Java in Chapter 2, "Java's Design Is Flexible and Dynamic." The HelloWorld program you saw in Chapter 2 was a Java applet, meaning that it ran within the confines of a Web page and printed text as graphical output. The HelloWorld program in this chapter is a Java application, which means that it runs within the Java interpreter as a stand-alone program and has text output.

Listing 12.1. The `HelloWorld` class.

```
class HelloWorld {
  public static void main (String args[]) {
    System.out.println("Hello, World!");
  }
}
```

After compiling the program with the Java compiler (`javac`), you are ready to run it in the Java interpreter. The Java compiler places the executable output in a file called `HelloWorld.class`. This naming convention might seem strange considering the fact that most programming languages use the .EXE file extension for executables. Not so in Java! Following the object-oriented nature of Java, all Java programs are stored as Java classes that are created and executed as objects in the Java run-time environment. To run the HelloWorld program, type `java HelloWorld` at the command prompt. As you may have guessed, the program responds by displaying "Hello, World!" on your screen. Congratulations—you just wrote and tested your first Java program!

As you might have guessed, HelloWorld is a very minimal Java program. Even so, there's still a lot happening in those few lines of code. To fully understand what is happening, you need to examine the program line by line. First, you need to understand that Java relies heavily on classes. In fact, the first statement of HelloWorld reminds you that HelloWorld is a class, not just a program. Furthermore, looking at the `class` statement in its entirety, the name of the class is defined as `HelloWorld`. This name is used by the Java compiler as the name of the executable output class. The Java compiler creates an executable class file for each class defined in a Java source file. If there is more than one class defined in a `.java` file, the Java compiler will store each one in a separate `.class` file. It isn't strictly necessary to give the source file the same name as the class file, but it is highly recommended as a style guideline.

The `HelloWorld` class contains one *method*, or member function. For now, you can think of this function as a normal procedural function that happens to be linked to the class. The details of methods are covered in Chapter 14, "Classes, Packages, and Interfaces." The single method in the `HelloWorld` class is called `main`, and should be familiar if you have used C or C++. The `main` method is where execution begins when the class is executed in the Java interpreter. The `main` method is defined as being `public static` with a `void` return type. `public` means that the method can be called from anywhere inside or outside of the class. `static` means that the method is the same for all instances of the class. The `void` return type means that `main` does not return a value.

The `main` method is defined as taking a single parameter, `String args[]`. `args` is an array of `String` objects that represents command-line arguments passed to the class upon execution. Because HelloWorld doesn't use any command-line arguments, you can ignore the `args` parameter. You'll learn a little more about strings later in this chapter.

The `main` method is called when the `HelloWorld` class is executed. `main` consists of a single statement that prints the message "Hello, World!" to the standard output stream, as follows:

```
System.out.println("Hello, World!");
```

This statement might look a little confusing at first because of the nested objects. To help make things clearer, examine the statement from right to left. First notice that the statement ends in a semicolon, which is standard Java syntax that has been borrowed from C/C++. Moving on to the left, you see that the "Hello, World!" string is in parentheses, which means it is a parameter to a function call. The method being called is actually the `println` method of the `out` object. The `println` method is similar to the `printf` method in C, except that it automatically appends a `newline` (\n) at the end of the string. The `out` object is a member variable of the `System` object that represents the standard output stream. Finally, the System object is a global object in the Java environment that encapsulates system functionality.

That pretty well covers the HelloWorld class—your first Java program. If you got lost a little in the explanation of the HelloWorld class, don't be too concerned. HelloWorld was presented with no prior explanation of the Java language and was only meant to get your feet wet with Java code. The rest of this chapter focuses on a more structured discussion of the fundamentals of the Java language.

Tokens

When you submit a Java program to the Java compiler, the compiler parses the text and extracts individual *tokens*. A token is the smallest element of a program that is meaningful to the compiler. This actually is true for all compilers, not just the Java compiler. These tokens define the structure of the Java language. All of the tokens that comprise Java are known as the Java *token set*. Java tokens can be broken down into five categories: identifiers, keywords, literals, operators, and separators. The Java compiler also recognizes and subsequently removes comments and whitespaces.

The Java compiler removes all comments and whitespaces while tokenizing the source file. The resulting tokens then are compiled into machine-independent Java bytecode that is capable of being run from within an interpreted Java environment. The bytecode conforms to the hypothetical Java Virtual Machine, which abstracts processor differences into a single virtual processor. For more information on the Java Virtual Machine, check out Chapter 39, "Java's Virtual Machine, Bytecodes, and More." Keep in mind that an interpreted Java environment can be either the Java command-line interpreter or a Java-capable browser.

Identifiers

Identifiers are tokens that represent names. These names can be assigned to variables, methods, and classes to uniquely identify them to the compiler and give them meaningful names to the programmer. HelloWorld is an identifier that assigns the name HelloWorld to the class residing in the HelloWorld.java source file developed earlier.

Although you can be creative in naming identifiers in Java, there are some limitations. All Java identifiers are case-sensitive and must begin with a letter, an underscore (_), or a dollar sign ($). Letters include both upper- and lowercase letters. Subsequent identifier characters can include the numbers 0 to 9. The only other limitation to identifier names is that the Java keywords, which are listed in the next section, cannot be used. Table 12.1 contains a list of valid and invalid identifier names.

Table 12.1. Valid and invalid Java identifiers.

Valid	Invalid
HelloWorld	Hello World
Hi_Mom	Hi_Mom!
heyDude3	3heyDude
tall	short
poundage	#age

The `Hello World` identifier is invalid because it contains a space. The `Hi_Mom!` identifier is invalid because it contains an exclamation point. The `3heyDude` identifier is invalid because it begins with a number. The `short` identifier is invalid because `short` is a Java keyword. Finally, the `#age` identifier is invalid because it begins with the # symbol.

Beyond the mentioned restrictions of naming Java identifiers, there are a few stylistic rules you should follow to make Java programming easier and more consistent. It is standard Java practice to name multiple-word identifiers in lowercase except for the beginning letter of words in the middle of the name. For example, the variable `toughGuy` is in correct Java style, whereas `toughguy`, `ToughGuy`, and `TOUGHGUY` are all in violation. This rule isn't etched in stone—it's just a good idea to follow because most other Java code you run into will follow this style. Another more critical naming issue regards the use of underscore and dollar sign characters at the beginning of identifier names. This is a little risky because many C libraries use the same naming convention for libraries, which can be imported into your Java code. To eliminate the potential problem of name clashing in these instances, it's better to stay away from the underscore and dollar sign characters at the beginning of your identifier names. A good usage of the underscore character is to separate words where you normally would use a space.

Keywords

Keywords are predefined identifiers reserved by Java for a specific purpose and are used only in a limited, specified manner. Java has a richer set of keywords than C or C++, so if you are learning Java with a C/C++ background, be sure to pay attention to the Java keywords. The following keywords are reserved for Java:

abstract	double	int	super
boolean	else	interface	switch
break	extends	long	synchronized
byte	false	native	this
byvalue	final	new	threadsafe
case	finally	null	throw

catch	float	package	transient
char	for	private	true
class	goto	protected	try
const	if	public	void
continue	implements	return	while
default	import	short	
do	instanceof	static	

Literals

Program elements that are used in an invariant manner are called *literals* or constants. Literals can be numbers, characters, or strings. Numeric literals include integers, floating-point numbers, and Booleans. Booleans are considered numeric because of the C influence on Java. In C, the Boolean values for true and false are represented by 1 and 0. Character literals always refer to a single Unicode character. Strings, which contain multiple characters, still are considered literals even though they are implemented in Java as objects.

> **NOTE**
>
> If you aren't familiar with the Unicode character set, it is a 16-bit character set that replaces the ASCII character set. Because it is 16 bit, there are enough entries to represent many symbols and characters from other languages. Unicode is quickly becoming the standard for modern operating systems.

Integer Literals

Integer literals are the primary literals used in Java programming and come in a few different formats: decimal, hexadecimal, and octal. These formats correspond to the base of the number system used by the literal. Decimal (base 10) literals appear as ordinary numbers with no special notation. Hexadecimal numbers (base 16) appear with a leading 0x or 0X, similar to C/C++. Octal (base 8) numbers appear with a leading 0 in front of the digits. For example, an integer literal for the decimal number 12 is represented in Java as 12 in decimal, 0xC in hexadecimal, and 014 in octal.

Integer literals default to being stored in the int type, which is a signed 32-bit value. If you are working with very large numbers, you can force an integer literal to be stored in the long type by appending an l or L to the end of the number, as in 79L. The long type is a signed 64-bit value.

Floating-Point Literals

Floating-point literals represent decimal numbers with fractional parts, such as 3.142. They can be expressed in either standard or scientific notation, meaning that the number 563.84 also can be expressed as 5.6384e2.

Unlike integer literals, floating-point literals default to the double type, which is a 64-bit value. You have the option of using the smaller 32-bit float type if you know the full 64 bits are not needed. You do this by appending an f or F to the end of the number, such as 5.6384e2f. If you are a stickler for details, you also can explicitly state that you want a double type as the storage unit for your literal, such as 3.142d. Because the default storage for floating-point numbers is double already, this isn't necessary.

Boolean Literals

Boolean literals are certainly a welcome addition if you are coming from the world of C/C++. In C, there is no Boolean type, and therefore no Boolean literals. The Boolean values True and False are represented by the integer values 1 and 0. Java fixes this problem by providing a boolean type with two possible states: true and false. Not surprisingly, these states are represented in the Java language by the keywords true and false.

Boolean literals are used in Java programming about as often as integer literals because they are present in almost every type of control structure. Any time you need to represent a condition or state with two possible values, a boolean is what you need. You'll learn a little more about the boolean type later in this chapter. For now, just remember the two Boolean literal values: true and false.

Character Literals

Character literals represent a single Unicode character and appear within a pair of single quotation marks. Similar to C/C++, special characters (control characters and characters that cannot be printed) are represented by a backslash (\) followed by the character code. A good example of a special character is \n, which forces the output to a new line when printed. Table 12.2 shows the special characters supported by Java.

Table 12.2. Special characters supported by Java.

Description	Representation
Backslash	\\
Continuation	\
Backspace	\b

continues

Table 12.2. continued

Description	Representation
Carriage Return	\r
Form Feed	\f
Horizontal Tab	\t
Newline	\n
Single Quote	\'
Double Quote	\"
Unicode Character	\udddd
Octal Number	\ddd

An example of a Unicode character literal is \u0048, which is a hexadecimal representation of the character H. This same character is represented in octal as \110.

String Literals

String literals represent multiple characters and appear within a pair of double quotation marks. Unlike all of the other literals discussed, string literals are implemented in Java by the String class. This is very different from the C/C++ representation of strings as an array of characters.

When Java encounters a string literal, it creates an instance of the String class and sets its state to the characters appearing within the double quotes. From a usage perspective, the fact that Java implements strings as objects is relatively unimportant. However, it is worth mentioning at this point because it is a reminder that Java is very object oriented in nature—much more than C++, which is widely considered the current object-oriented programming standard.

Operators

Operators, also known as *operands,* specify an evaluation or computation to be performed on a data object or objects. These operands can be literals, variables, or function return types. The operators supported by Java follow:

```
+        -        *        /        %        &        |

^        ~        &&       ||       !        <        >

<=       >=       <<       >>       >>>      =        ?

++       --       ==       +=       -=       *=       /=

%=       &=       |=       ^=       !=       <<=      >>=

>>>=     .        [        ]        (        )
```

Just seeing these operators probably doesn't help you a lot in determining how to use them. Don't worry—you'll learn a lot more about operators and how they are used in the next chapter, "Expressions, Operators, and Control Structures."

Separators

Separators are used to inform the Java compiler of how things are grouped in the code. For example, items in a list are separated by commas much like lists of items in a sentence. Java separators go far beyond commas, however, as you'll find out in the next chapter. The separators supported by Java follow:

```
{ } ; , :
```

Comments and Whitespace

Earlier you learned that comments and whitespace are removed by the Java compiler during the tokenization of the source code. You might be wondering, "What qualifies as whitespace and how are comments supported?" First, whitespace consists of spaces, tabs, and linefeeds. All occurrences of spaces, tabs, or linefeeds are removed by the Java compiler, as are comments. Comments can be defined in three different ways, as shown in Table 12.3.

Table 12.3. Types of comments supported by Java.

Type	Usage
/* comment */	All characters between /* and */ are ignored.
// comment	All characters after the // up to the end of the line are ignored.
/** comment */	Same as /* */, except that the comment can be used with the javadoc tool to create automatic documentation.

The first type of comment (/* comment */) should be familiar if you have programmed in C before. All characters inside the /* and */ comment delimiters are ignored by the compiler. Similarly, the second type of comment (// comment) also should be familiar if you have used C++. All characters appearing after the // comment delimiter up to the end of the line are ignored by the compiler. These two comment types are borrowed from C and C++. The final comment type (/** comment */) works in the same fashion as the C-style comment type, with the additional benefit that it can be used with the Java Automatic Documentation tool, javadoc, to create automatic documentation from the source code. The javadoc tool is covered in Chapter 37, "Java Documentation." The following are a few examples of using the various types of comments:

```
/* This is a C style comment. */
// This is a C++ style comment.
/** This is a javadoc style comment. */
```

Data Types

One of the fundamental concepts of any programming language is that of data types. Data types define the storage methods available for representing information, along with how the information is interpreted. Data types are linked tightly to the storage of variables in memory because the data type of a variable determines how the compiler interprets the contents of the memory. You already have received a little taste of data types in the discussion of literal types.

To create a variable in memory, you must declare it by providing the type of the variable as well as an identifier that uniquely identifies the variable. The syntax of the Java declaration statement for variables follows:

```
Type Identifier [, Identifier];
```

The declaration statement tells the compiler to set aside memory for a variable of type `Type` with the name `Identifier`. The optional bracketed `Identifier` indicates that you can make multiple declarations of the same type by separating them with commas. Finally, as in all Java statements, the declaration statement ends with a semicolon.

Java data types can be divided into two categories: simple and composite. Simple data types are core types that are not derived from any other types. Integer, floating-point, Boolean, and character types are all simple types. Composite types, on the other hand, are based on simple types, and include strings, arrays, and both classes and interfaces in general. You'll learn about arrays later in this chapter. Classes and interfaces are covered in Chapter 14, "Classes, Packages, and Interfaces."

Integer Data Types

Integer data types are used to represent signed integer numbers. There are four integer types: `byte`, `short`, `int`, and `long`. Each of these types takes up a different amount of space in memory, as shown in Table 12.4.

Table 12.4. Java integer types.

Type	Size
byte	8 bits
short	16 bits
int	32 bits
long	64 bits

To declare variables using the integer types, use the declaration syntax mentioned previously with the desired type. The following are some examples of declaring integer variables:

```
int i;
short rocketFuel;
long angle, magnitude;
byte red, green, blue;
```

Floating-Point Data Types

Floating-point data types are used to represent numbers with fractional parts. There are two floating-point types: `float` and `double`. The `float` type reserves storage for a 32-bit single-precision number and the `double` type reserves storage for a 64-bit double-precision number.

Declaring floating-point variables is very similar to declaring integer variables. The following are some examples of floating-point variable declarations:

```
float temperature;
double windSpeed, barometricPressure;
```

boolean Data Type

The `boolean` data type is used to store values with one of two states: `true` or `false`. You can think of the `boolean` type as a 1-bit integer value, because 1 bit can have only two possible values: 1 or 0. However, instead of using 1 and 0, you use the Java keywords `true` and `false`. `true` and `false` aren't just conveniences in Java; they are actually the only legal Boolean values. This means that you can't interchangeably use Booleans and integers like in C/C++. To declare a Boolean value, just use the `boolean` type declaration:

```
boolean gameOver;
```

Character Data Type

The character data type is used to store single Unicode characters. Because the Unicode character set is composed of 16-bit values, the `char` data type is stored as a 16-bit unsigned integer. You create variables of type `char` as follows:

```
char firstInitial, lastInitial;
```

Remember that the `char` type is useful only for storing single characters. If you come from a C/C++ background, you might be tempted to try to fashion a string by creating an array of `chars`. In Java this isn't necessary because the `String` class takes care of handling strings. This doesn't mean that you should never create arrays of characters, it just means that you shouldn't use a character array when you really want a string. C and C++ do not distinguish between character arrays and strings, but Java does.

Casting Types

There will inevitably be times when you need to convert from one data type to another. The process of converting one data type to another is called *casting*. Casting often is necessary when a function returns a type different than the type you need to perform an operation. For example, the read member function of the standard input stream (System.in) returns an int. You must cast the returned int type to a char type before storing it, as in the following:

```
char c = (char)System.in.read();
```

The cast is performed by placing the desired type in parentheses to the left of the value to be converted. The System.in.read function call returns an int value, which then is cast to a char because of the (char) cast. The resulting char value is then stored in the char variable c.

The storage size of the types you are attempting to cast is very important. Not all types will safely cast to other types. To understand this, consider the outcome of casting a long to an int. A long is a 64-bit value and an int is a 32-bit value. When casting a long to an int, the compiler chops off the upper 32 bits of the long value so it will fit into the 32-bit int. If the upper 32-bits of the long contain any useful information, it will be lost and the number will change as a result of the cast. Information loss also can occur when casting between different fundamental types, such as integer and floating-point numbers. For example, casting a double to a long would result in the loss of the fractional information, even though both numbers are 64-bit values.

When casting, the destination type should always be equal to or larger in size than the source type. Furthermore, you should pay close attention to casting across fundamental types, such as floating-point and integer types. Table 12.5 lists the casts that are guaranteed to result in no loss of information.

Table 12.5. Casts that result in no loss of information.

From Type	To Type
byte	short, char, int, long, float, double
short	int, long, float, double
char	int, long, float, double
int	long, float, double
long	float, double
float	double

Blocks and Scope

In Java, source code is broken up into parts separated by opening and closing curly braces ({ and }). Everything between curly braces is considered a block and exists more or less independently of everything outside of the braces. Blocks aren't important just from a logical sense—they are required as part of the syntax of the Java language. Without any braces, the compiler would have trouble determining where one section of code ends and the next section begins. From a purely aesthetic viewpoint, it would be very difficult for someone else reading your code to understand what was going on without the braces. For that matter, it wouldn't be very easy for you to understand your own code without the braces.

Braces are used to group related statements together. You can think of everything between matching braces as being executed as one statement. In fact, from an outer block, that's exactly what an inner block appears like: a single statement. But what's an outer block? Glad you asked, because it brings up another important point: Blocks can be hierarchical. One block can contain one or more nested subblocks.

It is standard Java programming style to identify different blocks with indentation. Every time you enter a new block you should indent your source code by a number of spaces, preferably two. When you leave a block you should move back, or *deindent,* two spaces. This is a fairly established convention in many programming languages. However, it is just a style and is not technically part of the language. The compiler would produce identical output even if you didn't indent anything. Indentation is used for the programmer, not the compiler; it simply makes the code easier to follow and understand. Following is an example of the proper indentation of blocks in Java:

```
for (int i = 0; i < 5; i++) {
  if (i < 3) {
    System.out.println(i);
  }
}
```

Following is the same code without any block indentations:

```
for (int i = 0; i < 5; i++) {
if (i < 3) {
System.out.println(i);
}
}
```

The first code listing clearly shows the breakdown of program flow through the use of indentation; it is obvious that the if statement is nested within the for loop. The second code listing, on the other hand, provides no visual cues as to the relationship between the blocks of code. Don't worry if you don't know anything about if statements and for loops; you'll learn plenty about them in the next chapter, "Expressions, Operators, and Control Structures."

The concept of *scope* is tightly linked to blocks and is very important when working with variables in Java. Scope refers to how sections of a program (*blocks*) affect the lifetime of variables.

Every variable declared in a program has an associated scope, meaning that the variable only is used in that particular part of the program.

Scope is determined by blocks. To better understand blocks, take a look again at the `HelloWorld` class in Listing 12.1. The `HelloWorld` class is composed of two blocks. The outer block of the program is the block defining the `HelloWorld` class:

```
class HelloWorld {
...
}
```

Class blocks are very important in Java. Almost everything of interest is either a class itself or belongs to a class. For example, methods are defined inside the classes they belong to. Both syntactically and logically, everything in Java takes place inside a class. Getting back to `HelloWorld`, the inner block defines the code within the `main` method as follows:

```
public static void main (String args[]) {
...
    }
```

The inner block is considered to be nested within the outer block of the program. Any variables defined in the inner block are local to that block and are not visible to the outer block; the scope of the variables is defined as the inner block.

To get an even better idea behind the usage of scope and blocks, take a look at the `HowdyWorld` class in Listing 12.2.

Listing 12.2. The `HowdyWorld` class.

```
class HowdyWorld {
  public static void main (String args[]) {
    int i;
    printMessage();
  }
  public static void printMessage () {
    int j;
    System.out.println("Howdy, World!");
  }
}
```

The `HowdyWorld` class contains two methods: `main` and `printMessage`. `main` should be familiar to you from the `HelloWorld` class, except in this case it declares an integer variable `i` and calls the `printMessage` method. `printMessage` is a new method that declares an integer variable `j` and prints the message "Howdy, World!" to the standard output stream, much like the `main` method did in HelloWorld.

You've probably figured out already that HowdyWorld results in basically the same output as HelloWorld, because the call to `printMessage` results in a single text message being displayed.

What you might not see right off is the scope of the integers defined in each method. The integer i defined in main has a scope limited to the body of the main method. The body of main is defined by the curly braces around the method (the method block). Similarly, the integer j has a scope limited to the body of the printMessage method. The importance of the scope of these two variables is that the variables aren't visible beyond their respective scopes; the HowdyWorld class block knows nothing about the two integers. Furthermore, main doesn't know anything about j, and printMessage knows nothing about i.

Scope becomes more important when you start nesting blocks of code within other blocks. The GoodbyeWorld class shown in Listing 12.3 is a good example of variables nested within different scopes.

Listing 12.3. The GoodbyeWorld class.

```
class GoodbyeWorld {
  public static void main (String args[]) {
    int i, j;
    System.out.println("Goodbye, World!");
    for (i = 0; i < 5; i++) {
      int k;
      System.out.println("Bye!");
    }
  }
}
```

The integers i and j have scopes within the main method body. The integer k, however, has a scope limited to the for loop block. Because k's scope is limited to the for loop block, it cannot be seen outside of that block. On the other hand, i and j still can be seen within the for loop block. What this means is that scoping has a top-down hierarchical effect—variables defined in outer scopes still can be seen and used within nested scopes, but variables defined in nested scopes are limited to those scopes. Incidentally, don't worry if you aren't familiar with for loops, you'll learn all about them in the next chapter, "Expressions, Operators, and Control Structures."

For more reasons than visibility, it is important to pay attention to the scope of variables when you declare them. Along with determining the visibility of variables, the scope also determines the lifetime of variables. This means that variables actually are destroyed when program execution leaves their scope. Looking at the GoodbyeWorld example again, storage for the integers i and j is allocated when program execution enters the main method. When the for loop block is entered, storage for the integer k is allocated. When program execution leaves the for loop block, the memory for k is freed and the variable destroyed. Similarly, when program execution leaves main, all of the variables in its scope are freed and destroyed (i and j). The concept of variable lifetime and scope becomes even more important when you start dealing with classes. You'll get a good dose of this in Chapter 14, "Classes, Packages, and Interfaces."

Arrays

An array is a construct that provides for the storage of a list of items of the same type. Array items can be of either a simple or composite data type. Arrays also can be multidimensional. Java arrays are declared with square brackets ([]). The following are a few examples of arrays in Java:

```
int numbers[];
char[] letters;
long grid[][];
```

If you are familiar with arrays in another language, you might be puzzled by the absence of a number between the square brackets specifying the number of items in the array. Java doesn't allow you to specify the size of an empty array when declaring the array. You always must explicitly set the size of the array with the new operator or by assigning a list of items to the array on creation. The new operator is covered in the next chapter, "Expressions, Operators, and Control Structures."

> **NOTE**
>
> It might seem like a hassle to always have to explicitly set the size of an array with the new operator. The reason for doing this is because Java doesn't have pointers like C or C++ and therefore doesn't allow you to just point anywhere in an array and create new items. By handling memory management this way, the bounds checking problems common with C and C++ have been avoided in the Java language.

Another strange thing you might notice about Java arrays is the optional placement of the square brackets in the array declaration. You are allowed to place the square brackets either after the variable type or after the identifier.

The following are a couple of examples of arrays that have been declared and set to a specific size by using the new operator or by assigning a list of items in the array declaration:

```
char alphabet[] = new char[26];
int primes = {7, 11, 13};
```

More complex structures for storing lists of items, such as stacks and hashtables, are also supported by Java. Unlike arrays, these structures are implemented in Java as classes. You'll get a crash course in some of these other storage mechanisms in Chapter 19, "The Utilities Package."

Strings

In Java, strings are handled by a special class called String. Even literal strings are managed internally by an instantiation of a String class. An instantiation of a class is simply an object that has been created based on the class description. This method of handling strings is very different from languages like C and C++, where strings are represented simply as an array of characters. The following are a few strings declared using the Java String class:

```
String message;
String name = "Mr. Blonde";
```

At this point it's not that important to know the String class inside and out. You'll learn all the gory details of the String class in Chapter 18, "The Language Package."

Summary

In this chapter, you have taken a look at the core components of the Java language. It is hoped that you now have a better insight about why Java has become popular in such a relatively short time. With vast improvements over the weaknesses of the C and C++ languages—arguably the industry language standards—Java will no doubt become more important in the near future. The language elements covered in this chapter are just the tip of the iceberg when it comes to the benefits of programming in Java.

Now that you are armed with the fundamentals of the Java language, it is hoped that you are ready to press onward and learn more about the Java language. The next chapter, "Expressions, Operators, and Control Structures," covers exactly what its title suggests. In it you will learn how to work with and manipulate much of the information you learned about in this chapter. In doing so, you will be able to start writing programs that do a little more than display cute messages on the screen.

Expressions, Operators, and Control Structures

13

by Michael Morrison

In the previous chapter you learned about the basic components of a Java program. This chapter focuses on how to use these components to do more useful things. Data types are interesting, but without expressions and operators you can't do much with them. Even expressions and operators alone are somewhat limited in what they can do. Throw in control structures and you have the ability to do some interesting things.

This chapter covers all of these issues and pulls together many of the missing pieces of the Java programming puzzle you've begun to assemble. You'll not only expand your knowledge of the Java language a great deal, but also learn what it takes to write some more interesting programs.

Expressions and Operators

Once you have created variables, you typically want to do something with them. Operators enable you to perform an evaluation or computation on a data object or objects. Operators applied to variables and literals form *expressions*. An expression can be thought of as a programmatic equation. More formally, an expression is a sequence of one or more data objects (operands) and zero or more operators that produce a result. An example of an expression follows:

```
x = y / 3;
```

In this expression, x and y are variables, 3 is a literal, and = and / are operators. This expression states that the y variable is divided by 3 using the division operator (/), and the result is stored in x using the assignment operator (=). Notice that the expression was described from right to left. This is the standard technique for breaking down and understanding expressions in Java, as well as most other programming languages. This right-to-left evaluation of expressions isn't just a technique for your own understanding of expressions—it's how the compiler itself analyzes expressions to generate code.

Operator Precedence

Even with the compiler analyzing expressions right to left, there still are many times when the result of an expression would be indeterminate without any other rules. The following expression illustrates the problem:

```
x = 2 * 5 + 12 / 4
```

Strictly using the right-to-left evaluation of the expression, the division operation 12 / 4 is carried out first, which leaves a result of 3. The addition operation 5 + 3 is then performed, which gives you a result of 8. The multiplication operation 2 * 8 is then performed, which gives you a result of 16. Finally, the assignment operation x = 16 is handled, in which case the number 16 is assigned to the variable x.

If you have some experience with operator precedence from another language, you might already be questioning the evaluation of this expression, and for good reason—it's wrong! The problem is that using a simple right-to-left evaluation of expressions can yield inconsistent results, depending on the order of the operators. The solution to this problem lies in operator precedence, which determines the order in which operators are evaluated. Every Java operator has an associated precedence. Following is a listing of all the Java operators from highest to lowest precedence:

.	[ ]	( )	
++	- -	!	~
*	/	%	
+	-		
<<	>>	>>>	
<	>	<=	>=
==	!=		
&			
^			
&&			
||			
? :			
=			

In this list of operators, all of the operators in a particular row have equal precedence. The precedence level of each row decreases from top to bottom. This means that the [ ] operator has a higher precedence than the * operator, but the same precedence as the ( ) operator.

Expression evaluation still moves from right to left, but only when dealing with operators that have the same precedence. Otherwise, operators with a higher precedence are evaluated before operators with a lower precedence. Knowing this, take a look at the same equation again:

```
x = 2 * 5 + 12 / 4
```

Before using the right-to-left evaluation of the expression, first look to see if any of the operators have differing precedence. Indeed they do! The multiplication (*) and division (/) operators both have the highest precedence, followed by the addition operator (+), and then the assignment operator (=). Because the multiplication and division operators share the same precedence, evaluate them from right to left. Doing this, you perform the division operation 12 / 4 first, resulting in 3. You then perform the multiplication operation 2 * 5, which results in 10. After performing these two operations, the expression looks like this:

```
x = 10 + 3;
```

Because the addition operator has a higher precedence than the assignment operator, you perform the addition 10 + 3 next, resulting in 13. Finally, the assignment operation x = 13 is processed, resulting in the number 13 being assigned to the variable x. As you can see, evaluating the expression using operator precedence yields a completely different result.

Just to get the point across, take a look at another expression that uses parentheses for grouping purposes:

```
x = 2 * (11 - 7);
```

Without the grouping parentheses, you would perform the multiplication first and then the subtraction. However, referring back to the precedence list, the () operator comes before all other operators. So, the subtraction 11 - 7 is performed first, yielding 4 and the following expression:

```
x = 2 * 4;
```

The rest of the expression is easily resolved with a multiplication and an assignment to yield a result of 8 in the variable x.

Integer Operators

There are three types of operations that can be performed on integers: unary, binary, and relational. Unary operators act only on single integer numbers, and binary operators act on pairs of integer numbers. Both unary and binary integer operators return integer results. Relational operators, on the other hand, act on two integer numbers but return a Boolean result rather than an integer.

Unary and binary integer operators typically return an int type. For all operations involving the types byte, short, and int, the result is always an int. The only exception to this rule is if one of the operands is a long, in which case the result of the operation also will be of type long.

Unary

Unary integer operators act on a single integer. Table 13.1 lists the unary integer operators.

Table 13.1. The unary integer operators.

Description	Operator
Increment	++
Decrement	- -
Negation	-
Bitwise complement	~

The increment and decrement operators (++ and - -) increase and decrease integer variables by one. Similar to their complements in C and C++, these operators can be used in either prefix or postfix form. A prefix operator takes effect prior to the evaluation of the expression it is in, and a postfix operator takes effect after the expression has been evaluated. Prefix unary operators are placed immediately before the variable and postfix unary operators are placed immediately following the variable. Following is an example of each type of operator:

```
y = ++x;
z = x--;
```

In the first example, x is *prefix incremented*, which means that it is incremented before being assigned to y. In the second example, x is *postfix decremented*, which means that it is decremented after being assigned to z. In the latter case, z is assigned the value of x prior to x being decremented. Listing 13.1 contains the IncDec program, which uses both types of operators. Please note that the IncDec program is actually implemented in the Java class IncDec. This is a result of the object-oriented structure of Java, which requires programs to be implemented as classes. So, when you see a reference to a Java program, keep in mind that it is really referring to a Java class.

Listing 13.1. The IncDec class.

```
class IncDec {
  public static void main (String args[]) {
    int x = 8, y = 13;
    System.out.println("x = " + x);
    System.out.println("y = " + y);
    System.out.println("++x = " + ++x);
    System.out.println("y++ = " + y++);
    System.out.println("x = " + x);
    System.out.println("y = " + y);
  }
}
```

The IncDec program produces the following results:

```
x = 8
y = 13
++x = 9
y++ = 13
x = 9
y = 14
```

The negation unary integer operator (-) is used to change the sign of an integer value. This operator is as simple as it sounds, as indicated by the following example:

```
x = 8;
y = -x;
```

In this example, x is assigned the literal value 8 and then is negated and assigned to y. The resulting value of y is -8. To see this code in a real Java program, check out the Negation program in Listing 13.2.

Listing 13.2. The `Negation` class.

```
class Negation {
  public static void main (String args[]) {
    int x = 8;
    System.out.println("x = " + x);
    int y = -x;
    System.out.println("y = " + y);
  }
}
```

The last Java unary integer operator is the bitwise complement operator (~), which performs a bitwise negation of an integer value. *Bitwise negation* means that each bit in the number is toggled. In other words, all of the binary zeros become ones and all the binary ones become zeros. Take a look at an example very similar to the one for the negation operator:

```
x = 8;
y = ~x;
```

In this example x is assigned the literal value 8 again, but it is bitwise complemented before being assigned to y. What does this mean? Well, without getting into the details of how integers are stored in memory, it means that all of the bits of the variable x are flipped, yielding a decimal result of -9. This result has to do with the fact that negative numbers are stored in memory using a method known as *two's complement* (see the following note). If you're having trouble believing any of this, try it yourself with the `BitwiseComplement` program shown in Listing 13.3.

> **NOTE**
>
> Integer numbers are stored in memory as a series of binary bits that can each have a value of 0 or 1. A number is considered negative if the highest-order bit in the number is set to 1. Because a bitwise complement flips all the bits in a number, including the high-order bit, the sign of a number is reversed.

Listing 13.3. The `BitwiseComplement` class.

```
class BitwiseComplement {
  public static void main (String args[]) {
    int x = 8;
    System.out.println("x = " + x);
    int y = ~x;
    System.out.println("y = " + y);
  }
}
```

Binary

Binary integer operators act on pairs of integers. Table 13.2 lists the binary integer operators.

Table 13.2. The binary integer operators.

Description	Operator
Addition	+
Subtraction	-
Multiplication	*
Division	/
Modulus	%
Bitwise AND	&
Bitwise OR	¦
Bitwise XOR	^
Left Shift	<<
Right Shift	>>
Zero-Fill Right Shift	>>>

The addition, subtraction, multiplication, and division operators (+, -, *, and /) all do what you would expect them to. An important thing to note is how the division operator works; because you are dealing with integer operands, the division operator returns an integer divisor. In cases where the division results in a remainder, the modulus operator (%) can be used to get the remainder value. Listing 13.4 contains the `Arithmetic` program, which shows how the basic binary integer arithmetic operators work.

Listing 13.4. The `Arithmetic` class.

```
class Arithmetic {
  public static void main (String args[]) {
    int x = 17, y = 5;
    System.out.println("x = " + x);
    System.out.println("y = " + y);
    System.out.println("x + y = " + (x + y));
    System.out.println("x - y = " + (x - y));
    System.out.println("x * y = " + (x * y));
    System.out.println("x / y = " + (x / y));
    System.out.println("x % y = " + (x % y));
  }
}
```

The results of running the `Arithmetic` program follow:

```
x = 17
y = 5
x + y = 22
x - y = 12
x * y = 85
x / y = 3
x % y = 2
```

These results shouldn't surprise you too much. Just notice that the division operation x / y, which boils down to 17 / 5, yields the result 3. Also notice that the modulus operation x % y, which is resolved down to 17 % 5, ends up with a result of 2, which is the remainder of the integer division.

Mathematically, a division by zero results in an infinite result. Because representing infinite numbers is a big problem for computers, division or modulus operations by zero result in an error. To be more specific, a runtime exception is thrown. You'll learn a lot more about exceptions in Chapter 16, "Exception Handling."

The bitwise AND, OR, and XOR operators (&, |, and ^) all act on the individual bits of an integer. These operators sometimes are useful when an integer is being used as a bit field. An example of this is when an integer is used to represent a group of binary flags. An int is capable of representing up to 32 different flags, because it is stored in 32 bits. Listing 13.5 contains the program `Bitwise`, which shows how to use the binary bitwise integer operators.

Listing 13.5. The `Bitwise` class.

```
class Bitwise {
  public static void main (String args[]) {
    int x = 5, y = 6;
    System.out.println("x = " + x);
    System.out.println("y = " + y);
    System.out.println("x & y = " + (x & y));
    System.out.println("x | y = " + (x | y));
    System.out.println("x ^ y = " + (x ^ y));
  }
}
```

The output of running `Bitwise` follows:

```
x = 5
y = 6
x & y = 4
x | y = 7
x ^ y = 3
```

To understand this output, you must first understand the binary equivalents of each decimal number. In `Bitwise`, the variables x and y are set to 5 and 6, which correspond to the binary numbers 0101 and 0110. The bitwise AND operation compares each bit of each number to see if they are the same. It then sets the resulting bit to 1 if both bits being compared are 1, and 0 otherwise. The result of the bitwise AND operation on these two numbers is 0100 in binary, or decimal 4. The same logic is used for both of the other operators, except that the rules for comparing the bits are different. The bitwise OR operator sets the resulting bit to 1 if either of the bits being compared is 1. For these numbers, the result is 0111 binary, or 7 decimal. Finally, the bitwise XOR operator sets resulting bits to 1 if exactly one of the bits being compared is 1, and 0 otherwise. For these numbers, the result is 0011 binary, or 3 decimal.

The left-shift, right-shift, and zero-fill-right-shift operators (<<, >>, and >>>) shift the individual bits of an integer by a specified integer amount. The following are some examples of how these operators are used:

```
x << 3;
y >> 7;
z >>> 2;
```

In the first example, the individual bits of the integer variable x are shifted to the left three places. In the second example, the bits of y are shifted to the right seven places. Finally, the third example shows z being shifted to the right two places, with zeros shifted into the two leftmost places. To see the shift operators in a real program, check out Shift in Listing 13.6.

Listing 13.6. The Shift class.

```
class Shift {
  public static void main (String args[]) {
    int x = 7;
    System.out.println("x = " + x);
    System.out.println("x >> 2 = " + (x >> 2));
    System.out.println("x << 1 = " + (x << 1));
    System.out.println("x >>> 1 = " + (x >>> 1));
  }
}
```

The output of Shift follows:

```
x = 7
x >> 2 = 1
x << 1 = 14
x >>> 1 = 3
```

The number being shifted in this case is the decimal 7, which is represented in binary as 0111. The first right-shift operation shifts the bits two places to the right, resulting in the binary number 0001, or decimal 1. The next operation, a left shift, shifts the bits one place to the left, resulting in the binary number 1110, or decimal 14. Finally, the last operation is a zero-fill right shift, which shifts the bits 1 place to the right, resulting in the binary number 0011, or decimal 3. Pretty simple, huh? And you probably thought it was difficult working with integers at the bit level!

Based on these examples, you may be wondering what the difference is between the right-shift (>>) and zero-fill-right-shift operators (>>>). The right-shift operator appears to shift zeros into the leftmost bits, just like the zero-fill-right-shift operator, right? Well, when dealing with positive numbers, there is no difference between the two operators; they both shift zeros into the upper bits of a number. The difference arises when you start shifting negative numbers. Remember that negative numbers have the high-order bit set to 1. The right-shift operator preserves the high-order bit and effectively shifts the lower 31 bits to the right. This behavior yields results for negative numbers similar to those for positive numbers. That is, -8 shifted right by one will result in -4. The zero-fill-right-shift operator, on the other hand, shifts zeros into all the upper bits, including the high-order bit. When this shifting is applied to negative numbers, the high-order bit becomes 0 and the number becomes positive.

Relational

The last group of integer operators is the relational operators, which all operate on integers but return a type `boolean`. Table 13.3 lists the relational integer operators.

Table 13.3. The relational integer operators.

Description	Operator
Less Than	<
Greater Than	>
Less Than Or Equal To	<=
Greater Than Or Equal To	>=
Equal To	==
Not Equal To	!=

These operators all perform comparisons between integers. Listing 13.7 contains the `Relational` program, which demonstrates the use of the relational operators with integers.

Listing 13.7. The `Relational` class.

```
class Relational {
  public static void main (String args[]) {
    int x = 7, y = 11, z = 11;
    System.out.println("x = " + x);
    System.out.println("y = " + y);
    System.out.println("z = " + z);
    System.out.println("x < y = " + (x < y));
    System.out.println("x > z = " + (x > z));
    System.out.println("y <= z = " + (y <= z));
    System.out.println("x >= y = " + (x >= y));
    System.out.println("y == z = " + (y == z));
    System.out.println("x != y = " + (x != z));
  }
}
```

The output of running `Relational` follows:

```
x = 7
y = 11
z = 11
x < y = true
x > z = false
y <= z = true
x >= y = false
y == z = true
x != y = true
```

As you can see, the `println` method is smart enough to print Boolean results correctly as `true` and `false`.

Floating-Point Operators

Similar to integer operators, there are three types of operations that can be performed on floating-point numbers: unary, binary, and relational. Unary operators act only on single floating-point numbers, and binary operators act on pairs of floating-point numbers. Both unary and binary floating-point operators return floating-point results. Relational operators, however, act on two floating-point numbers but return a Boolean result.

Unary and binary floating-point operators return a `float` type if both operands are of type `float`. If one or both of the operands is of type `double`, however, the result of the operation is of type `double`.

Unary

The unary floating point operators act on a single floating-point number. Table 13.4 lists the unary floating-point operators.

Table 13.4. The unary floating-point operators.

Description	Operator
Increment	++
Decrement	--

As you can see, the only two unary floating point operators are the increment and decrement operators. These two operators respectively add and subtract `1.0` from their floating-point operand.

Binary

The binary floating-point operators act on a pair of floating-point numbers. Table 13.5 lists the binary floating-point operators.

Table 13.5. The binary floating-point operators.

Description	Operator
Addition	+
Subtraction	-
Multiplication	*
Division	/
Modulus	%

The binary floating-point operators consist of the four traditional binary operations (+, -, *,), along with the modulus operator (%). You might be wondering how the modulus operator fits in here, considering that its usage as an integer operator relied on an integer division. If you recall, the integer modulus operator returned the remainder of an integer division of the two operands. But a floating-point division never results in a remainder, so what does a floating-point modulus do? The floating-point modulus operator returns the floating-point equivalent of an integer division. What this means is that the division is carried out with both floating-point operands, but the resulting divisor is treated as an integer, resulting in a floating-point remainder. Listing 13.8 contains the `FloatMath` program, which shows how the floating-point modulus operator works along with the other binary floating-point operators.

Listing 13.8. The `FloatMath` class.

```
class FloatMath {
  public static void main (String args[]) {
    float x = 23.5F, y = 7.3F;
    System.out.println("x = " + x);
    System.out.println("y = " + y);
    System.out.println("x + y = " + (x + y));
    System.out.println("x - y = " + (x - y));
    System.out.println("x * y = " + (x * y));
    System.out.println("x / y = " + (x / y));
    System.out.println("x % y = " + (x % y));
  }
}
```

The output of `FloatMath` follows:

```
x = 23.5
y = 7.3
```

```
x + y = 30.8
x - y = 16.2
x * y = 171.55
x / y = 3.21918
x % y = 1.6
```

The first four operations no doubt performed as you expected, taking the two floating-point operands and yielding a floating-point result. The final modulus operation determined that 7.3 divides into 23.5 an integral amount of 3 times, leaving a remaining result of 1.6.

Relational

The relational floating-point operators compare two floating-point operands, leaving a Boolean result. The floating-point relational operators are the same as the integer relational operators listed in Table 13.3, except that they work on floating-point numbers.

Boolean Operators

Boolean operators act on Boolean types and return a Boolean result. The Boolean operators are listed in Table 13.6.

Table 13.6. The Boolean operators.

Description	Operator
Evaluation AND	&
Evaluation OR	¦
Evaluation XOR	^
Logical AND	&&
Logical OR	¦¦
Negation	!
Equal To	==
Not Equal To	!=
Conditional	?:

The evaluation operators (&, ¦, and ^) evaluate both sides of an expression before determining the result. The logical operators (&& and ¦¦) avoid the right-side evaluation of the expression if it is not needed. To better understand the difference between these operators, take a look at the following two expressions:

```
boolean result = isValid & (Count > 10);
boolean result = isValid && (Count > 10);
```

The first expression uses the evaluation AND operator (&) to make an assignment. In this case, both sides of the expression always are evaluated, regardless of the values of the variables involved. In the second example, the logical AND operator (&&) is used. This time, the isValid Boolean value is first checked. If it is false, the right side of the expression is ignored and the assignment is made. This is more efficient because a false value on the left side of the expression provides enough information to determine the false outcome.

Although the logical operators are more efficient, there still may be times when you want to use the evaluation operators to ensure that the entire expression is evaluated. The following code shows how the evaluation AND operator is necessary for the complete evaluation of an expression:

```java
while ((++x < 10) && (++y < 15)) {
  System.out.println(x);
  System.out.println(y);
}
```

In this example, the second expression (++y > 15) is evaluated after the last pass through the loop because of the evaluation AND operator. If the logical AND operator had been used, the second expression would not have been evaluated and y would not have been incremented after the last time around.

The Boolean operators negation, equal-to, and not-equal-to (!, ==, and !=) perform exactly as you might expect. The negation operator toggles the value of a Boolean from false to true or from true to false, depending on the original value. The equal-to operator simply determines whether two Boolean values are equal (both true or both false). Similarly, the not-equal-to operator determines whether two Boolean operands are unequal.

The conditional Boolean operator (?:) is the most unique of the Boolean operators, and is worth a closer look. This operator also is known as the *ternary operator* because it takes three items: a condition and two expressions. The syntax for the conditional operator follows:

```
Condition ? Expression1 : Expression2
```

The Condition, which itself is a Boolean, is first evaluated to determine whether it is true or false. If Condition evaluates into a true result, Expression1 is evaluated. If Condition ends up being false, Expression2 is evaluated. To get a better feel for the conditional operator, check out the Conditional program in Listing 13.9.

Listing 13.9. The Conditional class.

```java
class Conditional {
  public static void main (String args[]) {
    int x = 0;
    boolean isEven = false;
    System.out.println("x = " + x);
    x = isEven ? 4 : 7;
    System.out.println("x = " + x);
  }
}
```

The results of the Conditional program follow:

```
x = 0
x = 7
```

The integer variable x is first assigned a value of 0. The Boolean variable isEven is assigned a value of false. Using the conditional operator, the value of isEven is checked. Because it is false, the second expression of the conditional is used, which results in the value 7 being assigned to x.

String Operators

Along with integers, floating-point numbers, and Booleans, strings also can be manipulated with operators. Actually, there is only one string operator: the concatenation operator (+). The concatenation operator for strings works very similarly to the addition operator for numbers—it adds strings together. The concatenation operator is demonstrated in the Concatenation program shown in Listing 13.10.

Listing 13.10. The Concatenation class.

```
class Concatenation {
  public static void main (String args[]) {
    String firstHalf = "What " + "did ";
    String secondHalf = "you " + "say?";
    System.out.println(firstHalf + secondHalf);
  }
}
```

The output of Concatenation follows:

```
What did you say?
```

In the Concatenation program, literal strings are concatenated to make assignments to the two string variables, firstHalf and secondHalf, upon creation. The two string variables are then concatenated within the call to the println method.

Assignment Operators

One final group of operators that you haven't seen yet is the assignment operators. Assignment operators actually work with all of the fundamental data types. Table 13.7 lists the assignment operators.

Table 13.7. The assignment operators.

Description	Operator
Simple	=
Addition	+=
Subtraction	-=
Multiplication	*=
Division	/=
Modulus	%=
AND	&=
OR	¦=
XOR	^=

With the exception of the simple assignment operator (=), the assignment operators function exactly like their nonassignment counterparts, except that the resulting value is stored in the operand on the left side of the expression. Take a look at the following examples:

```
x += 6;
x *= (y - 3);
```

In the first example, x and 6 are added and the result stored in x. In the second example, 3 is subtracted from y and the result multiplied by x. The final result is then stored in x.

Control Structures

Although performing operations on data is very useful, it's time to move on to the issue of program flow control. The flow of your programs is dictated by two different types of constructs: branches and loops. Branches enable you to selectively execute one part of a program instead of another. Loops, on the other hand, provide a means to repeat certain parts of a program. Together, branches and loops provide you with a powerful means to control the logic and execution of your code.

Branches

Without branches or loops, Java code executes in a sequential fashion, as shown in Figure 13.1.

In Figure 13.1, each statement is executed sequentially. What if you don't always want every single statement executed? Then you use a branch. Figure 13.2 shows how a conditional branch gives the flow of your code more options.

FIGURE 13.1.

A program executing sequentially.

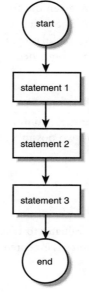

FIGURE 13.2.

A program executing with a branch.

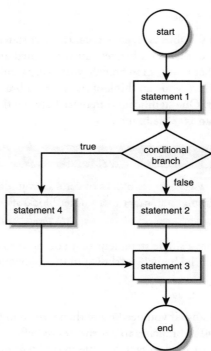

By adding a branch, you've given the code two optional routes to take, based on the result of the conditional expression. The concept of branches might seem trivial, but it would be difficult if not impossible to write useful programs without them. Java supports two types of branches: `if-else` branches and `switch` branches.

if-else

The `if-else` branch is the most commonly used branch in Java programming. It is used to select conditionally one of two possible outcomes. The syntax for the `if-else` statement follows:

```
if (Condition)
  Statement1
else
  Statement2
```

If the Boolean `Condition` evaluates to `true`, `Statement1` is executed. Likewise, if the `Condition` evaluates to `false`, `Statement2` is executed. The following example should make it a little more clear:

```
if (isTired)
  timeToEat = true;
else
  timeToEat = false;
```

If the Boolean variable `isTired` is `true`, the first statement is executed and `timeToEat` is set to `true`. Otherwise, the second statement is executed and `timeToEat` is set to `false`. You might have noticed that the `if-else` branch works very similarly to the conditional operator (`?:`) you saw earlier. In fact, you can think of the `if-else` branch as an expanded version of the conditional operator. One significant difference between the two is that you can include compound statements in an `if-else` branch.

> **NOTE**
>
> *Compound statements* are blocks of code surrounded by curly braces {} that appear as a single, or simple, statement to an outer block of code.

If you have only a single statement that you need to execute conditionally, you can leave off the `else` part of the branch, as shown in the following example:

```
if (isThirsty)
  pourADrink = true;
```

On the other hand, if you need more than two conditional outcomes, you can string together a series of `if-else` branches to get the desired effect. The following example shows multiple `if-else` branches used to switch between different outcomes:

```
if (x == 0)
  y = 5;
else if (x == 2)
  y = 25;
else if (x >= 3)
  y = 125;
```

In this example, three different comparisons are made, each with its own statement that is executed upon a true conditional result. Notice, however, that subsequent if-else branches are in effect nested within the prior branch. This ensures that at most one statement is executed.

The last important topic to cover in regard to if-else branches is compound statements. As mentioned earlier, a compound statement is a block of code surrounded by curly braces that appears to an outer block as a single statement. The following is an example of a compound statement used with an if branch:

```
if (performCalc) {
  x += y * 5;
  y -= 10;
  z = (x - 3) / y;
}
```

Sometimes, when nesting if-else branches, it is necessary to use curly braces to distinguish which statements go with which branch. The following example illustrates the problem:

```
if (x != 0)
  if (y < 10)
    z = 5;
else
  z = 7;
```

In this example, the style of indentation indicates that the else branch belongs to the first (outer) if. However, because there was no grouping specified, the Java compiler assumes that the else goes with the inner if. To get the desired results, you need to modify the code as follows:

```
if (x != 0) {
  if (y < 10)
    z = 5;
}
else
  z = 7;
```

The addition of the curly braces tells the compiler that the inner if is part of a compound statement, and more importantly, it completely hides the else branch from the inner if. Based on what you learned from the discussion of blocks and scope in the last chapter, you can see that code within the inner if has no way of accessing code outside its scope, including the else branch.

Listing 13.11 contains the source code for the IfElseName class, which uses a lot of what you've learned so far.

Listing 13.11. The IfElseName class.

```
class IfElseName {
  public static void main (String args[]) {
    char firstInitial = (char)-1;
    System.out.println("Enter your first initial:");
    try {
      firstInitial = (char)System.in.read();
    }
    catch (Exception e) {
      System.out.println("Error: " + e.toString());
    }
    if (firstInitial == -1)
      System.out.println("Now what kind of name is that?");
    else if (firstInitial == 'j')
      System.out.println("Your name must be Jules!");
    else if (firstInitial == 'v')
      System.out.println("Your name must be Vincent!");
    else if (firstInitial == 'z')
      System.out.println("Your name must be Zed!");
    else
      System.out.println("I can't figure out your name!");
  }
}
```

When typing the letter v in response to the input message, IfElseName yields the following results:

```
Your name must be Vincent!
```

The first thing in IfElseName you probably are wondering about is the read method. The read method simply reads a character from the standard input stream (System.in), which is typically the keyboard. Notice that a cast is used because read returns an int type. Once the input character has been successfully retrieved, a succession of if-else branches are used to determine the proper output. If there are no matches, the final else branch is executed, which notifies users that their names could not be determined. Notice that the value read is checked to see if it is equal to −1. The read method returns −1 if it has reached the end of the input stream.

NOTE

You may have noticed that the call to the read method in IfElseName is enclosed within a try-catch clause. The try-catch clause is part of Java's support for exception handling and is used in this case to trap errors encountered while reading input from the user. You'll learn more about exceptions and the try-catch clause in Chapter 16, "Exception Handling."

Switch

Similar to the if-else branch, the switch branch specifically is designed to conditionally switch among multiple outcomes. The syntax for the switch statement follows:

```
switch (Expression) {
  case Constant1:
    StatementList1
  case Constant2:
    StatementList2
  ...
  default:
    DefaultStatementList
}
```

The switch branch evaluates and compares *Expression* to all of the case constants and branches the program's execution to the matching case statement list. If no case constants match *Expression*, the program branches to the *DefaultStatementList*, if one has been supplied (the *DefaultStatementList* is optional). You might be wondering what a statement list is. A statement list is simply a series, or *list*, of statements. Unlike the if-else branch, which directs program flow to a simple or compound statement, the switch branch directs the flow to a list of statements.

When the program execution moves into a case statement list, it continues from there in a sequential manner. To better understand this, take a look at Listing 13.12, which contains a switch version of the name program that you developed earlier with if-else branches.

Listing 13.12. The SwitchName1 class.

```
class SwitchName1 {
  public static void main (String args[]) {
    char firstInitial = (char)-1;
    System.out.println("Enter your first initial:");
    try {
      firstInitial = (char)System.in.read();
    }
    catch (Exception e) {
      System.out.println("Error: " + e.toString());
    }
    switch(firstInitial) {
      case (char)-1:
        System.out.println("Now what kind of name is that?");
      case 'j':
        System.out.println("Your name must be Jules!");
      case 'v':
        System.out.println("Your name must be Vincent!");
      case 'z':
        System.out.println("Your name must be Zed!");
      default:
        System.out.println("I can't figure out your name!");
    }
  }
}
```

When typing the letter v in response to the input message, SwitchName1 produces the following results:

```
Your name must be Vincent!
Your name must be Zed!
I can't figure out your name!
```

Hey, what's going on here? That output definitely does not look right. The problem lies in the way the switch branch controls program flow. The switch branch matched the v entered with the correct case statement, as shown in the first string printed. However, the program continued executing all of the case statements from that point onward, which is not what you wanted. The solution to the problem lies in the break statement. The break statement forces a program to break out of the block of code it is currently executing. Check out the new version of the program in Listing 13.13, with break statements added where appropriate.

Listing 13.13. The SwitchName2 class.

```java
class SwitchName2 {
  public static void main (String args[]) {
    char firstInitial = (char)-1;
    System.out.println("Enter your first initial:");
    try {
      firstInitial = (char)System.in.read();
    }
    catch (Exception e) {
      System.out.println("Error: " + e.toString());
    }
    switch(firstInitial) {
      case (char)-1:
        System.out.println("Now what kind of name is that?");
        break;
      case 'j':
        System.out.println("Your name must be Jules!");
        break;
      case 'v':
        System.out.println("Your name must be Vincent!");
        break;
      case 'z':
        System.out.println("Your name must be Zed!");
        break;
      default:
        System.out.println("I can't figure out your name!");
    }
  }
}
```

When you run SwitchName2 and enter v, you get the following output:

```
Your name must be Vincent!
```

That's a lot better! You can see that placing break statements after each case statement kept the program from falling through to the next case statements. Although you will use break statements in this manner the majority of the time, there might still be some situations where you will want a case statement to fall through to the next one.

Loops

When it comes to program flow, branches really only tell half of the story; loops tell the other half. Put simply, loops enable you to execute code repeatedly. There are three types of loops in Java: for loops, while loops, and do-while loops.

Just as branches alter the sequential flow of programs, so do loops. Figure 13.3 shows how a loop alters the sequential flow of a Java program.

FIGURE 13.3.

A program executing with a loop.

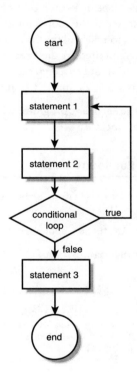

for

The for loop provides a means to repeat a section of code a designated number of times. The for loop is structured so that a section of code is repeated until some limit has been reached. The syntax for the for statement follows:

```
for (InitializationExpression; LoopCondition; StepExpression)
  Statement
```

The `for` loop repeats the *Statement* the number of times that is determined by the *InitializationExpression*, the *LoopCondition*, and the *StepExpression*. The *InitializationExpression* is used to initialize a loop control variable. The *LoopCondition* compares the loop control variable to some limit value. Finally, the *StepExpression* specifies how the loop control variable should be modified before the next iteration of the loop. The following example illustrates how a `for` loop can be used to print the numbers from one to ten:

```
for (int i = 1; i < 11; i++)
  System.out.println(i);
```

First, `i` is declared as an integer. The fact that `i` is declared within the body of the `for` loop might look strange to you at this point. Don't despair—this is completely legal. `i` is initialized to 1 in the *InitializationExpression* part of the `for` loop. Next, the conditional expression `i < 11` is evaluated to see if the loop should continue. At this point, `i` is still equal to 1, so *LoopCondition* evaluates to `true` and the *Statement* is executed (the value of `i` is printed to standard output). `i` is then incremented in the *StepExpression* part of the `for` loop, and the process repeats with the evaluation of *LoopCondition* again. This continues until *LoopCondition* evaluates to `false`, which is when x equals 11 (ten iterations later).

Listing 13.14 shows the `ForCount` program, which shows how to use a `for` loop to count a user-entered amount of numbers.

Listing 13.14. The `ForCount` class.

```java
class ForCount {
  public static void main (String args[]) {
    char input = (char)-1;
    int  numToCount;
    System.out.println("Enter a number to count to between 0 and 10:");
    try {
      input = (char)System.in.read();
    }
    catch (Exception e) {
      System.out.println("Error: " + e.toString());
    }
    numToCount = Character.digit(input, 10);
    if ((numToCount > 0) && (numToCount < 10)) {
      for (int i = 1; i <= numToCount; i++)
        System.out.println(i);
    }
    else
      System.out.println("That number was not between 0 and 10!");
  }
}
```

When the `ForCount` program is run and the number 4 is entered, the following output results:

```
1
2
3
4
```

`ForCount` first prompts the user to enter a number between zero and ten. A character is read from the keyboard using the `read` method and the result stored in the `input` character variable. The static `digit` method of the `Character` class then is used to convert the character to its base 10 integer representation. This value is stored in the `numToCount` integer variable. `numToCount` is then checked to make sure that it is in the range zero to ten. If so, a `for` loop is executed that counts from 1 to `numToCount`, printing each number along the way. If `numToCount` is outside of the valid range, an error message is printed.

Before you move on, there is one small problem with `ForCount` that you might not have noticed. Run it and try typing in a number greater than nine. What happened to the error message? The problem is that `ForCount` is grabbing only the first character it sees from the input. So if you type in `300`, it will just get the `3` and think everything is fine. You don't need to worry about fixing this problem right now, as it will be resolved when you learn more about input and output in Chapter 20, "The I/O Package."

while

Like the `for` loop, the `while` loop has a loop condition that controls the execution of the loop statement. Unlike the `for` loop, the `while` loop has no initialization or step expressions. The syntax for the `while` statement follows:

```
while (LoopCondition)
  Statement
```

If the Boolean `LoopCondition` evaluates to `true`, the `Statement` is executed and the process starts over. It is important to understand that there is no step expression, as in a `for` loop. This means that the `LoopCondition` must somehow be affected by code in the `Statement` or the loop will infinitely repeat, which is a bad thing. This is bad because an infinite loop causes a program to never exit, which hogs processor time and can ultimately hang the system.

Another important thing to notice about the `while` loop is that its `LoopCondition` occurs before the body of the loop `Statement`. This means that if the `LoopCondition` initially evaluates to `false`, the `Statement` never will be executed. This might seem trivial, but it is in fact the only thing that differentiates the `while` loop from the `do-while` loop, which is discussed in the next section.

To better understand how the `while` loop works, take a look at Listing 13.15, which shows how a counting program works using a `while` loop.

Listing 13.15. The WhileCount class.

```
class WhileCount {
  public static void main (String args[]) {
    char input = (char)-1;
    int  numToCount;
    System.out.println("Enter a number to count to between 0 and 10:");
```

continues

Listing 13.15. continued

```java
try {
    input = (char)System.in.read();
}
catch (Exception e) {
    System.out.println("Error: " + e.toString());
}
numToCount = Character.digit(input, 10);
if ((numToCount > 0) && (numToCount < 10)) {
    int i = 1;
    while (i <= numToCount) {
        System.out.println(i);
        i++;
    }
}
else
    System.out.println("That number was not between 0 and 10!");
}
}
```

Arguably, `WhileCount` doesn't demonstrate the best usage of a `while` loop. Loops that involve counting almost should always be implemented with `for` loops. However, seeing how a `while` loop can be made to imitate a `for` loop can give you insight into the structural differences between the two.

Because `while` loops don't have any type of initialization expression, you first have to declare and initialize the variable `i` to 1. Next, the loop condition for the `while` loop is established as `i <= numToCount`. Inside the compound `while` statement, you can see a call to the `println` method, which outputs the value of `i`. Finally, `i` is incremented and program execution resumes back at the `while` loop condition.

do-while

The `do-while` loop is very similar to the `while` loop, as you can see in the following syntax:

```java
do
    Statement
while (LoopCondition);
```

The major difference between the `do-while` loop and the `while` loop is that the *LoopCondition* is evaluated after the `Statement` is executed. This difference is important because there might be times when you want the *Statement* code to be executed at least once, regardless of the *LoopCondition*. The syntax for the `do-while` loop follows:

The *Statement* is executed initially, and from then on it is executed as long as the *LoopCondition* evaluates to `true`. Like the `while` loop, you must be careful with the `do-while` loop to avoid creating an infinite loop. An infinite loop occurs when the *LoopCondition* remains true indefinitely. The following example illustrates a very obvious infinite `do-while` loop:

```
do
  System.out.println("I'm stuck!");
while (true);
```

Because the *LoopCondition* is always true, the message I'm Stuck! is printed forever, or at least until you hit Ctrl+C and break out of the program.

break and continue

You've already seen how the break statement works in regard to the switch branch. The break statement is also useful when dealing with loops. You can use the break statement to jump out of a loop and effectively bypass the loop condition. Listing 13.16 shows how the break statement can help you out of the infinite loop problem shown earlier.

Listing 13.16. The BreakLoop class.

```
class BreakLoop {
  public static void main (String args[]) {
    int i = 0;
    do {
      System.out.println("I'm stuck!");
      i++;
      if (i > 100)
        break;
    }
    while (true);
  }
}
```

In BreakLoop, a seemingly infinite do-while loop is created by setting the loop condition to true. However, the break statement is used to exit the loop when i is incremented past 100.

Another useful statement that works similarly to the break statement is the continue statement. Unlike break, the continue statement is only useful when working with loops and has no real application to the switch branch. The continue statement works like the break statement in that it jumps out of the current iteration of a loop. The difference with continue is that program execution is restored to the test condition of the loop. Remember, break jumps completely out of a loop. Use break when you want to jump out and terminate a loop, and use continue when you want to jump immediately to the next iteration of the loop.

Summary

A lot of territory has been covered in this chapter. You started off by learning about expressions and then moved right into operators, learning how they work and how they affect each data type. You won't regret the time spent working with operators in this chapter—they are at the core of almost every mathematical or logical Java expression.

From operators, you moved on to control structures, learning about the various types of branches and loops. Branches and loops provide the means to alter the flow of Java programs and are just as important as operators in the whole realm of Java programming.

With the concepts presented in this chapter firmly set in your mind, you are ready to dig a little deeper into Java. Next stop: object-oriented programming with classes, packages, and interfaces!

Classes, Packages, and Interfaces

14

by Michael Morrison

IN THIS CHAPTER

So far, you've managed to avoid the issue of object-oriented programming and how it relates to Java. This chapter aims to remedy that problem. It begins with a basic discussion of object-oriented programming in general. With this background in place, you can then move into the rest of the chapter, which covers the specific elements of the Java language that provide support for object-oriented programming—namely, classes, packages, and interfaces.

You can think of this chapter as the chapter that finishes helping you to your feet in regard to learning the Java language. Classes are the final core component of the Java language that you need to learn to be a proficient Java programmer. Once you have a solid understanding of classes and how they work in Java, you'll be ready to write some serious Java programs. So, what are you waiting for, read on!

Object-Oriented Programming Primer

If you've been anywhere near the computer section of a bookstore or picked up a programming magazine in the last five years, you've no doubt seen the hype surrounding object-oriented programming. It's the most popular, yet generally least understood programming technology to come about in a while, and it all revolves around the concept of an *object*.

You may have been wondering what the big deal is with objects and object-oriented technology. Is it something you should be concerned with, and if so, why? If you sift through the hype surrounding the whole object-oriented issue, you'll find a very powerful technology that provides a lot of benefits to software design. The problem is that object-oriented concepts can be difficult to grasp. And you can't embrace the benefits of object-oriented design if you don't completely understand what they are. Because of this, a complete understanding of the theory behind object-oriented programming is usually developed over time through practice.

A lot of the confusion among developers in regard to object-oriented technology has led to confusion among computer users in general. How many products have you seen that claim they are object-oriented? Now, considering the fact that object-orientation is a software design issue, what can this statement possibly mean to a software consumer? In many ways, "object-oriented" has become to the software industry what "new and improved" is to the household cleanser industry. The truth is that the real world is already object-oriented, which is no surprise to anyone. The significance of object-oriented technology is that it enables programmers to design software in much the same way that they perceive the real world.

Now that you've come to terms with some of the misconceptions surrounding the object-oriented issue, try to put them aside and think of what the term object-oriented might mean to software design. This primer lays the groundwork for understanding how object-oriented design makes writing programs faster, easier, and more reliable. And it all begins with the object. Even though this chapter ultimately focuses on Java, this object-oriented primer section really applies to all object-oriented languages.

Objects

Objects are software bundles of data and the procedures that act on that data. The procedures are also known as methods. The merger of data and methods provides a means of more accurately representing real-world objects in software. Without objects, modeling a real-world problem in software requires a significant logical leap. Objects, on the other hand, enable programmers to solve real-world problems in the software domain much easier and more logically.

As evident by its name, objects are at the heart of object-oriented technology. To understand how software objects are beneficial, think about the common characteristics of all real-world objects. Lions, cars, and calculators all share two common characteristics: state and behavior. For example, the state of a lion might include color, weight, and whether the lion is tired or hungry. Lions also have certain behaviors, such as roaring, sleeping, and hunting. The state of a car includes the current speed, the type of transmission, whether it is two- or four-wheel drive, whether the lights are on, and the current gear, among other things. The behaviors for a car include turning, braking, and accelerating.

As with real-world objects, software objects also have these two common characteristics (state and behavior). To relate this back to programming terms, the state of an object is determined by its data and the behavior of an object is defined by its methods. By making this connection between real-world objects an-d software objects, you begin to see how objects help bridge the gap between the real world and the world of software inside your computer.

Because software objects are modeled after real-world objects, you can more easily represent real-world objects in object-oriented programs. You could use the lion object to represent a real lion in an interactive software zoo. Similarly, car objects would turn out very useful in a racing game. However, you don't always have to think of software objects as modeling physical real-world objects; software objects can be just as useful for modeling abstract concepts. For example, a thread is an object used in multithreaded software systems that represents a stream of program execution. You'll learn a lot more about threads and how they are used in Java in the next chapter, "Threads and Multithreading."

Figure 14.1 shows a visualization of a software object, including the primary components and how they relate.

FIGURE 14.1.

A software object.

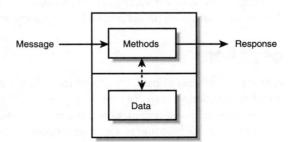

The software object in Figure 14.1 clearly shows the two primary components of an object: data and methods. The figure also shows some type of communication, or access, between the data and the methods. Additionally, it shows how messages are sent through the methods, which result in responses from the object. You'll learn more about messages and responses a little later in this chapter.

The data and methods within an object express everything that the object represents (state), along with what all it can do (behavior). A software object modeling a real-world car would have variables (data) that indicate the car's current state: It's traveling at 75 mph, it's in 4th gear, and the lights are on. The software car object would also have methods that allow it to brake, accelerate, steer, change gears, and turn the lights on and off. Figure 14.2 shows what a software car object might look like.

FIGURE 14.2.

A software car object.

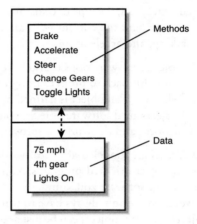

In both Figures 14.1 and 14.2 you probably noticed the line separating the methods from the data within the object. This line is a little misleading because methods have full access to the data within an object. The line is there to illustrate the difference between the visibility of the methods and the data to the outside. In this sense, an object's visibility refers to what parts of the object another object has access. Because object data defaults to being invisible, or inaccessible to other objects, all interaction between objects must be handled through methods. This hiding of data within an object is called encapsulation.

Encapsulation

Encapsulation is the process of packaging an object's data together with its methods. A powerful benefit of encapsulation is the hiding of implementation details from other objects. This means that the internal portion of an object has more limited visibility than the external portion. This results in a safeguarding of the internal portion against unwanted external access.

The external portion of an object is often referred to as the object's *interface,* because it acts as the object's interface to the rest of the program. Because other objects must communicate with the object only through its interface, the internal portion of the object is protected from outside tampering. And because an outside program has no access to the internal implementation of an object, the internal implementation can change at any time without affecting other parts of the program.

So, you've learned that encapsulation provides two primary benefits to programmers:

- Implementation hiding
- Modularity

Implementation hiding refers to the protection of the internal implementation of an object. An object is composed of a public interface and a private section that can be a combination of internal data and methods. The internal data and methods are the sections of the object hidden. The primary benefit is that these sections can change without affecting other parts of the program.

Modularity means that an object can be maintained independently of other objects. Because the source code for the internal sections of an object is maintained separately from the interface, you are free to make modifications with confidence that your object won't cause problems. This makes it easier to distribute objects throughout a system.

Messages

An object acting alone is rarely very useful; most objects require other objects to do much of anything. For example, the car object is pretty useless by itself with no other interaction. Add a driver object, however, and things get more interesting! Knowing this, it's pretty clear that objects need some type of communication mechanism in order to interact with each other.

Software objects interact and communicate with each other through messages. When the driver object wants the car object to accelerate, it sends the car object a message. If you want to think of messages more literally, think of two people as objects. If one person wants the other person to come closer, they send the other person a message. More accurately, they may say to the other person "Come here, please." This is a message in a very literal sense. Software messages are a little different in form, but not in theory—they tell an object what to do.

Many times the receiving object needs—along with a message—more information so that it knows exactly what to do. When the driver tells the car to accelerate, the car must know by how much. This information is passed along with the message as *message parameters.*

From this discussion, you can see that messages consist of three things:

1. The object to receive the message (car)
2. The name of the action to perform (accelerate)
3. Any parameters the method requires (15 mph)

These three components are sufficient information to fully describe a message for an object. Any interaction with an object is handled by passing a message. This means that objects anywhere in a system can communicate with other objects solely through messages.

So you don't get confused, understand that "message passing" is another way of saying "method calling." When an object sends another object a message, it is really just calling a method of that object. The message parameters are actually the parameters to a method. In object-oriented programming, messages and methods are synonymous.

Because everything that an object can do is expressed through its methods (interface), message passing supports all possible interactions between objects. In fact, interfaces allow objects to send and receive messages to each other even if they reside in different locations on a network. Objects in this scenario are referred to as *distributed objects*. Java is specifically designed to support distributed objects.

Classes

Throughout this discussion of object-oriented programming, you've only dealt with the concept of an object already existing in a system. You may be wondering how objects get into a system in the first place. This question brings you to the most fundamental structure in object-oriented programming: the class. A *class* is a template or prototype that defines a type of object. A class is to an object what a blueprint is to a house. Many houses may be built from a single blueprint; the blueprint outlines the makeup of the houses. Classes work exactly the same way, except that they outline the makeup of objects.

In the real world, there are often many objects of the same kind. Using the house analogy, there are many different houses around the world, but houses all share common characteristics. In object-oriented terms, you would say that your house is a specific instance of the class of objects known as houses. All houses have states and behaviors in common that define them as houses. When a builder starts building a new neighborhood of houses, he typically builds them all from a set of blueprints. It wouldn't be as efficient to create a new blueprint for every single house, especially when there are so many similarities shared between each one. The same thing goes in object-oriented software development; why rewrite tons of code when you can reuse code that solves similar problems?

In object-oriented programming, as in construction, it's also common to have many objects of the same kind that share similar characteristics. And like the blueprints for similar houses, you can create blueprints for objects that share certain characteristics. What it boils down to is that classes are software blueprints for objects.

As an example, the car class discussed earlier would contain several variables representing the state of the car, along with implementations for the methods that enable the driver to control the car. The state variables of the car remain hidden underneath the interface. Each instance, or instantiated object, of the car class gets a fresh set of state variables. This brings you to another important point: When an instance of an object is created from a class, the variables declared by that class are allocated in memory. The variables are then modified through the object's methods. Instances of the same class share method implementations but have their own object data.

Where objects provide the benefits of modularity and information hiding, classes provide the benefit of reusability. Just as the builder reuses the blueprint for a house, the software developer reuses the class for an object. Software programmers can use a class over and over again to create many objects. Each of these objects gets its own data but shares a single method implementation.

Inheritance

So, what happens if you want an object that is very similar to one you already have, but with a few extra characteristics? You just inherit a new class based on the class of the similar object. Inheritance is the process of creating a new class with the characteristics of an existing class, along with additional characteristics unique to the new class. Inheritance provides a powerful and natural mechanism for organizing and structuring programs.

So far, the discussion of classes has been limited to the data and methods that make up a class. Based on this understanding, all classes are built from scratch by defining all the data and all the associated methods. Inheritance provides a means to create classes based on other classes. When a class is based on another class, it inherits all the properties of that class, including the data and methods for the class. The class doing the inheriting is referred to as the subclass (child class), and the class providing the information to inherit is referred to as the superclass (parent class).

Using the car example, child classes could be inherited from the car class for gas powered cars and cars powered by electricity. Both new car classes share common "car" characteristics, but they also add a few characteristics of their own. The gas car would add, among other things, a fuel tank and a gas cap, where the electric car might add a battery and a plug for recharging. Each subclass inherits state information (in the form of variable declarations) from the superclass. Figure 14.3 shows the car parent class with the gas and electric car child classes.

FIGURE 14.3.
Inherited car objects.

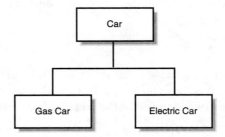

Inheriting the state and behaviors of a superclass alone wouldn't do all that much for a sub-class. The real power of inheritance is the ability to inherit properties and add *new* ones; subclasses can add variables and methods to the ones they inherited from the superclass. Re-member, the electric car added a battery and a recharging plug. Additionally, subclasses have the ability to override inherited methods and provide different implementations for them. For example, the gas car would probably be able to go much faster than the electric car. The accel-erate method for the gas car could reflect this difference.

Class inheritance is designed to allow as much flexibility as possible. You can create inherit-ance trees as deep as necessary to carry out your design. An inheritance tree, or class hierarchy, looks much like a family tree; it shows the relationships between classes. Unlike a family tree, the classes in an inheritance tree get more specific as you move down the tree. The car classes in Figure 14.3 are a good example of an inheritance tree.

By using inheritance, you've learned how subclasses can allow specialized data and methods in addition to the common ones provided by the superclass. This enables programmers to reuse the code in the superclass many times, thus saving extra coding effort and therefore eliminat-ing potential bugs.

One final point to make in regard to inheritance: It is possible and sometimes useful to create superclasses that act purely as templates for more usable subclasses. In this situation, the super-class serves as nothing more than an abstraction for the common class functionality shared by the subclasses. For this reason, these types of superclasses are referred to as abstract classes. An abstract class cannot be instantiated, meaning that no objects can be created from an abstract class. The reason an abstract class can't be instantiated is that parts of it have been specifically left unimplemented. More specifically, these parts are made up of methods that have yet to be implemented—abstract methods.

Using the car example once more, the accelerate method really can't be defined until the car's acceleration capabilities are known. Of course, how a car accelerates is determined by the type of engine it has. Because the engine type is unknown in the car superclass, the accelerate method could be defined but left unimplemented, which would make both the accelerate method and the car superclass abstract. Then the gas and electric car child classes would implement the accelerate method to reflect the acceleration capabilities of their respective engines or motors.

Classes

No doubt you're probably about primered out by now and ready to get on with how classes work in Java. Well, wait no longer! In Java, all classes are subclassed from a superclass called Object. Figure 14.4 shows what the Java class hierarchy looks like in regard to the Object su-perclass.

FIGURE 14.4.
Classes derived from the
`Object` *superclass.*

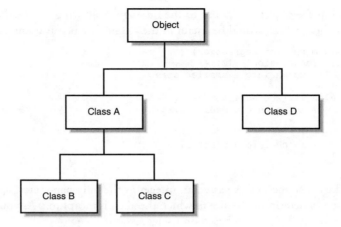

As you can see, all the classes fan out from the `Object` base class. In Java, `Object` serves as the superclass for all derived classes, including the classes that make up the Java API.

Declaring Classes

The syntax for declaring classes in Java follows:

```
class Identifier {
  ClassBody
}
```

`Identifier` specifies the name of the new class, which is by default derived from `Object`. The curly braces surround the body of the class, `ClassBody`. As an example, take a look at the class declaration for an `Alien` class, which could be used in a space game:

```
class Alien {
  Color color;
  int   energy;
  int   aggression;
}
```

The state of the `Alien` object is defined by three data members, which represent the color, energy, and aggression of the alien. It's important to notice that the `Alien` class is inherently derived from `Object`. So far, the `Alien` class isn't all that useful; it needs some methods. The most basic syntax for declaring methods for a class follows:

```
ReturnType Identifier(Parameters) {
  MethodBody
}
```

`ReturnType` specifies the data type that the method returns, `Identifier` specifies the name of the method, and `Parameters` specifies the parameters to the method, if there are any. As with class bodies, the body of a method, `MethodBody`, is enclosed by curly braces. Remember that in object-oriented design terms a method is synonymous with a message, with the return type being the object's response to the message. Following is a method declaration for the morph method, which would be useful in the Alien class because some aliens like to change shape:

```
void morph(int aggression) {
  if (aggression < 10) {
    // morph into a smaller size
  }
  else if (aggression < 20) {
    // morph into a medium size
  }
  else {
    // morph into a giant size
  }
}
```

The morph method is passed an integer as the only parameter, aggression. This value is then used to determine the size to which the alien is morphing. As you can see, the alien morphs to smaller or larger sizes based on its aggression.

If you make the morph method a member of the Alien class, it is readily apparent that the aggression parameter isn't necessary. This is because aggression is already a member variable of Alien, to which all class methods have access. The Alien class with the addition of the morph method looks like this:

```
class Alien {
  Color color;
  int    energy;
  int    aggression;

  void morph() {
    if (aggression < 10) {
      // morph into a smaller size
    }
    else if (aggression < 20) {
      // morph into a medium size
    }
    else {
      // morph into a giant size
    }
  }
}
```

Deriving Classes

So far, the discussion of class declaration has been limited to creating new classes inherently derived from Object. Deriving all your classes from Object isn't a very good idea, because you would have to redefine the data and methods for each class. The way you derive classes from classes other than Object is by using the extends keyword. The syntax for deriving a class using the extends keyword follows:

```
class Identifier extends SuperClass {
  ClassBody
}
```

Identifier refers to the name of the newly derived class, *SuperClass* refers to the name of the class you are deriving from, and *ClassBody* is the new class body.

Using the `Alien` class as the basis for a derivation example, what if you had an `Enemy` class that defined information for all enemies? You would no doubt want to derive the `Alien` class from `Enemy`. Following is the `Enemy`-derived `Alien` class using the `extends` keyword:

```
class Alien extends Enemy {
  Color color;
  int    energy;
  int    aggression;

  void morph() {
    if (aggression < 10) {
      // morph into a smaller size
    }
    else if (aggression < 20) {
      // morph into a medium size
    }
    else {
      // morph into a giant size
    }
  }
}
```

This declaration assumes that the `Enemy` class declaration is readily available in the same package as `Alien`. In reality, you will likely derive from classes in a lot of different places. To derive a class from an external superclass, you must first import the superclass using the `import` statement.

NOTE

You'll get to packages a little later in this chapter. For now, just think of a package as a group of related classes.

If you had to import the `Enemy` class, you would do so like this:

```
import Enemy;
```

Overriding Methods

There are times when it is useful to override methods in derived classes. For example, if the `Enemy` class had a `move` method, you would want the movement to vary based on the type of enemy. Some types of enemies may fly around in specified patterns, while other enemies may crawl in a random fashion. To allow the `Alien` class to exhibit its own movement, you would override the `move` method with a version specific to alien movement. The `Enemy` class would then look something like this:

```
class Enemy {
...
```

```
   void move() {
     // move the enemy
   }
}
```

Likewise, the Alien class with the overridden move method would look something like this:

```
class Alien {
  Color color;
  int    energy;
  int    aggression;

  void move() {
    // move the alien
  }

  void morph() {
    if (aggression < 10) {
      // morph into a smaller size
    }
    else if (aggression < 20) {
      // morph into a medium size
    }
    else {
      // morph into a giant size
    }
  }
}
```

When you create an instance of the Alien class and call the move method, the new move method in Alien is executed rather than the original overridden move method in Enemy. Method overriding is a simple, yet powerful usage of object-oriented design.

Overloading Methods

Another powerful object-oriented technique is method overloading. Method overloading enables you to specify different types of information (parameters) to send to a method. To overload a method, you declare another version with the same name but different parameters.

For example, the move method for the Alien class could have two different versions: one general movement and one for moving to a specific location. The general version is the one you've already defined, which moves the alien based on its current state. The declaration for this version follows:

```
void move() {
  // move the alien
}
```

To enable the alien to move to a specific location, you overload the move method with a version that takes x and y parameters, which specify the location to move. The overloaded version of move follows:

```
void move(int x, int y) {
  // move the alien to position x,y
}
```

Notice that the only difference between the two methods is the parameter lists; the first move takes no parameters while the second move takes two integers.

You may be wondering how the compiler knows which method is being called in a program, when they both have the same name. The compiler keeps up with the parameters for each method along with the name. When a call to a method is encountered in a program, the compiler checks the name and the parameters to determine which overloaded method is being called. In this case, calls to the move methods are easily distinguishable by the absence or presence of the integer parameters.

Access Modifiers

Access to variables and methods in Java classes is accomplished through access modifiers. Access modifiers define varying levels of access between class members and the outside world (other objects). Access modifiers are declared immediately before the type of a member variable or the return type of a method. There are four access modifiers: default, public, protected, and private.

Access modifiers not only affect the visibility of class members, but also of classes themselves. However, class visibility is tightly linked with packages, which are covered later in this chapter.

Default

The default access modifier specifies that only classes in the same package can have access to a class's variables and methods. So, class members with default access have a visibility limited to other classes within the same package. There is no actual keyword for declaring the default access modifier; it is applied by default in the absence of an access modifier. For example, the Alien class members all had default access, because no access modifiers were specified. Examples of a default access member variable and method follow:

```
long length;
void getLength() {
   return length;
}
```

Notice that neither the member variable or the method supply an access modifier, so they take on the default access modifier implicitly.

public

The public access modifier specifies that class variables and methods are accessible to anyone, both inside and outside the class. This means that public class members have global visibility and can be accessed by any other objects. Some examples of public member variables follow:

```
public int count;
public boolean isActive;
```

protected

The protected access modifier specifies that class members are accessible only to methods in that class and subclasses of that class. This means that protected class members have visibility limited to subclasses. Examples of a protected variable and a protected method follow:

```
protected char middleInitial;
protected char getMiddleInitial() {
  return middleInitial;
}
```

private

Finally, the private access modifier, which is the most restrictive, specifies that class members are only accessible by the class they are defined in. This means that no other class has access to private class members, even subclasses. Some examples of private member variables follow:

```
private String firstName;
private double howBigIsIt;
```

The static Modifier

There are times when you need a common variable or method for all objects of a particular class. The static modifier specifies that a variable or method is the same for all objects of a particular class.

Typically, new variables are allocated for each instance of a class. When a variable is declared as being static, it is only allocated once regardless of how many objects are instantiated. The result is that all instantiated objects share the same instance of the static variable. Similarly, a static method is one whose implementation is exactly the same for all objects of a particular class. This means that static methods only have access to static variables.

Following are some examples of a static member variable and a static method:

```
static int refCount;
static int getRefCount() {
  return refCount;
}
```

A beneficial side effect of static members is that they can be accessed without having to create an instance of a class. Remember the System.out.println method used in the last chapter? Do you recall ever instantiating a System object? Of course not. out is a static member variable of the System class, which means you can access it without having to actually instantiate a System object.

The `final` Modifier

Another useful modifier in regard to controlling class member usage is the `final` modifier. The `final` modifier specifies that a variable has a constant value or that a method cannot be overridden in a subclass. To think of the `final` modifier literally, it means that a class member is the final version allowed for the class.

Following are some examples of `final` member variables:

```
final public int numDollars = 25;
final boolean amIBroke = false;
```

If you are coming from the world of C++, `final` variables may sound kind of familiar. In fact, `final` variables in Java are very similar to `const` variables in C++; they must always be initialized upon declaration and their value can't change any time afterward.

The `synchronized` Modifier

The `synchronized` modifier is used to specify that a method is thread safe. This basically means that only one path of execution is allowed into a `synchronized` method at a time. In a multithreaded environment like Java, it is possible to have many different paths of execution running through the same code. The `synchronized` modifier changes this rule by only allowing a single thread access to a method at once, forcing the others to wait their turn. If the concept of threads and paths of execution are totally new to you, don't worry; they are covered in detail in the next chapter, "Threads and Multithreading."

The `native` Modifier

The `native` modifier is used to identify methods that have native implementations. The `native` modifier informs the Java compiler that a method's implementation is in an external C file. It is for this reason that `native` method declarations look different from other Java methods; they have no body. Following is an example of a `native` method declaration:

```
native int calcTotal();
```

Notice that the method declaration simply ends in a semicolon; there are no curly braces containing Java code. This is because `native` methods are implemented in C code, which resides in external C source files. To learn more about `native` methods, check out Chapter 38, "Native Methods and Libraries."

Abstract Classes and Methods

In the object-oriented primer earlier in this chapter, you learned about abstract classes and methods. To recap, an abstract class is a class that is partially implemented and whose purpose is solely as a design convenience. Abstract classes are made up of one or more abstract methods, which are methods that are declared but left bodiless (unimplemented).

The Enemy class discussed earlier is an ideal candidate to become an abstract class. You would never want to actually create an enemy object because it is too general. However, it serves a very logical purpose being a superclass for more specific enemy classes, like the Alien class. To turn the Enemy class into an abstract class, you use the abstract keyword, like this:

```
abstract class Enemy {
  abstract void move();
  abstract void move(int x, int y);
}
```

Notice the usage of the abstract keyword before the class declaration for Enemy. This tells the compiler that the Enemy class is abstract. Also notice that both move methods are declared as being abstract. Because it isn't clear how to move a generic enemy, the move methods in Enemy have been left unimplemented (abstract).

There are a few limitations to using abstract of which you should be aware. First, you can't make creation methods abstract. (You'll learn about creation methods in the next section covering object creation.) Second, you can't make static methods abstract. This stems from the fact that static methods are declared for all classes, so there is no way to provide a derived implementation for an abstract static method. Finally, you aren't allowed to make private methods abstract. At first this limitation may seem to be a little picky, but think about what it means. When you derive a class from a superclass with abstract methods, you must override and implement all the abstract methods or you won't be able to instantiate your new class, and it will remain abstract itself. Now consider that derived classes can't see private members of their superclass, methods included. This results in you not being able to override and implement private abstract methods from the superclass, which means you can't implement (non-abstract) classes from it. If you are limited to only deriving new abstract classes, you won't be able to accomplish much!

Casting

Although casting between different data types was discussed in Chapter 12, "Java Language Fundamentals," the introduction of classes puts a few new twists on casting. Casting between classes can be broken down into three different situations:

- Casting from a subclass to a superclass
- Casting from a superclass to a subclass
- Casting between siblings

In the case of casting from a subclass to a superclass, you can cast either implicitly or explicitly. Implicit casting simply means you do nothing, whereas explicit casting means you have to provide the class type in parentheses, just as with casting fundamental data types. The cast from subclass to superclass is completely reliable, because subclasses contain information tying them to their superclasses. In the case of casting from a superclass to a subclass, you are required to cast explicitly. This cast isn't completely reliable, because the compiler has no way of knowing if the class being cast to is a subclass of the superclass in question. Finally, the cast from sibling to sibling isn't allowed in Java. If all this casting sounds a little confusing, check out the following example:

```
Double d1 = new Double(5.238);
Number n = d1;
Double d2 = (Double)n;
Long l = d1;  // this won't work!
```

In this example, data type wrapper objects are created and assigned to each other. If you aren't familiar with the data type wrapper classes, don't worry, you'll learn about them in Chapter 18, "The Language Package." For now, all you need to know is that the `Double` and `Long` sibling classes are both derived from the `Number` class. In the example, after the `Double` object `d1` is created, it is assigned to a `Number` object. This is an example of implicitly casting from a subclass to a superclass, which is completely legal. Another `Double` object, `d2`, is then assigned the value of the `Number` object. This time, an explicit cast is required because you are casting from a superclass to a subclass, which isn't guaranteed to be reliable. Finally, a `Long` object is assigned the value of a `Double` object. This is a cast between siblings and is not allowed in Java; it will result in a compiler error.

Object Creation

Although most of the design work in object-oriented programming is creating classes, you don't really benefit from that work until you create instances (objects) of those classes. To use a class in a program, you must first create an instance of it.

The Creation Method

Before getting into the details of how to create an object, there is an important method you need to know about: the creation method. When you create an object, you will typically want to initialize its member variables. The creation method is a special method you can implement in all of your classes that allows you to initialize variables and perform any other operations when an object is created from the class. The creation method is always given the same name as the class.

Listing 14.1 contains the complete source code for the `Alien` class, which contains two creation methods.

Listing 14.1. The `Alien` class.

```
class Alien extends Enemy {
  protected Color color;
  protected int   energy;
  protected int   aggression;

  public Alien() {
    color = Color.green;
```

continues

Listing 14.1. continued

```
    energy = 100;
    aggression = 15;
  }

  public Alien(Color c, int e, int a) {
    color = c;
    energy = e;
    aggression = a;
  }

  public void move() {
    // move the alien
  }

  public void move(int x, int y) {
    // move the alien to the position x,y
  }

  public void morph() {
    if (aggression < 10) {
      // morph into a smaller size
    }
    else if (aggression < 20) {
      // morph into a medium size
    }
    else {
      // morph into a giant size
    }
  }
}
```

The Alien class uses method overloading to provide two different creation methods. The first creation method takes no parameters and initializes the member variables to default values. The second creation method takes the color, energy, and aggression of the alien and initializes the member variables with them. Along with containing the new creation methods, this version of Alien uses access modifiers to explicitly assign access levels for each member variable and method. This is a good habit to get into.

This version of the Alien class is located in the source file Enemy1.java on the CD-ROM, which also includes the Enemy class. Keep in mind that these classes are just example classes with little functionality. However, they are good examples of Java class design and can be compiled into Java classes.

The new Operator

To create an instance of a class, you declare an object variable and use the new operator. When dealing with objects, a declaration merely states what type of object a variable is to represent. The object isn't actually created until the new operator is used. Following are two examples of using the new operator to create instances of the Alien class:

```
Alien anAlien = new Alien();
Alien anotherAlien;
anotherAlien = new Alien(Color.red, 56, 24);
```

In the first example, the variable `anAlien` is declared and the object is created by using the `new` operator with an assignment directly in the declaration. In the second example, the variable `anotherAlien` is first declared, then the object is created and assigned in a separate statement.

> **NOTE**
>
> If you have some C++ experience, you no doubt recognize the `new` operator. Even though the `new` operator in Java works in a somewhat similar fashion as its C++ counterpart, keep in mind that you must *always* use the `new` operator to create objects in Java. This is in contrast to the C++ version of `new`, which is only used when you are working with object pointers. Because Java doesn't support pointers, the `new` operator must always be used to create new objects.

Object Destruction

When an object falls out of scope, it is removed from memory, or deleted. Similar to the creation method that is called when an object is created, Java provides the ability to define a destruction method that is called when an object is deleted. Unlike the creation method, which takes on the name of the class, the destruction method is called `finalize`. The `finalize` method provides a good place to perform any type of cleanup for the object, and is defined as

```
void finalize() {
  // cleanup
}
```

An example of cleanup typically performed by Java objects is closing files. It is worth noting that the `finalize` method is not guaranteed to be called by Java as soon as an object falls out of scope. The reason for this is that Java deletes objects as part of its system garbage collection, which occurs at inconsistent intervals. Because an object isn't actually deleted until Java performs a garbage collection, the `finalize` method for the object isn't called until then either.

Packages

Java provides a powerful means of grouping related classes and interfaces together in a single unit: packages. You'll learn about interfaces a little later in this chapter. Put simply, packages are groups of related classes and interfaces. Packages provide a convenient mechanism for managing a large group of classes and interfaces, while avoiding potential naming conflicts. The Java API itself is implemented as a group of packages.

As an example, the `Alien` and `Enemy` classes developed earlier would fit nicely into an `Enemy` package, along with any other enemy objects. By placing classes into a package, you also allow them to benefit from the default access modifier, which provides classes in the same package access to each other's class information.

Declaring Packages

The syntax for the `package` statement follows:

```
package Identifier;
```

This statement must be placed at the beginning of a compilation unit (source file), before any class declarations. Every class located in a compilation unit with a package statement is considered part of that package. You can still spread classes out among separate compilation units; just be sure to include a package statement in each.

Packages can be nested within other packages. In this case, the Java interpreter expects the directory structure containing the executable classes to match the package hierarchy.

Importing Packages

When it comes time to use classes outside of the package you are working in, you must use the `import` statement. The `import` statement enables you to import classes from other packages into a compilation unit. You can import individual classes or entire packages of classes at once if you wish. The syntax for the `import` statement follows:

```
import Identifier;
```

`Identifier` is the name of the class or package of classes you are importing. Going back to the `Alien` class, the `color` member variable is an instance of the `Color` object, which is part of the Java AWT class library. For the compiler to understand this member variable type, you must import the `Color` class. This is accomplished with either of the following statements:

```
import java.awt.Color;
import java.awt.*;
```

The first statement imports the specific class `Color`, which is located in the `java.awt` package. The second statement imports all of the classes in the `java.awt` package. Note that the following statement doesn't work:

```
import java.*;
```

This statement doesn't work because you can't import nested packages with the * specification. This only works when importing all of the classes in a particular package, which is still very useful.

There is one other way to import objects from other packages: explicit package referencing. By explicitly referencing the package name each time you use an object, you can avoid using an import statement. Using this technique, the declaration of the `color` member variable in `Alien` would like this:

```
java.awt.Color color;
```

Explicitly referencing the package name for an external class is generally not required; it usually only serves to clutter up the class name and can make the code harder to read. The exception to this rule is when two packages have classes with the same name. In this case, you are required to explicitly use the package name with the class names.

Class Visibility

Earlier in this chapter you learned about access modifiers, which affect the visibility of classes and class members. Because class member visibility is determined relative to classes, you're probably wondering what visibility means for a class. Class visibility is determined relative to packages.

For example, a `public` class is visible to classes in other packages. Actually, `public` is the only explicit access modifier allowed for classes. Without the `public` access modifier, classes default to being visible to other classes in a package but not visible to classes outside of the package.

Interfaces

The last stop on this object-oriented whirlwind tour of Java is interfaces. An interface is a prototype for a class and is useful from a logical design perspective. This description of an interface may sound vaguely familiar... Remember abstract classes?

Earlier in this chapter you learned that an abstract class is a class that has been left partially unimplemented due to abstract methods, which are themselves unimplemented. Interfaces are abstract classes that are left completely unimplemented. Completely unimplemented in this case means that *no* methods in the class have been implemented. Additionally, interface member data is limited to static final variables, which means that they are constant.

The benefits of using interfaces are much the same as the benefits of using abstract classes. Interfaces provide a means to define the protocols for a class without worrying with the implementation details. This seemingly simple benefit can make large projects much easier to manage; once interfaces have been designed, the class development can take place without worrying about communication among classes.

Another important usage of interfaces is the capacity for a class to implement multiple interfaces. This is a twist on the concept of multiple inheritance, which is supported in C++, but not in Java. Multiple inheritance enables you to derive a class from multiple parent classes. Although powerful, multiple inheritance is a complex and often tricky feature of C++ that the Java designers decided they could do without. Their workaround was to allow Java classes to implement multiple interfaces.

The major difference between inheriting multiple interfaces and true multiple inheritance is that the interface approach only enables you to inherit method descriptions, not implementations. So, if a class implements multiple interfaces, that class must provide all of the functionality for the methods defined in the interfaces. Although this is certainly more limiting than multiple inheritance, it is still a very useful feature. It is this feature of interfaces that separate them from abstract classes.

Declaring Interfaces

The syntax for creating interfaces follows:

```
interface Identifier {
   InterfaceBody
}
```

Identifier is the name of the interface and *InterfaceBody* refers to the abstract methods and static final variables that make up the interface. Because it is assumed that all the methods in an interface are abstract, it isn't necessary to use the `abstract` keyword.

Implementing Interfaces

Because an interface is a prototype, or template, for a class, you must implement an interface to arrive at a usable class. To implement an interface, you use the `implements` keyword. The syntax for implementing a class from an interface follows:

```
class Identifier implements Interface {
   ClassBody
}
```

Identifier refers to the name of the new class, *Interface* is the name of the interface you are implementing, and *ClassBody* is the new class body. Listing 14.2 contains the source code for Enemy2.java, which includes an interface version of Enemy, along with an Alien class that implements the interface.

Listing 14.2. The Enemy interface and Alien class.

```
package Enemy;

import java.awt.Color;

interface Enemy {
  abstract public void move();
  abstract public void move(int x, int y);
}

class Alien implements Enemy {
  protected Color  color;
  protected int    energy;
  protected int    aggression;
```

```
public Alien() {
  color = Color.green;
  energy = 100;
  aggression = 15;
}

public Alien(Color c, int e, int a) {
  color = c;
  energy = e;
  aggression = a;
}

public void move() {
  // move the alien
}

public void move(int x, int y) {
  // move the alien to the position x,y
}

public void morph() {
  if (aggression < 10) {
    // morph into a smaller size
  }
  else if (aggression < 20) {
    // morph into a medium size
  }
  else {
    // morph into a giant size
  }
}
}
```

Summary

This chapter covered the basics of object-oriented programming, along with the specific Java constructs that enable you to carry out object-oriented concepts: classes, packages, and interfaces. You learned the benefits of using classes, along with how to implement objects from them. The communication mechanism between objects, messages (methods), were covered. You also learned how inheritance provides a powerful means of reusing code and creating modular designs. You then learned how packages enable you to logically group similar classes together, making large sets of classes easier to manage. Finally, you saw how interfaces provide a template for deriving new classes in a structured manner.

You are now ready to move on to more advanced features of the Java language, such as threads and multithreading. The next chapter covers exactly these topics.

Threads and Multithreading

15

by Charles L. Perkins

IN THIS CHAPTER

This chapter is about threads—what they are and how they can make your applets work better with other applets and with the Java system in general. We discuss how to "think multithreaded," how to protect your methods and variables from unintended thread conflicts, how to create, start, and stop threads and threaded classes, and how the scheduler works in Java.

First, let's begin by motivating the need for threads.

Threads are a relatively recent invention in the computer science world. Although processes, their larger parent, have been around for decades, threads have only recently been accepted into the mainstream. What's odd about this is that they are extremely valuable, and programs written with them are noticeably better, even to the casual user. In fact, some of the best individual, Herculean efforts over the years have involved implementing a threads-like facility by hand to give a program a more friendly feel to its users.

Imagine that you're using your favorite text editor on a large file. When it starts up, does it need to examine the entire file before it lets you edit? Does it need to make a copy of the file? If the file is huge, this can be a nightmare. Wouldn't it be nicer for it to show you the first page, enabling you to begin editing, and somehow (in the background) complete the slower tasks necessary for initialization? Threads allow exactly this kind of within-the-program parallelism.

Perhaps the best example of threading (or lack of it) is a Web browser. Can your browser download an indefinite number of files and Web pages at once while still enabling you to continue browsing? While these pages are downloading, can your browser download all the pictures, sounds, and so forth in parallel, interleaving the fast and slow download times of multiple Internet servers? HotJava can do all of these things—and more—by using the built-in threading of the Java language.

Threads: What They Are and Why You Need Them

Depending on your experience with operating systems and with environments within those systems, you may or may not have run into the concept of threads. Let's start from the beginning with some definitions.

When a program runs, it starts executing, runs its initialization code, calls methods or procedures, and continues running and processing until it's complete or until the program is exited. That program uses a single thread—where the thread is a single locus of control for the program.

Multithreading, as in Java, enables several different execution threads to run at the same time inside the same program, in parallel, without interfering with each other.

Here's a simple example. Suppose you have a long computation near the start of a program's execution. This long computation may not be needed until later on in the program's execution—it's actually tangential to the main point of the program, but it needs to get done eventually. In a single-threaded program, you have to wait for that computation to finish before the rest of the program can continue running. In a multithreaded system, you can put that computation into its own thread, enabling the rest of the program to continue running independently.

Using threads in Java, you can create an applet so that it runs in its own thread, and it will happily run all by itself without interfering with any other part of the system. Using threads, you can have lots of applets running at once on the same page. Depending on how many you have, you may eventually exhaust the system so that all of them will run slower, but all of them will run independently.

Even if you don't have lots of applets, using threads in your applets is good Java programming practice. The general rule of thumb for well-behaved applets: Whenever you have any bit of processing that is likely to continue for a long time (such as an animation loop, or a bit of code that takes a long time to execute), put it in a thread.

Writing Applets with Threads

How do you create an applet that uses threads? There are several things you need to do. Fortunately, none of them are difficult, and a lot of the basics of using threads in applets is just boilerplate code that you can copy and paste from one applet to another. Because it's so easy, there's almost no reason *not* to use threads in your applets, given the benefits.

There are four modifications you need to make to create an applet that uses threads:

- Change the signature of your applet class to include the words `implements Runnable`.
- Include an instance variable to hold this applet's thread.
- Modify your `start()` method to do nothing but spawn a thread and start it running.
- Create a `run()` method that contains the actual code that starts your applet running.

The first change is to the first line of your class definition. You've already got something like this:

```
public class MyAppletClass extends java.applet.Applet {
...
}
```

You need to change it to the following :

```
public class MyAppletClass extends java.applet.Applet  implements Runnable {
...
}
```

What does this do? It includes support for the `Runnable` interface in your applet. Interfaces, as discussed in Chapter 14, "Classes, Packages, and Interfaces," are a way to collect method names common to different classes, which can then be mixed in and implemented inside different classes that need to implement that behavior. Here, the `Runnable` interface includes the behavior your applet needs to run a thread; in particular, it gives you a default definition for the run() method.

The second step is to add an instance variable to hold this applet's thread. Call it anything you like; it's a variable of the type Thread (Thread is a class in java.lang, so you don't have to import it):

```
Thread runner;
```

Third, add a start() method or modify the existing one so that it does nothing but create a new thread and start it running. Here's a typical example of a start() method:

```
public void start() {
        if (runner == null); {
            runner = new Thread(this);
            runner.start();
        }
    }
```

If you modify start() to do nothing but spawn a thread, where does the body of your applet go? It goes into a new method, run(), which looks like this:

```
public void run() {
    // what your applet actually does
}
```

run() can contain anything you want to run in the separate thread: initialization code, the actual loop for your applet, or anything else that needs to run in its own thread. You also can create new objects and call methods from inside run(), and they'll also run inside that thread. The run method is the real heart of your applet.

Finally, now that you've got threads running and a start method to start them, you should add a stop() method to suspend execution of that thread (and therefore whatever the applet is doing at the time) when the reader leaves the page. stop(), like start(), is usually something along these lines:

```
public void stop() {
        if (runner != null) {
            runner.stop();
            runner = null;
        }
    }
```

The stop() method here does two things: it stops the thread from executing and also sets the thread's variable (runner) to null. Setting the variable to null makes the Thread object it previously contained available for garbage collection so that the applet can be removed from memory after a certain amount of time. If the reader comes back to this page and this applet, the start method creates a new thread and starts up the applet once again.

And that's it! Four basic modifications, and now you have a well-behaved applet that runs in its own thread.

The Problem with Parallelism

If threading is so wonderful, why doesn't every system have it? Many modern operating systems have the basic primitives needed to create and run threads, but they are missing a key ingredient. The rest of their environment is not *thread-safe*. Imagine that you are in a thread, one of many, and each of you is sharing some important data managed by the system. If you were managing that data, you could take steps to protect it (as you'll see later in this chapter), but the system is managing it. Now visualize a piece of code in the system that reads some crucial value, thinks about it for a while, and then adds 1 to the value:

```
if (crucialValue > 0) {
    . . .                   // think about what to do
    crucialValue += 1;
}
```

Remember that any number of threads may be calling upon this part of the system at once. The disaster occurs when two threads have both executed the `if` test before either has incremented the `crucialValue`. In that case, the value is clobbered by them both with the same `crucialValue + 1`, and one of the increments has been lost. This may not seem so bad to you, but imagine instead that the crucial value affects the state of the screen as it is being displayed. Now, unfortunate ordering of the threads can cause the screen to be updated incorrectly. In the same way, mouse or keyboard events can be lost, databases can be inaccurately updated, and so forth.

This disaster is inescapable if any significant part of the system has not been written with threads in mind. Therein lies the barrier to a mainstream threaded environment—the large effort required to rewrite existing libraries for thread safety. Luckily, Java was written from scratch with this is mind, and every Java class in its library is thread-safe. Thus, you now have to worry only about your own synchronization and thread-ordering problems, because you can assume that the Java system will do the right thing.

NOTE

Some readers may wonder what the fundamental problem really is. Can't you just make the . . . area in the example smaller and smaller to reduce or eliminate the problem? Without atomic operations, the answer is no. (*Atomic operations* are a series of instructions that cannot be interrupted by another thread. They can be thought of as operations that appear to happen "all at once.") Even if the . . . took zero time, you must first look at the value of some variable to make any decision and then change something to reflect that decision. These two steps can never be made to happen at the same time without an atomic operation. Unless you're given one by the system, it's literally impossible to create your own.

Even the one line `crucialValue += 1` involves three steps: Get the current value, add one to it, and store it back. (Using `++crucialValue` doesn't help either.) All three steps need to happen "all at once" (atomically) to be safe. Special Java primitives, at the lowest levels of the language, provide you with the basic atomic operations you need to build safe, threaded programs.

Thinking Multithreaded

Getting used to threads takes a little while and a new way of thinking. Rather than imagining that you always know exactly what's happening when you look at a method you've written, you have to ask yourself some additional questions. What will happen if more than one thread calls into this method at the same time? Do you need to protect it in some way? What about your class as a whole? Are you assuming that only one of its methods is running at the same time?

Often you make such assumptions, and a local instance variable will be messed up as a result. Let's make a few mistakes and then try to correct them. First, the simplest case:

```java
public class  ThreadCounter {
    int  crucialValue;

    public void  countMe() {
        crucialValue += 1;
    }

    public int    howMany() {
        return crucialValue;
    }
}
```

This code suffers from the most pure form of the "synchronization problem:" the += takes more than one step, and you may miscount the number of threads as a result. (Don't be too concerned about the specifics of how threads are created yet; just imagine that a whole bunch of them are able to call `countMe()`, at once, at slightly different times.) Java enables you to fix this:

```java
public class  SafeThreadCounter {
    int  crucialValue;

    public synchronized void  countMe() {
        crucialValue += 1;
    }

    public              int   howMany() {
        return crucialValue;
    }
}
```

The `synchronized` keyword tells Java to make the block of code in the method thread-safe. Only one thread will be allowed inside this method at once, and others have to wait until the currently running thread is finished with it before they can begin running it. This implies that synchronizing a large, long-running method is almost always a bad idea. All your threads would end up stuck at this bottleneck, waiting single file to get their turn at this one slow method.

It's even worse than you might think for unsynchronized variables. Because the compiler can keep them around in registers during computations, and a thread's registers can't be seen by other threads (especially if they're on another processor in a true multiprocessor computer), a variable can be updated in such a way that *no possible order* of thread updates could have produced the result. This is completely incomprehensible to the programmer. To avoid this bizarre case, you can label a variable `volatile`, meaning that you know it will be updated asynchronously by multiprocessor-like threads. Java then loads and stores it each time it's needed and does not use registers.

> **NOTE**
>
> In earlier releases, variables that were safe from these bizarre effects were labeled `threadsafe`. Because most variables are safe to use, however, they are now assumed to be thread-safe unless you mark them `volatile`. Using `volatile` is an extremely rare event. In fact, in the 1.0 release, the Java class library does not use `volatile` anywhere.

Points About `Points`

The method `howMany()` in the last example doesn't need to be `synchronized`, because it simply returns the current value of an instance variable. Someone higher in the call chain may need to be `synchronized`, though—someone who uses the value returned from the method. Here's an example:

```
public class  Point {      // redefines class Point from package java.awt
    private float  x, y;  // OK since we're in a different package here

    public  float  x() {         // needs no synchronization
        return x;
    }

    public  float  y() {         // ditto
        return y;
    }
    . . .      // methods to set and change x and y
}

public class  UnsafePointPrinter {
    public void  print(Point p) {
        System.out.println("The point's x is " + p.x()
                              + " and y is " + p.y() + ".");
    }
}
```

The analogous methods to howMany() are x() and y(). They need no synchronization because they just return the values of instance variables. It is the responsibility of the caller of x() and y() to decide whether it needs to synchronize itself—and in this case, it does. Although the method print() simply reads values and prints them out, it reads *two* values. This means that there is a chance that some other thread, running between the call to p.x() and the call to p.y(), could have changed the value of x and y stored inside the Point p. Remember, you don't know how many other threads have a way to reach and call methods in this Point object! "Thinking multithreaded" comes down to being careful any time you make an assumption that something has *not* happened between two parts of your program (even two parts of the same line, or the same expression, such as the string + expression in this example).

TryAgainPointPrinter

You could try to make a safe version of print() by simply adding the synchronized keyword modifier to it, but instead, let's try a slightly different approach:

```
public class  TryAgainPointPrinter {
    public void  print(Point p) {
        float  safeX, safeY;

        synchronized(this) {
            safeX = p.x();      // these two lines now
            safeY = p.y();      // happen atomically
        }
        System.out.print("The point's x is " + safeX
                              + " y is " + safeY);
    }
}
```

The synchronized statement takes an argument that says what object you would like to lock to prevent more than one thread from executing the enclosed block of code at the same time. Here, you use this (the instance itself), which is exactly the object that would have been locked by the synchronized method as a whole if you had changed print() to be like your safe countMe() method. You have an added bonus with this new form of synchronization: You can specify exactly what part of a method needs to be safe, and the rest can be left unsafe.

Notice how you took advantage of this freedom to make the protected part of the method as small as possible, while leaving the String creations, concatenations, and printing (which together take a small but nonzero amount of time) outside the "protected" area. This is both good style (as a guide to the reader of your code) and more efficient, because fewer threads get stuck waiting to get into protected areas.

SafePointPrinter

The astute reader, though, may still be worried by the last example. It seems as if you made sure that no one executes *your* calls to x() and y() out of order, but have you prevented the Point p from changing out from under you? The answer is no, you still have not solved the problem. You really do need the full power of the synchronized statement:

```
public class  SafePointPrinter {
    public void  print(Point p) {
        float  safeX, safeY;

        synchronized(p) {      // no one can change p
            safeX = p.x();     // while these two lines
            safeY = p.y();     // are happening atomically
        }
        System.out.print("The point's x is " + safeX
                            + " y is " + safeY);
    }
}
```

Now you've got it. You actually needed to protect the Point p from changes, so you lock it by giving it as the argument to your synchronized statement. Now when x() and y() happen together, they can be sure to get the current x and y of the Point p, without any other thread being able to call a modifying method between. You're still assuming, however, that the Point p has properly protected *itself.* (You can always assume this about system classes—but *you* wrote this Point class.) You can make sure by writing the only method that can change x and y inside p yourself:

```
public class  Point {
    private float  x, y;

    . . .          // the x() and y() methods

    public synchronized void  setXAndY(float  newX,  float  newY) {
        x = newX;
        y = newY;
    }
}
```

By making the only "set" method in Point synchronized, you guarantee that any other thread trying to grab the Point p and change it out from under you has to wait: You've locked the Point p with your synchronized(p) statement, and any other thread has to try to lock the same Point p via the implicit synchronized(this) statement p now executes when entering setXAndY(). Thus, at last, you are thread-safe.

> **NOTE**
>
> By the way, if Java had some way of returning more than one value at once, you could write a synchronized getXAndY() method for Points that returns both values safely. In

> the current Java language, such a method could return a new, unique Point to guaran-
> tee to its callers that no one else has a copy that might be changed. This sort of trick
> can be used to minimize the parts of the system that need to be concerned with
> synchronization.

ReallySafePoint

An added benefit of the use of the synchronized modifier on methods (or of synchronized(this)
{. . .}) is that only one of these methods (or blocks of code) can run at once. You can use that
knowledge to guarantee that only one of several crucial methods in a class will run at once:

```
public class  ReallySafePoint {
    private float  x, y;

    public synchronized Point  getUniquePoint() {
        return new Point(x, y);    // can be a less safe Point
    }                              // because only the caller has it

    public synchronized void   setXAndY(float  newX,  float  newY) {
        x = newX;
        y = newY;
    }

    public synchronized void   scale(float  scaleX,  float  scaleY) {
        x *= scaleX;
        y *= scaleY;
    }

    public synchronized void   add(ReallySafePoint  aRSP) {
        Point  p = aRSP.getUniquePoint();

        x += p.x();
        y += p.y();
    }   // Point p is soon thrown away by GC; no one else ever saw it
}
```

This example combines several of the ideas mentioned previously. To avoid a caller's having to
synchronize(p) whenever getting your x and y, you give them a synchronized way to get a
unique Point (like returning multiple values). Each method that modifies the object's instance
variables is also synchronized to prevent it from running between the x and y references in
getUniquePoint() and from stepping on one another as they modify the local x and y. Note
that add() itself uses getUniquePoint() to avoid having to say synchronized(aRSP).

Classes that are this safe are a little unusual; it is more often your responsibility to protect yourself from other threads' use of commonly held objects (such as Points). You can fully relax when
you know for certain that you're the only one that knows about an object. Of course, if you
created the object yourself and gave it to no one else, you *can* be that certain.

Protecting a Class Variable

Finally, suppose you want a class variable to collect some information across all a class's instances:

```
public class  StaticCounter {
    private static int  crucialValue;

    public synchronized void  countMe() {
        crucialValue += 1;
    }
}
```

Is this safe? If `crucialValue` were an instance variable, it would be. Because it's a class variable, however, and there is only one copy of it for all instances, you can still have multiple threads modifying it by using different *instances* of the class. (Remember, the `synchronized` modifier locks the object `this`—an instance.) Luckily, you already know the tools you need to solve this:

```
public class  StaticCounter {
    private static int  crucialValue;

    public void  countMe() {
        synchronized(getClass()) {   // can't directly name StaticCounter
            crucialValue += 1;       // the (shared) class is now locked
        }
    }
}
```

The trick is to "lock" on a different object—not on an instance of the class, but on the class itself. Because a class variable is "inside" a class, just as an instance variable is inside an instance, this shouldn't be all that unexpected. In a similar way, classes can provide global resources that any instance (or other class) can access directly by using the class name, and lock by using that same class name. In the last example, `crucialValue` was used from within an instance of `StaticCounter`, but if `crucialValue` were declared `public` instead, from anywhere in the program, it would be safe to say the following:

```
synchronized(Class.for.Name("StaticCounter")) {
    StaticCounter.crucialValue += 1;
}
```

> **NOTE**
>
> The direct use of another class's (or object's) variable is really bad style—it's used here simply to demonstrate a point quickly. `StaticCounter` would normally provide a `countMe()`-like class method of its own to do this sort of dirty work.

You can now begin to appreciate how much work the Java team has done for you by thinking all these hard thoughts for each and every class (and method!) in the Java class library.

Creating and Using Threads

Now that you understand the power (and the dangers) of having many threads running at once, how are those threads actually created?

> **CAUTION**
>
> The system itself always has a few so-called *daemon* threads running, one of which is constantly doing the tedious task of garbage collection for you in the background. There is also a main user thread that listens for events from your mouse and keyboard. If you're not careful, you can sometimes lock up this main thread. If you do, no events are sent to your program and it appears to be dead. A good rule of thumb is that whenever you're doing something that *can* be done in a separate thread, it probably *should* be. Threads in Java are relatively cheap to create, run, and destroy, so don't use them too sparingly.

Because there is a class `java.lang.Thread`, you might guess that you could create a thread of your own by subclassing it—and you are right:

```
public class  MyFirstThread extends Thread { // a.k.a., java.lang.Thread
    public void  run() {
        . . .                   // do something useful
    }
}
```

You now have a new type of `Thread` called `MyFirstThread`, which does something useful (unspecified) when its `run()` method is called. Of course, no one has created this thread or called its `run()` method, so it does absolutely nothing at the moment. To actually create and run an instance of your new thread class, you write the following:

```
MyFirstThread  aMFT = new MyFirstThread();

aMFT.start();     // calls our run() method
```

What could be simpler? You create a new instance of your thread class and then ask it to start running. Whenever you want to stop the thread, you use this:

```
aMFT.stop();
```

Besides responding to `start()` and `stop()`, a thread can also be temporarily suspended and later resumed:

```
Thread  t = new Thread();

t.suspend();
. . .             // do something special while t isn't running
t.resume();
```

A thread will automatically `suspend()` and then `resume()` when it's first blocked at a synchronized point and then later unblocked (when it's that thread's "turn" to run).

The `Runnable` Interface

This is all well and good if every time you want to create a thread you have the luxury of being able to place it under the `Thread` class in the single-inheritance class tree. What if it more naturally belongs under some other class, from which it needs to get most of its implementation? Interfaces come to the rescue:

```
public class  MySecondThread extends ImportantClass implements Runnable {
    public void  run() {
        . . .                   // do something useful
    }
}
```

By implementing the interface `Runnable`, you declare your intention to run in a separate thread. In fact, the class `Thread` itself implements this. As you also might guess from the example, the interface `Runnable` specifies only one method: `run()`. As in `MyFirstThread`, you expect someone to create an instance of a thread and somehow call your `run()` method. Here's how this is accomplished:

```
MySecondThread  aMST = new MySecondThread();
Thread          aThread = new Thread(aMST);

aThread.start();    // calls our run() method, indirectly
```

First, you create an instance of `MySecondThread`. Then, by passing this instance to the constructor making the new `Thread`, you make it the target of that `Thread`. Whenever that new `Thread` starts up, its `run()` method calls the `run()` method of the target it was given (assumed by the `Thread` to be an object that implements the `Runnable` interface). When `start()` is called, `aThread` (indirectly) calls your `run()` method. You can stop `aThread` with `stop()`. If you don't need to talk to the `Thread` explicitly or to the instance of `MySecondThread`, here's a one line shortcut:

```
new Thread(new MySecondThread()).start();
```

> **NOTE**
>
> As you can see, the class name, `MySecondThread`, is a bit of a misnomer—it does not descend from `Thread`, nor is it actually the thread that you `start()` and `stop()`. It probably should have been called `MySecondThreadedClass` or `ImportantRunnableClass`.

`ThreadTester`

Here's a longer example:

```
public class  SimpleRunnable implements Runnable {
    public void  run() {
        System.out.println("in thread named '"
                          + Thread.currentThread().getName() + "'");
```

```
    } // any other methods run() calls are in current thread as well
}

public class ThreadTester {
    public static void main(String argv[]) {
        SimpleRunnable aSR = new SimpleRunnable();

        while (true) {
            Thread t = new Thread(aSR);

            System.out.println("new Thread() " + (t == null ?
                                          "fail" : "succeed") + "ed.");
            t.start();
            try { t.join(); } catch (InterruptedException ignored) {}
                // waits for thread to finish its run() method
        }
    }
}
```

> **NOTE**
>
> You may be worried that only one instance of the class SimpleRunnable is created, but many new Threads are using it. Don't they get confused? Remember to separate in your mind the aSR instance (and the methods it understands) from the various threads of execution that can pass through it. aSR's methods provide a template for execution, and the multiple threads created are sharing that template. Each remembers where it is executing and whatever else it needs to make it distinct from the other running threads. They all share the same instance and the same methods. That's why when adding synchronization, you need to be so careful to imagine numerous threads running rampant over each of your methods.

The class method currentThread() can be called to get the thread in which a method is currently executing. If the SimpleRunnable class were a subclass of Thread, its methods would know the answer already (*it* is the thread running). Because SimpleRunnable simply implements the interface Runnable, however, and counts on someone else (ThreadTester's main()) to create the thread, its run() method needs another way to get its hands on that thread. Often, you'll be deep inside methods called by your run() method when suddenly you need to get the current thread. The class method shown in the example works, no matter where you are.

> **CAUTION**
>
> You can do some reasonably disastrous things with your knowledge of threads. For example, if you're running in the main thread of the system and, because you think you are in a different thread, you accidentally say the following:
>
> Thread.currentThread().stop();
>
> it has unfortunate consequences for your (soon-to-be-dead) program!

The example then calls `getName()` on the current thread to get the thread's name (usually something helpful, such as `Thread-23`) so it can tell the world in which thread `run()` is running. The final thing to note is the use of the method `join()`, which, when sent to a thread, means "I'm planning to wait forever for you to finish your `run()` method." You don't want to do this lightly: If you have anything else important you need to get done in your thread any time soon, you can't count on how long the `join()`ed thread may take to finish. In the example, its `run()` method is short and finishes quickly, so each loop can safely wait for the previous thread to die before creating the next one. (Of course, in this example, you didn't have anything else you wanted to do while waiting for `join()` anyway.) Here's the output produced:

```
new Thread() succeeded.
in thread named 'Thread-1'
new Thread() succeeded.
in thread named 'Thread-2'
new Thread() succeeded.
in thread named 'Thread-3'
^C
```

Ctrl+C was pressed to interrupt the program, because it otherwise would continue forever.

NamedThreadTester

If you want your threads to have particular names, you can assign them yourself by using a two-argument form of `Thread`'s constructor

```
public class NamedThreadTester {
    public static void main(String argv[]) {
        SimpleRunnable aSR = new SimpleRunnable();

        for (int i = 1; true; ++i) {
            Thread t = new Thread(aSR, "" + (100 - i)
                                    + " threads on the wall...");

            System.out.println("new Thread() " + (t == null ?
                                        "fail" : "succeed") + "ed.");
            t.start();
            try { t.join(); } catch (InterruptedException ignored) {}
        }
    }
}
```

which takes a target object, as before, and a `String`, which names the new thread. Here's the output:

```
new Thread() succeeded.
in thread named '99 threads on the wall...'
new Thread() succeeded.
in thread named '98 threads on the wall...'
new Thread() succeeded.
in thread named '97 threads on the wall...'
^C
```

Naming a thread is one easy way to pass it some information. This information flows from the parent thread to its new child. It's also useful, for debugging purposes, to give threads meaningful names (such as `network input`) so that when they appear during an error—in a stack trace, for example—you can easily identify which thread caused the problem. You might also think of using names to help group or organize your threads, but Java actually provides you with a `ThreadGroup` class to perform this function. A `ThreadGroup` allows you to group threads, to control them all as a unit, and to keep them from being able to affect other threads (useful for security).

Knowing When a Thread Has Stopped

Let's imagine a different version of the last example, one that creates a thread and then hands the thread off to other parts of the program. Suppose it would then like to know when that thread dies so that it can perform some cleanup operation. If `SimpleRunnable` were a subclass of `Thread`, you might try to catch `stop()` whenever it's sent—but look at `Thread`'s declaration of the `stop()` method:

```
public final void  stop() { . . . }
```

The `final` here means that you can't override this method in a subclass. In any case, `SimpleRunnable` is *not* a subclass of `Thread`, so how can this imagined example possibly catch the death of its thread? The answer is to use the following magic:

```
public class  SingleThreadTester {
    public static void  main(String argv[]) {
        Thread  t = new Thread(new SimpleRunnable());

        try {
            t.start();
            someMethodThatMightStopTheThread(t);
        } catch (ThreadDeath  aTD) {
            . . .              // do some required cleanup
            throw aTD;      // re-throw the error
        }
    }
}
```

All you need to know is that if the thread created in the example dies, it `throws` an error of class `ThreadDeath`. The code `catches` that error and performs the required cleanup. It then rethrows the error, allowing the thread to die. The cleanup code is not called if the thread exits normally (its `run()` method completes), but that's fine; you posited that the cleanup was needed only when `stop()` was used on the thread.

> **NOTE**
>
> Threads can die in other ways—for example, by throwing exceptions that no one catches. In these cases, `stop()` is never called, and the previous code is not sufficient. (If the cleanup always has to occur, even at the normal end of a thread's life, you can

put it in a `finally` clause.) Because unexpected exceptions can come out of nowhere to kill a thread, multithreaded programs that carefully `catch` and handle all their exceptions are more predictable, robust, and easier to debug.

Thread Scheduling

You might wonder exactly what order your threads will be run in, and how you can control that order. Unfortunately, the current implementations of the Java system cannot precisely answer the former, though with a lot of work, you can always do the latter.

> **NOTE**
>
> The part of the system that decides the real-time ordering of threads is called the *scheduler*.

Preemptive Versus Nonpreemptive

Normally, any scheduler has two fundamentally different ways of looking at its job: nonpreemptive scheduling and preemptive time-slicing.

> **NOTE**
>
> With *nonpreemptive scheduling*, the scheduler runs the current thread forever, requiring that thread explicitly to tell it when it is safe to start a different thread.
>
> With *preemptive time-slicing*, the scheduler runs the current thread until it has used up a certain tiny fraction of a second, and then "preempts" it, `suspend()`s it, and `resume()`s another thread for the next tiny fraction of a second.

Nonpreemptive scheduling is very courtly, always asking for permission to schedule, and is quite valuable in extremely time-critical, real-time applications where being interrupted at the wrong moment, or for too long, could mean crashing an airplane.

Most modern schedulers use preemptive time-slicing, because except for a few time-critical cases, it has turned out to make writing multithreaded programs much easier. For one thing, it does not force each thread to decide exactly when it should "yield" control to another thread. Instead, every thread can just run blindly on, knowing that the scheduler will be fair about giving all the other threads their chance to run.

It turns out that this approach is still not the ideal way to schedule threads. You've given a little too much control to the scheduler. The final touch many modern schedulers add is to enable you to assign each thread a priority. This creates a total ordering of all threads, making some threads more "important" than others. Being higher priority often means that a thread gets run more often (or gets more total running time), but it always means that it can interrupt other, lower-priority threads, even before their "time-slice" has expired.

The current Java release does not precisely specify the behavior of its scheduler. Threads can be assigned priorities, and when a choice is made between several threads that all want to run, the highest-priority thread wins. However, among threads that are all the same priority, the behavior is not well-defined. In fact, the different platforms on which Java currently runs have different behaviors—some behaving more like a preemptive scheduler, and some more like a nonpreemptive scheduler.

> **NOTE**
>
> This incomplete specification of the scheduler is terribly annoying and, presumably, will be corrected in later releases. Not knowing the fine details of how scheduling occurs is perfectly all right, but not knowing whether equal priority threads must explicitly yield or face running forever is not all right. For example, all the threads you have created so far are equal priority threads, so you don't know their basic scheduling behavior!

Testing Your Scheduler

To find out what kind of scheduler you have on your system, try the following:

```java
public class RunnablePotato implements Runnable {
    public void run() {
        while (true)
            System.out.println(Thread.currentThread().getName());
    }
}

public class PotatoThreadTester {
    public static void main(String argv[]) {
        RunnablePotato aRP = new RunnablePotato();

        new Thread(aRP, "one potato").start();
        new Thread(aRP, "two potato").start();
    }
}
```

For a nonpreemptive scheduler, this prints the following

```
one potato
one potato
```

```
one potato
. . .
```

forever, until you interrupt the program. For a preemptive scheduler that time-slices, it repeats the line one potato a few times, followed by the same number of two potato lines, over and over

```
one potato
one potato
...
one potato
two potato
two potato
...
two potato
. . .
```

until you interrupt the program. What if you want to be sure the two threads will take turns, no matter what the system scheduler wants to do? You rewrite RunnablePotato as follows:

```
public class  RunnablePotato implements Runnable {
    public void  run() {
        while (true) {
            System.out.println(Thread.currentThread().getName());
            Thread.yield();  // let another thread run for a while
        }
    }
}
```

> **TIP**
>
> Normally you would have to say Thread.currentThread().yield() to get your hands on the current thread, and then call yield(). Because this pattern is so common, however, the Thread class provides a shortcut.

The yield() method explicitly gives any other threads that want to run a chance to begin running. (If there are no threads waiting to run, the thread that made the yield() simply continues.) In our example, there's another thread that's just *dying* to run, so when you now execute the class ThreadTester, it should output the following:

```
one potato
two potato
one potato
two potato
one potato
two potato
. . .
```

even if your system scheduler is nonpreemptive, and would never normally run the second thread.

PriorityThreadTester

To see whether priorities are working on your system, try this:

```
public class  PriorityThreadTester {
    public static void  main(String argv[]) {
        RunnablePotato   aRP = new RunnablePotato();
        Thread           t1  = new Thread(aRP, "one potato");
        Thread           t2  = new Thread(aRP, "two potato");

        t2.setPriority(t1.getPriority() + 1);
        t1.start();
        t2.start();    // at priority Thread.NORM_PRIORITY + 1
    }
}
```

> **TIP**
>
> The values representing the lowest, normal, and highest priorities that threads can be assigned are stored in class variables of the Thread class: Thread.MIN_PRIORITY, Thread.NORM_PRIORITY, and Thread.MAX_PRIORITY. The system assigns new threads, by default, the priority Thread.NORM_PRIORITY. Priorities in Java are currently defined in a range from 1 to 10, with 5 being normal, but you shouldn't depend on these values; use the class variables, or tricks like the one shown in the preceding example.

If one potato is the first line of output, your system does not preempt using priorities.

Why? Imagine that the first thread (t1) has just begun to run. Even before it has a chance to print anything, along comes a higher-priority thread (t2) that wants to run right away. That higher-priority thread should preempt (interrupt) the first, and get a chance to print two potato before t1 finishes printing anything. In fact, if you use the RunnablePotato class that never yield()s, t2 stays in control forever, printing two potato lines, because it's a higher priority than t1 and it never yields control. If you use the latest RunnablePotato class (with yield()), the output is alternating lines of one potato and two potato as before, but starting with two potato.

Here's a good, illustrative example of how complex threads behave:

```
public class  ComplexThread extends Thread {
    private int   delay;

    ComplexThread(String  name,  float  seconds) {
        super(name);
        delay = (int) seconds * 1000;   // delays are in milliseconds
        start();                        // start up ourself!
    }

    public void  run() {
        while (true) {
            System.out.println(Thread.currentThread().getName());
```

```
            try {
                Thread.sleep(delay);
            } catch (InterruptedException e) {
                return;
            }
        }
    }

    public static void  main(String argv[]) {
        new ComplexThread("one potato",    1.1F);
        new ComplexThread("two potato",    1.3F);
        new ComplexThread("three potato", 0.5F);
        new ComplexThread("four",          0.7F);
    }
}
```

This example combines the thread and its tester into a single class. Its constructor takes care of naming (itself) and of starting (itself), because it is now a `Thread`. The `main()` method creates new instances of its own class, because that class is a subclass of `Thread`. `run()` is also more complicated because it now uses, for the first time, a method that can `throw` an unexpected exception.

The `Thread.sleep()` method forces the current thread to `yield()` and then waits for at least the specified amount of time to elapse before allowing the thread to run again. Another thread, however, might interrupt the sleeping thread. In such a case, it throws an `InterruptedException`. Now, because `run()` is not defined as throwing this exception, you must "hide" the fact by `catching` and handling it yourself. Because interruptions are usually requests to stop, you should exit the thread, which you can do by simply returning from the `run()` method.

This program should output a repeating but complex pattern of four different lines, where every once in a great while you see the following:

```
. . .
one potato
two potato
three potato
four
. . .
```

You should study the pattern output to prove to yourself that true parallelism is going on inside Java programs. You may also begin to appreciate that, if even this simple set of four threads can produce such complex behavior, many more threads must be capable of producing near chaos if not carefully controlled. Luckily, Java provides the synchronization and thread-safe libraries you need to control that chaos.

Summary

This chapter showed that parallelism is desirable and powerful, but introduces many new problems—such as methods and variables now need to be *protected* from thread conflicts—that can lead to chaos if not carefully controlled.

By "thinking multithreaded," you can detect the places in your programs that require synchronized statements (or modifiers) to make them thread-safe. A series of Point examples demonstrated the various levels of safety you can achieve, while ThreadTesters showed how subclasses of Thread, or classes that implement the Runnable interface, are created and run() to generate multithreaded programs.

You also learned how to yield(), how to start(), stop(), suspend(), and resume() your threads, and how to catch ThreadDeath whenever it happens.

Finally, you learned about preemptive and nonpreemptive scheduling, both with and without priorities, and how to test your Java system to see which of them your scheduler is using.

This wraps up the description of threads. You now know enough to write the most complex of programs: multithreaded ones. As you get more comfortable with threads, you may begin to use the ThreadGroup class or to use the enumeration methods of Thread to get your hands on all the threads in the system and manipulate them. Don't be afraid to experiment; you can't permanently break anything, and you only learn by trying.

Exception Handling

16

by Charles L. Perkins

IN THIS CHAPTER

This chapter covers exceptional conditions in Java. You learn how to handle them, how to create them, and how your code is limited—yet made more robust—by them.

Let's begin by discussing why new ways of handling exceptions were invented.

Programming languages have long labored to solve the following common problem:

```
int   status = callSomethingThatAlmostAlwaysWorks();

if (status == FUNNY_RETURN_VALUE) {
    . . .           // something unusual happened, handle it
    switch(someGlobalErrorIndicator) {
        . . .           // handle more specific problems
    }
} else {
    . . .           // all is well, go your merry way
}
```

Somehow this seems like a lot of work to do to handle a rare case. What's worse, if the function called returns an int as part of its normal answer, you must distinguish one special integer (FUNNY_RETURN_VALUE) to indicate an error. What if that function really needs all the integers? You must do something even uglier.

Even if you manage to find a distinguished value (such as NULL in C for pointers, -1 for integers, and so forth), what if there are multiple errors that must be produced by the same function? Often, some global variable is used as an error indicator. The function stores a value in it and prays that no one else changes it before the caller gets to handle the error. Multiple errors propagate badly, if at all, and there are numerous problems with generalizing this to large programs, complex errors, and so forth.

Luckily, there is an alternative: using exceptions to help you handle abnormal conditions in your program, making the normal, nonexceptional code cleaner and easier to read.

> **NOTE**
>
> An *exception* is any object that is an instance of the class Throwable (or any of its subclasses).

Programming in the Large

When you begin to build complex programs in Java, you discover that after designing the classes and interfaces, and their methods' descriptions, you still have not defined all the behavior of your objects. After all, an interface describes the normal way to use an object and doesn't include any strange, exceptional cases. In many systems, the documentation takes care of this problem by explicitly listing the distinguished values used in "hacks" like the previous example.

Because the system knows nothing about these hacks, it cannot check them for consistency. In fact, the compiler can do nothing at all to help you with these exceptional conditions, in contrast to the helpful warnings and errors it produces if a method is used incorrectly.

More importantly, you have not captured in your design this important aspect of your program. Instead, you are forced to make up a way to describe it in the documentation and hope you have not made any mistakes when you implement it later. What's worse, everyone else makes up a different way of describing the same thing. Clearly, you need some uniform way of declaring the intentions of classes and methods with respect to these exceptional conditions. Java provides just such a way:

```
public class  MyFirstExceptionalClass {
    public void  anExceptionalMethod() throws MyFirstException {
        . . .
    }
}
```

Here, you warn the reader (and the compiler) that the code . . . may throw an exception called `MyFirstException`.

You can think of a method's description as a contract between the designer of that method (or class) and you, the caller of the method. Usually, this description tells the types of a method's arguments, what it returns, and the general semantics of what it normally does. You are now being told, as well, what abnormal things it can do. This is a promise, just like the method promises to return a value of a certain type, and you can count on it when writing your code. These new promises help to tease apart and make explicit all the places where exceptional conditions should be handled in your program, and that makes large-scale design easier.

Because exceptions are instances of classes, they can be put into a hierarchy that can naturally describe the relationships among the different types of exceptions. In fact, if you take a moment to glance in Appendix B, "Class Hierarchy Diagrams," at the diagrams for `java.lang` errors and `java.lang` exceptions, you'll see that the class `Throwable` actually has two large hierarchies of classes beneath it. The roots of these two hierarchies are subclasses of `Throwable` called `Exception` and `Error`. These hierarchies embody the rich set of relationships that exist between exceptions and errors in the Java run-time environment.

When you know that a particular kind of error or exception can occur in your method, you are supposed to either handle it yourself or explicitly warn potential callers about the possibility using the `throws` clause. Not all errors and exceptions must be listed; instances of either class `Error` or `RuntimeException` (or any of their subclasses) do not have to be listed in your `throws` clause. They get special treatment because they can occur anywhere within a Java program and are usually conditions that you, as the programmer, did not directly cause. One good example is the `OutOfMemoryError`, which can happen anywhere, at any time, and for any number of reasons.

> **NOTE**
>
> You can, of course, choose to list these errors and run-time exceptions if you like, but the callers of your methods will not be forced to handle them; only in your `throws` clause non-run-time exceptions *must* be handled.
>
> Whenever you see the word "exception" by itself, it almost always means "exception or error" (that is, an instance of `Throwable`). The previous discussion makes it clear that `Exceptions` and `Errors` actually form two separate hierarchies, but except for the `throws` clause rule, they act exactly the same.

If you examine the diagrams in Appendix B more carefully, you'll notice that there are only six types of exceptions (in `java.lang`) that must be listed in a `throws` clause (remember that all `Errors` and `RuntimeExceptions` are exempt):

- `ClassNotFoundException`

- `CloneNotSupportedException`

- `IllegalAccessException`

- `InstantiationException`

- `InterruptedException`

- `NoSuchMethodException`

Each of these names suggests something that is explicitly caused by the programmer, not some behind-the-scenes event such as `OutOfMemoryError`.

If you look further in Appendix B, near the bottom of the diagrams for `java.util` and `java.io`, you'll see that each package adds some new exceptions. The former is adding two exceptions somewhat akin to `ArrayStoreException` and `IndexOutOfBoundsException`, and so decides to place them under `RuntimeException`. The latter is adding a whole new tree of `IOExceptions`, which are more explicitly caused by the programmer, and so they are rooted under `Exception`. Thus, `IOExceptions` must be described in `throws` clauses. Finally, package `java.awt` (in diagram `java.awt-components`) defines one of each style, implicit and explicit.

The Java class library uses exceptions everywhere, and to good effect. If you examine the detailed API documentation in your Java release, you see that many of the methods in the library have `throws` clauses, and some of them even document (when they believe it will make something clearer to the reader) when they may throw one of the implicit errors or exceptions. This is just a nicety on the documenter's part, because you are not required to catch conditions like that. If it wasn't obvious that such a condition could happen there, and for some reason you really cared about catching it, this would be useful information.

Programming in the Small

Now that you have a feeling for how exceptions can help you design a program and a class library better, how do you actually use exceptions? Let's try to call anExceptionalMethod() defined in this chapter's first example:

```
public void  anotherExceptionalMethod() throws MyFirstException {
    MyFirstExceptionalClass  aMFEC = new MyFirstExceptionalClass();

    aMFEC.anExceptionalMethod();
}
```

Let's examine this example more closely. If you assume that MyFirstException is a subclass of Exception, it means that if you don't handle it in anotherExceptionalMethod()'s code, you must warn your callers about it. Because your code simply calls anExceptionalMethod() without doing anything about the fact that it may throw MyFirstException, you must add that exception to your throws clause. This is perfectly legal, but it does defer to your caller something that perhaps you should be responsible for doing yourself. (It depends on the circumstances, of course.)

Suppose that that you feel responsible today and decide to handle the exception. Because you're now declaring a method without a throws clause, you must "catch" the expected exception and do something useful with it:

```
public void  responsibleMethod() {
    MyFirstExceptionalClass  aMFEC = new MyFirstExceptionalClass();

    try {
        aMFEC.anExceptionalMethod();
    } catch (MyFirstException m) {
        . . .      // do something terribly significant and responsible
    }
}
```

The try statement says basically: "Try running the code inside these braces, and if there are exceptions thrown, I will attach handlers to take care of them." You can have as many catch clauses at the end of a try as you need. Each allows you to handle any and all exceptions that are instances of the class listed in parentheses, of any of its subclasses, or of a class that implements the interface listed in parentheses. In the catch in this example, exceptions of the class MyFirstException (or any of its subclasses) are being handled.

What if you want to combine both the approaches shown so far? You'd like to handle the exception yourself, but also reflect it up to your caller. This can be done by explicitly rethrowing the exception:

```
public void  responsibleExceptionalMethod() throws MyFirstException {
    MyFirstExceptionalClass  aMFEC = new MyFirstExceptionalClass();

    try {
        aMFEC.anExceptionalMethod();
    } catch (MyFirstException m) {
        . . .            // do something responsible
```

```
        throw m;      // re-throw the exception
    }
}
```

This works because exception handlers can be nested. You handle the exception by doing something responsible with it, but decide that it is too important to not give an exception handler that might be in your caller a chance to handle it as well. Exceptions float all the way up the chain of method callers this way (usually not being handled by most of them) until at last, the system itself handles any uncaught ones by aborting your program and printing an error message. In a stand-alone program, this is not such a bad idea; but in an applet, it can cause the browser to crash. Most browsers protect themselves from this disaster by catching all exceptions themselves whenever they run an applet, but you can never tell. If it's possible for you to catch an exception and do something intelligent with it, you should.

Let's see what throwing a new exception looks like. Let's flesh out this chapter's first example:

```
public class  MyFirstExceptionalClass {
    public void  anExceptionalMethod() throws MyFirstException {
        . . .
        if (someThingUnusualHasHappened()) {
            throw new MyFirstException();
            // execution never reaches here
        }
    }
}
```

> **NOTE**
>
> throw is a little like a break statement—nothing "beyond it" is executed.

This is the fundamental way that all exceptions are generated; someone, somewhere, has to create an exception object and throw it. In fact, the whole hierarchy under the class Throwable would be worth much less if there were not throw statements scattered throughout the code in the Java library at just the right places. Because exceptions propagate up from any depth down inside methods, any method call you make might generate a plethora of possible errors and exceptions. Luckily, only the ones listed in the throws clause of that method need be thought about; the rest travel silently past on their way to becoming an error message (or being caught and handled "higher up" in the system).

Here's an unusual demonstration of this, where the throw, and the handler that catches it, are very close together:

```
System.out.print("Now ");
try {
    System.out.print("is ");
    throw new MyFirstException();
    System.out.print("a ");
```

```
} catch (MyFirstException m) {
    System.out.print("the ");
}
System.out.print("time.\n");
```

It prints out Now is the time.

Exceptions are really a quite powerful way of partitioning the space of all possible error conditions into manageable pieces. Because the first catch clause that matches is executed, you can build chains such as the following:

```
try {
    someReallyExceptionalMethod();
} catch (NullPointerException n) {  // a subclass of RuntimeException
    . . .
} catch (RuntimeException r) {       // a subclass of Exception
    . . .
} catch (IOException i) {            // a subclass of Exception
    . . .
} catch (MyFirstException m) {       // our subclass of Exception
    . . .
} catch (Exception e) {              // a subclass of Throwable
    . . .
} catch (Throwable t) {
    . . .  // Errors, plus anything not caught above are caught here
}
```

By listing subclasses before their parent classes, the parent catches anything it would normally catch that's also *not* one of the subclasses above it. By juggling chains like these, you can express almost any combination of tests. If there's some really obscure case you can't handle, perhaps you can use an interface to catch it instead. That would enable you to design your (peculiar) exceptions hierarchy using multiple inheritance. Catching an interface rather than a class can also be used to test for a property that many exceptions share but that cannot be expressed in the single-inheritance tree alone.

Suppose, for example, that a scattered set of your exception classes require a reboot after being thrown. You create an interface called NeedsReboot, and all these classes implement the interface. (None of them needs to have a common parent exception class.) Then, the highest level of exception handler simply catches classes that implement NeedsReboot and performs a reboot:

```
public interface  NeedsReboot { }    // needs no contents at all

try {
    someMethodThatGeneratesExceptionsThatImplementNeedsReboot();
} catch (NeedsReboot n) {     // catch an interface
    . . .                     // cleanup
    SystemClass.reboot();     // reboot using a made-up system class
}
```

By the way, if you need really unusual behavior during an exception, you can place the behavior into the exception class itself! Remember that an exception is also a normal class, so it can contain instance variables and methods. Although using them is a little unusual, it might be valuable on a few occasions. Here's what this might look like:

```
try {
    someExceptionallyStrangeMethod();
} catch (ComplexException e) {
    switch (e.internalState()) {     // probably returns an instance variable value
        case e.COMPLEX_CASE:         // a class variable of the exception's class
            e.performComplexBehavior(myState, theContext, etc);
            break;
        . . .
    }
}
```

The Limitations Placed on the Programmer

As powerful as all this sounds, isn't it a little limiting, too? For example, suppose you want to override one of the standard methods of the Object class, toString(), to be smarter about how you print yourself:

```
public class  MyIllegalClass {
    public String  toString() {
        someReallyExceptionalMethod();
        . . .            // returns some String
    }
}
```

Because the superclass (Object) defined the method declaration for toString() without a throws clause, any implementation of it in any subclass must obey this restriction. In particular, you cannot just call someReallyExceptionalMethod(), as you did previously, because it will generate a host of errors and exceptions, some of which are not exempt from being listed in a throws clause (such as IOException and MyFirstException). If all the exceptions thrown were exempt, you would have no problem, but because some are not, you have to catch at least those few exceptions for this to be legal Java:

```
public class  MyLegalClass {
    public String  toString() {
        try {
            someReallyExceptionalMethod();
        } catch (IOException e) {
        } catch (MyFirstException m) {
        }
        . . .            // returns some String
    }
}
```

In both cases, you elect to catch the exceptions and do absolutely nothing with them. Although this is legal, it is not always the right thing to do. You may need to think for a while to come up with the best, nontrivial behavior for any particular catch clause. This extra thought and care makes your program more robust, better able to handle unusual input, and more likely to work correctly when used by multiple threads.

MyIllegalClass's toString() method produces a compiler error to remind you to reflect on these issues. This extra care will richly reward you as you reuse your classes in later projects and in larger and larger programs. Of course, the Java class library has been written with exactly this degree of care, and that's one of the reasons it's robust enough to be used in constructing all your Java projects.

The `finally` Clause

Finally, for `finally`. Suppose there is some action that you absolutely must do, no matter what happens. Usually, this is to free some external resource after acquiring it, to close a file after opening it, or something similar. To be sure that "no matter what" includes exceptions as well, you use a clause of the `try` statement designed for exactly this sort of thing, `finally`:

```
SomeFileClass  f = new SomeFileClass();

if (f.open("/a/file/name/path")) {
    try {
        someReallyExceptionalMethod();
    } finally {
        f.close();
    }
}
```

This use of `finally` behaves very much like the following

```
SomeFileClass  f = new SomeFileClass();

if (f.open("/a/file/name/path")) {
    try {
        someReallyExceptionalMethod();
    } catch (Throwable t) {
        f.close();
        throw t;
    }
}
```

except that `finally` can also be used to clean up not only after exceptions but after `return`, `break`, and `continue` statements as well. Here's a complex demonstration:

```
public class  MyFinalExceptionalClass extends ContextClass {
    public static void  main(String argv[]) {
        int  mysteriousState = getContext();

        while (true) {
            System.out.print("Who ");
            try {
                System.out.print("is ");
                if (mysteriousState == 1)
                    return;
                System.out.print("that ");
                if (mysteriousState == 2)
                    break;
                System.out.print("strange ");
                if (mysteriousState == 3)
                    continue;
                System.out.print("but kindly ");
```

```
                    if (mysteriousState == 4)
                        throw new UncaughtException();
                    System.out.print("not at all ");
                } finally {
                    System.out.print("amusing man?\n");
                }
                System.out.print("I'd like to meet the man ");
            }
        System.out.print("Please tell me.\n");
    }
}
```

Here is the output produced depending on the value of mysteriousState:

```
1    Who is amusing man?
2    Who is that amusing man?
     Please tell me
3    Who is that strange amusing man?
     ...
4    Who is that strange but kindly amusing man?
5    Who is that strange but kindly not at all amusing man?
     I'd like to meet the man Who is that strange...?
     ...
```

> **NOTE**
>
> In cases 3 and 5, the output never ends until you press Ctrl+C. In 4, an error message generated by the UncaughtException is also printed.

Summary

This chapter discussed how exceptions aid your program's design, robustness, and multithreading capability.

You also learned about the vast array of exceptions defined and thrown in the Java class library, and how to try methods while catching any of a hierarchically ordered set of possible exceptions and errors. Java's reliance on strict exception handling does place some restrictions on the programmer, but you learned that these restrictions are light compared to the rewards.

Finally, the finally clause was discussed, which provides a fool-proof way to be certain that something is accomplished, no matter what.

PART

IN THIS PART

The Java Class Libraries

Overview of the Class Libraries

17

by Michael Morrison

IN THIS CHAPTER

Code reuse is one of the most significant benefits of using object-oriented design practices. Creating reusable, inheritable classes can save amazing amounts of time and energy, which in turn greatly boosts productivity. Java itself takes code reuse to heart in its implementation of a wide variety of standard objects that are available to Java programmers. The standard Java objects are known collectively as the Java class libraries.

The Java class libraries are implemented as packages, which contain groups of related classes. Along with classes, the standard Java packages also include interfaces, exception definitions, and error definitions. Java is composed of three class libraries, or packages: the language package, the utilities package, and the I/O package. In this chapter, you learn what these packages are and what classes and interfaces comprise each.

> **NOTE**
>
> There actually are three other standard packages that are important in Java programming, but they aren't technically considered part of the basic Java class libraries. You'll learn about these packages in Part V, "Applet Programming," and Part VI, "Network Programming."

The Language Package

The Java language package, which is also known as `java.lang`, provides classes that make up the core of the Java language. The language package contains classes at the lowest level of the Java class libraries. For example, the `Object` class, which all classes are derived from, is located in the language package.

It's impossible to write a Java program without dealing with at least a few of the elements of the language package. You'll learn much more about the inner workings of the language package in the next chapter. The most important classes contained in the language package follow:

- The `Object` Class
- Data Type Wrapper Classes
- The `Math` Class
- String Classes
- `System` and `Runtime` Classes
- Thread Classes
- `Class` Classes
- Exception Handling Classes
- Process Classes

The `Object` Class

The `Object` class is the superclass for all classes in Java. Because all classes are derived from `Object`, the methods defined in `Object` are shared by all classes. This results in a core set of methods that all Java classes are guaranteed to support. `Object` includes methods for making copies of an object, testing objects for equality, and converting the value of an object to a string.

Data Type Wrapper Classes

The fundamental data types (`int`, `char`, `float`, and so on) in Java are not implemented as classes. Many times it is useful, however, to know more information about a fundamental type than just its value. By implementing class wrappers for the fundamental types, additional information can be maintained, as well as methods defined that act on the types. The data type wrapper classes serve as class versions of the fundamental data types, and are named similarly to the types they wrap. For example, the type wrapper for `int` is the `Integer` class. Following are the Java data type wrapper classes:

- ■ `Boolean`
- ■ `Character`
- ■ `Double`
- ■ `Float`
- ■ `Integer`
- ■ `Long`

Type wrappers are also useful because many of Java's utility classes require classes as parameters, not simple types. It is worth pointing out that type wrappers and simple types are not interchangeable. However, you can get a simple type from a wrapper through a simple method call, which you'll learn about in the next chapter.

The `Math` Class

The `Math` class serves as a grouping of mathematical functions and constants. It is interesting to note that all the variables and methods in `Math` are `static`, and the `Math` class itself is `final`. This means you can't derive new classes from `Math`. Additionally, you can't instantiate the `Math` class. It's best to think of the `Math` class as just a conglomeration of methods and constants for performing mathematical computations.

The `Math` class includes the `E` and `PI` constants, methods for determining the absolute value of a number, methods for calculating trigonometric functions, and minimum and maximum methods, among others.

String Classes

For various reasons (mostly security related), Java implements text strings as classes, rather than forcing the programmer to use character arrays. The two Java classes that represent strings are String and StringBuffer. The String class is useful for working with constant strings that can't change in value or length. The StringBuffer class is used to work with strings of varying value and length.

The System and Runtime Classes

The System and Runtime classes provide a means for your programs to access system and runtime environment resources. Like the Math class, the System class is final and is entirely composed of static variables and methods. The System class basically provides a system-independent programming interface to system resources. Examples of system resources include the standard input and output streams, System.in and System.out, which typically model the keyboard and monitor.

The Runtime class provides direct access to the runtime environment. An example of a runtime routine is the freeMemory method, which returns the amount of free system memory available.

Thread Classes

Java is a multithreaded environment and provides various classes for managing and working with threads. Following are the classes and interfaces used in conjunction with multithreaded programs:

- Thread
- ThreadDeath
- ThreadGroup
- Runnable

The Thread class is used to create a thread of execution in a program. The ThreadDeath class is used to clean up after a thread has finished execution. As its name implies, the ThreadGroup class is useful for organizing a group of threads. Finally, the Runnable interface provides an alternate means of creating a thread without subclassing the Thread class. Threads and multithreading are covered in detail in Chapter 15, "Threads and Multithreading."

Class Classes

Java provides two classes for working with classes: Class and ClassLoader. The Class class provides runtime information for a class, such as the name, type, and parent superclass. Class is useful for querying a class for runtime information, such as the class name. The ClassLoader class provides a means to load classes into the runtime environment. `ClassLoader` is useful for loading classes from a file or for loading distributed classes across a network connection.

Error-Handling Classes

Runtime error handling is a very important facility in any programming environment. Java provides the following classes for dealing with runtime errors:

- Throwable
- Exception
- Error

The `Throwable` class provides low-level error-handling capabilities such as an execution stack list. The `Exception` class is derived from `Throwable` and provides the base level of functionality for all the exception classes defined in the Java system. The `Exception` class is used for handling normal errors. The `Error` class is also derived from `Throwable`, but it is used for handling abnormal errors that aren't expected to occur. Very few Java programs worry with the `Error` class; most use the `Exception` class to handle runtime errors. Error handling with exceptions is covered in detail in Chapter 16, "Exception Handling."

Process Classes

Java supports system processes with a single class, `Process`. The `Process` class represents generic system processes that are created when you use the `Runtime` class to execute system commands.

The Utilities Package

The Java utilities package, which is also known as `java.util`, provides various classes that perform different utility functions. The utilities package includes a class for working with dates, a set of data structure classes, a class for generating random numbers, and a string tokenizer class, among others. You'll learn much more about the classes that make up the utilities package in Chapter 19, "The Utilities Package." The most important classes contained in the utilities package follow:

- The `Date` Class
- Data Structure Classes
- The `Random` Class
- The `StringTokenizer` Class
- The `Properties` Class
- The `Observer` Interface
- The `Enumeration` Interface

The Date Class

The Date class represents a calendar date and time in a system-independent fashion. The Date class provides methods for retrieving the current date and time as well as computing days of the week and month.

Data Structure Classes

The Java data structure classes and interfaces implement popular data structures for storing data. The data structure classes and interfaces are as follows:

- BitSet
- Dictionary
- Hashtable
- Properties
- Vector
- Stack
- Enumeration

The BitSet class represents a set of bits, which is also known as a bitfield. The Dictionary class is an abstract class that provides a lookup mechanism for mapping keys to values. The Hashtable class derives from Dictionary and provides additional support for working with keys and values. The Properties class is derived from Hashtable and provides the additional functionality of being readable and writable to and from streams. The Vector class implements an array that can dynamically grow. The Stack class derives from Vector and implements a classic stack of last-in-first-out (LIFO) objects. Finally, the Enumeration interface specifies a set of methods for counting (iterating) through a set of values.

The Random Class

Many programs, especially programs that model the real world, require some degree of randomness. Java provides randomness by way of the Random class. The Random class implements a random-number generator by providing a stream of pseudo-random numbers. A slot machine program is a good example of one that would make use of the Random class.

The StringTokenizer Class

The StringTokenizer class provides a means of converting text strings into individual tokens. By specifying a set of delimiters, you can parse text strings into tokens using the StringTokenizer class. String tokenization is useful in a wide variety of programs, from compilers to text-based adventure games.

The Observer Classes

The model-view paradigm is becoming increasingly popular in object-oriented programming. This model breaks a program down into data and views on the data. Java supports this model with the Observable class and the Observer interface. The Observable class is subclassed to define the observable data in a program. This data is then connected to one or more observer classes. The observer classes are implementations of the Observer interface. When an Observable object changes state, it notifies all of its observers of the change.

The I/O Package

The Java I/O package, also known as java.io, provides classes with support for reading and writing data to and from different input and output devices, including files. The I/O package includes classes for inputting streams of data, outputting streams of data, working with files, and tokenizing streams of data. You'll learn a lot more about the classes that make up the I/O package in Chapter 20, "The I/O Package." The most important classes contained in the I/O package follow:

- Input Stream Classes
- Output Stream Classes
- File Classes
- The StreamTokenizer Class

Input Stream Classes

Java uses input streams to handle reading data from an input source. An input source can be a file, a string, memory, or anything else that contains data. The input stream classes follow:

- InputStream
- BufferedInputStream
- ByteArrayInputStream
- DataInputStream
- FileInputStream
- FilterInputStream
- LineNumberInputStream
- PipedInputStream
- PushbackInputStream
- SequenceInputStream
- StringBufferInputStream

The InputStream class is an abstract class that serves as the base class for all input streams. The InputStream class defines an interface for reading streamed bytes of data, finding out the number of bytes available for reading, and moving the stream position pointer, among other things. All the other input streams provide support for reading data from different types of input devices.

Output Stream Classes

Output streams are the counterpart to input streams and handle writing data to an output source. Similar to input sources, output sources include files, strings, memory, and anything else that can contain data. The output stream classes defined in java.io follow:

- OutputStream
- BufferedOutputStream
- ByteArrayOutputStream
- DataOutputStream
- FileOutputStream
- FilterOutputStream
- PipedOutputStream
- PrintStream

The OutputStream class is an abstract class that serves as the base class for all output streams. OutputStream defines an interface for writing streamed bytes of data to an output source. All the other output streams provide support for writing data to different output devices. Data written by an output stream is formatted to be read by an input stream.

File Classes

Files are the most widely used method of data storage in computer systems. Java supports files with two different classes: File and RandomAccessFile. The File class provides an abstraction for files that takes into account system-dependent features. The File class keeps up with information about a file including the location where it is stored and how it can be accessed. The File class has no methods for reading and writing data to and from a file; it is only useful for querying and modifying the attributes of a file. In actuality, you can think of the File class data as representing a filename, and the class methods as representing operating system commands that act on filenames.

The RandomAccessFile class provides a variety of methods for reading and writing data to and from a file. RandomAccessFile contains many different methods for reading and writing different types of information, namely the data type wrappers.

The StreamTokenizer Class

The StreamTokenizer class provides the functionality for converting an input stream of data into a stream of tokens. StreamTokenizer provides a set of methods for defining the lexical syntax of tokens. Stream tokenization can be useful in parsing streams of textual data.

Summary

This chapter provided a thumbnail sketch of the contents of the three Java class libraries: the language package, the utilities package, and the I/O package. Although you didn't learn a lot of gritty details, or how to use any classes in a real program, you hopefully now have a broad picture in your mind of what these packages can do. The Java class libraries provide a rich set of classes for overcoming a wide variety of programming obstacles.

A common problem when using programming environments with a lot of support libraries is knowing what functionality is provided and what functionality you must write yourself. This chapter hopefully has given you an idea of what standard classes you can reuse in your own Java programs, and what classes you will have to implement yourself.

Having seen what each package in the Java class libraries contain, you're probably eager to get busy learning how to use the classes in each. The next three chapters each focus on one of the three packages that make up the Java class libraries.

The Language Package

18

by Michael Morrison

The Java language package is at the heart of the Java language. In this chapter you learn more about some of the classes that make up the language package (`java.lang`). You'll find many of the classes in the language package to be indispensable in writing Java programs.

The language package contains many classes, each with a variety of member variables and methods. You won't learn about every class and every method in this chapter, as it would simply be too much material to cover in a single chapter. Rather, you will focus on the most important classes in the language package; classes that will come in the most useful as you begin developing your own Java classes. Please note that although the multithreading and error-handling classes are part of the language package, they aren't covered in this chapter. This is because Chapters 15 and 16 are devoted to them.

The `Object` Class

The `Object` class is probably the most important of all Java classes, simply because it is the superclass of all Java classes. It is important to have a solid understanding of the `Object` class, as all the classes you develop will inherit the variables and methods of `Object`. The `Object` class implements the following important methods:

- `Object clone()`
- `boolean equals(Object obj)`
- `int hashCode()`
- `final Class getClass()`
- `String toString()`

The `Object clone()` creates a clone of the object it is called on. `clone` creates and allocates memory for the new object that is being copied to. `clone` actually creates a new object and then copies the contents of the calling object to the new object. An example of using the clone method follows:

```
Circle circle1 = new Circle(1.0, 3.5, 4.2);
Circle circle2 = circle1.clone();
```

In this example, the `circle1` object is created, but the `circle2` object is only declared. `circle2` is not created by using the `new` operator; it is created by `circle1` calling the `clone` method to create a clone of itself.

The `equals` method compares two objects for equality. `equals` is only applicable when both objects have been stored in a `Hashtable`. The `hashCode` method returns the hashcode value for an object. `Hashcodes` are integers that uniquely represent objects in the Java system.

The `getClass` method returns the runtime class information for an object in the form of a `Class` object. If you recall, the `Class` object keeps up with runtime class information, such as the name of a class and the parent superclass.

The toString method returns a string representing the value of an object. Because the value of an object varies depending on the class type, it is assumed that each class will override the toString method to display information specific to that class. The information returned by toString could be very valuable for determining the internal state of an object when debugging.

Data Type Wrapper Classes

The data type wrapper classes serve to provide object versions of the fundamental Java data types. Type wrapping is important because many Java classes and methods operate on classes rather than fundamental types. Furthermore, by creating object versions of the simple data types, it is possible to add useful member functions for each. Following are the type wrapper classes supported by Java:

- Boolean
- Character
- Double
- Float
- Integer
- Long

Although each wrapper implements methods specific to each data type, there are a handful of methods applicable to all the wrappers. These methods follow:

- ClassType(*type*)
- *type* *type*Value()
- int hashCode()
- String toString()
- boolean equals(Object obj)
- static boolean valueOf(String s)

> **NOTE**
>
> Actually, the valueOf method isn't implemented in the Character class, but it is implemented in all the other wrapper classes.

The ClassType method is actually the creation method for each class. The wrapper creation methods take as their only parameter the *type* of data they are wrapping. This enables you to create a type wrapper from a fundamental type. For example, you would use the creation method for the Character class like this:

```
Character c1 = new Character('x');
```

The *type*Value method is used to get the fundamental type back from a wrapper. *type*Value returns a value of the same type as the fundamental type it wraps. Following is an example of how a fundamental type can be extracted from a wrapper object:

```
char c2 = c1.charValue();
```

> **NOTE**
>
> Remember, fundamental types are not represented in Java by classes or objects. Data type wrapper classes provide a means of representing a fundamental type as an object, which is often useful. Wrapper classes are different from other Java classes in that their only purpose is to allow fundamental types to be represented as objects.

The hashCode method returns the hashcode for a type wrapper object. This hashCode method is simply an overridden version of the hashCode method contained in the Object class.

The toString method is used to get a string representation of the internal state of an object. toString is typically overridden in each class so as to reflect unique state implementations. Following is an example of how you might output the state of a wrapper variable using toString:

```
System.out.println(c1.toString());
```

The equals method is used to test for equality between two wrapper objects. This is the same equals method implemented in Object and inherited by all other objects in Java. The valueOf method is implemented in all of the type wrappers except Character. valueOf, which is static, is used to convert a string to a value of a particular wrapper type. valueOf parses the String parameter s and returns the value of it.

Now that you have an idea of what functionality all of the wrapper classes share, it's time to take a look at some of the specifics of each class.

The Boolean Class

The Boolean class   wraps the boolean fundamental data type. Boolean implements only one method in addition to the common wrapper methods already mentioned:

```
static boolean getBoolean(String name)
```

getBoolean returns a type boolean that represents the boolean property value of the String parameter name. The name parameter refers to a property name that represents a boolean property value. Because getBoolean is static, it is typically meant to be used without actually instantiating a `Boolean` object.

The `Boolean` class also includes two `final static` (constant) data members: `TRUE` and `FALSE`. `TRUE` and `FALSE` represent the two possible states that the `Boolean` class can represent. It is important to note the difference between `true` and `false`, and `Boolean.TRUE` and `Boolean.FALSE`. The first pair applies to `boolean` fundamental types, while the second pair applies to `Boolean` classes; they cannot be interchanged.

The Character Class

The `Character` class wraps the `char` fundamental type and provides some useful methods for manipulating characters. The methods implemented by `Character`, beyond the common wrapper methods, follow:

- `static boolean isLowerCase(char ch)`
- `static boolean isUpperCase(char ch)`
- `static boolean isDigit(char ch)`
- `static boolean isSpace(char ch)`
- `static char toLowerCase(char ch)`
- `static char toUpperCase(char ch)`
- `static int digit(char ch, int radix)`
- `static char forDigit(int digit, int radix)`

All these methods are `static`, which means that they can be used without instantiating a `Character` object. The `isLowerCase` and `isUpperCase` methods return whether or not a character is an uppercase or lower case character. An example of using the `isLowerCase` method follows:

```
Character c = new Character('g');
boolean isLower = Character.isLowerCase(c);
```

In this case, the `boolean` variable `isLower` is set to `true`, because `'g'` is a lowercase character.

The `isDigit` method simply returns whether or not a character is a digit (0-9). Following is an example of how to use the `isDigit` method:

```
boolean isDigit = Character.isDigit('7');
```

The `boolean` variable `isDigit` is set to `true` here because `'7'` is in fact a numeric digit.

The `isSpace` method returns whether or not a character is whitespace. (Whitespace is defined as any combination of the space, tab, newline, carriage return, or linefeed characters.) Following is an example of how to use `isSpace`:

```
boolean isSpace = Character.isSpace('\t');
```

In this example, the `isSpace` `boolean` variable is set to `true` because the tab character is considered whitespace.

The `toLowerCase` and `toUpperCase` methods convert a character to a lower or uppercase character. If a character is already lowercase and `toLowerCase` is called, the character is not changed. Similarly, `toUpperCase` does nothing to uppercase characters. Following are a few examples of using these methods:

```
char c1 = Character.toUpperCase('g');
char c2 = Character.toLowerCase('M');
```

In the first example, `c1` is converted from `'g'` to `'G'` because of the call to the `toUpperCase` method. In the second example, `c2` is converted from `'M'` to `'m'` because of the call to `toLowerCase`.

The `digit` method returns the numeric (integer) value of a character digit in base 10. The `radix` parameter specifies the base of the character digit for conversion. If the character is not a valid digit, `-1` is returned. Following are a few examples of using the `digit` method:

```
char c1 = '4';
char c2 = 'c';
int four = Character.digit(c1, 10);
int twelve = Character.digit(c2, 16);
```

In the first example, the character `'4'` is converted to the integer number `4` using the `digit` method. In the second example, the hexadecimal number represented by the character `'c'` is returned as the base 10 integer number `12`.

The `forDigit` method performs the reverse of the `digit` method; it returns the character representation of an integer digit. Once again, `radix` specifies the base of the integer number. Following is an example of how to use `forDigit`:

```
int i = 9;
char c = Character.forDigit(i, 10);
```

In this example, the integer number `9` is converted to the character `'9'` by the `forDigit` method.

The `Character` class provides two `final` `static` data members for specifying the radix limits for conversions: `MIN_RADIX` and `MAX_RADIX`. `MIN_RADIX` specifies the minimum radix (2) for performing numeric to character conversions and vice-versa. Likewise, `MAX_RADIX` specifies the maximum radix (36) for conversions.

Integer Classes

The Integer and Long classes wrap the fundamental integer types int and long and provide a variety of methods for working with integer numbers. The methods implemented by Integer follow:

- ■ static int parseInt(String s, int radix)
- ■ static int parseInt(String s)
- ■ long longValue()
- ■ float floatValue()
- ■ double doubleValue()
- ■ static Integer getInteger(String name)
- ■ static Integer getInteger(String name, int val)
- ■ static Integer getInteger(String name, Integer val)

The parseInt methods parse strings for an integer value, and return the value as an int. The version of parseInt with the radix parameter enables you to specify the base of the integer; the other version of parseInt assumes a base of 10.

The longValue, floatValue, and doubleValue methods return the values of an integer converted to the appropriate type. For example, the following code shows how to convert an Integer to a double:

```
Integer i = new Integer(17);
float f = i.floatValue();
```

In this example, the value of the Integer variable i is converted to a float value and stored in the float variable f. The result is that the integer value 17 is converted to the float value 17.0.

The getInteger methods return an integer property value specified by the String property name parameter name. Notice that all three of the getInteger methods are static, which means you don't need to instantiate an Integer object to use these methods. The differences between these methods is what happens if the integer property isn't found. The first version returns 0 if the property isn't found, the second version returns the int parameter val, and the last version returns the Integer value val.

The Integer class also includes two final static (constant) data members: MINVALUE and MAXVALUE. MINVALUE and MAXVALUE specify the smallest and largest numbers that can be represented by an Integer object.

The Long object is very similar to the Integer object except it wraps the fundamental type long. Long actually implements similar methods as Int, with the exception that they act on long type numbers rather than int type numbers.

Floating Point Classes

The Float and Double classes wrap the fundamental floating point types float and double. These two classes provide a group of methods for working with floating point numbers. The methods implemented by the Float class follow:

- `boolean isNaN()`
- `static boolean isNaN(float v)`
- `boolean isInfinite()`
- `static boolean isInfinite(float v)`
- `int intValue()`
- `long longValue()`
- `double doubleValue()`
- `static int floatToIntBits(float value)`
- `static float intBitsToFloat(int bits)`

The isNaN methods return whether or not the Float value is the special not-a-number (NaN) value. The first version of isNaN operates on the value of the calling Float object. The second version is static and takes the float to test as its parameter, v.

The isInfinite methods return whether or not the Float value is infinite, which is represented by the special NEGATIVE_INFINITY and POSITIVE_INFINITY final static member variables. Like the isNaN methods, isInfinity comes in two versions: a class value version and a static version that takes a float as an argument.

The intValue, longValue, and doubleValue methods return the values of a floating point number converted to the appropriate type. For example, the following code shows how to convert a Float to a long:

```
Float f = new Float(5.237);
long l = f.longValue();
```

In this example, the value of the Float variable f is converted to a long and stored in the long variable l. This results in the floating point value 5.237 being converted to the long value 5.

The last two methods implemented by the Float class are floatToIntBits and intBitsToFloat. The floatToIntBits and intBitsToFloat methods convert floating point values to their integer bit representations and back.

The Float class also has a group of final static (constant) data members: MINVALUE, MAXVALUE, NEGATIVE_INFINITY, POSITIVE_INFINITY, and NaN. MINVALUE and MAXVALUE specify the smallest and largest numbers that can be represented by a Float object. NEGATIVE_INFINITY and POSITIVE_INFINITY represent negative and positive infinity, while NaN represents the special not-a-number condition.

The Double object is very similar to the Float object. The only difference is that Double wraps the fundamental type double instead of float. Double implements similar methods as Float, with the exception that the methods act on double rather than float type numbers.

The Math Class

The Math class contains many invaluable mathematical functions along with a few useful constants. The Math class isn't intended to be instantiated; it is basically just a holding class for mathematical functions. Additionally, the Math class is declared as final so you can't derive from it. The most useful methods implemented by the Math class follow:

- static double sin(double a)
- static double cos(double a)
- static double tan(double a)
- static double asin(double a)
- static double acos(double a)
- static double atan(double a)
- static double exp(double a)
- static double log(double a)
- static double sqrt(double a)
- static double pow(double a, double b)
- static double ceil(double a)
- static double floor(double a)
- static int round(float a)
- static long round(double a)
- static double rint(double a)
- static double atan2(double a, double b)
- static synchronized double random()
- static int abs(int a)
- static long abs(long a)
- static float abs(float a)
- static double abs(double a)
- static int min(int a, int b)
- static long min(long a, long b)
- static float min(float a, float b)
- static double min(double a, double b)

- ▪ `static int max(int a, int b)`
- ▪ `static long max(long a, long b)`
- ▪ `static float max(float a, float b)`
- ▪ `static double max(double a, double b)`

The trigonometric methods `sin`, `cos`, `tan`, `asin`, `acos`, and `atan` perform the standard trigonometric functions on `double` values. All the angles used in the trigonometric functions are specified in radians. Following is an example of calculating the sine of an angle:

```
double dSine = Math.sin(Math.PI / 2);
```

Notice in the example that the `PI` constant member of the `Math` class was used in the call to the `sin` method. You'll learn about the `PI` constant member variable of `Math` at the end of this section.

The `exp` method returns the exponential number `E` raised to the power of the `double` parameter a. Similarly, the `log` method returns the natural logarithm (base `E`) of the number passed in the parameter a. The `sqrt` method returns the square root of the parameter number a. The `pow` method returns the result of raising a number to a power. `pow` returns a raised to the power of b. Following are some examples of using these math methods:

```
double d1 = 12.3;
double d2 = Math.exp(d1);
double d3 = Math.log(d1);
double d4 = Math.sqrt(d1);
double d5 = Math.pow(d1, 3.0);
```

The `ceil` and `floor` methods return the "ceiling" and "floor" for the passed parameter a. The ceiling is the smallest whole number greater than or equal to a, where the floor is the largest whole number less than or equal to a. The `round` methods round `float` and `double` numbers to the nearest integer value, which is returned as type `int` or `long`. Both `round` methods work by adding `0.5` to the number and then returning the largest integer that is less than or equal to the number. The `rint` method returns an integral value, similar to `round`, that remains a type `double`. Following are some examples of using these methods:

```
double d1 = 37.125;
double d2 = Math.ceil(d1);
double d3 = Math.floor(d1);
int i = Math.round((float)d1);
long l = Math.round(d1);
double d4 = Math.rint(d1);
```

Notice in the first example of using `round` that the `double` value d1 must be explicitly cast to a `float`. This is necessary because this version of `round` takes a `float` and returns an `int`.

The `atan2` method converts rectangular coordinates to polar coordinates. The `double` parameters a and b represent the rectangular x and y coordinates to be converted to polar coordinates, which are returned as a `double` value.

The `random` method generates a pseudo-random number between 0.0 and 1.0. `random` is useful for generating random floating point numbers. To generate random numbers of different types, you should use the `Random` class, which is located in the utilities package, `java.util`. The utilities package, including the `Random` class, is covered in the next chapter.

The `abs` methods return the absolute value of numbers of varying types. There are versions of `abs` for working with the following types: `int`, `long`, `float`, and `double`. Following is an example of using the `abs` method to find the absolute value of an integer number:

```
int i = -5, j;
j = Math.abs(i);
```

The `min` and `max` methods return the minimum and maximum numbers given a pair of numbers to compare. Like the `abs` methods, the `min` and `max` methods come in different versions for handling the types `int`, `long`, `float`, and `double`. Following is an example of using the `min` and `max` methods:

```
double d1 = 14.2, d2 = 18.5;
double d3 = Math.min(d1, d2);
double d4 = Math.max(d1, 11.2);
```

Beyond the rich set of methods provided by the `Math` class, there are also a couple of important constant member variables: `E` and `PI`. The `E` member represents the exponential number (`2.7182...`) used in exponential calculations, where `PI` represents the value of Pi (`3.1415...`).

String Classes

Unlike C and C++, text strings in Java are represented with classes rather than character arrays. The two classes that model strings in Java are `String` and `StringBuffer`. The reason for having two string classes is that the `String` class represents constant (immutable) strings and the `StringBuffer` class represents variable (mutable) strings.

The `String` Class

The `String` class is used to represent constant strings. The `String` class has less overhead than `StringBuffer`, which means you should try to use it if you know that a string is constant. The creation methods for the `String` class follow:

- `String()`
- `String(String value)`
- `String(char value[])`
- `String(char value[], int offset, int count)`
- `String(byte ascii[], int hibyte, int offset, int count)`
- `String(byte ascii[], int hibyte)`
- `String(StringBuffer buffer)`

It is readily apparent from the number of creation methods for String that there are many ways to create String objects. The first creation method simply creates a new string that is empty. All of the other creation methods create strings that are initialized in different ways from various types of text data. Following are examples of using some of the String creation methods to create String objects:

```
String s1 = new String();
String s2 = new String("Hello");
char cArray[] = {'H', 'o', 'w', 'd', 'y'};
String s3 = new String(cArray);
String s4 = new String(cArray, 1, 3);
```

In the first example, an empty String object (s1) is created. In the second example, a String object (s2) is created from a literal String value, "Hello". The third example shows a String object (s3) being created from an array of characters. Finally, the fourth example shows a String object (s4) being created from a subarray of characters. The subarray is specified by passing 1 as the offset parameter and 3 as the count parameter. This means that the subarray of characters is to consist of the first three characters starting at one character into the array. The resulting subarray of characters in this case consists of the characters 'o', 'w', and 'd'.

Once you have some String objects created, you are ready to work with them using some of the powerful methods implemented in the String class. Some of the most useful methods provided by the String class follow:

- `int length()`
- `char charAt(int index)`
- `boolean startsWith(String prefix)`
- `boolean startsWith(String prefix, int toffset)`
- `endsWith(String suffix)`
- `int indexOf(int ch)`
- `int indexOf(int ch, int fromIndex)`
- `int indexOf(String str)`
- `int indexOf(String str, int fromIndex)`
- `int lastIndexOf(int ch)`
- `int lastIndexOf(int ch, int fromIndex)`
- `int lastIndexOf(String str)`
- `int lastIndexOf(String str, int fromIndex)`
- `String substring(int beginIndex)`
- `String substring(int beginIndex, int endIndex)`
- `boolean equals(Object anObject)`
- `boolean equalsIgnoreCase(String anotherString)`
- `int compareTo(String anotherString)`

- `String concat(String str)`
- `String replace(char oldChar, char newChar)`
- `String trim()`
- `String toLowerCase()`
- `String toUpperCase()`
- `static String valueOf(Object obj)`
- `static String valueOf(char data[])`
- `static String valueOf(char data[], int offset, int count)`
- `static String valueOf(boolean b)`
- `static String valueOf(char c)`
- `static String valueOf(int i)`
- `static String valueOf(long l)`
- `static String valueOf(float f)`
- `static String valueOf(double d)`

The `length` method simply returns the length of a string, which is the number of Unicode characters in the string. The `charAt` method returns the character at a specific index of a string specified by the `int` parameter `index`. The `startsWith` and `endsWith` methods determine whether or not a string starts or ends with a prefix or suffix string, as specified by the `prefix` and `suffix` parameters. The second version of `startsWith` enables you to specify an offset to begin looking for the string prefix. Following are some examples of using these methods:

```
String s1 = new String("This is a test string!");
int len = s1.length();
char c = s1.charAt(8);
boolean b1 = s1.startsWith("This");
boolean b2 = s1.startsWith("test", 10);
boolean b3 = s1.endsWith("string.");
```

In this series of examples, a `String` object is first created with the value `"This is a test string!"`. The length of the string is calculated using the `length` method, and stored in the integer variable `len`. The length returned is `22`, which specifies how many characters are contained in the string. The character at offset `8` into the string is then obtained using the `charAt` method. Like C and C++, Java offsets start at `0`, not `1`. If you count eight characters into the string, you can see that `charAt` returns the `'a'` character. The next three examples use the `startsWith` method to determine if specific strings are located in the `String` object. The first `startsWith` example looks for the string `"This"` at the beginning of the `String` object. This returns `true` because the string is in fact located at the beginning of the `String` object. The second `startsWith` example looks for the string `"test"` beginning at offset `10` into the `String` object. This call also returns `true` because the string `"test"` is located ten characters into the `String` object. The last example uses the `endsWith` method to check for the occurrence of the string `"string."` at the end of the `String` object. This call returns `false` because the `String` object actually ends with `"string!"`.

The indexOf methods return the location of the first occurrence of a character or string within a String object. The first two versions of indexOf determine the index of a single character within a string, while the second two versions determine the index of a string of characters within a string. Each pair of indexOf methods contain a version for finding a character or string based on the beginning of the String object, as well a version that enables you to specify an offset into the string to begin searching for the first occurrence. If the character or string is not found, indexOf returns -1. The lastIndexOf methods work very much like indexOf, with the exception that lastIndexOf searches backwards through the string. Following are some examples of using these methods:

```
String s1 = new String("Saskatchewan");
int i1 = s1.indexOf('t');
int i2 = s1.indexOf("chew");
int i3 = s1.lastIndexOf('a');
```

In this series of examples, a String object is created with the value "Saskatchewan". The indexOf method is then called on this string with the character value 't'. This call to indexOf returns 5, since the first occurrence of 't' is five characters into the string. The second call to indexOf specifies the string literal "chew". This call returns 6, since the substring "chew" is located six characters into the String object. Finally, the lastIndexOf method is called with a character parameter of 'a'. The call to lastIndexOf returns 10, indicating the third 'a' in the string. Remember, lastIndexOf searches backward through the string to find the first occurrence of a character.

The substring methods return a substring of the calling String object. The first version of substring returns the substring beginning at the index specified by beginIndex, through the end of the calling String object. The second version of substring returns a substring beginning at the index specified by beginIndex and ending at the index specified by endIndex. Following is an example of using one of the substring methods:

```
String s1 = new String("sasquatch");
String s2 = s1.substring(3);
String s3 = s1.substring(2, 7);
```

In this example, a String object is created with the value "sasquatch". A substring of this string is then retrieved using the substring method and passing 3 as the beginIndex parameter. This results in the substring "quatch", which begins at the string index of three and continues through the rest of the string. The second version of substring is then used with starting and ending indices of 2 and 7, yielding the substring "squat".

There are two methods for determining equality between String objects: equals and equalsIgnoreCase. The equals method returns a Boolean value based on the equality of two strings. isEqualNoCase performs a similar function, except it compares the strings with case insensitivity. Similarly, the compareTo method compares two strings and returns an integer value that specifies whether the calling String object is less than, greater than, or equal to the anotherString parameter. The integer value returned by compareTo specifies the numeric difference between the two strings; it is a positive value if the calling String object is greater, and negative if the passed String object is greater. If the two strings are equal, the return value is 0.

Wait a minute—if strings are just text, how can you get a numeric difference between two strings, or establish which one is greater than or less than the other? When strings are compared using the `compareTo` method, each character is compared to the character at the same position in the other string, until they don't match. When two characters are found that don't match, `compareTo` converts them to integers and finds the difference. This difference is what is returned by `compareTo`. Check out the following example to get a better idea of how this works:

```
String s1 = new String("abcfj");
String s2 = new String("abcdz");
System.out.println(s1.compareTo(s2));
```

Each pair of characters is compared until two are encountered that don't match. In this example, the `'f'` and `'d'` characters are the first two that don't match. Since the `compareTo` method is called on the `s1` `String` object, the integer value of `'d'` (`100`) is subtracted from the integer value of `'f'` (`102`) to determine the difference between the strings. Notice that all characters following the two nonmatching characters are ignored in the comparison.

The `concat` method is used to concatenate two `String` objects. The string specified in the `str` parameter is concatenated onto the end of the calling `String` object. Following are a few examples of string concatenation:

```
String s1 = new String("I saw sasquatch ");
String s2 = new String(s1 + "in Saskatchewan.");
String s3 = s1.concat("in Saskatchewan.");
```

In these concatenation examples, a `String` object is first created with the value `"I saw sasquatch"`. The first concatenation example shows how two strings can be concatenated using the addition operator (`+`). The second example shows how two strings can be concatenated using the `concat` method. In both examples, the resulting string is the sentence `"I saw sasquatch in Saskatchewan."`.

The `replace` method is used to replace characters in a string. All occurrences of `oldChar` are replaced with `newChar`. Using the strings from the previous concatenation examples, you could replace all of the s characters with m characters like this:

```
String s4 = s3.replace('s', 'm');
```

This results in the string `"I maw mamquatch in Samkatchewan."`. Notice that the uppercase `'S'` character wasn't replaced.

The `trim` method trims leading and trailing whitespace off of a `String` object. The `toLowerCase` and `toUpperCase` methods are used to convert all of the characters in a `String` object to lower and uppercase. Following are some examples of using these methods using the strings from the previous two examples:

```
String s5 = new String("\t  Yeti\n");
String s6 = s5.trim();
String s7 = s3.toLowerCase();
String s8 = s4.toUpperCase();
```

In this example, the `trim` method is used to strip off the leading and trailing whitespace, resulting in the string `"Yeti"`. The call to `toLowerCase` results in the string `"i saw sasquatch in saskatchewan."`. The only character modified was the `'I'` character, which was the only uppercase character in the string. The call to `toUpperCase` results in the string `"I MAW MAMQUATCH IN SAMKATCHEWAN."`. All of the lowercase characters were converted to uppercase, as you might have guessed!

Finally, the `valueOf` methods all return `String` objects that represent the particular type taken as a parameter. For example, the `valueOf` method that takes an `int` will return the string `"123"` when passed the integer number 123.

The `StringBuffer` Class

The `StringBuffer` class is used to represent variable, or non-constant, strings. The `StringBuffer` class is useful when you know that a string will change in value or in length. The creation methods for the `StringBuffer` class follow:

- `StringBuffer()`
- `StringBuffer(int length)`
- `StringBuffer(String str)`

The first creation method simply creates a new string buffer that is empty. The second creation method creates a string buffer that is `length` characters long, initialized with spaces. The third creation method creates a string buffer from a `String` object. This last creation method is useful when you need to modify a constant `String` object. Following are examples of using the `StringBuffer` creation methods to create `StringBuffer` objects:

```
String s1 = new String("This is a string!");
String sb1 = new StringBuffer();
String sb2 = new StringBuffer(25);
String sb3 = new StringBuffer(s1);
```

Some of the most useful methods implemented by `StringBuffer` follow:

- `int length()`
- `int capacity()`
- `synchronized void setLength(int newLength)`
- `synchronized char charAt(int index)`
- `synchronized void setCharAt(int index, char ch)`
- `synchronized StringBuffer append(Object obj)`
- `synchronized StringBuffer append(String str)`
- `synchronized StringBuffer append(char c)`
- `synchronized StringBuffer append(char str[])`
- `synchronized StringBuffer append(char str[], int offset, int len)`

■ StringBuffer append(boolean b)

■ StringBuffer append(int I)

■ StringBuffer append(long l)

■ StringBuffer append(float f)

■ StringBuffer append(double d)

■ synchronized StringBuffer insert(int offset, Object obj)

■ synchronized StringBuffer insert(int offset, String str)

■ synchronized StringBuffer insert(int offset, char c)

■ synchronized StringBuffer insert(int offset, char str[])

■ StringBuffer insert(int offset, boolean b)

■ StringBuffer insert(int offset, int I)

■ StringBuffer insert(int offset, long l)

■ StringBuffer insert(int offset, float f)

■ StringBuffer insert(int offset, double d)

■ String toString()

The length method is used to get the length, or number of characters in the string buffer. The capacity method is similar to length except it returns how many characters a string buffer has allocated in memory, which is sometimes greater than the length. Characters are allocated for a string buffer as they are needed. Many times more memory is allocated for a string buffer than is actually being used. In these cases, the capacity method will return the amount of memory allocated for the string buffer. You can explicitly change the length of a string buffer using the setlength method. An example of using setLength would be to truncate a string by specifying a shorter length. The following example illustrates the effects of using these methods:

```
StringBuffer s1 = new StringBuffer(14);
System.out.println("capacity = " + s1.capacity());
System.out.println("length = " + s1.length());
s1.append("Bigfoot");
System.out.println(s1);
System.out.println("capacity = " + s1.capacity());
System.out.println("length = " + s1.length());
s1.setLength(3);
System.out.println(s1);
System.out.println("capacity = " + s1.capacity());
System.out.println("length = " + s1.length());
```

The resulting output of this example follows:

```
capacity = 14
length = 0
Bigfoot
capacity = 14
length = 7
Big
capacity = 14
length = 3
```

In this example, the newly created string buffer shows a capacity of 14 (based on the value passed in the creation method) and a length of 0. After appending the string "Bigfoot" to the buffer, the capacity remains the same but the length grows to 7, which is the length of the string. Calling setLength with a parameter of 3 truncates the length down to 3, but leaves the capacity unaffected at 14.

The charAt method returns the character at the location in the string buffer specified by the index parameter. You can change characters at specific locations in a string buffer using the setCharAt method. The setCharAt method replaces the character at index with the ch character parameter. The following example illustrates these two methods:

```
StringBuffer s1 = new StringBuffer("I saw a Yeti in Yellowstone.");
char c1 = s1.charAt(9);
System.out.println(c1);
s1.setCharAt(4, 'r');
System.out.println(s1);
```

In this example, the call to charAt results in the character 'e', which is located 9 characters into the string. The call to setCharAt results in the following output, based on the 'w' in "saw" being replaced by 'r':

```
I sar a Yeti in Yellowstone.
```

The StringBuffer class implements a variety of overloaded append methods. The append methods allow you to append various types of data onto the end of a String object. Each append method returns the String object that it was called on. The insert methods enable you to insert various data types at a specific offset in a string buffer. insert works very similar to append, with the exception of where the data is placed. Following are some examples of using append and insert:

```
StringBuffer sb1 = new StringBuffer("2 + 2 = ");
StringBuffer sb2 = new StringBuffer("The tires make contact ");
sb1.append(2 + 2);
sb2.append("with the road.");
sb2.insert(10, "are the things on the car that ");
```

In this set of examples, two string buffers are first created using the creation method for StringBuffer that takes a string literal. The first StringBuffer object initially contains the string "2 + 2 = ". The append method is used to append the result of the integer calculation 2 + 2. In this case, the integer result 4 is converted by the append method to the string "4" before it is appended to the end of the StringBuffer object. The value of the resulting StringBuffer object is "2 + 2 = 4". The second string buffer object begins life with the value "The tires make contact ". The string "with the road." is then appended onto the end of the string buffer using the append method. Then the insert method is used to insert the string "are the things on the car that ". Notice that this string is inserted at index 10 within the StringBuffer object. The resulting string after these two methods are called follows:

```
The tires are the things on the car that make contact with the road.
```

The last method of interest in StringBuffer is the toString method. toString returns the String object representation of the calling StringBuffer object. toString is useful when you have a StringBuffer object but need a String object.

System and Runtime Classes

The System and Runtime classes provide access to the system and runtime environment resources. The System class is defined as final and is composed entirely of static variables and methods, which means you will never actually instantiate an object of it. The Runtime class provides direct access to the runtime environment, and is useful for executing system commands and determining things like the amount of available memory.

The System Class

The System class contains the following useful methods:

- `static long currentTimeMillis()`
- `static void arraycopy(Object src, int src_position, Object dst, int dst_position, int length)`
- `static Properties getProperties()`
- `static String getProperty(String key)`
- `static String getProperty(String key, String def)`
- `static void setProperties(Properties props)`
- `static void gc()`
- `static void loadLibrary(String libname)`

The currentTimeMillis method returns the current system time in milliseconds. The time is specified in GMT (Greenwich Mean Time), and reflects the number of milliseconds that have elapsed since midnight on January 1, 1970. This is a standard frame of reference for computer time representation.

The arraycopy method copies data from one array to another. arraycopy copies length elements from the src array beginning at position src_position to the dst array starting at dst_position.

The getProperties method gets the current system properties and returns them via a Properties object. There are also two getProperty methods in System that allow you to get individual system properties. The first version of getProperty returns the system property matching the key parameter passed into the method. The second version of getProperty does the same as the first except it returns the default def parameter if the property isn't found. The setProperties method takes a Properties object and sets the system properties with it.

The gc method stands for garbage collection and does exactly that. gc forces the Java runtime system to perform a memory garbage collection. You can call gc if you think the system is running low on memory, since a garbage collection will usually free up memory.

The Java system supports executable code in dynamic link libraries. A dynamic link library is a library of Java classes that can be accessed at runtime. The loadLibrary method is used to load a dynamic link library. The name of the library to load is specified in the libname parameter.

The System class contains three member variables that are very useful for interacting with the system: in, out, and err. The in member is an InputStream object that acts as the standard input stream. The out and err members are PrintStream objects that act as the standard output and error streams.

The Runtime Class

The Runtime class is another very powerful class for accessing Java system-related resources. Following are a few of the more useful methods in the Runtime class:

- static Runtime getRuntime()
- long freeMemory()
- long totalMemory()
- void gc()
- synchronized void loadLibrary(String libname)

The static method getRuntime returns a Runtime object representing the runtime system environment. The freeMemory method returns the amount of free system memory in bytes. Because freeMemory returns only an estimate of the available memory, it is not completely accurate. If you need to know the total amount of memory accessible by the Java system, you can use the totalMemory method. The totalMemory method returns the number of bytes of total memory, where the freeMemory method returns the number of bytes of available memory. Listing 18.1 contains the source code for the Memory program, which displays the available free memory and total memory.

Listing 18.1. The Memory class.

```
class Memory {
  public static void main (String args[]) {
    Runtime runtime = Runtime.getRuntime();
    long freeMem = runtime.freeMemory() / 1024;
    long totalMem = runtime.totalMemory() / 1024;
    System.out.println("Free memory : " + freeMem + "KB");
    System.out.println("Total memory : " + totalMem + "KB");
  }
}
```

An example of the output of running the Memory program follows:

```
Free Memory : 3068KB
Total Memory : 3071KB
```

The Memory class uses the getRuntime, freeMemory, and totalMemory methods of the Runtime class. Note that the amount of memory returned by each method is converted from bytes to kilobytes by dividing by 1024.

The other two methods of importance in the Runtime class, gc and loadLibrary, work exactly the same as the versions belonging to the System class.

Class **Classes**

Java provides two classes in the language package for dealing with classes: Class and ClassLoader. The Class class allows you access to the runtime information for a class. The ClassLoader class provides support for dynamically loading classes at runtime.

The Class **Class**

Some of the more useful methods implemented by the Class class follow:

- ■ static Class forName(String className)
- ■ String getName()
- ■ Class getSuperclass()
- ■ ClassLoader getClassLoader()
- ■ boolean isInterface()
- ■ String toString()

The forName method is a static method used to get the runtime class descriptor object for a class. The String parameter className specifies the name of the class you want information for. forName returns a Class object containing runtime information for the specified class. Notice that forName is static and is the method you typically will use to get an instance of the Class class for determining class information. Following is an example of how to use the forName method to get information about the StringBuffer class:

```
Class info = Class.forName("java.lang.StringBuffer");
```

The getName method retrieves the string name of the class represented by a Class object. Following is an example of using the getName method:

```
String s = info.getName();
```

The getSuperclass method returns a Class object containing information about the super-class of an object. The getClassLoader method returns the ClassLoader object for a class, or null if no class loader exists. The isInterface method returns a Boolean indicating whether or not a class is an interface.

Finally, the toString method returns the name of a class or interface. toString automatically prepends the string "class" or "interface" to the name based on whether the Class object represents a class or an interface.

The ClassLoader Class

The ClassLoader class provides the framework for enabling you to dynamically load classes into the runtime environment. Following are the methods implemented by ClassLoader:

- ◼ abstract Class loadClass(String name, boolean resolve)
- ◼ final Class defineClass(byte data[], int offset, int length)
- ◼ final void resolveClass(Class c)
- ◼ final Class findSystemClass(String name)

The loadClass method is an abstract method that must be defined in a subclass of ClassLoader. loadClass resolves a class name passed in the String parameter name into a Class runtime object. loadClass returns the resulting Class on success, or null if not successful. The defineClass method converts an array of byte data into a Class object. The class is defined by the data parameter beginning at offset and continuing for length bytes. A class defined with defineClass must be resolved before it can be used. You can resolve a class by using the resolveClass method, which takes a Class object as its only parameter.

Finally, the findSystemClass method is used to find and load a system class. A system class is a class that uses the built in (primordial) class loader, which is defined as null.

Summary

In this chapter you learned a great deal about the classes and interfaces that make up the Java language package. The language package lays out the core classes, interfaces, and errors of the Java class libraries. Although some of the classes implemented in the language package are fairly low-level, a solid understanding of these classes is necessary to move on to other areas of the Java class libraries.

You learned in this chapter how fundamental data types can become objects using the data type wrappers. You then learned about the many mathematical functions contained in the Math class. And don't forget about the string classes, which provide a powerful set of routines for working with strings of text. You finished up with a tour of how to access the system and runtime resources of Java, along with the lower-level runtime and dynamic class support.

The next chapter provides the next stop on this guided tour of the Java class libraries, which is the Java utilities package.

The Utilities Package

IN THIS CHAPTER

package provides a collection of classes that implement various standard program-
ructures. These classes are useful in a variety of ways and are the fundamental
ks of the more complicated data structures used in the other Java packages and in
plications. Unless otherwise noted, all of the interfaces and classes discussed in
xtend the java.lang.Object class. Table 19.1 lists the classes and interfaces imple-
is package along with a brief description of each.

Utilities package interfaces and classes.

ion	Interface for classes that can enumerate a vector.
	Interface for classes that can observe observable objects.

	Used to store a collection of binary values.
	Used to store date and time data.
y	Used to store a collection of key and value pairs.
	Used to store a hash table.
e	Used to store observable data.
s	Used to store a properties list that can be saved.
	Used to generate a pseudo-random number.
	Used to store a stack.
enizer	Used to tokenize a string.
	Used to store a vector data type.

ices

package has two interfaces that can be used in classes of your own design—Enu-
Observer. *Interfaces* are a set of methods that must be written for any class that
plement" the interface. This provides a consistent way of using all classes that
e interface.

tion interface is used for classes that can retrieve data from a list, element by ele-
mple, there is an Enumeration class in the Utilities package that implements the
interface for use in conjunction with the Vector class. The Observer interface is
gning classes that can watch for changes that occur in other classes.

Enumeration

This interface specifies a set of methods used to enumerate—that is, iterate through—a list. An object that implements this interface may be used to iterate through a list only once because the `Enumeration` object is consumed through its use.

For example, an `Enumeration` object can be used to print all the elements of a `Vector` object, `v`, as follows:

```
for (Enumeration e=v.elements();e.hasMoreElements();)
    System.out.print(e.nextElement()+" ");
```

The Enumeration interface specifies only two methods—`hasMoreElements()` and `nextElement()`. The `hasMoreElements()` method must return True if there are elements remaining in the enumeration. The `nextElement()` method must return an object representing the next element within the object that is being enumerated. The details of how the Enumeration interface is implemented and how the data is represented internally are left up to the implementation of the specific class.

See also: `Dictionary`, `Hashtable`, `Properties`, `Vector`.

Observer

This interface, if implemented by a class, allows an object of the class to observe other objects of the class `Observable`. The observer is notified whenever the `Observable` object that it is watching has been changed.

The interface only specifies one method, `update(Observable, Object)`. This method is called by the observed object to notify the observer of changes. A reference to the observed object is passed along with any additional object that the observed object wishes to pass to the observer. The first argument enables the observer to operate on the observed object, while the second argument is used to pass information from the observed to the observer.

Classes

The Utilities package supplies ten different classes that provide a wide variety of functionality. While these classes don't generally have much in common, they all provide support for the most common data structures used by programmers.

BitSet

This class implements a data type that represents a collection of bits. The collection will grow dynamically as more bits are required. It is useful for representing a set of True/False values. Specific bits are identified using non-negative integers. The first bit is bit 0 (see Figure 19.1).

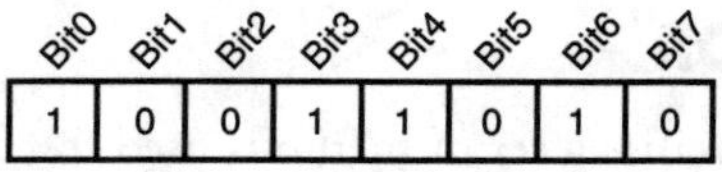

FIGURE 19.1.

Example of a BitSet
object.

This class is most useful for storing a group of related True/False values such as user responses to Yes/No questions. Individual bits in the set are turned on or off with the set() and clear() methods, respectively. Individual bits are queried with the get() method. These methods all take the specific bit number as their only argument. The basic Boolean operations AND, OR, and XOR can be performed on two BitSets using the and(), or(), and xor() methods. Because these methods modify one of the BitSets, one generally will use the clone() method to create a duplicate of one, and then AND, OR, or XOR the clone with the second BitSet. The result of the operation then will end up in the cloned BitSet. The BitSet1 program in Listing 19.1 illustrates the basic BitSet operations, whereas Table 19.2 summarizes all the various methods available in the BitSet class.

Listing 19.1. BitSet1.java—**BitSet example program.**

```java
import java.io.DataInputStream;
import java.util.BitSet;

class BitSet1 {
    public static void main(String args[])
        throws java.io.IOException
    {
        DataInputStream dis=new DataInputStream(System.in);
        String bitstring;
        BitSet set1,set2,set3;
        set1=new BitSet();
        set2=new BitSet();

        // Get the first bit sequence and store it
        System.out.println("Bit sequence #1:");
        bitstring=dis.readLine();
        for (short i=0;i<bitstring.length();i++){
            if (bitstring.charAt(i)=='1')
                set1.set(i);
            else
                set1.clear(i);
        }
        // Get the second bit sequence and store it
        System.out.println("Bit sequence #2:");
        bitstring=dis.readLine();
        for (short i=0;i<bitstring.length();i++){
            if (bitstring.charAt(i)=='1')
                set2.set(i);
            else
                set2.clear(i);
        }
        System.out.println("BitSet #1: "+set1);
        System.out.println("BitSet #2: "+set2);

        // Test the AND operation
        set3=(BitSet)set1.clone();
```

```
        set3.and(set2);
        System.out.println("set1 AND set2: "+set3);

        // Test the OR operation
        set3=(BitSet)set1.clone();
        set3.or(set2);
        System.out.println("set1 OR set2: "+set3);

        // Test the XOR operation
        set3=(BitSet)set1.clone();
        set3.xor(set2);
        System.out.println("set1 XOR set2: "+set3);
    }
}
```

The output from this program looks like this:

```
Bit sequence #1:
1010
Bit sequence #2:
1100
BitSet #1: {0, 2}
BitSet #2: {0, 1}
set1 AND set2: {0}
set1 OR set2: {0, 1, 2}
set1 XOR set2: {1, 2}
```

Table 19.2. The `BitSet` interface.

Constructors	
BitSet()	Constructs an empty BitSet.
BitSet(int)	Constructs an empty BitSet of a given size.

Methods	
and(BitSet)	Logically ANDs the object's bit set with another BitSet.
clear(int)	Clears a specific bit.
clone()	Creates a clone of the BitSet object.
equals(Object)	Compares this object against another BitSet object.
get(int)	Returns the value of a specific bit.
hashCode()	Returns the hash code.
or(BitSet)	Logically ORs the object's bit set with another BitSet.
set(int)	Sets a specific bit.
size()	Returns the size of the set.
toString()	Converts bit values to a string representation.
xor(BitSet)	Logically XORs the object's bit set with another BitSet.

In addition to extending the java.lang.Object class, BitSet implements the java.lang.Cloneable interface.

Date

This class is used to represent dates and times in a system-independent fashion. For example, the current date or a specific date can be printed as shown in Listing 19.2.

Listing 19.2. Date1.java—Date example program.

```java
import java.util.Date;

public class Date1{
    public static void main (String args[]){
        Date today=new Date();
        System.out.println("Today is "+today.toLocaleString()+
            " ("+today.toGMTString()+")");

        Date birthday=new Date(89,10,14,8,30,00);
        System.out.println("My birthday is"+
            birthday.toString()+" ("+birthday.toGMTString()+")");

        Date anniversary=new Date("Jun 21, 1986");
        System.out.println("My anniversary is "+
            anniversary+" ("+anniversary.toGMTString()+")");
    }
}
```

The output from this program looks like this:

```
Today is 01/21/96 19:55:17 (22 Jan 1996 01:55:17 GMT)
My birthday is Thu Nov 14 08:30:00  1989 (14 Nov 1989 14:30:00 GMT)
My anniversary is Sat Jun 21 00:00:00  1989 (21 Jun 1986 05:00:00 GMT)
```

The default constructor is used when the current date and time are needed. A specific date and time can be used to initialize a Date object using the constructors that take three, five, and six integers. These constructors allow the date and time to be specified using YMD, YMDHM, or YMDHMS. Any parts of the time not specified by the three- and five-integer constructors will be set to zero.

> **NOTE**
>
> Date/time formats can be conveniently summarized using notations of the form YMD, YMDHMS, HMS, or MDY. These abbreviated formats indicate in what order the various numeric parts of the date will appear. Each letter refers to a specific component of the date/time: year (Y), month (M), day (D), hour (H), minute (M), and second (S). Whether the letter M refers to month or minute depends on the context.

Alternately, a Date object can be constructed using a single string that represents a date and time using a variety of different syntax. One of the most important is the international standard date syntax of the form, "Sun, 14 Aug 1995 9:00:00 GMT." Continental U.S. time zone abbreviations are understood, but time zone offsets should be considered for general use—for example, "Sun, 14 Aug 1995 9:00:00 GMT+0600" (six hours west of the Greenwich meridian). The local time zone is assumed if none is supplied.

> **NOTE**
>
> This class intends to store date and time information in UTC (Coordinated Universal Time). However, it does not necessarily achieve this goal exactly. The implementation of the class is limited by the underlying time system of the operating system. Because modern operating systems typically assume that a day is always 86,400 seconds, the extra leap seconds that are needed about once a year to accurately reflect UTC usually are not added. UTC is a time standard based on an atomic clock. Time specifications using UTC are considered equal to GMT (Greenwich Mean Time).

The date can be converted to a text representation using the methods toString(), toGMTString(), and toLocaleString(), which convert the date and time to the standard UNIX, GMT, or local time formats, respectively. When a date is being converted to a string by an automatic coercion, the toString() method will be used.

The Date class also has methods for setting and querying the date and time component values once the Date object is constructed. The individual parts of the date (month, date, year) and time (hours, minutes, seconds) always are specified in local time. When referring to the various parts of the date and time, the first letter of each part typically is used as an abbreviation. For example, YMDHMS would be used to indicate that all six parts (year, month, date, hour, minute, second) are present. Each of these parts of the date and time have a specific range of acceptable values, as illustrated in Table 19.3.

Table 19.3. Date component ranges.

Year	Year minus 1900
Month	0-11 (January=0)
Date	1-31
Day	0-6 (Sunday=0)
Hour	0-23
Minute	0-59
Second	0-59

The date and time also can be specified using a single integer UTC value that represents the number of milliseconds that have elapsed since a specific starting date (which might vary from system to system). For UNIX systems this date is January 1, 1970. The program Date2 in Listing 19.3 shows how this single value corresponds to the normal YMDHMS representation.

Listing 19.3. Date2.java—Date example program.

```java
import java.util.Date;

public class Date2{
    public static void main (String args[]){
        Date beginning=new Date(0);
        Date anniversary=new Date("Jun 21, 1986");
        Date today=new Date();

        System.out.println(beginning+"="+beginning.getTime());
        System.out.println(anniversary+"="+anniversary.getTime());
        System.out.println(today+"="+today.getTime());
    }
}
```

The output from this program looks like this:

```
Wed Dec 31 18:00:00  1969=0
Sat Jun 21 00:00:00  1986=519714000000
Sun Jan 21 19:55:17  1996=822275717000
```

Dates can be compared to each other by using this UTC value or by using the methods after(), before(), or equals().

Table 19.4 summarizes the complete interface of the Date class.

Table 19.4. The Date interface.

Constructors	
Date()	Constructs a date using today's date and time.
Date(long)	Constructs a date using a single UTC value.
Date(int, int, int)	Constructs a date using YMD.
Date(int, int, int, int, int)	Constructs a date using YMDHM.
Date(int, int, int, int, int, int)	Constructs a date using YMDHMS.
Date(string)	Constructs a date from a string.
Static Methods	
UTC(int, int, int, int, int, int)	Calculates a UTC value from YMDHMS.
parse(string)	Returns the single UTC value of a date in text format.

Methods	
`after(Date)`	True if the date is later than the specified date.
`before(Date)`	True if the date is earlier than the specified date.
`equals(Object)`	True if the date and the specified date are equal.
`getDate()`	Returns the day of the month.
`getDay()`	Returns the day of the week.
`getHours()`	Returns the hour.
`getMinutes()`	Returns the minute.
`getMonth()`	Returns the month.
`getSeconds()`	Returns the second.
`getTime()`	Returns the time as a single UTC value.
`getTimezoneOffset()`	Returns the time zone offset, in minutes, for this locale.
`getYear()`	Returns the year after 1900.
`hashCode()`	Computes a hash code for the date.
`setDate(int)`	Sets the date.
`setHours(int)`	Sets the hours.
`setMinutes(int)`	Sets the minutes.
`setMonth(int)`	Sets the month.
`setSeconds(int)`	Sets the seconds.
`setTime(long)`	Sets the time using a single UTC value.
`setYear(int)`	Sets the year.
`toGMTString()`	Converts a date to text using Internet GMT conventions.
`toLocaleString()`	Converts a date to text using locale conventions.
`toString()`	Converts a date to text using UNIX `ctime()` conventions.

Random

This class implements a pseudo-random number data type used to generate a stream of seemingly random numbers. To create a sequence of different pseudo-random values each time the application is run, create the Random object as follows:

```
Random r=new Random();
```

This will seed the random generator with the current time. On the other hand, consider the following statement:

```
Random r=new Random(326);    // Pick any value
```

This will seed the random generator with the same value each time, resulting in the same sequence of pseudo-random numbers each time the application is run. The generator can be reseeded at any time using the setSeed() method.

Pseudo-random numbers can be generated by using one of the functions: nextInt(), nextLong(), nextFloat(), nextDouble(), or nextGaussian(). For example, the program Random1 in Listing 19.4 will print out five pseudo-random uniformly distributed values using these functions.

Listing 19.4. Random1.java—Random **example program.**

```java
import java.lang.Math;
import java.util.Date;
import java.util.Random;

class Random1 {
    public static void main(String args[])
        throws java.io.IOException
    {
        int count=6;
        Random randGen=new Random();

        System.out.println("Uniform Random Integers");
        for (int i=0;i<count;i++)
        System.out.print(randGen.nextInt()+" ");
        System.out.println("\n");

        System.out.println("Uniform Random Floats");
        for (int i=0;i<count;i++)
        System.out.print(randGen.nextFloat()+" ");
        System.out.println("\n");

        System.out.println("Gaussian Random Floats");
        for (int i=0;i<count;i++)
            System.out.print(randGen.nextGaussian()+" ");
        System.out.println("\n");

        System.out.println("Uniform Random Integers [1,6]");
        for (int i=0;i<count;i++)
            System.out.print((Math.abs(randGen.nextInt())%6+1)+" ");
        System.out.println("\n");
        }
}
```

The output from the preceding program looks like this:

```
Uniform Random Integers
1704667569 -1431446235 1024613888 438489989 710330974 -1689521238

Uniform Random Floats
0.689189 0.0579988 0.0933537 0.748228 0.400992 0.222109

Gaussian Random Floats
-0.201843 -0.0111578 1.63927 0.205938 -0.365471 0.626304
```

```
Uniform Random Integers [1,6]
4 6 1 6 3 2
```

If you need to generate uniformly distributed random integers within a specific range, the output from nextInt(), nextLong(), or nextDouble() can be scaled to match the required range. A simpler approach is to take the remainder of the result of nextInt() divided by the number of different values plus the first value of the range. For example, if the values 10 to 20 are needed one can use the formula nextInt()%21+10. Unfortunately, though this method is much simpler than scaling the output of nextInt(), it only is guaranteed to work on truly random values. Because the pseudo-random generator might have various undesired correlations, the modulus operator might not provide acceptable results—one might get all odd numbers, for example.

NOTE

The uniformly distributed random numbers are generated using a modified linear congruential method with a 48-bit seed. Uniformly distributed random numbers within a given range will all appear with the same frequency. This class can also generate random numbers from a Gaussian or Normal distribution. The Gaussian frequency distribution curve is also referred to as a bell curve. For information on this, see Donald Knuth, *The Art of Computer Programming, Volume 2*, Section 3.2.1.

Table 19.5 summarizes the complete interface of the Random class.

Table 19.5. The Random interface.

Constructors	
Random()	Creates a new random number generator.
Random(long)	Creates a new random number generator using a seed.
Methods	
nextDouble()	Returns a pseudo-random uniformly distributed Double.
nextFloat()	Returns a pseudo-random uniformly distributed Float.
nextGaussian()	Returns a pseudo-random Gaussian distributed Double.
nextInt()	Returns a pseudo-random uniformly distributed Int.
nextLong()	Returns a pseudo-random uniformly distributed Long.
setSeed(long)	Sets the seed of the pseudo-random number generator.

Refer also to Random().

StringTokenizer

The StringTokenizer class breaks up a string into tokens. The delimiter set can be specified when the StringTokenizer object is created or can be specified on a per-token basis. The default delimiter set is the set of whitespace characters. For example, the StringTokenizer1 code in Listing 19.5 prints out each word of the string on a separate line.

Listing 19.5. StringTokenizer1.java—StringTokenizer example program.

```java
import java.io.DataInputStream;
import java.util.StringTokenizer;

class StringTokenizer1 {
    public static void main(String args[])
        throws java.io.IOException
    {
        DataInputStream dis=new DataInputStream(System.in);

        System.out.println("Enter a sentence: ");
        String s=dis.readLine();
        StringTokenizer st=new StringTokenizer(s);
        while (st.hasMoreTokens())
            System.out.println(st.nextToken());
    }
}
```

The output from this listing will look like this:

```
Enter a sentence:
Four score and seven
Four
score
and
seven
```

The method countTokens() returns the number of tokens remaining in the string using the current delimiter set—that is, the number of times nextToken() can be called before generating an exception. This is an efficient method because it does not actually construct the substrings that nextToken() must generate.

In addition to extending the java.lang.object class, the StringTokenizer class implements the java.util.Enumeration interface. Table 19.6 summarizes the methods of the StringTokenizer class.

Table 19.6. The StringTokenizer interface.

Constructors

StringTokenizer(string)	Constructs a StringTokenizer given a string using whitespace as delimiters.
StringTokenizer(string, string)	Constructs a StringTokenizer given a string and a delimiter set.
StringTokenizer(string, string, boolean)	Constructs a StringTokenizer given a string and a delimiter set.

Methods

countTokens()	Returns the number of tokens remaining in the string.
hasMoreTokens()	Returns True if more tokens exist.
nextToken()	Returns the next token of the string.
nextToken(string)	Returns the next token, given a new delimiter set.
hasMoreTokens()	Returns True if more elements exist in the enumeration.
nextElement()	Returns the next element of the enumeration using the current delimiter set.

Vector

The Vector class implements a dynamically allocated list of objects. It attempts to optimize storage by increasing the storage capacity of the list when needed by increments larger than just one object. With this mechanism, there typically is some excess capacity in the list. When this capacity is exhausted, the list is reallocated to add another block of objects at the end of the list. Setting the capacity of the Vector object to the needed size before inserting a large number of objects will reduce the need for incremental reallocation. Because of this mechanism, it is important to remember that the capacity (available elements in the Vector object) and the size (number of elements currently stored in the Vector object) usually are not the same.

For example, in Figure 19.2, a Vector with capacityIncrement equal to three has been created. As objects are added to the Vector, new space is allocated in chunks of three objects. After five elements have been added, there still will be room for one more element without the need for any additional memory allocation. After the sixth element has been added, there is no more excess capacity. When the seventh element is added, a new allocation will be made that adds three additional elements, giving a total capacity of nine. After the seventh element is added, there will be two remaining unused elements.

FIGURE 19.2.

Vector *objects with varying number of elements.*

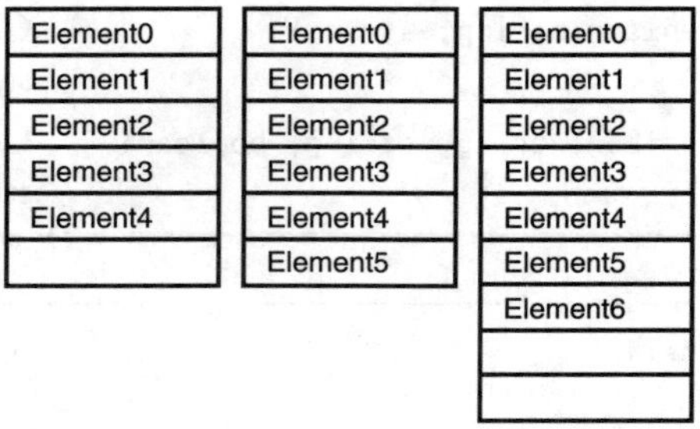

Element0	Element0	Element0
Element1	Element1	Element1
Element2	Element2	Element2
Element3	Element3	Element3
Element4	Element4	Element4
	Element5	Element5
		Element6

The initial storage capacity and the capacity increment both can be specified in the constructor. Even though the capacity is automatically increased as needed, the ensureCapacity() method can be used to increase the capacity to a specific minimum number of elements, whereas trimToSize() can be used to reduce the capacity to the minimum needed to store the current elements. New elements can be added to the Vector using the addElement() and insertElementAt() methods. The elements passed to be stored in the Vector must be derived from type Object. Elements can be changed using the setElementAt() method. Removal of elements is accomplished with the removeElement(), removeElementAt(), and removeAllElements() methods. Elements can be accessed directly using the elementAt(), firstElement(), and lastElement() methods, whereas elements can be located using the indexOf() and lastIndexOf() methods. Information about the size and the capacity of the Vector are returned by the size() and capacity() methods respectively. The setSize() method can be used to directly change the size of the Vector.

For example, the Vector1 code in Listing 19.6 creates a Vector of integers by adding new elements to the end. It then, using a variety of techniques, prints the Vector.

Listing 19.6. Vector1.java—Vector **example program.**

```
import java.lang.Integer;
import java.util.Enumeration;
import java.util.Vector;

class Vector1 {
    public static void main(String args[]){
        Vector v=new Vector(10,10);
        for (int i=0;i<20;i++)
            v.addElement(new Integer(i));

        System.out.println("Vector in original order using an Enumeration");
        for (Enumeration e=v.elements();e.hasMoreElements();)
            System.out.print(e.nextElement()+" ");
```

```
        System.out.println();

        System.out.println("Vector in original order using elementAt");
        for (int i=0;i<v.size();i++)
            System.out.print(v.elementAt(i)+" ");
        System.out.println();

        // Print out the original vector
        System.out.println("\nVector in reverse order using elementAt");
        for (int i=v.size()-1;i>=0;i--)
            System.out.print(v.elementAt(i)+" ");
        System.out.println();

        // Print out the original vector
        System.out.println("\nVector as a String");
        System.out.println(v.toString());
    }
}
```

The output from this program looks like this:

```
Vector in original order using an Enumeration
0 1 2 3 4 5 6 7 8 9 10 11 12 13 14 15 16 17 18 19
Vector in original order using elementAt
0 1 2 3 4 5 6 7 8 9 10 11 12 13 14 15 16 17 18 19

Vector in reverse order using elementAt
19 18 17 16 15 14 13 12 11 10 9 8 7 6 5 4 3 2 1 0

Vector as a String
[0, 1, 2, 3, 4, 5, 6, 7, 8, 9, 10, 11, 12, 13, 14, 15, 16, 17, 18, 19]
```

> **NOTE**
>
> The expression new Integer() was used to create integer objects to store because the
> fundamental types, such as int, are not objects in Java. This technique is used many
> times throughout this chapter.

Notice the use of the Enumeration object as one way to access the elements of a Vector. Look at the following lines:

```
for (Enumeration e=v.elements();e.hasMoreElements();)
    System.out.print(e.nextElement()+" ");
```

One can see that an Enumeration object that represents all of the elements in the Vector is created and returned by the Vector method elements(). With this Enumeration object, the loop can check to see if there are more elements to process using the Enumeration method hasMoreElements() and can get the next element in the Vector using the Enumeration method nextElement().

The Vector2 program in Listing 19.7 illustrates some of the vector-accessing techniques. It first generates a vector of random integers, then allows the user to search for a specific value. The location of the first and last occurrences of the value is printed by the program using the indexOf() and lastIndexOf() methods.

Listing 19.7. Vector2.java—Vector example program.

```
import java.io.DataInputStream;
import java.lang.Integer;
import java.lang.Math;
import java.util.Enumeration;
import java.util.Random;
import java.util.Vector;

class Vector2 {
    public static void main(String args[])
        throws java.io.IOException
    {
        int numElements;
        DataInputStream dis=new DataInputStream(System.in);
        Vector v=new Vector(10,10);
        Random randGen=new Random();

        System.out.println("How many random elements? ");
        numElements=Integer.valueOf(dis.readLine()).intValue();
        for (int i=0;i<numElements;i++)
            v.addElement(new Integer(Math.abs(
                randGen.nextInt())%numElements));

        System.out.println(v.toString());

        Integer searchValue;
        System.out.println("Find which value? ");
        searchValue=Integer.valueOf(dis.readLine());
        System.out.println("First occurrence is element "+
            v.indexOf(searchValue));
        System.out.println("Last occurrence is element "+
            v.lastIndexOf(searchValue));
    }
}
```

The output from this program looks like this:

```
How many random elements?
10
[0, 2, 8, 4, 9, 7, 8, 6, 3, 2]
Find which value?
8
First occurrence is element 2
Last occurrence is element 6
```

In addition to extending the java.lang.Object class, the Vector class implements the java.lang.Cloneable interface. Table 19.7 summarizes the methods of the Vector class.

Table 19.7. `Vector` interface.

Variables	
`capacityIncrement`	Size of the incremental allocations, in elements.
`elementCount`	Number of elements in `Vector`.
`elementData`	Buffer where the elements are stored.

Constructors	
`Vector()`	Constructs an empty vector.
`Vector(int)`	Constructs an empty vector with the specified storage capacity.
`Vector(int, int)`	Constructs an empty vector with the specified storage capacity and `capacityIncrement`.

Methods	
`addElement(Object)`	Adds the specified object at the end of the `Vector`.
`capacity()`	Returns the capacity of the `Vector`.
`clone()`	Creates a clone of the `Vector`.
`contains(Object)`	True if the specified object is in the `Vector`.
`copyInto(Object[])`	Copies the elements of this vector into an array.
`elementAt(int)`	Returns the element at the specified index.
`elements()`	Returns an `Enumeration` of the elements.
`ensureCapacity(int)`	Ensures that the `Vector` has the specified capacity.
`firstElement()`	Returns the first element of the `Vector`.
`indexOf(Object)`	Returns the index of the first occurrence of the specified object within the `Vector`.
`indexOf(Object, int)`	Returns the index of the specified object within the `Vector` starting the search at the index specified and proceeding toward the end of the `Vector`.
`insertElementAt(Object, int)`	Inserts an object at the index specified.
`isEmpty()`	True if the `Vector` is empty.
`lastElement()`	Returns the last element of the `Vector`.
`lastIndexOf(Object)`	Returns the index of the last occurrence of the specified object within the `Vector`.
`lastIndexOf(Object, int)`	Returns the index of the specified object within the `Vector` starting the search at the index specified and proceeding toward the beginning of the `Vector`.

continues

Table 19.7. continued

Methods	
removeAllElements()	Removes all elements of the Vector.
removeElement(Object)	Removes the specified object from the Vector.
removeElementAt(int)	Removes the element with the specified index.
setElementAt(Object, int)	Stores the object at the specified index in the Vector.
setSize(int)	Sets the size of the Vector.
size()	Returns the number of elements in the Vector.
toString()	Converts the Vector to a string.
trimToSize()	Trims the Vector's capacity down to the specified size.

Refer also to Vector, Hashtable.

Stack

This class implements a *Last In, First Out* (LIFO) stack of objects. Even though it is based on (extends) the Vector class, Stacks are typically not accessed in a direct fashion. Instead, values are pushed onto and popped off of the top of the stack. The net effect is that values that were most recently pushed are the first ones to be popped. For example, the Stack1 code in Listing 19.8 pushes strings onto the stack, and then retrieves them. The strings will end up being printed in the reverse order that they were stored.

Listing 19.8. Stack1.java—Stack **example program.**

```
import java.io.DataInputStream;
import java.util.Stack;
import java.util.StringTokenizer;

class Stack1 {
    public static void main(String args[])
        throws java.io.IOException
    {
        DataInputStream dis=new DataInputStream(System.in);

        System.out.println("Enter a sentence: ");
        String s=dis.readLine();
        StringTokenizer st=new StringTokenizer(s);
        Stack stack=new Stack();
        while (st.hasMoreTokens())
            stack.push(st.nextToken());
```

```
        while (!stack.empty())
            System.out.print((String)stack.pop()+" ");
        System.out.println();
    }
}
```

The output from this program looks like this:

```
Enter a sentence:
The quick brown fox jumps over the lazy dog
dog lazy the over jumps fox brown quick The
```

Even though `Stack` objects normally are not accessed in a direct fashion, it is possible to search the `Stack` for a specific value using the `search()` method. It accepts an object to find and returns the distance from the top of the `Stack` where the object was found. It will return -1 if the object is not found.

The method `peek()` will return the top object on the `Stack` without actually removing it from the `Stack`. The `peek()` method will throw an `EmptyStackException` if the `Stack` has no items.

Table 19.8 summarizes the complete interface of the `Stack` class.

Table 19.8. `Stack` interface.

Constructors	
`Stack()`	Constructs an empty `Stack`.
Methods	
`empty()`	True if the `Stack` is empty.
`peek()`	Returns the top object on the `Stack`.
`pop()`	Pops an element off the `Stack`.
`push(Object)`	Pushes an element onto the `Stack`.
`search(Object)`	Finds an object on the `Stack`.

Dictionary

This class is an abstract class that is used as a base for the `Hashtable` class. It implements a data structure that allows a collection of key and value pairs to be stored. Any type of object can be used for the keys or the values. Typically, the keys are used to find a particular corresponding value. Figure 19.3 illustrates a `Dictionary` where product codes and names are stored.

FIGURE 19.3.

Example of a Dictionary *object.*

Key	Value
342	Widget
124	Gadget
754	FooBar
383	Wadget
843	Dongle
543	Snippet

Because this class is an abstract class that cannot be used directly, the code examples presented cannot actually be run. They are presented only to illustrate the purpose and use of the methods declared by this class. The following code would, hypothetically, be used to create a Dictionary with these values illustrated:

```
Dictionary products = new Dictionary();
products.put(new Integer(342), "Widget");
products.put(new Integer(124), "Gadget");
products.put(new Integer(754), "FooBar");
```

The put() method is used to insert a key and value pair into the Dictionary. The two arguments both must be derived from the class Object. The key is the first argument and the value is the second.

A value can be retrieved using the get() method and a specific key to find. It returns the null value if the specified key is not found. For example:

```
String name = products.get(new Integer(124));
if (name != null) {
    System.out.println("Product name for code 124 is " + name);
}
```

While an individual object can be retrieved with the get() method, sometimes it is necessary to access all of the keys or all of the values. There are two methods, keys() and elements(), that will return Enumerations that can be used to access the keys and the values, respectively.

Table 19.9 summarizes the complete interface of the Dictionary class.

Table 19.9. Dictionary **interface.**

Constructors	
Dictionary()	Constructs an empty Dictionary.

Methods	
elements()	Returns an Enumeration of the values.
get(Object)	Returns the object associated with the specified key.
isEmpty()	True if the Dictionary has no elements.
keys()	Returns an Enumeration of the keys.

Methods	
put(Object, Object)	Stores the specified key and value pair in the Dictionary.
remove(Object)	Removes an element from the Dictionary by its key.
size()	Returns the number of elements stored.

Refer also to Enumeration, Hashtable, Properties.

Hashtable

This class implements a hash table storage mechanism for storing key and value pairs. Hash tables are designed to quickly locate and retrieve information stored using a key. Keys and values may be of any object type but the key object's class must implement the hashCode() and equals() methods.

The example Hashtable1 in Listing 19.9 creates a Hashtable object and stores 10 key and value pairs using the put() method. It then uses the get() method to return the value corresponding to a key entered by the user.

Listing 19.9. Hashtable1.java—Hashtable **example program.**

```
import java.io.DataInputStream;
import java.lang.Integer;
import java.lang.Math;
import java.util.Random;
import java.util.Hashtable;

class Hashtable1 {
    public static void main(String args[])
        throws java.io.IOException
    {
        DataInputStream dis=new DataInputStream(System.in);
        int numElements=10;
        String keys[]={"Red","Green","Blue","Cyan","Magenta",
            "Yellow","Black","Orange","Purple","White"};
        Hashtable ht;
        Random randGen=new Random();

        ht=new Hashtable(numElements*2);
        for (int i=0;i<numElements;i++)
            ht.put(keys[i],new Integer(Math.abs(
                randGen.nextInt())%numElements));

        System.out.println(ht.toString());

        String keyValue;
        System.out.println("Which key to find? ");
        keyValue=dis.readLine();
```

continues

Listing 19.9. continued

```
        Integer value=(Integer)ht.get(keyValue);
        if (value!=null) System.out.println(keyValue+" = "+value);
    }
}
```

The output from this program looks like this:

```
{Cyan=4, White=0, Magenta=4, Red=5, Black=3, Green=8, Purple=3, Orange=4, Yellow=2,
➥Blue=6}
Which key to find?
Red
Red = 5
```

In addition to the get() method, the contains() and containsKey() methods can be used to search for a particular value or key respectively. Both return True or False depending on whether or not the search was successful. The contains() method must perform an exhaustive search of the table and is not as efficient as the containsKey() method, which can take advantage of the hash table's storage mechanism to find the key quickly.

Because hash tables need to allocate storage for more data than actually is stored, a measurement called the load factor is used to indicate the number of used storage spaces as a fraction of the total available storage spaces. It is expressed as a value between 0 and 100 percent. Typically the load factor should not be higher than about 50 percent for efficient retrieval of data from a hash table. When specifying the load factor in a program, a fractional value in the range 0.0 to 1.0 should be used to represent load factors in the range 0 to 100 percent.

Hash tables can be constructed in three different ways: by specifying the desired initial capacity and load factor, by specifying only the initial capacity, or by specifying neither. If the load factor is not specified, the Hashtable will be rehashed into a larger table when it is full; otherwise it is rehashed when it exceeds the load factor. The constructors will throw an IllegalArgumentException if the initial capacity is less than or equal to zero, or if the load factor is less than or equal to zero.

The clone() method can be used to create a copy (*clone*) of the Hashtable. However, it creates a shallow copy of the Hashtable—that is, the keys and values themselves are not clones. It overrides the inherited clone() method.

CAUTION

The clone() method is a relatively expensive operation to perform in terms of memory utilization and execution time. Because the new Hashtable still refers directly to the objects (keys and values) stored in the old table, caution should be used to avoid making changes that will disrupt the original Hashtable.

The Hashtable class extends the java.util.Dictionary class and implements the java.lang.Cloneable interface. Table 19.10 summarizes the methods of the Hashtable class.

Table 19.10. The Hashtable interface.

Constructors	
Hashtable()	Constructs an empty Hashtable.
Hashtable(int)	Constructs an empty Hashtable with the specified capacity.
Hashtable(int, float)	Constructs an empty Hashtable given capacity and load factor.

Methods	
clear()	Deletes all elements from the Hashtable.
clone()	Creates a clone of the Hashtable.
contains(Object)	True if the specified object is an element of the Hashtable.
containsKey(Object)	True if the Hashtable contains the specified key.
elements()	Returns an Enumeration of the Hashtable's values.
get(Object)	Returns the object associated with the specified key.
isEmpty()	True if the Hashtable has no elements.
keys()	Returns an Enumeration of the keys.
put(Object, Object)	Stores the specified key and value pair in the Hashtable.
rehash()	Rehashes the contents of the table into a bigger table.
remove(Object)	Removes an element from the Hashtable by its key.
size()	Returns the number of elements stored.
toString()	Converts the contents to a very long string.

Refer also to hashCode, equals.

Properties

This class is a Hashtable that can be stored and restored from a stream. It is used to implement persistent properties. It also allows for an unlimited level of nesting by searching a default property list if the required property is not found.

The example program Properties1 in Listing 19.10 creates two Properties lists. One will be the default property list and the other will be the user-defined property list. When the user property list is created, the default Properties object is passed. When the user property list is searched, if the key value is not found, the default Properties list will be searched.

Listing 19.10. `Properties1.java`—Properties example program.

```java
import java.io.DataInputStream;
import java.lang.Integer;
import java.util.Properties;

class Properties1 {
    public static void main(String args[])
        throws java.io.IOException
    {
        int numElements=4;
        String defaultNames[]={"Red","Green","Blue","Purple"};
        int defaultValues[]={1,2,3,4};
        String userNames[]={"Red","Yellow","Orange","Blue"};
        int userValues[]={100,200,300,400};
        DataInputStream dis=new DataInputStream(System.in);
        Properties defaultProps=new Properties();
        Properties userProps=new Properties(defaultProps);

        for (int i=0;i<numElements;i++){
            defaultProps.put(defaultNames[i],
                Integer.toString(defaultValues[i]));
            userProps.put(userNames[i],
                Integer.toString(userValues[i]));
        }
        System.out.println("Default Properties");
        defaultProps.list(System.out);
        System.out.println("\nUser Defined Properties");
        userProps.list(System.out);

        String keyValue;
        System.out.println("\nWhich property to find? ");
        keyValue=dis.readLine();
        System.out.println("Property '"+keyValue+"' is '"+
            userProps.getProperty(keyValue)+"'");
    }
}
```

Notice that the `getProperties()` method is used instead of the inherited `get()` method. The `get()` method only searches the current `Properties` object. The `getProperties()` method must be used in order to have the default `Properties` list searched. An alternative form of the `getProperties()` method has a second argument that is a default `Properties` list to search instead of the default specified when the `Properties` object was created.

The `propertyNames()` method can be used to return an `Enumeration` that can be used to index through all of the property names. This `Enumeration` includes the property names from the default `Properties` list. Likewise, the `list()` method, which prints the `Properties` list to the standard output, will list all of the properties of the current `Properties` object and those in the default `Properties` object.

Properties objects can be written to and read from a stream using the save() and load() methods respectively. In addition to the output or input stream, the save method has an additional string argument that will be written to the beginning of the stream as a header comment.

The Properties class extends the Hashtable class. Table 19.11 summarizes the methods of the Properties class.

Table 19.11. The Properties interface.

Variables	
defaults	Default Properties list to search.

Constructors	
Properties()	Constructs an empty property list.
Properties(Properties)	Constructs an empty property list with specified default.

Methods	
getProperty(string)	Returns a property given the key.
getProperty(string, string)	Returns a property given the specified key and default.
list(PrintStream)	Lists the properties to a stream for debugging.
load(InputStream)	Reads the properties from an InputStream.
propertyNames()	Returns an Enumeration of all of the keys.
save(OutputStream, string)	Writes the properties to an OutputStream.

Observable

This class acts as a base class for objects that wish to be observed by other objects that implement the Observer interface. An Observable object can notify its Observers whenever the Observable object is modified using the notifyObservers() method. This method accomplishes the notification by invoking the update() method of all of its Observers, optionally passing a data object which is passed to notifyObservers. Observable objects may have any number of Observers.

Table 19.12 summarizes the complete interface of the Observable class.

Table 19.12. `Observable` interface.

Constructors	
`Observable()`	

Methods	
`addObserver(Observer)`	Adds an `Observer` to the observer list.
`clearChanged()`	Clears an observable change.
`countObservers()`	Returns the number of `Observer`s.
`deleteObserver(Observer)`	Deletes an `Observer` from the observer list.
`deleteObservers()`	Deletes all `Observer`s from the observer list.
`hasChanged()`	True if an observable change occurred.
`notifyObservers()`	Notifies all observers if an observable change occurred.
`notifyObservers(Object)`	Notifies all observers of a specific observable change.
`setChanged()`	Sets a flag to indicate that an observable change occurred.

Refer also to `Observer`.

Summary

This chapter has described the classes that make up the Java Utilities package. This package provides complete implementations of some of the most useful data types (other than the fundamental numeric types) and the basic data structures needed by programmers. Many of the data types and data structures that you will develop using Java will be based on the classes found in the Utilities package. This chapter should be a good starting point for understanding the utility of these important Java classes and for understanding how to use them effectively.

The I/O Package

20

*by Michael
Morrison*

It would be impossible for a program to do anything useful without performing some kind of input or output of data. Most programs require input from the user and in return output information to the screen, printer, and often to files. The Java I/O package provides an extensive set of classes for handling input and output to and from many different devices. In this chapter you learn about the primary classes contained in the I/O package, along with some examples that show off the capabilities of these classes.

The I/O package, which is also known as java.io, contains many classes, each with a variety of member variables and methods. This chapter does not take an exhaustive look at every class and method contained in the I/O package. Instead, you may view this chapter as a tutorial on how to perform basic input and output using the more popular I/O classes. Armed with the information learned in this chapter, you will be ready to begin using the Java I/O classes in your own programs. And should you choose to explore the more complex I/O classes supported by Java, you will be prepared for the challenge.

Input Stream Classes

The Java input model is based on the concept of an input stream. An input stream can be thought of much like a physical (and certainly more literal) stream of water flowing from a water plant into the pipes of a water system. The obvious difference is that an input stream deals with binary computer data rather than physical water. The comparison is relevant, however, because the data going into an input stream flows like the water being pumped into a pipe. Data that is pumped into an input stream can be directed in many different ways, much like water is directed through the complex system of pipes that make up a water system. The data in an input stream is transmitted a byte at a time, which is roughly analogous to individual drops of water flowing into a pipe.

More practically speaking, Java uses input streams as the means of reading data from an input source, such as the keyboard. The basic input stream classes supported by Java follow:

- `InputStream`
- `BufferedInputStream`
- `DataInputStream`
- `FileInputStream`
- `StringBufferInputStream`

The `InputStream` Class

The `InputStream` class is an abstract class that serves as the base class for all the other input stream classes. `InputStream` defines a basic interface for reading streamed bytes of information. The methods defined by the `InputStream` class will become very familiar to you because they serve a similar purpose in every `InputStream` derived class. This design approach enables you to learn the protocol for managing input streams once, and then apply it to different devices using an InputStream derived class.

The typical scenario when using an input stream is to create an InputStream derived object and tell it you want to input information (by calling an appropriate method). If no input information is currently available, the InputStream uses a technique known as "blocking" to wait until input data becomes available. An example of when blocking will take place is the case of using an input stream to read information from the keyboard. Until the user has typed in information and pressed Return, there is no input available to the InputStream object. The InputStream object then waits (blocks) until the user presses Return, in which case the input data becomes available and the InputStream object can process it as input.

The InputStream class defines the following methods:

- `abstract int read()`
- `int read(byte b[])`
- `int read(byte b[], int off, int len)`
- `long skip(long n)`
- `int available()`
- `synchronized void mark(int readlimit)`
- `synchronized void reset()`
- `boolean markSupported()`
- `void close()`

InputStream defines three different read methods for reading input data in various ways. The first read method takes no parameters and simply reads a byte of data from the input stream and returns it as an integer. This version of read returns -1 if the end of the input stream is reached. Because this version of read returns a byte of input as an int, you will need to cast it to a char if you are reading characters. The second version of read takes an array of bytes as its only parameter, enabling you to read multiple bytes of data at once. You have to make sure that the byte array passed into read is large enough to hold the information being read, or an IOException will be thrown. This version of read returns the actual number of bytes read, or -1 if the end of the stream is reached. The last version of read takes a byte array, an integer offset, and an integer length as parameters. This version of read is very similar to the second version, except it enables you to specify where in the byte array you want the new information placed. The off parameter specifies the offset into the byte array to start placing new data, and the len parameter specifies the maximum number of bytes to read.

The skip method is used to skip over bytes of data in the input stream. skip takes a long value n as its only parameter, which specifies how many bytes of input to skip. It returns the actual number of bytes skipped, or -1 if the end of the input stream is reached.

The available method is used to determine the number of bytes of input data that can be read without blocking. available takes no parameters and returns the number of available bytes.

This method is useful if you want to ensure that there is input data available so as to avoid the blocking mechanism.

The mark method marks the current position in the stream. This position can later be returned to using the reset method. The mark and reset methods are useful in situations where you want to read ahead in the stream but not lose your original position. An example of this situation is verifying a file type, such as an image file. You would probably read the file header first and mark the position at the end of the header. You would then read some of the data to make sure it follows the format expected for that file type. If the data doesn't look right, you can reset the read pointer and try a different technique.

Notice that the mark method takes an integer parameter, readlimit. readlimit specifies how many bytes can be read before the mark becomes invalidated. In effect, readlimit determines how far you can read ahead and still be able to reset the marked position. The markSupported method returns a Boolean value representing whether or not an input stream supports the mark/reset functionality.

Finally, the close method closes an input stream and releases any resources associated with the stream. It is not necessary to explicitly call close, since input streams are automatically closed when the InputStream object is destroyed. Although it is not necessary, calling close immediately after you are finished using a stream is a good programming practice. The reason for this is that close causes the stream buffer to be flushed, which helps avoid file corruption.

The System.in Object

The keyboard is the most standard input device for retrieving user input. The System class contained in the language package contains a member variable that represents the keyboard, or standard input stream. This member variable is called in and is an instance of the InputStream class. This variable is useful for reading user input from the keyboard. Listing 20.1 contains the ReadKeys1 program, which shows how the System.in object can be used along with the first version of the read method. This program can be found on the CD-ROM in the file ReadKeys1.java.

> **NOTE**
>
> I mentioned the keyboard as being the standard input stream. This isn't totally true, because the standard input stream can receive input from any number of sources. Although the keyboard certainly is the most common method of feeding input to the standard input stream, it is not the only method. An example of the standard input stream being driven by a different input source is the redirection of a file into a stream.

Listing 20.1. The `ReadKeys1` class.

```
class ReadKeys1 {
  public static void main (String args[]) {
    StringBuffer s = new StringBuffer();
    char c;
    try {
      while ((c = (char)System.in.read()) != '\n') {
        s.append(c);
      }
    }
    catch (Exception e) {
      System.out.println("Error: " + e.toString());
    }
    System.out.println(s);
  }
}
```

The `ReadKeys1` class first creates a `StringBuffer` object called `str`. It then enters a `while` loop that repeatedly calls the `read` method until a newline character is detected (the user hits Return). Notice that the input data returned by `read` is cast to a `char` type before being stored in the character variable `c`. Each time a character is read, it is appended to the string buffer using the `append` method of `StringBuffer`. It is important to see how any errors caused by the `read` method are handled by the `try/catch` exception handling blocks. The `catch` block simply prints an error message to the standard output stream based on what error occurred. Finally, when a newline character is read from the input stream, the `println` method of the standard output stream is called to output the string to the screen. You'll learn more about the standard output stream a little later in this chapter.

Listing 20.2 contains `ReadKeys2`, which is similar to `ReadKeys1` except that it uses the second version of the `read` method. This `read` method takes an array of bytes as a parameter to store the input that is read. `ReadKeys2` can be found on the CD-ROM in the file `ReadKeys2.java`.

Listing 20.2. The `ReadKeys2` class.

```
class ReadKeys2 {
  public static void main (String args[]) {
    byte buf[] = new byte[80];
    try {
      System.in.read(buf);
    }
    catch (Exception e) {
      System.out.println("Error: " + e.toString());
    }
    String s = new String(buf, 0);
    System.out.println(s);
  }
}
```

In ReadKeys2, an array of bytes is created that is 80 bytes long. A single read method call is performed that reads everything the user has typed. The input is blocked until the user presses Return, in which case the input becomes available and the read method fills the byte array with the new data. A String object is then created to hold the constant string previously read. Notice that the creation method, or constructor, used to create the String object takes an array of bytes (buf) as the first parameter and appends the high byte value specified in the second parameter to each byte, thus forming 16-bit Unicode characters. Because the standard ASCII characters map to Unicode characters with zeros in the high byte, passing 0 as the high byte to the constructor works perfectly. Finally, println is again used to output the string.

The ReadKeys3 program in Listing 20.3 shows how to use the last version of the read method. This version of read again takes an array of bytes, as well as an offset and length for determining how to store the input data in the byte array. ReadKeys3 can be found on the CD-ROM in the file ReadKeys3.java.

Listing 20.3. The ReadKeys3 class.

```
class ReadKeys3 {
  public static void main (String args[]) {
    byte buf[] = new byte[10];
    try {
      System.in.read(buf, 0, 10);
    }
    catch (Exception e) {
      System.out.println("Error: " + e.toString());
    }
    String s = new String(buf, 0);
    System.out.println(s);
  }
}
```

ReadKeys3 is very similar to ReadKeys2, with one major difference: the third version of the read method is used to limit the maximum number of bytes read into the array. The size of the byte array is also shortened to ten bytes to show how this version of read handles it when more data is available than the array can hold. Remember that this version of read can also be used to read data into a specific offset of the array. In this case, the offset is specified as 0 so that the only difference is the maximum number of bytes that can be read (10). This is a useful technique of guaranteeing that you don't overrun a byte array.

The BufferedInputStream Class

The BufferedInputStream class, as its name implies, provides a buffered stream of input. This means that more data is read into the buffered stream than you might have requested, meaning that subsequent reads come straight out of the buffer, rather than the input device. This can result in much faster read access, because reading from a buffer is really just reading from memory. BufferedInputStream implements all of the same methods defined by InputStream.

As a matter of fact, it doesn't implement any new methods of its own. However, the `BufferedInputStream` class does have two different constructors, which follow:

■ `BufferedInputStream(InputStream in)`

■ `BufferedInputStream(InputStream in, int size)`

Notice that both constructors take an `InputStream` object as the first parameter. The only difference between the two is the size of the internal buffer. In the first constructor, a default buffer size is used, whereas in the second constructor you specify the buffer size with the `size` integer parameter. To support buffered input, the `BufferedInputStream` class also defines a handful of member variables, which follow:

■ `byte buf[]`

■ `int count`

■ `int pos`

■ `int markpos`

■ `int marklimit`

The `buf` byte array member is the buffer where input data is actually stored. The `count` member variable keeps up with how many bytes are stored in the buffer. The `pos` member variable keeps up with the current read position in the buffer. The `markpos` member variable specifies the current mark position in the buffer as set using the `mark` method. `markpos` is equal to `-1` if no mark has been set. And finally, the `marklimit` member variable specifies the maximum number of bytes that can be read before the mark position is no longer valid. `marklimit` is set by the `readlimit` parameter passed into the `mark` method. All these member variables are specified as `protected`, so you will probably never actually use any of them. However, seeing these variables should give you some insight into how the `BufferedInputStream` class implements the methods defined by `InputStream`.

Listing 20.4 contains the `ReadKeys4` program, which uses a `BufferedInputStream` object instead of `System.in` to read input from the keyboard. `ReadKeys4` can be found in the file `ReadKeys4.java` on the CD-ROM.

Listing 20.4. The `ReadKeys4` class.

```
import java.io.*;

class ReadKeys4 {
  public static void main (String args[]) {
    BufferedInputStream in = new BufferedInputStream(System.in);
    byte buf[] = new byte[10];
    try {
      in.read(buf, 0, 10);
    }
    catch (Exception e) {
      System.out.println("Error: " + e.toString());
```

continues

Listing 20.4. continued

```
    }
    String s = new String(buf, 0);
    System.out.println(s);
  }
}
```

Notice first that the `BufferedInputStream` class must be imported from the I/O package. Actually, in this case the * qualifier is used to import all the classes in the I/O package. The `BufferedInputStream` object is created by passing the `System.in` `InputStream` into its constructor. From there on, the program is essentially the same as `ReadKeys3`, except that the `read` method is called on the `BufferedInputStream` object rather than `System.in`.

The `DataInputStream` Class

The `DataInputStream` class is useful for reading primitive Java data types from an input stream in a portable fashion. There is only one constructor for `DataInputStream`, which simply takes an `InputStream` object as its only parameter. This constructor is defined as follows:

`DataInputStream(InputStream in)`

`DataInputStream` implements the following useful methods beyond those defined by `InputStream`:

- `final int skipBytes(int n)`
- `final void readFully(byte b[])`
- `final void readFully(byte b[], int off, int len)`
- `final String readLine()`
- `final boolean readBoolean()`
- `final byte readByte()`
- `final int readUnsignedByte()`
- `final short readShort()`
- `final int readUnsignedShort()`
- `final char readChar()`
- `final int readInt()`
- `final long readLong()`
- `final float readFloat()`
- `final double readDouble()`

The `skipBytes` method works very similarly to `skip`, with the exception being that `skipBytes` blocks until all bytes are skipped. The number of bytes to skip is determined by the integer parameter n. There are two `readFully` methods implemented by `DataInputStream`. These methods are similar to the `read` methods, except that they block until all data has been read. The normal read methods only block until *some* data is available, not all. The readFully methods are to the read methods what skipBytes is to skip.

The readLine method is used to read a line of text that has been terminated with a newline (\n), carriage return (\r), carriage return/newline (\r\n), or end-of-file character sequence (EOF). readLine returns the line of text in a String object. Listing 20.5 contains the ReadFloat program, which uses the readLine method to read a floating point value from the user.

Listing 20.5. The ReadFloat class.

```
import java.io.*;

class ReadFloat {
  public static void main (String args[]) {
    DataInputStream in = new DataInputStream(System.in);
    String s = new String();
    try {
      s = in.readLine();
      float f = Float.valueOf(s).floatValue();
      System.out.println(f);
    }
    catch (Exception e) {
      System.out.println("Error: " + e.toString());
    }
  }
}
```

In ReadFloat, a DataInputStream object is first created based on System.in. A String object is then created to hold the input line of text. The readLine method is called with the resulting line of text being stored in the String object s. A floating point number is extracted from the string by first getting a Float object from the string by using the valueOf static method of the Float class. The floatValue method is then called on the Float object to get a float value, which is then stored in the float variable f. This value is then output to the screen using println.

The rest of the methods implemented by DataInputStream are variations of the read method for different fundamental data types. The type read by each method is easily identifiable by the name of the method.

The FileInputStream Class

The FileInputStream class is useful for performing simple file input. For more advanced file input operations, you will more than likely want to use the RandomAccessFile class, which is discussed a little later in this chapter. The FileInputStream class can be instantiated using one of three following constructors:

- FileInputStream(String name)
- FileInputStream(File file)
- FileInputStream(FileDescriptor fdObj)

The first constructor takes a String object parameter called name, which specifies the name of the file to use for input. The second constructor takes a File object parameter that specifies the file to use for input. You'll learn more about the File object near the end of this chapter. The third constructor for FileInputStream takes a FileDescriptor object as its only parameter.

The FileInputStream class functions exactly like the InputStream class, except that it is geared toward working with files. Listing 20.6 contains the ReadFile program, which uses the FileInputStream class to read data from a text file. ReadFile can be found in the file ReadFile.java on the CD-ROM.

Listing 20.6. The ReadFile class.

```
import java.io.*;

class ReadFile {
  public static void main (String args[]) {
    byte buf[] = new byte[64];
    try {
      FileInputStream in = new FileInputStream("Grocery.txt");
      in.read(buf, 0, 64);
    }
    catch (Exception e) {
      System.out.println("Error: " + e.toString());
    }
    String s = new String(buf, 0);
    System.out.println(s);
  }
}
```

In ReadFile, a FileInputStream object is first created by passing a string with the name of the file ("Grocery.txt") as the input file. The read method is then called to read from the input file into a byte array. The byte array is then used to create a String object, which is in turn used for output. Pretty simple!

The StringBufferInputStream Class

The StringBufferInputStream class, aside from having a very long name, is a pretty neat class. StringBufferInputString enables you to use a string as a buffered source of input. StringBufferInputStream implements all the same methods defined by InputStream, and no more. The StringBufferInputStream class has a single constructor, which follows:

```
StringBufferInputStream(String s)
```

The constructor takes a String object, which it constructs the string buffer input stream out of. Although StringBufferInputStream doesn't define any additional methods, it does provide a few of its own member variables, which follow:

■ String buffer

■ int count

■ int pos

The buffer string member is the buffer where the string data is actually stored. The count member variable specifies the number of characters to use in the buffer. Finally, the pos member variable keeps up with the current position in the buffer. Like the BufferedInputStream class, you will probably never see these member variables, but they are important in understanding how the StringBufferInputStream class is implemented.

Listing 20.7 contains the ReadString program, which uses a StringBufferInputStream to read data from a string of text data. ReadString can be found in the file ReadString.java on the CD-ROM.

Listing 20.7. The ReadString class.

```
import java.io.*;

class ReadString {
  public static void main (String args[]) {
    // Get a string of input from the user
    byte buf1[] = new byte[64];
    try {
      System.in.read(buf1, 0, 64);
    }
    catch (Exception e) {
      System.out.println("Error: " + e.toString());
    }
    String s1 = new String(buf1, 0);

    // Read the string as a string buffer and output it
    StringBufferInputStream in = new StringBufferInputStream(s1);
    byte buf2[] = new byte[64];
    try {
      in.read(buf2, 0, 64);
    }
    catch (Exception e) {
      System.out.println("Error: " + e.toString());
    }
    String s2 = new String(buf2, 0);
    System.out.println(s2);
  }
}
```

The ReadString program enables the user to type in text, which is read and stored in a string. This string is then used to create a StringBufferInputStream that is read into another string for output. Obviously, this program goes to a lot of trouble to do very little; it's only meant as a demonstration of how to use the StringBufferInputStream class. Knowing this, it's up to you to find an interesting application to apply this class to.

The first half of the ReadString program should look pretty familiar; it's essentially the guts of the ReadKeys3 program, which reads data entered by the keyboard into a string. The second half of the program is where you actually get busy with the StringBufferInputStream object. A StringBufferInputStream object is created using the String object (s1) containing the text entered from the keyboard. The contents of the StringBufferInputStream object are then read into a byte array using the read method. The byte array is in turn used to construct another String object (s2), which is output to the screen.

Output Stream Classes

In Java, output streams are the logical counterparts to input streams and handle writing data to output sources. Using the water analogy from the discussion of input streams earlier, an output stream would be equivalent to the water spout on your bathtub. Just as water travels from a water plant through the pipes and out of the spout into your bathtub, so must data flow from an input device through the operating system and out of an output device. A leaky water spout is an even better way to visualize the transfer of data out of an output stream; each drop of water falling out of the spout represents a byte of data. Each byte of data flows to the output device just like the drops of water falling one after the next out of the bathtub spout.

Getting back to Java, you use output streams to output data to various different output devices, such as the screen. The primary output stream classes used in Java programming follow:

- OutputStream
- PrintStream
- BufferedOutputStream
- DataOutputStream
- FileOutputStream

The Java output streams provide a variety of ways to output data. The OutputStream class defines the core behavior required of an output stream. The PrintStream class is geared toward outputting text data, such as the data sent to the standard output stream. The BufferedOutputStream class is an extension to the OutputStream class that provides support for buffered output. The DataOutputStream class is useful for outputting primitive data types such as int or float. And finally, the FileOutputStream class provides the support necessary to output data to files.

The OutputStream Class

The OutputStream class is the output counterpart to InputStream and serves as an abstract base class for all the other output stream classes. OutputStream defines the basic protocol for writing streamed data to an output device. Like the methods for InputStream, you will become accustomed to the methods defined by OutputStream, because they act very much the same in every

OutputStream derived class. The benefit of this common interface is that you can essentially learn a method once and then be able to apply it to different classes without starting the learning process over again.

You will typically create an OutputStream derived object and call an appropriate method to tell it you want to output information. The OutputStream class uses a technique similar to the one used by InputStream; it will block until data has been written to an output device. While blocking (waiting for the current output to be processed), the OutputStream class will not allow any further data to be output.

The OutputStream class implements the following methods:

- abstract void write(int b)
- void write(byte b[])
- void write(byte b[], int off, int len)
- void flush()
- void close()

OutputStream defines three different write methods for writing data in a few different ways. The first write method writes a single byte to the output stream, as specified by the integer parameter b. The second version of write takes an array of bytes as a parameter and writes them to the output stream. The last version of write takes a byte array, an integer offset, and a length as parameters. This version of write is very much like the second version, except it uses the other parameters to determine where in the byte array to begin outputting data, along with how much data to output. The off parameter specifies an offset into the byte array to begin outputting data from, and the len parameter specifies how many bytes are to be output.

The flush method is used to flush the output stream. Calling flush will force the OutputStream object to output any pending data.

Finally, the close method closes an output stream and releases any resources associated with the stream. Like InputStream objects, it isn't usually necessary to call close on an OutputStream object, because streams are automatically closed when they are destroyed.

The PrintStream Class

The PrintStream class is derived from OutputStream and is designed primarily for printing output data as text. PrintStream has two different constructors:

- PrintStream(OutputStream out)
- PrintStream(OutputStream out, boolean autoflush)

Both PrintStream constructors take an OutputStream object as their first parameter. The only difference between the two methods is how the newline character is handled. In the first constructor, the stream is flushed based on an internal decision by the object. In the second constructor, you can specify that the stream be flushed every time it encounters a newline character. You specify this through the Boolean `autoflush` parameter.

The `PrintStream` class also implements a rich set of methods, which follow:

- `boolean checkError()`
- `void print(Object obj)`
- `synchronized void print(String s)`
- `synchronized void print(char s[])`
- `void print(char c)`
- `void print(int i)`
- `void print(long l)`
- `void print(float f)`
- `void print(double d)`
- `void print(boolean b)`
- `void println()`
- `synchronized void println(Object obj)`
- `synchronized void println(String s)`
- `synchronized void println(char s[])`
- `synchronized void println(char c)`
- `synchronized void println(int I)`
- `synchronized void println(long l)`
- `synchronized void println(float f)`
- `synchronized void println(double d)`
- `synchronized void println(boolean b)`

The `checkError` method flushes the stream and returns whether or not an error has occurred. The return value of `checkError` is based on an error ever having occurred on the stream, meaning that once an error occurs, `checkError` will always return `true` for that stream.

`PrintStream` provides a variety of `print` methods to handle all your printing needs. The version of `print` that takes an `Object` parameter simply outputs the results of calling the `toString` method on the object. The other `print` methods each take a different type parameter that specifies which data type is printed for each.

The `println` methods implemented by `PrintStream` are very similar to the `print` methods. The only difference is that the `println` methods print a newline character following the data that is printed. The `println` method that takes no parameters simply prints a newline character by itself.

The `System.out` Object

The monitor is the primary output device on modern computer systems. The `System` class has a member variable that represents the standard output stream, which is typically the monitor. The member variable is called `out` and is an instance of the `PrintStream` class. `out` is very useful for outputting text to the screen. But you already know this because you've seen the `out` member variable in most of the sample programs developed thus far.

The `BufferedOutputStream` Class

The `BufferedOutputStream` class, which is very similar to the `OutputStream` class, provides a buffered stream of output. This enables you to write to a stream without causing a bunch of writes to an output device. The `BufferedOutputStream` class maintains a buffer that is written to when you write to the stream. When the buffer gets full or when it is explicitly flushed, it is written to the output device. This output approach is much more efficient since most of the data transfer is taking place in memory. And when it does come time to output the data to a device, it all happens at once.

The `BufferedOutputStream` class implements the same methods defined in `OutputStream`, meaning that there are no additional methods, except for constructors. The two constructors for `BufferedOutputStream` follow:

- `BufferedOutputStream(OutputStream out)`
- `BufferedOutputStream(OutputStream out, int size)`

Both constructors for `BufferedOutputStream` take an `OutputStream` object as their first parameter. The only difference between the two is the size of the internal buffer used to store the output data. In the first constructor, a default buffer size is used, where in the second constructor you specify the buffer size with the `size` integer parameter. The buffer itself within the `BufferedOutputStream` class is managed by two member variables, which follow:

- `byte buf[]`
- `int count`

The `buf` byte array member variable is the actual data buffer where output data is stored. The `count` member keeps up with how many bytes are in the buffer. These two member variables are sufficient to represent the state of the output stream buffer.

Listing 20.8 contains the `WriteStuff` program, which uses a `BufferedOutputStream` object to output a byte array of text data. `WriteStuff` can be found in the file `WriteStuff.java` on the CD-ROM.

Listing 20.8. The `WriteStuff` class.

```java
import java.io.*;

class WriteStuff {
  public static void main (String args[]) {
    // Copy the string into a byte array
    String s = new String("Dance, spider!\n");
    byte[] buf = new byte[64];
    s.getBytes(0, s.length(), buf, 0);

    // Output the byte array (buffered)
    BufferedOutputStream out = new BufferedOutputStream(System.out);
    try {
      out.write(buf, 0, 64);
      out.flush();
    }
    catch (Exception e) {
      System.out.println("Error: " + e.toString());
    }
  }
}
```

The `WriteStuff` program fills a byte array with text data from a string and outputs the byte array to the screen using a buffered output stream. `WriteStuff` begins by creating a `String` object containing text, and a byte array. The `getBytes` method of `String` is used to copy the bytes of data in the string to the byte array. The `getBytes` method copies the low byte of each character in the string to the byte array. This works because the Unicode representation of ASCII characters has zeros in the high byte. Once the byte array is ready, a `BufferedOutputStream` object is created by passing `System.out` into the constructor. The byte array is then written to the output buffer using the `write` method. Since the stream is buffered, it is necessary to call the `flush` method to actually output the data.

The `DataOutputStream` Class

The `DataOutputStream` class is useful for writing primitive Java data types to an output stream in a portable way. `DataOutputStream` only has one constructor, which simply takes an `OutputStream` object as its only parameter. This constructor is defined as follows:

`DataOutputStream(OutputStream out)`

The `DataOutputStream` class implements the following useful methods beyond those inherited from `OutputStream`:

- `final int size()`
- `final void writeBoolean(boolean v)`
- `final void writeByte(int v)`
- `final void writeShort(int v)`
- `final void writeChar(int v)`

- ■ final void writeInt(int v)
- ■ final void writeLong(long v)
- ■ final void writeFloat(float v)
- ■ final void writeDouble(double v)
- ■ final void writeBytes(String s)
- ■ final void writeChars(String s)

The size method is used to determine how many bytes have been written to the stream thus far. The integer value returned by size specifies the number of bytes written.

The rest of the methods implemented in DataOutputStream are all variations on the write method. Each different version of write*Type* takes a different data type that is in turn written as output.

The FileOutputStream Class

The FileOutputStream class provides a means to perform simple file output. For more advanced file output, you should check out the RandomAccessFile class, which is discussed a little later in this chapter. A FileOutputStream object can be created using one of the three following constructors:

- ■ FileOutputStream(String name)
- ■ FileOutputStream(File file)
- ■ FileOutputStream(FileDescriptor fdObj)

The first constructor takes a String parameter, which specifies the name of the file to use for input. The second constructor takes a File object parameter that specifies the input file. You'll learn about the File object a little later in this chapter. The third constructor takes a FileDescriptor object as its only parameter.

The FileOutputStream class functions exactly like the OutputStream class, except that it is specifically designed to work with files. Listing 20.9 contains the WriteFile program, which uses the FileOutputStream class to write user input to a text file. WriteFile can be found in the file WriteFile.java on the CD-ROM.

Listing 20.9. The WriteFile class.

```
import java.io.*;

class WriteFile {
  public static void main (String args[]) {
    // Read the user input
    byte buf[] = new byte[64];
    try {
      System.in.read(buf, 0, 64);
    }
```

continues

Listing 20.9. continued

```
      catch (Exception e) {
        System.out.println("Error: " + e.toString());
      }

      // Output the data to a file
      try {
        FileOutputStream out = new FileOutputStream("Output.txt");
        out.write(buf);
      }
      catch (Exception e) {
        System.out.println("Error: " + e.toString());
      }
    }
  }
}
```

In WriteFile, user input is read from the standard input stream into a byte array using the read method of InputStream. A FileOutputStream object is then created with a filename of "Output.txt", which is passed in as the only parameter to the constructor. The write method is then used to output the byte array to the stream. You can see that working with output file streams is just as easy as working with input file streams.

File Classes

If the FileInputStream and FileOutputStream classes don't quite meet up to your file handling expectations, don't despair! Java provides two more classes for working with files that are sure to meet your needs. These two classes are File and RandomAccessFile. The File class basically models an operating system directory entry, enabling you access to information about a file including file attributes and the full path where the file is located, among other things. The RandomAccessFile class, on the other hand, provides a variety of methods for reading and writing data to and from a file.

The File Class

The File class can be instantiated using one of three constructors, which follow:

- File(String path)
- File(String path, String name)
- File(File dir, String name)

The first constructor takes a single String parameter that specifies the full path name of the file. The second constructor takes two String parameters: path and name. The path parameter specifies the directory path where the file is located, while the name parameter specifies the name of the file. The third constructor is similar to the second, except it takes another `File` object as the first parameter instead of a string. The `File` object in this case is used to specify the directory path of the file.

The most important methods implemented by the `File` class follow:

- `String getName()`
- `String getPath()`
- `String getAbsolutePath()`
- `String getParent()`
- `boolean exists()`
- `boolean canWrite()`
- `boolean canRead()`
- `boolean isFile()`
- `boolean isDirectory()`
- `boolean isAbsolute()`
- `long lastModified()`
- `long length()`
- `boolean mkdir()`
- `boolean mkdirs()`
- `boolean renameTo(File dest)`
- `boolean delete()`
- `String[] list()`
- `String[] list(FilenameFilter filter)`

The `getName` method gets the name of a file and returns it as a string. The `getPath` method returns the path of a file, which may be relative, as a string. The `getAbsolutePath` method returns the absolute path of a file. The `getParent` method returns the parent directory of a file, or `null` if a parent directory is not found.

The `exists` method returns a Boolean specifying whether or not a file actually exists. The `canWrite` and `canRead` methods return Boolean values the specify whether a file can be written to or read from. The `isFile` and `isDirectory` methods return Boolean values the specify if a file is valid and if the directory information is valid. The `isAbsolute` method returns a Boolean value specifying if a filename is absolute.

The `lastModified` method returns a `long` value that specifies the time in which a file was last modified. The `long` value returned is only useful in determining differences between modification times; it has no meaning as an absolute time and is not suitable for output. The `length` method returns the length of a file in bytes.

The mkdir method creates a directory based on the current path information. mkdir returns a Boolean indicating the success of creating the directory. The mkdirs method is similar to mkdir, except that it can be used to create an entire directory structure. The renameTo method renames a file to the name specified by the File object passed as the dest parameter. The delete method deletes a file. Both renameTo and delete return a Boolean value indicating success or failure.

Finally, the list methods of the File object obtain listings of the directory contents. Both list methods return a list of filenames in a String array. The only difference between the two is that the second version takes a FilenameFilter object that enables you to filter out certain files from the list.

Listing 20.10 contains the source code for the FileInfo program, which uses a File object to determine information about a file in the current directory. The FileInfo program is located in the FileInfo.java source file on the CD-ROM.

Listing 20.10. The FileInfo class.

```java
import java.io.*;

class FileInfo {
  public static void main (String args[]) {
    System.out.println("Enter file name: ");
    char c;
    StringBuffer buf = new StringBuffer();
    try {
      while ((c = (char)System.in.read()) != '\n')
        buf.append(c);
    }
    catch (Exception e) {
      System.out.println("Error: " + e.toString());
    }
    File file = new File(buf.toString());
    if (file.exists()) {
      System.out.println("File Name  : " + file.getName());
      System.out.println("      Path  : " + file.getPath());
      System.out.println("Abs. Path  : " + file.getAbsolutePath());
      System.out.println("Writable   : " + file.canWrite());
      System.out.println("Readable   : " + file.canRead());
      System.out.println("Length     : " + (file.length() / 1024) + "KB");
    }
    else
      System.out.println("Sorry, file not found.");
  }
}
```

The FileInfo program uses the File object to get information about a file in the current directory. The user is first prompted to type in a filename, with the resulting input being stored in a String object. The String object is then used as the parameter to the File object's constructor. A call to the exists method determines if the file actually exists. If so, information about the file is obtained through the various File methods and the results output to the screen.

The `RandomAccessFile` Class

The `RandomAccessFile` class provides a multitude of methods for reading and writing to files. Although you can certainly use `FileInputStream` and `FileOutputStream` for file I/O, `RandomAccessFile` provides many more features and options. Following are the constructors for RandomAccessFile:

- `RandomAccessFile(String name, String mode)`
- `RandomAccessFile(File file, String mode)`

The first constructor takes a `String` parameter specifying the name of the file to access, along with a `String` parameter specifying the type of mode (read or write). The mode type can be either `"r"` for read mode, or `"rw"` for read/write mode. The second constructor takes a `File` object as the first parameter, which specifies the file to access. The second parameter is a mode string, which works exactly the same as in the first constructor.

The `RandomAccessFile` class implements a variety of powerful file I/O methods. Following are some of the most useful ones:

- `int skipBytes(int n)`
- `long getFilePointer()`
- `void seek(long pos)`
- `int read()`
- `int read(byte b[])`
- `int read(byte b[], int off, int len)`
- `final boolean readBoolean()`
- `final byte readByte()`
- `final int readUnsignedByte()`
- `final short readShort()`
- `final int readUnsignedShort()`
- `final char readChar()`
- `final int readInt()`
- `final long readLong()`
- `final float readFloat()`
- `final double readDouble()`
- `final String readLine()`
- `final void readFully(byte b[])`
- `final void readFully(byte b[], int off, int len)`
- `void write(byte b[])`

- ■ `void write(byte b[], int off, int len)`
- ■ `final void writeBoolean(boolean v)`
- ■ `final void writeByte(int v)`
- ■ `final void writeShort(int v)`
- ■ `final void writeChar(int v)`
- ■ `final void writeInt(int v)`
- ■ `final void writeLong(long v)`
- ■ `void writeFloat(float v)`
- ■ `void writeDouble(double v)`
- ■ `void writeBytes(String s)`
- ■ `void writeChars(String s)`
- ■ `long length()`
- ■ `void close()`

From looking at this method list, you no doubt are thinking that many of these methods look familiar. And they should look familiar; most of the methods implemented by `RandomAccessFile` are also implemented by either `FileInputStream` or `FileOutputStream`. The fact that `RandomAccessFile` combines them into a single class is a convenience in and of itself. But you already know how to use these methods because they work just like they do in `FileInputStream` and `FileOutputStream`. What you are interested in are the new methods implemented by `RandomAccessFile`.

The first new method you might have noticed is the `getFilePointer` method. `getFilePointer` returns the current position of the file pointer as a `long` value. The file pointer indicates the location in the file where data will be read from or written to next. In read mode, the file pointer is analogous to the needle on a phonograph or the laser in a CD player. The `seek` method is the other new method that should catch your attention. `seek` sets the file pointer to the absolute position specified by the `long` parameter pos. Calling `seek` to move the file pointer is analogous to moving the phonograph needle with your hand. In both cases, the read point of the data or music is being moved. It is a similar situation when you are writing data as well.

Listing 20.11 contains the source code for `FilePrint`, which is a program that uses the `RandomAccessFile` class to print a file to the screen. The source code for the `FilePrint` program can be found in the file `FilePrint.java` on the CD-ROM.

Listing 20.11. The `FilePrint` class.

```
import java.io.*;

class FilePrint {
  public static void main (String args[]) {
    System.out.println("Enter file name: ");
```

```
    char c;
    StringBuffer buf = new StringBuffer();
    try {
      while ((c = (char)System.in.read()) != '\n')
        buf.append(c);
      RandomAccessFile file = new RandomAccessFile(buf.toString(), "rw");
      while (file.getFilePointer() < file.length())
        System.out.println(file.readLine());
    }
    catch (Exception e) {
      System.out.println("Error: " + e.toString());
    }
  }
}
```

The FilePrint program begins very much like the FileInfo program in that it prompts the user to type in a filename and stores the result in a string. It then uses that string to create a RandomAccessFile object in read/write mode, which is specified by passing "rw" as the second parameter to the constructor. A while loop is then used to repeatedly call the readLine method until the entire file has been read. The call to readLine is performed within a call to println so that each line of the file is output to the screen.

Summary

Whew, this chapter covered a lot of ground! Hopefully you've managed to make it this far relatively unscathed. On the up side, you've learned about all there is to know about fundamental Java I/O and the most important classes in the I/O package. That's not to say that there isn't still a wealth of information inside the I/O package that you haven't seen. The point is that the Java class libraries are very extensive, which means that some of the classes will only be useful under very special circumstances. The goal of this chapter was to highlight the more mainstream classes and methods within the I/O package.

If you think you've had enough talk about I/O, then maybe you're ready for the next phase of Java: applet programming. You've survived this far, so you might as well push on and start reaping the real benefits of knowing the Java language and class libraries inside and out. The next section of the book is focused on applet programming, which enables you to embed graphical Java applications into HTML pages. Have fun!

V

PART

IN THIS PART

Applet Programming

Applet Programming Overview

21

by David Gulbransen and Kenrick Rawlings

One of the major uses of Java is the creation of miniapplications, or *applets*, which are designed to be small, fast, and easily transferable over network resources. These applets can be thought of as small programs that might be more focused in scope than a full-blown application. For example, an application might be a spreadsheet. A full-blown spreadsheet would enable users to specify a variety of calculations and functions, from amortizing loans to keeping full financial records for a small business. An applet, on the other hand, might be limited to a loan calculator, figuring interest and loan payments. Rather than trying to do it all, like an application, applets generally focus on one small task or a component of a task. Instead of being limited and narrow, applets are streamlined and more efficient.

What Is an Applet?

Quite simply, applets are compiled Java programs that are run using the Applet Viewer or through any World Wide Web browser that supports Java. What an applet does is up to you. It can display graphics, play sounds, accept user input, and manipulate data just like any program. This section is designed to help you understand what goes into creating an applet and how applets can function in conjunction with the Internet and the World Wide Web.

Technically an applet is a subclass of `java.awt.Panel`. Being such, an applet can contain features from the Abstract Window Toolkit and the Java Language Package. To aid in the creation of applets, Sun also has developed the Java Applet Package, a collection of constructs and methods designed to make a number of useful features accessible to programmers.

Applets and the World Wide Web

Applets were not conceived for use with the Internet, instead they were designed for use with hand-held computing devices, or Personal Digital Assistants. However, the basic properties of applets have made them a perfect fit for use on the Internet and the World Wide Web. Because applets are small, they are downloaded and launched very quickly. Applets can add new levels of functionality and interactivity to Web pages without the overhead of full-scale applications. With the recent introduction of Java-capable browsers such as Netscape, applets have begun to make a serious impact on the World Wide Web.

More Web pages are now featuring Java applets for a variety of uses. Some of the ways applets are currently being used on the World Wide Web include the following:

- Animation
- Displaying images with sound
- Graphic effects, such as scrolling text
- Interactive programming, such as games

Java applets take special advantage of the features already built into Web browsers, enabling programmers to obtain a rich feature set with a minimum of code. For example, to incorporate

GIF or JPEG files into a Java applet, it is not necessary to write any decoding methods for the image files. Applets can use the browser's decoder to display image files. Using the browser to display images makes applets easily extensible. If a new image format becomes popular and is incorporated into a browser, the Java applet will automatically be able to handle that format. It isn't necessary for the applet programmer to change the applet significantly to access new formats. Applets are well-suited to the World Wide Web because they leverage browser features to decrease size, increase download speed, and simplify applet programming.

NOTE

At the time of this writing, the only browser currently supporting Java is the Netscape Navigator 2.0. Because of this, the text concentrates on how Java takes advantage of Netscape's features, some of which are currently unique to Netscape. This is not meant to be an endorsement of Netscape, and certainly as Java begins to broaden its scope other browsers will add to Java's functionality as well.

How Applets Differ from Applications

Applets can be quite robust programs; however, there are significant differences between applets and applications. Applets are not full-featured applications. There are concrete and implicit limitations that need to be considered in designing and creating applets. For example:

- Applets leverage browsers
- Applets have limited file access
- Applets have limited network access

We've already described how applets leverage Web browsers to provide functionality over applications. However, the nature of applets warrants some important restrictions on their functionality in the interest of security.

The Limits of Applets

Because applets can be downloaded over the Web, they are, by nature, not secure. Applets are precompiled bytecode. The compiled bytecode is downloaded to your machine and executed locally. Because of this, both Sun and browser manufacturers have placed some restrictions on the functionality of applets. Unfortunately, while these restrictions limit what an applet is capable of, they are not meant to hinder the development of applets. Instead, these restrictions are meant to ensure the security of machines that will run applets by preventing applets from being used maliciously. This security was implemented to help them gain wide acceptance on the Net.

Functional Limits

Applets are downloaded from their home servers as bytecode. This is what makes Java easily portable from platform to platform. The bytecode is platform-independent, and is executed through the Applet Viewer or a Java-capable Web browser. Because the bytecode is executed on a user's local machine, there needs to be some level of security to make sure that the integrity of the machine is not compromised.

One of the ways that Java accomplishes this is through a verification process to ensure that the bytecode does not violate any Java language conventions. In order to perform verification, any methods or variables must be called by name. Calling methods by name allows verification of all the methods and variables in the bytecode, and ensures that an applet is not accessing memory areas that might contain the OS or other applications. Limiting functions to call-by-name also has the advantage of eliminating memory pointers, and anyone who has struggled with pointers in C or C++ can testify that pointers are one of the most commonly misunderstood aspects of programming. The elimination of pointers is not without a price—implementing all methods and variables by name slows down Java applets when compared to other programming languages.

Applets are not given full access to the local machine's file system. Applets currently do not have the means to save files out to a user's local machine, and they can't read files off the local machine either. Though this does limit the functionality of applets significantly, allowing applets access to a local file system would represent a serious security hole. For example, if an applet could read files on a system, it could potentially send information from those files back to the applet's author. If an applet could write files to a system, it could potentially become a carrier for viruses. Rather than risk security, applets are simply prevented from accessing files. Undoubtedly, file access would increase the functionality of applets and the end goal is to allow applets to read and save files. There are various ways this might be accomplished, but until more security methods are implemented, applets are prevented from file system access.

Applets also are restricted from loading dynamic or shared libraries from other programming languages. Java has the capability to declare methods as being *native*, which allows the virtual machine to take advantage of other language libraries such as C or C++. However, because these libraries can't be verified and they would require access to the file system, applets are not allowed to use dynamic libraries. The end goal is to optimize Java to the point where all of the dynamic libraries could be written in Java and the need for other language libraries would be eliminated. As the language grows and evolves, many of these limitations will be removed. For now, they are the price of participating so closely in the evolution of a new language.

Limitations Imposed by the Browser

In addition to the limitations imposed by the language itself, the browser that executes applet bytecode also places some restrictions on applets. A Web browser is a *trusted application*—a user has chosen to load the browser on the local machine and trusts that it will not damage any files or the operating system. Applets are untrusted applications. They are downloaded immediately and are executed on a machine without receiving the user's consent. (The user might choose to use a Java-capable browser, and therefore imply consent, but the user can't approve individual applets.) Because of this, Java-capable browsers have placed some restrictions on applets in order to ensure that they don't violate system integrity inadvertently.

The most important limitation placed on an applet by the Web browser is network connectivity. Applets currently are limited to network connections with their host machines. This means your Java applet can communicate directly back to the Web server that it's downloaded from, but it cannot contact any other servers on the Net. Networking also comes back to the issue of security. By restricting access back to the applet's original host, applets are provided basic network functionality with a minimum security risk. If applets were allowed to contact any server on the Net, applets could perform some potentially dangerous tasks.

For example, if an applet was allowed to contact any server, it would be possible to make a connection to any e-mail server. An applet could then masquerade as your machine and send forged mail that would appear to be coming from you. The issue of network connectivity for applets is widely debated among Java developers. It is still possible to write a number of applets that take advantage of network connections to their own servers. Though restricting network connectivity imposes some limits on applets, it is being done in the interest of security. Certainly, as better security methods are developed, network connectivity will increase and applets will become more functional. For more information on Java security issues, see Chapter 40.

Applet Basics

The object-oriented nature of Java is instrumental in understanding what defines an applet from a technical standpoint. Because of the hierarchy of the Java classes, an applet is an extension of the `Panel` object in the Abstract Windows Toolkit (AWT). A panel is a subclass of the `Container` class (see Figure 21.1), and as such can contain any Java language components, such as buttons, menus, scroll bars, and so on.

Because an applet actually is a class, applets can be used to build other applets or full-blown applications. Just as your applets can be used within other applets, they also inherit features from the classes above them.

Applets also have distinct stages in their lifetime. These stages include `init`, `start`, `stop`, and `destroy`. All of these methods can be overwritten by the applet programmer to accomplish specific tasks during each stage in an applet's lifetime.

FIGURE 21.1.
The Java class hierarchies.

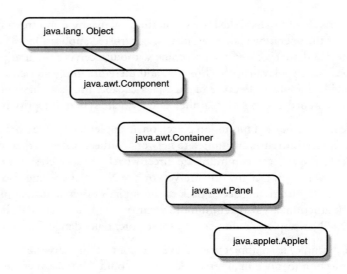

Here is a breakdown of the four stages:

`init();`

The `init` stage consists of initializing any methods and variables the applet needs to function, such as images to be loaded. The `init` method is called when the applet is first loaded.

`start();`

The `start` stage starts the primary functions of an applet. For example, if an applet plays a sound, it could start playing during the `start` stage. The `start` method is called when the `init` method has finished and the applet is ready to execute.

`stop();`

The `stop` stage can be used to stop any actions that might still be in progress from the `start` stage when an applet is exited. For example, a sound loop would need to be stopped when a person left the Web page containing a sound applet. The `stop` method is called when the page is left, or the browser is minimized.

`destroy();`

`Destroy` is called automatically, and completes any memory cleanup or garbage collection that needs to be done when an applet is destroyed. It can be overwritten, but this is not generally necessary. The `destroy` method is called when you quit a browser.

Inheriting from the `Applet` Class

Applets inherit the properties of the `Panel` object in the AWT, and the `Applet` class attributes from `java.applet.Applet`. This is evident in the way that all Java applets are structured. In defining the initial applet,

```
public class Classname extends java.applet.Applet { }
```

the code shows how your applet class is an extension of the `Applet` class. There are a number of methods that are built into the `Applet` class to make developing applets easier and these are the subject of Chapter 23, "The Applet Package and Graphics."

The idea of inheritance is fundamental to the structure of applets. Applets inherit the capability to contain user interface objects because all applets are `Panels`. Applets inherit a great deal of their functionality from the `Applet` class.

Applet HTML

Applets currently can be viewed on several UNIX platforms, Windows 95, and Windows NT. The Java world is continuing to expand, and soon Java will be available for more popular platforms. Once your Java code has been compiled, it can be executed with the Applet Viewer, or through any Java-capable browser. Applets require the following two components to execute:

- The compiled bytecode
- An HTML file containing basic applet information and parameters

The compiled bytecode is the executable component of the applet. The HTML file is required by both the Applet Viewer and any Web browser in order to execute the code properly. The HTML file is based on the `<applet>` tag and takes the following basic structure:

```
<html>
    <applet codebase=location of code code=filename.class width=100 height=150
alt=alternate>
    <param name="parameter" value="accepted value">
    </applet>
    </html>
```

The `<applet>` tag contains the filename of your executable code, in the format of `filename.class`, followed by the dimensions of your applet. The initial dimensions of the applet need to be given in pixels. This is because the applet has to fit into the conventions of HTML page layout. The `<param>` tag accepts the parameter name and its associated value. The parameter tag is only necessary if the applet is designed to take parameters, and it can be repeated as many times as necessary to establish the parameter values. Here is a list of the tags and values that can be used in an applet HTML file:

param

The parameter tag also takes name and value tags to specify the values for any parameters an applet accepts (see the preceding HTML example).

The following are actually parameters to the `<applet>` tag, and are used to give the browser information about the applet itself.

`codebase`

The codebase is the base URL location of the Java bytecode. This enables you to have your code in a different directory than the page your applet appears on.

`alt`

Identical to the HTML `<alt>` tag, this tag enables you to provide an alternate image or text for Web browsers that are not Java-capable. Alternate options can also be specified by placing HTML code between the `<applet>` and `</applet>` tags.

`name`

The `<name>` tag enables you to specify a symbolic name for an applet. The name is used as a reference to communicate by other applets on the same page.

`align`

Identical to the standard HTML `<align>` tag. This tag enables you to specify right, left, or center alignment of your applet.

`vspace` and `hspace`

These tags enable you to specify the amount of vertical and horizontal space around an applet when it is aligned to the left or right with the `<align>` tag.

`code`

The `code` parameter is required with the `<applet>` tag. It specifies the location of the actual compiled applet.

`width`

The `width` parameter is used with the `<applet>` tag to specify the width of the window that should be opened when the applet is added to the page. It is required by the `<applet>` tag.

`height`

The `height` parameter is similar to width, specifying the height of the applet window. It is also required.

A Basic Applet Example

The following applet example is called `Speaker`. It displays a static graphic image and plays an audio file.

```
/*      Speaker
        This applet displays a gif or jpeg while playing a sound (.au) file.
*/

import java.awt.*;
import java.applet.*;
import java.lang.*;
import java.net.URL;

public class Speaker extends java.applet.Applet {

        Image image;
        AudioClip sound;
        String graphic;
        String clip;

        public String[][] getParameterInfo() {
                String[][] info = {
                        {"graphic",     "string",       "The image file to be displayed."},
                        {"clip",        "string",       "The sound file to be played."},
                };
        return info;
        }

        public void init() {

                graphic = getParameter("graphic");
                clip = getParameter("clip");
                image = getImage(getDocumentBase(), graphic);
                sound = getAudioClip(getDocumentBase(), clip);
        }

        public void paint(Graphics g) {
                        g.drawImage(image, 0, 0, this);
                }

        public void start() {
                repaint();

                // This could also be sound.loop(); to loop the sound.
                sound.play();
        }

        public void stop() {
                sound.stop();
        }
}
```

The User Interface

Because of the nature of this applet, the user interface is fairly limited. It doesn't accept interactive input from users, so it really isn't necessary to include elements from the AWT. For the purpose of starting with an applet in its most simple form, this applet does not deal with issues of user input or event handling. Those topics are covered later in this section in Chapter 22, "The Windowing Package." However, if the image and sound file were hard-coded, it would seriously impair the general usefulness of this applet.

In order to make this a functional applet, Speaker is designed to accept the image file and sound file from parameters specified in the <applet> tag. Parameters are a function of user interface. They enable the user to specify changeable elements of an applet—in this case the image and the sound. The following code allows the Speaker applet to read parameters and convert them into variables for use:

```
public String[][] getParameterInfo() {
        String[][] info = {
                {"graphic",    "string",     "The image file to be displayed."},
                {"clip",     "string",     "The sound file to be played."},
        };
    return info;
    }

    public void init() {

        graphic = getParameter("graphic");
        clip = getParameter("clip");
        image = getImage(getDocumentBase(), graphic);
        sound = getAudioClip(getDocumentBase(), clip);
    }
```

The applet is passed the information from the HTML file and enters that information in an array where it can be queried by other methods, such as getParameter(). Using getParameter, the applet can use the user-provided filenames to load the image file and the sound file.

The General Design

The overall design of this applet is very simple. Once the parameters are parsed, it is only a matter of downloading the image and sound files and displaying them.

To download the files, the applet uses getImage() and getAudioClip() from the Applet Package. The image files can be either GIF or JPEG files. Because applets are capable of displaying either format with the same method, it isn't necessary to specify what type of image the files are. The same is true with the sound file. Applets only can deal with sound in the AU format right now, so dealing with file information is easy.

```
public void paint(Graphics g) {
     g.drawImage(image, 0, 0, this);
}

public void start() {
    repaint();
    sound.play();
}

public void stop() {
    sound.stop();
}
```

Summary

As you can see, it does not take a ton of Java code to make some great enhancements to your Web pages. With a few short lines of code you can add graphics and sound easily—just by linking an applet to your pages with a few lines of HTML. Now that you have an idea about the basic workings of applets, we'll move on to some more advanced topics to help you program applets with a broader range of features and functionality.

Applet Programming

The following outlines the basic tools for creating your own applets.

Chapter 22, "The Windowing Package," covers the Abstract Window Toolkit. The AWT enables you to create user interfaces for your applets and create key components such as buttons and text fields. The chapter also covers event handling and other components important in the creation of interactive applets.

Chapter 23, "The Applet Package and Graphics," discusses some of the features that are included in the Applet Package. It covers some aspects of applet control, the structure of applets, and methods included in the Applet Package.

Chapter 24, "Programming Applets," wraps up the discussion of applets with some practical examples of assembling your own applets. This chapter builds some applets from the ground up—from user interfaces to data structures.

Unfortunately, even with this comprehensive coverage, there are still many aspects of Java and applet programming that will not be covered. This section tries to cover all of the basic topics needed to get you started and enough advanced topics to get you programming robust, feature-rich applets. Java is a full-featured programming language and undoubtedly the subject of applet programming could fill an entire book on its own. Java is also in a constant state of evolution. As the language becomes more complete, changes will be made. In order to learn about all of the necessary changes, updates, and features that could not be covered here, you should consult the official Sun documentation of the Java language. Most of the API and other Java-related documentation can be found at http://www.javasoft.com. Keep in mind that the Sun documentation is quite technical and often requires an advanced understanding of Java, but as a technical reference source it can be invaluable.

The Windowing Package

22

by David Gulbransen and Kenrick Rawlings

The Abstract Window Toolkit (normally referred to as the AWT) is a well-thought-out and very portable windowing library. It is a standard part of the Java environment and provides all of the basic functionality one would expect to use in a modern windowing system.

The AWT delivers on the promise made by many cross-platform windowing libraries, allowing your application to run on completely different windowing systems. Moreover, it manages to preserve the look and feel of the user's system, so AWT-based applications won't get a reputation for having a Java look.

The bulk of the basic AWT is subclassed from one basic class: Component (see Figure 22.1).

FIGURE 22.1.

AWT Component class hierarchy.

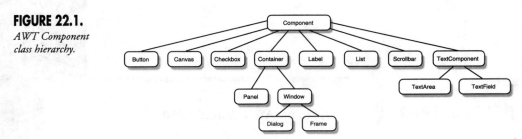

The AWT has most of the graphical components that are standard in graphical user interfaces (GUIs). Thankfully, it also is relatively easy to use standard components to derive new components for extra functionality.

This chapter covers all of the core concepts of the AWT. First, an example of a simple applet that uses the AWT is provided. Next, event handling (controlling interactions between components) is covered in detail. There is a large palette of components available, and the common ones are covered next. Finally, a complete user interface is be developed using the AWT.

A Simple AWT Applet

First, let's look at a simple AWT applet that contains a Button as shown in Listing 22.1.

Listing 22.1. A simple AWT applet

```
import java.awt.*;
import java.applet.Applet;

public class Example1 extends Applet {
    Button hiButton;

    public void init() {
        hiButton = new Button("Click Me!");
        add(hiButton);
    }
}

<applet code=Example1.class width=250 height=100></applet>
```

Figure 22.2 shows what is produced when the code is compiled and viewed in the AppletViewer.

FIGURE 22.2.

A simple AWT applet.

It is not important at this point to understand exactly what every line means. Instead, try to get a general feel for what is going on. The example is doing the following:

1. A `Button` component is created with the label, `Click Me!`
2. The `Button` is added to the container (in this case an applet).

For a program with a user interface that produces output, there is surprisingly little code here. Almost all the real work of handling the user interface is hidden behind the scenes. If you are using basic components, it's relatively easy to keep things simple. However, if you want to extend the functionality of the basic components, the complexity of your code increases.

When a component is created, it usually is added to a container. A container is simply an area of the screen in which components (and even other containers) can be placed. This can go on endlessly: A component is added to a container, which is added to another container, and so on. We will, in fact, be doing just this in the calculator example at the end of the chapter.

This flexibility is one of the biggest advantages of programming the AWT. In an object-oriented programming environment, it makes sense to think of the user interface as actual objects and concentrate on relationships between objects. This is exactly what the AWT lets you do.

> **NOTE**
>
> This chapter deals primarily with the AWT and applets. Features of the AWT are not limited to applet programming. Windowing is an important feature of applications as well. Our focus on applets enables us to take advantage of the fact that all applets are a subclass of `Panel`, which simplifies some of the concepts of programming a user interface.

Don't Panic

Programming any graphical interface can be a daunting task due to the number of things you need to keep track of. For this reason, the AWT is one of the most difficult parts of Java to master. However, as long as you keep in mind a few basic tenets from the outset, it's certainly manageable.

First, every viewable item in the AWT is subclassed from `Component`. This provides a core set of methods that work across all components (things like setting color, and so on). Always make sure what the class being used is subclassed from. Usually, the function you are looking from is a step or two up the chain.

Second, everything in the AWT is event-driven. This means that unlike many styles of programming, you do not construct your program to proceed in a linear manner, but to respond to user actions. Although this adds a level of complexity to your programs, it also makes them much more usable.

Third, components are never placed on the page in absolute positions. Java was designed from the beginning to run on many different platforms, keeping the look and feel consistent with the operating system's native environment. The size and precise shape of a button, for example, isn't known to an interface designer. Therefore, all components are placed inside containers that are relative to other components. Although this seems strange at first, it turns out to be a powerful technique, and one that will make your applications more robust.

> **NOTE**
>
> If you've done Windows or Macintosh programming before, many of the underlying concepts are very similar here, especially if you've used a class library such as OWL or MFC. The major difference is simplicity. Most concepts in the AWT are much more straightforward than in other development environments.

Event Handling

An event is a communication from the outside world to the program that something has occurred. The following are a few basic event types:

- Mouse clicks

  Generated when the mouse button is clicked while positioned over a component.

- Mouse movement

  Whenever the mouse is moved over a component, many events are sent to the component informing it what coordinates in the component the mouse has moved to.

- Action events

  When a component that an action can be performed upon is used, an `Action` event is created by default and the owner of the component (usually the container in which the component is placed) is notified that something happened.

One of the most important things to understand about the AWT is how events are handled. Without events, your application will not be able to respond to user actions.

Let's add basic event handling to the example from earlier in the chapter. (See Listing 22.2.)

Listing 22.2. Adding event handling to the sample applet.

```java
import java.awt.*;
    import java.applet.Applet;

    public class Example2 extends Applet {
        Button hiButton;

        public void init() {
            hiButton = new Button("Click Me!");
            add(hiButton);
        }

        public boolean action(Event evt, Object what) {
            if (evt.target == hiButton) {
                hiButton.setLabel("Clicked!");
                return true;
            }
            else
                return false;
        }
    }

<applet code=Example2.class width=250 height=100></applet>
```

The resulting applet is shown in Figure 22.3. All that has been changed is the addition of the `action()` method. When a component that has an action associated with it (that is, a button) is manipulated by the user, the `action()` method of that component is called.

FIGURE 22.3.

Using event handling.

In this case we are using the default `Button` instead of subclassing our own. The default event handler tries to handle the action event inside of the `Button`, but cannot find a handler that will take the event. It then passes the event up the chain of components, to the container that holds the component. It keeps doing this until it finds a handler that accepts the event or hits the top of the chain.

Let's break the `action()` method down line by line:

```java
public boolean action(Event evt, Object what) {
```

All event handlers have a form similar to this. They accept a parameter of type `Event` that provides detailed information about the event. Second, they return a Boolean value indicating True if the event was handled, or False if it was not.

```java
if (evt.target == hiButton) {
```

Here the target of the event is being checked to see whether or not it is the button. Because `evt.target` and `hiButton` are both objects, we can check to see if they are the same object.

```
hiButton.setLabel("Clicked!");
```

Because the button was clicked, we change the button to reflect that.

```
    return true;
}
else
    return false;
```

Finally, if the event was handled, return `true`, or else return `false`. This is an important concept to keep in mind: The event handler keeps searching for a method that will accept the `Event`. Accepting the `Event` is signaled by returning `true`.

Event Handling in Detail

In almost all cases, you will want to use the event-handling methods that Sun has provided for you. These are summarized in Table 22.1. Remember that everything is relative to the component. For example, the `mouseMove()` method of a component is called when the mouse is moved inside that component.

Table 22.1. Java events.

Event Type	Method
Action taken	action(Event evt, Object what)
Mouse button pressed	mouseDown(Event evt, int x, int y)
Mouse button released	mouseUp(Event evt, int x, int y)
Mouse moved	mouseMove(Event evt, int x, int y)
Mouse dragged	mouseDrag(Event evt, int x, int y)
Mouse enters component	mouseEnter(Event evt, int x, int y)
Mouse exits component	mouseExit(Event evt, int x, int y)
Key pressed	keyDown(Event evt, int key)
Key released	keyUp(Event evt, int key)

When would you want to use other methods than `action()`? The answer is that when you actually want to change the behavior of a component (as opposed to just using the component as is was originally designed) `action()` isn't quite enough. It only reports events that are essential to the utility of the component, such as a mouse click on a button.

Let's add new behavior to the previous example (see Listing 22.3 and Figure 22.4).

Listing 22.3. Adding new behavior to the sample applet.

```
import java.awt.*;
import java.applet.Applet;

public class Example3 extends Applet {
    Button hiButton;

    public void init() {
        hiButton = new Button("Click Me!!!");
        add(hiButton);
    }


    public boolean mouseEnter(Event evt, int x, int y) {
        hiButton.setLabel("Go Away!");
        return true;
    }

    public boolean mouseExit(Event evt, int x, int y) {
        hiButton.setLabel("Stay Away!");
        return true;
    }


    public boolean action(Event evt, Object what) {
        if (evt.target == hiButton) {
            hiButton.setLabel("Clicked!");
            return true;
        }
        else
            return false;
    }
}

<applet code=Example3.class width=250 height=100></applet>
```

FIGURE 22.4.

Changing the behavior of a component.

Now, whenever the mouse moves over the applet, the user is informed that perhaps clicking on the button isn't such a good idea. This is a fundamentally different behavior than the previous example. Before, we were using a button in a completely standard manner. Here, we wished to change that functionality. This is important to remember—otherwise, you might end up subclassing components where you don't need to, making your program slower and more difficult to understand and maintain.

handleEvent() or action()

Generally, a combination of action() and the other built-in event handlers will do the job nicely. For those times when you want to take complete control of the process yourself, handleEvent() is available.

handleEvent() has advantages and disadvantages. On the positive side, you have complete control. On the negative side, you have complete control. This means that you must be very careful overriding the default handleEvent() or your application can become buggy and confusing very quickly.

For example, let's say you overrode handleEvent() in your class for whatever reason, but you had used mouseEnter() earlier in the development of the program, as shown in the following:

```
class MyLabel extends Label {
    MyLabel(String label) {
        super(label);
    }

    public boolean mouseEnter(Event evt, int x, int y) {
        setText("Not Again");
    }

    public boolean handleEvent(Event evt) {
        if (Event.id == KEY_PRESS) {
            setText("Keypress");
            return true;
        } else return false;
    }
}
```

You would expect the mouseEnter() you had written to keep working. Unfortunately that's not the case. Because the default handleEvent() has been overridden, mouseEnter() never gets called. Luckily there is an easy solution to this problem for many cases. Add the following to your handleEvent() in place of return false;:

```
return super.handleEvent(evt);
```

This has the benefit of keeping all of the functionality of the old handleEvent() while letting you manipulate things first. Note, however, that you can also override handleEvent() to remove functionality, in which case you wouldn't want to call the parent's handleEvent(). It's all up to you.

Delivering Events

Occasionally the ability of the program to manufacture its own events comes in quite handy. Although it may seem strange to fake an event, in reality it makes the design of a program much simpler.

For example, if you were designing a calculator you might decide to write an event handler in the main container that deciphers the action events from the button, as follows:

```
public boolean action(Event evt, obj What) {
    if (evt.target == oneKey)
    ...        // Append 1 to the current number
    }
    ...
}
```

However, it might make sense to add the ability to handle keyboard input, because a user of the calculator would expect that functionality from a calculator. Although you could just copy the code from the `action()` handler to a new `keyDown()` handler, you would then have two copies of the same code in the same program to maintain and keep track of. The solution is to deliver your own event. A simple event can be created with the following form:

```
Event aEvent = new Event(target, id, obj);
```

Where target is the `Object` that you would like the event delivered to, id is an integer representing the event type (see Table 22.2), and `obj` is an arbitrary argument to append to the event if there is extra information that you would like the handler to receive.

Then, to deliver the event, you just need to call `deliverEvent()` as follows:

```
deliverEvent(aEvent);
```

So, in the previous example, you could add another handler that does the following:

```
public boolean keyDown(Event evt, int key) {
    if (key == 49) {            // If the 1 key was pressed
        deliverEvent(new Event(oneKey,Event.MOUSE_DOWN, null));
        return true;
    }
    ...
}
```

Now you can manage the rest of the program without worrying about handling keyboard input differently—the same event is generated whether the button is clicked or the corresponding key is pressed. Table 22.2 shows the event types available in the AWT.

Table 22.2. AWT event types.

Event type	*Event ID's*
The Action event	ACTION_EVENT
Mouse button pressed	MOUSE_DOWN
Mouse dragged	MOUSE_DRAG
Mouse entered	MOUSE_ENTER

continues

Table 22.2. continued

Event type	Event ID's
Mouse exited	MOUSE_EXIT
Mouse button released	MOUSE_UP
Mouse moved	MOUSE_MOVE
Key pressed	KEY_PRESS
Key released	KEY_RELEASE

Dealing with Focus

When a user clicks a user interface component, that item becomes in a sense "selected." This is as known as the *input focus*. For instance, when a text field is clicked on, the user then can type in the field because it has the input focus.

When a component receives the input focus, the gotFocus() method of that component is called, as follows:

```
public boolean gotFocus(Event evt, Object what) {
    ...
}
```

When a component loses the input focus, the lostFocus() method of that component is called, as follows:

```
public boolean lostFocus(Event evt, Object what) {
    ...
}
```

It is not uncommon for a program to desire to keep the focus. For example, if a text-entry field was being used to display output rather than to accept input, you probably would not want it to be able to receive the focus. Using a text-entry field to display output enables you to take advantage of the field's text-handling abilities. In that case, the requestFocus() method exists, as shown in the following:

```
public void requestFocus() {
    ...
}
```

This could be placed in the container that the text field has been used in and would bar that field from receiving the focus.

Components

Components are the building blocks from which all programs using the AWT are built. There are many other classes to handle the components and the interactions between them, but if it's on the screen, it's a component.

This enables us to say a number of things about all components:

- All components have a screen position and a size
- All components have a foreground and background color
- Components are either enabled or disabled
- There is a standard interface for components to handle events

AWT components can be conceptually broken down into three major categories:

Interface components

Interface components encompass all of the standard widgets or controls normally associated with a windowing system. Examples of these include buttons, text labels, scrollbars, pick lists, and text-entry fields.

Containers

Containers encompass areas in which components can be placed. This allows groups of components to be grouped together to form a more cohesive object to be manipulated. A `Panel` is an example of this type of component.

Windows

Windows are a very special case of the `Component` class. All other components are added onto a container that already exists, whereas a `Window` is an actual, separate window with a completely new area to create an interface upon. Normally with applet programming, windows are not used. `Dialogs` and `Frames` are examples of this type of component.

Interface Components

Interface components are components specifically designed to give information to, or get information from, the user.

Button

A `Button` is a standard clickable button. (See Figure 22.5.) It can be customized to either have a text label or be blank. Buttons can be used for myriad uses in an applet—whenever there needs to be confirmation from the user that they are ready to move on, a `Button` is the obvious choice.

FIGURE 22.5.

The Button *component.*

Location:

`java.awt.Button`

Constructors:

`Button()`

Creates a `Button` with no label.

`Button(String lbl)`

Creates a `Button` with the label `lbl`.

Core component-specific methods:

`String getLabel()`

Returns the label of the `Button`.

`void setLabel(String lbl)`

Sets the label of the `Button` to `lbl`.

Action:

`Sends an action event when pressed.`

Example:

`Button aButton = new Button("Ok");`

Canvas

A `Canvas` is a completely generic component. It is provided as a foundation to subclass interesting graphics components. Canvases are not very useful for beginning- or intermediate-level Java programs, but extremely useful if you need to create your own component from the ground up.

Location:

`java.awt.Canvas`

Constructors:

`Canvas()`

Creates a `Canvas`.

Core component-specific methods:

```
void paint(Graphics g)
```

Paints the Canvas in the default background color.

Action:

```
None by default.
```

Example:

```
Canvas aCanvas = new Canvas();
```

Checkbox

A Checkbox is a small box with an optional label that the user can either click on or off (see Figure 22.6). This can be useful if you have an applet that has a variety of attributes that the user can set at once. Moreover, more than one Checkbox can be grouped together within a CheckboxGroup to allow only one attribute to be set at a time.

FIGURE 22.6.

The Checkbox *component.*

Location:

```
java.awt.Checkbox
```

Constructors:

```
Checkbox()
```

Creates a blank Checkbox set to false.

```
Checkbox(String lbl)
```

Creates a Checkbox set to false with the label lbl.

```
Checkbox(String lbl, CheckboxGroup group, boolean state)
```

Creates a Checkbox set to state with the label lbl, contained in group CheckboxGroup.

Core component-specific methods:

```
String getLabel()
```

Returns the label of the Checkbox.

```
String setLabel(String lbl)
```

Sets the label of the Checkbox to lbl.

```
boolean getState()
```

Returns the state of the Checkbox.

```
void setState(boolean st)
```

Sets the state of the Checkbox to st.

```
CheckboxGroup getCheckboxGroup()
```

Returns the CheckboxGroup that the Checkbox belongs to, if any.

```
void setCheckboxGroup(CheckboxGroup g)
```

Sets the CheckboxGroup of the Checkbox to g.

Action:

Sends an action event when the state changes.

Example:

```
Checkbox aBox = new Checkbox("Show");
```

Label

A Label is simply a piece of text that can be placed on a component (see Figure 22.7). Although a Label doesn't do much, it can be quite useful to add text to an applet to clarify its functionality.

FIGURE 22.7.

The Label *component.*

Location:

```
java.lang.Label
```

Constructors:

```
Label()
```

Creates an empty Label.

```
Label(String lbl)
```

Creates a Label with the text set to lbl.

```
Label(String lbl, int align)
```

Creates a Label with the text set to lbl and the alignment of the text set to one of the following:

Label.LEFT	Left alignment
Label.CENTER	Center alignment
Label.RIGHT	Right alignment

Core component-specific methods:

```
int getAlignment()
```

Returns the alignment of the `Label`.

```
void setAlignment(int align)
```

Sets the alignment of the `Label` to align.

```
String getText()
```

Returns the text of the `Label`.

```
void setText(String lbl)
```

Sets the text of the `Label` to lbl.

Action:

None, by default.

Example:

```
Label aLabel = new Label("Hello!");
```

List

A `List` is a scrollable list of text items that a user can choose from (see Figure 22.8). This can be useful in circumstances where the applet you are creating can do multiple things. For instance, if you were writing a loan calculator, you might have a `List` that contained different loan lengths (12 month, 36 month, and so on). A `List` can allow one selection at a time or multiple selections.

FIGURE 22.8.

The List *component.*

Constructors:

```
List()
```

Creates a new `List` with no visible lines, disallowing multiple selections.

```
List(int vlines, boolean scr)
```

Creates a new scrolling list with the number of visible lines set to vlines and also set to allow multiple selections based upon the Boolean scr.

Core component-specific methods:

```
void addItem(String item)
```

Add item at end of the List.

```
void addItem(String item, int index)
```

Add item at position index.

```
void clear()
```

Clears the List.

```
int countItems()
```

Returns the number of items currently in the List.

```
void delItem(int index)
```

Deletes item at index.

```
String getItem(int index)
```

Returns the item at index.

```
void replaceItem(String new_item, int index)
```

Replace item at index with new_item.

Example:

```
List aList = new List();
aList.addItem("First");
aList.addItem("Second");
```

Scrollbar

A Scrollbar is a slideable bar that can be used for a variety of uses (see Figure 22.9). A Scrollbar is often used when it would be useful to enable the user to move quickly over a large area by sliding the scrollbar up and down. They can also be used to allow a proportional way to set a value. Additionally, a scrollbar can be oriented either horizontally or vertically.

FIGURE 22.9.

The Scrollbar
component.

Constructors:

```
Scrollbar()
```

Creates a Scrollbar oriented vertically.

```
Scrollbar(int orn)
```

Creates a Scrollbar oriented to orn, which can be one of the following:

```
Scrollbar.HORIZONTAL
Scrollbar.VERTICAL
```

```
Scrollbar(int orn, int val, int vis, int min, int max)
```

Creates a Scrollbar with orientation orn, default value val, page size vis, minimum value min, and maximum value max.

Core Component-specific methods:

```
int getOrientation()
```

Returns the orientation of the Scrollbar.

```
setValue(int val)
```

Sets the value of the Scrollbar to val.

```
int getMinimum()
```

Returns the minimum value of the Scrollbar.

```
int getMaximum()
```

Returns the maximum value of the Scrollbar.

```
int getVisible()
```

Returns the visible amount (page size) of the Scrollbar.

```
void setValue(int value)
```

Sets the value of the Scrollbar to val.

Example:

```
ScrollBar aScrollbar = new Scrollbar(Scrollbar.HORIZONTAL);
```

TextField

A TextField is a component that lets the user enter a single line of text (see Figure 22.10). This should be sufficient for almost all data entry that applets will need. Although the name implies that this component is oriented towards text, remember that numbers are text as well and a TextField does a wonderful job for entering numerical data.

FIGURE 22.10.

The TextField
component.

Constructors:

```
public TextField()
```

Creates a `TextField`.

```
public TextField(int cols)
```

Creates a `TextField` with `cols` number of columns.

```
public TextField(String txt)
```

Creates a `TextField` set to the string `txt`.

```
public TextField(String txt, int cols)
```

Creates a `TextField` set to `txt` with `cols` number of columns.

Core component-specific methods:

```
int getColumns()
```

Returns the number of columns in the `TextField`.

```
String getText()
```

Returns the text contained in this `TextField`.

```
void setText(String txt)
```

Sets the text of the `TextField` to `txt`.

Example:

```
TextField aTextField = new TextField("37", 5);
```

TextArea

A `TextArea` is a text-editing component that is much like a `TextField` except that it allows multiple lines (see Figure 22.11). It is mainly useful for things such as comment fields or any other application that needs the user to manipulate a significant amount of text.

FIGURE 22.11.

The TextArea *component.*

Constructors:

```
TextArea()
```

Creates a `TextArea`.

`TextArea(int rw, int cl)`

Creates a `TextArea` with `rw` number of rows and `cl` number of columns.

`TextArea(String txt)`

Creates a `TextArea` with the text set to `txt`.

`TextArea(String text, int rw, int cl)`

Creates a `TextArea` set with text set to `txt`, with `rw` number of rows and `cl` number of columns.

Core component-specific methods:

`int getColumns()`

Returns the number of columns in the `TextField`.

`int getRows()`

Returns the number of rows in the `TextField`.

`String getText()`

Returns the text contained in this `TextComponent`.

`void setText(String txt)`

Sets the text of the `TextField` to `txt`.

Example:

`TextArea aTextArea = new TextArea("Ok", 5, 40);`

Component Example

Earlier it was mentioned that straightforwardness was one of the hallmarks of the design of the AWT. Here's a good example of that straightforwardness: an applet that contains all of the components just covered—except `Canvas`, which by default has no real visual representation. (See Figure 22.12.) The source is provided in Listing 22.4.

Listing 22.4. Adding many components to an applet.

```
import java.awt.*;
import java.applet.Applet;
public class ManyComp extends Applet {
    Button aButton;
    Canvas aCanvas;
    Checkbox aBox;
    Label aLabel;
    List aList;
```

continues

Listing 22.4. continued

```
        Scrollbar aScrollbar;
        TextField aTextField;
        TextArea aTextArea;
        public void init() {
                aButton = new Button("Ok");
                aCanvas = new Canvas();
                aBox = new Checkbox("Show");
                aLabel = new Label("Hello!");
                aList = new List();
                aScrollbar = new Scrollbar(Scrollbar.HORIZONTAL);
                aTextField = new TextField("37", 5);
                aTextArea = new TextArea("Ok", 5, 40);
                aList.addItem("First");
                aList.addItem("Second");
                 add(aButton);
                add(aCanvas);
                add(aBox);
                add(aLabel);
                add(aList);
                add(aScrollbar);
                add(aTextField);
                add(aTextArea);
        }

    }
<applet code=ManyComp.class width=250 height=600></applet>
```

FIGURE 22.12.

An example applet with many components.

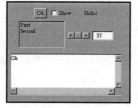

Containers

Containers are simply components that can contain other components. They are themselves components and can thus contain other containers. Think of them as a way to subdivide an area to construct the user interface into plots into which components can be placed, or even subdivided further.

There are two general types of containers: Panels and Windows. The major difference between them is that a Panel is a defined area on a window that already exists, whereas a Window is an entirely new window (see the next section). Also, the Applet class is a subclass of Panel, so an Applet can be treated just like a Panel. (See Figure 22.13.)

Let's look at an example:

```
import java.awt.*;
    import java.applet.Applet;
```

```
public class Example4 extends Applet {
    Button button1, button2;
    public void init() {
        button1 = new Button("First");
            add(button1);
        button2 = new Button("Second");
        add(button2);
    }
}
```

```
<applet code=Example4.class width=250 height=100></applet>
```

FIGURE 22.13.

Using containers.

After the component is created, all that needs to be done is to call the `add()` method for the container with the specified component. If your interface is quite simple, adding components to a container in this manner might be enough. However, if you desire to have some control over the placement of the components a Layout can be used.

Layouts

A Layout can be thought of as a template that is placed over a container to define how components will be added. The most common layout is BorderLayout(), which orients components according to compass points, except center which gets the space left over. All the layouts are listed in Table 22.3.

Table 22.3. Standard AWT layouts.

Layout Name	Function
BorderLayout	Layout according to compass points
GridLayout	Layout on a grid
GridBagLayout	Layout on a grid where elements can be different sizes
CardLayout	Layout that contains a series of "cards" that can be flipped through
FlowLayout	Layout that arranges components left to right

The Layout of a Panel is established with the setLayout() method and then new components are added using the add() method with an argument indicating placement before the component to be added, which can be one of "North," "South," "East," "West," or "Center," demonstrated in Listing 22.5. (See Figure 22.14.)

Listing 22.5. Using `layouts`.

```java
import java.awt.*;
    import java.applet.Applet;

    public class Example5 extends Applet {
        Button button1, button2;

        public void init() {
            setLayout(new BorderLayout());
            button1 = new Button("First");
            add("North", button1);
            button2 = new Button("Second");
            add("South", button2);
        }
    }

<applet code=Example5.class width=250 height=100></applet>
```

FIGURE 22.14.

Adding a Layout *to an applet*

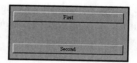

Frames and Windows

A `Window` is a special kind of container: A completely separate window from the base is constructed when one is created. A `Frame` is a subclass of `Window` that allows menus to be added to the window. See Listing 22.6 and Figure 22.15.

Listing 22.6. An applet that brings up a `Window`.

```java
import java.awt.*;
import java.applet.Applet;

public class FrameExample extends Applet {
    Frame aFrame;

    public void init() {
        aFrame = new Frame("Example Frame");
        aFrame.show();
    }
}

<applet code=FrameExample.class width=250 height=100></applet>
```

When the `Frame` is created it is by default invisible. It is a good idea to resize it to the desired shape first with `resize()`, add the desired components (if any), then call the `show()` method of the `Frame`, which displays the `Frame`.

FIGURE 22.15.
Adding a Window *to an applet.*

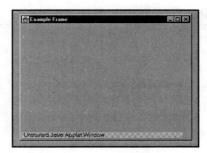

Common Methods of All Components

The bulk of the AWT is subclassed from the Component class. Thankfully, the Component class contains a great deal of functionality that is available to all of the subclassed components.

Sizing and Moving

Unfortunately, the AWT currently does not include the concept of machine-independent sizing, so it is not possible to specify movement or sizing in real world measurements (inches, centimeters, and so on). In current implementations of Java you can expect the coordinates used to correspond to machine pixels.

To change the size of a component, use the resize() method:

```
void resize(int width, int height)
```

To move the component use the move() method:

```
void move(int x, int y)
```

Foreground and Background Color

Color in Java is abstracted into the Color class, which has a number of static variables to represent color (see Table 22.4), along with the ability to specify an arbitrary color with an instance of the Color object, as follows:

```
Color aColor = new Color(int r, int g, int b)
```

r, g, and b, are the red, green, and blue components specified in a 24-bit palette.

TIP

Remember that static variables do not require an instance of the class to use them, so the color black can be generated just by using Color.black.

Table 22.4. Standard Java color variables.

black
blue
cyan
darkGray
gray
green
lightGray
magenta
orange
pink
red
white
yellow

The foreground color of a component can be set with the `setForeground` method, as follows:

```
setForeground(Color.green)
```

The background color can be set with the `setBackground` method, as follows:

```
void setBackground(Color.black)
```

Disabling and Enabling

A component can effectively be turned on or turned off by setting it enabled or disabled. To disable a component, use the enable method as follows:

```
enable()
```

To enable the component, use the disable method as follows:

```
disable()
```

Designing a User Interface

Suppose we wanted to create simple calculator applet. It would make sense to build the user interface first, then add functionality step by step. Thus, let's start with the main `Applet`. A calculator would definitely require a display, so let's add that first, as follows:

```
import java.awt.*;
import java.applet.Applet;
```

```
public class Calculator extends Applet {
    Label display;

    public void init() {
        setLayout(new BorderLayout());
        display = new Label("0", 10);
        add("North", display);
    }
}
```

A `BorderLayout` makes sense here because the display will always be at the top of the screen. Adding the keyboard is a bit trickier. There will need to be 10 number buttons and 4 operation keys grouped together. This calls for a few more panels with the appropriate keys added. This is implemented in Listing 22.7.

Listing 22.7. A prototype for an interface for a calculator.

```
public class Calculator extends Applet {
    Label display;
    Panel bottom;
    Panel num_panel;
    Panel func_panel;
    Button number[] = new Button[10];
    Button function[] = new Button[6];

    public void init() {
        setLayout(new BorderLayout());
        display = new Label("0", Label.RIGHT);
        add("North", display);

        bottom = new Panel();
        bottom.setLayout(new BorderLayout());

        num_panel = new Panel();
        num_panel.setLayout(new GridLayout(4,3));

        for (int x=9; x>=0; x--) {
            number[x] = new Button((new String()).valueOf(x));
            num_panel.add(number[x]);
        }

        function[4] = new Button(".");
        num_panel.add(function[4]);

        function[5] = new Button("=");
        num_panel.add(function[5]);

        bottom.add("Center", num_panel);

        func_panel = new Panel();
        func_panel.setLayout(new GridLayout(4,1));

        function[0] = new Button("+");
```

continues

Listing 22.7. continued

```
          function[1] = new Button("-");
          function[2] = new Button("*");
          function[3] = new Button("/");

          for (int x=0; x<4; x++)
              func_panel.add(function[x]);

          bottom.add("East", func_panel);

          add("Center", bottom);
      }
  }

<applet code=Calculator.class width=135 height=140></applet>
```

Figure 22.16 shows the applet. The original panel has been subdivided twice. At the top of the applet is the label for the display; below that is a panel for all of the keys. However, this panel must be again subdivided to group the number and function keys separately. Thus, a number panel and a function panel are added.

FIGURE 22.16.

A calculator user interface.

Because the lower panels contain keys, it makes sense to use a layout that is conducive to this. The GridLayout fits the purpose perfectly: It allows a grid to be specified and then components are added left to right and top to bottom until it is full.

The function panel then is added to the "East" (right) side of the lower panel, leaving the rest of the space to the number keys. The number keys are specified to be "Center," and thus use up all of the space remaining in the panel.

This provides a mock-up of how the final calculator will work and gives an idea of user-interface considerations that need to be considered and also design decisions that are integral to the whole applet. For example, should all of the processing be contained in the main applet class, or should the panels become separate classes to isolate functionality and promote code reuse? These and other issues will be discussed in Chapter 24, "Programming Applets," where the calculator applet is completed.

Summary

In this chapter the most important topics of the AWT have been covered. The two most important things to remember are components and events. First, all user interface items (Button, Checkbox, and so on) are called components and are subclassed from the Component class. This gives a core set of functionality to all interface components in the AWT.

Second, when the user interacts with a component in the AWT, an Event is generated and is sent to that component. Think of an Event as the language the AWT uses to communicate.

The AWT is certainly a complex topic, and building user interfaces in it is not trivial. However, because it leverages Java's strong support for object-oriented programming, it is certainly manageable.

The Applet Package and Graphics

V

Applet Package consists of several interfaces and the Applet class. (See Table 23.1.) The
ods found in this class are used to construct applets and to provide basic functionality
as image and audio manipulation.

e 23.1. The Applet Package.

terfaces	AppletContext
	AppletStub
	AudioClip
lass	Applet

AppletContext interface contains methods to access an applet's environment, such as chang-
ie URL displayed by the browser.

etStub is an interface that contains methods used to write an applet viewer, such as the
etViewer provided by Sun in the Java Development Kit. Because these methods are nec-
y for interpreting applets, this interface is not used by applet programmers for creating the
ts themselves.

Clip contains methods for manipulating audio from within your applets. Although the
Clip interface is currently limited, it does offer basic sound capabilities. Future versions
a undoubtedly will expand on the basic functionality of this interface.

Graphics() class is a subclass of the AWT, and it contains the graphics methods. The
ods found here can be used to create graphics primitives and perform simple graphics
pulations. This chapter only touches briefly on the Graphics class. Chapter 25,
nation Programming," will address some of the more advanced things you can do with
raphics() methods.

OTE

hen programming graphics, most complex images can actually be broken down into
aller components known as *primitives*. These simple graphics building blocks such as
oint, line, rectangle, oval, and polygon can be used in conjunction with each other
create more detailed shapes or images.

aracteristics of Applets

ted in the overview, applets have limited functionality compared to full applications. For
ple, applets viewed on the web cannot do the following:

- Access files from the local file system
- Access network hosts other than their base host

However, you still can use applets to create a variety of programs and enhance Web services. Keep in mind that for their limitations, applets do offer some advantages over applications. Because applets are executed within the AppletViewer or a Java-capable Web browser, some advanced features such as audio and image processing are utilized from the browser. This makes creating functional, visually interesting applets even easier.

The most important aspect of applets stems from the object-oriented nature of Java. Applets are objects. They are subclassed from the `Panel` object, which is in turn subclassed from `Container`. All of this subclassing has some advantages. Methods are passed down from one class to the next, and that means that you have a wide variety of methods available to you when programming your applets.

> **TIP**
>
> Keep Java's object-oriented nature in mind when consulting the API documentation. If you are searching for a particular method for an object and are unable to find it, be sure to search up the class hierarchy. Because objects inherit the methods of classes they are subclassed from, if you travel up the hierarchy, you are apt to find the method you are looking for.

Applet Lifecycles

Applets have four lifecycle methods: `init()`, `start()`, `stop()`, and `destroy()`. These lifestyle methods can be used to control an applet at various stages of execution, and are called automatically. You can override any of these methods to perform specific tasks during execution, but it is not necessary to declare any of these methods.

init()

`init()` is the first method called by an applet once it has been loaded by the AppletViewer or browser. Because it is called before the applet begins execution, it can be overridden to perform any initialization tasks, such as loading images, establishing the layout, or parsing parameter information. For example,

```
public void init() {

    clip = getAudioClip(getDocumentBase(), soundfile.au);

    setLayout(new FlowLayout());
```

```
    play = new Button("Play Clip");
    add(play);

}
```

will load a specified audio file and create a layout with the button Play Clip. By loading any necessary files before the applet starts, you can avoid conflicts such as the applet trying to display an image that is not yet loaded.

start()

When an applet has been loaded into the AppletViewer or browser, start() is called automatically to begin the actual execution of the applet. Start() generally will contain the core of an applet. For example, the following code plays an audio file (clip).

```
public void start() {

    clip.play();
}
```

stop()

stop() is similar to start(). It is called automatically when an applet should stop execution—for example, when you leave an applet's web page. stop() could be used to stop a sound file that is playing in a loop, or to stop any threads that might be executing.

```
public void stop() {

    clip.stop();
}
```

destroy()

destroy() is called when an applet has completely finished executing, and any resources allocated by the applet need to be returned to the system. Because Java takes care of garbage collection and memory allocation, it generally is not necessary to override destroy().

Leveraging the Browser

Because applets are executed within the environment of the AppletViewer or a Java-capable browser, applets can use some functions of the browser to their advantage. For example, applets use an HTML tag to specify parameters and pass information about the applet's location. Applets also can use a browser's capability to display images.

Locating Files

The HTML tag `<applet>` is used to place an applet on a web page or to invoke the AppletViewer. The applet, therefore, has a code base, and a document base.

The code base is the base URL of an applet itself, and the document base is the base URL of the HTML file that contains the applet. You can use the methods `getCodeBase` and `getDocumentBase` to obtain the base URLs to be used when loading image files or audio files. For example:

```
image = getImage(getDocumentBase(), graphic);
```

will use the base URL of the applet HTML file to load image files.

Images

One of the biggest advantages applets gain by utilizing the browser is the ability to display images using the browser's image decoder. This means that you can take advantage of GIF and JPEG file formats within your applets without writing any special code.

The two primary methods used in conjunction with images are `getImage()` and `drawImage()`. The method `getImage(URL, string)` will accept a URL and a filename, and use that information to load a graphic file from the applet's host machine into memory. For example,

```
image = getImage(getDocumentBase(), "Me.gif");
```

will load the file `Me.gif` from the host specified by the `getDocumentBase()` method. That image then can be used at will by the applet.

In order to view the image on the screen, it is necessary to use the method `drawImage()`, which is actually a part of the `Graphics` class in the AWT.

```
//Draw an image on screen

import java.awt.*;
import java.applet.*;
import java.net.URL;

public class Pict extends java.applet.Applet {

    Image image;

    public void init() {
        image = getImage(getDocumentBase(), "me.gif");
    }

    public void paint(Graphics g) {
        g.drawImage(image, 0, 0, this);
    }
```

```
    public void start() {
        repaint();
    }
}
```

In the preceding example, the applet follows some simple guidelines:

- The image is loaded during Init() using the getImage() method.

  This helps to make sure that the image has at least started to load before it is drawn. Later we will discuss a method to ensure that images are loaded before being drawn.

- The paint() method is overridden to utilize drawImage. When repaint() is called in Start, the update() method is automatically called, which in turn calls paint().

  The result is your image on screen. Keep in mind that images have a high overhead. If your applet uses more than a few images, you might want to make sure that all of the images are loaded properly before executing the rest of the code. Loading the images during init() is a good start, but might not always be sufficient. For example, if we were to write a slide show applet that cycled through a series of images, it would be best to ensure that all of the images were loaded properly before beginning the slide show. Thankfully, there is a utility class designed for just such a purpose: MediaTracker.

Using MediaTracker

The MediaTracker class enables you to establish a media tracking object that can monitor the status of loading images and inform your applet when the task is complete. Let's take a look at the code necessary to utilize the MediaTracker class.

```
MediaTracker LoadImages;
Image slides[];
int images;

public void init() {
    for (int i = 0; i < images; i++) {
        slides[i] = getImage(getDocumentBase(), imagefile + i + "." + type);
            if (i > 0)
                LoadImages.addImage(slides[i], 1);
            else
                LoadImages.addImage(slides[i], 0);
    }

    try {
        LoadImages.waitForID(0);
    } catch (InterruptedException e) {
        System.out.println("Image Loading Failed!");
    }

    showStatus(imagefile + " Images Loaded");
    index = 0;
    repaint();
    LoadImages.checkID(1,true);
}
```

In the preceding code, we create a media tracking object called `LoadImages` which will be responsible for tracking the loading of our images. We've created an array, `slides[]`, to store the images that are loaded, and created an `int` variable `images` to represent the total number of images. The next step is to use our media tracking object in conjunction with `getImage()` to load our slides. We use the `MediaTracker` method `addImage()` to add each image to the list of images being tracked, and then we use `checkID()` with the true boolean to make sure that the images are loaded before proceeding.

Using `MediaTracker` to help you monitor status can be a safeguard for your applets. If you have an image-based animation, or some other graphics-intensive applet, it might be wise to use `MediaTracker`. As the name implies, `MediaTracker` is designed to be used with any media—graphics, audio, and so on. However, the current implementation of `MediaTracker` only supports images.

Audio

The Applet Package also contains methods for working with audio files. (See Table 23.2.)

Table 23.2. Audio methods.

`getAudioClip()`
`play()`
`loop()`
`stop()`

The `getAudioClip()` method can be found in `java.applet.Applet` and is used in the same manner as `getImage()`. The remaining audio methods are contained in the `AudioClip` interface and exist to manipulate the file itself. These functions include the following:

`play()`	Play an audio file until the end of the file.
`loop()`	Play an audio file until the end, and repeat.
`stop()`	Stop playing a sound file.

Loading and playing an audio file operates much like loading and playing images, as shown in the following:

```
import java.applet.*;
import java.lang.*;
import java.net.URL;

public class PlaySound extends Applet {

    AudioClip sound;

    public void init() {
```

```
        sound = getAudioClip(getDocumentBase(), "hi.au");
    }

    public void start() {
    sound.play();
    }
}
```

Audio Limitations

Unfortunately, the methods currently provided for audio are quite limited. The audio methods currently only support .au format sound files. Additionally, the methods provided aren't very robust. You only can play a sound file. There is no way to pause the file or clip a sound file. The lack of audio context methods means that your applets only can incorporate limited audio features, but the AudioClip interface is certainly an area that will be slated for improvement in future releases of the JDK.

Applet Contexts

The AppletContext interface contains methods that are useful for manipulating an applet's environment. These methods allow the applet to exchange information with the browser to update web pages and to communicate applet status to the browser. The Applet Package contains the method getAppletContext(), which allows the applet to obtain information about its environment, the AppletViewer, or a Web browser. This context information can then be used by the applet to the environment.

Using showDocument()

Applets can be used to manipulate the browser itself. For example, an applet could function as an animated button on a Web page. An applet also could serve as a dynamic image map, providing users with instant status updates about the URLs contained in the map. In order to do that, an applet needs to be able to issue instructions to the browser. One of those instructions is showDocument(). The showDocument() method can be used to send the browser to a new URL. It is evoked in the following manner:

```
try {
    getAppletContext().showDocument(new URL(url));
} catch (java.net.MalformedURLException e) {
    System.out.println("URL Unreachable");
}
```

This line of code obtains information about the environment that the applet running in and instructs that environment to go to another URL. Because of the nature of showDocument(), it is important to monitor for errors. The try and catch syntax is very important when using showDocument(). Because the method causes the browser to search over the Net for a URL, the success of this method depends on the availability of the given URL. Should the browser not be able to reach the specified URL, your applet needs to be instructed to catch any errors that might be generated.

Using `showStatus()`

Often, an applet will want to communicate the status of an operation to the user. This can be accomplished with the `showStatus()` method. For example, when we looked at loading images using `MediaTracker`, the code contained the following line:

```
showStatus(imagefile + " Images Loaded");
```

This line of code called the `showStatus()` method to report when the images were finished loading. When an applet engages in tasks that might take a long time, `showStatus()` can be used to keep users informed of an applet's progress. This can be advantageous when troubleshooting, and adds a level of user friendliness to your applets.

Getting Parameters

One of the most important aspects of the HTML files that evoke Java applets is the `<param>` tag. The parameter tag allows the applet user to specify the value of variables that will be passed to the applet. When your applet loads images or sound files, using parameters to pass the filenames to the applet can make your applet more flexible. Parameters also can be used to change the functionality of your applet. For example, the amount of delay between images in the `SlideShow` applet is defined by a parameter. The format for specifying parameters in an HTML files is as follows:

```
<HTML>
<applet code="SlideShow.class"  width=400 height=250>
<param name="caption" value="A Sample Photo Album">
</applet>
</HTML>
```

`name` specifies the parameter name and `value` specifies the parameter value passed to the applet. Parameters are established with the `getParameterInfo()` method. This method establishes an array containing an applet's parameters and an information string that describes each parameter's function. Let's add the capability to accept parameters to our `SlideShow` example:

```
public class SlideShow extends Applet implements Runnable {

    String imagefile, soundfile, type, caption;
    int images, delay;

    public String[][] getParameterInfo() {
        String[][] info = {
            {"caption", "string", "Title of the Slide Viewer"},
            {"imagefile", "string", "Base Image File Name (ex. picture)"},
                {"soundfile", "string", "Sound File Name (ex. audio.au)"},
                    {"images", "int", "Total number of image files"},
                    {"delay", "int", "Delay in between images (in ms.)"},
                    {"type", "string", "Image File Type(gif, jpg, etc)"},
```

```
    };
    return info;
}

public void init() {

caption   = getParameter("caption");
imagefile = getParameter("imagefile");
soundfile = getParameter("soundfile");
type      = getParameter("type");
images    = Integer.valueOf(getParameter("images")).intValue();
delay     = Integer.valueOf(getParameter("delay")).intValue();
}
}
```

For example, in the code above, the line

```
{"caption", "string", "Title of the Slide Viewer"},
```

establishes the caption parameter, which is a string that represents the title of the SlideShow. Once parameters have been defined, they can be accessed using the getParameter() method. This method is used to obtain the value of a parameter and assign it to a variable within your applet. In the case of the SlideShow, parameters are used to specify the base imagefile name, the soundfile name, the number of images, the title of the viewer, and the delay between slides for the automatic slideshow option.

Graphics

One of Java's primary attractions is the ability to spice up Web pages. What is a better way to spice up Web pages than animation and interaction? Before we can cover animation in Chapter 25 it is necessary to cover some basics concerning graphics in Java.

NOTE

The Graphics() methods are actually a part of the Abstract Windows Toolkit. However, because the AWT's scope is so broad, we've broken the AWT up to make it a little more manageable. Keep in mind that graphics are listed under the AWT when consulting the API.

Java contains a number of graphics primitives that can enable you to begin creating basic shapes and minimal on-screen graphics quite quickly. Table 23.3 is a summary of some of the more useful Graphics methods. Keep in mind that these methods must be called within a graphics context. Java needs to be made aware of the graphics object you are manipulating in order to draw an on-screen graphic. For example

```
//Draw a Line

import java.awt.*;
```

```
import java.applet.*;

public class Line extends java.applet.Applet {

    public void paint(Graphics g) {
        g.drawLine(50,50,100,150);
    }

    public void start() {
        repaint();
    }
}
```

produces the following output shown in Figure 23.1.

FIGURE 23.1.

A line drawn using the
`drawLine()` *method.*

Here, the `drawLine()` method is used to draw a line between the points x1,y1 and x2,y2. The `drawLine()` method is evoked with the following line:

`g.drawLine(50,50,100,150);`

This line specifies the default graphics context (graphics object g), and a line from the point (50,50) to (100,150).

Table 23.3. A summary of Graphics contexts.

Method	Result
`Graphics()`	Constructs a new `Graphics` object.
`create()`	Creates a new `Graphics` object.
`dispose()`	Disposes of the current graphics context.
`clearRect()`	Clears the specified rectangle using the current background color.
`clipRect()`	Clips to a rectangle.
`drawLine()`	Draws a line between two points (x1,y1) and (x2,y2).
`drawRect()`	Draws a rectangle using the current color.

continues

Table 23.3. continued

Method	Result
drawRoundRect()	Draws a rounded corner rectangle using the current color.
draw3DRect()	Draws a 3-D rectangle.
drawOval()	Draws an oval using the current color.
drawPolygon()	Draws a polygon using an array of x points and y points.
drawString()	Draws a string using the current font and color.
fillRect()	Fills a rectangle using the current color.
fillRoundRect()	Draws a filled rounded rectangle.
fill3DRect()	Paints a 3-D rectangle filled with the current color.
fillOval()	Fills an oval using the current color.
fillPolygon()	Fills a polygon with the current color.
getColor()	Gets the current color value.
setColor()	Sets the current color value.
getFont()	Gets the current font name.
setFont()	Sets the font for all text operations.

The methods used to create ovals and rectangles are called in a similar fashion. Each method accepts four integer values to specify the starting point of the shape and its dimensions. Here are some examples (see Figures 23.2 and 23.3) of drawRect() and drawOval():

```
//Draw a Rectangle

import java.awt.*;
import java.applet.*;

public class Rectangle extends java.applet.Applet {

    public void paint(Graphics g) {
        g.drawRect(50,50,100,150);
    }

    public void start() {
        repaint();
    }
}
```

## Chapter 23

FIGURE 23.2.

A rectangle drawn with `drawRect()`.

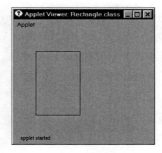

```
//Draw an Oval
public void paint(Graphics g) {
    g.drawOval(50,50,100,150);
}
```

FIGURE 23.3.

An oval drawn with `drawOval()`.

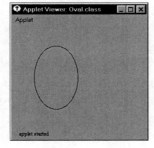

Just as these methods can be used to create oval and rectangle outlines, `fillRect()` and `fillOval()` can be used to create solid shapes. (See Figure 23.4.) The code is quite similar:

```
//Draw Filled Shapes

import java.awt.*;
import java.applet.*;

public class Fills extends java.applet.Applet {

    public void paint(Graphics g) {
        g.setColor(Color.blue);
        g.fillRect(50,50,100,150);
        g.setColor(Color.red);
        g.fillOval(200,50,100,150);
    }

    public void start() {
        repaint();
    }
}
```

FIGURE 23.4.

A filled oval and filled rectangle drawn using fillRect() *and* fillOval().

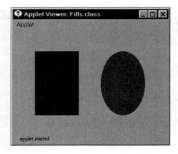

In addition to the basic rectangle and oval, the Graphics class also contains a method for creating polygons. The drawPolygon() method and fillPolygon() method can be used to create polygons containing any number of points. The methods accept integer arrays for the x and y values of the points, as in the following:

```
drawPolygon(int[], int[], int)
fillPolygon(int[], int[], int)
```

The last integer accepted is the total number of points contained in the polygon and the closing point. When creating polygons, keep in mind the following caveats:

- The integer arrays represent all of the x points and all of the y points, not the point pairs. This can be confusing at first, so keep careful track of the arrays.

- Any polygon you create must contain a closing point. Java does not automatically close polygons, so be sure to list all points including a common beginning and ending point.

Keeping those ideas in mind, drawing a polygon (see Figure 24.5) can actually be quite easy, as in the following:

```
//Draw a Polygon and Filled Polygon
import java.awt.*;
import java.applet.*;

public class Poly extends java.applet.Applet {

    int x[] = {100,200,250,50,100};
    int y[] = {50,50,200,200,50};
    int a[] = {300,350,400,300};
    int b[] = {200,50,200,200};

    public void paint(Graphics g) {
        g.drawPolygon(x,y,5);
        g.setColor(Color.blue);
        g.fillPolygon(a,b,4);
    }

    public void start() {
        repaint();
    }
}
```

FIGURE 23.5.
Examples of filled and unfilled polygons.

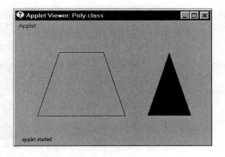

In the preceding examples, we've also used the setColor() method. The setcolor method can be used to change the drawing color used by any method in the Graphics class. The setColor() method can accept a number of predefined color variables (such as red and blue) or can accept RGB color values.

These are the basic graphics methods you need to get started creating images in your applets. Chapter 25 will discuss some more advanced uses for these methods, such as animation.

A Sample Applet: SlideShow

SlideShow is a simple photo gallery application that can be used to set up a slide show of images (see Figure 23.6). The application accepts the following several parameters:

- caption

  caption is the title that is displayed above the control buttons. You can use this parameter to personalize your slide show.

- imagefile

  This is the base filename for the images to shown. The images should all share the same base filename and be numbered sequentially starting with zero. For example, image0.gif, image1.gif, and so on. It is not necessary to give the image numbers or extension type in this parameter, as they will be specified later.

- soundfile

  This is the name of the soundfile to be played during the automatic slideshow. It should be the full filename, complete with extension. For example, sound.au.

- images

  This is an integer value specifying the total number of images to be displayed.

- delay

  This is an integer value for the delay between images in the AutoShow.

- type

  This parameter specifies if the images are GIF or JPEG files.

FIGURE 23.6.

The SlideShow *in action: an image of the author hard at work.*

The structure of this applet is fairly straightforward. The layout consists of the image to be displayed and some simple controls. The "AutoCycle images" button enables and disables the automatic slide show feature, and the "Sound On" button enables the user to turn the sound off. Previous and Next buttons are provided to enable users to cycle through the slides at their own pace.

The applet itself loads the images using MediaTracker during the Init() state, and then begins a thread for the automatic show. The activity of the thread is then controlled by the check box.

The check boxes and buttons are monitored for *action events*. If an action event is detected from one of the check boxes, the thread and audio are stopped or started as appropriate. The buttons also are monitored for action events, which simply increment or decrement the index counter. The end result is a simple SlideShow applet that enables you to have an automatic show or control your own images.

The HTML file for the SlideShow applet is as follows:

```
<HTML>
<applet code="SlideShow.class"  width=400 height=250>
<param name="caption" value="A Sample Photo Album">
<param name="imagefile" value="image">
<param name="soundfile" value="song.au">
<param name="images" value="5">
<param name="delay" value="5000">
<param name="type" value="gif">
</applet>
</HTML>
```

Listing 23.1 is the complete code for the SlideShow applet.

Listing 23.1. The complete `SlideShow` applet.

```
/* A simple Slide Viewer */

import java.awt.*;
import java.lang.*;
import java.applet.*;
import java.net.URL;

public class SlideShow extends Applet implements Runnable {

    MediaTracker LoadImages;
    Image slides[];
    String imagefile, soundfile, type, caption;
    Thread AutoShow;
    int images, delay;
    int index = 0;
    Button forward, backward;
    Checkbox auto, sound;
    Label title;
       AudioClip clip;
    Panel marquee, control;

    public String[][] getParameterInfo() {
        String[][] info = {
            {"caption", "string", "Title of the Slide Viewer"},
            {"imagefile", "string", "Base Image File Name (ex. picture)"},
                 {"soundfile", "string", "Sound File Name (ex. audio.au)"},
                      {"images", "int", "Total number of image files"},
                      {"delay", "int", "Delay in between images (in ms.)"},
                      {"type", "string", "Image File Type(gif, jpg, etc)"},
        };
        return info;
    }

    public void init() {

    //Parse the parameters from the HTML file

    LoadImages = new MediaTracker(this);

    caption = getParameter("caption");
    imagefile = getParameter("imagefile");
    soundfile = getParameter("soundfile");
    type    = getParameter("type");
    images  = Integer.valueOf(getParameter("images")).intValue();
    slides = new Image[images];
    delay   = Integer.valueOf(getParameter("delay")).intValue();

    //Use MediaTracker to load the images

    for (int i = 0; i < images; i++) {
        slides[i] = getImage(getDocumentBase(), imagefile + i + "." + type);
            if (i > 0)
                LoadImages.addImage(slides[i], 1);
```

continues

Listing 23.1. continued

```
            else
                LoadImages.addImage(slides[i], 0);
    }

    try {
        LoadImages.waitForID(0);
    } catch (InterruptedException e) {
        System.out.println("Image Loading Failed!");
    }

    showStatus(imagefile + " Images Loaded");
    index = 0;
    repaint();
    LoadImages.checkID(1,true);

    clip = getAudioClip(getDocumentBase(), soundfile);

    //Create the SlideViewer layout

    setLayout(new BorderLayout());

    forward = new Button("Next");
    backward = new Button("Previous");
    auto = new Checkbox("AutoCycle Images");
    auto.setState(true);
    sound = new Checkbox("Sound On");
    sound.setState(true);
    title = new Label(caption);

    Panel marquee = new Panel();
    marquee.setLayout(new BorderLayout());

    marquee.add("North", title);

    Panel control = new Panel();
    control.setLayout(new FlowLayout());

    control.add(auto);
    control.add(sound);
    control.add(backward);
    control.add(forward);

    setFont(new Font("Helvetica", Font.BOLD, 18));
    add("South", marquee);
    setFont(new Font("Helvetica", Font.PLAIN, 14));
    marquee.add("South", control);
    }

    //Monitor checkboxes and buttons for actions

    public boolean action(Event evt, Object what) {
        if (evt.target == sound) {
            if (sound.getState() == true)
                clip.loop();
```

```
        else
            clip.stop();
        return true;
    } else if (evt.target == backward) {
        if (index !=0) {
            index--;
            repaint();
        }
        return true;
    } else if (evt.target == forward) {
        index++;
        repaint();
        return true;
        } else
        return false;
}

public void start() {
    images = 0;
    repaint();

    clip.loop();
    AutoShow = new Thread(this);
    AutoShow.start();
}

public void stop() {
    index = 0;
    repaint();
    if (AutoShow!= null) AutoShow.stop();
    AutoShow= null;
}

public void run() {
    Thread running = Thread.currentThread();
    while (AutoShow==running) {
        try {
            Thread.sleep(delay);
        } catch (InterruptedException e) {
            break;
        }
            if (auto.getState() == true) {
                if (LoadImages.checkID(1,true))
                    synchronized (this) {
                        if (index == (slides.length - 1))
                            index = 0;
                        else
                            index++;
                    }

                    repaint();
            }
    }
}
```

continues

Listing 23.1. continued

```
//Update is called by repaint()

public void update(Graphics g) {
    try {
        paint(g);
    } catch (ArrayIndexOutOfBoundsException e) {
        if(index < 0)
            index = 0;
        else if (index > images)
            index = images;
        System.out.println("No more Images!");
    }
}

//Paint the slide image on the screen
//and account for missing images

public void paint(Graphics g) {
    if (LoadImages.isErrorAny()) {
        g.setColor(Color.black);
        g.fillRect(0, 0, size().width, size().height);
        return;
    }

    g.drawImage(slides[index], 0, 0, this);
}
}
```

Summary

With the methods found in the AWT and in the Applet Package you have all the tools you need to create applets on your own. Understanding the lifecycle of applets can help you make your applets more efficient and ensure they function correctly. You should also be able to handle images and audio files and have a basic understanding of graphics. Now that the building blocks for applets are under your command, let's move on to Chapter 24, "Programming Applets," and look at some practical implementations of these techniques.

Programming Applets

24

by David Gulbransen and Kendrick Rawlings

IN THIS CHAPTER

Previous chapters have covered all the separate elements needed to program applets. In this chapter we bring these concepts together. We first cover general applet design and then construct two practical applets.

Basic Applet Design

Although applets can be programmed by trial and error, putting some effort into design ahead of time can save headaches later in the programming process.

You wouldn't build a house without a floor plan, so why jump into building an applet? Designing any program is not a trivial task, but if you take some time to figure out the major foundations of your applet, the coding will be much smoother.

There are many facets to program design. What do you want your program to do? Who is the program being written for? This chapter assumes that you've already answered these fundamental questions and are ready to code your applet. We'll concentrate on two very important aspects of applet design: user interface and class design.

User Interface

Almost all applets involve some sort of visual interaction with the user. It is important to structure the interface near the beginning of the design process because changing the user interface later can be difficult. User interface (UI) is the subject of many books, and there are as many approaches to user interface as there are modern religions. For the sake of simplicity, we've tried to keep the applets in this section functional. When your are designing your UI, always keep functionality mind. Some other major areas to consider are layout, grouping, and user interaction.

Layout

Choosing the wrong layout on a container can make the job of laying out the user interface painful. Different layouts have different strengths:

- `GridLayout` is a natural choice when the designer needs to lay out the components in a rigid order. Because the layout follows the form of a grid, it's a natural choice for elements such as keypads.

- `BorderLayout` fits better when there is a main working area to place in the center with toolbars on the periphery. Because the element in the center is allocated all remaining layout space, it can be useful for elements such as pictures.

- `FlowLayout` is a catch-all layout. You can add elements sequentially, and it spaces elements automatically. It can be suited to a variety of control situations.

Grouping

The judicious use of containers is extremely important in applet programming. If there is a logical distinction between user interface components, group them in a container. Remember, there are no restrictions on the number of elements and layouts you use in your applet. Grouping similar elements together and nesting layouts might be the most effective way to achieve the UI you want. It can also make moving or modifying elements later much more manageable.

User Interaction

Any applet, no matter how big or small, should react logically to a user's actions. For instance, if the applet's main function is to play sound, clicking the mouse button should probably toggle the sound on and off. Always try to anticipate ways users will want to interact with your applet. Try to make your applets consistent with industry standards so users are not surprised by idiosyncratic quirks in the UI.

Class Design

Because Java is an object-oriented environment, it's natural to split a program up into classes. Once you start to break applets down into different classes, however, you add to an applets complexity. Because a majority of applets are reasonably simple, most applets need only one class.

Class design is a sensitive subject. Class design is a near-religious issue among many object-oriented programmers. The subject can be broken into two camps:

■ Minimalist

With this approach you ask yourself, "Do I really need another class here?" If an applet is small and no part of it will likely be used in the future, it usually makes sense to try to keep things as simple as possible and the number of classes to a minimum. This doesn't mean trying to cram everything into one class, but using only enough to get the job done. Whenever another class is made, instances of it need to be declared and there will need to be interactions with it. Complexity is the bane of programming, and it makes sense to avoid it when possible.

■ Complete

With this approach you attempt to model the desired program as a series of instances of classes, and design those classes to interact in ways to produce the desired response. This is arguably a superior approach to the minimalist approach, because reusable components tend to accumulate through its use.

There is no right or wrong answer to class design. The correct answer is probably somewhere in between the extremes. If a project is large or may contain large components that could be reused in later projects, try to break it up into its natural class structure. If it will just be a small one-time applet, it probably makes more sense to keep things simple.

In this chapter, we concentrate on two working applets. Each concentrates on a different important aspect of programming applets:

- ■ `Calculator`

  The `Calculator` applet finishes the applet started in Chapter 22, "The Windowing Package." It is extended to be a fully functional four-function algebraic calculator. It's a good example of programming an applet with only one class, using the AWT components feature of passing events to keep things simple.

- ■ `ColorPicker`

  The `ColorPicker` enables you to display a specified RGB color in real time. This could be used to find the value of colors that could be used with an applet in the browser. It uses multiple classes and shows the strengths and weaknesses of that approach.

The Calculator

At the end of Chapter 22 we developed a sample user interface for an algebraic calculator. Luckily, creating prototypes like this is often quite fruitful. With some minor modifications, we can use that prototype code as the interface of a working applet. Listing 24.1 shows the code we start with.

Listing 24.1. The original `Calculator` code.

```
import java.awt.*;
import java.applet.Applet;

public class Calculator extends Applet {
    Label display;
    Panel bottom;
    Panel num_panel;
    Panel func_panel;
    Button number[] = new Button[10];
    Button function[] = new Button[6];

    public void init() {
      setLayout(new BorderLayout());
      display = new Label("0", Label.RIGHT);
      add("North", display);

      bottom = new Panel();
      bottom.setLayout(new BorderLayout());
```

```
        num_panel = new Panel();
        num_panel.setLayout(new GridLayout(4,3));

        for (int x=9; x>=0; x--) {
          number[x] = new Button((new String()).valueOf(x));
          num_panel.add(number[x]);
        }

        function[4] = new Button(".");
        num_panel.add(function[4]);

        function[5] = new Button("=");
        num_panel.add(function[5]);

        bottom.add("Center", num_panel);

        func_panel = new Panel();
        func_panel.setLayout(new GridLayout(4,1));

        function[0] = new Button("+");
        function[1] = new Button("-");
        function[2] = new Button("*");
        function[3] = new Button("/");

        for (int x=0; x<4; x++)
          func_panel.add(function[x]);

        bottom.add("East", func_panel);

        add("Center", bottom);
    }
}
```

User Interface

The final version of the calculator should appear similar to the one shown in Figure 24.1. It contains three main panels that are added to the applet:

1. bottom

    Container to group the number pad and the key pad so they can be added as a group

2. num_panel

    The number keys, decimal point, and equal sign

3. func_panel

    The four function keys: addition, subtraction, multiplication, and division

The construction of the basic user interface was discussed in Chapter 22.

FIGURE 24.1.

Early prototype of
`Calculator` *keyboard.*
(Note incorrect key order.)

Listing 24.2 shows the modified code we are going to use for the final version.

Listing 24.2. The `Calculator` code modified to correct the key placement.

```
import java.awt.*;
import java.applet.Applet;

public class Calculator extends Applet {
    Label display;
    Panel bottom;
    Panel num_panel;
    Panel func_panel;
    Button number[] = new Button[10];
    Button function[] = new Button[6];

    public void init() {
      setLayout(new BorderLayout());
      display = new Label("0", Label.RIGHT);
      add("North", display);

      bottom = new Panel();
      bottom.setLayout(new BorderLayout());

      num_panel = new Panel();
      num_panel.setLayout(new GridLayout(4,3));

      for (int i=7; i>0;i = i - 3)
        for (int j=0; j<3; j++) {
          number[i+j] = new Button((new String()).valueOf(i+j));
          num_panel.add(number[i+j]);
        }

      number[0] = new Button((new String()).valueOf(0));
      num_panel.add(number[0]);

      function[4] = new Button(".");
      num_panel.add(function[4]);

      function[5] = new Button("=");
      num_panel.add(function[5]);

      bottom.add("Center", num_panel);
```

```
      func_panel = new Panel();
      func_panel.setLayout(new GridLayout(4,1));

      function[0] = new Button("+");
      function[1] = new Button("-");
      function[2] = new Button("*");
      function[3] = new Button("/");

      for (int x=0; x<4; x++)
        func_panel.add(function[x]);

      bottom.add("East", func_panel);

      add("Center", bottom);
    }
  }
```

The basic code is essentially the same. There is, however, one section of code that is different and a bit tricky:

```
for (int i=7; i>0;i = i - 3)
  for (int j=0; j<3; j++) {
    number[i+j] = new Button((new String()).valueOf(i+j));
    num_panel.add(number[i+j]);
  }
```

In the Chapter 22 version, the keyboard (although functional) looks a bit odd (refer to Figure 24.1): the keys don't look like a normal calculator (see Figure 24.2).

This is a result of how GridLayout adds components to the container: left-to-right, top-to-bottom. When the buttons are added, they need to be added in the sequence 7→8→9→4→5→6→1→2→3. That's exactly what the nested for loop does. Our prototyping in Chapter 22 paid off with code that is usable for the calculator with only a slight modification.

FIGURE 24.2.

The finalized Calculator *applet.*

Class Design

In order to keep things simple, only one class is used in the Calculator applet: the applet itself. If the applet were going to be extended greatly and pieces of it were going to be pulled out and used in other projects (say for a scientific calculator or a numeric keypad in another application), it would make sense to break it up into classes. This could be accomplished relatively easily, because there are concrete elements that could be pulled out, such as Display and Numeric Keypad. In fact, this is exactly what happens in the `ColorPicker` example.

In order to perform calculations with our calculator, the current number is stored in the `display` `Label` and converted when necessary. But the calculator also needs to retain its state in order to remember the last number entered and the last function called. Thus, the following variables are added to the `Calculator` class:

```
float last_num = 0;
  char last_func = ' ';
```

These come into play when any function key on the calculator is pressed. For example, if we wanted to add 2 and 3, we would press the 2 button, the + button, the 3 button, and finally the = button. By the time the = is pressed, there needs to be a way to find out what the first argument is (the second is stored in the label) and the function that needs to be processed.

Finishing the Applet

Because there will be no additional classes in the program, a method is needed to handle all the events caused by the user pressing different buttons. Luckily, this is provided. Whenever a button is pressed, an `ACTION` event is generated and the `action()` method of the panel that contains it is called. If it's not handled in the component, the event is passed up to the container that holds the component. Thus, all we need is an `action()` event handler:

```
public boolean action(Event evt, Object what) {
```

The only events that need to be handled are button clicks. Everything else can be ignored. What we need is a simple way to filter out everything that is not a button. Luckily, Java includes run-time time checking:

```
if (evt.target instanceof Button) {
```

At this point, the applet knows that a button has been clicked. Which button? The simplest way is to just get the label of the button, which has purposely been made only one character, and perform a `switch()` on it:

```
char but_val = ((Button) evt.target).getLabel().charAt(0);

switch (but_val) {
```

The typecast, although bothersome, is necessary because the target of the event can be any object. A specific method of class button [`getLabel()`] needs to be called, however. This returns a `String`, on which in turn `charAt(0)` is called, which gives the character desired.

First, check to see if a function button was pressed:

```
case '+':
case '*':
case '-':
case '/':      last_num = Float.valueOf(display.getText()).floatValue();
```

```
        last_func = but_val;
        display.setText("");
        break;
```

Because this is an algebraic calculator, no functions are performed until the user presses the "equal" key. This means we need a way to keep track of the last number selected and the function to be performed. This is accomplished with the assigning of last_num and last_func.

The last_num assignment may look a bit strange. However, all that's happening is that the text of the label (a String) is converted into a Float, and then that Float is converted into the float base data type. Remember that Float and float are not the same.

When the equal key is pressed, things get a bit more complicated:

```
case '=':  float curr_num = 0;
        float result = 0;
        curr_num = Float.valueOf(display.getText()).floatValue();
        if (last_func != ' ') {
          switch (last_func) {
            case '+':  result = last_num + curr_num;
                       break;
            case '*':  result = last_num * curr_num;
                       break;
            case '-':  result = last_num - curr_num;
                       break;
            case '/':  result = last_num / curr_num;
                       break;
        }

        last_num = result;
          display.setText(String.valueOf(result));
        }
        break;
```

First, the current number is stored as a floating-point number. Then, if a function key was pressed, perform that function on the current and last numbers and set the display to the result.By default last_func is a space, so if equal is pressed before a function is pressed, nothing happens.

Finally, when a number is pressed, it is appended to the current label, unless the label has the default "0" in it, in which case the display is set to the number just pressed. Finally, True is returned because a button was pressed. If a button was not pressed (evt.target wasn't an instance of Button) return False.

```
        default:  if (display.getText() == "0")
                display.setText("");
                display.setText(display.getText() + but_val);

    }

    return true;

  }

  return false;
}
```

That's it. There is a surprising amount of functionality for such a small amount of code. This illustrates an important point about the Abstract Window Toolkit (discussed in Chapter 22) and Java in general: It is tempting to try and handle everything yourself when programming, but looking at the framework and figuring out how things work together pay off in the end. For example, coming from programming on a different platform it would be easy to miss the `action()` handler and to end up using `handleEvent()` for everything. Using `handleEvent()` would make the calculator much more difficult to write.

Listing 24.3 shows the final code for the `Calculator`.

Listing 24.3. The final version of the `Calculator`.

```java
import java.awt.*;
import java.applet.Applet;

public class Calculator extends Applet {
  Label display;
  float last_num = 0;
  char last_func = ' ';

  Panel bottom;
  Panel num_panel;
  Panel func_panel;
  Button number[] = new Button[10];
  Button function[] = new Button[6];

  public boolean action(Event evt, Object what) {

    if (evt.target instanceof Button) {
      char but_val = ((Button) evt.target).getLabel().charAt(0);

      switch (but_val) {
        case '+':
        case '*':
        case '-':
        case '/':  last_num = Float.valueOf(display.getText()).floatValue();
              last_func = but_val;
              display.setText("");
              break;

        case '=':  float curr_num = 0;
              float result = 0;
              curr_num = Float.valueOf(display.getText()).floatValue();
              if (last_func != ' ') {
                switch (last_func) {
                  case '+':  result = last_num + curr_num;
                        break;
                  case '*':  result = last_num * curr_num;
                        break;
                  case '-':  result = last_num - curr_num;
                        break;
                  case '/':  result = last_num / curr_num;
                        break;
```

```
                }
                last_num = result;
                display.setText(String.valueOf(result));
            }
            break;

    default:  if (display.getText() == "0")
                display.setText("");
              display.setText(display.getText() + but_val);

    }

    return true;

  }
  return false;
}


public void init() {
  setLayout(new BorderLayout());
  display = new Label("0", Label.RIGHT);
  add("North", display);

  bottom = new Panel();
  bottom.setLayout(new BorderLayout());

  num_panel = new Panel();
  num_panel.setLayout(new GridLayout(4,3));

  for (int i=7; i>0;i = i - 3)
    for (int j=0; j<3; j++) {
      number[i+j] = new Button((new String()).valueOf(i+j));
      num_panel.add(number[i+j]);
    }

  number[0] = new Button((new String()).valueOf(0));
  num_panel.add(number[0]);

  function[4] = new Button(".");
  num_panel.add(function[4]);

  function[5] = new Button("=");
  num_panel.add(function[5]);

  bottom.add("Center", num_panel);

  func_panel = new Panel();
  func_panel.setLayout(new GridLayout(4,1));

  function[0] = new Button("+");
  function[1] = new Button("-");
  function[2] = new Button("*");
  function[3] = new Button("/");

  for (int x=0; x<4; x++)
    func_panel.add(function[x]);
```

continues

Listing 24.3. continued

```
    bottom.add("East", func_panel);

    add("Center", bottom);
  }
}
```

Finally, here is the HTML applet tag for the calculator:

```
<applet code="Calculator.class" width=135 height=140>
```

The `ColorPicker`

Although the standard colors (`Color.black`, `Color.red`, and so on) are fine for basic applets, it would be great to be able to see how different RGB colors are represented. `ColorPicker` is an interactive applet that enables you to do this. Figure 24.3 shows the user interface of the `ColorPicker`.

Unlike the `Calculator`, the `ColorPicker` is broken up into many different classes. This complicates the programming slightly but does fit much more closely into the object-oriented paradigm.

User Interface

The `ColorPicker` has two main panels:

1. A color selector panel
2. A panel that contains the current color

FIGURE 24.3.

The user interface of the
`ColorPicker`.

The color selector panel in turn holds three RGB choosers, one for Red, Green, and Blue. In addition, a label is added at the bottom to display the hex representation of the current color, which is used directly in browsers (to set the background color or bgcolor, for example).

Each RGB selector in turn contains a scrollbar and a text field that interact with one another to give a graphical and textual readout of the current value. In this way each color component selector can be thought of as one component that holds the current value, with two interfaces to allows changes: text entry and sliding the scrollbar.

A BorderLayout is used throughout the applet, except in the placing of the RGB choosers, where a 3×1 GridLayout would be more natural.

Class Design

Whereas the calculator is contained in one class, the ColorPicker contains a class for each of the containers listed in the "User Interface" section.

The ColorPicker Class

The ColorPicker is the class that represents the applet itself, although here it is little more than a launch point for the other objects that make up the applet:

```
public class ColorPicker extends Applet {
  ColorPanel out;
  ColorSelector select;

  public void init() {
    setLayout(new BorderLayout() );

    out = new ColorPanel();
    select = new ColorSelector(out,255,204,102);
    add("West", select);
    add("Center", out);
  }

}
```

All that is really happening here is the layout is defined and an instance of a ColorPanel and ColorSelector (see the following classes) are created. Note that a handle to the ColorPanel, out, is passed to the ColorSelector, which allows the objects to communicate back and forth directly.

The ColorPanel Class

The ColorPanel is the representation of the current color. Luckily, the AWT provides a class that visually does the job perfectly: Panel. The only other significant aspect to the class is that it needs to have a method to change the color:

```
class ColorPanel extends Panel {

  void change(Color new_c) {
    setBackground(new_c);
    repaint();
  }
}
```

This, aside from some cosmetic considerations later, is the entire `ColorPanel` class.

The `ColorSelector` class

The `ColorSelector` constitutes the entire input portion of the applet. Although the bulk of the actual interface coding lies lower in the hierarchy (in the `RGBChooser` class). It needs to contain three `RGBChoosers`, a `Label` for the HTML (hex) representation of the current color, and finally a reference to the `ColorPanel` to allow it to change its color:

```
class ColorSelector extends Panel {
  ColorPanel controller;
  Label html;
  RGBChooser red, green, blue;

  ColorSelector(ColorPanel myController, int r, int g, int b) {
    super();

    controller = myController;
    setLayout(new BorderLayout());

    Panel controls = new Panel();
    controls.setLayout(new GridLayout(3,1));
    red = new RGBChooser(this, r, "Red");
    controls.add(red);
    green = new RGBChooser(this, g, "Green");
    controls.add(green);
    blue = new RGBChooser(this, b,"Blue");
    controls.add(blue);
    add("Center", controls);
    html = new Label("#000000");
    html.setBackground(Color.gray);
    add("South", html);

    colorChange();
  }

}
```

The bulk of this code is pretty straightforward. Notice that a reference to the instance of the `ColorSelector` class is passed down to each `RGBChooser`, along with their default value and a text label to identify them. Also, the HTML label is constructed using a dummy string to ensure that the layout manager doesn't resize it to be too small to hold the requisite color information.

However, the `colorChange()` method seems a bit strange. The need for it arises from the need for the `ColorChoose` to be notified that the color has changed from three separate places. If either the red, green, or blue component change, the whole color changes, which must be re-flected in the new color. The applet could be designed to require the user to press an "update" button when they want to see the color they have chosen, but it would be much more satisfy-ing that whenever an RGB component is changed the color panel changes automatically. And that is exactly what is done.

```
void colorChange() {
    Color new_c = getColor();
    int col[] = new int[3];
    StringBuffer text;

    text = new StringBuffer("");
    col[0] = new_c.getRed();
    col[1] = new_c.getGreen();
    col[2] = new_c.getBlue();

    for(int i=0;i<3;i++) {
        if (col[i] < 16)
            text.append('0');
        text.append(Integer.toString(col[i],16));
    }

    controller.change(new_c);
    html.setText("#" + text.toString());
}
```

First a call to getColor() is made. Although this could be placed inline in the colorChange() method, it makes more sense to abstract it out as a method of its own because it represents an essential state of the class that would be of use were it to be used in other programs:

```
Color getColor() {
  return new Color(red.value(), green.value(), blue.value());
}
```

The bulk of the rest of the code in colorChange() pertains to massaging the color into the HTML representation: a six-digit number representing the color in three hex pairs. The current color is broken down into red, green, and blue through the respective methods in the Color package. Then, each is converted to a hex string representation (prefixing a '0' if necessary). Finally, the ColorPanel and HTML label are updated to reflect the change.

The RGBChooser class

The three RGBChooser objects are the only way in which the user can interact with the ColorPicker applet. Thus, they should be as flexible as possible while keeping their function as obvious as possible.

Each object needs to continually hold the state of one piece of information: an integer value between 0 and 255. It is natural to be able to type the number in, so a TextField is an obvious component to add. However, a linear way to change the number by sliding the mouse would make it possible to quickly inspect a wide variety of colors. A Scrollbar would do this job nicely.

Let's take a first crack at the class definition:

```
class RGBChooser extends Panel {
  ColorSelector controller;
  Scrollbar colorScroll;
  TextField colorField;
  int c_value;

  RGBChooser(ColorSelector myController, int initial, String caption) {
    super();
    controller = myController;

    setLayout(new BorderLayout());

    colorField = new TextField();
    colorScroll = new Scrollbar(Scrollbar.VERTICAL, initial, 0, 0, 255);
    set_value(initial);
    add("East", colorScroll);

    Panel temp_panel = new Panel();
    temp_panel.setLayout(new GridLayout(3,1));
    Label label1 = new Label(caption);
    temp.add(label1);
    temp.add(colorField);
    add("Center", temp_panel);
  }
}
```

First, we set up a handle to the `ColorSelector` that contains the `RGBChooser`. This allows the `RGBChooser` to inform the `ColorSelector` when the value of the component has changed.

Next, we set up the `TextField` and `ScrollBar`. Unfortunately for this application, a scrollbar is at its minimum value when at the top of its area and maximum at the bottom. Thus, there needs to be conversion from scrollbar values to actual values (when the scrollbar is 0 the desired value is 255 since the scrollbar is at the top of its allowable area, for example).

Much like the `ColorPanel`, it would be nice to have an interface to the state of the object, so we will add both a method to change its value and to return it:

```
int value() {
  return c_value;
}

void set_value(int initial) {
  c_value = initial;
}
```

All that's left in the class is the handling of events. Because the Calculator used ACTION events, we will purposely use raw event handling here to show a different way to do things. Doing your own raw event handling is fine, but remember that you are responsible for dispatching events if they are not handled by the overridden `handleEvent`.

Here's the event handler:

```
public boolean handleEvent(Event evt) {
  Integer in;

  if (evt.target == colorScroll) {
    in = (Integer) evt.arg;
    colorField.setText(String.valueOf(255-in.intValue()));
    set_value(255 - in.intValue());
    controller.colorChange();
    return true;
  } else if (evt.target == colorField) {
    String tmp;
    tmp = (String) evt.arg;
    in = Integer.valueOf(tmp);
    set_value(in.intValue());
    colorScroll.setValue(-1 * (in.intValue() - 255));
    controller.colorChange();
    return true;
  } else {
    return super.handleEvent(evt);
  }
}
```

First, if the scrollbar has been moved, get its current value (which is passed along in the event as its argument), and then set the value of the RGBChooser to that value (remembering to change from scrollbar values).

Second, if the user has changed the value of the colorField, its value is converted to an integer and then the RGBChooser is set to that value.

In either case, if the user updates the scrollbar, the text field is altered as well, and vice versa. This helps to avoid a discrepancy between the different types of input. With the data in sync, the ColorSelector is notified and the color is updated.

Finally, if the event was not handled, call the default event handler. This insures that if new code is added later everything will work at planned (calls to action(), mouseUp(), and so on).

Finishing the Applet

Believe it or not, the applet is now finished. By deriving classes from the components and adding behavior as we went down the class hierarchy, all the needed functionality has been added. This reflects one of the wonderful things about object-oriented programming: If the design is proper to the project at hand at the beginning of the project, and each component does its job correctly, a working program falls out at the end.

Listing 24.4 shows the finished working applet.

Listing 24.4. The final code for the `ColorPicker` applet.

```java
import java.awt.*;
import java.applet.Applet;
import java.lang.Integer;

public class ColorPicker extends Applet {
  ColorPanel out;
  ColorSelector select;

  public void init() {
    setLayout(new BorderLayout() );

    out = new ColorPanel();
    select = new ColorSelector(out,255,204,102);
    add("West", select);
    add("Center", out);
  }
}

class ColorPanel extends Panel {

    void change(Color new_c) {
    setBackground(new_c);
    repaint();
  }

}

class ColorSelector extends Panel {
  ColorPanel controller;
  Label html;
  RGBChooser red, green, blue;

  ColorSelector(ColorPanel myController, int r, int g, int b) {
    super();

    controller = myController;
    setLayout(new BorderLayout());

    Panel controls = new Panel();
    controls.setLayout(new GridLayout(3,1));
    red = new RGBChooser(this, r, "Red");
    controls.add(red);
    green = new RGBChooser(this, g, "Green");
    controls.add(green);
    blue = new RGBChooser(this, b, "Blue");
    controls.add(blue);
    add("Center", controls);
    html = new Label("#000000");
    html.setBackground(Color.gray);
    add("South", html);

    colorChange();
  }

  void colorChange() {
    Color new_c = getColor();
```

```
    int col[] = new int[3];
    StringBuffer text;

    text = new StringBuffer("");
    col[0] = new_c.getRed();
    col[1] = new_c.getGreen();
    col[2] = new_c.getBlue();

    for(int i=0;i<3;i++) {
      if (col[i] < 16)
      text.append('0');
      text.append(Integer.toString(col[i],16));
    }

    controller.change(new_c);
    html.setText("#" + text.toString());
  }

  Color getColor() {
    return new Color(red.value(), green.value(), blue.value());

  }
}


class RGBChooser extends Panel {
  ColorSelector controller;
  Scrollbar colorScroll;
  TextField colorField;
  int c_value;

  RGBChooser(ColorSelector myController, int initial, String caption) {
    super();
    controller = myController;

    setLayout(new BorderLayout());

    colorField = new TextField(String.valueOf(initial));
    colorScroll = new Scrollbar(Scrollbar.VERTICAL, 255-initial, 0, 0, 255);
    set_value(initial);
    add("East", colorScroll);

    Panel temp_panel = new Panel();
    temp_panel.setLayout(new GridLayout(3,1));
    Label label1 = new Label(caption);
    temp_panel.add(label1);
    temp_panel.add(colorField);
    add("Center", temp_panel);
  }


  public boolean handleEvent(Event evt) {
    Integer in;

    if (evt.target == colorScroll) {
      in = (Integer) evt.arg;
      colorField.setText(String.valueOf(255-in.intValue()));
```

continues

Listing 24.4. continued

```
        set_value(255 - in.intValue());
        controller.colorChange();
        return true;
    } else if (evt.target == colorField) {
        String tmp;
        tmp = (String) evt.arg;
        in = Integer.valueOf(tmp);
        set_value(in.intValue());
        colorScroll.setValue(-1 * (in.intValue() - 255));
        controller.colorChange();
        return true;
    } else {
        return super.handleEvent(evt);
    }
}

int value() {
    return c_value;
}

void set_value(int initial) {
    c_value = initial;
}
}
```

Here is the HTML applet tag for the `ColorPicker`:

```
<applet code="ColorPicker.class" width=400 height=300 alt="Color Picker">
</applet>
```

Applets In the Real World

The possibilities for applets are wide open. The ability to seamlessly deliver applications over a network to widely different operating system and computer types is a grand opportunity that will surely be exploited in many unforeseen ways. However, even with the potential Java represents, there are a few general considerations and future developments that should be kept in mind when developing applets.

Applets Must Be Small

Upon learning Java it is easy to envision large applets that could replace many of the functions of current programs. However, it is important to keep in mind the main limitation involved with Java applets: bandwidth. Currently, whenever an applet is run it must be downloaded from the network. Although this isn't a problem for smaller applets, imagine using a a 14.4 modem and trying to run an applet that is several megabytes.

Responding to the User

Many early applets suffer from a lack of user interaction. Audio players that drone on incessantly and animations that cannot be stopped that use large amounts of CPU time are just two examples of this problem. If you don't want large amounts of negative user feedback, spend some time up from thinking about issues like this.

JavaScript

Finally, Sun and Netscape have announced that there will be hooks from the JavaScript scripting language (available in Netscape Navigator and many more products soon) into Java to allow JavaScript to control applets as disparate objects. This could quite likely spur a move in applet development to program small reusable components made to be scripted rather than run by themselves. JavaScript is explored in detail in Part IX, "JavaScript."

Summary

We've covered a lot of ground in this chapter. We've looked at interface design, class design, and other applet programming issues. Nothing compares to experience when it comes to any kind of programming. Working on your own applets and learning through trial and error often provides invaluable experience. We've tried, however, to give you some examples of issues that will arise when you start programming your own applets. As your applets grow in complexity, you will likely encounter your own unique problems. The lesson to be learned here is that a time investment in planning pays off. Hopefully, keeping these basic design tenets in mind will enable you to create a variety of applets that can serve you and other users well. A little preplanning and forethought can save you time and frustration, and help you create innovative new applets.

Animation Programming

25

by Chris Seguin

History, as the cliché claims, repeats itself. Consider this.

Between 4000 and 6000 years ago, the Sumerians began communicating using pictograms. In 1827, Joseph Niepce produced the first photographs on a metal plate. Eighty-eight years later, the motion picture camera was created, and in 1937 the first full-length animation feature was released. Since then, animation has transformed from a novelty to an art form. We regularly see animation in commercials, television, and movies.

The history of the Web is similar. When it was first released, Web pages could only contain text and links to other pages. In the early 1990s, a browser called Mosaic was released that added the ability to incorporate pictures and sound. This started a flurry of interest in the Internet. But after a while, even the carefully designed web pages with elaborate background images and colored text began to grow stale. Java, the most recent extension to the World Wide Web, allows programs to be added to Web pages.

Animations have been available on the Web since early versions of Mosaic, where Mosaic would download the MPEG file and launch a separate viewer. With the release of Netscape version 1.1, CGI files could use a push-and-pull method of creating animations. The browser would receive instructions to reread the information or read the next URL address after a set delay. The client could keep the connection open, and push new information onto the browser every so often. However, this type of animation was only available on Netscape, and it was slow. One of the popular uses of Java is to create animations. Because the Java animations are on the page, they serve to call attention to the Web page, rather than away from the page in the manner that a separate viewer does. Java is also faster than the Netscape method and will work on any browser that supports the Java.

This chapter covers

- The `Animator` class
- Design of simple animation systems
- Double buffering
- Advanced animation techniques

The design of simple animation systems is illustrated with animated text and images. This chapter covers double buffering, which is the easiest way to eliminate animation flicker. The advanced animation techniques include alternate designs to keep track of time, inbetweens, and backgrounds.

The Animator Class

Before we dive into the programming of animation applets, let's start with the hands down easiest way to create an animation: use someone else's applet. Herb Jellinek at Sun Microsystems has created an `Animator` class, an applet that creates an animation. This class is provided as a demonstration program with the Java Developer's Kit.

To use the `Animator` applet, do the following:

1. Copy the following three files to your classes directory: `Animator.class`, `ParseException.class`, and `ImageNotFoundException.class`.
2. Create the image and sound files for your animations.
3. Put the applet tag on your web page. Table 25.1 shows the parameters that the `Animator` applet reads from your HTML file.

Table 25.1. `Animator` **applet parameters.**

TAG	*Description*	*Default*
IMAGESOURCE	The directory that contains the image files	The same directory that contains the HTML file
STARTUP	The image to be displayed while the program loads the other images	None
BACKGROUND	The image to be displayed in the background	A filled, light gray rectangle that covers the entire applet
STARTIMAGE	The number of the first image	1
ENDIMAGE	The number of the last image	1
IMAGES	A list of indexes of the images to be displayed in the order that they are to be displayed	None
PAUSE	The number of milliseconds for the pause between frames	3900
PAUSES	The number of milliseconds for the pause between each frame	The value of PAUSE
REPEAT	A Boolean value: Does the animation cycle through the images? (yes or true/no or false)	True
POSITIONS	The coordinates of where each image will be displayed in the applet	(0,0)
SOUNDSOURCE	The directory that contains the sound files	The value of IMAGESOURCE
SOUNDTRACK	The background music	None
SOUNDS	The sounds to be displayed for each image in the animation	None

Most of the tags are straightforward in their use, but some tags need additional explanation. We'll begin with the images, and then describe how to use the tags that accept multiple inputs.

All image files used by the `Animator` class must start with the letter T followed by a number. For instance, if you have three GIF files that form the changing part of the animation, you could name them `T1.gif`, `T2.gif`, and `T3.gif`. The background image and startup image have no constraints on their names.

There are two ways to specify the order of the images. First, you could specify the first and last image with the `STARTIMAGE` and `ENDIMAGE` tags. If the value of the `STARTIMAGE` tag is greater than the value of the `ENDIMAGE` tag, the images are displayed starting `STARTIMAGE` and decrementing to `ENDIMAGE`. Second, you could specify the order of the images with the `IMAGES` tag. This tag takes multiple inputs, so let's consider how to give multiple inputs to the `Animator` applet.

Several tags take multiple inputs. The `Animator` class has implemented these using a ¦ as a separator between values. For instance, `IMAGES` requires the list of numbers of the images to be displayed. If you wanted to display the images 1, 3, and 2 in that order, you would write

```
<PARAM NAME=IMAGES VALUE=1¦3¦2>
```

`SOUNDS` works that same way except that values can be left blank. A blank value in the `SOUNDS` tag means that no sound is played for that image. `PAUSES` also takes multiple inputs, but if an input is left out, it defaults to the standard pause between images. For instance

```
<PARAM NAME=PAUSE VALUE=250>
<PARAM NAME=PAUSES VALUE=1000¦¦4>
```

displays the first image for 1000ms (1000 milliseconds), the second image for 250ms, and the third image for 4ms.

The `POSITION` tag is a set of coordinates. As in the `IMAGES` and `SOUNDS` tags, the coordinates are separated by a ¦ character. The x and y values of the coordinate are separated by an @ character. If a coordinate is left blank, the image remains in the same location as the previous image. For example, if you wanted to draw the first and second images at (30,25), and the third image at (100, 100), you would write

```
<PARAM NAME=POSITION VALUE=30@25¦¦100@100>
```

TIP

You may want to add the following code to the `Animator` class after the `paint()` method and recompile the `Animator` class.

```
void update (Graphics g)
    {
    paint (g);
    }
```

The reason for this addition is that the default `update()` method clears the applet drawing area to `lightGray` before it calls the `paint()` method. Clearing the applet to gray first may cause your animation to flicker.

The `Animator` class enables you to create an animation quickly and easily. If, however, you have more than one moving object or you would like to draw your objects as the animation runs, you will have to write your own animation applet. The next section begins with the design of an animator and gives four examples.

Simple Animation

Let's dive right into programming simple animations in Java. These animations might not be perfectly smooth in their presentation but will illustrate the basic design of an animation. We will also look at what makes a good animation. We'll begin with creating an abstract animated object class, and then create several examples of the animation in action.

AnimationObject class

When writing a program in an object-oriented language, the first step is to decompose the problem into things that interact. The things, called *objects,* are grouped into classes of similar things. The class holds all the information about an object. Sometimes, classes are very similar, and a class can be created to represent the similarities of the class. This is called a *base class.* If the base class doesn't actually store information, but provides a list of methods that all the members of the class have, the class is called a *abstract class.*

Java is an objected-oriented language, so in creating a design for a program, first find similarities in the components of the program. When designing an animation, we will begin by looking for similarities. Each image or text message that moves is an object. But if you consider these objects, you find that they are very similar. Each object needs to be able to paint itself in the applet window. In addition to painting the object, something about the objects is changing, or it wouldn't be an animation. So the object must know when to change.

Let's create a class with the following two methods:

- `paint()`—directs the object to paint itself
- `clockTick()`—tells the object to change

Because a moving text object and an image have nothing in common other than these methods, I have created an abstract class as follows:

```
AnimationObject extends Object {
    public void paint (Graphics G)
    {
```

```
//  Draw the object here
        }

        public void clockTick ()
        {
        //  Modify the object
        }
}
```

This skeleton enables you to simplify the design of the applet object. For instance, the paint() routine just erases the screen and sends each animation object a paint() method:

```
public void paint (Graphics g) {
        update (g);
        }
    public void update (Graphics g) {
        //  Erase the screen
        g.setColor (Color.lightGray);
        g.fillRect (0, 0, nWidth, nHeight);
        g.setColor (Color.black);

        //  Paint each object
        for (int ndx = 0; ndx < AnimatedObjects.length; ndx++)
            AnimatedObjects[ndx].paint (g, this);
        }
```

For now, we'll assume that the update() method and the paint() method are essentially the same, although a description of the difference is given in the section on double buffering. The update() method is straightforward, but it may cause your animation to flicker. Code to fix the flicker is given in the section on double buffering.

The run() method is only three steps. First, the applet tells each object that one time unit has passed, and then the applet repaints itself. Finally, the program pauses.

```
public void run() {
        int ndx = 0;

        //  Set the priority of the thread
        Thread.currentThread().setPriority(Thread.MIN_PRIORITY);

        //  Do the animation
        while (size().width > 0 &&
               size().height > 0 &&
               kicker != null) {

            for (ndx = 0; ndx < AnimatedObjects.length; ndx++)
                AnimatedObjects[ndx].clockTick ();

            repaint();

            try { Thread.sleep(nSpeed); }
                catch (InterruptedException e) {}
            }
        }
```

The hard part is initially creating the applet, and that depends on how difficult it is to create each of the animation objects. So let's start with moving text.

Moving Text

NOTE

The code in this section is in Example 25.1 in file `exmp25_1.java`.

Everyone has seen animated text, such as weather warnings that slide across the bottom of the TV screen during storms. We'll start with an animation object that moves a text message around the applet drawing area and consider why this is effective.

Java provides the `drawString (String s, int x, int y)` routine in the `java.awt.Graphics` class that draws a string at a specific location. To animate text, the applet repeatedly draws the string at a different location.

If we wanted to scroll text across the applet, what would we need to store? First, you need a text message. For this example, let's assume that the message only slides to the left. It's easy to extend this code so that the message would also slide right, up, or down. In addition to the message, you would need some internal variables to store the x and y location of where the message should be printed next.

The next question is, "How do you compute when the message is no longer visible?" We need to know about the length of the message and the width of the applet to determine when the message disappears from view and where it should reappear. We won't be able to determine the length of the message until we have the `java.awt.Graphics` object, so we'll postpone this computation until the first time we `paint()` the text message.

Let's begin by creating an object that stores each of these values:

```
class TextScrolling extends AnimationObject {

    //  Internal Variables
    String pcMessage;

    int nXPos;
    int nYPos;
    int nAppletWidth;
    int nMessageWidth;
```

Now we need to initialize these variables in the constructor method. The constructor needs the text message and the applet width. The other values are computed in the `paint` method.

```
public TextScrolling (String pcMsg, int nWide) {
        pcMessage = pcMsg;

        nAppletWidth = nWide;
        nMessageWidth = -1;

        nXPos = nWide;
        nYPos = -1;
        }
```

Use the drawString() method to draw the text message. The paint() routine is more complex, however, because we need to compute nYPos and nMessageWidth. The constructor assigned both of these variables the value -1 to flag them as unknown values. Now that a Graphics object is available, their values can be computed:

```
public void paint (Graphics g, Applet parent) {
        if (nYPos < 0) {
            //  Determine the y position
            nYPos = (g.getFontMetrics ()).getHeight ();

            //  Determine the size of the message
            char pcChars [];
            pcChars = new char [pcMessage.length() + 2];
            pcMessage.getChars (0, pcMessage.length() - 1,
                                pcChars, 0);
            nMessageWidth = (g.getFontMetrics ()).charsWidth
                            (pcChars, 0, pcMessage.length());
        }

        //  Draw the object here
        g.drawString (pcMessage, nXPos, nYPos);
        }
```

> **TIP**
>
> Drawing in an applet is easy because the applet only draws graphics that fall inside its boundaries. This process is called *clipping*—limiting the drawing area to a specific rectangle. All graphics output that falls outside the rectangle is not displayed. You can further limit the region where the graphics are drawn using
> `java.awt.Graphics.clipRect()`.

Now, whenever the clock ticks, the message shifts to the left. You can do this by adjusting the nXPos variable. We reset the nXPos whenever the message is no longer visible:

```
public void clockTick () {
        //  Do nothing until the message width is known
        if (nMessageWidth < 0)
            return;

        //  Move Right
        nXPos -= 10;
        if (nXPos < -nMessageWidth)
            nXPos = nAppletWidth - 10;
        }

//  END of TextScrolling Object
}
```

At this point, I could point out a lack of computation in the `paint()` and `clockTick()` methods and launch into a lecture on how it is important to avoid extensive computations. But either you already know that, or you would discover it very quickly with the first complex animation you write.

How can you avoid complex computations? Two possibilities follow:

- Perform the computations off-line
- Do each computation once, and save the results

In this animation object, the value of the variables `nMessageWidth` and `nYPos` were computed once in the `paint()` routine. Before then, the information wasn't available.

Let's consider some more examples. First, we will write two programs to display a series of images in an applet and to move a single image around an applet. These programs demonstrate the first possibility. For the second possibility, we draw and copy a stick person.

Images

In the past ten years, computer animations of many different objects have been created using the physical equations that model movement. Interactions between rigid bodies are the easy to animate, but more advanced techniques have created realistic animations of rubber bands and elastic cubes that deform as they interact. The computations required for these are extensive and are not suitable for the online nature of applets.

The first animation object uses the flipbook principle of animation. For this method, generate all the pictures in advance, and allow Java to display the images in sequence to create the illusion of motion. The second method is useful for rigid body motion and interactions, where we take a single image and move it around the applet drawing area.

But first, let's review some information about images.

MediaTracker

Images take a while to load into the computer's memory, and they look very strange if you display them before they are completely ready. Have you ever seen the top of a head bouncing around a Web page? Very unnerving :-) To avoid this gruesome possibility, the creators of Java have provided a `MediaTracker` class. A `MediaTracker` object enables you to determine if an image is correctly loaded.

> **NOTE**
>
> Though a `MediaTracker` will eventually be able to determine if an audio objects has loaded correctly, it currently only supports images.

The MediaTracker object provides three types of methods:

- register or check-in images
- start loading images
- determine if the images are successfully loaded

The methods that register images are named AddImage:

- AddImage (Image img, int groupNumber)—begins tracking an image and includes the image in the specified group
- AddImage (Image img, int groupNumber, int width, int height) —begins tracking a scaled image

You can organize images with the group number. This enables you to check logical groups of images at once.

The methods to start the images loading follow:

- checkAll (true)—starts loading all the images, returns immediately
- checkID (int groupNumber, true)—starts loading all the images in the group specified by groupNumber, returns immediately
- waitForAll()—starts loading all images, returns when all images are loaded
- waitForID(int groupNumber)—starts loading all images in the group specified by groupNumber, returns when all images in the group are loaded

> **NOTE**
>
> In checkAll() and checkID(), the last input is true. This is not a variable, but the Boolean constant.

Because the routines that start with check return immediately, you can continue with other processing and occasionally check the progress with checkID(groupNumber) and checkAll().

The final two methods follow:

- isErrorAny()—returns true if any errors were encountered loading any image
- isErrorID(int groupNumber)—returns true if any errors were encountered loading the images in the specified group

Now we are ready to start working with the image object animators. We'll begin with a changing image animation, and then we'll create a moving image animation.

Changing Images

The flipbook method of animation in Java is the most popular on Web sites. Flipbooks contain pictures but no words. The first picture is slightly different from the second, and the second picture is slightly different from the third. When you thumb through a flipbook as shown in Figure 25.1, the pictures appear to move. In this section, we create an applet that takes a series of images, and repeatedly displays them in the applet window to create the illusion of motion.

> **NOTE**
>
> The code in this section is in Example 25.2 in file `exmp25_2.java` on the CD-ROM.

FIGURE 25.1.

Thumbing through a flipbook creates the illusion of motion.

This program needs to store two values: the images to be displayed and the `MediaTracker` to determine if the images are ready. Internally, we will also keep track of the number of the image to be displayed next:

```
class ChangingImage extends AnimationObject {

    //  Internal Variables
    Image ImageList [];
    int nCurrent;
    MediaTracker ImageTracker;
```

The constructor initializes the variables with the constructor's inputs, and starts the animation sequence with the first image:

```
public ChangingImage (Image il[], MediaTracker md,
               Applet parent) {
       ImageList = il;
       nCurrent = 0;
       ImageTracker = md;
       }
```

As mentioned earlier, it is important to check that the image is available before it is drawn:

```
public void paint (Graphics g, Applet Parent) {
       //  Draw the object here
       if (ImageTracker.checkID(1)) {
           g.drawImage (ImageList [nCurrent], 100, 100, Parent);
           }
       else
           System.out.println
               ("Not Ready Yet " + (nCurrent+1));
       }
```

Remember that this object is only one part of a possibly large animation, and you may need to sacrifice the first few pictures to keep all the parts of the animation together. Therefore, the object doesn't check the `ImageTracker` to see if the images are ready in the `clockTick` method:

```
public void clockTick () {
       nCurrent++;
       if (nCurrent >= ImageList.length)
           nCurrent = 0;
       }

//  END of ChangingImage Object
}
```

With this approach, most of the work is done ahead of time, either as you draw all the images or by a computer program which generates and saves the images. This method is how you animate objects with elastic properties or realistic lighting in Java because of the amount of computation involved.

Moving Images

> **NOTE**
>
> The code in this section is in Example 25.3 in file `exmp25_3.java`.

For rigid bodies, there is an easier way to create a 2D animation: you can take an image of the object and move it around the applet drawing area. An example of a rigid body is a rock or a table because they don't deform or change while they move. A cube of gelatin wiggles as it moves, and deforms when it runs into another object.

The MovingImage class is very similar to the ChangingImage class in previous section. The variables are a picture and the X and Y locations where it will be drawn. In this object, the nCurrent variable keeps track of the location in the object's path, rather than the image:

```
class MovingImage extends AnimationObject {
    //  Internal Variables
    Image Picture;
    MediaTracker ImageTracker;
    int nCurrent;

    int pnXPath [];
    int pnYPath [];
```

The constructor for MovingImage is nearly identical to the constructor for ChangingImage, except it has two extra variables to save:

```
public MovingImage (Image img, MediaTracker md,
                int pnXs [], int pnYs [],
                Applet parent) {
        Picture = img;
        nCurrent = 0;

        ImageTracker = md;

        pnXPath = pnXs;
        pnYPath = pnYs;
        }
```

Now instead of changing images, we simply draw the image at the next location in the path:

```
public void paint (Graphics g, Applet Parent) {
        //  Draw the object here
        if (ImageTracker.checkID(1))
            g.drawImage (Picture,
                        pnXPath[nCurrent], pnYPath[nCurrent],
                        Parent);
        }
```

The clockTick() program is nearly identical to the method written for the ChangingImage object.

Copy Area

> **NOTE**
>
> The code in this section is in Example 25.4 in file exmp25_4.java.

Remember that we are trying to minimize the amount of computation that we perform during an animation. If we don't have an image that we can use, we have to draw the image using graphic primitives. So let's say that we want to slide a stick figure across the applet. Here is a small method that draws a stick person at a specified location:

```
public void drawStickFigure (Graphics g, int nX, int nY) {
        g.drawOval (nX +  10, nY +  20, 20, 40);
        g.drawLine (nX +  20, nY +  60, nX +  20, nY + 100);
        g.drawLine (nX +  10, nY +  70, nX +  30, nY +  70);
        g.drawLine (nX +  10, nY + 150, nX +  20, nY + 100);
        g.drawLine (nX +  20, nY + 100, nX +  30, nY + 150);
        }
```

The original stick figure is drawn in black on a lightGray background. To continue the animation, we can erase it by redrawing the figure in lightGray over the black figure, then draw a new figure in black a little to the right. For such an uncomplicated drawing, this method is effective. For the purpose of this illustration, however let's animate the stick figure using the copyArea() method:

```
public void paint (Graphics g, Applet Parent) {
        if (bFirstTime) {
            bFirstTime = false;
            drawStickFigure (g, nX, nY);
            }
        else {
            g.copyArea (nX, nY, 35, 155, 5, 0);
            }
        }
```

The first time the paint() method is called, the figure is drawn using the drawStickFigure routine. After the first time, the paint() routine recopies the stick figure a few pixels to the right. To erase the old copy of the figure, some blank space is copied with the stick figure. The result: the figure slides across the applet.

There is one problem with this animation so far. Our previous animations would repeatedly cycle across the screen. Once our little figure is out of the viewing area, it is gone for good. If only there was a way to draw an image in Java, and save it. Then we could use the animation techniques in the previous section to move the image around the applet drawing area.

Fortunately, such a facility is available in Java. In addition to enabling us to create an image off-line so that it can be used repeatedly, this facility generates a cleaner flicker-free animation.

Double-Buffered Animation

In order to double buffer your animation, you

- create an off-screen image and get the associated graphics object
- draw using the off-screen graphics object
- copy the off-screen image onto the applet's graphic object

> **NOTE**
>
> An example illustrating the flickering effect and the improvement created by using double buffering is in Example 25.5 in file `exmp25_5.java` on the CD-ROM.

The first step requires that you create an image in which you will do all the work. To create the off-screen image, you must know the height and width of the drawing area. Once that is determined, you can get the graphics object from the image with the `getGraphics()` method:

```
offScreenImage = createImage(width, height);
    offScreenGraphic = offScreenImage.getGraphics();
```

The graphics object extracted from the image is now used for all drawing. This part is the same as the `paint()` program in the "Simple Animation" section, except instead of using g you use `offScreenGraphic`:

```
//  Erase the screen
    offScreenGraphic.setColor (Color.lightGray);
    offScreenGraphic.fillRect (0, 0, width, height);
    offScreenGraphic.setColor (Color.black);

    //  Paint each object
    for (int ndx = 0; ndx < AnimatedObjects.length; ndx++)
        AnimatedObjects[ndx].paint (offScreenGraphic, this);
```

Finally, you need to copy the off screen image into the applet's graphics object:

```
g.drawImage(offScreenImage, 0, 0, this);
```

And you have now succeeded in improving the clarity of your animation. You might be wondering why this would improve the animation. After all, the number of pixels that are drawn has increased! There are three reasons for this improvement:

- Most machines have an efficient way to copy a block of bits onto the screen, and an image is just a block of bits.
- There are no extra computations interrupting the drawing of the picture. These extra computations come from drawing lines, determining the boundaries of a filled area, and looking up fonts.
- Video memory cannot be cached in the CPU, while an image can be anywhere in memory.
- All of the image appears at once, so even though more work was done between frames a human perceives that all the work is done instantaneously.

Now we have reduced the flicker by creating an off-screen image. In the first section, the theme was to reduce the computation that the applet performed. Using the off-screen image increased the computations, but improves the visual effect. Now we will eliminate extra computations in the program using the off-screen image.

update() and paint()

Earlier, I said that paint() and update() were essentially the same. In fact, most of the sample code that Sun Microsystems provides does exactly what I did in the "Simple Animation" section: the paint() method calls the update() method. So what is the difference?

The paint() method is called when the applet begins execution and when the applet is exposed. An applet is said to be exposed when more area or different area can be viewed by the user. For example, when an applet is partially covered by a window, it needs to be redrawn after the covering window is removed. The removal of the covering window exposes (change the screen to enable the user to see more of a viewing area of a window) the applet. See Figure 25.2 for an example.

FIGURE 25.2.

Moving another window exposes the applet.

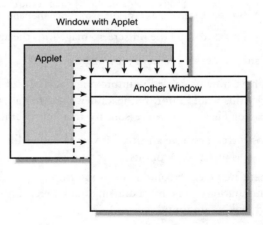

Update is called whenever a repaint() method is called. For instance, in the run() method of the applet, a repaint() method is called on every iteration through the loop.

So what does that mean? If the paint() method calls update() method, the applet does extra work by recomputing what the image should be. Yet less than a second ago, update() created a perfectly good picture, and it is still available for paint() to use. It is better if the paint() method copies the image created by update() onto the screen again.

Here is a more efficient pairing of `paint()` and `update()`:

```
public void paint (Graphics g) {
      if (offScreenImage != null)
          g.drawImage(offScreenImage, 0, 0, this);
          }

   public void update (Graphics g) {
      if (offScreenImage != null) {
          // Erase the screen
          offScreenGraphic.setColor (Color.lightGray);
          offScreenGraphic.fillRect (0, 0, nWidth, nHeight);
          offScreenGraphic.setCOlor (Color.black);

          // Paint each object
          for (int ndx = 0; ndx < AnimatedObjects.length; ndx++)
              AnimatedObjects[ndx].paint (offScreenGraphic,
                                    this);

          g.drawImage(offScreenImage, 0, 0, this);
          }
      }
```

TIP

One problem with this approach is that the `paint()` method is called as the applet begins running. At this time in the execution of the applet, there is no image to display because `update()` has not yet been called. The effect: the first screen that the user sees is a filled white rectangle that covers the entire applet. You can remedy this by printing a text message in the off-screen image when it is created.

The double buffered approach is one of the most widely used algorithms to improve animation. Part of the reason that this algorithm is widely used is the ease of implementing it. The next section discusses other widely used algorithms that help improve your animation.

Alternate Designs for a Two-Dimensional Animator

Here you learn about three tactics for better animations. First, time is essential to animations, and how you organize it can greatly simplify the program. Second, you learn about inbetweens, which reduce the amount of time you spend creating the animation. Third, backgrounds provide an alternative method to erase the screen and spice up the animation.

Time

The single most obvious feature in animation is that objects move. To have motion, there must be a concept of time. In this section, we'll consider three ways of implementing time and when they should be used.

Informing Objects

The animation in the first section of this chapter, each moving object received a `clockTick` method for each time period. This is very useful for most animations, where objects are continually changing and there is a cycle in the object.

One example of this type of animation is juggling a ball. Each ball follows a single path. The motions of the hands also follow a path. But the lengths of the ball path and the hand path are different. Therefore, each object should store where it is in its path.

You can use the design described in the Simple Animation section for this type of design.

Time Object

For other objects, what the object draws is easy to compute from the length of time the animation has run. An animation of a space ship entering the atmosphere or a running stop watch would be good examples of this type.

To use this type of time, you should create an `AnimationTime` object. This object receives `clockTick()` methods from the applet's `run` method. It will also return the current time when a `now()` method is sent to it. This code follows:

```
public class AnimationTime {
    int nCurrentTime = 0;

    public void clockTick () {
        nCurrentTime++;
        }

    public int now () {
        return nCurrentTime;
        }
    }
```

The `run()` method in your applet is elementary, because you only need to send a `clockTick()` method to the `AnimationTime` object. The changing objects in the animation no longer receive a `clockTick()` method from the run method. In the `paint()` method of the changing objects, the current time is queried from the `AnimationTime` object with the `now()` method.

Event Queues

An event queue is a commonly used technique of keeping track of time in a simulation. An event queue is an ordered list of actions. The list is ordered according to when the action will occur. If multiple actions occur at the same time, they are stored in the order that they were added to the event queue. In other words, an event queue queues up the events in chronological order. This approach is very useful for simulations in which actions may occur at irregular times. An event queue animation is useful if the changes in the applet do not occur in even intervals.

These implementations of time ease the creation of animation applets. There are two other common animation algorithms that can reduce the amount of time you spend creating the animation. The first is the use of inbetweens. When using inbetweens, you don't need to specify where the image will be at every time step. Instead, the computer determines where to draw the image. The second is the use of background images.

Inbetweens

When the first movie length animation was finished, it required over two million hand-drawn pictures. Because there were only four expert artists, it would have been impossible for these people to create the entire film. Instead, these artists drew the main or key frames (the frames specified by the creator of the animation). Other artists drew the inbetween frames (frames created to move objects between their key positions).

This approach is used today to create animations, except now the computer creates the inbetween frames. Generally, a computer needs more key frames than a human artist, because computers don't have common sense knowledge about how something should move. For instance, a falling rock increases speed as it falls, which is obvious, but a computer does not know this obvious fact. You can compensate for the computer's lack of common sense by specifying how the objects move between key positions. Four common trajectories are shown in Figure 25.3.

FIGURE 25.3.

These graphs show four different trajectories for moving objects.

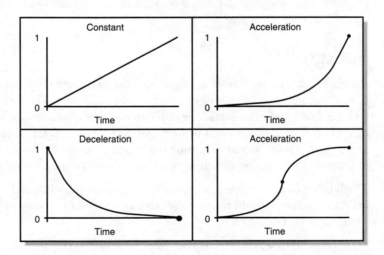

To see how inbetweens work, consider Figure 25.4, which shows a ball moving upwards using the acceleration trajectory from Figure 25.3. At first, the ball object moves slowly, but the distance between successive positions of the ball slowly increases. The successive positions of the balls are numbered, with 1 being the starting image, and 10 being the final image.

FIGURE 25.4.

The motion of an image corresponds to the location on the trajectory graph.

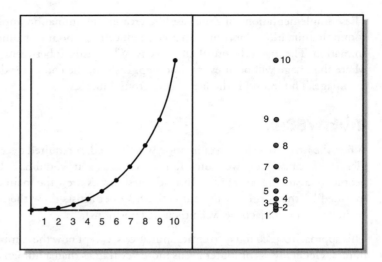

Inbetweens reduce the amount of information an animation artist must enter to create the desired animation. The next section presents a few hints for using a background image. Basically, a background image is a combination all the unchanging pictures into one image which is displayed in the background. Using a background can reduce the computations involved in the animation.

Background

Another trick that animators use is to draw the background on one sheet of paper, and then draw the characters and moving objects on a piece of plastic. The background remains the same and it is drawn once. By overlaying different the plastic pictures, the illusion of movement can be created. The same trick can be used with a computer. You first create a background image and save it. Then, instead of erasing the image with the `fillRect()`, you use `copyArea()` or `drawImage()` to initialize the off-screen image and draw the moving parts on top.

The borders of your moving images should be transparent just as if the characters were drawn on plastic. One program to erase the borders is called `giftrans`, and it is available at anonymous ftp sites. One site is

`http://www-genome.wi.mit.edu/WWW/tools/graphics/giftrans/`

This site contains a DOS executable file, for computers that can open a DOS window, and the C source code for other systems that have a C compiler. Many more sites have this file, and you can find at least 20 more by searching Lycos with the keyword giftrans.

Example Object Animator

Now let's take all the ideas that we have discussed in this chapter and make a multiple object animator. (The full source code is provided in the CD-ROM.) In this section, we'll see some of the highlights. First, we want the code to be able to read from the HTML file the number and motion of the animation objects. Second, I'll review how some of the advanced animation techniques are used in this example.

To enable the program to read the motion specifications from the applet tag, we need to do the following:

- store the images and animation objects in a vector
- generalize the ChangingImage and MovingImage to a single object
- add routines to the init() method to load the required information

The first step is to store the images and the animation objects in a vector. The applet then dynamically stores however many objects or images there will be in the animation. For more information about how to use a vector, see Chapter 31, "Extending Java with Content and Protocol Handlers."

The effect of an AnimatedImage object is a moving changing picture. It needs an array of images and two arrays for the path the object travels. However, the AnimatedImage object sometimes is used as a ChangingImage object, and it would be easier on the user if numbers could be passed for the path variables. The constructor has been overloaded for this purpose. The other change is the use of a vector to store the images, which allows us to store an arbitrary number of images.

The init() method is standard, but the applet generates the tags it needs as it runs. It does this by concatenating strings with numbers:

```
String at = getParameter ("IL" + 3);
```

This enables us to load an arbitrary number of animation objects. For the tags and what they mean, consult Table 25.2.

Table 25.2. Tags for Example 25.7.

TAG	Description
IL?	Image letter, what should prefix the image file names
IC?	The number of images
IO?	Image offset, which image should you start with
KF?	The number of key frames

continues

Table 25.2. continued

TAG	Description
X?_?	The x coordinates of the key frame
Y?_?	The y coordinates of the key frame
XT?_?	The type of motion between X values
YT?_?	The type of motion between Y values
W?_?	The number of points between values

The first ? in the tag refers to the number of the animated object. The second ? in the tag is the number of the frame. For instance, X3_7 refers to the x value of the third animated object in the seventh key frame.

Now, let's consider some of the advanced techniques and how they were used in this example. This program provides the functionality to create inbetweens and to use a background image. To keep the animation from flickering, this code also uses the double buffered approach to painting the image.

The paths of the moving objects are specified in the HTML file, but they are filled in as suggested by the user with the InBetweenGenerator object. This object requires three values: the key locations, how many frames to produce between each set of key locations, and the type of motion between each key location. It then generates an array of integers that represent the path that object traverses. To extend the InBetweenGenerator object to create another type of motion between end points, rewrite the interpolation() method to include your new motion. All the equations in this method take a number between 0 and 1, and return a number between 0 and 1. However, if you want the object to overshoot the source or the destination, you can create equations that produce values outside of that range.

Notice that a background image is an image that doesn't move and doesn't change. So to create a background for the animation, you just make the background image the first animated object.

Summary

In this chapter, we created the AnimationObject base class that simplifies the design. This animation class was then used to create moving text, flipbook style animation, and moving image animation. Double buffering was used to eliminate flicker, and we discussed the difference between the paint() and update() methods. Alternate designs for time keeping were discussed briefly. The final algorithms discussed were the use of inbetweens and background images.

What really launched Java into the spotlight for many people was the ability to perform animations on the World Wide Web. With the release of Netscape 2.0, Java is not the only way to create animations on Web pages. Increasingly, there are specialized programs that help you create animations that can be visible on Web pages. One of these is Shockwave for Director, which enables you to create animations in director, and Shockwave allows the animations to be viewed. VRML is language to specifies three dimensional animations, by specifying the locations objects and a viewing path. VRML currently requires special graphics hardware to view. Thus, Java is still the least expensive way to create an animation.

For More Information

Here are some web sites that you can browse that have more information about animations. The best collections of Java applets is Gamelan, and it has a page on animations. The URL is

```
http://www.gamelan.com/Gamelan.animation.html
```

These sites have many links to animations. Viewing some of these sites can give you ideas for your animations:

- `http://www.xm.com/cafe/AnimatePLUS/slideshow.html`—Description of the slideshow applet
- `http://www.auburn.edu/~harshec/WWW/Cinema.html`—An example of the slideshow in action
- `http://www-itg.lbl.gov/vbart/`—BART Schedule Animation
- `http://www.intrinsa.com/personal/steve/ClickBoard/ClickBoard.html`—Interactive Animation
- `http://www.sealevelsoftware.com/sealevel/javademo.htm`—Animation of Falling Rain Drops
- `http://www.dimensionx.com/dnx/StreamingAnimation/index.html`—Smooth loading Animation
- `http://www.geom.umn.edu/~daeron/apps/flag.html`—United States Flag blowing in the wind

More information about animation can be found at

```
http://java.sun.com/people/avh/javaworld/animation/
```

Phone Book and Telephone Dialer Applications

26

by Gene Leybzon

IN THIS CHAPTER

In this chapter we go through the design of an interactive online telephone book application. First of all, we need to decide which features we want to include in the online telephone book. Of course, we want it to display names and telephone numbers. It would be a nice feature to have a telephone book applet that dials selected numbers. Also, we will want to keep all telephone information on the Internet so that it will be easier to keep this information up-to-date and enable users to access this information from different computer platforms.

We can summarize features we want to be implemented in the telephone book application:

■ display telephone numbers

■ interactively search for phone numbers

■ provide a platform-independent interface to access information

■ display a friendly user interface

■ dial selected phone numbers and enter numbers the user wishes to dial

Here are the implementation-specific details:

■ take a client/server approach

■ use Web technology

■ develop the applet with Java

Application Design

Strategic decisions we need to make:

■ where and how to store data

■ how to dial a phone number

■ what controls to use for the user interface

Once we selected Java and Web technology as our implementation base, the answer about where to store the data apparently is clear: We will keep it as a document on a Web server. The format does not make a big difference. It could be an HTML document or simply a text file, as long as we can access it over the Net. We will use a very simple format. Name or address information will be delimited from the phone numbers by space or tab symbols. Separate records will be delimited by end-of-line markers. Here is an example of a data file:

```
Jim  (314) 935-81-34 <EOL>
Gene 0-117-095-158-5544 <EOL>
```

How can we dial a phone number? Our first idea would be to simply send the AT command sequence to a modem and have it dial the number over the interface with a telephone line. But what if you do not have a modem attached to your computer or it is busy because you are connected to a BBS or an Internet service provider? A better way would be to dial the number by playing telephone dialing tones on the computer speaker. We always can create or record dialing tones (also called DTMF tones, for *Dual Tone Multi-Frequency*) and use them when we need to dial a number.

Now let's think about the user interface. Definitely, we will need to display telephone numbers and a searchable list where the user can select a name or address. We will need a dial button. Also, it would be nice to have something like a telephone button pad so that users could enter a phone number that is not found in the telephone book.

We can start designing application components and creating a skeleton for our program. First of all, to have a valid Java application accessible from the Internet browser, we need to include an Applet class. Then, we need a class that incorporates user controls: buttons, edit boxes, and list boxes. Let's call it PhoneControls. To include the functionality of the telephone button pad, we will create a third class called ButtonPad.

The PhoneDial class, derived from the Java Applet class, implements the functionality of Java interactive application capable of communicating with Java-enabled Internet browsers. We will need to customize the default behavior of the Applet class in order to bring telephone book functionality to our users. At this time, the PhoneDial applet does almost nothing. It creates a PhoneControls class that will have telephone book controls, adding this to the center of its own window. Then it passes start and stop notification events to the PhoneControl class in order to enable controls when Applet is started and disable them when it is about to finish.

```java
public class PhoneDial extends Applet {
    PhoneControls controls;
    public void init() //applet initialization function
        {
                String strParam = getParameter("PHONEBOOK"); //get argument
"PHONEBOOK"
                    String strPhoneBook = (strParam == null) ? "phonebook.html" :
strParam; //use the default telephone book document name if  argument not found
                controls = new PhoneControls();  //create controls
                add("Center", controls); //add controls to the applet
    }

      public void start() //applet starting
        {
          controls.enable(); //enable controls on applet start
        }

      public void stop() //applet is about to be closed
        {
          controls.disable(); //disable controls
        }

    public static void main(String args[])
        {
        Frame f = new Frame("PhoneDial"); //create applet frame
        PhoneDial     phoneDial = new PhoneDial(); //create a new applet class

        phoneDial.init(); //init applet
        phoneDial.start(); //start applet
```

```
        f.add("Center", phoneDial); //add applet to the center of allocated window
        f.resize(150, 200); //resize to preferred dimensions
        f.show(); //show applet
         }
}
```

The function `main()` does a very important job for the applet: It creates a frame for our application and starts a thread where the application actually is running. At first it might seem a little strange. Why should we care about creating a thread for an application if it already is running? The key to understanding this is in the fact that we should return control from the `main` function, and must do it as fast as possible in order to free up the Internet browser for other useful tasks. At the same time, we will need to keep our application running to process user input, update the screen when necessary, and so on. Luckily, we do not need to write any code to start a thread. This is the default behavior of the `Applet` class.

We want to add a frame and possibly resize the applet to the dimensions we think would be optimal for our application. We do not expect that we will always get these dimensions. Actually, the browser will negotiate the real size to allocate for the applet during initialization. The application-desired size might be overridden when the actual space available is not large enough or when dimensions are specified in the HTML document that includes calls to the applet.

The last function call we want to add to the `main` function is `show()`. It will send a request to the Internet browser notifying it that our application is ready to be displayed and will cause it to update the part of the screen allocated for our applet.

Two other classes, `PhoneControls` and `ButtonPad`, are derived from the `Panel` class and inherit the functionality of that group of controls. `ButtonPad` will include telephone buttons and `PhoneControls` class will include all other elements of user interface: text box for telephone number, list box for selection telephone number from the list of persons and organizations, and the "dial" button that initiate process of dialing selected number.

```
class PhoneControls extends Panel      //class that will incorporate user controls
{
 ButtonPad controlsButtonPad; //declare class with telephone-style buttons

    public PhoneControls() // PhoneControls  class constructor
    {
        //TO DO: Add buttons "0" to "9", "*" and "#"
    }
}

class ButtonPad extends Panel  //class with telephone button pad keys
{
    public ButtonPad() // ButtonPad class constructor
    {
        //TO DO: Add text box for telephone number, list box and "Dial" button
    }
}
```

At this time, we included only empty constructors for `PhoneControls` and `ButtonPad` classes and placed the `ButtonPad` variable declaration into the `PhoneControls`. Note that we have not actually created a new `ButtonPad` class. We do not need that unless we actually have some buttons in it.

At this time we can compile our project and create an HTML file to test it out. We do not need to have anything in this page but a call to the `PhoneDial` applet:

```
<title>PhoneBook</title>
<hr>
<applet code=PhoneDial.class width=400 height=400>
</applet>
<hr>
```

It is no surprise that our application does nothing at this point except display a gray square.

Interface Design

Now we need to forget that we are computer programmers and become an artist for a moment. We need to place our controls so that they will be easy to find. We do not have too many of them—just a button pad, a window where we want to edit the phone number, and a box where we can select a person or organization we want to call. The more people involved in interface design, the more solutions you will have. One of the possible solutions for the user interface is shown on Figure 26.1.

FIGURE 26.1.

User interface for the Phone Book and Telephone Dialer application.

Now we can go back to coding and start from the button pad control. First, we need to select the layout. Because all buttons have the same size, `GridLayout` is the natural choice. We create a `GridLayout` class and declare the dimensions (four rows and three columns as on your telephone pad) and a gap between buttons.

```
GridLayout bag = new GridLayout(4, 3, 1, 1);
```

Now we can assign this layout to our panel as follows:

```
setLayout(bag);
```

At this time we can add buttons. To do this, we will create a button, set a label for it, and then add this button into our control panel. We use a small `case` statement to handle labels for the buttons on the bottom row differently—instead of sequential numbers we need to add `*`, `0`, and `#` to these buttons.

```
for(int i= 0; i<12; i++)
{
      Button b = new Button(" ");
      if (i<9)
         setLabel("   "+String.valueOf(i+1)+"   ");
      else
         switch(i)
         {
           case 9:
               b.setLabel("*");
               break;
           case 10:
               b.setLabel("0");
               break;
           case 11:
               b.setLabel("#");
               break;
         }
      add(b);
}
```

Now when the button pad is ready, we can place it on the `main` control panel and start adding other controls. First, we need to declare control elements in the `PhoneControl` class as follows:

```
TextField textPhone;
   Button        buttonDial;
   List          listPhone;
```

We will use the variable `textPhone` for the text control with the phone number, `buttonDial` for the large Dial button on the bottom of our form, and `listPhone` for the list box control where the user can look up the person or organization to call.

For the `PhoneControl`, we cannot select the same layout used for the button pad because all controls are of different sizes. We have a choice between `CardLayout`, `GridBagLayout`, `FlowLayout`, and `BorderLayout`. Of course, `CardLayout` does not fit—we do not want to have the user flipping cards until finding the right control; it is more appropriate for options in setup dialogs. `FlowLayout` just places controls one after another—we do not want that either. With the `GridBagLayout`, you have the most control over the placement of interface elements, but for this flexibility you will have to pay with extra coding. You will have to set up values that control placement to the `GridBagConstraints` class. It is not entirely a complex job but just a little boring. We will use `BorderLayout` because it is simple enough and allows us to control component placement in terms of North, South, East, West, and Center. Now we can set up layout and add our controls to the `PhoneControls` panel, as follows:

```
setLayout(new BorderLayout());
    htPhones = new Hashtable();
    listPhone = new List(5, false);
    add("East", listPhone);
    add("North", textPhone =  new TextField("", 12));
    add("West", controls = new ButtonPad());
    add("South", buttonDial =  new Button("Dial"));
```

The whole program at this point is shown in Listing 26.1.

Listing 26.1. The Phone Book application.

```
/*
 *  Phone Book Application
 */
import java.awt.*;
import java.applet.*;

public class PhoneDial extends Applet
{
    PhoneControls controls;

     public void init()
    {
        setLayout(new BorderLayout());
        controls = new PhoneControls();
        add("Center", controls);
    }

    public void start()
    {
        controls.enable();
    }

    public void stop()
    {
        controls.disable();
    }
}



    public static void main(String args[])
    {

      Frame f = new Frame("PhoneDial"); //create an application frame
      PhoneDial     phoneDial = new PhoneDial();

      phoneDial.init(); //init application
      phoneDial.start(); //start application

      f.add("Center", phoneDial); //add application to the frame
      f.resize(150, 200); //resize frame
      f.show(); //show frame
    }
}

class PhoneControls extends Panel
{
   Applet     appletParent;
   ButtonPad controls;
   TextField textPhone;
   Button     buttonDial;
   List       listPhone;

   public  PhoneControls(Applet appParent, String strPhBook)
   {
```

continues

Listing 26.1. continued

```java
        appletParent= appParent;

    setLayout(new BorderLayout());

    htPhones = new Hashtable(); //create a hash table for phone numbers
    listPhone = new List(5, false); //create a list to display names
        add("East", listPhone); //add list box control


    add("North", textPhone =  new TextField("", 12)); //create and add field for
                                                //the telephone number
    add("West", controls = new ButtonPad());//add button pad panel
    add("South", buttonDial =  new Button("Dial")); //create "Dial" button
    }
}

class ButtonPad extends Panel
{
    public ButtonPad()
    {
    //create GridBag layout with 4 rows and 3 columns, 1 pixel gap between
    //elements
    GridLayout bag = new GridLayout(4,3, 1, 1);

    //set layout to ButtonPad panel
    setLayout(bag);

    for(int i= 0; i<12; i++)
    {
      //create a new button
      Button b = new Button(" ");

      //set labels to button
      if (i<9)
        b.setLabel("   "+String.valueOf(i+1)+"   ");
      else
        switch(i)
        {
        case 9:
                b.setLabel("*");
            break;
        case 10:
                b.setLabel("0");
            break;
            case 11:
                b.setLabel("#");
            break;
        }
    //add button to the ButtonPad
    add(b);
    }

    }

}
```

Handling User Input

Now, when we have all of our controls in place, we can start adding some real functionality to our applet. First, we need to handle user input. We can do this by handling events that take place when the user pushes buttons or selects an item from the list box.

To do this we will create an Action()method in the PhoneControl applet. It will replace the default Action() method in the Control class that does nothing but pass event notification to the parent class. This function has two arguments. The first argument is the instance of the Event class that includes information about the type of the event, coordinates of the pointer, and event time stamp as well as a bunch of other useful data. The second argument is an event-dependent argument. For the push button events, this argument is a string with a button label that tell us which button causes the event to be fired.

The action method should return a true value when it processes an event, and no other action needs to be done based on this event. It should return a false value when the parent class needs to be notified in order to process the event again. For example, if we wanted to see which button was pressed in the ButtonPad class and at the same time wanted to handle the same push-the-button events in the PhoneControls class, we would implement the action method in the ButtonPad class so that it returned a false value on button notification events.

Here is the code that handles button events:

```
public boolean action(Event ev, Object arg)
{
        if (ev.target instanceof Button)
        {
                String label = (String)arg;
            if (label.equals("Dial"))
              DialPhone(textPhone.getText().trim());
            else
              textPhone.setText(textPhone.getText().trim()+label.trim());

                return true;
        }
}
```

First we determine what kind of event we are working with and whether this event is caused by pushing a dial button. We will call the function DialPhone() that will dial a phone number shown by textPhone control. Because the user can enter some spaces around the phone number, we want to trim them out before passing the argument to the DialPhone function. Don't worry about the implementation for the DialPhone function at this time—we will code it later.

If the user selects a button from the button pad, we will append the label from this button to the phone number in textControl. This simply enters the data from the button pad into the phone number field.

Before writing the code that will handle the selection of the list box, we need to think how the phone numbers are stored in our application. Probably, we do not want to show both phone numbers and names at the same time in the `listPhone` control. It makes more sense to show just the name of the person or organization and leave the phone number information off-screen unless a particular item in the list is selected.

To store the association between names and phone numbers, we will use a hash table. We can populate it from the phone book file and then do a lookup in this table to find the phone number associated with the selected name. To use a hash table we need to import the `java.util.Hashtable` class into our project and include a variable of `Hashtable` type called `htPhones` into the `PhoneControl` class.

To handle events resulting from the phone number selection on the button pad, we will add the following code to the action method:

```
if (ev.target instanceof List)
{
textPhone.setText((String)htPhones.get(listPhone.getSelectedItem()));
      return true;
}
```

After detecting that the event was created by the list box control we look up the item that is selected on the `listPhone`. We then use the selected name to get the phone number associated with it from the hash table and pass this phone number to the `textPhone` control.

This is all we need to do to handle user input.

How to Get Names and Phone Numbers Over the Net

Our goal is to write a function that will get a document with phone information over the Net.

To create a network connection, we will need to create an instance of the `URL` class. There are several constructors for the `URL` class, and we will choose one with two arguments: base network address and relative address. For the base address we will use the address of our applet, which we can obtain through the call to the `getDocumentBase()` method of applet class. The relative address will be the actual name for the file we want to get and it will be an argument passed to our applet.

After creating a URL connection, we can open a stream to get access to the data.

The following code will open an input stream to the network file `strPhoneBook`:

```
//declare an input stream object
    InputStream is = null;
    //declare URL
    URL urlPhBook;

    try
    {
```

```
            //open connection to file with name strPhoneBook
        urlPhBook = new URL(appletParent.getDocumentBase(), strPhoneBook);

                //open an input stream
          is = urlPhBook.openStream();

        /*
                *   Do something useful here
        */

                //close input stream
                is.close();

    }

    catch (MalformedURLException e)
    {
        //report exception
    }
```

Note that we have to catch and handle `MalformedURLException` in our application because the applet does not have a default handler for most network exceptions. We will not perform any detailed processing of the exception, but will just report it to the user.

Parsing Names and Phone Numbers

The file with names and phone numbers that we keep on the Net will have a very simple format. Each record in this file has two fields: a name or an address, and a phone number. Records will be separated by line separators, either carriage return or a combination of carriage return and line feed so that both UNIX and PC users can use their favorite text editors. Fields in a record will be separated by space or tab symbols. Also, we want to have comments in our file so we will ignore all lines starting with the # symbol and everything after double forward slashes. Here is an example of the phone file acceptable by the applet:

```
#Our simple phone book
work   (314) 994 1976
home (314) 863-6688
FAX   314-537-5542     // my work FAX number
```

To parse the file with phone records, we will use the `StreamTokenizer` class. `StreamTokenizer` incorporates a simple parser that will help us to split an input stream into the sequence of tokens. The tokenizer requires a buffered stream on the input so we need to construct a `BufferedInputStream` based on our `InputStream` class.

The following code creates a buffered input stream with 4KB of memory allocated for the buffer and an instance of the `StreamTokenizer` class called `st`.

```
StreamTokenizer st = new StreamTokenizer(new BufferedInputStream(is, 4000));
```

Before the `StreamTokenizer` can do any useful jobs, we need to define what symbols will be acceptable as regular characters, how we want to designate comments, and whether we want to handle end-of-line symbols differently from others:

```
st.eolIsSignificant(true);        //end of line is a significant symbol
st.commentChar('#');              //comments will start with '#' symbol
st.slashSlashComments(true); //allow C++ -style comments (//)
st.wordChars('(', ')');    //  '(' and  ')' are regular characters
st.wordChars('-', 'z');    //  '-', numbers and letters are regular characters
```

Now we can write an input stream-parsing function that will put name information into the list control and phone numbers into the hash table, as follows:

```
int nCnt = 0;    //record counter
     htPhones.clear(); //clear the hash table
 scan:
     while (true)   //main paring loop
         switch (st.nextToken()) //what is our next token?
         {
          case StreamTokenizer.TT_EOF: //end of file
               break scan;  //get out of the loop
          default: //unknown token
             break;
               case StreamTokenizer.TT_WORD: //word (any sequence of
                                             //characters from the union of
                                             //intervals 0..9, A-Z, a-z, or
                                             //characters ')', '(' or '-')

          String strRecord = st.sval; //text: name or address
          String strValue = "";

          st.nextToken();  //get next token
          while (st.ttype != StreamTokenizer.TT_EOL &&
     st.ttype != StreamTokenizer.TT_EOF) //parse to the end of line or to the
                                         //end of file - whichever comes first
          {
     if (st.ttype == StreamTokenizer.TT_WORD)  //text characters from the
                                               //phone number: '-', '(' or ')'
                                               //symbols
          {
                 strValue = strValue + st.sval;
          }
          else
             if (st.ttype == StreamTokenizer.TT_NUMBER) //numbers from the
                                                        //phone number
             {
                 strValue = strValue + String.valueOf(st.nval);
             }
          st.nextToken();
          }

          nCnt++; //increment phone records counter
          lb.addItem(strRecord, nCnt); //add name or address to the list box
          htPhones.put(strRecord, strValue); //add phone number to the hash
                                             //table

          break; //parse next record
     }//end of parsing loop
```

It's Time to Dial a Number—the DialPhone() Function

The only major piece of code we need to write at this point is the `DialPhone()` function. This function is called when a user presses the Dial button. The only argument for this function is the phone number the user wants to dial. This function should play the DTMF tones corresponding to this number.

The DTMF signal is a direct algebraic summation of the amplitudes of two waves of different frequencies. For instance, 1 is coded as the sum of the 1209 Hz and 697 Hz signals. A full list of DTMF tones is shown in Table 26.1. We do not want to generate and mix tones on the sound card, so we will use prerecorded audio files with DTMF signals. It is possible to use WaveGen or a similar sound file generating program to generate these files. Assume that you already have audio files and have placed those files in the /audio/ subdirectory.

Table 26.1. DTMF tones.

Telephone key	High tone [Hz]	Low tone [Hz]	Filename
0	1336	941	0.au
1	1209	697	1.au
2	1336	697	2.au
3	1477	697	3.au
4	1209	770	4.au
5	1336	770	5.au
6	1477	770	6.au
7	1209	852	7.au
8	1336	852	8.au
9	1477	852	9.au
*	1209	941	star.au
#	1477	941	pound.au

To play a DTMF sequence corresponding to a telephone number, we want to separate the string with the telephone number into the array of characters and then play the sequence of audio clips with tones based on the appropriate characters.

To separate a string `Phone` into array `sepPhone[]`, we will use the `getChars()` function from the `String` class:

```
char sepPhone[];
sepPhone =  new char [phone.length()];
phone.getChars(0, phone.length(), sepPhone, 0);
```

To play an audio clip from the Java applet you need to call the `play()` function, which takes two arguments: the URL that specifies the directory on the Web server with the audio file and the string with the name of the audio file. To get the URL we can call `getCodeBase()`, which returns the URL of our applet. The filename we use is based on the telephone key we want to play.

Of course, we do not want to play anything other than the keys from the telephone panel, so we ignore all of the characters from the `sepPhone` array other than numbers or * and # characters.

```
for (int i = 0; i < phone.length(); i++)  //loop throughout all keys from sepPhone
                                           //array
{
   if ((sepPhone[i] >= '0') && (sepPhone[i] <= '9')) //if we have a valid numeric
                                                      //key
        appletParent.play(appletParent.getCodeBase(), "audio/"+sepPhone[i]+".au");
//play one of files 0.au to 9.au base on sepPhone[i] character
   else if (sepPhone[i] == '*') //star key
        appletParent.play(appletParent.getCodeBase(), "audio/star.au");
//play star.au file
        else if (sepPhone[i] == '#') //pound key
            appletParent.play(appletParent.getCodeBase(), "audio/pound.au");
//play pound.au file
}
```

Add Information Functions

Like in an auto body shop when the work is almost done, a little more effort needs to be done to make the results look nice. For our application, we will add `getAppletInfo()` and `getParameterInfo()` functions, and add functions to show the current application status—it always pays to be nice to users.

The function `getAppletInfo()` should return a string with copyright, version, and author information. It potentially could be used by Internet browsers to identify applets that could cause problems and reject them. The code is as follows:

```
public String getAppletInfo()
{
    return "Phone Book and Dialer. Copyright (C) 1995, 1996 Gene Leybzon";
}
```

The function `getParameterInfo()` returns a two-dimensional string array with a description of applet arguments. Each row of this array has a parameter name, type, and description. Because we have just one parameter for our applet, we will return the 1-by-3 array, as follows:

```
public String[][] getParameterInfo()
{
      String[][] info =
      {
        {"phonebook",        "url",              "phone directory file"}
      };
      return info;
}
```

To show applet messages we will use the ShowStatus() function that takes a string and puts it into the Applet context. Depending on the Internet browser this information could be shown as a browser information panel or in a separate window with the Java applet log.

Add some more comments and we are done. Listing 26.2 contains the final revision of PhoneDial applet source code.

Listing 26.2. Source code for the final revision of the PhoneDial applet.

```
/* Phone Book Applet
 */
import java.awt.*;
import java.applet.*;
import java.io.StreamTokenizer;
import java.io.InputStream;
import java.io.BufferedInputStream;
import java.net.URL;
import java.net.MalformedURLException;
import java.util.Hashtable;

public class PhoneDial extends Applet {
/* Phone Book applet */
    PhoneControls controls;

    public void init()
    {
          String strParam = getParameter("PHONEBOOK");
          String strPhoneBook = (strParam == null) ? "phonebook.html" : strParam;

          setLayout(new BorderLayout());
          controls = new PhoneControls(this, strPhoneBook);
          add("Center", controls);
    }

    public void start()
    {
          controls.enable();
    }

    public void stop()
    {
          controls.disable();
    }

    public String getAppletInfo()
    {
```

continues

Listing 26.2. continued

```
            return "Phone Book and Dialer. Copyright (C) Gene Leybzon, 1995, 1996";
    }

    public String[][] getParameterInfo()
    {
        String[][] info =
        {
            {"phonebook",       "url",              "phone directory file"},
        };
        return info;
    }

    public boolean handleEvent(Event e)
    {
        if (e.id == Event.WINDOW_DESTROY)
        {
            System.exit(0);
        }

        return false;
    }

    public static void main(String args[])
    {
        Frame f = new Frame("PhoneDial");
        PhoneDial      phoneDial = new PhoneDial();

        phoneDial.init();
        phoneDial.start();

        f.add("Center", phoneDial);
        f.resize(150, 200);
        f.show();
    }
}

class PhoneControls extends Panel
/* Phone Book Controls */
{
    Applet     appletParent;
    ButtonPad controls;
    TextField textPhone;
    Button     buttonDial;
    List       listPhone;
    Hashtable htPhones;

    public  PhoneControls(Applet appParent, String strPhBook)
    {
        appletParent= appParent;

        setLayout(new BorderLayout());

        htPhones = new Hashtable();
        listPhone = new List(5, false);
        add("East", listPhone);
```

```
    FillListBox(listPhone, strPhBook);
    listPhone.select(1);

    add("North", textPhone =  new TextField("", 12));
    add("West", controls = new ButtonPad());
    add("South", buttonDial =  new Button("Dial"));
}

public boolean action(Event ev, Object arg)
{
    if (ev.target instanceof Button)
    {
        String label = (String)arg;
        if (label.equals("Dial"))
            DialPhone(textPhone.getText().trim());
        else
            textPhone.setText(textPhone.getText().trim()+label.trim());

        return false;

    }

    if (ev.target instanceof List)
    {
        textPhone.setText((String)htPhones.get(listPhone.getSelectedItem()));
        return false;
    }

    return false;
}

public void DialPhone(String phone)
/* Play DTMF tone sequence */
{
    char sepPhone[];
    sepPhone =  new char [phone.length()];
    phone.getChars(0, phone.length(), sepPhone, 0);

    appletParent.showStatus("Dial in progress ..." + phone);
    for (int i = 0; i < phone.length(); i++)
    {
        if ((sepPhone[i] >= '0') && (sepPhone[i] <= '9'))
        {
            appletParent.play(appletParent.getCodeBase(),"audio"+sepPhone[i]+".au");
        }
        else
            if (sepPhone[i] == '*')
                appletParent.play(appletParent.getCodeBase(), "audio/star.au");
        else
            if (sepPhone[i] == '#')
                appletParent.play(appletParent.getCodeBase(), "audio/pound.au");
    }
}

public void FillListBox(List lb, String strPhoneBook)
/* Get document strPhoneBook from the net and fill list box control */
{
```

continues

Listing 26.2. continued

```
        InputStream is = null;

        URL urlPhBook;
        try
        {
        urlPhBook = new URL(appletParent.getDocumentBase(), strPhoneBook);

        try
        {
        is =  urlPhBook.openStream();

        StreamTokenizer st = new StreamTokenizer(new BufferedInputStream(is, 4000));
        st.eolIsSignificant(true);
        st.commentChar('#');
        st.slashSlashComments(true);
        st.wordChars('(', ')');
        st.wordChars('-', 'z');

        int nCnt = 0;
        htPhones.clear();
scan:
      while (true)
          switch (st.nextToken())
          {
          case StreamTokenizer.TT_EOF:
                                break scan;
          default:
                        break;
          case StreamTokenizer.TT_WORD:
              String strRecord = st.sval;
              String strValue = "";

              st.nextToken();
              while (st.ttype != StreamTokenizer.TT_EOL &&
                      st.ttype != StreamTokenizer.TT_EOF)
              {
                if (st.ttype == StreamTokenizer.TT_WORD)
                {
                        strValue = strValue + st.sval;
                }
                else
                  if (st.ttype == StreamTokenizer.TT_NUMBER)
                  {
                        strValue = strValue + String.valueOf(st.nval);
                  }
                st.nextToken();
              }

              nCnt++;
              lb.addItem(strRecord, nCnt);
              htPhones.put(strRecord, strValue);

              break;
          }

          is.close();
```

```
          }

      catch(Exception e)
      {
        String message = e.toString();
        appletParent.showStatus("Exception ..." + message);
      }
      }

      catch (MalformedURLException e)
      {
          String message = e.toString();
          appletParent.showStatus("Exception ..." + message);
      }
      }
}

class ButtonPad extends Panel
/* Telephone button pad controls */
{
    public ButtonPad()
    {
     GridLayout bag = new GridLayout(4,3, 1, 1);
     setLayout(bag);

     for(int i= 0; i<12; i++)
     {
       Button b = new Button(" ");
       if (i<9)
          b.setLabel("   "+String.valueOf(i+1)+"   ");
       else
          switch(i)
          {
           case 9:
               b.setLabel("*");
               break;
           case 10:
               b.setLabel("0");
               break;
           case 11:
               b.setLabel("#");
               break;
          }

          add(b);
     }
    }
}
```

Summary

In this chapter we get through the process of designing and implementing a real-world Java application — telephone book and phone number dialer. We have used Java AWT library to create a user interface, and Java applet methods to get information from the Internet and play sound files. Other topics we have discussed include interface layout management, input stream parsing, and event handling.

Network Programming

Introduction to Java Network Programming

27

by Mike Fletcher

One of the best features of Java is its networking support. Java has classes that range from low-level TCP/IP connections to ones that provide instant access to resources on the World Wide Web. Even if you have never done any network programming before, Java makes it easy.

The following chapters introduce you to the networking classes and how to use them. A guide to what is covered by each chapter follows:

- Chapter 27, "Introduction to Java Network Programming"

  The chapter you are reading contains an introduction to TCP/IP networking and a list of the concepts you should be familiar with before reading the rest of the networking section.

- Chapter 28, "The java.net Package"

  This chapter is a tour of the classes that make up the Java networking package java.net. The exceptions raised by the networking classes also are covered, as are the interfaces specified by the package.

- Chapter 29, "Network Programming"

  This chapter, the meat of the networking chapters, contains examples of how to use the networking classes. There also is a section about deciding which Java classes best suit your networking needs.

- Chapter 30, "Overview of Content and Protocol Handlers"

  The chapter discusses what protocol and content handlers are, how they can be applied, and provides an introduction to writing your own.

- Chapter 31, "Extending Java with Content and Protocol Handlers"

  New classes can be written to allow the URL class to deal with new protocols and content types. For example, a Web browser written in Java could be extended to deal with a new image format. This chapter details how to write and use these classes.

Prerequisites

Though networking with Java is fairly simple, there are a few concepts and classes from other packages that you should be familiar with before reading this part of the book. If you are only interested in writing an applet that interacts with an HTTP daemon, you probably can just concentrate on the URL class for now. For the other network classes, you will need at least a passing familiarity with the World Wide Web, java.io classes, threads, and TCP/IP networking.

World Wide Web Concepts

If you are using Java you probably already have a familiarity with the Web. Knowledge of how Uniform Resource Locators (URLs) work is needed to use the URL and URLConnection classes.

`java.io` Classes

Once you have a network connection established using one of the low-level classes, you will be using `java.io.InputStream` and `java.io.OutputStream` objects or appropriate subclasses of the objects to communicate with the other endpoint. Also, many of the `java.net` classes throw `java.io.IOException` when they encounter a problem.

Threads

Although not strictly needed for networking, threads make using the network classes easier. Why tie up your user interface waiting for a response from a server when a separate communication thread can wait rather than the interface thread? Server applications also can service several clients simultaneously by spawning off a new thread to handle each incoming connection.

TCP/IP Networking

Before using the networking facilities of Java, you need to be familiar with the terminology and concepts of the TCP/IP networking model. The last part of this chapter should serve to get you up to speed.

Internet Networking: A Quick Overview

TCP/IP (Transmission Control Protocol/Internet Protocol) is the set of networking protocols used by Internet hosts to communicate with other Internet hosts. If you have ever had any experience with networks or network programming in general you should be able to just skim this section and check back when you find a term you are not familiar with. A list of references is given at the end of this section if you would like more detailed information.

TCP/IP and Networking Terms

Like any other technical field, computer networking has its own set of jargon. These definitions should clear up what the terms mean.

- **host**

  An individual machine on a network. Each host on a TCP/IP network has at least one unique address (see *IP number*).

- **hostname**

  A symbolic name that can be mapped into an IP number. Several methods exist for performing this mapping, such as DNS (Domain Name Service) and Sun's NIS (Network Information Services).

- **IETF**

  The Internet Engineering Task Force, a group responsible for maintaining Internet standards and defining new ones.

- **internet**

  A network of networks. When capitalized as the Internet it refers to the globally interconnected network of networks.

- **IP number**

  A unique address for each host on the Internet (unique in the sense that a given number may only be used by one particular machine, but a particular machine may be known by multiple IP numbers). This currently is a 32-bit number that consists of a network part and a host part. The network part identifies the network the host resides on and the host part is the specific host on that network. Sometimes the IP number is referred to as the *IP address* of a host.

- **packet**

  A single message sent over a network. Sometimes a packet is referred to as a *datagram*, but the former term usually refers to data at the network layer and the latter refers to a higher-layer message.

- **protocol**

  A set of data formats and messages used to transmit information. Different network entities must speak the same protocol in order to understand each other.

- **protocol stack**

  Networking services can be thought of as different layers that use lower-level services to provide services to higher-level services. This set of layers providing network functionality is known as a *protocol stack*.

- **RFC**

  Request For Comments—documents in which proposed Internet standards are released. Each RFC is issued a sequential number, which is how they are usually referenced. Examples are RFC 791, which specifies the Internet Protocol (the IP of TCP/IP), and RFC 821, which specifies the protocol used for transferring e-mail between Internet hosts (SMTP).

- **router**

  A host that knows how to forward packets between different networks. A router can be a specialized piece of network hardware or can be something as simple as a machine with two network interfaces (each on a different physical network).

- **socket**

  A communications *endpoint* (that is, one end of a conversation). In the TCP/IP context, a socket usually is identified by a unique pair consisting of the source IP address and port number and the destination IP address and port number.

The Internet Protocols

TCP/IP is a set of communications protocols for communicating between different types of machines and networks (hence the name *internet*). The name TCP/IP comes from two of the protocols: the Transmission Control Protocol and the Internet Protocol. Other protocols in the TCP/IP suite are the User Datagram Protocol (UDP), the Internet Control Message Protocol (ICMP), and the Internet Group Multicast Protocol (IGMP).

These protocols define a standard format for exchanging information between machines (known as *hosts*) regardless of the physical connections between them. TCP/IP implementations exist for almost every type of hardware and operating system imaginable. Software exists to transmit IP datagrams over network hardware ranging from modems to fiber-optic cable.

TCP/IP Network Architecture

There are four layers in the TCP/IP network model. Each of the protocols in the TCP/IP suite provides for communication between entities in one of these layers. These lower-level layers are used by higher-level layers to get data from host to host. The layers are as follows, with examples of what protocols live at each layer:

- Physical (Ethernet, Token Ring, PPP)
- Network (IP)
- Transport (TCP, UDP)
- Application (Telnet, HTTP, FTP, Gopher)

FIGURE 27.1.

The TCP/IP protocol stack.

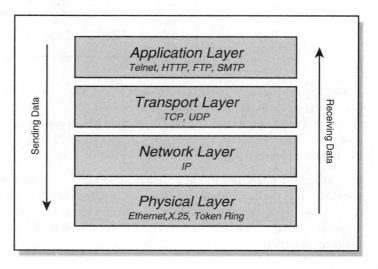

Each layer in the stack takes data from the one above it and adds the information needed to get the data to their destination, using the services of the layer below. One way to think of this layering is like the layers of an onion. Each protocol layer adds a layer to the packet going down the protocol stack. When the packet is received, each layer peels off its addressing to determine where to send the packet next.

As an example, suppose that your Web browser wants to retrieve something from a Web server running on a host on the same physical network. The browser sends an HTTP request using the TCP layer. The TCP layer asks the IP layer to send the data to the proper host. The IP layer then would use the physical layer to send the data to the appropriate host.

At the receiving end, each layer strips off the addressing information that the sender added and determines what to do with the data. Continuing the example, the physical layer would pass the received IP packet to the IP layer. The IP layer would determine that the packet is a TCP packet and pass it to the TCP layer. The TCP layer would pass the packet to the HTTP daemon process. The HTTP daemon then processes the request and sends the data requested back through the same process to the other host.

FIGURE 27.2.

Addressing information is added and removed at each layer.

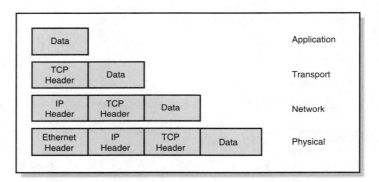

In a case where the hosts are not on the same physical network, the IP layer would handle routing the packet through the correct series of hosts (known as *routers*) until it reaches its destination. One of the nice features of the IP protocol is that individual hosts do not have to know how to reach every host on the Internet. The host simply passes to a default router any packets for networks it does not know how to reach.

For example, a university might only have one machine with a physical connection to the Internet. All of the campus routers would know to forward all packets destined for the Internet to this host. Similarly, any host on the Internet only has to know to get packets to this one router to reach any host at the university. The router would forward the packets to the appropriate local routers.

FIGURE 27.3.

An example of IP routing.

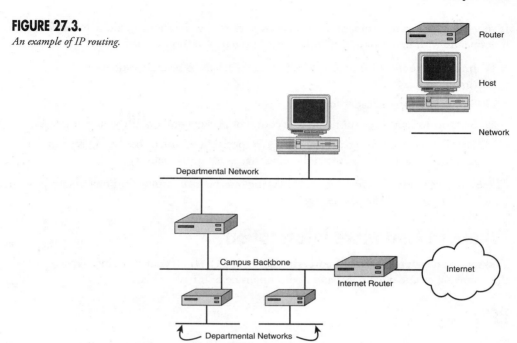

There is a publicly available program for UNIX platforms called `traceroute` that is useful if you want to find out what routers actually are responsible for getting a packet from one host to another and how long each hop takes. The source for `traceroute` can be found by consulting an Archie server for an FTP site near you, or from `ftp://ee.lbl.gov`.

The Future: IP Version 6

Back when the TCP/IP protocols were being developed in the early 1970s, 32-bit IP numbers seemed more than capable of addressing all the hosts on an internet. Though there currently is not a lack of IP numbers, the explosive growth of the Internet in recent years is rapidly consuming the remaining unassigned addresses. To address this lack of IP numbers a new version of the IP protocols is being developed by the IETF. This new version, known as either IPv6 or IPng (IP Next Generation), will provide for a much larger address space of 128 bits. This address space will allow for approximately 3.4×10^{38} different IP addresses.

IPv6 will be backward compatible with current IP implementations to allow older clients to interoperate with newer ones. Other benefits of the new version are as follows:

- Improved support for *multicasting* (sending packets to several destinations at one time).
- Simplified packet header formats.
- Support for authentication and encryption of packet contents at the network layer.
- Support for designating a connection as a special flow which should be given special treatment (such as real-time audio data that needs quick delivery).

These enhancements to TCP/IP should allow the Internet to continue the phenomenal growth it has experienced over the past few years.

Where to Find More Information

This was not meant to completely cover the subject of TCP/IP. If your curiosity has been piqued, the following online documents and books might be of interest to you.

RFCs

The first and definitive source of information on the IP protocol family are the Request For Comments documents defining the standards themselves. An index of all of RFC documents is available through the Web at `http://ds.internic.net/ds/rfc-index.html`. This page has pointers to all currently available RFCs (organized in groups of 100) as well as a searchable index.

Table 27.1 gives the numbers of some relevant RFCs and what they cover. Keep in mind that a given RFC might have been made obsolete by a subsequent RFC. The InterNIC site's index will note in the description any documents that were made obsolete by a subsequent RFC.

Table 27.1. RFC documents.

RFC Number	Topic
791	The Internet Protocol (IP)
793	The Transmission Control Protocol (TCP)
768	The User Datagram Protocol (UDP)
894	Transmission of IP Datagrams over Ethernet Networks
1171	The PPP Protocol
1883	IP Version 6

RFC Number	Topic
1602	The Internet Standards Process: How an RFC Becomes a Standard
1880	Current Internet Standards

Books

A good introduction to TCP/IP is the book *TCP/IP Network Administration* by Craig Hunt (O'Reilly and Associates, ISBN 0-937175-82-X). Though written as a guide for system administrators of UNIX machines, the book contains an excellent introduction to all aspects of TCP/IP, such as routing and the Domain Name Service (DNS).

Another book worth checking out is *The Design and Implementation of the 4.3BSD UNIX Operating System* by Samuel J. Leffler et al. (Addison-Wesley, ISBN 0-201-06196-1). In addition to covering how a UNIX operating system works, it contains a chapter on the TCP/IP implementation.

If you are a beginner, another way to get started get started with TCP/IP is by reading *Teach Yourself TCP/IP in 14 Days* by Timothy Parker (Sams Publishing, ISBN 0-672-30549-6).

Summary

This chapter is a roadmap to the next three chapters. It has shown what concepts you need to be familiar with before you dive into network programming in Java. You should be comfortable with how TCP/IP networking operates in general (or at least know where to look for more information).

The java.net Package

28

by Mike Fletcher

This chapter serves as an introduction to the package containing Java's networking facilities. It covers the classes, interfaces, and exceptions that make up the `java.net` package.

Unless otherwise noted, classes, exceptions, and interfaces are members of the `java.net` package. The full package name will be given for members of other classes such as `java.io.IOException`. Method names will be shown followed by `()`, such as `close()`.

These descriptions are not intended to be a complete reference. For a more detailed description of the components of the `java.net` package and the arguments of their various methods, see Appendix A, "Java Language Summary."

Classes

The classes in the networking package fall into three general categories:

■ Web interface classes

The `URL` and `URLConnection` classes provide a quick and easy way to access content using Uniform Resource Locators. This content may be located on the local machine, or anywhere on the WWW. The `URLEncoder` class provides a way to convert text for use as arguments for CGI scripts. The `URL` class is covered in Chapter 29, "Network Programming."

■ Raw network interface classes

`Socket`, `ServerSocket`, `DatagramSocket`, and `InetAddress` are the classes that provide access to plain, bare-bones networking facilities. They are the building blocks for implementing new protocols, talking to preexisting servers, and the like. Chapter 29 covers using these classes in detail.

■ Extension classes

The `ContentHandler` and `URLStreamHandler` abstract classes are used to extend the capabilities of the `URL` class. Chapter 31, "Extending Java with Content and Protocol Handlers," explains how to write handlers for new protocols and content types.

Keep in mind that some of the `java.net` classes (such as `URLConnection` and `ContentHandler`) are abstract classes and cannot be directly instantiated. Subclasses provide the actual implementations for the different protocols and contents.

The following table lists all of the classes in the package along with a brief description of what functionality each provides.

Table 28.1. Classes of the `java.net` package.

Class	Purpose
URL	Represents a Uniform Resource Locator
URLConnection	Retrieves content addressed by URL objects
Socket	Provides a TCP (connected, ordered stream) socket
ServerSocket	Provides a server (listening) TCP socket
DatagramSocket	Provides a UDP (connectionless datagram) socket
DatagramPacket	Represents a datagram to be sent using a DatagramSocket
InetAddress	Represents a host name and its corresponding IP number or numbers
URLEncoder	Encodes text in the x-www-form-urlencoded format
URLStreamHandler	Subclasses implement communications streams for different URL protocols
ContentHandler	Subclasses know how to turn MIME objects into corresponding Java objects
SocketImpl	Subclasses provide access to TCP/IP facilities

The description of each class is given in the following format:

- A general description of the class and its purpose
- A description of the class constructors and their arguments
- An overview of the methods provided
- A description of the member variables of the class, if any

URL

The URL class represents a web Uniform Resource Locator. Along with the URLConnection class, this class provides access to resources located on the World Wide Web via the HTTP protocol or on the local machine through file: URLs.

Constructors

The constructors for the URL class provide for creating absolute and relative URLs. There is a constructor that takes a whole String as a URL, as well as constructors allowing the protocol, host, and file to be specified in separate String objects. The class also provides for relative URLs with a constructor that takes another URL object for context and a String as the relative part.

Methods

The URL class provides methods for retrieving individual components of the represented URL (such as the protocol and the host name). It also provides comparison methods for determining if two URL objects reference the same content.

Probably the most important method is getContent(). This returns an object representing the contents of the URL. There also is an openConnection() method that returns a URLConnection object that will provide a connection to the remote content. The connection object then can be used to retrieve the content, as with the getContent() method.

URLConnection

The URLConnection class does the actual work of retrieving content that is specified by URL objects. This class is an abstract class, and as such cannot be directly instantiated. Instead, subclasses of the class provide the implementation to handle different protocols. The subclasses know how to use the appropriate subclasses of the URLStreamHandler class to connect and retrieve the content.

Constructors

The only constructor provided takes a URL object and returns a URLConnection object for that URL. However, because this is an abstract class it cannot be directly instantiated. Instead of using a constructor you probably will use the URL class openConnection() method. The Java runtime system will create an instance of the proper connection subclass to handle the URL.

Methods

The getContent() method acts just like the URL class method of the same name. The class also provides methods to get information such as the content type of the resource or HTTP header information sent with the resource. Examples of these methods are getContentType(), which returns what the HTTP Content-Type header contained, and the verbosely named guessContentTypeFromStream(), which will try to determine the content type by observing the incoming data stream.

Methods also are provided to obtain an InputStream object that reads data from the connection. For URLs that provide for output there is a corresponding getOutputStream() method. The remaining URLConnection methods deal with retrieving or setting class variables.

Variables

There are several protected members that describe aspects of the connection, such as the URL connected to and whether the connection supports input or output. A variable also notes whether the connection will use a cached copy of the object or not.

Socket

A socket object is the Java representation of a TCP connection. When a socket is created, a connection is opened to the specified destination. Stream objects can be obtained to send and receive data to the other end.

Constructors

The constructors for the socket class take two arguments: the name (or IP address) of the host to connect to, and the port number on that host to connect to. The host name may be given as either a String or as an InetAddress object. In either case the port number is specified as an integer.

Methods

The two most important methods are getInputStream() and getOutputStream(), which return stream objects that can be used to communicate through the socket. A close() method is provided to tell the underlying operating system to terminate the connection. Methods also are provided to retrieve information about the connection such as the local and remote port numbers and an InetAddress representing the remote host.

ServerSocket

The ServerSocket represents a listening TCP connection. Once an incoming connection is requested, the ServerSocket object will return a socket object representing the connection. In normal use, another thread would be spawned off to handle the connection. The ServerSocket then is free to listen for the next connection request.

Constructors

Both constructors take as an argument the local port number to listen for connection requests. A constructor is provided that also takes the maximum time to wait for a connection as a second argument.

Methods

The most important method is accept(). This method will block the calling thread until a connection is received. A socket object is returned representing this new connection. The close() method tells the operating system to stop listening for requests on the socket. Also provided are methods to retrieve the host name the socket is listening on (in InetAddress form) and the port number being listened to.

DatagramSocket

The `DatagramSocket` represents a connectionless datagram socket. This class works with the `DatagramPacket` class to provide for communication using the UDP protocol.

Constructors

Because UDP is a connectionless protocol, you do not need to specify a host name when creating a `DatagramSocket`—only the port number on the local host. There is a second constructor which takes no arguments. When this constructor is used the port number will be assigned arbitrarily by the operating system.

Methods

The two most important methods are `send()` and `receive()`. Each takes as an argument an appropriately constructed `DatagramPacket` (described in the following section). In the case of the `send()` method, the data contained in the packet is sent to the specified host and port. The `receive()` method will block execution until a packet is received by the underlying socket, at which time the data will be copied into the packet provided.

The other methods provided are a `close()` method to ask for the underlying socket to be shut down, and a `getLocalPort()` method that will return the local port number associated with the socket. This last method is particularly useful when you let the system pick the port number for you.

DatagramPacket

`DatagramPacket` objects represent one packet of data that is sent using the UDP protocol (using a `DatagramSocket`).

Constructors

The `DatagramPacket` class provides two constructors: one for outgoing packets and one for incoming packets. The incoming version takes as arguments a `byte` array to hold the received data and an `int` specifying the size of the array. The outgoing version also takes the remote host name (as an `InetAddress` object) and the port number on that host to send the packet to.

Methods

There are four methods in the class allowing the data, datagram length, and addressing (`InetAdress` and port number) information for the packet to be extracted. The methods are named, respectively, `getData()`, `getLength()`, `getAddress()`, and `getPort()`.

InetAddress

The InetAddress class represents a host name and its IP numbers. The class itself also provides the functionality to obtain the IP number for a given host name—similar to the C gethostbyname() function on UNIX and UNIX-like platforms.

Constructors

There are no explicit constructors for InetAddress objects. Instead, you use the static class method getByName(), which returns a reference to an InetAddress. Because some hosts might be known by more than one IP address, there also is a method getAllByName(), which returns an array of InetAddress objects.

Methods

Aside from the preceding static methods, there are methods that will return a String representation of the host name that the InetAddress represents (getHostName()) and an array of the raw bytes of the address (getAddress()). There also is an equals() method for the comparison of address objects. The class also supports a toString() method for printing out the host name and IP address textually.

URLEncoder

This class provides a method to encode arbitrary text in the x-www-form-urlencoded format. The primary use for this is in encoding arguments in URLs for CGI scripts. Nonprinting or punctuation characters are converted to a two-digit hexadecimal number preceded by a % character. Space characters are converted to a + character.

Constructors

There is no constructor for this class. All of the functionality is provided by means of a static method.

Methods

There is one static class method, encode(), which takes a String representing the text to encode and returns the translated text as a String.

URLStreamHandler

The subclasses of this class provide the implementation of objects that know how to open communications streams for different URL protocol types. More information on how to write handlers for new protocols can be found in Chapter 31, "Extending Java with Content and Protocol Handlers."

Constructors

The constructor for the URLStreamHandler class cannot be called because it is an abstract class.

Methods

Each subclass provides its own implementation of the openConnection() method, which opens an input stream to the URL specified as an argument. The method should return an appropriate subclass of the URLConnection class.

ContentHandler

Subclasses of the ContentHandler abstract class are responsible for turning a raw data stream for a MIME type into a Java object of the appropriate type. Writing handlers for new content types will be covered in detail in Chapter 31.

Constructors

Because ContentHandler is an abstract class, ContentHandler objects cannot be instantiated. An object implementing ContentHandlerFactory interface decides what the appropriate subclass is for a given MIME content type.

Methods

The important method for ContentHandler objects is the getContent() method, which does the actual work of turning data read using a URLConnection into a Java object. This method takes as its argument a reference to a URLConnection that will provide an InputStream at the beginning of the representation of an object.

SocketImpl

This abstract class provides a mapping from the raw networking classes to the native TCP/IP networking facilities of the host. This means that the Java application does not need to concern itself with the operating system specifics of creating network connections. The Java runtime loads the proper native code for the implementation, which is accessed by means of a SocketImpl object. Each Socket or ServerSocket then uses the SocketImpl object to access the network.

This scheme also allows for flexibility in different network environments. An application does not need to bother with details such as being behind a firewall, because the runtime takes care of loading the proper socket implementation (such as one that knows how to use the SOCKS proxy TCP/IP service).

Unless you are porting Java to a new platform or adding support for something such as connecting through a firewall, you probably will never see or use SocketImpl.

Constructors

There is one constructor that takes no arguments.

Methods

The methods provided by the SocketImpl class will look very familiar to anyone who has done socket programming under a UNIX variant. All of the methods are protected and may only be used by subclasses of SocketImpl that provide specific socket implementations.

The create() method creates a socket with the underlying operating system. It takes one boolean argument that specifies whether the created socket should be a stream (TCP) or datagram (UDP) socket. Two calls, connect() and bind(), cause the socket to be associated with a particular address and port.

For server sockets there is the listen() method, which tells the operating system how many connections may be pending on the socket. The accept() method waits for an incoming connection request. It takes another SocketImpl object as a parameter, which will represent the new connection once it has been established.

To allow reading and writing from the socket, the class provides the getInputStream() and getOutputStream() methods, which will return a reference to the corresponding stream. Once communication on a socket is finished, the close() method may be used to ask the operating system to close the connection. The remaining methods allow read access to the member variables, as well as a toString() method for printing a textual representation of the object.

Variables

Each SocketImpl object has four protected members:

- fd

  A java.io.FileDescriptor object that is used to access the underlying operating system network facilities.
- address

  An InetAddress object representing the host at the remote end of the connection.

- port

  The remote port number, stored as an `int`.

- localport

  The local port number, stored as an `int`.

Exceptions

Java's exception system allows for flexible error handling. The `java.net` package defines five new exceptions that are discussed in the following sections. All of these exceptions provide the same functionality as any `java.lang.Exception` object. Each exception is a subclass of `java.io.IOException`, so they may be handled with code such as the following fragment:

```
try {
    // Code that might cause an exception goes here
} catch( java.net.IOException e ) {
    System.err.println( "Error on socket operation:\n" + e );
    return;
}
```

This code could be put inside a `for` loop—for example, when trying to create a `Socket` to connect to a heavily loaded host.

UnknownHostException

This exception is thrown when a host name cannot be resolved into a machine address. The most probable causes for this are the following:

- The host name is misspelled.
- The host does not actually exist.
- There is a problem with the network and the host, or the host that is providing name-to-IP number mapping is unreachable.

> **TIP**
>
> If you are sure that you are using the right host name and are still getting this exception, you might need to fix the name-to-IP number mapping. How to go about this depends on the platform you are using. If you are using DNS, you will need to contact the administrator for the domain. If you are using Sun's NIS, you will need to have the system administrator change the entry on the NIS server. Finally, you might need to change the local machine's host file, usually named `hosts` or `HOSTS` (`/etc/hosts` on UNIX variants, `\WINDOWS\HOSTS` on Windows 95). In any case, using the IP number itself to connect to the host should work.

UnknownServiceException

The URLConnection class uses this exception to signal that a given connection does not support a requested facility such as input or output. If you write your own protocol or content handlers and do not override the default methods for getting input or output stream objects, the inherited method will throw this exception. An application that a user can give an arbitrary URL to should watch for this exception (users being the malicious creatures they are!).

SocketException

This exception is thrown when there is a problem using a socket. One possible cause is that the local port you are asking for is already in use (that is, another process already has the socket open). Some operating systems might wait for a period of time after a socket has been closed before allowing it to be reopened.

Another cause is that the user cannot bind to that particular port. On most UNIX systems, ports numbered less than 1,024 cannot be used by users other than the root or superuser account. This is a security measure, because most well-known services reside on ports in this range. Normal users are not able to start their own server in place of the system version. While you are developing a service, you might want to run the server on a higher numbered port. Once the service has been developed and debugged, you can move it to the normal port.

This exception also is thrown if you try to use the setSocketImplFactory() method of the Socket or ServerSocket classes when the SocketImplFactory already has been set. Usually the Java runtime will set this to a reasonable value for you, but if you are writing your own socket factory (for example, to provide sockets through a firewall) this exception could get thrown.

ProtocolException

This exception is raised by the underlying network support library. It is thrown by a native method of the PlainSocketImpl class when the underlying socket facilities returns a protocol error.

MalformedURLException

The URL class throws this exception if it is given a syntactically invalid URL. One cause can be that the URL specifies a protocol that the URL class does not support. Another cause is that the URL cannot be parsed. A URL for the HTTP or FILE protocols should have the following general form:

protocol://*hostname/path*[*/path/…/path*]*/object*

Where:

- ■ *protocol* is the protocol to use to connect to the resource.
- ■ *hostname* is the host name to contact, optionally followed by a : and the port number to connect to (for example, `kremvax.gov.su:8000`). The host name also may be given as an IP address.
- ■ *path[/path/…/path]* is the path to the object separated by / characters.
- ■ *object* is the name of the actual object itself.

This syntax for a URL depends upon the protocol. The complete URL specification can be found in RFC 1738 (see Chapter 27, "Introduction to Java Network Programming," for details on retrieving RFC documents), or check out the World Wide Web Consortium's site at `http://www.w3.org/` for the latest version.

Other Exceptions

In addition to the exceptions in the `java.net` package, several methods throw exceptions from the `java.io` package. The most common of these is `java.io.IOException`—which, for example, is thrown when there is a problem reading a Web resource by the URL class or if there is a problem creating a `Socket`.

Interfaces

The `java.net` package defines three interfaces. These primarily are used behind the scenes by the other networking classes rather than by user classes. Unless you are porting Java to a new platform or are extending it to use a new socket protocol, you probably will have no need to implement these interfaces in a class. They are included here for completeness, and for those people who like to take off the cover and poke around the innards to find out how things work.

SocketImplFactory

This interface defines a method that returns a `SocketImpl` instance appropriate to the underlying operating system. The socket classes use an object implementing this interface to create the `SocketImpl` objects they need to use the network.

URLStreamHandlerFactory

Classes that implement this interface provide a mapping from protocols such as HTTP or FTP into the corresponding `URLStreamHandler` subclasses. The URL class uses this factory object to obtain a protocol handler.

ContentHandlerFactory

The URLStreamHandler class uses this interface to obtain ContentHandler objects for different content types. The interface specifies one method, createContentHandler(), which takes the MIME type for which a handler is desired as a String.

Summary

This chapter has been a quick introduction to get you acquainted with the networking facilities that Java provides. Appendix C, "The Java Class Library," contains more detailed information on the specific arguments and return types for the various methods. Sun also provides complete API documentation on its Web site at http://www.javasoft.com/JDK-1.0/api/packages.html (a PostScript version for printing is also available).

The next chapter, "Network Programming," contains examples that show how to use these classes in more detail. Several classes are developed that show how to use the networking facilities covered here to create your own network applications and applets.

Network Programming

29

by Mike Fletcher

This chapter shows how to put Java's networking classes to use in applets and applications. Before getting into the examples, a short overview is presented of the capabilities and limitations of the different network classes. If you have never done any network programming, this should help you decide on what type of connection class you need to base your application. This overview should help you to pick the Java classes that will best fit your networking application. An overview of Java security, as it relates to network programming, is also given.

The examples show you what each of the Java networking classes does and how to use them. The first example is an applet that retrieves a specified URL and displays the contents in a window using the URL and URLConnection classes. Next is a client for the Finger protocol that demonstrates the use of Socket objects. The TCPServer example shows how to use a ServerSocket to write a simple TCP-based server. The last two examples use the DatagramSocket and DatagramPacket in both server and client roles.

Which Class Is Right for Me?

The answer to this question depends on what you are trying to do and what type of application you are writing. The different network protocols have their own advantages and disadvantages. If you are writing a client for someone else's protocol, the decision probably has been made for you. If you are writing your own protocol from scratch, the following should help you decide what transport method (and hence, what Java classes) best fit your application.

URL

This class is an example of what can be accomplished using the other, lower-level network objects. The URL class is best suited for applications or applets that need to access content on the World Wide Web. If all you need to use Java for is writing Web browser applets, the URL and URLConnection classes in all likelihood will handle your network communications needs.

The URL class enables you to retrieve a resource from the Web by specifying the Uniform Resource Locator for it. The content of the URL is fetched and turned into a corresponding Java object (such as a String containing the text of an HTML document). If you are fetching arbitrary information, the URLConnection object provides methods that will try to deduce the type of the content either from the filename in the URL or from the content stream itself.

Socket

The Socket class provides a reliable, ordered stream connection (that is, a TCP/IP socket connection). The host and port number of the destination are specified when the Socket is created.

The connection is reliable because the transport layer (the TCP protocol layer) acknowledges the receipt of sent data. If one end of the connection does not get an acknowledgment back within a reasonable period of time, it will resend the unacknowledged data (a technique known as *Positive Acknowledgment with Retransmission*, often abbreviated as PAR). Once you have written data into a Socket, you can assume that the data will get to the other side (unless you receive an IOException, of course).

Ordered stream means that the data arrive at the opposite end in the exact same order that you write the data. However, because the data are a stream, write boundaries are not preserved. What this means is that if you write 200 characters, the other side might read all 200 at once. It might get the first 10 characters one time and the next 190 the next time data are received from the socket. In either case the receiver cannot tell where each group of data was written.

The reliable stream connection provided by Socket objects is well suited for interactive applications. Examples of protocols that use TCP as their transport mechanism are telnet and FTP. The HTTP protocol used to transfer data for the Web also uses TCP to communicate between hosts.

ServerSocket

A ServerSocket object represents what Socket-type connections communicate with. Server sockets listen on a given port for connection requests when their accept() method is called. The ServerSocket offers the same connection-oriented, ordered stream protocol (TCP) that the Socket object does. In fact once a connection has been established, the accept() method will return a Socket object to talk with the remote end.

DatagramSocket

A DatagramSocket provides an unreliable, connectionless, datagram connection (that is, a UDP/IP socket connection).

Unlike the reliable connection provided by a Socket, there is no guarantee that what you send over a UDP connection actually gets to the receiver. The TCP connection provided by the Socket class takes care retransmitting any packets that might get lost. Packets sent through UDP simply are sent out and forgotten, which means that if you need to know that the receiver got the data, you will have to send back some sort of acknowledgment. This does not mean that your data will never get to the other end of a UDP connection. If a network error happens (your cat jiggles the Ethernet plug out of the wall, for instance) then the UDP layer will not try to send it again or even know that the packet did not get to the recipient.

Connectionless means that the socket does not have a fixed receiver. You may use the same DatagramSocket to send packets to different hosts and ports, whereas a Socket connection is only to a given host and port. Once a Socket is connected to a destination it cannot be changed. The fact that UDP sockets are not bound to a specific destination also means that the same socket can listen for packets as well as originating them. There is no UDP DatagramServerSocket equivalent to the TCP ServerSocket.

Datagram refers to the fact that the information is sent as discrete packets rather than a continuous ordered stream. The individual packet boundaries are preserved. It might help to think of it as dropping fixed-size postcards in a mailbox. For example, if you send four packets, the order in which they arrive at the destination is not guaranteed to be the same in which they were sent. The receiver could get them in the same order they were sent or they could arrive in reverse order. In any case, each packet will be received whole.

Given the above constraints, why would anyone want to use a `DatagramSocket`? There are several advantages to using UDP, as follows:

- You need to communicate with several different hosts. Because a `DatagramSocket` is not bound to a particular host, you may use the same object to communicate with different hosts by specifying the `InetAddress` when you create each `DatagramPacket`.

- You are not worried about reliable delivery. If the application you are writing does not need to know that the data it sends get to the other end, using a UDP socket eliminates the overhead of acknowledging each packet that TCP does. Another case would be if the protocol you are using has its own method of handling reliable delivery and retransmission.

- The amount of data being sent does not merit the overhead of setting up a connection and the reliable delivery mechanism. An application that is only sending 100 bytes for each transaction every 10 minutes would be an example of this situation.

The NFS (Network File System) protocol version two, originally developed by Sun with implementations available for most operating systems, is an example application that uses UDP for its transport mechanism. Another example of an application where a `DatagramSocket` might be appropriate would be a multiplayer game. The central server would need to communicate to all of the players involved, and would not necessarily need to know that a position update got to the player.

> **NOTE**
>
> An actual game that uses UDP for communication is Netrek, a space combat simulation loosely based on the *Star Trek* series. Information on Netrek can be found using the Yahoo subject catalog at `http://www.yahoo.com/Recreation/Games/Internet_Games/Netrek/`. There is also a Usenet newsgroup, `news:rec.games.netrek`.

Decisions, Decisions

Now that you know what the classes are capable of, you can choose the one that best fits your application. Table 29.1 sums up what type of connection each of the base networking classes creates. The direction column indicates where a connection originates: "Outgoing" indicates that your application is opening a connection out to another host; and "Incoming" indicates that some other application is initiating a connection to yours.

Table 29.1. Low-level connection objects summarized.

Class	Connection Type	Direction
Socket	Connected, ordered byte stream (TCP)	Outgoing
ServerSocket	Connected, ordered byte stream (TCP)	Incoming
DatagramSocket	Connectionless datagram (UDP)	Incoming or Outgoing

You need to look at the problem you are trying to solve, any constraints you have, and the transport mechanism that best fits your situation. If you are having problems choosing a transport protocol, take a look at some of the RFCs that define Internet standards for applications (such as HTTP or SMTP). One of them might be similar to what you are trying to accomplish. As an alternative, you could be indecisive and provide both TCP and UDP versions of your service, duplicating the processing logic and customizing the network logic. Trying both transport protocols with a pared-down version of your application might give you an indication that better serves your purposes. Once you've looked at these factors you should be able to decide what class to use.

A Note on Java Security and the Network Classes

One of the purposes of Java is to enable executable content from an arbitrary network source to be retrieved and run securely. To enable this, the Java runtime enforces certain limitations on what classes obtained through the network may do. You should be aware of these constraints because they will affect the design of applets and how the applets must be loaded. You will need to take into consideration whatever security constraints are imposed by your target environment and your development environment, as well, when designing your application or applet.

For example, Netscape Navigator 2.0 allows code loaded from local disk more privileges than code loaded over a network connection. A class loaded from an HTTP daemon may only create outgoing connections back to the host from which it was loaded. If the class had been loaded from the local host (that is, it was located somewhere in the class search path on the machine running Navigator), it would be able to connect to an arbitrary host. Contrast this with the appletviewer provided with Sun's Developer's Kit. The appletviewer can be configured to act similarly to Navigator or to enforce no restrictions on network connectivity.

If you need full access to all of Java's capabilities, there is always the option of writing a stand-alone application. A stand-alone application (that is, one not running in the context of a Web browser) has no restrictions on what it is allowed to do. Sun's HotJava Web browser is an example of a stand-alone application.

> **NOTE**
>
> For a more detailed discussion of Java security and how it is designed into the language and runtime, take a look at Chapter 40, "Java Security."
>
> In addition, Sun has several white paper documents and a collection of frequently asked questions available at `http://www.javasoft.com/sfaq/`.

These checks are implemented by a subclass of `java.lang.SecurityManager`. Depending on the security model, the object will allow or deny certain actions. You can check beforehand whether a capability your applet needs is present by calling the `SecurityManager` yourself. The `java.lang.System` object provides a `getSecurityManager()` method that returns a reference to the `SecurityManager` active for the current context. If your applet needs to open a `ServerSocket`, for instance, you can call the `checkListen()` method yourself and print an error message (or pop up a dialog box) alerting the users and referring them to installation instructions.

Using the URL Class

The `URL` class lets your Java code access resources from anywhere on the World Wide Web. We'll start off by creating an applet that fetches a URL and displays the raw contents in a window. This first applet will use the `URLConnection` class method `getInputStream()` to read in the raw data.

Next, we'll modify the applet to use the `getContent()` method to convert the resource into an appropriately typed Java object.

The urlFetcher Applet

FIGURE 29.1.

The urlFetcher *applet.*

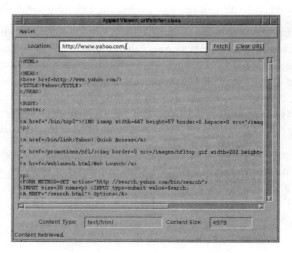

Design

The applet will be relatively straightforward. The user interface will be a location field for the entry of the URL to fetch along with two buttons: one to fetch the URL, and one to clear out the URL field. Below this will be a `java.awt.TextArea` object that will hold the content retrieved. Two read-only fields will go below the text to show the content type and size. These fields and the area will be member variables so that their `setText()` methods can be used to indicate changes when a new URL is retrieved. To let the user know what is happening, we'll use the `Applet` method `showStatus()`.

Functionally the applet will be broken into four parts:

- A `makeUI()` method that will construct the user interface
- The `init()` method that will call `makeUI()` and then see whether a starting URL was specified as a parameter
- The `doFetch()` method that will do the actual work of fetching a URL and updating the display
- The `handleEvent()` method that will be responsible for processing UI events and calling the proper methods.

Applet Skeleton

We'll start by outlining the overall structure of the applet. Specific methods or blocks of code will be represented by comments, and the exact code will be shown as it is developed. This format will be used for the examples throughout the rest of the chapter. The member variables of the class are used to hold the different text fields and the main text area so that methods can update them as necessary. They are set to `null` to start with, and the UI objects are allocated in `makeUI()`, as follows:

```java
import java.applet.Applet;
import java.awt.*;
import java.net.*;
import java.io.*;

public class urlFetcher extends Applet {
  TextField urlField = null;
  TextArea contentArea = null;
  TextField contentType = null;
  TextField contentSize = null;

  // init() Method

  // makeUI() Method

  // doFetch() Method

  // handleEvent() Method

}
```

init()

All the initialization needed for this applet is to call our method to construct the user interface and then see whether a starting URL was specified as a parameter to the applet. If a URL was specified, we'll set the text of urlField and call our doFetch() method to have it loaded, as follows:

```
public void init( ) {
  makeUI( );

  if( getParameter( "URL" ) != null ) {
    urlField.setText( getParameter( "URL" ) );
    doFetch( );
  }
```

makeUI()

This method allocates all of the user interface objects and inserts them into our applet's window. No networking code is used here, just AWT objects, so there won't be any commentary.

```
public void makeUI( ) {
  setLayout( new BorderLayout( ) );

  Panel p = new Panel( );

  contentArea = new TextArea( 24, 80 );

  Font fCourier = new Font( "Courier", Font.PLAIN, 12 );
  contentArea.setFont( fCourier );

  contentArea.setEditable( false );

  p.add( contentArea );

  add( "Center", p );

  p = new Panel( );

  p.add( new Label( "Location:" ) );

  urlField = new TextField( 40 );
  p.add( urlField );

  p.add( new Button( "Fetch" ) );
  p.add( new Button( "Clear URL" ) );

  add( "North", p );

  p = new Panel( );
  p.add( new Label( "Content Type:" ) );

  contentType = new TextField( 20 );
  contentType.setEditable( false );

  p.add( contentType );
```

```
  p.add( new Label( "Content Size:" ) );

  contentSize = new TextField( 10 );
  contentSize.setEditable( false );

  p.add( contentSize );

  add( "South", p );

  repaint( );
}
```

doFetch()

This method is where we put the URL and URLConnection classes to use, so we'll go into a bit more detail. First we will rough out the skeleton for the method.

```
public void doFetch( ) {
  URL target = null;

  // Construct a URL

  try {
    // Get a URLConnection and InputStream

    // Read and Display the content
  } catch( IOException e ) {
    showStatus( "Error fetching \"" + target
      + "\": " + e );
    return;
  }
}
```

Construct a URL

The first step in fetching the resource is to construct a URL from the text that the user entered in the urlField. If the URL is valid, we'll display a status to let the user know what is happening. Otherwise, the constructor will throw a MalformedURLException. In this case we'll take the exception text and display that and then return. If the applet is being loaded through the network, the URL cannot point to a host other than the one that the class was loaded from. To cope with this, we'll catch any SecurityExceptions that might occur and display an appropriate message.

```
try {
  target = new URL( urlField.getText( ) );
  showStatus( "Fetching \"" + target + "\"" );
} catch( MalformedURLException e ) {
  showStatus( "Bad URL \"" + urlField.getText( ) + "\": "
            + e.getMessage( ) );
  return;
} catch( SecurityException e ) {
  showStatus( "Security Error: " + e.getMessage( ) );
  return;
}
```

Get a `URLConnection` and `InputStream`

The next step is to get a `URLConnection` from the `URL` just created. This object provides information about the stream being retrieved. It also has methods for obtaining an `InputStream` (and `OutputStream`, where appropriate) for the connection. At the same time we will allocate a `byte` array, an `int`, and a `String` for use reading the data. Remember that this code is contained inside a `try` and `catch` block that will handle any `IOExceptions` that might occur, as follows:

```
String content = "";
URLConnection con = target.openConnection( );
byte b[] = new byte[ 1024 ];
int nbytes;

BufferedInputStream in =
  new BufferedInputStream( con.getInputStream( ), 2048 );
```

Read and Display the Content

First, we will read all of the data from the `BufferedInputStream` just created. Before doing this, the `setText()` method will be called with an empty string to clear out the previous contents, if any. The following `while` loop then reads 1024 bytes at a time. We use the `String` constructor, which takes the number of bytes to read from array. The `read()` method returns the amount of data that actually were read, and this number is passed to the constructor. This string then is appended to the text already in the `TextArea`.

```
contentArea.setText( "" );

while( (nbytes = in.read( b, 0, 1024 )) != -1 ) {
  content = new String( b, 0, 0, nbytes );
  contentArea.appendText( content );
}
```

Next, we will use the `URLConnection` that was obtained to find the content type of the data (see Chapter 31, "Extending Java with Content and Protocol Handlers," for a discussion of MIME types) and the length of the data. In general, these methods will return null or -1 to indicate that the attribute can't be determined. Finally, we will display a status method to let the user know that the content has been retrieved.

```
String type = con.getContentType( )
if( type == null ) {
  type = "Unknown";
}
contentType.setText( type );

int size = con.getContentLength( );
if( size == -1 ) {
  size = content.length( );
}
contentSize.setText( Integer.toString( size ) );
```

handleEvent()

As the final step, we'll write the event dispatcher for our applet. All that our applet is interested in are action events. These will be generated either by the user pressing the Enter key in the URL field or by pressing one of the two buttons. For any other event we will return `false` because we don't handle it.

```java
public boolean handleEvent( Event e ) {
  switch( e.id ) {
  case Event.ACTION_EVENT:
    {
      if( e.target instanceof TextField
          ¦¦ e.arg.equals( "Fetch" ) ) {
        doFetch( );
        return true;
      }

      if( e.arg.equals( "Clear URL" ) ) {
        urlField.setText( "" );
        return true;
      }
    }

  default:
    return false;
  }
}
```

urlFetcher Notes

That's all there is to using URL objects. All the source code is available on the CD-ROM as `urlFetcher`. Keep in mind that if you load this applet from an HTTP daemon rather than from local disk, you will only be allowed to fetch URLs from the same server. This applet is used again in Chapter 31, "Extending Java with Content and Protocol Handlers."

Using the Socket Class

The `Socket` class probably will solve most of your raw network access needs. In this section, we'll demonstrate how to use the class with a client for a standard Internet service. The example also will lay the groundwork for writing TCP servers with `ServerSockets`, as well as being the basis for the protocol handler example in Chapter 31.

A Client for the Finger Protocol

The first example of using `Socket` objects will be a client for the Finger protocol. This protocol is used to request information about users from a multiuser system, such as the last time they accessed the system or their real names. Most UNIX variants provide a Finger server to handle requests, and there are programs for Windows and Macintosh platforms that provide the same service. There is a client program, usually called Finger, or the service can be accessed by connecting to the server's port with a telnet application.

The Finger protocol is defined in RFC 762. The server listens on TCP port 79. It expects either a user name to retrieve information about, followed by ASCII carriage return and linefeed characters, or just the carriage return and linefeed characters if information is sought on all users currently logged in. The information will be returned as ASCII text in a system-dependent format (although most UNIX variants will give similar information).

Design

The `fingerClient` class will be very simple. It will have a member to hold the `Socket` we use to communicate, and two `String` objects to hold the user name and host we want information about. Because the protocol is so simple, we'll do all of the communication in a method called `getInfo()`. This method will send the query and return the results to the caller as a `String`. Instead of throwing any exceptions, we will catch them and return an error message to the caller.

To illustrate how to use the `client` class, we'll have a `fingerApplet` that will display for whom Finger is being used, what host we are querying, and a `TextArea` to display the results of the `getInfo()` call.

`fingerClient` Source

FIGURE 29.2.

The finished `fingerClient` *applet.*

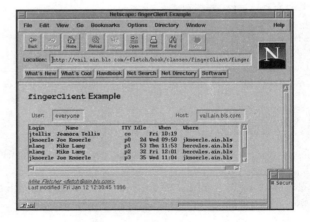

Skeleton

The first thing to do is lay out the overall skeleton of the client class.

```
import java.net.*;
import java.io.*;
```

```
public class fingerClient {
  Socket s;
  String host = null;
  String user = null;

  public static final int fingerPort = 79;

  // Constructors

  // The getInfo() method
}
```

Constructors

We will have two constructors: one that takes only a host name, and one that takes a host name and the name of a user. The constructors simply will copy the information into the appropriate member variables, as follows:

```
fingerClient( String h ) {
  host = h;
  user = "";
}

fingerClient( String h, String u ) {
  host = h;
  user = u;
}
```

The getInfo() Method

This is the method that does the actual work of contacting the Finger daemon and reading back the information. It will throw an UnknownHostException if it cannot open a Socket to the specified host. If an error occurs while reading data from the socket, an IOException will be thrown. We'll start as follows by declaring the method and defining local variables: a String to hold our return value and a StringBuffer to build the return value in; a PrintStream to send our request to the Finger daemon; and a BufferedInputStream to read the response.

```
public String getInfo( )
   throws IOException, UnknownHostException {
  String retval = "";
  StringBuffer strBuf = new StringBuffer();

  BufferedInputStream in = null;
  PrintStream out = null;
```

Next, we will create a Socket object to the Finger port on the host specified. After doing so, we will create our I/O streams using the getOutputStream() and getInputStream() methods of the Socket, as follows:

```
s = new Socket( host, fingerPort );

out = new PrintStream( s.getOutputStream( ) );
in = new BufferedInputStream( s.getInputStream( ) );
```

The next step is to send our request and read back the results. The request is sent by sending the user name we want information about, followed by a carriage return and linefeed. The `PrintStream` method `println()` takes care of appending the carriage return and linefeed pair for us. After the request has been sent, we read back data from the server with a `while` loop into our `StringBuffer`. If an I/O error occurs, we'll print an error message to `System.err` and throw the exception again.

```
out.println( user );

try {
  byte b[] = new byte[ 1024 ];
  int nbytes;

  while( (nbytes = in.read( b, 0, 1024 )) != -1 ) {
    strBuf.append( new String( b, 0, 0, nbytes ) );
  }
} catch( IOException e ) {
  System.err.println( "Error during read: "
                      + e );
  throw e;
}
```

All that is left to do now is to close our socket and return the `String` (constructed from the `StringBuffer`) to our caller, as follows:

```
  s.close( );
  s = null;

  retval = strBuf.toString( );

  return retval;
}
```

`fingerApplet` Source

The following source code is an applet that uses the `fingerClient` developed earlier. This applet can be embedded in your home page to let people know the last time you logged in and whether you currently are online. It will default to using Finger for everyone on the host the page is loaded from. Keep in mind that because of Java's security constraints, you only will be able to ask the machine running the HTTP daemon for Finger information if the `fingerClient` class is loaded over the network. One way around this is to have the `fingerClient.class` file located on your local machine somewhere in the `CLASSPATH` searched by your browser. The complete source for the `fingerApplet` class is given in Listing 29.1 (as well as on the CD-ROM).

Listing 29.1. `fingerApplet` Source Code.

```
import java.applet.Applet;
import java.awt.*;

public class fingerApplet extends Applet {
  public void init( ) {
```

```
fingerClient c = null;
String info = null;
String host = null;
String user = null;

if( getParameter( "host" ) != null ) {
  host = getParameter( "host" );
} else {
  host = "localhost";
}

if( getParameter( "user" ) != null ) {
  user = getParameter( "user" );
} else {
  user = "";
}

c = new fingerClient( host, user );

try {
  info = c.getInfo( );
} catch( Exception e ) {
  info = "Problem fingering "
    + (user.equals( "" ) ? "everyone" : user)
    + "@" + host + "\n" + e );
}

setLayout( new BorderLayout( ) );

TextField tmp = null;

Panel lp = new Panel( );
lp.add( new Label( "User:" ) );

tmp = new TextField( (user.equals("") ? "everyone" : user ) );
tmp.setEditable( false );
lp.add( tmp );

Panel rp = new Panel( );
rp.add( new Label( "Host:" ) );

tmp = new TextField( host );
tmp.setEditable( false );
rp.add( tmp );

Panel p = new Panel( );

p.setLayout( new BorderLayout( ) );

p.add( "West", lp );
p.add( "East", rp );

add( "North", p );

TextArea t = new TextArea( 80, 4 );

Font fCourier = new Font( "Courier", Font.BOLD, 12 );
```

continues

Listing 29.1. continued

```
    t.setFont( fCourier );
    t.setEditable( false );

    add( "Center", t );

    t.setText( info );

    repaint( );
}
```

Example Applet Tag

An example of the HTML tags needed to use the `fingerApplet` follows. The parameters should be changed to reflect the user and host you want information for. Remember that if no user name is given, the `fingerClient` will retrieve information about all users logged in. If no host name is given, the applet will default to using Finger on the host that the applet code was retrieved from.

```
<applet code="fingerApplet.class" width="500" height="300">
<param name="host" value="kremvax.gov.su">
<param name="user" value="gorby">
</applet>
```

Using the `ServerSocket` Class

This section will build on the concepts established in the previous one. You can't use `ServerSocket` objects very well unless you know how to handle the `Socket` objects that represent the individual connections your server receives. If you skipped over the discussion using the `Socket` class, go back and read it.

> **NOTE**
>
> Any clients that want to connect to your server must know what port it will be listening on. For standard services such as HTTP or FTP, there are assigned, well-known port numbers. You will need to make sure that your service is on an unused port number; otherwise, your server either will not run or will get requests for the wrong service. The Internet Assigned Numbers Authority (IANA) is responsible for maintaining a list of services and the ports they live on. The current list of assigned port numbers is available from `ftp://ftp.isi.edu/in-notes/iana/assignments/`.
>
> Another concern to keep in mind when choosing the port that your server will listen on is that ports numbered under 1024 cannot be listened on through most variants of

UNIX unless the owner of the process is the root or superuser account. This is because most of the well-known system services have been assigned ports in the under 1024 range. As long as you pick a number well above 1024, you shouldn't be interfering with another service.

A Simple TCP Server

Our example TCP server will listen for incoming connections on a given port (5000 by default—a nice, high port number). When it receives a connection, it will read data from the socket and write the data back. Figure 29.4 shows what the finished client applet will look like.

FIGURE 29.3.

The finished TCPServer *applet.*

Design

The server will run in its own thread. It will open a ServerSocket when it is constructed. The constructor will accept the port number to listen for connections on. The server object will implement the Runnable interface. This allows other threads to continue while the server thread is blocked waiting for an incoming connection. In addition to the normal start() and stop() methods, we also will implement a join() method to allow another thread to wait for us to exit.

The run() method will call the accept() method on our socket. This method will return a Socket representing the incoming connection. The server will display a message showing where the connection originated to System.err. It next will obtain I/O streams for the Socket and display a welcome message. We then will enter a while loop reading data from the Socket and writing it back until one of two strings are received: bye, which will cause the connection to be closed and the server to wait for the next connection; and DIE!, which will cause the server thread to exit. We also will have an applet wrapper to allow the server to be started inside of a Web browser environment.

TCPServer **Skeleton**

We'll start out by outlining the overall structure of the server class.

```
import java.io.*;
import java.net.*;

public class TCPServer implements Runnable {
  Thread serverThread = null;
  ServerSocket s = null;
  int port = 5000;

  // Constructor

  // Runnable / Thread methods

  // run() Method
}
```

Constructor

The constructor will take one argument: the port number to listen for connections on. It then will try to allocate a ServerSocket on that port. If an exception occurs, we will display an error message and then throw the exception again.

```
public TCPServer( int p ) throws IOException {
  port = p;

  try {
    s = new ServerSocket( port );
  } catch( IOException e ) {
    System.err.println( "Exception allocating ServerSocket: "
                        + e );

    throw e;
  }
```

Runnable Methods

Next, we will implement the methods to start and stop the server thread. These will be used again and again in the rest of the classes in this chapter, so we'll go into a bit of detail here. All of these methods are defined as synchronized so that only one thread of execution may be accessing a given TCPServer object at a time. This prevents one thread from calling the stop() method while another is in the start() method (which could cause a NullPointerException). The first method will start a new server thread running if one is not already. The method also will allocate a new ServerSocket if s does not hold one already. This allows for the server to be stopped and restarted.

```
public synchronized void start( ) {
  if( serverThread == null ) {
    serverThread = new Thread( this );
    serverThread.setPriority( Thread.MAX_PRIORITY / 4 );
    serverThread.start( );
  }

  if( s == null ) {
    try {
      s = new ServerSocket( port );
    } catch( IOException e ) {
      System.err.println( "Exception allocating ServerSocket: "
                          + e );

      return;
    }
  }
}
```

The next method stops a server thread of execution, if one exists. It also will close our
ServerSocket if we have one.

```
public synchronized void stop( ) {
  if( serverThread != null ) {
    serverThread.stop( );
    serverThread = null;
  }

  if( s != null ) {
    try {
      s.close( );
      s = null;
    } catch( IOException e ) {
      System.err.println( "Exception closing ServerSocket: "
                          + e );

      return;
    }
  }
}
```

Last, we have the join() method. This method will block the calling thread until the
serverThread finishes its execution. It does not need to be marked as synchronized because
multiple threads may all be waiting for our thread to exit, and we do not manipulate any member variables. The method will throw InterruptedException if another thread interrupts the
one trying to join. If there is no thread to wait for, the method will return immediately.

```
public final void join( ) throws InterruptedException {
  if( serverThread != null ) {
    serverThread.join( );
  }

  return;
}
```

run( ) **Method**

The run( ) method is where all of the server work is done.

```
public void run( ) {
  InputStream in = null;
  PrintStream out = null;
  Socket con = null;

  while( serverThread != null ) {
    // Wait for an incoming connection

    // Get I/O Streams for the Socket

    // Talk to the client
  }

  // Close the ServerSocket
}
```

Wait for an Incoming Connection

Once the server is up and running, the first thing to do is hurry up and wait. The ServerSocket accept( ) method will block our thread until a client contacts our port requesting a connection. When one does, the method will return a Socket object representing the new connection. We'll print where the connection is coming from to System.err. If there is an error accepting the connection, we'll print an error message and return, terminating the server thread.

```
try {
  con = s.accept( );
} catch( IOException e ) {
  System.err.println( "Error on accept: " + e );
  return;
}

System.err.println( "Got connection from "
                    + con.getInetAddress() + ":"
                    + con.getPort( ) );
```

Get I/O Streams for the Socket

Now that we have someone to talk to, we need to allocate stream objects so that the server can send and receive information to the client. We'll use a plain InputStream to receive information from the other end, and a PrintStream for writing back to the client.

```
try {
  out = new PrintStream( con.getOutputStream( ) );
  in = con.getInputStream( );
} catch( Exception e ) {
  System.err.println( "Error building streams: " + e );
}
```

Talk to the Client

We will start by printing a welcome message to the client. This message also will inform the client how to end the connection.

```
out.println(
  "Hi there! Enter 'bye' to exit, 'DIE!' to stop server." );
```

Having welcomed the user, we go into a `while` loop, reading whatever they send us and parroting it back to them. We check each group of data to see whether it contains either of the commands we understand (`bye` or `DIE!`). If it does, we take the appropriate action and set the `done` flag to `true`.

```
try {
  int nbytes;
  boolean done = false;
  byte b[] = new byte[ 1024 ];

  while( !done && ((nbytes = in.read( b, 0, 1024 )) != -1 ) {
    String str = new String( b, 0, 0, nbytes );

    out.println( "Received:\n" + str );

    if( str.trim().compareTo( "bye" ) == 0 ) {
      System.err.println( "Got bye.  Closing Connection." );
      done = true;
    }

    if( str.trim().compareTo( "DIE!" ) == 0 ) {
      System.err.println( "Exiting." );
      stop( );
      return;
    }

    out.println( "Bye!" );
    out.flush( );
  }
} catch( Exception e ) {
  System.err.println( "Error reading: " + e );
}
```

Close the `ServerSocket`

The last thing to do before going back to listen for the next connection is to close the `Socket` for the current connection. The `while` loop then will go back to the top and start over again.

```
try {
  con.close( );
} catch( Exception e ) {
  System.err.println( "Error on close: " + e );
}
```

TCPServerApplet **Source**

We now will show the source for the wrapper applet in its entirety in Listing 29.2. The code is also on the CD-ROM in the TCPServer directory.

Listing 29.2. The complete TCPServerApplet **source.**

```java
import java.applet.Applet;
import java.awt.*;
import java.io.*;

// Wrapper for Listen class
public
class TCPServerApplet extends Applet {
  TCPServer serv = null;

  public void init( ) {
    int port = 5000;

    try {
      String param = getParameter( "port" );
      if( param != null ) {
        port =
          Integer.valueOf( param ).intValue();
      }
    } catch( Exception e ) {
      ;
    }

    try {
      serv = new TCPServer( port );
    } catch( IOException e ) {
      System.err.println( "Error starting server: " + e );
      return;
    }

    serv.start( );

    TextArea statusArea = new TextArea( 80, 4 );

    setLayout( new BorderLayout( ) );

    statusArea.setText( statusMessage );
    statusArea.setEditable( false );

    add( "Center", statusArea );

    System.err.println( "Thread started" );
    System.err.println( "Waiting for 1 to die" );

    // Join with server thread
    try {
      serv.join();
    } catch ( InterruptedException e ) {
```

```
     System.err.println( "join interrupted: " + e );
   }

   serv = null;

 }

 public static void main( String args[] ) {

   (new TCPServerApplet()).init( );

   System.exit( 0 );
 }

}
```

TCPServer Notes

Keep in mind that this is a single threaded server (that is, there's only one thread handling clients). This means that only one client at a time may talk to the server. Any other clients will not receive a connection until after the current client has been serviced. In a real server application, you would want to be able to handle multiple clients simultaneously. For an example of how to do this, see the echoUDPServer example later in this chapter.

Another detail to remember is that Java's security system will not let code loaded over the network open a ServerSocket in an applet context. If your applet needs access to ServerSocket objects, it must be loaded from the local disk.

Using the DatagramSocket Class

Communicating with a DatagramSocket takes a different mindset from the TCP-based Socket and ServerSocket classes. Whereas the latter two classes function similarly to reading data from a file, the fixed-size messages of the UDP protocol are an entirely different matter. With a stream socket, you have to provide some means of delineating the beginning and end of messages. But when you use UDP, each message arrives in its own discrete package.

A Meager Beginning: The Echo Service

Our first example application using the DatagramSocket is to create a client that talks to a server process for the Echo Service. This service, defined in RFC 862, accepts connections through TCP and UDP. Whatever you send to the server is copied and sent back verbatim. It is mainly a sanity-checking mechanism. You can connect to the server and make sure that traffic is reaching the destination host.

FIGURE 29.4.

The finished
echoUDPClient *applet.*

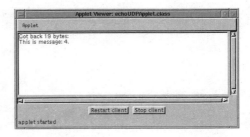

Design

This example will consist of two classes: a class to communicate with the echo server, and a subclass of Applet to provide a user interface.

The first class, which we'll call echoUDPClient, will handle all interaction with the server. In order to display our status, the constructor will take a reference to a java.awt.TextComponent. The constructor also will accept a host name to connect to, defaulting to the local host if it is unavailable. The class will implement the Runnable interface so that the user interface can continue processing events. The run() method will perform the following steps:

1. Allocate a DatagramSocket, and an InetAddress object for the host we are contacting.

2. Set a counter to zero.

3. While the thread is running:

    Create a DatagramPacket to be sent to the destination host containing a message This is packet #, with "#" being the current value of the counter.

    Use the send() method to transmit this packet to the destination.

    Create another DatagramPacket to receive the echo server's reply.

    Call the receive() method to wait for the reply packet.

    Insert the reply into the TextContainer.

    Increment the counter, and sleep for three seconds.

    Close the DatagramSocket.

The second class, which will be called echoUDPApplet, will have three UI components: a TextArea for the echoUDPClient to display its results in, a Button to stop the client object, and a second Button to start a new echoUDPClient object.

echoUDPClient **Source**

We'll develop the client UDP class first. After the skeleton and constructors, the miscellaneous utility methods will be given. Next the methods implementing the Runnable interface and the run() method are shown.

Skeleton

We'll start off the class with the requisite `import` statements. All of the I/O and networking packages will be included, as well as the AWT `TextComponent` so that we know how to display results.

```
import java.io.*;
import java.net.*;
import java.awt.TextComponent;
```

Next, set up the skeleton for the class and the member variables. A static final member will be defined to specify the port that the echo service listens on (from the RFC).

```
public class echoUDPClient implements Runnable {
  Thread echoThread = null;
  TextComponent results;
  InetAddress targetHost;

  public static final int echoPort = 7;

  // Constructors

  // Misc. methods

  // Thread control methods

  // run() Method
}
```

Constructors

The `echoUDPClient` has two constructors, both requiring a `TextComponent` where results will be shown, and one allowing the host to be contacted to be specified. Both constructors may throw the `UnknownHostException` if the host name cannot be resolved into an IP address by the `InetAddress` class.

```
echoUDPClient( TextComponent r, String host ) throws UnknownHostException {
 results = r;
  targetHost = InetAddress.getByName( host );
}

echoUDPClient( TextComponent r) throws UnknownHostException {
  results = r;
  targetHost = InetAddress.getLocalHost();
}
```

Miscellaneous Methods

In the miscellaneous methods section there is one entry, the `setMessage()` method that will display our status in the `TextComponent` passed when the object was constructed.

```
public void setMessage( String msg ) {
  results.setText( msg );
}
```

Thread Controls

Before getting into the run() method, the start() and stop() methods need to be defined. The start method will create a new thread from the object (if one does not already exist), set the created thread's priority to a low value, and start the thread executing. The stop method will stop the thread associated with the object if it is running, set the echoThread member to null (so we know that a thread isn't currently running), and display a message using setMessage() to let the user know we're stopping. Keep in mind that both of these methods need to be synchronized to prevent creating multiple threads by accident.

```
public synchronized void start( ) {
  if( echoThread == null ) {
    echoThread = new Thread( this );
    echoThread.setPriority( Thread.MAX_PRIORITY / 4 );
    echoThread.start( );
  }
}

public synchronized void stop( ) {
  if( echoThread != null ) {
    echoThread.stop( );
    echoThread = null;
  }

  setMessage( results.getText( ) + "\nEcho Client Stopping." );
}
```

run( ) Method

The run() method does all of the work in the echoUDPClient class. You might want to refer back to the design section to refresh your memory. The first thing to do is to declare the method and local variables. The two local variables are a DatagramSocket to hold our connection, and a counter to keep track of how many packets we send.

```
public void run( ) {
  DatagramSocket s = null;
  int counter = 0;

  // Allocate a DatagramSocket

  while( echoThread != null ) {
    // Allocate and Send a DatagramPacket

    // Wait For Reply DatagramPacket

    // Display Results and Sleep Three Seconds
  }

  return;
}
```

Allocate a `DatagramSocket`

Because our object is not a server, we do not care what local port number our socket is connected on. If a socket cannot be created and an exception is thrown, we will display the error message using `setMessage()` and `return` (which will cause the client thread to terminate).

```
try {
  s = new DatagramSocket( );
} catch( Exception e ) {
  String errorMessage =
    "Error creating DatagramSocket: " + e;

  setMessage( errorMessage );

  return;
}
```

Allocate and Send `DatagramPacket`

The next code fragment will increment the counter, create a message and `DatagramPacket` to hold it, and send the message to the destination. Our error handling is rather simple: Ignore it and go back to the top of the `while` loop. In a real application you would want to try to resend the message.

To create the message from a `String`, we'll be using the `getBytes()` method of that class. Next we'll create a `DatagramPacket` using this `byte` array, the `InetAddress` we found in the constructor, and the class constant `echoPort`.

```
counter++;

String messageText = "This is message: " + counter + ".";

byte messageBytes[] = new byte[ messageText.length() ];
messageText.getBytes( 0, messageText.length(), messageBytes, 0 );

DatagramPacket sendPacket =
  new DatagramPacket( messageBytes, messageBytes.length,
                      targetHost, echoUDPClient.echoPort );
```

Now that we have our datagram, we need to send it off. In case there is a problem sending the packet, we'll watch for an `IOException` with a `try` and `catch` block.

```
try {
  s.send( sendPacket );
} catch( IOException e ) {
  String errorMessage =
    "Error receiving packet: " + e;
  setMessage( errorMessage );

  continue;
}
```

Wait for Reply `DatagramPacket`

Now that the echo request has been sent, we need to prepare a `DatagramPacket` to receive the reply from the server.

```
Byte receiveBuf[] = new byte[ 1024 ];
DatagramPacket receivePacket =
  new DatagramPacket( receiveBuf, 1024 );
```

You probably noticed that the buffer allocated is much larger than any reply we're likely to receive. Because we sent the message and know the exact size of the reply (the same message), why not allocate a buffer of that same size? In general, you might not know the exact size of the datagram you will be receiving. It almost never hurts to overestimate and make the buffer a bit larger.

The code to receive a message from the socket looks almost identical to that for sending. Again, if the `receive()` method throws an exception we print the error in our results window and go back to the beginning of the `while` loop.

```
try {
  s.receive( receivePacket );
} catch( IOException e ) {
  String errorMessage =
    "Error receiving packet: " + e;
  setMessage( errorMessage );

  continue;
}
```

Display Results and Sleep Three Seconds

If we get to this point, we successfully have sent a packet to the echo server and gotten a reply back. We will create a `String` from the raw `byte` array of the packet and display it using `setMessage()`.

```
String replyMessage = "Got back " + receivePacket.getLength()
  + " bytes:\n"
  + (new String( receivePacket.getData(), 0 ));

setMessage( replyMessage );
```

Before looping, we need to put in a bit of a delay so we don't overwhelm the machine we're asking to echo back to us (and so the network administrator doesn't come hunting for the person flooding the network with traffic). We'll use the `Thread` class method `sleep()` to put the client thread to sleep for 3,000 milliseconds (three seconds). The call will be enclosed in a `try` and `catch` block in case an `InterruptedException` is thrown, but we'll just ignore these exceptions if they do occur.

```
try {
  Thread.sleep( 3000 );
} catch( InterruptedException e ) {
  ;     // Ignore interruption
}
```

echoUDPApplet **Source**

The applet wrapper for the echoUDPClient does not do any networking on its own, so again we'll just have a listing of its source instead of a play-by-play explanation.

Listing 29.3. The complete echoUDPApplet code.

```java
import java.applet.Applet;
import java.awt.*;

public
class echoUDPApplet extends Applet {
  TextArea resultsText;
  String host;
  echoUDPClient c;

  public void init( ) {
    String param;

    // Get parameters, setting to defaults if needed
    param = getParameter( "host" );
    if( param != null ) {
      host = param;
    } else {
      host = "localhost";
    }

    makeUI();
    restartClient( );
  }

  public void destroy( ) {
    // Stop the client if it is running
    if( c != null ) {
      c.stop();
    }
  }

  public boolean handleEvent( Event e ) {
    switch( e.id ) {
    case Event.ACTION_EVENT:
      {
        if( e.arg.equals( "Restart client" ) ) {
          restartClient();
          return true;
        }
        if( e.arg.equals( "Stop client" ) ) {
          stopClient();
          return true;
        }
      }
    default:
      return false;                // Signal that we didn't handle it
    }
  }
```

continues

Listing 29.3. continued

```
    public void stopClient( ) {
      if( c != null ) {
        c.stop();
        c = null;
      }
    }

    public void restartClient( ) {
      stopClient();
      try {
        c = new echoUDPClient( resultsText, host );
        c.start();                          // Start the echo thread running
      } catch( Exception e ) {
        String errorMessage = "Error creating echoUDPClient: " + e;
        resultsText.setText( errorMessage );
      }
    }

void makeUI( ) {
    setLayout( new BorderLayout() );
    resultsText = new TextArea( 80, 4 );
    add( "Center", resultsText );

    Panel buttonPanel = new Panel();
    buttonPanel.add( new Button( "Restart client" ) );
    buttonPanel.add( new Button( "Stop client" ) );

    add( "South", buttonPanel );
  }

}
```

echoUDPClient **Notes and Observations**

Because UDP is an unreliable protocol, we'll have no idea from the send() call alone whether our packet gets to the remote host. It could go wandering off into the ether(net) and never reach the destination. If the echo server never receives a packet from us, we certainly won't be getting a reply. But wait—the call to the receive() method blocks the calling thread. If the echo server never sends us a packet, the client will be stuck waiting for a message that will never come.

For this simple example it is acceptable to ignore this unlikely situation, but a real application would need to watch out for it and take appropriate action. One possible solution would be to put a wrapper class that runs in its own thread around the network client object. The calling thread could stop the thread of the wrapper class after a time-out and check for received data.

Example Applet Tag

The following applet tag shows how the UDP client could be embedded in an HTML page. Remember that the Java security constraints might keep the applet from working unless the code is loaded from the local disk.

```
<applet code="echoUDPApplet.class" width="500" height="200">
<param name="host" value="www.fnord.net">
</applet>
```

A `DatagramSocket`-Based Server

Server applications using UDP sockets do not look much different from client applications. The last example in this chapter will be a server for the same echo protocol the preceding client was created for. This application will listen for packets on a port and send them back verbatim. The final applet is shown in Figure 29.5.

FIGURE 29.5.

The output from the `echoUDPServer` *in the console window.*

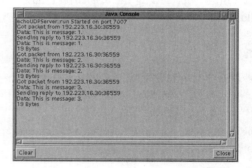

Design

This application will be split into three classes: an `echoUDPServer` class that will handle receiving packets, an `echoObject` class that will return replies to their source, and an applet wrapper `echoUDPServerApplet` that will run a server in an applet context (security constraints permitting). Because servers are most often run in a stand-alone context, the server will use `System.err` to display all output rather than a GUI interface. With the AppletViewer this output will be shown on the terminal or DOS shell where it was started, while Netscape Navigator will print the output to the Java console window.

The `echoUDPServer` class will open a socket on a port specified in the constructor (in order to enable us to run on any port we want). This will enable the server to run on UNIX platforms without disturbing the system's echo service or requiring the server to be run by `root`.

> **NOTE**
>
> The default port setting for our client object is the official echo port, port seven. For the server the default will be port 7007. To use the client together with the server, you need to change the `echoPort` constant in the `echoUDPClient` class and recompile it. If you are using a Windows 95 or Windows NT platform, you should be able to specify the default port (7) when you run the server applet and use the client unmodified.

Each `echoObject` will run in its own thread. Although this is not strictly needed for such a simple service, a more complex server might want to allocate a new socket for each client and let that thread handle all communications with that particular host.

echoObject **Class**

We will start off by developing the `echoObject` class that will respond to echo requests. This class should go in the same source file as `echoUDPServer`.

Skeleton

The `echoObject` will have one constructor that will take the server's `DatagramSocket` (to send the reply with) and the datagram that we are replying to (which has the address and port the packet came from). These objects will be copied into member variables.

Because the object is `Runnable`, we also need to define `start()` and `stop()` methods and a `Thread` variable to hold the thread for the object.

```
import java.io.*;
import java.net.*;

class echoObject implements Runnable {
  Thread echoThread = null;
  DatagramSocket s = null;
  DatagramPacket source = null

  public echoObject( DatagramSocket s, DatagramPacket src ) {
    this.s = s;
    source = src;
  }

  public synchronized void start( ) {
    if( echoThread == null ) {
      echoThread = new Thread( this );
      echoThread.setPriority( Thread.MAX_PRIORITY / 8 );
      echoThread.start( );
    }
  }
}
```

```
public synchronized void stop( ) {
  if( echoThread != null ) {
    echoThread.stop( );
    echoThread = null;
  }
}

// run() Method

}
```

run( ) Method

The run() method first retrieves the data from the received packet and prints it to System.err. We use the getLength() method rather than the length member of the byte[] because the DatagramSocket will set it to the number of bytes actually received rather than the size of the buffer.

```
public synchronized void run( ) {
  String messageText = new String( source.getData( ), 0,
                                    0, source.getLength( ) );

  System.err.print( "Sending reply to " );
  System.err.println( source.getAddress( )
                      + ":" + source.getPort() );
  System.err.println( "Data: " + messageText );
  System.err.println( messageText.length() + " Bytes" );
```

Next, we will allocate a new DatagramPacket to send back to the source. We first allocate a byte[] to hold the data and copy the bytes from the String. Then we allocate the packet using the InetAddress and port number from the source packet.

```
  Byte messageBytes[] = new byte[ source.getLength( ) ];
  messageText.getBytes( 0, messageText.length(), messageBytes, 0 );

  DatagramPacket reply =
    new DatagramPacket( messageBytes, messageText.length( ),
                        source.getAddress( ), source.getPort( ) );
```

Finally, we will use the socket to send the reply back. If there is an exception sending the packet we will print it out to the error stream. After sending the datagram the method returns, ending the thread.

```
  try {
    s.send( reply );
  } catch( IOException e ) {
    System.err.print( "Error sending reply to " );
    System.err.print( source.getAddress( ) + ":"
                      + source.getPort( ) );
    System.err.println( ",.Exception was: " + e );
  }

  return;
}
```

echoUDPServer **Class**

The UDP server class will look familiar after having developed the echoUDPClient and TCPServer classes. Each server object will run in its own thread, with the run() method containing the bulk of the code. The server will create an echoObject to service the request.

Skeleton

The constructor takes the port number to run on as the argument and allocates the socket to listen on. The port number isn't stored in a member because the socket provides it through the getLocalPort() method. We also define the usual thread variable, and start and stop methods.

```java
import java.io.*;
import java.net.*;

// echoObject code goes here

public
class echoUDPServer implements Runnable {
  Thread serverThread = null;
  DatagramSocket s = null;

  public static final int echoPort = 7007;

  public echoUDPServer( int port ) throws SocketException {
    s = new DatagramSocket( port );
  }

  public synchronized void start( ) {
    if( serverThread == null ) {
      serverThread = new Thread( this );
      serverThread.setPriority( Thread.MAX_PRIORITY / 4 );
      serverThread.start( );
    }
  }

  public synchronized void stop( ) {
    if( serverThread != null ) {
      serverThread.stop( );
      serverThread = null;
    }
  }

  // run() Method

}
```

run() **Method**

The run method loops forever until the thread is stopped. It starts by printing a message to System.err, noting what port it is listening on. Next is the main while loop where incoming packets are dispatched. Finally, the socket is closed before returning.

```
public synchronized void run( ) {
  System.err.println( "echoUDPServer Started on port "
                      + s.getLocalPort( ) );

  while( serverThread != null ) {
    // Allocate a packet to receive into

    // Wait for a packet

    // Print out the packet

    // Allocate an echoObject and start it.
  }

  try {
    s.close( );
  } catch( Exception e ) {
    System.err.println( "Error closing socket: " + e );
  }

  return;
}
```

Allocate a Packet to Receive Into

The first thing to do in the while loop is to allocate a packet so that the socket has something to receive data into.

```
byte   recvBytes[] = new byte[ 8192 ];

DatagramPacket incomingPacket =
  new DatagramPacket( recvBytes, recvBytes.length );
```

Wait for a Packet

Now that we have somewhere to put it, we will call the receive() method and wait for a packet to come in. The method will block the executing thread until a packet is received. Keep this in mind when using the receive() method in a thread that you don't want blocked (such as the same thread as your user interface). If there is an error while receiving a packet, we simply print the exception and continue back to the top of the while loop.

```
try {
  s.receive( incomingPacket );
} catch( IOException e ) {
  System.err.println( "Error receiving: " + e );

  continue;
}
```

Print the Packet

The next bit of code prints the received packet to System.err.

```
System.err.print( "Got packet from " );
System.err.println( incomingPacket.getAddress()
                    + ":" + incomingPacket.getPort( ) );
```

```
String str = new String( incomingPacket.getData( ), 0 );
System.err.println( "Data: " + str );
```

Allocate an echoObject

The last step the while loop takes is to create a new echoObject to send back the reply. This object will send the echo reply back to the client while the server thread goes back to listening for new requests.

```
echoObject handler =
  new echoObject( s, incomingPacket );

handler.start( );
```

echoUDPServerApplet

Because the echoUDPServer class prints all messages to the System.err stream, we don't need much of an interface. The following applet does nothing more than creating a new server object and printing a message telling the user where to look.

```
import java.applet.Applet;
import java.awt.TextArea;
import java.awt.BorderLayout;

public
class echoUDPServerApplet extends Applet {
  public void init( ) {
    echoUDPServer srv = null;
    String statusMessage = null;
    int port = 0;

    if( getParameter( "port" ) != null ) {
      port = Integer.valueOf( getParameter( "port" ) ).intValue( );
    } else {
      port = echoUDPServer.echoPort;
    }

    try {
      srv = new echoUDPServer( port );

      srv.start( );
      statusMessage = "Server running on port " + port + ".\n";
      statusMessage += "Watch the Java console for information.";
    } catch( Exception e ) {
      statusMessage = "Error creating server: " + e;
    }

    TextArea statusArea = new TextArea( 80, 4 );

    setLayout( new BorderLayout( ) );

    statusArea.setText( statusMessage );
    statusArea.setEditable( false );
```

```
    add( "Center", statusArea );
  }
}
```

Example Applet Tag

The following tag will start an echo server running on port 7007. Remember that the compiled class files need to be located somewhere in the CLASSPATH for wherever you are using to view the applet. Otherwise, you will get a SecurityException when the echoUDPServer tries to allocate a DatagramSocket.

```
<applet code="echoUDPServerApplet.class" width="500" height="200">
<param name="port" value="7007">
</applet>
```

Summary

You now should know enough to strike out on your own and develop networking applets and applications. For simple Web-based applets, the urlFetcher example should show you all you need to know. The other examples can be altered and used as the core of new applications. For example, the TCPServer could be rewritten to service Finger requests for hosts that don't already have a finger daemon (such as Windows 95 boxes).

To see more examples of how to put the networking classes to use, check out Chapter 31, "Extending Java with Content and Protocol Handlers." The fingerClient is used to enable Java to understand URLs of the form finger://hostname/user, and the urlFetcher applet is extended.

Overview of Content and Protocol Handlers

30

by Suresh Jois

IN THIS CHAPTER

The first section of this chapter is a note on the history and evolution of protocol and content handler architecture within Java. The second section discusses protocol handlers—their definition, potential applications where they can be used as a very effective and powerful design and implementation tool, and general guidelines for writing your own protocol handlers. The third section of this chapter discusses the same issues for content handlers.

Historical and Evolutionary Note

The Alpha version of Java had a standardized API for handlers. This was possible because the only Java-enabled Web browser at that time was Sun's own HotJava. Within HotJava, Sun had full control over the architecture and deployment of handlers—both standard handlers as well as custom user-designed handlers.

Beginning with Java Beta, however, Sun is evolving the Java API, including the protocol and content handler APIs, with the objective of integrating it with other vendors' Web browsers, including Netscape Navigator. The next chapter provides examples of code written to illustrate protocol and content handlers using the latest release of the JDK.

Java Protocol Handlers

This section starts with a definition of protocol handlers. We then examine dynamic protocol handlers in the Java language, followed by a discussion of potential application scenarios. This section concludes with a set of guidelines for designing and implementing protocol handlers in Java.

Definition of a Protocol Handler

In the context of client-server software design, a *protocol* is a predefined set of sequences in which information is exchanged between the client and the server software. It is the common language that they have been designed (by the programmer) to use to communicate with each other.

A *protocol handler* is a piece of code that is used (both by the server and client programs), to perform the function of shuttling data to and from the server and client applications. In the *read* mode, protocol handlers listen for incoming data on a network connection, verify if the data sequence conforms to the predefined protocol, and if it does, pass the data on to other parts of the program. In the *write* mode, they shuttle data in the opposite direction.

In conventional languages like C and C++, protocol handlers have to be designed and integrated into the system architecture up front, along with other components of a client-server system. This means that when the protocol has to be changed for business or engineering reasons, the handler and other related parts of the client and server systems have to go through a complete implementation and release cycle. This limits the shelf life of the handler and thereby the return-on-investment of the implementation effort.

Dynamic Protocol Handlers in Java

The Java language eliminates all constraints of static design on protocol handlers and their deployment in client-server systems. Unlike a static/frozen protocol handler in conventional languages, a protocol handler in Java has the following elements of dynamism:

- A client or a server program need not possess the protocol handler code in advance—the code can be loaded on the fly.
- If a client program needs a new (and hitherto unknown) protocol handler, it can query the server (which initiated the transaction) and get the handler code from across the network.
- Design changes in the handler can be propagated on the fly without affecting other parts of the system and going through a full implementation-release cycle.

The following features of Java make this possible:

- version-checked loading of classes
- ability to fetch classes from across the network

Given these two Java language features, you can easily make protocol handlers dynamically loadable, given that you design and implement the handlers as a Java class hierarchy.

Detailed guidelines for exploiting the previous Java features to construct dynamic protocol handlers are presented in a later section (*Guidelines for Designing Dynamic Protocol in Java*). In the next section, we'll explore application scenarios where dynamic protocol handlers are a powerful and even necessary design mechanism.

Application Scenarios for Dynamic Protocol Handlers

In this section we examine some client-server application scenarios where dynamic protocol handling is shown to be much more effective and powerful than traditional static handler design.

Dynamically Extensible Web Browsers

Most Web browsers can handle the http, FTP, gopher and other popular Internet protocols. In addition, some browsers can handle secure/encrypted protocols. Let's say, for example, a browser vendor or the W3O (the organization that sets and arbitrates standards for the World Wide Web) makes some changes to an existing protocol or creates a new protocol. Any such new development triggers a new cycle of product design and implementation and distribution of new browsers. Users are also forced to keep abreast of announcements and releases, periodically download new browsers, and install them on their machines.

Therefore, any change or improvement in a Web protocol forces the entire industry and the user community to swallow the change whole. This problem can be solved by using dynamically loadable protocol handlers.

A commonly used protocol for secure data transmission on the Web is HTTPS. A standard Web URL such as `http://someserver.com/info.html` will initiate a nonsecure network connection between the server and the browser. A secure server URL such as `https://someserver.com/secretinfo.html`, however, will cause both the browser and the server to encrypt or scramble all transactions. Of course for this to work, both the browser and the server have to be "aware" of this protocol and incorporate the actual protocol code.

Now imagine that the federal government comes up with a new standard for secure financial transmission, called (for example) HTTP-FED and expects all Web browsers and servers to incorporate the new protocol. This would require

- vendors to design and distribute new versions of their products
- users to upgrade their installations
- servers to constantly check and warn any stragglers who have not upgraded their browsers

Going through this change can be tiresome, expensive, and error prone, especially when the technology is rapidly changing and evolving. This problem can be alleviated by separating the design of the browser (and the server) from that of the protocol and making the protocol dynamically loadable. This is very easy to do in Java, as opposed to other conventional languages such as C or C++.

To make a product, such as a Web browser, automatically protocol-adaptive to the previously mentioned hypothetical new protocol HTTP-FED, a designer needs to

- implement the protocol-dependent part of the browser in Java and make it aware of a "Home" server, where new handlers will be found
- host the actual HTTP-FED protocol handling code on the "Home" server

When the browser user tries to access a URL with the new HTTP-FED protocol, the browser will see that it does not understand HTTP-FED. This will cause the Java-implemented part of the browser to access the "Home" server and automatically download the new protocol handler. All this will be transparent to the user.

Multiprotocol Financial Transaction Systems

A rapidly emerging technology in the Internet arena is the ability to conduct financial transactions on the Internet. The scope of this technology includes home banking, online shopping, online bill payment, and so on. The theory is that, using a Web browser, you will be able to conduct any sort of transaction that involves the transfer of money. The reality of implementing this, however, is a bit more complex.

There are several industry groups and individual companies that are involved in creating protocols and standards for online financial transactions. Each is interested in having some or all of their favorite proposals gain pervasive acceptance by the industry and end users. Because most of us pay for almost anything we do, there is a lot of money to be made in being a primary enabler or carrier of these transactions.

While the industry players fight it out, what is the best product design strategy to follow, from the perspective of the following users of this technology:

- first-tier product vendors (such as browser makers)?
- second-tier vendors (such as makers of financial and tax utilities, pay-per-access service providers, online retailers)?
- end users who wish to conduct online transactions now?

In the short run, the standards and protocol situation is going to remain fragmented and rapidly changing.

Given the shifting sands of online transaction technology, the best bet is to design applications that are immune or adaptive in relation to multiple and emerging protocols and standards. Again, the only way to do this is to implement dynamic protocol handlers in Java.

Multiplayer Games

Imagine that you are in charge of designing the protocols for a networked multiplayer electronic game. Such games enable multiple people to participate in a game session through a network.

Such games are usually designed as a client-server system, with

- a game client program that runs on each user's machine and provides the visual interface to the game
- game server software that runs on a gaming server computer and keeps track of the number of people, their game moves, scores, and so on
- a game protocol that enables the server and multiple clients to exchange game data and to remain in sync with each other during a game session

To make the example concrete, let's assume you are designing some sort of a wagering game, which requires players to make a wager before each move. The person who makes the move wins or loses money depending on whether the move was good or bad within the rules of the game.

This means that for every move, the protocol for this game has to carry information about (among other things)

- the value of the wager
- the actual move made by a player
- the net gain or loss for each player

Now, for an interesting twist to this scenario, let's say you wish to allow your target consumer to try the game before he or she buys it. This means you would have to distribute two versions of your game: a paid licensed version that allows actual wagering and financial transaction, and another free version that allows people to play but not actually wager and exchange money. Depending on whether the player is using a free version or paid version of the client, the protocol code in the client has to transmit or block wagering information during the game session.

If you were coding the game in C or C++, you would have to distribute physically two separate versions of the game—one with a fully functional protocol and the other with the wagering part of the protocol turned off. This would create the overhead of two separate tracks of the product-cycle that spans coding, documentation, maintenance, advertising, distribution, support, and maintenance mechanisms.

If you implement your game in Java, you can merge the two product-cycle tracks and implement a fully automated try-before-you-buy mechanism. This is accomplish by doing the following:

- design and distribute a single client program, with no protocol code included
- design the protocol as a class hierarchy to segment the handling of wagering data from other parts of the protocol
- host the protocol code on the gaming server

Then, when the user runs the client program and connects to the gaming server, the server can authenticate the client for a valid license code and send the appropriate protocol code—the fully functional version for licensed clients and the wager-disabled version for unlicensed clients.

It is pretty obvious that the Java-based implementation with dynamically loadable protocol handlers is much cleaner and effective than a C- or C++-based implementation with no such flexibility.

Guidelines for Designing Dynamic Protocol Handlers in Java

From the earlier application scenarios, you might already have a good idea of how to go about designing a dynamic protocol handler and how to deploy it within a client-server application.

Here is a set of guidelines that will help consolidate the ideas and provide a strategy for implementing Java-based dynamic protocol handlers in diverse design situations.

- Identify all the client and program states during which some transactions will occur between the client and the server. Let's call this the set of transactional states of the system. This set of transactional states should be carefully chosen so there is no duplication of functionality between members of this set.

- For each such transactional state, identify the one or more protocols that will be used.

- Create detailed specifications for each protocol in the proposed protocol suite.

- Parameterize the protocol specifications per the different transactional states in the system and partition them into a Java class hierarchy that corresponds to your parameterization.

- Create a single generic protocol loader class within both the client and server programs. The class should accept a set of parameters that identify a transactional state and load the appropriate protocol from the protocol class hierarchy.

- If you wish to add a new protocol to the system, as stated, identify the transactional state that will use it and add the protocol code at an appropriate place in the exiting protocol class hierarchy.

- For both existing and new protocols, the generically designed loader will use a local version of the protocol. If it does not find one on the local file system, it will go across to a specified "Home" server and download an appropriate handler from there.

Java Content Handlers

Much of what has been said for protocol handlers in the previous section also applies to content handlers. Thus, some material here is similar to material in prior sections. There is, however, a fundamental difference between content and protocol handlers that becomes clear as we go along.

Definition of a Content Handler

The Internet is used to exchange diverse types of data—images, plain text, audio clips, executable programs, and so on. Each type of data is encoded in a specific format. Common examples of such encoding formats include, among others

- JPEG and GIF formats for images
- AU, AIFF, and WAV formats for audio data
- PLAIN and DOC for documents
- HTML for Web pages

Such encoded data is targeted for consumption by one or more applications on users' computers. Content Type, also sometimes called MIME Type, specifies what format the data is encoded in and what class of applications can potentially consume this data. Using this information, a client program such as a Web browser or an e-mail reader can collect incoming data and spawn an appropriate module of internal code or an external "Helper" program to consume the data.

In the context of a client-server software system, a protocol is a predefined set of sequences in which information is exchanged between the client and the server software, while content type specifies the exact nature and format of the data being transmitted through the protocol. The content type is physically a part of a protocol sequence and is often transmitted in the header portion of the protocol. The protocol header might include other information such as the length (in bytes) of the data. All this information is used in tandem by the recipient program to decode and use the data.

A protocol handler is a piece of code that is used (both by the server and client programs) to perform the function of shuttling data to and from each other. A content handler is a piece of code that kicks in after the protocol handler has done its job. The content handler either directly consumes the incoming data or spawns an external application to use the data.

In conventional languages such as C and C++, content handlers, like protocol handlers, have to be designed and integrated along with other components of the system. This means that when a data-encoding format changes, or a new content type has to be supported for business or engineering reasons, the entire application has to go through a complete implementation and release cycle.

Dynamic Content Handlers in Java

The Java language eliminates the need for tightly coupled and static design of content handlers and their deployment in client-server systems. Unlike a static/frozen content handler in conventional languages, a content handler in Java has the following elements of dynamism:

- A client or a server program need not possess the handler code in advance—the code can be loaded on the fly.
- If a client program needs a new (and hitherto unknown) content handler, it can query the server (which initiated the transaction) and get the handler code from across the network.
- Design changes in the handler can be propagated on the fly without affecting other parts of the system and going through a full implementation-release cycle.

Just as with protocol handlers, the following features of Java make this possible:

- version-checked loading of classes
- ability to fetch classes from across the network

Given these two Java language features, you can easily make content handlers dynamically loadable if you design and implement the handlers as a Java class hierarchy.

Detailed guidelines for exploiting the previous Java features to construct dynamic content handlers is be presented in the "Guidelines for Designing Dynamic Content Handlers in Java" section a little later in this chapter. In the next section, however, we'll explore application scenarios where dynamic content handlers are useful and even necessary.

Application Scenarios for Dynamic Content Handlers

In this section we explore some client-server application scenarios where dynamic content handling is shown to be much more effective and powerful than traditional static handler design.

Dynamically Extensible Web Browsers, E-mail Readers, and News Readers

Most Web browsers can handle a limited set of content types, such as HTML, Plain Text, GIF images, and so on. When a Web browser cannot itself handle a particular data type, it calls an external "Helper" application to handle it.

E-mail and news readers can only display plain ASCII textual data. All MIME data types attached to the e-mail or news article have to be saved on disk to be handled later by another program.

For the purpose of the following discussion, we'll refer to Web browsers, mail readers, and news readers collectively as browser programs (they all let the user "browse" information coming through the Net).

In all the previous cases, the browser program has to do one of the following:

- understand the content type internally
- assume an external program exists on the user's computer that can be called to handle the data

What if neither of the above is true? What if the incoming content type is totally new, so that neither the browser program understands it nor can an external program use it? Well, so far the solution using conventional languages has been this:

- incorporate more and more content type handlers into the browser
- ship external helper applications for every new content type

Each such new development triggers a new cycle of product design, implementation, and distribution of new browser programs so that the new features can reach end users. Also, with each new release and new sets of features, applications tend to bloat and consume more hardware resources. Users are also forced to keep abreast of announcements and releases and must periodically download new browser and helper programs and install them on their machines.

Thus, any change or improvement in a content type forces the entire industry and the user community to scramble to keep up. This problem can be solved using dynamically loadable content handlers.

Let us imagine the MPEG committee comes up with a new MPEG-encoding format called MPEG-2000, and expects all browser programs to understand and render this new format correctly. This would require

■ MPEG-encoded content vendors to design and distribute new versions of their content, along with appropriate helper applications

■ browser vendors with built-in handlers to update their code to handle the new format

■ users to upgrade their current versions of helper apps and browsers, and tweak all the configuration files so both old MPEG-encoded content and newer content can be seamlessly handled

Going through this is a chore. As with protocol handlers, this problem can be alleviated by separating the design of the browser from that of the content handler, and making the content handler dynamically loadable. This is very easy to do in Java, as opposed to other conventional languages such as C or C++.

To make a product such as a Web browser automatically adaptive to the hypothetical new MPEG content type

■ implement the content handler part of the browser in Java

■ host the Java code to handle the new content type on the same server from which you plan to serve the data encoded in the proposed new content type

When the browser tries to decode data that is encoded in the new content type, the Java-implemented part will access the same server where the data came from and automatically download the appropriate handler. All this will be transparent to the user.

Other Nonbrowser Applications

The concept of dynamic content handling can be extended to several other application domains. A generic potential application domain is to use content handlers to mediate "computing-resource-for-rent" type applications.

Let's say a hypothetical company, TronGlut, Inc., has an enormous array of powerful computers, and a hypothetical compression technology researcher—Dr. Pix—has invented a new compression algorithm. This algorithm is very advanced, but requires enormous computing power to test. Thus, Dr. Pix contracts with TronGlut, Inc. to send test data (such as images, sounds, and text) and algorithms to TronGlut's computers, which will run the algorithm and return compressed data to Dr. Pix.

In this scenario, Dr. Pix will host the data and host the corresponding handler code (the compression algorithms to be tested) on a server. TronGlut's computer runs an automatic browser-type application that sequentially accesses uncompressed data and corresponding handler code from Dr. Pix's server. After running the handler on each data item, the results are e-mailed back to Dr. Pix, who evaluates the results visually and algorithmically with another browser.

Guidelines for Designing Dynamic Content Handlers in Java

From the earlier application scenarios, you may already have a good idea of how to go about designing a dynamic content handler.

Here is a set of guidelines that will help consolidate the ideas and provide a strategy for implementing Java-based dynamic content handlers in diverse design situations:

- Create a Java class for each content type you need to handle in your application, and organize them into a suitable class hierarchy.

- Create a single generic content handler loader class within both the client and server programs that accepts a set of parameters that identify a specific content type and loads the appropriate content handler from the content handler class hierarchy.

- If you are a content vendor and wish to create a new content type, create a Java class that handles the new type, and host the code on the same server from which you plan to serve data.

- For both existing and new content types, the generically designed content handler loader will use a local version of the handler. If it doesn't find one on the local file system, it will go access the specified content server and download an appropriate handler from there.

Summary

In this chapter, we examined the concept of dynamically loadable protocol and content handlers in Java. With specific application scenarios and design guidelines, we saw how these twin features of Java empower software designers to implement client-server applications in a modular, adaptive, and extensible way. In the light of these features, we contrasted client-server design using Java against using other languages like C and C++.

The next chapter expands the material presented in this chapter and presents specific code samples illustrating the design of protocol and content handlers in Java.

Extending Java with Content and Protocol Handlers

3 1

by Mike Fletcher

Java's URL class gives applets and applications easy access to the World Wide Web using the HTTP protocol. This is fine and dandy if you can get the information you need into a format that a Web server or CGI script can access. However, wouldn't it be nice if your code could talk directly to the server application without going through an intermediary CGI script or some sort of proxy? Wouldn't you like your Java-based Web browser to be able to display your wonderful new image format? This is where protocol and content handlers come in.

What Are Protocol and Content Handlers?

Handlers are classes that extend the capabilities of the standard URL class. A protocol handler provides an InputStream (and OutputStream, where appropriate) that retrieves the content of a URL. Content handlers take an InputStream for a given MIME type and convert it into a Java object of the appropriate type.

MIME Types

MIME, or *Multipurpose Internet Mail Extensions*, is the Internet standard for specifying what type of content a resource contains. As you might have guessed from the name, it originally was proposed for the context of enclosing nontextual components in Internet e-mail. This allows different platforms (PCs, Macintoshes, UNIX workstations, and others) to exchange multimedia content in a common format.

The MIME standard, described in RFC 1521, defines an extra set of headers similar to those on Internet e-mail. The headers describe attributes such as the method of encoding the content and the MIME content type. MIME types are written as *type/subtype*, where *type* is a general category such as text or image and *subtype* is a more specific description of the format such as html or jpeg. For example, when a Web browser contacts an HTTP daemon to retrieve an HTML file, the daemon's response looks something like the following:

```
Content-type: text/html

<HEAD><TITLE>Document moved</TITLE></HEAD>
<BODY><H1>Document moved</H1>
```

The Web browser parses the Content-type: header and sees that the data is text/html—an HTML document. If it was a GIF image the header would have been Content-type: image/gif.

IANA (Internet Assigned Numbers Authority), the group that maintains the lists of assigned protocol numbers and the like, is responsible for registering new content types. A current copy of the official MIME types is available from ftp://ftp.isi.edu/in-notes/iana/assignments/media-types/. This site also has specifications or pointers to specifications for each type.

Getting Java to Load New Handlers

The exact procedure for loading a protocol or content handler depends on the Java implementation. The following instructions are based on Sun's Developer's Kit and should work for any implementation derived from Sun's. If you have problems, check the documentation for your particular Java version.

In the JDK implementation, the URL class and helpers look for classes in the sun.net.www package. Protocol handlers should be in a package called sun.net.www.protocol.*ProtocolName*, where *ProtocolName* is the name of the protocol (such as ftp or http). The handler class itself should be named Handler. For example, the full name of the HTTP protocol handler class, provided by Sun with the JDK, is sun.net.www.protocol.http.Handler. In order to get your new protocol handler loaded, you need to construct a directory structure corresponding to the package names and add the directory to your CLASSPATH environment variable. Assume that you have a handler for a protocol—we'll call it the foo protocol. Your Java library directory is *…/java/lib/* (*…\java\lib* on Windows machines). You will need to take the following steps:

- Make directories *…/java/lib/sun*, *…/java/lib/sun/net*, and so on.
  The last directory should be called *./java/lib/sun/net/www/protocol/foo*.

- Place your Handler.java file in the last directory (that is, it should be named *…/java/lib/sun/net/www/protocol/foo/Handler.java*).

- Compile the Handler.java file.

If you place the ZIP file of network classes from the CD-ROM in your CLASSPATH, the example handlers should load correctly.

Creating a Protocol Handler

We will start extending Java by using the fingerClient class developed in Chapter 29, "Network Programming," to implement a handler for the Finger protocol. Our handler will take URLs of the form finger:*user@hostname*, where *user* is the user name we want information for (or all users, if omitted) and *hostname* is the host to query. The urlFetcher applet will be used to demonstrate the protocol handler.

Design

The first decision that needs to be made is how to structure URLs for our protocol. We'll imitate the HTTP URL and specify that Finger URLs should be of the following form:

finger://*host*/*user*

host is the host to contact and *user* is an optional user to ask for information about. If the user name is omitted, we will return information about all users. This is the same behavior as the `fingerClient` developed in Chapter 29. The only modification to the `fingerClient` class that needs to be made is to insert the `package` statement to put the class in the correct package.

Because we already have the `fingerClient`, we only need to write subclasses to `URLStreamHandler` and `URLConnection`. Our stream handler will use the client object to format the returned information using HTML. The handler will write the content into a `StringBuffer`, which will be used to create a `StringBufferInputStream`. The `fingerConnection`, a subclass of `URLConnection`, will take this stream and implement the `getInputStream()` and `getContent()` methods.

In our implementation, the protocol handler object does all the work of retrieving the remote content while the connection object simply retrieves the data from the stream provided. Usually, you would have the connection object handler retrieving the content. The `openConnection()` method would open a connection to the remote location, and the `getInputStream()` would return a stream to read the contents.

Copying the `fingerClient`

The first thing to do is copy the `fingerClient` source from Chapter 29 into the right subdirectory. The only modification that needs to be made to the class is to add the following statement to the top of the file:

```
package sun.net.www.protocol.finger;
```

Everything else in the file remains the same. You just need to recompile the source so that you get a class file with the correct package information.

`fingerConnection` Source

We'll go ahead and present the source for the `URLConnection` subclass. This class should go in the same file as the `Handler` class. The constructor will copy the `InputStream` passed and call the `URLConnection` constructor. It also sets the `URLConnection` member to indicate that the connection cannot take input. Listing 31.1 contains the source for this class.

Listing 31.1. The `fingerConnection` class.

```
class fingerConnection extends URLConnection {
  InputStream in;

  fingerConnection( URL u, InputStream in ) {
    super( u );
    this.in = in;
    this.setDoInput( false );
  }

  public void connect( ) {
    return;
  }
```

```
public InputStream getInputStream( ) throws IOException {
  return in;
}

public Object getContent( ) throws IOException {
  String retval;
  int nbytes;
  byte buf[] = new byte[ 1024 ];

  try {
    while( (nbytes = in.read( buf, 0, 1024 )) != -1 ) {
      retval += new String( buf, 0, 0, nbytes );
    }
  } catch( Exception e ) {
    System.err.println(
      "fingerConnection::getContent: Exception\n" + e );

    e.printStackTrace( System.err );
  }

  return retval
}
}
```

Handler **Source**

First we'll rough out the skeleton of the `Handler.java` file. We need the package statement so that our classes are compiled into the package where the runtime handler will be looking for them. We also import the `fingerClient` object here. The outline of the class is shown in Listing 31.2.

Listing 31.2. Protocol handler skeleton.

```
package sun.net.www.protocol.finger;

import java.io.*;
import java.net.*;
import sun.net.www.protocol.finger.fingerClient;


// fingerConnection source goes here

public class Handler extends URLStreamHandler {
  // openConnection() Method
}
```

openConnection() **Method**

Now we'll develop the method responsible for returning an appropriate `URLConnection` object to retrieve a given URL. Our method starts out by allocating a `StringBuffer` to hold our return data. We also will parse out the host name and user name from the URL argument. If the host was omitted, we default to localhost. The code for openConnection() is given in Listings 31.3 through 31.6.

Listing 31.3. The openConnection() method, part one.

```
public synchronized URLConnection openConnection( URL u ) {
  StringBuffer sb = new StringBuffer( );

  String host = u.getHost( );
  String user = u.getFile( ).substring( 1, u.getFile( ).length() );

  if( host.equals( "" ) ) {
    host = "localhost";
  }
```

Next, the method will write an HTML header into the buffer. This will allow a Java-based Web browser to display the Finger information in a nice-looking format.

Listing 31.4. The openConnection() method, part two.

```
sb.append( "<HTML><head>\n");
sb.append( "<title>Fingering " );
sb.append( (user.equals("") ? "everyone" : user) );
sb.append( "@" + host );
sb.append( "</title></head>\n" );

sb.append( "<body>\n" );
sb.append( "<pre>\n" );
```

We now will use the fingerClient class to get the information into a String and then append it to our buffer. If there is an error while getting the Finger information, we will put the error message from the exception into the buffer instead.

Listing 31.5. The openConnection() method, part three.

```
try {
  String info = null;
  info = (new fingerClient( host, user )).getInfo( );

  sb.append( info )
} catch( Exception e ) {
  sb.append( "Error fingering: " + e );
}
```

Finally we'll close off the open HTML tags and create a fingerConnection object which will be returned to the caller, as follows:

Listing 31.6. The `openConnection()` method, part four.

```
  sb.append( "\n</pre></body>\n</html>\n" );

  return new fingerConnection( u,
    (new StringBufferInputStream( sb.toString( ) ) ) );
}
```

Using the Handler

Once you have all of the code compiled and in the right locations, load the `urlFetcher` applet from Chapter 29 and enter a Finger URL. If everything loads right, you should see something that looks like Figure 31.1. If you get an error that says Finger is an unknown protocol, check that you have your `CLASSPATH` set correctly.

FIGURE 31.1.

The `urlFetcher` *applet displaying a Finger URL.*

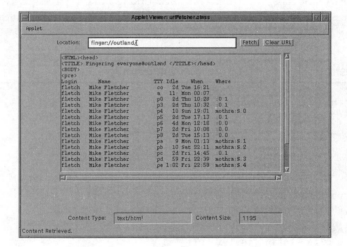

Creating a Content Handler

This content handler example will be for the MIME type `text/tab-separated-values`. This type will be familiar if you have ever used a spreadsheet or database program. Many such applications can import and export data in an ASCII text file, with each column of data in a row separated by a Tab character (`"\t"`). The first line is interpreted as the names of the fields, and the remaining lines are the actual data.

Design

Our first design decision is to figure out what type of Java object or objects to map the tab-separated values. Because this is a textual content, some sort of `String` object would seem to be the best solution. The spreadsheet characteristics of rows and columns of data can be represented by arrays. Putting these two facts together gives us a data type of String[][], or an array of arrays of String objects. The first array is an array of String[] objects, each representing one row of the data. Each of these arrays consists of a String for each cell of the data.

Also, we'll need to have some way of breaking the input stream into the separate fields. We will make a subclass of java.io.StreamTokenizer to handle this task. The StreamTokenizer class provides methods for breaking an InputStream into individual tokens. You might want to browse over the entry for StreamTokenizer in the API reference if you are not familiar with it.

Content Handler Skeleton

Content handlers are implemented by subclassing the java.net.ContentHandler class. These subclasses are responsible for implementing a getContent() method. We'll start with the skeleton of the class. We'll import the networking and I/O packages, as well as the java.util.Vector class. We also will define the skeleton for our tabStreamTokenizer class. This is shown in Listing 31.7.

Listing 31.7. Content handler skeleton.

```
/*
 * Handler for text/tab-separated-values MIME type.
 */

// This needs to go in this package for JDK-derived
// Java implementations

package sun.net.www.content.text;

import java.net.*;
import java.io.*;

class tabStreamTokenizer extends StreamTokenizer {
  public static final int TT_TAB = ''\t'

  // Constructor
}

import java.util.Vector;

public
  class tab_separated_values extends ContentHandler {

  // getContent method

}
```

The `tabStreamTokenizer` Class

First we will define the class that will break the input up into the separate fields. Most of the functionality we need is provided by the `StreamTokenizer` class, so we only need to define a constructor that will specify the character classes needed to get the behavior we want. For the purposes of this content handler there are three types of tokens: `TT_TAB` tokens, which will represent fields; `TT_EOL` tokens, which signal the end of a line (that is, the end of a row of data); and `TT_EOF`, which signals the end of the input file. Because this class is relatively simple it will be presented in its entirety in Listing 31.8.

Listing 31.8. The `tabStreamTokenizer` class.

```
class tabStreamTokenizer extends StreamTokenizer {
  public static final int TT_TAB = '\t';

  tabStreamTokenizer( InputStream in ) {
    super( in );

    // Undo parseNumbers() and whitespaceChars(0, ' ')
    ordinaryChars( '0', '9' );
    ordinaryChar( '.' );
    ordinaryChar( '-' );
    ordinaryChars( 0, ' ' );

    // Everything but TT_EOL and TT_TAB is a word
    wordChars( 0, ('\t'-1) );
    wordChars( ('\t'+1), 255 );

    // Make sure TT_TAB and TT_EOL get returned verbatim.
    whitespaceChars( TT_TAB, TT_TAB );
    ordinaryChar( TT_EOL );
  }

}
```

The `getContent` Method

Subclasses of `ContentHandler` need to provide an implementation of `getContent()` that returns a reference to an `Object`. The method takes as its parameter a `URLConnection` object from which the class can obtain an `InputStream` to read the resource's data.

`getContent` Skeleton

First, we'll define the overall structure and method variables. We need a flag, which will be called `done`, to signal when we've read all of the field names from the first line of text. The number of fields (columns) in each row of data will be determined by the number of fields in the first line of text, and will be kept in an int variable numFields. We also will declare another integer, index, for use while inserting the rows of data into a String[].

We will need some method of holding an arbitrary number of objects because we cannot tell the number of data rows in advance. To do this we'll use the java.util.Vector object, which we'll call lines, to keep each String[]. Finally, we will declare an instance of our tabStreamTokenizer, using the getInputStream() method from the URLConnection passed as an argument to the constructor. Listing 31.9 shows the skeleton code for the method.

Listing 31.9. The getContent() skeleton.

```
public Object getContent( URLConnection con )
  throws IOException
{
  boolean done = false;
  int numFields = 0;
  int index = 0;
  Vector lines = new Vector();

  tabStreamTokenizer in =
    new tabStreamTokenizer( con.getInputStream( ) );

  // Read in the first line of data (Listing 31.10 & 31.11)

  // Read in the rest of the file (Listing 31.12)

  // Stuff all data into a String[][] (Listing 31.13)
}
```

Reading the First Line

The first line of the file will tell us the number of fields and the names of the fields in each row for the rest of the file. Because we don't know beforehand how many fields there are, we'll be keeping each field in a Vector firstLine. Each TT_WORD token that the tokenizer returns is the name of one field. We know we are done once it returns a TT_EOL token and can set the flag done to true. We will use a switch statement on the ttype member of our tabStreamTokenizer to decide what action to take. This is done in the code in Listing 31.10.

Listing 31.10. Reading the first line of data.

```
Vector firstLine = new Vector( );

while( !done && in.nextToken( ) != in.TT_EOF  ) {
  switch( in.ttype ) {
  case in.TT_WORD:
    firstLine.addElement( new String( in.sval ) );
    numFields++;
    break;
```

```
  case in.TT_EOL:
    done = true;
    break;
  }
}
```

Now that we have the first line in memory, we need to build an array of `String` objects from those stored in the `Vector`. To accomplish this we'll first allocate the array to the size just determined. Then we will use the `copyInto()` method to transfer the strings into the array just allocated. Finally, the array will be inserted into `lines`. (See Listing 31.11.)

Listing 31.11. Copying field names into an array.

```
// Copy first line into array
  String curLine[] = new String[ numFields ];
  firstLine.copyInto( curLine );
  lines.addElement( curLine );
```

Read the Rest of the File

Before reading the remaining data, we need to allocate a new array to hold the next row. Then we loop until encountering the end of the file, signified by `TT_EOF`. Each time we retrieve a `TT_WORD`, we will insert the `String` into `curLine` and increment `index`.

The end of the line will let us know when a row of data is done, at which time we will copy the current line into our `Vector`. Then we will allocate a new `String[]` to hold the next line and set `index` back to zero (to insert the next item starting at the first element of the array). The code to implement this is given in Listing 31.12.

Listing 31.12. Reading in the rest of the data.

```
curLine = new String[ numFields ];

while( in.nextToken( ) != in.TT_EOF ) {
  switch( in.ttype ) {
  case in.TT_WORD:
    curLine[ index++ ] = new String( in.sval );
    break;

  case in.TT_EOL:
    lines.addElement( curLine );
    curLine = new String[ numFields ];
    index = 0;
    break;
  }
}
```

Stuff All Data Into `String[][]`

At this point all of the data has been read in. All that remains is to copy the data from `lines` into an array of arrays of `String`, as follows in Listing 31.13.

Listing 31.13. Returning TSV data as `String[][]`.

```
String retval[][] = new String[ lines.size() ][];
lines.copyInto( retval );

return retval;
```

Using the Content Handler

In order to show how the content handler works, we'll be modifying the `urlFetcher` applet from Chapter 29. We'll be changing it to use the `getContent()` method to retrieve the contents of a resource rather than reading the data from the stream returned by `getInputStream()`. Because we're only changing the `doFetch()` method, we won't include the entire applet again, only the portions that change. The first change is to call the `getContent()` method and get an `Object` back rather than getting an `InputStream`. Listing 31.14 shows this change.

Listing 31.14. Modified `urlFetcher.doFetch()` code, part one.

```
try {
  boolean displayed = false;
  URLConnection con = target.openConnection();
  Object obj = con.getContent( );
```

Next come tests using the `instanceof` operator. We handle `String` objects and arrays of `String` objects by placing the text into the `TextArea`. Arrays are printed item by item. If the object is a subclass of `InputStream`, we read the data from the stream and display it. `Image` content will just be noted as being an `Image`. For any other content type, we simply throw our hands up and remark that we cannot display the content (because we're not a full-fledged Web browser). The code to do this is shown below in Listing 31.15.

Listing 31.15. Modified `urlFetcher.doFetch()` code, part two.

```
  if( obj instanceof String ) {
    contentArea.setText( (String) obj );
    displayed = true;
  }

  if( obj instanceof String[] ) {
    String array[] = (String []) obj;
    StringBuffer buf = new StringBuffer( );
```

```
      for( int i = 0; i < array.length; i++ )
        buf.append( "item " + i + ": " + array[i] + "\n" );

      contentArea.setText( buf.toString( ) );
      displayed = true;
    }

  if( obj instanceof String[][] ) {
    String array[][] = (String [][]) obj;
    StringBuffer buf = new StringBuffer( );

    for( int i = 0; i < array.length; i++ ) {
      buf.append( "Row " + i + ":\n\t" );
      for( int j = 0; j < array[i].length; j++ )
        buf.append( "item " + j + ": "
                  + array[i][j] + "\t" );
      buf.append( "\n" );
    }

    contentArea.setText( buf.toString() );
    displayed = true;
  }

  if( obj instanceof Image ) {
    contentArea.setText( "Image" );
    diplayed = true;
  }

  if( obj instanceof InputStream ) {
    int c;
    StringBuffer buf = new StringBuffer( );

    while( (c = ((InputStream) obj).read( )) != -1 )
      buf.append( (char) c );

    contentArea.setText( buf.toString( ) );
    displayed = true;
  }

  if( !displayed ) {
    contentArea.setText( "Don't know how to display "
      obj.getClass().getName( ) );
  }

  // Same code to display content type and length

} catch( IOException e ) {
  showStatus( "Error fetching \"" + target + "\": " + e );
  return;
}
```

The complete modified applet source is on the CD as `urlFetcher_Mod.java` in the `tsvContentHandler` directory. Figure 31.2 illustrates what it will show when displaying `text/tab-separated-values`.

FIGURE 31.2.

The urlFetcher_Mod
applet.

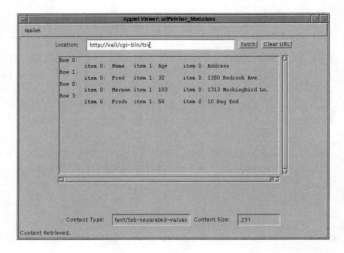

The file displayed is included as example.tsv. Most HTTP daemons should return the correct content type for files ending in .tsv. If the data does not show up as text/tab-separated-values, you might need to try one of the following things:

- Ask your Webmaster to look at the MIME configuration file for your HTTP daemon. The Webmaster will be able to either tell you the proper file suffix or modify the daemon to return the proper type.

- If you can install CGI scripts on your Web server, there is a sample script with the content handler example that returns data in the proper format.

Summary

After reading this chapter you should have an understanding of how Java can be extended fairly easily to deal with new application protocols and data formats. You should know what classes you have to derive your handlers from (URLConnection and URLStreamHandler for protocol handlers, ContentHandler for content handlers), and how to get Java to load the new handler classes.

If you want to try your hand at writing a handler, try something simple at first. For a protocol handler you could try the echo protocol shown in Chapter 28. A more challenging task might be writing a content handler for application/postscript which prints the file out (this would more than likely need some native code, or some way to use the java.lang.Runtime.exec() method to call a local printing program).

PART

Games, Multimedia, and VRML

Game Programming With Java

32

by Tim Macinta

Creating games with Java is a lot like creating games with other languages. You need to deal with the design of movable objects (often referred to as *sprites*), the design of a graphics engine to keep track of the movable objects, and double buffering to make movement look smooth. This chapter will cover methods for creating these standard building blocks of games using Java.

Thankfully, Java takes care of a lot of the dirty work that you would need to do if you were writing a game in another language. For instance, Java provides built-in support for transparent pixels, making it easier to write a graphics engine that can draw nonrectangular objects. Java also has built-in support for allowing several different programs to run at once—perfect for creating a world with a lot of creatures, each with its own special methods for acting. However, the added bonuses of Java can turn into handicaps if they are not used properly. This chapter will deal with using the advantages of Java to write games and how to avoid the pitfalls that accompany the power.

Graphics: Creating a Graphics Engine

A *graphics engine* is essential to a well-designed game in Java. A graphics engine is an object that is given the duty of painting the screen. The graphics engine keeps track of all objects that are on the screen at one time, the order in which to draw the objects, and the background to be drawn. By far, the most important function of the graphics engine is the maintenance of movable object blocks.

Movable Object Blocks in Java

So what's the big fuss about movable object blocks (MOBs)? Well, they make your life infinitely easier if you're interested in creating a game that combines graphics and user interaction, as most games do. The basic concept of a movable object is that the object contains both a picture that will be drawn on the screen and information that tells you where it is on the screen. To make the object move, you simply tell it which way to move and you're done—it takes care of the redrawing.

The bare-bones method for making a movable object block in Java is illustrated by Listing 32.1. As you can see, the movable object consists merely of an image and a set of coordinates. You might be thinking, "Movable objects are supposed to take care of all the redrawing that needs to be done when they are moved. How is that possible with just the code from Listing 32.1?" Redrawing will be the graphics engine's job. Don't worry about it for now; we'll cover it a little later.

Listing 32.1. Use this code to create a bare-bones movable object (MOB). This code should be saved in a file called `MOB.java`.

```java
import java.awt.*;

public class MOB {
    public int x = 0;
    public int y = 0;
    public Image picture;

        public MOB(Image pic) {
            picture=pic;
        }
}
```

As you can see in Listing 32.1, the constructor for our movable object block (MOB) takes an `Image` and stores it away to be drawn when needed. After we've instantiated an MOB (that is, after we've called the constructor), we have a movable object that we can move around the screen just by changing its x and y values. The engine will take care of redrawing the movable object in the new position, so what else is there to worry about now?

One thing to consider is the nature of the picture that is going to be drawn every time the movable object is drawn. Consider the place where the image probably will originate. In all likelihood the picture either will come from a GIF or JPEG file, which has one very important consequence—it will be rectangular. So what? Think about what your video game will look like if all of your movable objects are rectangles. Your characters would be drawn, but so would their backgrounds. Chances are, you'll want to have a background for the entire game, so it would be unacceptable if the unfilled space on character images covered up your background just because the images were rectangular and the characters were of another shape.

When programming games in other languages, this problem often is resolved by examining each pixel in a character's image before drawing it to see whether it's part of the background. If the pixel is not part of the background, it's drawn as normal. If the pixel is part of the background, it's skipped and the rest of the pixels are tested. Pixels that aren't drawn usually are referred to as transparent pixels. If this seems like a laborious process to you, that's because it is. Fortunately, Java has built-in support for transparent colors in images, which simplifies your task immensely. You don't have to check each pixel for transparency before it's drawn because Java can do that automatically! Java even has built-in support for different levels of transparency. For example, you can create pixels that are 20 percent transparent to give your images a ghostlike appearance. For now, though, we'll just deal with fully transparent pixels.

Java's capability to draw transparent pixels makes the task much easier of painting movable objects on the screen. But how do you tell Java what pixels are transparent and what pixels aren't? You could load the image and run it through a filter that changes the `ColorModel`, but that would be doing it the hard way. Fortunately, Java supports transparent GIF files. Whenever a transparent GIF file is loaded, all of the transparency is preserved by Java. That means your job just got a lot easier.

Now the problem becomes how to make transparent GIFs. This part is easier than you think. Simply use your favorite graphics package to create a GIF file (or a picture in some other format that you eventually can convert to a GIF file). Select a color that doesn't appear anywhere in the picture and fill all areas that you want to be transparent with the selected color. Make a note of the RGB value of the color that you use to fill in the transparent places. Now you can use a program to convert your GIF file into a transparent GIF file. I personally use Giftool, available at `http://www.homepages.com/tools/index.html`, to make transparent GIF files. You simply pass to Giftool the RGB value of the color you selected for transparency and Giftool makes that color transparent inside the GIF file. Giftool also is useful for making your GIF files *interlaced*. Interlaced GIF files are the pictures that appear with block-like edges initially and keep getting more defined as they continue to load.

Construction of a Graphics Engine

Now you have movable objects that know where they're supposed to be and don't eat up the background as they go there. The next step is to design something that will keep track of your movable objects and draw them in the proper places when necessary. This will be the job of our `GraphicsEngine` class. Listing 32.2 shows the bare bones of a graphics engine. This is the minimum that you would need to handle multiple movable objects. Even this leaves out several things that nearly all games need, but we'll get to those things later. For now, we'll concentrate on how this bare-bones system works in order to give you a solid grasp of the basic concepts.

Listing 32.2. This is a bare-bone graphics engine that tracks of your movable objects. The code should be saved in a file called `GraphicsEngine.java`.

```java
import java.awt.*;
import java.awt.image.*;

public class GraphicsEngine {
  Chain mobs = null;

  public GraphicsEngine() {}

  public void AddMOB (MOB new_mob) {
    mobs = new Chain(new_mob, mobs);
  }

  public void paint(Graphics g, ImageObserver imob) {
    Chain temp_mobs = mobs;
    MOB mob;
```

```
      while (temp_mobs != null) {
        mob = temp_mobs.mob;
        g.drawImage(mob.picture, mob.x, mob.y, imob);
        temp_mobs = temp_mobs.rest;
      }
    }
}

class Chain {
  public MOB mob;
  public Chain rest;

  public Chain(MOB mob, Chain rest) {
    this.mob = mob;
    this.rest = rest;
  }

}
```

Before we detail how the GraphicsEngine class works, let's touch on the Chain class. The Chain class looks rather simple—and it can be—but don't let that fool you. Entire languages such as LISP and Scheme have been built around data structures that have the same function as the Chain class. The class is simply a data structure that holds two objects. Here, we're calling those two objects item and rest because we are going to use Chain to create a linked list. The power of the Chain structure—and those structures like it—is that they can be used as building blocks to create a multitude of more complicated structures. These structures include circular buffers, binary trees, weighted di-graphs, and linked lists, to name a few. Using the Chain class to create a linked list will be suitable for our purposes.

To understand what a linked list is, think of a train as an example of a linked list: The train could be considered to be the first car followed by the rest of the train. The rest of the train could be described as the second car followed by the remaining cars. This description could continue until you reached the last car which would be described as the caboose followed by nothing. To compare this analogy with the code for the class Chain, a Chain is analogous to a train. A Chain can be described as a movable object followed by the rest of the Chain, just as a train could be described as a car followed by the rest of the train. And just as the rest of the train could be considered a train by itself, the rest of the Chain can be considered a Chain itself, and that's why the rest is of type Chain.

From the looks of the constructor for Chain, it appears that you need an existing Chain to make another Chain. This makes sense when you already have a Chain and want to add to it, but how do you start a new Chain? To do this, create a Chain that is an item linked to nothing. How do you link an item to nothing? Use the Java symbol for nothing—null—to represent the rest Chain. If you take a look at the code, that's exactly what we did. Our instance variable mobs is of type Chain and it is used to hold a linked list of movable objects. Look at the method AddMOB from Listing 32.2. Whenever we want to add another movable object to the list of movable objects that we're controlling, we simply make a new list of movable objects that has the new movable object as the first item and the old Chain as the rest of the list. Notice that the initial value of mobs is null, which is used to represent nothing.

How do we use the list of movable objects once AddMOB has been called for all of the movable objects we want to handle? Take a look at the paint method. The first thing to do is copy the pointer to mobs into a temporary Chain called temp_mobs. Note that the pointer is copied, not the actual contents. If the contents were copied instead of the pointer, this approach would take much longer and would be much more difficult to implement. "But I thought Java doesn't have pointers," you might be thinking at this point. That's not exactly true; Java doesn't have pointer arithmetic, but pointers still are used to pass arguments, although the programmer never has direct access to these pointers.

temp_mobs now contains a pointer to the list of all of the movable objects to be drawn. The task at hand is to go through the list and draw each movable object. The variable mob will be used to keep track of each movable object as we get to it. The variable temp_mobs will represent the list of movable objects we have left to draw (that's why we started it off pointing to the whole list). We'll know all of our movable objects have been drawn when temp_mobs is null, because that will be like saying the list of movable objects left to draw is empty. That's why the main part of the code is encapsulated in a while loop that terminates when temp_mobs is null.

Take a look at the code inside the while loop of the paint method. The first thing that is done is assigning mob to the movable object at the beginning of the temp_mobs Chain so that there is an actual movable object to deal with. Now it's time to draw the movable object. The g.drawImage command draws the movable object in the proper place. The variable mob.picture is the picture stored earlier when the movable object was created. The variables mob.x and mob.y are the screen coordinates where the movable object should be drawn; notice that these two variables are looked at every time the movable object is drawn, so changing one of these coordinates while the program is running has the same effect as moving it on the screen. The final argument passed to g.drawImage, imob, is an ImageObserver that is responsible for redrawing an image when it changes or moves. Don't worry about where to get an ImageObserver from; chances are, you'll be using the GraphicsEngine class to draw inside a Component (or a subclass of Component such as Applet), and a Component implements the ImageObserver interface so that you can just pass the Component to GraphicsEngine whenever you want to repaint.

The final line inside the while loop shortens the list of movable objects that need to be drawn. It points temp_mobs away from the Chain that it just drew a movable object off the top of and points it to the Chain that contains the remainder of the MOBs. As we continue to cut down the list of MOBs by pointing to the remainder, temp_mobs will eventually wind up as null, which will end the while loop with all of our movable objects drawn. (See Figure 32.1 for a graphical explanation.)

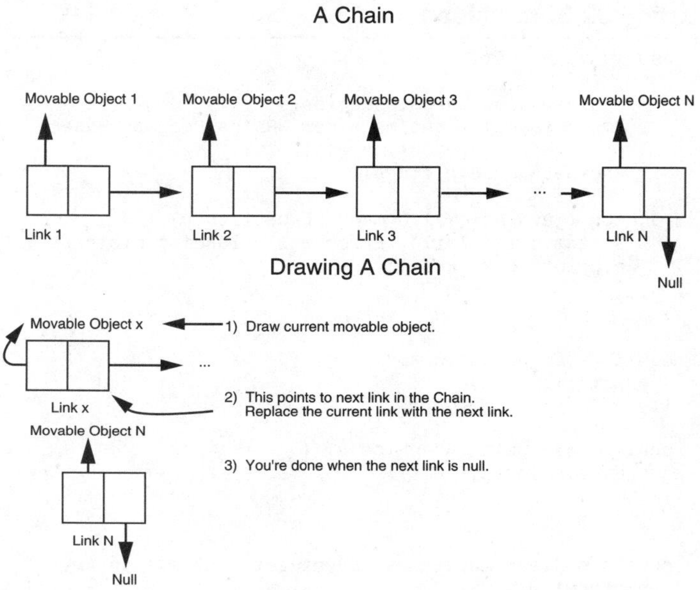
A Chain
Movable Object 1
Movable Object 2
Movable Object 3
Movable Object N
Link 1
Link 2
Link 3
Link N
Null
Drawing A Chain
Movable Object x
1) Draw current movable object.
Link x
2) This points to next link in the Chain.
Replace the current link with the next link.
Movable Object N
3) You're done when the next link is null.
Link N
Null

FIGURE 32.1.
A graphical representation of a `Chain`.

Installing the `GraphicsEngine`

The graphics engine we just built certainly had some important things left out, but it will work. Let's go over how to install the `GraphicsEngine` inside a `Component` first, and then go back and improve on the design of the graphics engine and the `MOB`. It would be a good idea to type in and compile Listings 32.1 through 32.3 now so that you can get an idea of what the code does. Compile the code by saving each listing into its own file and then using the `javac` command. In addition to compiling the code in Listings 32.1 through 32.3, you also will need to create an HTML file as shown in Listing 32.4. As the final step, you will need to place a small image file to be used as the movable object in the same directory as the code and either rename it to `one.gif` or change the line inside the `init` method in Listing 32.3 that specifies the name of the picture being loaded.

Listing 32.3. This is a sample applet that illustrates the `GraphicEngine` class. The code should be saved in a file named `Game.java`.

```
import java.awt.*;
import java.applet.Applet;
import java.net.URL;

public class Game extends Applet {
  GraphicsEngine engine;
  MOB picture1;
```

continues

Listing 32.3. continued

```
public void init() {
  try {
    engine = new GraphicsEngine();
    Image image1 = getImage(new URL(getDocumentBase(), "one.gif"));
    picture1 = new MOB(image1);
    engine.AddMOB(picture1);
  }
  catch (java.net.MalformedURLException e) {
    System.out.println("Error while loading pictures...");
    e.printStackTrace();
  }
}

public void update(Graphics g) {
  paint(g);
}

public void paint(Graphics g) {
  engine.paint(g, this);
}


public boolean mouseMove (Event evt, int mx, int my) {
  picture1.x = mx;
  picture1.y = my;
  repaint();
  return true;
}

}
```

Listing 32.4. This is the code that must be put into an HTML file in order to view the applet. Use a Java-enabled browser or the JDK AppletViewer to view this file once you have compiled everything.

```
<html>
<head>
<title>GraphicsEngine Example</title>
</head>

<body>
<h1>GraphicsEngine Example</h1>

<applet code="Game.class" width=200 height=200>
</applet>
</body>
</html>
```

Once you have the example up and running, the image you selected should appear in the upper-left corner of the applet's window. Pass your mouse over the applet's window. The image you have chosen should follow your pointer around the window.

Let's go over how the code works that linked the `GraphicsEngine` into the applet called `Game`. Our instance variables are `engine`, which controls all of the movable objects we can deliver, and `picture1`, a movable object that draws the image chosen.

The `init` method is fairly straightforward. You initialize `engine` by setting it equal to a new `GraphicsEngine`. Next, the image that you chose is loaded with a call to `getImage`. This line creates the need for the `try` and `catch` statements that surround the rest of the code in order to catch any invalid URLs. After the image is loaded, it is used to create a new `MOB`, and `picture1` is initialized to this new `MOB`. The work is completed by adding the movable object to `engine` so that `engine` will draw it in the future. The remaining lines (the lines inside the `catch` statement) are just there to provide information about any errors that occur.

The `update` method is used to avoid flickering. By default, applets use the `update` method to clear the window that they live in before they repaint themselves with a call to their `paint` method. This can be a useful feature if you're changing the display only once in a while, but with graphics-intensive programs this can create a lot of flicker because the screen refreshes itself frequently. Because the screen refreshes itself so frequently, once in a while it will catch the applet at a point where it has just cleared its window and hasn't had a chance to redraw itself yet. This will result in a flicker.

The flicker was eliminated here simply by leaving out the code that clears the window and going straight to the `paint` method. If you have run this example applet, you probably have already noticed that not clearing the screen might solve the problem of flickering, but it creates another problem—your movable object is leaving streaks! Don't worry, though, the streaks will be eliminated a little later when we introduce double buffering into our graphics engine.

As you can see, the `Game.paint` method consists of one line—a call to the `paint` method in `engine`. It might seem like a waste of time going from `update` to `paint` to `engine.paint` just to draw one image. Once you have a dozen or more movable objects on the screen at once, however, you'll appreciate the simplicity of being able to add the object in the `init` method and then forget about it the rest of the time, letting the `engine.paint` method take care of everything.

Finally, we have the `mouseMove` method. This is what provides the tracking motion so that the movable object follows your pointer around the window. There are, of course, other options for user input that will be discussed later. The tracking is accomplished simply by setting the coordinates of the movable object to the position of the mouse. The call to `repaint` just tells the painting thread that something has changed, and the painting thread will call `paint` when it gets around to it, so you don't need to worry about redrawing any more. To finish up, `true` is returned to inform the caller that the `mouseMove` event was taken care of.

Improving the Bare-Bones Engine

Now that the framework has been laid for a functional graphics engine, it's time to make improvements. Let's start with movable objects. What should be considered when thinking about the uses that movable objects have in games? Chances are, sooner or later you'll want to write a game with a lot of movable objects. It would be much easier to come up with some useful properties that you want all your movable objects to have now so that you don't have to deal with each movable object individually later.

One area that merits improvement is the order in which movable objects are painted. What if you had a ball (represented by a movable object) that was bouncing along the screen, and you wanted it to travel in front of a person (also represented by a movable object)? How could you make sure that the ball was drawn after the person every time, thus making it look like the ball is in front? You could make sure that the ball is the first movable object added to the engine, thus ensuring that it's always the last movable object painted. However, that could get hairy if you have 10 or 20 movable objects that all need to be in a specific order. Also, what if you wanted the same ball to bounce back across the screen later on, but this time behind the person? The method of adding movable objects in the order you want them drawn obviously wouldn't work, because you would be switching the drawing order in the middle of the program.

What is needed is some sort of prioritization scheme. The improved version of the graphics engine implements a scheme where each movable object has an integer that represents its priority. The movable objects with the highest priority number get drawn last and thus appear in front.

Listing 32.5 shows the changes that need to be made to the MOB class to implement prioritization. Listing 32.6 shows the changes that need to be made to the GraphicsEngine class, and Listing 32.7 shows the changes that need to be made to the Game applet. Several other additional features also have been added, and we'll touch on those later.

The heart of the prioritization scheme lies in the new version of GraphicsEngine.paint. The basic idea is that before any movable objects are drawn, the complete list of movable objects is sorted by priority each time. The highest priority objects are put at the end of the list so that they are drawn last and appear in front, and the lowest priority objects are put at the beginning of the list so that they are drawn first and appear in back. A bubble sort algorithm is used to sort the objects. Bubble sort algorithms usually are slower than other algorithms, but they tend to be easier to implement. In this case, the extra time taken by the bubble sort algorithm is relatively negligible because the majority of time within the graphics engine is eaten up just by displaying the images.

Compile and run the extended versions of the code in Listings 32.5, 32.6, and 32.7. After doing so, look at the init method in the Game class and pay particular attention to the priorities assigned to each movable object. From looking at the mouseMove method, you should be able to see that the first five movable objects line up in a diagonal line of sorts as long as you move your mouse slowly. If you move your mouse slowly, you should see that three of the first five movable objects are noticeably in front of the other two. This should make sense if you examine the priorities they were assigned inside the Game.init method.

You also will notice that the bouncing object is always in front of the objects that you control with your mouse. This is because it was assigned a higher priority than all of the other objects. Try hitting the S key. The first object that your mouse controls now should be displayed in front of the bouncing object. Take a look at the Game.keyDown method to see why this occurs. You will see that pressing the S key toggles the priority of picture1 between a priority that is lower than the bouncing object and a priority that is higher than the bouncing object.

Listing 32.5. This is the enhanced version of the MOB class. Save this code in a file named MOB.java.

```java
import java.awt.*;

public class MOB {
  public int x = 0;
  public int y = 0;
  public Image picture;
  public int priority = 0;
  public boolean visible = true;

  public MOB(Image pic) {
    picture=pic;
  }
}
```

Listing 32.6. This code listing is the enhanced version of the GraphicsEngine class. Save the code in a file called GraphicsEngine.java.

```java
import java.awt.*;
import java.awt.image.*;

public class GraphicsEngine {
  Chain mobs = null;
  public Image background;
  public Image buffer;
  Graphics pad;

  public GraphicsEngine(Component c) {
    buffer = c.createImage(c.size().width, c.size().height);
    pad = buffer.getGraphics();
  }

  public void AddMOB (MOB new_mob) {
    mobs = new Chain(new_mob, mobs);
  }
```

continues

Listing 32.6. continued

```java
public void paint(Graphics g, ImageObserver imob) {

  /* Draw background on top of buffer for double buffering. */

  if (background != null) {
    pad.drawImage(background, 0, 0, imob);
  }

  /* Sort MOBs by priority */

  Chain temp_mobs = new Chain(mobs.mob, null);
  Chain ordered = temp_mobs;
  Chain unordered = mobs.rest;
  MOB mob;
  while (unordered != null) {
    mob = unordered.mob;
    unordered = unordered.rest;
    ordered = temp_mobs;
    while (ordered != null) {
    if (mob.priority < ordered.mob.priority) {
      ordered.rest = new Chain(ordered.mob, ordered.rest);
      ordered.mob = mob;
      ordered = null;
    }
    else if (ordered.rest == null) {
      ordered.rest = new Chain(mob, null);
      ordered = null;
    }
    else {
      ordered = ordered.rest;
    }
    }
  }

  /* Draw sorted MOBs */

  while (temp_mobs != null) {
    mob = temp_mobs.mob;
    if (mob.visible) {
    pad.drawImage(mob.picture, mob.x, mob.y, imob);
    }
    temp_mobs = temp_mobs.rest;
  }

  /* Draw completed buffer to g */

  g.drawImage(buffer, 0, 0, imob);

  }
}

class Chain {
  public MOB mob;
  public Chain rest;
```

```
    public Chain(MOB mob, Chain rest) {
      this.mob = mob;
      this.rest = rest;
    }

}
```

Listing 32.7. This is an extended example that illustrates the properties of the GraphicsEngine class. Save this code in a file called Game.java.

```java
import java.awt.*;
import java.applet.Applet;
import java.net.URL;

public class Game extends Applet implements Runnable {
  Thread kicker;
  GraphicsEngine engine;
  MOB picture1, picture2, picture3, picture4, picture5, picture6;

  public void init() {
    try {
      engine = new GraphicsEngine(this);
      engine.background = getImage(new URL(getDocumentBase(), "background.jpg"));
      Image image1 = getImage(new URL(getDocumentBase(), "one.gif"));
      picture1 = new MOB(image1);
      picture2 = new MOB(image1);
      picture3 = new MOB(image1);
      picture4 = new MOB(image1);
      picture5 = new MOB(image1);
      picture6 = new MOB(image1);
      picture1.priority = 5;
      picture2.priority = 1;
      picture3.priority = 4;
      picture4.priority = 2;
      picture5.priority = 3;
      picture6.priority = 6;
      engine.AddMOB(picture1);
      engine.AddMOB(picture2);
      engine.AddMOB(picture3);
      engine.AddMOB(picture4);
      engine.AddMOB(picture5);
      engine.AddMOB(picture6);
    }
    catch (java.net.MalformedURLException e) {
      System.out.println("Error while loading pictures...");
      e.printStackTrace();
    }
  }

  public void start() {
    if (kicker == null) {
      kicker = new Thread(this);
    }
    kicker.start();
  }
```

continues

Listing 32.7. continued

```java
public void run() {
  while (true) {
    picture6.x = (picture6.x+3)%size().height;
    int tmp_y = (picture6.x % 40 - 20)/3;
    picture6.y = size().width/2 - tmp_y*tmp_y;
    repaint();
    try {
  kicker.sleep(50);
    }
    catch (InterruptedException e) {
    }
  }
}

public void stop() {
  if (kicker != null && kicker.isAlive()) {
    kicker.stop();
  }
}


public void update(Graphics g) {
  paint(g);
}

public void paint(Graphics g) {
  engine.paint(g, this);
}


public boolean mouseMove (Event evt, int mx, int my) {
  picture5.x = picture4.x-10;
  picture5.y = picture4.y-10;
  picture4.x = picture3.x-10;
  picture4.y = picture3.y-10;
  picture3.x = picture2.x-10;
  picture3.y = picture2.y-10;
  picture2.x = picture1.x-10;
  picture2.y = picture1.y-10;
  picture1.x = mx;
  picture1.y = my;
  return true;
}

public boolean keyDown (Event evt, int key) {
  switch (key) {
  case 'a':
    picture6.visible = !picture6.visible;
    break;
  case 's':
    if (picture1.priority==5) {
   picture1.priority=7;
      }
    else {
    picture1.priority=5;
```

```
        }
      break;
    }
    return true;
  }


}
```

Two big features also implemented in the improved code were double buffering and the addition of a background image. This is accomplished entirely in `GraphicsEngine`. Notice the changes in the constructor for `GraphicsEngine`. The graphics engine now creates an image so that it can do off-screen processing before it's ready to display the final image. The off-screen image is named `buffer`, and the `Graphics` context that draws into that image is named `pad`.

Now take a look at the changes to the `paint` method in `GraphicsEngine`. Notice that up until the end, all of the drawing is done into the `Graphics` context `pad` instead of the `Graphics` context `g`. The background is drawn into `pad` at the beginning of the `paint` method and then the movable objects are drawn into `pad` after they have been sorted. Once everything is drawn into `pad`, the image buffer contains exactly what we want the screen to look like; so we draw `buffer` to `g`, which displays it on the screen.

Another feature that was added to the extended version of the movable objects was the capability to make your movable objects disappear when they aren't wanted. This was accomplished by giving `MOB`s a flag called `visible`. Take a look at the end of `GraphicsEngine.paint` to see how this works. This feature would come in handy if you had an object that you only wanted to show part of the time. For instance, you could make a bullet as a movable object. Before the bullet is fired, it is in a gun and should not be visible, so you set `visible` to `false` and the bullet isn't shown. Once the bullet is fired it can be seen, so you set `visible` to `true` and the bullet is shown. Run the `Game` applet and try pressing the A key a few times. As you can see from the `keyDown` method, hitting the A key toggles the `visible` flag of the bouncing object between `true` and `false`.

By no means do the features shown in Listings 32.5, 32.6, and 32.7 exhaust the possibilities of what can be done with the structure of movable objects. Several additional features could easily be added, such as a centering feature for movable objects so that they are placed on the screen based on their center rather than edge, an animation feature so that a movable object could step through several images instead of just displaying one, the addition of velocity and acceleration parameters, or even a collision-detection method that would allow you to tell when two movable objects have hit each other. Feel free to extend the code as needed to accommodate your needs.

We haven't actually written a game in this chapter, but we have laid the foundation for writing games. You now have objects that you can move around the screen simply by changing their coordinates. These tools have been the building blocks for games since the beginning of graphics-based computer games. Use your imagination and experiment. If you need more help extending the concepts described here concerning the creation of games with movable objects and their associated graphics engines, pick up a book that's devoted strictly to game programming. *Tricks of the Game-Programming Gurus,* (Sams Publishing) is a good example.

Sounds

We've spent all this time learning how to do the graphics for a game in Java, but what about sounds? Sound in Java is not yet complicated. The Java development team worked hard on the first release of Java, but they unfortunately didn't have time to incorporate a lot of sound support.

Check out `java.applet.AudioClip` to discover the full extent of sound use in the 1.0 release of Java. There are only three methods: `loop`, `play`, and `stop`. This makes life somewhat easier because the interface is so simple. Use `Applet.getAudioClip` to load an `AudioClip` in the AU format and you have two choices: Use the `play` method to play it at specific times or the `loop` method to play it continuously. The applications for each are obvious. Use the `play` method for something that's going to happen once in a while, such as the firing of a gun, and use the `loop` method for something that should be heard all of the time, such as background music or the hum of a car engine.

Java-Specific Game Design Issues

When thinking about the design of your game, there are some Java-specific design issues that you must consider. One of Java's most appealing characteristics is that it can be downloaded through the Web and run inside a browser. This networking aspect brings several new considerations into play. Java also is meant to be a cross-platform language, which has important ramifications in the design of the user interface and games that rely heavily on timing.

Picking a User Interface

When picking a user interface, there are several things you should keep in mind. Above all, remember that your applet should be able to work on all platforms because Java is a cross-platform language. If you choose to use the mouse as your input device, keep in mind that regardless of how many buttons your mouse has, a mouse in Java only has one button. Java can read from any button on a mouse, but it considers all the buttons to be the same button. The Java development team made the design choice to have only one button so that Macintosh users wouldn't get the short end of the stick.

If you use the keyboard as your input device it is even more critical for you to remember that although the underlying platforms might be vastly different, Java is platform-independent. This becomes a problem because the different machines that Java can run on might interpret keystrokes differently when more than one key is held down at once. It might seem worthwhile to throw a *supermove* in your game that knocks an opponent off the screen, activated by holding down four secret keys at the same time. However, doing this might destroy the platform independence of your program, because there could be other platforms that don't handle four keystrokes at once. The best way to go would be to design a user interface that doesn't call into question whether it is truly cross-platform. Try to get by with only one key at a time, and stay away from control and function keys in general since they could be interpreted as browser commands by different browsers that your applet runs in.

Limiting Factors

Because one of the main features of Java is that it can be downloaded and run across the Net, the limitations imposed by this method bear some investigation. First, please keep in mind that most people with a network connection aren't on the fastest lines in the world. You might be ready to develop the coolest animation ever for a Java game, but keep in mind that nobody will want to see it if it takes forever to download. It is a good idea to avoid extra frills when they are going to be costly in terms of downloading time.

One trick that you can use to get around a lengthy download time is to send everything that you can for downloading in the background. For instance, you could send level one of your game for downloading, start the game, and while the user plays level one, levels two and up could be sent for downloading in a background thread. This task is simplified considerably with the `java.awt.MediaTracker`. To use the `MediaTracker` class, simply add all of your images to a `MediaTracker` with the `addImage` method and then call `checkAll` with `true` as an argument.

Opening a network connection can take a significant amount of time. If you have 32 or 40 pictures to send for downloading, the time this takes can quickly add up. One trick that will help you decrease the number of network connections you have to open is to combine several smaller pictures into one big picture. This decreases the number of pictures you have to send for downloading. You can use a paint program or image editing program to create a large image that is made up of your smaller images placed side by side. You then can send for downloading the large image only. This decreases the number of network connections you need to open and might also decrease the total number of bytes contained in the image data. Depending on the type of compression used, if the smaller images that make up your larger image are similar, you probably will achieve better compression by combining them into one picture. Once the larger picture has been loaded from across the network, the smaller pictures can be extracted by using the `java.awt.image.CropImageFilter` class to crop the image for each of the original smaller images.

Another thing that needs to be kept in mind with applets is timing. Java is remarkably fast for an interpreted language, but graphics handling usually leaves something to be desired when it comes to rendering speed. Your applet probably will be rendered inside a browser, which slows it down even more. If you are developing your applets on a state-of-the-art workstation, please keep in mind that there are a large number of people who will be running Java inside a Web browser on much slower PCs. When your applets are graphics-intensive it's always a good idea to test them on slower machines to make sure that the performance is acceptable. If you find that an unacceptable drop in performance occurs when you switch to a slower platform, try shrinking the Component that your graphics engine draws into. You also might want to try shrinking the images used inside your movable objects because the difference in rendering time is most likely the cause of the drop in performance.

Another thing to watch out for is poor threading. A top-of-the-line workstation might allow you to push your threads to the limit, but on a slow PC computation time is often far too precious, and improperly handled threading can lead to some bewildering results. Notice in the run method in Listing 32.7 that we tell the applet's thread to sleep for 50 milliseconds. You might want to try taking this line out and seeing what happens. If you're using the AppletViewer or a browser, it will probably lock up or at least appear to respond very slowly to mouse clicks and keystrokes. This happens because the applet's thread, kicker, is eating up all of the computation time and there's not much time left over for the painting thread or the user input thread. Threads can be extremely useful, but you have to make sure that they are put to sleep once in a while to give other threads a chance to run.

Summary

In this chapter we developed a basic graphics engine with Java that can be used for game creation. This graphics engine incorporated movable objects with prioritization and visibility settings, double buffering, and a background image. Creating the graphics engine itself didn't actually accomplish the construction of a game because constructing one game would have been of limited use. The construction of a tool that can be expanded to produce a multitude of games is far more useful.

This chapter also touched on issues that need to be kept in mind when developing games with Java. It is important to remember that Java is a cross-platform language and therefore will be run on different platforms. This basically means that when you develop your games you should be aware that people will want to run them on machines that might not be as capable as your machine.

Multimedia and Java

33

by Ben Bloch

Java's multimedia capabilities are currently primitive and sometimes inadequate or nonexistent. Nevertheless, Java is positioned as an important technology for Internet-based multimedia, particularly for distributing multimedia content on demand. Furthermore, as bandwidth increases—both within corporate intranets and throughout the Internet—and Java matures and is more widely supported, its importance will grow. Sun has already promised more extensive multimedia features in future releases of Java.

This chapter presents the big picture of multimedia and how it relates to Java. You can think of this chapter as your tour guide through the world of Java multimedia. Some topics are covered here in detail, while other topics have already been covered in prior chapters. In the case of topics being covered in prior chapters, you will see clear references to those chapters in case you happened upon this chapter first. Still other topics are on the horizon and can only be covered in a general sense. Nevertheless, you should finish this chapter with a solid understanding of what type of support Java currently has for multimedia, and where it's headed in the future.

Because Java has some competition in bringing multimedia to the Web, this chapter also briefly discusses alternatives to Java. In particular, the Macromedia Director movie player, Shockwave, is covered. Macromedia Director is a popular multimedia tool that enables multimedia developers to create interactive movies. More information on Macromedia Director is available at `http://www.macromedia.com`.

Bandwidth Limitations

Before getting into multimedia as it affects Java, it's important to look into a major limitation in dealing with multimedia on the Web: bandwidth. Bandwidth refers to the amount of information that can be sent over a network connection at a time. The multimedia potential of any Web-based media application is directly inhibited by the bandwidth of the connection. Most users across the public Internet access the Net at between 9600 and 28,800 bps.

A variety of emerging technologies in the near future will aid in providing a bandwidth that enables the delivery of multimedia applications in real time. In the meantime, you must consider all the available techniques to minimize file size and ensure that your applications are compelling. In other words, no matter how cool your multimedia content is, if it takes 10 minutes to transfer to an end user's machine, it's basically worthless. So, you should use all the tools at your disposal to deal with the bandwidth limitation as it exists today.

Java

Although more mature tools exist for creating and viewing multimedia on the Web, Java is very important even now for distributed multimedia applications on the Internet. It will be increasingly important both as its support for multimedia grows, and as bandwidth increases on the Web. Java's main contribution will be a robust environment delivering *all code* necessary to run multimedia content on demand by the user. This eliminates the growing problem of the plethora of browser and plug-in providers, with each provider having multiple versions and proprietary MIME types. Java will help simplify this by requiring the client to have only the necessary Java interpreter downloaded and configured.

In addition, Java also enables lower-level data handling and network access, thus raising the level of site interactivity in terms of interaction with back-end data. Presentations using Java, unlike those based on some other technologies, need not be as stand-alone.

Java Multimedia Features

Although primitive, Java currently has multimedia features, which include the following:

- Extensive graphics support, including support for drawing primitives and bitmapped images
- Basic digital audio support
- A multithreaded environment, which aids in timing and animation
- A media tracker for keeping up with distributed media content

These multimedia features are provided in the standard Java API. Sun also provides an animation class for creating simple animations in addition to the multimedia support in the API classes.

Graphics

Java provides a wide range of graphics support in its standard API. Java graphics features can be broken down roughly into two groups: primitive drawing routines and bitmapped image routines.

Primitive Drawing

Lest you think I'm referring to etchings on a cave wall, primitive drawing simply refers to the most basic drawing functions such as lines and points. Java provides its primitive drawing support through the `Graphics` class. The Java `Graphics` class provides support for many types of primitive drawing functions, including lines, ovals, arcs, and polygons, to name a few. The `Graphics` class was covered in detail in Chapter 23, "The Applet Package and Graphics."

Building Your Own Graphics Class Using Primitives

Because the Java technology is still immature, even simple tasks such as drawing a simple grid could require creating a class with several methods. In the following example, we create `GridDraw.class` to draw a grid using primitives.

The first thing we do is to import `java.applet.Applet` and the `java.awt.*`. Then, the class `GridDraw` is created as an extension of `Panel.class`. Once all variables are initialized, the `GridDraw` method sets the layout using `BorderLayout` and sets background color to white.

Public method `setGrid` is created as void because no result is returned. This method can then be invoked by any other class that creates an instance of type `GridDraw`. This method receives values to determine where to start drawing (`xstart`, `ystart`), desired width and height (`width`, `height`), and number of rows and columns (`numrows`, `numcols`).

The `paint()` method is invoked to draw a rectangle starting at (`xstart`, `ystart`) with a width specified by `width` and a height specified by `height`. The grid is created by drawing horizontal and vertical lines at every `height`/`numrows` and `width`/`numcols` interval throughout the loop.

The last method, `Dimension preferredSize()` specifies a default size for the grid, and is set to 250×250. This method listing can be seen in Listing 33.1.

Listing 33.1. `GridDraw.java`.

```java
import java.applet.Applet;
import java.awt.*;

public class GridDraw extends Panel{
    int i,j;
    public int xstart=0, ystart=0, width=0, height=0, numrows=0, numcols=0;

    GridDraw() {
        setLayout(new BorderLayout());
        setBackground(Color.white);
    }

    public void setGrid(int x, int y, int w, int h, int rows, int cols){
        xstart=x;
        ystart=y;
        width=w;
        height=h;
        numrows=rows;
        numcols=cols;
    }

    public void paint(Graphics g){
        g.setColor(Color.black);
        g.drawRect(xstart, ystart, width, height);
        for (int i=1; i<numrows; i++){
            g.drawLine(xstart, ystart+(i*height/numrows),
xstart+width,ystart+(i*height/numrows));
        }
        for (int j=1; j<numcols; j++){
            g.drawLine(xstart+(j*width/numcols), ystart, xstart+(j*width/
numcols), ystart+height);
        }

    }

    public Dimension preferredSize(){
        return (new Dimension(250,250));
    }

}
```

Using this class to draw a 5×5 grid in a 100 pixel by 100 pixel box is fairly simple, as shown in Listing 33.2.

Listing 33.2. `GridExample.java.`

```java
import java.applet.Applet;
import java.awt.*;

public class GridExample extends Applet {
    GridDraw gridDraw;

    public void init() {
        resize(250,250);
        setBackground(Color.black);

        add(gridDraw = new GridDraw());
        gridDraw.setGrid(20,20,100,100,5,5);
    }
}
```

An HTML file to view this, called `GridExample.html` (see Listing 33.3), can then be created.

Listing 33.3. `GridExample.html.`

```html
<title>Grid Example</title>
<hr>
<applet code=GridExample width=250 height=250>
</applet>
<hr>
```

The applet, when run as shown, will appear as shown in Figure 33.1.

FIGURE 33.1.

Output from `GridExample` *class.*

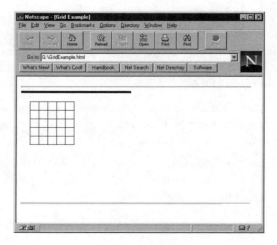

In the near future, many development tools will enable the user to quickly create graphical classes without much work. But until these tools become readily available, simple classes such as GridDraw can be coded fairly easily. The object-oriented nature of Java enables such classes to be used over and over.

Bitmapped Images

Although primitive graphics are useful for drawing graphs and charts, most realistic graphics require the use of bitmapped images. Bitmapped images are composed of pixels of different colors and can be created directly from scanned photographs and artwork. The majority of graphics viewed on the Web is in the form of bitmapped images. Java provides support for bitmapped images in a variety of ways.

The most fundamental support for bitmapped images in Java is the Image class, which represents an image in memory. The Graphics class also provides support for drawing images using the Image class. Furthermore, there is a whole set of classes for manipulating and working with images. This set of classes consists of an image filter framework, which enables you to perform transformations on images, such as brightening, sharpening, and scaling.

The Java programming aspects of bitmapped images were also covered in Chapter 23, "The Applet Package and Graphics," and Chapter 25, "Animation Programming."

Audio

The current release of Java provides fairly limited support for audio. However, within this support is the capability to play multiple, digital waveform audio sounds. This section examines how Java handles audio and is illustrated with some examples.

Audio Classes

The current release of Java supports audio through classes that interface with the audio hardware. The standard Java API actually only contains one class for working with audio, AudioClip, which is located in the java.applet package. The AudioClip class represents a single piece of digital waveform audio.

There are also a variety of undocumented, unsupported audio classes in the sun.audio package. These audio classes will more than likely form the basis for future, more extensive audio features in future releases of Java.

The standard, and currently only supported, format for audio data in Java is Sun's AU format. This format is nice because the audio files are usually very small. Of course, the trade-off is that the quality of sound is usually somewhat lacking.

Example: `HelloWorldAudio`

For illustrative purposes, let's extend the familiar `HelloWorld` applet with audio. You saw this applet way back in Chapter 1, "Java Makes Executable Content Possible." This example assumes creation of an audio file named `helloworld.au` that has been placed in a directory called `audio`. Listing 33.4 contains `HelloWorldAudio` applet, which plays the audio file `helloworld.au`.

Listing 33.4. The `HelloWorldAudio` applet.

```java
import java.applet.*;
import java.awt.*;
public class HelloWorldAudio extends HelloWorld {

AudioClip audio;

  public void init () {
    super.init();
    audio = getAudioClip(getCodeBase(),"audio/helloworld.au");
  }

  public void start() {
    audio.play();
  }
}
```

The class `HelloWorldAudio` is an extension of the `HelloWorld` class. It is declared `public` so that it is visible to the Java runtime environment. The `AudioClip` object is initialized in the `init` method by calling the `getAudioClip` method. This method creates an `AudioClip` object in memory from an audio file. The `start()` method then is used to play the audio stream with a simple call to the `play` method.

Now, let's create an HTML file to play `HelloWorldAudio.class` and call it `HelloWorldAudio.html` (see Listing 33.5).

Listing 33.5. `HelloWorldAudio.html`.

```html
<html>
<head>
<title>Hello World Audio</title>
</head>
<BODY><P>"Hello World Audio" </P>
<applet code=HelloWorldAudio.class width=100 height=80> </applet>
</BODY>
</HTML>
```

Multithreading

At the core of the Java architecture is the concept of multithreading. *Multithreading* is basically the capability of the Java environment to support multiple paths of execution. More practically speaking, it means you can have multiple sections of code or even multiple programs running at the same time. The details of multithreading and how threads are handled in Java were covered in Chapter 15, "Threads and Multithreading."

In this chapter, however, you are interested in how multithreading impacts multimedia in Java. Multithreading actually plays a vital role in multimedia because it is essential in providing a means for animations to execute at a fast speed without monopolizing the processor.

Consider the situation of playing an animation at 12 frames per second. In this case, the Java applet displaying the animation must update and redraw its graphical output 12 times every second, or once every 83 milliseconds. For an applet to maintain this kind of frame rate, it has to constantly keep working at updating and redrawing the animation frames. If this work was handled in an environment without threads, the animation code would basically take over the processor. However, in a multithreaded environment like Java, you can assign the animation its own thread and it will coexist comfortably in the runtime system. The animation still requires as much processor overhead as before, but the Java runtime system makes sure other threads get a shot at the processor, too.

The Media Tracker

The Java media tracker is another unique feature of Java that aids in supporting multimedia on the Web. The Java media tracker is a class that provides a mechanism for keeping up with when multimedia content has been successfully transferred over a network connection.

The need for the media tracker goes back to the issue of bandwidth discussed earlier in this chapter. Because it sometimes takes a considerable amount of time to transfer multimedia content over an Internet connection, Java multimedia applets desperately need to know if and when the content is available to use. The media tracker solves this problem by providing Java applets a means to track when multimedia objects have finished loading.

The media tracker was used in a practical sample applet in Chapter 25, "Animation Programming."

Future of Java and Multimedia

Probably much more important than the present state of Java multimedia is what the future holds. There are so many emerging multimedia technologies related to or based on Java that it is difficult to see which ones will brave the storm and which will just fade away. One thing is for certain: The future of Java and multimedia holds both a lot of uncertainty and a lot of promise.

Shockwave

In this section, you'll take a close look at one of the more promising multimedia technologies that promises to provide some degree of Java support: Macromedia's Shockwave technology.

In short, Shockwave is a new technology developed by Macromedia that allows Macromedia Director movies to be embedded in Web pages. Shockwave is distributed in the form of a Web browser plug-in. Currently, Shockwave is supported by Netscape Navigator 2.0 for Windows 3.1, Windows 95, and Macintosh. It is expected to soon be supported by other browsers.

To understand the impact a technology like Shockwave could have on the Web, you must understand what Macromedia Director itself is all about. Macromedia Director is a leading multimedia development tool, originally developed for the Macintosh and later released for Windows 3.1, that provides a powerful movie paradigm and graphical approach for creating interactive multimedia presentations. Multimedia developers use Director to control the choreography and coordination among images, sound, video clips, and other media types to create a complete multimedia movie. The approach is similar in theory to a director coordinating actors, props, and a soundtrack when creating a motion picture.

Creating a Shockwave Movie

The process of creating a Shockwave movie begins by first creating the movie using Director as if it were a standard Director movie. Once the movie is working well under Director, it is processed by Afterburner, which is a tool distributed with Shockwave that compresses the movie into a form more suitable for the Web.

The resulting compressed movie is then embedded in a Web page as multimedia content. In Netscape Navigator 2.0, a Shockwave movie is embedded like this:

```
<EMBED SRC="path/file_name.ext" WIDTH=n HEIGHT=n TEXTFOCUS=focus>
```

The WIDTH and HEIGHT arguments specify the width and height of the movie window, in pixels, and TEXTFOCUS tells the Shockwave plug-in when to respond to input from the keyboard. Possible TEXTFOCUS settings include focus, onMouse, onStart, and never.

If the user's browser doesn't support the Shockwave plug-in, the NOEMBED tag enables you to substitute a JPEG or GIF image in place of the movie, like this:

```
<NOEMBED> <IMG SRC="path/file_name.ext"> </NOEMBED>
```

Shockwave and Java

Deciding when to use new technologies such as Shockwave, as opposed to developing your own classes in Java, is often difficult. There are no hard rules governing when to use certain technologies over others. All you can hope for is a future integration and convergence of technologies, which would allow more options for multimedia developers. For example, Macromedia has shown a serious interest in Java. In fact, they have even promised some degree of Java support in future releases of Shockwave. What this will mean to the Java multimedia programmer isn't yet clear, but there is certainly the potential for a leveraging of high-level multimedia development tools with custom Java code.

Getting Shockwave Information

To get the latest information regarding Shockwave, check out Macromedia's Web site at `http://www.macromedia.com`. You can also take a look at the Director Web at `http://www.mcli.dist.maricopa.edu/director/`, which is a good place to go for examples of Shockwave movies and technical details showing how commands are used.

Summary

As a multimedia technology, Java is still in its infancy. Although it currently supports some interesting multimedia features such as graphics, imaging, basic sound, and media tracking, it is still lacking in many ways. This situation really is to be expected, because the Web community in general has yet to figure out the best approach to take in handling distributed multimedia. There are many problems to be solved before any technology can successfully deliver a widely distributed multimedia solution. However, even in its young state, Java is quickly positioning itself as the driving multimedia technology for the Web.

Java, however, isn't alone. There are other technologies aiming to solve many of the multimedia problems facing the Web as well. One of these technologies, Macromedia Shockwave, which is based on the popular Macromedia Director multimedia authoring tool, actually shows signs of supporting some degree of integration with Java. This mixture of Java and new third-party technologies will more than likely pave the way for the future of multimedia on the Web. Either way, there doesn't appear to be much doubt that Java will play a key role in the evolution of multimedia on the Web.

VRML and Java

by A

Virtual Reality Modeling Language (VRML) is a way to describe virtual worlds on the Web, just as HTML describes Web pages. Soon, having a home page on the World Wide Web will not be enough. You'll need your own home world (home.wrl) as well! As Java becomes integrated with VRML, you'll be able to write Java scripts to animate and enliven VRML worlds.

In this chapter, you'll get an introduction to what Virtual Reality Modeling Language is, what it looks like (see Figure 34.1), what you can do with it, and how it works. We'll look at the most exciting developments so far in wedding Java to VRML—from such companies as Dimension X, Paper Software, SGI, and WorldMaker—and will include source code for Java/VRML examples. At this point, Java APIs for VRML still are being developed, so these examples are right at the cutting edge.

FIGURE 34.1.

Aereal Serch is a VRML world by Dennis McKenzie and Adrian Scott with links to other worlds inside the various buildings.

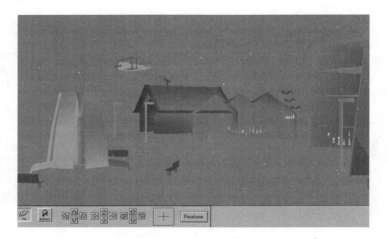

We also will look at designing a VRML site and what kinds of business models could work for VRML creators. In Appendix F, there is a VRML resources section with pointers to URLs relating to software, examples, converters, and other information.

The goal of virtual reality is to create an immersive experience so that you feel you are in the middle of a separate virtual world. Virtual reality generally relies upon three-dimensional computerized graphics plus audio. Virtual reality uses a first-person outlook. You move about in the virtual world rather than controlling a computer-generated figure moving around in the world.

HTML is a markup language, but VRML (pronounced "ver-mul") is not. We'll look at a simple world described in the standard VRML ASCII text representation, plus screen shots of what it actually looks like using a VRML browser.

What is a VRML browser? A VRML browser is to VRML what a standard browser such as Mosaic or Netscape Navigator is to HTML. The VRML browser loads in a virtual world described in VRML, and then renders it in three-dimensional graphics and lets you roam through the virtual world. You can select links in the virtual world that take you to other virtual worlds or any other URL such as an HTML page or GIF image.

Your VRML and standard Web browsers will communicate, so that when you select a link to an HTML file from a virtual world, your standard Web browser will load that URL. Conversely, when you select a link to a VRML file from your standard Web browser, the Web browser will recognize the MIME type and pass the URL or VRML file to your VRML browser. In the future we might see added capabilities in VRML browsers so that they can render an HTML page without having to switch to the standard Web browser.

One of the exciting developments in browsers has been the use of VRML plug-ins to other browsers, which was pioneered by Paper Software's WebFX VRML plug-in. Working as a plug-in, the VRML is displayed in the standard area of the Web browser where HTML is normally displayed. In some cases, such as Netscape's browser, there can be multiple VRML worlds showing at one time within an HTML page.

VRML files can be sent using the standard HTTP servers you use for your current HTML Web sites. In the future, we might see new kinds of servers with special capabilities suited to virtual reality applications, or these might be a part of HTTP-NG, a future version of HTTP.

So what can your home world look like? You might have a three-dimensional figure of yourself, or even of your living room (real or virtual). If you like windsurfing, you might have a windsurfer in some waves, linked to a map of your favorite windsurfing spots. Or you could have an art sculpture floating in midair.

History of VRML

At the first World Wide Web conference in 1994, Tim Berners-Lee (developer of the Web concept) and Dave Raggett organized a session known as a "Birds of a Feather" (BOF) session for interested people to discuss virtual reality and how it could be applied to the Web. Things took off rapidly, with the creation of an e-mail list for discussion of what was then called Virtual Reality Markup Language.

Because VRML isn't SGML (Standard Generalized Markup Language), and because of its graphical nature, the word "Markup" was later changed to "Modeling," though you can still find references to VR Markup Language floating around the Net. Memes are hard to kill.

The initial BOF meeting included several people who were working on 3D graphical interfaces to the Web. The e-mail list grew and grew: Within a week, there were more than one thousand members. The list moderator is Mark Pesce, one of the prime architects of VRML. Pesce announced the goal of having a draft version of the VRML specification ready for the fall 1994 WWW Conference.

Rather than reinvent the wheel, list members wanted to choose an existing technology as a starting point. Several proposals were put together. You can still see these proposals at the VRML

Repository (`http://www.sdsc.edu/vrml`). Eventually—try getting agreement among that many people—the list chose the Open Inventor ASCII file format developed by Silicon Graphics.

A subset of this format with extensions for Web hyperlinks came to form the initial VRML Specification. Gavin Bell of SGI adapted the Open Inventor format for VRML, with input from the list members. SGI allowed the format to be used in the open market, and also put a language parser into the public domain to help VRML gain momentum.

The three credited authors of the VRML 1.0 specification are Pesce, Bell, and Anthony Parisi of Intervista. Other major contributors are Chris Marrin of SGI and Jan Hardenbergh of Oki Advanced Products.

In December 1995, the first VRML Symposium was held in San Diego. It was the first exclusive VRML gathering, and excitement was everywhere. Several large companies not initially involved in VRML had become quite interested and came to the symposium with their own proposals for how VRML should evolve in the future.

A VRML consortium will most likely be created very shortly. In the meantime, the `www-vrml` e-mail list and a group known as the VAG, the VRML Architecture Group (`http://vag.vrml.org`), are leading the analysis of proposals for future versions of VRML. The VRML 2.0 Specification is currently under discussion. VRML 2.0 will define the exact mechanism of how VRML and Java will interact, such as tying Java scripts to 3D VRML geometry.

What You Need to Experience VRML

The very minimal setup for experiencing VRML is a computer and VRML browser software. An Internet connection is necessary to download worlds. However, VRML worlds stored on a computer disk can be viewed without an Internet connection. Actually, when I started out creating VRML software, I didn't have even VRML browser software, so I had to use wetware— my imagination—to visualize how my VRML worlds might look.

A very basic VRML/Java setup would include a 486/50 computer with 8MB RAM, VRML browser software such as WebFX, WebSpace, or WorldView, and an Internet connection with a 14.4KB modem. This will give you basic performance. Because the first versions of the VRML browsers are CPU-intensive and complicated, uncompressed VRML worlds can take up as much as 500KB, which takes a while to transfer over a 14.4KB Internet connection. However, world authors are learning how to create interesting worlds that can be as small as 20KB compressed.

Serious VRML/Java creators will want to move toward a UNIX workstation and a T1 connection. However, to create VRML worlds, all you really need is a text editor and knowledge of the VRML Specification!

There are many VRML browsers available. The most popular ones can be downloaded over the Internet, including:

- WebFX from Paper Software (http://www.paperinc.com)
- WebSpace from Silicon Graphics (http://webspace.sgi.com) and Template Graphics (http://www.tgs.com/~template)
- WorldView from Intervista (http://www.intervista.com)
- VR Scout from Chaco Communications (http://www.chaco.com)

To go beyond the basic system setup, you can start getting into fancy input and output devices. These can make the experience more immersive, but most people don't use them. Head-mounted displays (HMDs) bring virtual worlds closer to your eyes by displaying the worlds on two small screens that are part of glasses you wear. Head-tracking devices on the HMDs can figure out which direction you are facing and relay this information to the browser to change your orientation. Using a 3D mouse for input, you can move around in the three-dimensional virtual world, just as a standard mouse lets you move around in two dimensions.

Using the Browsers

Once you have downloaded a VRML browser from the Internet and installed the browser, you are ready to get started. (See Appendix F for URLs.)

Browsers come with some simple worlds that you can load into the VRML browser to begin with. Once you get familiar with the navigation commands, you can start moving out around the Web. A nice starting point on the Web is Aereal Serch, which is a VRML world with links to many other VRML worlds (http://www.virtpark.com/theme/serch/home.wrl.gz).

WebFX

In the main navigation mode, you can use a combination of keyboard and mouse to move around. For example, in WebFX from Paper Software (see Figure 34.2), the Fly mode uses arrow keys to affect the orientation of your head, and A and Z move you forward and backward. In Walk mode, the up and down arrow keys move you forward and backward, and the left and right keys turn you left or right. Holding down the Alt button with the arrow keys lets you pan to the sides. Several browsers feature an Examiner or Model mode, where you can spin around the world, rather than moving around inside it. In WebFX, this is accomplished by holding down the right mouse button and moving the mouse. A fun thing to do in WebFX and Webspace is to *fling* with the mouse: Hold down the button and quickly move the mouse and let go of the button while the mouse is moving. This will spin the world around and leave it spinning—very cool!

FIGURE 34.2.
WebFX from Paper Software.

In WebFX, if you tap the right mouse button for a moment, a menu appears that lets you change the settings or change cameras (that is, move to a different part of the world).

Webspace

Webspace from SGI and TGS features a unique user interface for the mouse. Examiner mode, where you spin the world around, is controlled with a trackball-style sphere (which will look familiar to fans of the old Centipede) and a roller that moves you forward into and backward out of the world. In Walk mode (see Figure 34.3), you move around a bar that looks like the handlebars of a tricycle. Somehow, it feels like driving a golf cart. Note that there is a little notch on the right side of the bar that attempts to give an indication of the vertical tilt of your viewpoint. This lets you set if you are looking up or down while you move around.

FIGURE 34.3.
*A VRML world viewed
with Webspace.*

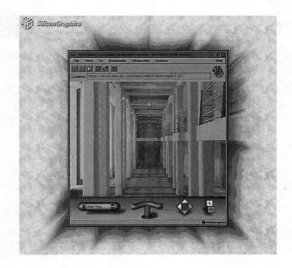

WorldView

WorldView from Intervista is geared towards using the mouse for navigation. (See Figure 34.4.) It has three boxes of buttons that correspond to panning, tilting, and flying. You also can choose between Fly and Inspect modes. Inspect mode is when you are spinning around the world itself rather than navigating in it. WorldView defaults to a blue background in worlds. Also, WorldView works as a standalone browser, so you can start navigating around VRML space without starting up a standard Web browser.

FIGURE 34.4.
*A virtual world viewed
with WorldView from
Intervista.*

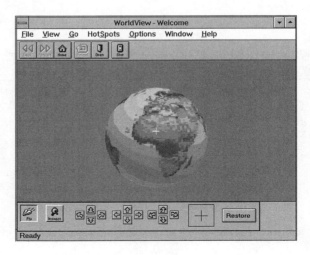

Introduction to Creating VRML Worlds

Creating VRML can be challenging at first. It's not as easy as HTML, nor are VRML browsers nearly as forgiving as HTML browsers. There are two ways to get started. First you can use a Web-based VRML authoring tool called Aereal Phonts to create VRML that uses 3D fonts. You can also learn to hand code simple VRML worlds.

Aereal Phonts

To give you a feeling for what VRML looks like, here's a short VRML world (see Listing 31.1), created with Aereal Phonts, a simple Web-based publicly accessible VRML authoring tool (see Figure 34.5) (`http://www.virtpark.com/theme/phonts.html`).

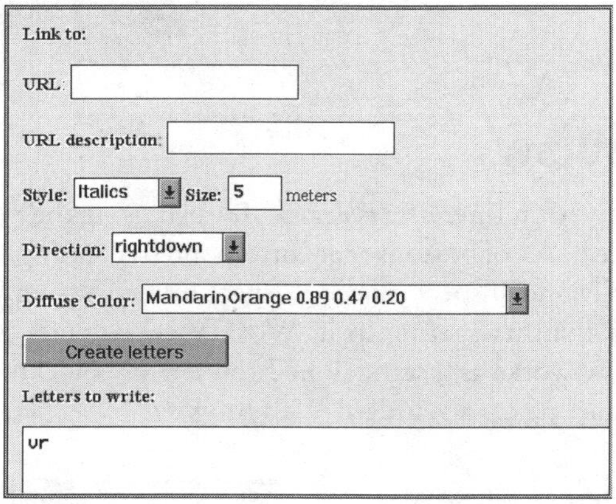

FIGURE 34.5.

Creating a simple VRML world with Aereal Phonts.

Listing 34.1. The letters vr in VRML, created with Aereal Phonts (reformatted for easy reading).

```
#VRML V1.0 ascii

Separator {
    Material { diffuseColor 0.89 0.47 0.20 }
    Scale { scaleFactor 5 5 5 }
    MatrixTransform { matrix 1 0 0 0 .3 1 0 0 0 0 1 0 0 0 0 1 }
    Separator {
        Translation { translation .1 .2 0 }
        Separator {
            Rotation { rotation 0 0 -1 -.4 }
            DEF a Cylinder { radius .05 height .45 }
        }
        Translation { translation .2 0 0 }
        Separator {
            Rotation { rotation 0 0 -1 .4 }
            USE a
        }
    }
```

```
    Translation { translation .5 0 0 }
    Separator {
        Translation { translation .05 .2 0 }
        Cylinder { radius .05 height .4 }
        Translation { translation .15 .12 0 }
        Separator {
            Rotation { rotation 0 0 -1 1.57 }
            Cylinder { radius .05 height .25 }
        }
    }

    Translation { translation .5 0 0 }
}
```

When you load this world into your VRML browser and spin it around, you'll see something similar to VRML World, shown in Figure 34.6.

FIGURE 34.6.

Wandering in VRML World created with Aereal Phonts.

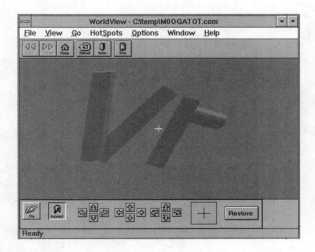

Creating a Simple Home World

The MIME type for VRML is x-world/x-vrml. If you haven't convinced your Web site administrator to add the VRML MIME type to your Web server yet, you can set up a simple CGI script that starts out with the following line (in Perl).

```
print "Content-type: x-world/x-vrml\n\n";
```

Or, for a Java server-side CGI:

```
System.out.println("Content-type: x-world/x-vrml");

System.out.println("");
```

After that, you can have the code print-out the rest of your VRML world.

As we saw above, a VRML world starts off with the following first line:

```
#VRML V1.0 ascii
```

Anything after a # in a line of a VRML script is considered a comment. For transmission purposes, comments can be stripped out of a VRML file before it is transmitted across a network. If you want anything like a copyright or other information to get to the viewer, you should use an INFO node. However, at the current time, none of the HTTP servers have been configured to strip the comments out, so you can be a bit sloppy in the near future!

Each VRML world consists of one node. Typically, that one node will be a Separator node that includes a grouping of various nodes inside it. Nodes can represent shapes like cubes and cones, properties like colors and textures, or groupings. Nodes can also give World Wide Web references, such as hyperlinks or in-line worlds, similar to HREFs and in-line graphics in HTML (shouldn't we call them in-space worlds?). As an example, the Material node is a property node that lets you assign colors and transparency properties.

For a detailed description of VRML nodes, refer to the VRML Specification at `http://www.hyperreal.com/~mpesce/vrml/vrml.tech/vrml10-3.html`. A VRML-enabled HTML version of the Specification is at `http://www.virtpark.com/theme/vrml/`.

Let's start by making a simple VRML home world from scratch by hand to illustrate how the language works. Figure 34.7 shows what it will look like in a VRML browser when we're done.

FIGURE 34.7.

A simple, hand-created VRML world.

We start off with the VRML header and a Separator node to hold the nodes we soon will add. (See Listing 34.2.)

Listing 34.2. A basic VRML file.

```
#VRML V1.0 ascii
Separator {
}
```

This is a valid VRML file. It will load into your VRML browser, but you won't see anything. Let's add a blue sphere. (See Listing 34.3.) We'll use a `Material` node to set the color to a blue, and then add a `Sphere` node with a radius of five meters.

Listing 34.3. A blue sphere in VRML.

```
#VRML V1.0 ascii
Separator {

    # blue sphere
    Material { diffuseColor 0 0 .7 } # sets the color to blue
    Sphere { radius 5 } # creates the sphere with radius 5 meters
}
```

Now that we have something showing up in the browser, let's add something with more visual depth to it. Find an image file on your computer or on the Web. Your VRML browser should support JPEG, GIF, and maybe BMP formats. Let's add a cube that uses the image as a texture. We'll locate it seven meters to the right (positive x axis) of the blue sphere by adding in a `Translation` node. (See Listing 34.4.)

Listing 34.4. A blue sphere and a texture-mapped cube.

```
#VRML V1.0 ascii
Separator {

    # blue sphere
    Material { diffuseColor 0 0 .7 } # sets the color to blue
    Sphere { radius 5 } # creates the sphere with radius 5 meters

    # textured cube
    Translation { translation 7 0 0 } # moves away from the sphere
    Texture2 { filename "image.jpg" } # sets the texture to image.jpg
    Cube { } # creates the cube
}
```

In Listing 34.4, `image.jpg` is the URL or filename of your image file. Now your home world is starting to get somewhere. As the final touch, let's add the VRML you created using Aereal Phonts. We do this using the `WWWInline` node and the URL for the VRML world you created with Aereal Phonts. We'll also use another `Translation` node to move from the center of the cube to the area above and between the sphere and cube. The world now becomes Listing 34.5.

Listing 34.5. The blue sphere and texture-mapped cube plus the letters vr in VRML as a WWWInline.

```
#VRML V1.0 ascii
Separator {

    # blue sphere
    Material { diffuseColor 0 0 .7 } # sets the color to blue
    Sphere { radius 5 } # creates the sphere with radius 5 meters

    # textured cube
    Translation { translation 7 0 0 } # moves away from the sphere
    Texture2 { filename "image.jpg" } # sets the texture to image.jpg
    Cube { } # creates the cube

    # WWWInline the Aereal Phonts world
    Translation { translation -3.5 6 0 } # move above the sphere & cube
    WWWInline { # render the following VRML world inside this world
        name "http://www.virtpark.com/theme/cgi-bin/world/Proteinman.wrl"
    }
}
```

Just replace the name URL in the WWWInline node with the URL of your Aereal Phonts world and your simple VRML home world is ready. As you can see in this example, WWWInline is a very powerful feature that taps into the power of the World Wide Web as a whole and differentiates VRML from non-Web attempts at VR.

Authoring Tools and Converters

There are a variety of tools becoming available to ease VRML world development. Trying to create VRML worlds by hand in a text editor can take quite a while and give you a headache as you try to spatially imagine your world. There are two categories of tools: authoring tools and converters.

Authoring tools are software packages that let you create worlds described in VRML. The HTML equivalent is software programs such as HoTMetaL and HTML Assistant. Hopefully, VRML authoring tools will let you develop and test your worlds in 3D. Most VRML authoring tools are still in very preliminary versions, though you can expect to see an explosion of these tools in the near future. Some that have been announced include Virtual Home Builder from Paragraph, Fountain from Caligari, EZ3D from Radiance, and Aereal Phonts from Aereal. For the latest authoring tool information, the best bet is to check the VRML repository Web sites.

Converters let you create a world using CAD or 3D modeling software and then translate a file from the 3D file format into the VRML format. Converters exist, or are being developed, for formats like DXF, 3DS, OFF, and IV. There are also commercial converter programs such as Interchange from Syndesis that convert between several 3D file formats and support—or are planning to support—VRML.

There's a problem with converters: they tend to generate huge, inefficient VRML files. In addition, the files may not be true, up-to-spec VRML. There are currently many .WRLs out on the Net that are not real VRML.

Optimizing Virtual Reality on the Web

In the beginning of VRML, many worlds took up large amounts of time to transfer on the Internet because their file sizes were so big. Then once you downloaded the file, it took forever to move around in it. If you would like to avoid these problems, you'll want to optimize your VRML for file size, rendering speed, and ease of navigation.

File Size

File size is a key factor for transmission over the Internet. If your Java code is creating VRML on the client solely for rendering on the client, file size is not a huge concern. However, in advanced Java/VRML code, you might want to create VRML avatars with geometry that is transported across the Internet for multiuser applications. In this case you will want to minimize the file size of the VRML that is transmitted for speed.

Creating efficient and effective VRML worlds is quite different than using a standard CAD package, so a niche will develop for VRML-specific authoring tools. In addition, standard CAD and 3D modeling packages are starting to include an export capability that lets people save or convert their files to VRML format.

As part of working with the Interactive Multimedia Festival, James Waldrop developed a script that reduces file size by about 75 percent. One file was reduced from 2.3MB down to 570KB. Information on the script is located at `http://vrml.arc.org/vrmltools/datafat.html`. It's important to understand what this script does before you use it, as the special optimizations it does might or might not be appropriate for your world. The script was developed for a VRML version of the Interactive Media Festival. (See Figure 34.8.) You can use the same file size optimization techniques to write Java code that produces small VRML file sizes.

Using these techniques and `gzip` compression, James, Mark Meadows, and others with the Interactive Multimedia Festival (`http://vrml.arc.org`) managed to compress their files by 94 percent. The techniques they used were the following:

- Turning infinitesimal numbers like 3.9e-09 into 0
- Trimming off long decimal expansions (3.4567890 -> 3.456)
- Getting rid of whitespace
- Getting rid of unnecessary normal information (VRML Normal nodes)

FIGURE 34.8.
Interactive Multimedia Festival in VRML.

Rendering Speed

The techniques above are useful for optimizing transmission time for users with low-speed network connections. The other main area for optimization is in rendering speed. These two concerns, transmission and rendering speeds, are sometimes at cross purposes, because improving rendering speed sometimes can result in a larger file.

Three important techniques for optimizing rendering time are the use of cameras, rendering hints, and levels of detail. Another concern is when to use texture maps.

The Future of VRML, Version 2.0 and Beyond

The four main enhancements that are expected for version 2.0 of Virtual Reality Modeling Language are interactivity, behaviors, 3D sound, and multiuser capabilities. The VRML community currently is considering proposals for VRML 2.0. Some of them, such as the Moving Worlds proposal from SGI/Sony/WorldMaker, build on VRML's 1.0 Open Inventor-inspired format. Proposals from Apple, Microsoft, and others depart from it significantly. Let's examine what these enhancements mean.

Interactivity

In an interactive virtual world, you can open doors, and watch them slowly open. You might move around the furniture in your apartment. Or hit the snooze button on your twitching, ringing alarm clock, after you get pulled out of a dream virtual world back into your home virtual world.

Designing this level of interactivity into VRML will be a challenge. It also might increase file sizes significantly.

Behaviors

Version 1.1 of VRML should include some limited capacity for animation. In version 2.0 and beyond you should be able to create behaviors, so that objects tend to have a minimal life of their own. Besides having some limited movements, such as a windmill turning, we might get objects that affect each other, so that when Don Quixote tries to joust with the windmill his horse shies away, or else the windmill shreds the tip of his lance. Behaviors are where Java will become most important, since most behaviors will be Java, with calls to an API that interfaces to the VRML browser. The interface mechanism is not defined yet. The behavior of an object will most likely be like a property of the geometry, with a URL link to the Java code. There is some discussion of including Java bytecodes in the VRML source.

Sound

3D sound gets very interesting and brings in a whole range of new possibilities. Sound has been a key feature in creating good immersive environments. In fact, people experimenting in VR have found that small improvements in sound will improve the immersive experience, as perceived by the user, more than small improvements in graphics quality.

Multiuser

Imagine playing football with a group of people in a virtual world in cyberspace, or imagine designing a new product with them. For these applications you need to have a multiuser capability in your virtual world. In multiuser VRML, people are shown using avatars, cyberspace representations people. VRML will allow support for multiuser worlds in the future. The initial multiuser support will most likely be through Java code, that actually sends the signals of avatar position and velocity. Some of the issues that need to be tackled include logging of who is currently in the world, including killing off *vampires* (people who have stopped being involved even if a message has not been sent to the server saying that they are signing off). Also, in some worlds you will want collision detection to prevent two avatars from existing in the same space. In addition, there needs to be a way to hand off avatars to other servers if someone chooses a hyperlink to another world. Other considerations will include how a person's avatar (cyberspace-representation) is created, how it is logged and transmitted, and what rules it might need to follow in various worlds.

Other VRML 2.0 Issues

In addition to the technical issues, probably the biggest challenge for VRML 2.0 (as Mark Pesce alludes to later) is getting a consensus for what VRML 2.0 should be. At this point, there are a lot of companies, money, and people involved in VRML, each with their own interests. It will be interesting to see how things work out.

Java Meets VRML

Java will drive multiuser interactions and behaviors in VRML 2.0 worlds. It is likely that other languages will be used in VRML 2.0 in addition to Java.

How Java Will Interact with VRML

Java can interact with VRML in at least two ways: describing extension nodes and as scripts loaded in-line to describe the interactions of VRML objects.

The first work combining VRML and Java resulted in Liquid Reality, a VRML tool kit written in Java by Dimension X. In Liquid Reality, if the Liquid Reality browser does not recognize a node, it requests the Java code describing the node from the server that served the file.

In most of the approaches being drafted for VRML 2.0, software code can be used to animate VRML objects. The Java code can be referenced in a URL attached to the geometry. The VRML 2.0 proposals are also considering allowing Java bytecodes to be inserted directly into a VRML file.

LEADING VRML/JAVA PIONEERS' THOUGHTS ON THE INTEGRATION OF JAVA AND VRML

Mark Pesce (`http://www.hyperreal.com/~mpesce`) is one of the creators of VRML and is author of *VRML-Browsing and Building Cyberspace* (New Riders, 1995), a book about VRML. According to Mark, "Java and VRML are perfect complements. Java is all about how things behave but says very little about how they appear. VRML is all about appearances, without speaking to how things behave. You could say that VRML is, while Java does. They need each other."

Mark sees Java and VRML developing, "Into a closer relationship—one where it becomes difficult to know where VRML ends and Java begins, and vice versa. I expect that when people want to talk about imaging Java, they'll use VRML, and when they think of motivating VRML, they'll use Java."

Mitra, the Chief Technology Officer of WorldMaker, sees VRML and Java remaining distinct. "I believe they will remain distinguishable for the foreseeable future; the equivalent is HTML and Java, where the HTML provides the structure and Java the functionality. In fact, in 3D they are likely to remain more distinguishable because the only way for the Java applets to influence the world is by manipulating a VRML scene graph."

Dimension X's Liquid Reality

Liquid Reality is a VRML tool kit written in Java, from Dimension X. Using extension nodes, you can create worlds with flying birds (see Figure 34.9) and bouncing apples (see Figure 34.10)!

INTERVIEW WITH KARL JACOBS AND SCOTT FRAIZE

Karl Jacobs is CEO of Dimension X (`http://www.dnx.com`) and Scott Fraize is Caffeinated Alchemist. Dimension X has developed Ice, a Java API for 3D, and Liquid Reality, a VRML tool kit for Java based on Ice.

Q: What is Liquid Reality?

Karl: It is a VRML tool kit. It provides everything you need to read in VRML and write out VRML and extend it with Java. It has all the mechanisms to do that on the fly. It's wrapped around Intel's 3DSound, which only took two days to add into Liquid Reality. You just use a `Directed Sound` node. Here's where you are in space, here's the sound file and there you are.

Liquid Reality is based on Ice, fully integrated with the tool kit. It differs from other APIs in that Liquid Reality is written in Java, so that it provides hardware independence. It's not as fast as Renderware and Reality Labs [the APIs other PC VRML browsers are written in] yet.

We'll be able to go to 2.0 relatively easily, whereas others will have to redesign. We can update the tool kit without re-releasing, by putting new Java classes up on the servers. Chris [Laurel of Dimension X, a Java/VRML guru] just ported Liquid Reality to SGI and Linux over the weekend.

Q: How will Sun's efforts to add 3D support to Java affect Liquid Reality?

Karl: Sun's 3D efforts are complementary to Liquid Reality. Rather than "canvas," you'll say "canvas3d."

Q: Will people need to be able to program in Java to do Java-enabled VRML?

Scott: Right now, you do have to program a bit. However, there's a library of plug-ins and effects, like `Rotor` node, that you can use.

Q: What business model do you foresee?

Karl: Ice is an API; we want to get it out there quickly and as widely as possible. The idea is that even if you want to put it up on your Web page as a free game, that's fine.

Liquid Reality is a tool kit so you have to pay a fee for updates and so on. The viewer is free. It's the try and buy that seems to be proven on the Internet.

FIGURE 34.9.

A Liquid Reality VRML world with flying birds, a flowing stream, and a spider that runs away from you when you get close to it.

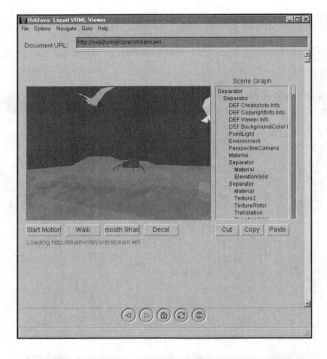

FIGURE 34.10.

A bouncing apple in a Liquid Reality VRML world.

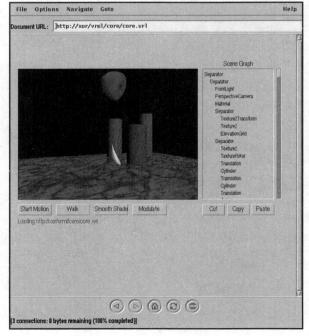

Listing 34.5 shows an example of a VRML world that has a rotating object in it, as referenced by the Rotor node.

Listing 34.5. A Liquid Reality Java-extended VRML file containing the extension Rotor.

```
#VRML V1.0 ascii

Separator {
   DEF BackgroundColor Info { string "0.5 0.5 0.5" }
   DEF Viewer Info { string "walk" }
   DEF ViewerSpeed Info { string "0.3" }

   Clock {}

#   PointLight { location 0 0 10 }
   PerspectiveCamera {
      position 0 0 8
      orientation 0 1 0 0
   }

   DirectionalLight { direction 1 0 0 }


   Material {
      ambientColor [ 0 0 0 ]
      diffuseColor [0.1 0.5 0.2 ]
#      specularColor [0.8 0.8 0.8]
      shininess 0.25
   }
   Separator {
#      Rotation { rotation 0 1 0 1.57 }
      Sphere { radius 1.1 }
   }

   Translation { translation -3 0 0 }

   Material {
      ambientColor [ 0 0 0 ]
      diffuseColor [ 0.7 0.1 0.1 ]
   }
   Cube { height 1.5 width 1.5 depth 1.5 }

   Translation { translation 6 0 0 }
   Material {
      ambientColor [ 0 0 0 ]
      diffuseColor [ 0.2 0.7 0.8 ]
#      specularColor [1 1 1]
      shininess 0.4
   }

   Separator {
      Rotor { rotation 1 0 0 1 }
      Cone {}
   }
#   Cylinder {}

}
```

Listing 34.6 shows the Java code that describes the Rotor extension node with calls to Liquid Reality's API.

Listing 34.6. Java code for the Liquid Reality Rotor node.

```java
// RotorNode.java
//
// Copyright  1995 Dimension X, Inc.
//    Chris Laurel 8-14-95

package ice.scene;

import ice.Matrix4;


// Rotor {
//     rotation   0 0 1 0      # SFRotation
//     speed      1            # SFFloat
// }

public class RotorNode extends ModelTransformationNode
{
    static String fieldnames[] = {
        "rotation",
        "speed"
    };
    static NodeField defaults[] = {
        new SFRotation(0, 0, 1, 0),
        new SFFloat(1)
    };

    public SFRotation rotation = new SFRotation((SFRotation) defaults[0], this);
    public SFFloat speed = new SFFloat((SFFloat) defaults[1], this);
    NodeField fields[] = {
        rotation, speed
    };


    public int numFields() { return fields.length; }
    public String fieldName(int n) { return fieldnames[n]; }
    public NodeField getDefault(int n) { return defaults[n]; }
    public NodeField getField(int n) { return fields[n]; }

    public void applyModelTransformation(Action a)
    {
        a.state.rotateModelMatrix(rotation.getAxisX(),
                rotation.getAxisY(),
                rotation.getAxisZ(),
                (float) (rotation.getAngle() +
                    speed.getValue() *
                    a.state.getTime() % (2 * Math.PI)));
    }

}
```

Paper Software

Paper Software is creating a Java API for VRML. The preliminary version is code-named Xpresso, and we'll look at a simple example to see the direction it is heading in. Expect it to be different when it is released.

INTERVIEW WITH MICK MCCUE

Mike McCue is the founder and CEO of Paper Software, creator of the WebFX VRML browser. Paper Software was acquired by Netscape for its VRML and VRML/Java technology. Paper Software is developing a Java API for VRML.

Q: How will world creators author Java-enabled VRML?

A: Our goal is that you will write a series of Java scripts that orchestrate behaviors. The behaviors themselves will probably be in DLLs initially. Right now the threading model is too slow for the performance people will want. Java will be an orchestrating mechanism for the overall world.

You kick off a canned behavior that exists native in our DLLs. That's the short term. Longer term, I think there will be a set of Java classes that will give you canned behaviors. As a world author, maybe I'll have a canned behavior that allows a man to run. I see that happening very soon after the first versions come out.

A few months later the canned Java behaviors will come out, and you will be able to drag and drop them onto VRML objects.

Longer term to that, eventually Java itself will become the behaviors engine, and you'll have some physics such as collision detection, gravity, and elasticity in the browser, but you'll have Java gradually implementing that too.

Q: How would you describe the future of Java and VRML? Will it even be possible to differentiate between Java and VRML?

A: Yes, I think it will be possible to differentiate between the two. That's because VRML is a file format and Java is a programming language.

You'll see VRML in OCXs and C++ APIs. There's a life beyond Java for VRML in a big way. I think it will be incorporated into Microsoft PowerPoint and Excel. I think it will be incorporated into your mission-critical applications.

Our goal is to begin with Java but to make sure we don't back ourselves into a corner by relying on it. We want to be language neutral.

On the Internet, Java and JavaScript will be the way to go.

Q: You've mentioned an interest in VRML as a starting point for multidimensional interfaces. What do you mean by that?

A: I gradually see the bulk of applications and operating systems today taking more advantage of 3D space to organize info rather than 2-D windows. I think 3D represents the next major user interface step. You will run all of these applications in a 3D environment. It will become a core, centralized part of the operating system.

This example is a bouncing ball, with the Java code `javaball.java`. It is referenced by putting the line

```
DEF BALL Sphere {}
```

in the VRML file. Figures 34.11 and 34.12 show screen shots of the ball in action.

FIGURE 34.11.

A bouncing ball in midair created with Paper's Java API.

FIGURE 34.12.

The bouncing ball is now squished on the ground.

This is what the Java code looks like. Notice that `import xpresso` brings in Paper's VRML API. You can see the calls to the API that start with `webfxObject`. (See Listing 34.7.)

Listing 34.7. Java code for the bouncing ball using Paper Software's preliminary API.

```
// Bring in some Java classes we will need
import java.awt.Graphics;
import java.util.Date;
import java.lang.Math;
import xpresso;

// A Java class that runs in its own thread as an applet
➡public class javaball extends java.applet.Applet implements Runnable {
```

```
        // variables
        Thread  ballThread;
        int     y = 0 ;
        float   fTemp = 0.0f;
        float   fHeight = 0.0f;
        int     object_id = 0 ;
        int     lSession = 0 ;
        int     lObjectID = 0 ;
        float   ff[] = new float[16] ;

        // Create an object to interface with VRML
        xpresso webfxObject = new xpresso() ;

/***********************************************************************
// init method
***********************************************************************/

    public void init()
    {

        // Initialize the VRML interface
        while (lSession == 0)
            lSession = webfxObject.XpressoInit() ;


        // Get pointers to the Ball object
        if (lSession != 0)
        {
            String strCube      = "Ball";
            String strFloor     = "Floor";

            while (lObjectID == 0)
                lObjectID = webfxObject.XpressoGetObject(lSession, 0, strCube) ;

        }


    }

/***********************************************************************
// start method
***********************************************************************/

    public void start()
    {
        if (ballThread == null)
        {
            ballThread = new Thread(this, "Ball");
            ballThread.start();
        }

        // Initialize to Identity matrix
        ff[0]=   1.0f;
        ff[1]=   0.0f;
        ff[2]=   0.0f;
        ff[3]=   0.0f;
```

continues

Listing 34.7. continued

```
        ff[4]=    0.0f;
        ff[5]=    1.0f;
        ff[6]=    0.0f;
        ff[7]=    0.0f;
        ff[8]=    0.0f;
        ff[9]=    0.0f;
        ff[10]=   1.0f;
        ff[11]=   0.0f;
        ff[12]=   0.0f;
        ff[13]=   0.0f;
        ff[14]=   0.0f;
        ff[15]=   1.0f;


    }

/**************************************************************************
// run method
**************************************************************************/

    public void run()
    {

        while (ballThread != null)
        {

            fHeight = 0.0f;

            // Ball falls down in 20 steps
            for (y = 1; y < 20; y++)
            {
                fTemp   = (float) y ;
                fHeight = fHeight + (1/fTemp);
                ff[13]  = fHeight;

                if (y>0)
                {
                    ff[0]    = 1f;
                    ff[5]    = 1f;
                    ff[10]   = 1f;
                }

                // Transform this ball to its new location and squoosh factor
                // then .... render the scene so we see the results
                if (lObjectID != 0)
                {

                    webfxObject.XpressoTransformObject(lSession, lObjectID, ff, 2) ;

                    webfxObject.XpressoRenderScene(lSession, 0) ;


                }

            }
```

```
            // Ball bounces up ... in 20 steps
            for (y = 20; y > 0; y—)
            {
                fTemp   = (float)y;
                fHeight = fHeight - (1/fTemp);
                ff[13]  = fHeight ;

                if (y==1)
                {
                    ff[0]  = 1.2f;
                    ff[5]  = .8f;
                    ff[10] = 1.2f;
                }

                if (y>1)
                {
                    ff[0]  = 1f;
                    ff[5]  = 1f;
                    ff[10] = 1f;
                }

                // Transform this ball to its new location and squoosh factor
                // then .... render the scene so we see the results
                if (lObjectID != 0)
                {
                    webfxObject.XpressoTransformObject(lSession, lObjectID, ff, 2) ;

                    webfxObject.XpressoRenderScene(lSession, 0) ;


                }

            }

            try {
                ballThread.sleep(5);
            } catch (InterruptedException e){
            }

        }
    }
/***********************************************************************
// stop method
***********************************************************************/

    public void stop()
    {
        ballThread.stop();
        ballThread = null;
    }

}
```

Summary

The explosion of interest in the World Wide Web has been incredible! VRML promises to ramp this exponential growth up to a new level of interactivity and feeling. Java will be the life force and pump to drive motion and interaction in advanced VRML worlds.

As VRML moves into its 2.0 version, and Java adds life to it, virtual reality on the Net will become as commonplace as HTML is today. Java-based interactivity, animations, and behaviors will enliven virtual worlds with personality and attitude.

Businesses will take advantage of virtual reality on the Web, starting with marketing efforts and graduating to original content.

Advanced Java

Multiuser Programming

by M⬛

Without doubt, Java is one of the more spectacular products to hit the computer market in recent years. Inasmuch as its initial support came from academia, most initial Java applets have been limited to decorative roles. However, now that Java's popularity has increased, Java has recently been utilized for more practical purposes. Applets have been used to enhance the speed of search engines and to create interactive environments for such purposes as retrieving financial information. In essence, by employing the power of Java in such applets, users are now able to do much of what they would think they should be able to do on the Internet.

Nevertheless, one of the more exciting powers of Java is that it gives programmers the ability to create multiuser environments in which many users can interact and share information. In a simple multiuser environment (see Figure 35.1), several users are connected to each other through a server running on a mutually accessible host. As a result, all actions by one user can instantaneously be displayed on the screens of other users across the world—without any requirement that the users know each other beforehand.

FIGURE 35.1.

A multiuser environment.

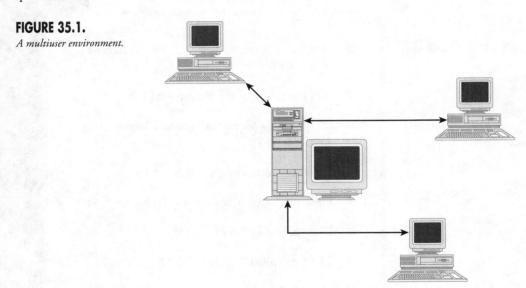

This feature enables Java programmers to accomplish feats never before possible in a Web page. A business can now set up such a system so that people who desire information could talk with a customer service representative directly on their Web page, rather than sending e-mail to a service department. Additionally, an enterprising company could allow people from around the world to participate in a real-time live auction. In general, by facilitating multiple-user environments that enable such sharing of information, Java has the power to revolutionize the Web.

WHY JAVA?

The concept of servers, sockets, and communication is nothing new, nor is the idea of linking many users together in a live-time environment. In fact, the Web, without Java, can be considered a multiuser environment inasmuch as multiple users can access the same information in the form of a simple HTML page. Furthermore, methods exist by which a user can directly affect what another user sees on a given page (such as the hit counters found on the bottom of many HTML pages).

What, then, does Java offer that is so revolutionary? It offers the capacity to perform actions *while the user is viewing the same HTML page.* The architecture of the Web enables users to view Web pages from around the world. However, once this page is displayed on your screen, it cannot change. In the example of the hit counters—although more users may access the given page—you will never be informed of this fact unless you reload that page. Java, however, brings life into Web pages (by means of applets), thus enabling them to perform actions such as communicating with a server. Java enables programmers to create applets as potent and effective as the applications on your own computer, and it is this capacity that enables us to create such multiuser environments.

In this chapter we discuss the elements required to create such a multiuser environment in Java. Although no entirely new topics in Java are presented, this chapter shows you how to bring several powerful aspects of Java together and highlights some of the more interesting applications of Java. Through explanation of the processes as well as sample code, this chapter enables you, the Java programmer, to code and establish your own multiuser environment. This chapter deals with subjects including the handling of the connections to the server, the graphical interface, and various animation and threading techniques necessary to make your applet Web-worthy. While each of these topics is illustrated with code, keep in mind that the essence of a multiuser environment is what you do, not how you do it. Furthermore, the code for each multiuser application is heavily dependent on the environment itself, and therefore significantly different in each. Consequently, while the code offered here can supply you with a suitable framework, it may be advisable to envision your own multiuser application. As each topic is presented, imagine how you would deal with each of the issues involved. Remember that in programming, and Java in particular, the limits of the language are the limits of your imagination. Be creative and have fun!

NOTE ON SOCKETS AND NETSCAPE

With any new technology comes new concerns and problems. Java is definitely not an exception to this rule. The chief concern of many has been the fact that Java applets can connect to servers from around the world and transmit information from the host that its owner might not want to make public. While there are several solutions to this problem, Netscape has chosen to place stringent restrictions on Java socket connections for now.

Currently, Java sockets can connect *only* to servers running on the host that served the applet. For example, an applet residing in `http://www.xyz.com/page.html` can only connect back to a server running on `www.xyz.com`. Therefore, when developing a multiuser environment as discussed in this chapter, make sure that the server to which the applet connects is running on the same host as the HTML page in which the applet resides. (See Chapter 40, "Java Security," for more details about applet security.)

Our Mission Should We Choose to Accept It...

In this chapter we develop a multiuser environment for a museum that is opening an exhibition of Haphazard Art. The museum believes that the most beautiful art is created by human-controlled whims, and thus has hired you to create an environment through which users from around the world can "weave" a quilt. The user should be able to access the Web page, select a color and a blank tile, and "paint" the tile. Not only should this tile change colors on the screen of the user, but it also should instantaneously become painted on the screens of all the users around the world who are working on that quilt. (The museum will then save these designs and display them at its upcoming exhibit.)

While this is a rather simplistic example of the power of multiuser environments, it is an excellent model for the explanation of the concepts involved.

Requirements of the Server

Although it is not of our direct concern, the server in this environment plays an extremely large role. Because this server can be written in virtually any language, we won't spend much time dealing with it here. However, it is necessary that we discuss the essentials for the server in a multiuser environment.

As you can see from the Figure 35.1, the server acts as the intermediate agent between the various users. Thus, the server must be able to do the following:

- Accept multiple connections from clients on a given port
- Receive information from the clients
- Send information to the clients

As the application becomes more involved, it is necessary to add additional functionality to the server. Even in the simple example of the museum quilt, it's necessary that the server keep track of the color of all the tiles. Furthermore, if a new client begins work on an in-progress quilt, it's necessary for the server to inform the client of the current status of the quilt.

Nevertheless, these subjects are extremely context-dependent and deal more with computer science than Java. Therefore, we now move on to more exciting matters, such as the socket communication required to provide the interaction.

Integrating a Communication Class in Your Applet

For an effective implementation, it's necessary to create a class that handles all the interaction with the server. This class manages such responsibilities as connecting and disconnecting from the server as well as the actual sending and receiving of data. By encapsulating this functionality in a separate class, we are able to deal with our problem in a more effective and logical manner.

A more important reason for encapsulating this functionality in a separate class, however, is the fact that in a multiuser environment the applet must do two things at the exact same time: listen for user interactions (such as a mouse click) *and* listen for new information from the server. The best way to do this is to create a separate class to handle the server interaction, and make that class a thread. (See Chapter 15, "Threads and Multithreading," for details on creating threads.) This threaded class will continually run for the lifetime of the applet, updating the quilt when required to do so. With this problem out of our hands, we can allow the applet class to respond to user interactions without worrying about the socket connection.

How to Connect to a Server

Assuming that we have a suitable server running, the actual communication is not a very complicated process. In essence, the applet need only to connect to the server and read and write information to the appropriate streams. Conveniently, Sun has wrapped most of these methods and variables in the `java.net.Socket` class.

Here is the beginning of our `Client` class that handles the actual communication:

```
import java.net.Socket;
import java.io.*;

public class Client extends Thread
{

    private Socket soc;
    public void connect ()
    {
      String        host = "www.museum.com";
```

```
    int         port = 2600;

    soc = new Socket(host, port);
  }
}
```

Note that it is necessary for you to know both the name of the host on which the server is running as well as the port on which the server can accept connections.

CHANGES IN THE JAVA LANGUAGE

Those programmers who have been involved with the Java language know that there were some changes to the Java language in going from the alpha to beta standards as well as in the transition from the beta1 to beta2 standards. While the transition from the beta1 to beta2 standards was not very dramatic, there was a very important change regarding private variables and their accessibility. Consequently, while much of the code required for a multiuser environment could be developed with the `sun.NetworkClient` class in the beta1 version, access restrictions to the `serverInput` and `serverOutput` streams have made this approach impossible in the beta2 version and all later versions, including the 1.0 JDK.

The best means to provide a multiuser environment using the 1.0 API is through the use of the `java.net.Socket` class. (You will note that the `java.net.Socket` class uses the methods `getInputStream()` and `getOutputStream()` to provide access to these restricted streams.) The code in this chapter has been tested with the 1.0 version of the JDK as well as the 2.0 version of Netscape, and should work with all later versions of Java and Netscape.

While in theory the previous method is sufficient to connect to a server on a known port, any experienced programmer knows that what works in theory does not always work in practice. Consequently, it is good practice to place all communication statements in a `try-catch` block. (Those unfamiliar with the `throw` and `try-catch` constructs can refer to Chapter 16, "Exception Handling.") In fact, forgetting to place all statements that deal with the server in a `try-catch` block will produce a compile-time error with the Java compiler.

Consequently, the precious method should actually look like this:

```
import java.net.Socket;
import java.io.*;

public class Client extends Thread
{
    private Socket soc;
    public boolean connect ()
    {
    String        host = "www.museum.com";
    int           port = 2600;
```

```
    try {
        soc = new Socket(host, port);
    }
    catch (Exception e)
        return(false);
    return(true);
}
```

Note that the method now returns a `boolean` variable in accordance to whether or not it was successful in connecting.

How to Communicate with the Server

Inasmuch as different situations require different constructs, Java supplies us with several options for the syntax of communication with a server. While all such approaches can work, some are more useful and flexible than others. Consequently, what follows is a rather generic method of communicating with a server, but keep in mind that there are some nice wrapper methods in the `java.io.InputStream` subclasses that you may wish to use to simplify the processing of the parsing involved with the communication.

Sending Information

Once we have established our connection, the output is then passed through the `java.net.Socket.outputStream`, which is a `java.io.outputStream`. Because this `OutputStream` is a protected variable, however, we cannot reference it as simply as one might imagine. In order to access this stream we must employ the `java.net.Socket.getOutputStream()` method. Thus, a simple method to send data would resemble the following:

```
public boolean SendInfo(int choice) {
    OutputStream out;
    try {
        out = soc.getOutputStream();
        out.write(choice);
        out.flush();
    }
    catch (Exception e)
        return(false);
    return(true);
}
```

Although the preceding code is sufficient to send information across a socket stream, communication will not be that simple in a true multiuser environment. Because we will have multiple clients in addition to the server, it is necessary to define a common protocol that all parties will speak. While this may be as simple as a specific order to a series of integers, it is nevertheless vital to the success of the environment.

A NOTE ON PROTOCOLS

While we will adopt a rather simple protocol for this applet, there are a few issues that one should keep in mind when developing more complex protocols:

- Preface each command by a title, such as a letter or short word. For example, B123 could be the command to buy property lot 123, and S123 could be the command to sell lot 123.

- Make all titles of the same format. This will make parsing of the input stream much easier. For example, B and S are good titles. B and Sell would cause some headaches.

- Terminate each command with a common character. This will signify the end of information and will also give you a starting point in the case that some of the information becomes garbled. For the sake of simplicity, the newline character (\n) is usually best.

In the case of our quilt-making applet for the museum, each update packet will consist of three things: the x-coordinate of the recently painted tile, the y-coordinate of the recently painted tile, and the color that is to be applied (which could also be represented by an integer). Additionally, we will use the newline character as our terminating character. All of this can be accomplished with the following method:

```java
public boolean SendInfo(int x, int y, int hue) {
   OutputStream out;

   try {
        out = soc.getOutputStream();
        out.write(x);
        out.write(y);
        out.write(hue);
        out.write('\n');
        out.flush();
      }
   catch (Exception e)
      return(false);
   return(true);
}
```

Reading Information

Another factor that complicates the reading of information from the socket is the fact that we have absolutely no idea when new information will travel across the stream. When we send data, we are in complete control of the stream and thus can employ a rather simple method as we did earlier. When reading from the socket, however, we do not know when new information will arrive. Thus we need to employ a method that will run constantly in a loop. As discussed previously, the best way to do this is to place our code in the run() method of a threaded class.

A REFRESHER ON THREADS

Before we proceed in our development of this threaded subclass, it is important to review a key concept. As presented in Chapter 15, a class that extends the definition of the `java.lang.Thread` class is able to continually execute code while other portions of the applet are running. Nevertheless, this is not true of all the methods of the threaded class.

Only the `run()` method has the power attributed to threads (namely the capacity to run independently of other operations). This method is automatically declared in every thread, but will have no functionality unless you override the original declaration in your code. While other methods can exist within the threaded subclass, remember that only the code contained in the `run()` method will have the capacity to execute concurrently with the rest of the processes in the application. Furthermore, remember that the `run()` method of class `foo` is begun by invoking `foo.start()` from the master class.

Also note that because we are overriding a method first declared in the `java.lang.Runnable` interface, we are forced to employ the original declaration: `public void run()`. Your code won't compile if you choose to use another declaration, such as `public boolean run()`. (We deal with ways of returning data in the section on sharing information later in this chapter.)

What results is the method shown in Listing 35.1. In reading it, pay attention to how we are able to stop the method from reading from the socket once the user is done; how the method would deal with garbled input; and how the method returns information to the main applet. (You will be quizzed later!)

Listing 35.1. Our method to read information from the socket.

```
public void run() {
   int spot = 0;
   int stroke[];
   stroke = new int[10];                    // an array for storing the commands
   DataInputStream in;

   in = new DataInputStream(soc.getInputStream());

   while (running) {
      do {                                  // reads the information
         try {
               stroke[spot] = in.readByte();
            }
         catch (Exception e)
               stroke[spot] = '\n';  // restarts read on error
      } while (  (stroke[spot] != '\n') && (++spot < 9) );
```

continues

Listing 35.1. continued

```
                                        // reads until the newline flag or limit of array
        spot = 0;                    // resets the counter
        quilt.sow(stroke[0],stroke[1],stroke[2]);
    }
}
```

Okay. Time is up. Here are the answers.

First of all, we must remember that we are designing this class to serve within a larger applet. It would be rather difficult for the Client class to decide when the "painting session" is over for it has no idea what is going on inside the applet. Thus, the applet, not the Client class, must have control of when the class will be looking for information. The best way to retain control of the run() method is to create a boolean field (running) inside the Client class itself. This variable can be set to true on connection to the server and can be set to false when the applet decides to close the connection. Thus, once the user has decided to close the connection, the run() method will exit the while loop and run through to its completion.

Second, we must remember that while we plan on receiving three integers followed by a newline character, in real life things do not always work as we plan them. Inasmuch as we do not know what exactly the error will be, there is no ideal way of handling garbled information. The previous method uses the newline character as its guide, and will continue to read until it reaches one. If, however, there are nine characters before a newline character, it will exit the do loop regardless and call the sow() method. This means that the sow() method in our main applet must be well constructed to handle such errors.

Third, and most important, is the means by which the class returns data to the applet. As we discussed earlier, this Client class will be a subclass of our main applet. Consequently, we will be able to call all public methods of the applet class. (In this example, the applet is referenced by the variable quilt.) While we will discuss this process in more detail later, keep in mind that the last line of code

```
quilt.sow(stroke[0],stroke[1],stroke[2]);
```

simply passes the appropriate values to a method in the applet that will in turn process them.

A NOTE FOR ADVANCED READERS

You will notice that in this case, all the information coming across the stream is read in the form of integers. Obviously, in the real world other data types such as characters, or even mixed data types such as three numbers and a letter, could be passed. While this would require slight alterations to the above code, it would not be a dramatic hack.

While you could deal with such a situation by having separate read() statements for each data type, keep in mind the ASCII relationship between characters and numbers. Because the ASCII value of a number is 48 more than that number (for example, '1' = 1 + 48), you can choose to read all the data in as integers and then translate certain values to their character equivalents, or vice versa depending on how you sent the information to the server.

Finally, keep in mind that serverInput is a basic java.lang.Inputstream that can be manipulated in several ways using the powers of the java.lang and java.io classes and methods. (See Chapter 18, "The Language Package," and Chapter 20, "The I/O Package," for more details on java.lang and java.io, respectively.)

Disconnecting

So far, we have been able to connect to the server and communicate with it. From the point of view of the user, we have begun the application and have successfully painted our quilt. We therefore have only one essential functionality that we haven't included in our Client class thus far: the capacity to disconnect from the server.

While the capacity to disconnect from the server may appear trivial, it is in fact very essential to a successful multiuser environment. A server can be constructed to accept numerous clients, but due to hardware constraints, there is an inherent limit to the number of clients that a server can have connected at the same time. Consequently, if the socket connections remain open even when the clients leave, the server will eventually become saturated with lingering sockets. In general, it's good practice to close sockets, for it benefits all aspects of the environment, ranging from the Internet-access software that the user is running to the person managing the server.

Without further ado, here is an appropriate disconnect() method for our Client class:

```
public boolean disconnect () {
   running = false;
   try {
         soc.close()
      }
   catch (Exception e)
      return(false);
   return(true);
}
```

While the code itself is nothing extraordinary, do note the use of the Boolean variable running (also used in the run() method). You will remember that the function of the running variable was to serve as a flag that allowed the client to listen to the socket stream. Inasmuch as we do not want the client to be listening to the socket stream after the user has decided to disconnect, we set the variable to be false in this method. Also note that, the running = false statement comes before the soc.close() statement. This is because regardless of the success of the disconnect statement, we no longer wish to listen to the stream.

The Graphical Interface

Now that we have developed the framework of our `Client` subclass, let's switch gears for a moment to develop the applet class that will act as the heart of our application. While not extremely intricate, the applet must be able to respond to user input and present the user with a friendly and attractive display. Fortunately, as a Web-based programming language, Java is very well suited for this. Each applet that you create inherits various methods that enable it to respond to virtually anything that the user can do. Furthermore, the `java.awt` package provides us with some excellent classes for creating good-looking interactive features such as buttons and text areas.

Responding to Input

The most important aspect of a graphical interface is its capacity to monitor the user's responses to the system. As you have seen in Chapter 22, "The Windowing Package," Java supplies us with an excellent system for doing this in the form of the `java.awt.Event` class. Additionally, the `java.awt.Component` class, of which `java.applet.Applet` is a subclass, provides us with many methods that we may use to catch and process events. These methods will seize control of the applet under appropriate conditions, thereby enabling the applet to react to specific user events.

For our museum quilt applet, the user must be able to change the current color, select a tile, and quit the application. If we decide that the user will select the tile through a mouse click and change colors and use the keyboard to quit, we would require two interactive methods from the `java.awt.Component` class: `keyDown(Event, int)` and `mouseDown(Event, int, int)`.

In this setup, the keyboard has two purposes: to enable the user to change colors and to enable him or her to quit. If we can choose to present the user with a pallet of numbered colors (0 to 9, for example), from which he or she can select, our `keyDown()` method could be as simple as

```
public boolean keyDown(Event evt, int key) {
    if ( (key >= '0') && (key <= '9') ) {          // if a valid key
        current_color = key - 48;                   // converts ASCII key to numeric
        return(true);                               // equivalent
    }
    else if ( key = 'Q') {
        leave();              // a method that will handle cleanup
        return(true);
    }
    return(false);
}
```

where `current_color` is a field that keeps track of the currently selected color.

If we declare museum to be an instance of the `Client` socket class (that we have almost completed), the `mouseDown()` method could be accomplished with the following code:

```
public boolean mouseDown(Event evt, int x, int y) {
    int x_cord, y_cord;
```

```
    if ( (x >= xoff) && (x =< xoff + xsize) && (y >= yoff) && (y =< yoff + ysize) {
                          // checks to see if the click was within the grid
        x_cord = (x - xoff)/scale;  // determines the x and y coordinates
        y_cord = (y- yoff)/scale;  //  of the click
        museum.sendInfo(x_cord, y_cord, current_color);  // makes use of the
                                     // sendInfo method to send the data
        return(true);                            // the click was valid
    }
    return(false);                   // the click was outside the bounds of the grid
}
```

Note that in the previous method it is necessary to have already declared the x and y offsets, the size of each tile (scale), and the size of the grid itself as global fields of the class.

Displaying Information

In Chapter 23, "The Applet Package and Graphics," you were given an overview of how to create a background and fill it in with whatever you would like. In a dynamic graphical interface, however, there will be various properties that will change and thus must be tracked in some manner. Our quilt application may consist of nothing more than a single colored background on which tiles of different colors are drawn. Consequently, the only information that we are concerned with is the color (if any) that has been assigned to the individual tiles.

A simple way of doing this is to create an array of java.awt.Color (hues[ ]) and assign each color to be used a given value (hues[1] = Color.blue, for example). Thus, we can store the design in simple array of integers: tiles[ ][ ], with each integer element representing a color. If we do so, our paint() method can be accomplished by the following code:

```
public void paint(Graphics g) {
   for (int i = 0; i < size; i++) {
      for(int j = 0; j < size; j++) {
         g.setColor(hues[ (tiles[i][j]) ]);
         g.fillRect( (i*scale+xoff) , (j*scale+yoff), scale,scale);
      }
   }
}
```

Note that in the preceding example, g.fillRect((i*scale+xoff) , (j*scale+yoff), scale,scale); will paint squares with length and width equal to a final field, scale, that are located on the grid with respect to the initial x and y offsets.

How to Thread the Client Class

Thus far, we have been successful in creating the interface that the user will find on our Web page, as well as some of the methods necessary to facilitate the user's interaction with the applet. We have also assembled a Client subclass that will serve as our means of communication. Our next step is to integrate the Client class within the applet class to produce a cohesive application.

Nevertheless, it is important to keep in mind that we are not using this subclass merely as a means of keeping the information separate. The main reason for creating a separate class is that by making it a thread as well, we are able to perform two tasks *at the exact same time*.

> **NOTE**
>
> Although it may seem as if we are able to perform two tasks at the exact same time, this is not entirely true on a standard single-processor computer. What Java (and other time-sharing applications such as Windows) does is portion "time-slices" to each thread, allowing each to run for a brief moment before switching control over to the other. Because this process is automatically done by the Java virtual machine and because the time for which a given thread is not running is so small, we can think of the two threads as running at the same time.

Although we almost forget about its existence, we must retain some control over the `Client` class. We do not want it checking for new commands before the socket connection has been opened or after it has been closed. Additionally, we want to be able to control such socket events as opening and closing in a manner that will isolate them from the main applet, but will also impact the status of our `run()` method. Conveniently for us, we developed the `Client` class in such a manner: keeping the `connect()` and `disconnect()` methods separate entities, both of which have control over the `run()` method (by means of the `boolean` variable `running`).

Consequently, within the applet class, the code necessary to control communications is quite simple:

```java
public class Project extends Applet {
   public Client museum;
         .
         .
         .
   public void init() {
      museum = new Client();
            .
            .
      museum.connect();
      museum.start();
   }
                        .
                        .
   public void leave() {
      museum.disconnect();
   }
}
```

First of all, note that this is the first time that we have dealt with the applet itself. Thus far its only important property is that it is named `Project`.

Also note the use of the constructor `Client()`. Like any other class, the `Client` class requires not only a declaration, but also a `new` statement to actually create and allocate memory for the class. We will deal with this constructor again in the next section.

Finally, note that in the previous example we established the connection by means of the `museum.connect()` statement located the `init()` method. Most likely (and in the case of the museum applet), we will want to establish the socket stream as soon as the applet starts up. Consequently, the most logical place for the `museum.connect()` statement is in the `init()` method. Nevertheless, you may place this code anywhere you may like in your applet. (You may, for example, have a "Connect to Server" button somewhere in your applet.)

> **WARNING**
>
> While giving the user the ability to initiate connection may be a good idea, be careful that you not do allow the same user to connect the server more than once without first disconnecting. This can lead to all sorts of headaches and improper results.

How to Share Information

We have created the framework of both the `Project` (applet) and `Client` classes and have begun the process of intertwining them by creating an instance of the `Client` class in the `Project` class. However, there is more to the interaction between the two classes than what we have thus far.

Remember that the purpose of the `Client` subclass is to provide information to the applet. Nevertheless, we are required to employ the `run()` method of the threaded `Client` class, which does not allow us to return information through a simple `return()` statement. Also, in most cases (as well as the museum application), we must return several pieces of information (the x and y coordinates of the tile being painted as well as its color).

However, with a little construction, we can easily solve this problem. First, we must enable the `Client` class to refer to the `Project` class. Thus, we must make a few alterations to the `Client` class. The changes will allow the `Client` class to accept the `Project` applet class in its constructor method and make use of it during its lifetime.

```
public class Client extends Thread
{
    private Project quilt;

    public Client (Project proj) {
        quilt = proj;
    }
...
}
```

Note that in this setup, the parent class is required to pass itself as an argument to the constructor method. Therefore the appropriate syntax would resemble the following:

```
museum = new Client(this);
```

What exactly does the previous code accomplish? First, it establishes a constructor method for the `Client` class. (Remember that as in C++, constructor methods must have the same name as the class itself.) While this constructor may serve other purposes, its most important function is to accept a reference to a `Project` class as one of its arguments.

Furthermore, we have created a public variable, `quilt`, of type `Project`. By doing so, each method of the `Client` class is now able to reference all public methods and variables in the `Project` class. For example, if we had the following definitions in the `Project` class

```
public int tiles_remaining;

public void sow(int x, int y, int hue) {
...
}
```

the `Client` subclass could reference `quilt.tiles_remaining`, and `quilt.sow()`.

The "Translating" Method

Okay, time for an assessment of where we stand. We are now able to

- Connect to the server
- Monitor the user's actions
- Display the current design
- Receive and send information
- Create a client "within" the main applet
- Enable the client to reference the main applet

As of now, whenever the user clicks on a square, the "request to paint" is immediately sent to the server by the `sendInfo()` method. Nevertheless, we have not yet developed a true method of translating a command after it comes back across the server stream.

We have, however, laid the foundation for such a process. By enabling the `Client` subclass to refer to all public variables and methods of the `Project` applet class, we have given ourselves access to all of the necessary information. In fact, we have many options for updating the data in the applet once it has been parsed from the server stream. Nevertheless, some approaches are much better than others.

The most secure and flexible approach is to create a "translating" method in the applet class, such as the sow() method in the Project class—mentioned several times in this chapter. This method will serve as the bridge between the client and applet classes. Why is this approach the best? Why can't we create some public variables in the Project class that can be changed by the Client class? There are several reasons.

Why Use a Translating Method?

The first such reason is that it makes life a great deal easier for the programmer. By employing a "translating" method, we are able to maintain the encapsulation enjoyed thus far in our application. The sow() method will be contained entirely within the Project class and thus will have all the necessary resources, such as private variables that would be hidden from the Client subclass. Furthermore, when we are actually coding the application, we will be able to focus on each class independently. When we code the Client class, we can effectively forget how the sow() method will work, and when we code the Project class, we can trust that the appropriate information will be sent to it.

The second reason for having the Client class rely on a foreign method is flexability. If we decided to revamp this application, thereby changing the manner in which we stored the data, we would have no need to drastically change the Client class. In fact, in the worst case, the only changes necessary would be to increase the amount of data being read from the stream and the number of parameters passed to the sow() method.

The third reason for employing a translating method is that by linking the two classes by a method rather than direct access, we are able to prevent the corruption and intermingling of data that can occur when two processes attempt to access the same data at the same time. For example, if we made tiles[ ][ ], the array that contained the design in the applet class to be public, we could change the colors with a statement such as this:

```
quilt.tiles[(stroke[0])][(stroke[1])] = stroke[2];
```

However, what would happen if at the exact moment that the paint() method was accessing tiles[1][2], the Client class were changing its value? What if more data had to be stored (the color, the design, the author's name, and so on)? Would the paint() method get the old data, the new data, a mixture, or none? As you can see, this could be a catastrophic problem. However, if we use a separate "translating" method in our applet class, this problem could easily be solved through use of the synchronized modifier. If our applet grew to the point that this problem presented itself, we could make the paint() method synchronized and place any necessary statements in a synchronized block. As a result, these portions of our code would never be able to run at the exact same time, thereby solving our problem.

How to Create a Translating Method

Now that we have seen why the sow() method is necessary, let us discuss its actual code. As we discussed earlier, each command in the museum application will consist of three integers: the x coordinate, the y coordinate, and the new color. Also remember that in our discussion of the `Client` class, we noted that the `sow()` method must be able to handle corrupted data. Consequently, the sow method could look something like this:

```
public void sow(int x, int y, int hue) {
    if ( (x>=0) && (x <= size) && ( y >= 0) && (y <= size) && (hue >= 0) && (hue <=
➡9) ) { // 9 colors
        tiles[x][y] = hue;
        repaint();
    }
}
```

While the first statement is self explanatory, the second statement deserves some comment, if not a complete explanation. The first statement performs the actual task of changing the color on the tile. However, the user will not see anything unless the `repaint()` method is called. Thus, by setting the array and calling `repaint()`, the `sow()` method updates the quilt in the mind of the computer as well as on the screen itself.

In a brief moment, we will also harness the `sow()` method to perform another vital function for us.

Finalizing the `Client` Class

Now that we have developed the entire functionality of the `Client` subclass, we will tie it together once and for all and put it aside. First look our final product over, as shown in Listing 35.2.

Listing 35.2. Our final version of the `Client` class.

```
import java.net.Socket;
import java.io.*;

public class Client extends Thread
{
    private Socket soc;
    private Boolean running;
    private Project quilt;

    public Client (Project proj) {
        quilt = proj;
    }
    public void connect () {
        String          host;
        int             port = 2600;

        host = "www.museum.com";
        try {
            soc = new  Socket(host, port);
        }
        catch (Exception e)
            return(false);
    }
```

```
public boolean SendInfo(int x, int y, int hue) {
  OutputStream out;

  try {
        out = soc.getOutputStream();
        out.write(x);
        out.write(y);
        out.write(hue);
        out.write('\n');
        out.flush();
     }
  catch (Exception e)
        return(false);
  return(true);
}

public void run() {
  int spot;
  int stroke[];
  stroke = new int[10];              // an array for storing the commands
  spot = 0;
  DataInputStream in;

  in = new DataInputStream(soc.getInputStream());

  while (running) {
        do {                                 // reads the information
           stroke[spot] = in.readByte();
        } while (  (stroke[spot] != '\n') && (++spot < 9) );
                                      // until the newline flag or limit of array
     spot = 0;            // resets counter
     quilt.sow(stroke[0],stroke[1],stroke[2]);
  }
}

public boolean disconnect () {
  running = false;
  try {
        soc.close()
     }
  catch (Exception e)
        return(false);
  return(true);
}
}
```

While none of the methods are new, there is a very important piece of the class that has been completely installed for the first time—namely the boolean field running. As a field, it is accessible to all methods within the Client subclass. Nevertheless, by making it private, we have assured that if it is changed, its change will be associated with an appropriate change in the status of the socket connection—a connection or disconnection, for example.

While the Client class may require application-dependent changes, the previous version is rather sufficient to satisfy most requirements. However, as of yet we have dealt rather little with the applet itself. This is primarily because each multiuser applet will inherently be very different.

Nevertheless, there are a few topics that should be discussed if you wish to develop a quality multiuser applet.

Advanced Topics

What we have developed thus far in the chapter is entirely sufficient to satisfy the demands of the museum. Nevertheless, there are several other topics regarding efficiency, architecture, and appearance that we have not dealt with yet. In the next few sections we will discuss such issues as well as those regarding the development of an effective server on the other end.

Animation and Dynamic Changes to the Screen

While a programmer may appreciate the intricacies of a multiuser environment, users are attracted to those applications that look nice and enable them to do interesting things. While a multiuser environment is certainly one of the latter, we must still keep in mind the first criteria of making our applet look nice and run smoothly.

Although this chapter's purpose is not to deal with such issues as the graphical layout of applets, the communication structures developed in this chapter do have a direct impact on the "smoothness" of the changes that will occur on the user's screen. In the case of the museum applet developed earlier in this chapter, every time that a user clicks on a tile, his or her request to paint must be sent to the server and then returned to the client. Once this information is finally returned to the client, the applet must then repaint each and every tile. While this process occurs in a matter of seconds—for the user who has to wait three seconds to see his change reflected, as well as the user who can actually observe each tile being repainted—this process may be a few seconds too slow.

> ### A SHOT OF JAVA JARGON
>
> As we have learned, the method that actually handles the creation of graphics in a Java applet is named `paint()`. While various actions such as drawing lines, changing the background color, and displaying messages may be performed in this method, this functionality is nevertheless commonly referred to as the "painting" of the applet.

This slow and choppy appearance, commonly referred to as "flickering," can nevertheless be easily remedied. While this requires a few changes to our applet, the main idea behind it is noticing that *we do not need to repaint those items that have not changed.* While this may seem rather elementary, when developing an applet, it would seem a great deal easier to simply repaint the entire screen. (In fact, if you take a look at some of the Java applets on the Web, you will notice that many applets exhibit the problem of flickering.)

In the case of our museum applet, you will see that we need only to paint the tile that has been changed. Because we know the coordinates and size of each tile, this should not be much of a problem at all. It would seem as if all that we had to do was modify the paint() method to paint only one tile. Thus when the sow() method calls repaint, only the most recently changed tile is changed.

Nevertheless, there are two problems with such a simplistic approach. First of all, the paint() method is not only called by explicit calls to repaint(). It is also called whenever the applet "appears," such as when it first starts up or after the browser has been hidden behind another application. Thus, if we change the paint() method to paint only one tile, we may be left with *only* one tile on our screen, rather than the full quilt.

Another problem is that we cannot pass information to the paint() method inasmuch as (like the run() method of threads) we are overriding an already created method.

Don't worry. These problems can be handled easily. Peruse the following additions to our code in Listing 35.3 and see if you can determine how the two problems were solved.

Listing 35.3. Revised code to provide smoother animation.

```
public class Project extends Applet {
   private boolean FullPaint;
   private java.awt.Point Changed;

   public void init() {
      ...
     FullPaint = true;
     Changed = new Point();
   }

   public void paint(Graphics g) {
     if (FullPaint) {
         for (int i = 0; i < size; i++)
            for(int j = 0; j < size; j++) {
                g.setColor(hues[ (tiles[i][j]) ]);
                g.fillRect( (i*scale+xoff) , (j*scale+yoff), scale,scale);
            }
      }
      else
         g.fillRect( (Changed.x*scale+xoff) , (Changed.y*scale+yoff), scale,scale);
      FullPaint = true;
   }

   public void sow(int x, int y, int hue) {
      if ( (x>=0) && (x <= size) && ( y >= 0) && (y <= size) && (hue >= 0) && (hue
➡<= 9) ) { // 9 colors
            tiles[x][y] = hue;
            Changed.x = x;
            Changed.y = y;
            FullPaint = false;
            repaint();
      }
   }
}
```

Not too bad, right? Let's see how the problems were solved.

Most notably, we have added two new variables, one for each problem. The first variable is a Boolean named FullPaint. As you can probably guess, its function is to inform the paint() method as to whether it should paint all the tiles over or just the newest one. Note that the key to this variable is that we want it to be true as much as possible so that we prevent the "one tile quilts" discussed earlier. In this setup, the FullPaint variable is set to false only one line before the call to repaint() and is reset to true at the end of the paint() method.

> **CAUTION**
>
> Remember to reset the FullPaint to true at the end of your paint() statement! If you don't you'll defeat the purpose of the variable—and ruin the appearance of your applet.

How did we deal with the second problem of being unable to inform the paint() method of what tile was changed? You will notice the use of the private Point Changed. Inasmuch as the field is accessible to all methods, by setting the x and y values of this variable in the sow() method, we are able to indirectly pass this information along to the paint() method.

> **A LOOK INSIDE THE EVOLUTION OF THE LANGUAGE**
>
> In the sample code, we employed Changed, a variable of type Point, which can be found in the java.awt package. While this is a useful class, it has not always been part of Java. When the alpha releases came out, authors (especially those who were making graphical interfaces) were forced to develop their own Point-type classes. While this was not much of a problem, Sun chose to respond to this need by including the Point class in the beta and later API libraries.

Ensuring that the Sockets Close Properly

Although we have developed a sufficient disconnect() method, we must remember that things do not always work as well as they should. In fact, the disconnect() method in the socket class has had some problems in Java further complicated by the fact that we are running our applet through a browser. As we discussed earlier, not closing sockets can become a serious problem in a multiuser environment. Thus, it is a good practice to develop into your protocol a "close" command. Although it should resemble the other commands in your protocol, it need not be anything elaborate. In the museum example, if 123 were the command to paint tile (1,2) color 3, sending ˉ123 could be the defined close command.

Are You Still There?

Another related issue is that some users may not tell the applet that they are leaving, and thus the disconnect() method will not have a chance to execute. For example, the user may go to another HTML page or his or her computer might be struck with a sudden power outage. In either case, it is thus advisable to have some method by which the server can ensure that all its clients are still active.

A simple way of doing this is to develop another command into your protocol, the semantics of which are irrelevant. Regardless of the syntax, the server should send out some kind of "Are you there?" command periodically. In terms of the applet itself, you should develop the translating method in such a manner that when such a command is received it will respond with an appropriate answer.

Consequently, if this functionality is built into the applet, the server will know that any client that does not respond within a reasonable amount of time (20 seconds, for example) is no longer active and can be closed.

Requests Versus Commands

In this chapter, we have continually referred to the information passed from each client to the server as a "request." Furthermore, you will note that in the system developed in this chapter, although a user may click a square, his or her screen is not updated until the request has been echoed back from the server. These two facts may seem a bit abnormal, for it may seem more natural to have the applet update itself and then inform the server of what was done. Nevertheless, as you will soon see, these two procedures are very necessary for the exact same reason.

In the example of the museum applet, users are only able to paint blank (unpainted) tiles. Thus, imagine for a moment what would happen if user A decided to paint tile (1,2) black, and a moment later user B decided to paint tile (1,2) yellow. User A's command would be received first, and thus B's command would be received second. (It is impossible for the server to receive two commands at the same time on the same socket. Subsequent commands are normally placed in a queue.) If the applets were designed to paint themselves *before* the commands were echoed, user A and user B would have different images of the same quilt at the same time. Disaster!

Consequently, in a multiuser environment where the status would be really important, or even a game, it is essential that you develop your environment in such a manner that the status of whatever is being displayed on the screen, such as the position of the players, is updated *only* by what is returned from the server. As a result, the server should be developed in such a manner that any invalid requests (such as a request to paint an already painted tile) are simply "sucked up" by the server and are not echoed to any clients. Thus, if two users attempt to paint the same tile, only the request of the first user would be honored, and the second request would simply be swallowed up by the server. Even better, you could enable your server to send user-specific error messages that would cause some form of error message on the user's screen.

Limiting and Keeping Track of Users

Several situations exist (such as error messages) wherein the server would like to speak with just one user. Furthermore, your situation might require that only five users may be in the environment at a given moment. These are real-world problems, but ones that are easily solved.

At the heart of these solutions is the idea of having more than one server for your multiuser environment. This may involve one central server that has the power to spawn other servers (on other ports), or a central server acting as a"gatekeeper," accepting clients only if there are openings.

Either case requires the development of a richer protocol, but also provides you with opportunities for greater power over your environment. For example, you can now establish several two-player games that will be managed by a central server. By designing the applet to connect on a given port (1626, for example) and request entrance to a game, the server on that port would act as a manager by beginning a new game on another port (1627, for example) and informing the applet of the new port number. Thus, the applet would disconnect from port 1626, connect to port 1627, and wait for the central server to send another user to the same port. Once the central server has sent two players to port 1627, it would start a new server on the next available port (1628, for example) and could continue indefinitely.

Also, in the case of the central server/children server system as well as the gatekeeper system, the server may assign each client an identification number upon connection. This will not only allow the server to keep track of who is sending the information, but also enable it to send user-specific messages (for example, "Player One—You can't do that"). Both of these tasks can be facilitated by appending a simple identification letter or number to each command in the protocol. (B112 could mean, for example, that player 1 just "b"ought plot 12.)

Summary

Although we have dealt with many topics in this chapter, keep in mind that the power of Java is its abstract capability to facilitate a multiuser environment, not its specific lexical constructs. Nevertheless, there are a few issues relating to the Java language that one should keep in mind when developing a multiuser environment:

- *Develop a user-friendly graphical interface.* By using the `java.awt.Event` class, you will be able to respond to the user's interactions in an effective manner.

- *Create a client class that extends the `java.lang.Thread` class.* While you are able to create as many methods as you wish within this class, the best approach is to harness the `run()` method's capacity to run concurrently to develop an effective means of reading data from the stream. Also, remember to use some form of a flag that will provide you with a way of controlling the lifetime of the `run()` method.

■ *Develop the framework by which the applet and client classes will be able to communicate.* This is best done by making an instance of the client class a field in the applet class. Making the appropriate methods of the client class public, your applet class will thus be able to perform such tasks as connecting, disconnecting, and sending data.

■ *Create a "translating" method in your applet class.* This will enable the client class to send the parsed data to the applet class to elicit the proper response.

Java Debugging

36

by Tim Park

Bugs are an unfortunate fact of life in software design. Similiar to most development environ-ments, Sun has included a debugger with the Java Development Kit (JDK) to help you fix your Java applets and applications. JDB (short for Java DeBugger) isn't a fancy visual debugging environment like the debuggers you might be familiar with in other professional development systems, but it does make the task of finding and exterminating bugs in your Java programs much easier.

JDB Commands

In this chapter, we use a simple Java applet to explain how to use JDB to help you debug your programs. As you can see from the output of the JDB help command (see Listing 36.1), the range of commands available in JDB is extensive.

Listing 36.1. JDB help output.

```
> help
** command list **
threads *threadgroup]     -- list threads
thread <thread id>        -- set default thread
suspend [thread id(s)]    -- suspend threads (default: all)
resume [thread id(s)]     -- resume threads (default: all)
where [thread id] ¦ all   -- dump a thread's stack
threadgroups              -- list threadgroups
threadgroup <name>        -- set current threadgroup

print <id> [id(s)]        -- print object or field
dump <id> [id(s)]         -- print all object information

locals                    -- print all local variables in current stack frame

classes                   -- list currently known classes
methods <class id>        -- list a class's methods

stop in <class id>.<method> -- set a breakpoint in a method
stop at <class id>:<line> -- set a breakpoint at a line
up [n frames]             -- move up a thread's stack
down [n frames]           -- move down a thread's stack
clear <class id>:<line>   -- clear a breakpoint
step                      -- execute current line
cont                      -- continue execution from breakpoint

catch <class id>          -- break for the specified exception
ignore <class id>         -- ignore when the specified exception

list [line number]        -- print source code
use [source file path]    -- display or change the source path

memory                    -- report memory usage
gc                        -- free unused objects

load classname            -- load Java class to be debugged
run <class> [args]        -- start execution of a loaded Java class
```

```
!!                          -- repeat last command
help (or ?)                 -- list commands
exit (or quit)              -- exit debugger
>
```

Using JDB to Debug Your Program

From our experience, the easiest way to learn JDB is to gain hands-on experience through using it. With this in mind, let's use JDB to debug the simple class that follows. We chose a simple class for the benefit of people skipping ahead to learn how to use the basic features of the debugger. But don't worry if you've read all of the previous chapters of this book—we'll still cover all the advanced features of JDB.

AddNumbers is a simple class that implements both the user interface and the algorithm to add two numbers together. Well, at least this is what it's supposed to do. In reality, the class has a simple bug that will be located using JDB. On the supplied CD-ROM, there are two Java classes: StartApplet, which is the requisite subclass of the Applet class that instantiates the AddNumbers class, and StartApplet.html, which is used by AppletViewer to load the applet.

Listing 36.2. AddNumbers.java.

```java
import java.awt.*;

public class AddNumbers extends Frame {

  int LeftNumber = 5;
  int RightNumber = 2;

  TextArea taResult;

  public AddNumbers() {

    setTitle("JDB Sample Java Program");
    setLayout(new BorderLayout());

    Panel p = new Panel();
    p.add(new Button("5"));
    p.add(new Button("1"));
    add("West", p);

    Panel g = new Panel();
    g.add(new Button("2"));
    g.add(new Button("3"));
    add("East", g);

    taResult = new TextArea(2,1);
    taResult.setEditable(false);
    add("South", taResult);
```

continues

640

Listing 36.2. continued

```
    pack();
    resize(300,200);
    show();

}

public void ComputeSum () {

  int Total = LeftNumber - RightNumber;

  String ConvLeft  = String.valueOf(LeftNumber);
  String ConvRight = String.valueOf(RightNumber);
  String ConvTotal = String.valueOf(Total);

    taResult.setText(ConvLeft + " + " + ConvRight + " = " +  ConvTotal);

}

public void paint(Graphics g) {

  ComputeSum();

}

public boolean handleEvent (Event evt) {

  switch (evt.id) {

    // Was the termination button pressed?

    case Event.WINDOW_DESTROY: {

      // Yes!  So exit gracefully.

      System.exit(0);
      return true;

    }

    default:

  }

  // Was the "5" button pressed?

  if ("5".equals(evt.arg)) {
    LeftNumber = 5;
    ComputeSum();
    return true;
  }

  // Was the "1" button pressed?

  if ("1".equals(evt.arg)) {
    LeftNumber = 1;
```

```
    ComputeSum();
    return true;
}

// Was the "2" button pressed?

if ("2".equals(evt.arg)) {
  RightNumber = 2;
  ComputeSum();
  return true;
}

// Was the "3" button pressed?

if ("3".equals(evt.arg)) {
  RightNumber = 3;
  ComputeSum();
  return true;
}

return false;

  }

}
```

Compiling for JDB

Before starting our debugging session, we need first to compile our Java applet to include extra information needed only for debugging. This information is needed so that the debugger can display information about your applet or application in a human comprehensible form, instead of a confusing wash of hexadecimal numbers (don't laugh—the first debuggers required you to do this translation—so count your lucky stars!).

In order to compile your program with debugging information enable, change to the `\java\classes\AddNumbers` directory and issue the following commands:

```
C:\java\classes\AddNumbers> javac_g -g AddNumbers.java
C:\java\classes\AddNumbers> javac_g -g StartApplet.java
```

The `javac_g` compiler is functionally identical to the `javac` compiler used in previous chapters, except that it doesn't perform any optimizations to your applet or application. Optimizations rearrange the statements in your applet or application to make them faster. This rearrangement makes it more difficult to conceptualize program flow when you are debugging, so using `javac_g` in conjunction with JDB is useful.

The `-g` command-line option tells the compiler to include line number and object names in the output file. This allows the debugger to reference objects and line numbers in a program by source code names instead of the Java interpreter's internal representations.

Setting Up a Debugging Session

The next step in debugging a Java application or applet is to start JDB. There are two ways to do this, depending on whether you are debugging an applet or an application. Because we are debugging a applet in our example, we will use the AppletViewer program supplied in the Java Development Kit to load JDB indirectly. If we were trying to debug an application instead, we would use the following command to start JDB:

```
C:\java\classes\AddNumbers> jdb MyApplication
```

Again, because we are debugging an applet in our example and not an application, we will not start JDB in the preceding manner. However, for future reference, after invoking the debugger, using JDB on a Java application is identical to using it on an applet.

With that important distinction covered, we start the AppletViewer with the following command:

```
C:\java\classes\AddNumbers> appletviewer -debug StartApplet.html
```

The `-debug` flag specifies to the AppletViewer that it should start up in JDB instead of directly executing the `AddNumbers` class.

Once AppletViewer loads, it will open its applet window and display something similar to the following in the command-line window:

```
C:\java\classes\AddNumbers> appletviewer -debug AddNumbers.html
Initializing jdb...
0x139f2f8:class(sun.applet.Appletviewer)
>_
```

The first thing you should notice about JDB is that it is command-line based. Although this makes the learning curve for JDB a little more steep, it doesn't prevent us from doing anything that you might be familiar with in a visual debugging environment.

Before going further, examine the third line of the preceding output. This indicates where the debugger is stopped in its execution of our applet. In this case, it is stopped during the execution of Sun's `applet.Appletviewer` class. This is logical, because `applet.Appletviewer` is the class that is transparently loaded and executed to load an applet (you're learning things by using JDB already!). The hexadecimal number that prefixes this on the third line is the ID number assigned to the `sun.applet.Appletviewer` object by the Java interpreter—aren't you glad now that you can see the English version because you used the `-g` option for `javac`?). The > prompt on the fourth line indicates that there is currently no default thread that we are watching—more on this later.

To understand the bug in `AddNumbers`, we will start the applet running in the debugger as follows:

```
> run
run sun.applet.AppletViewer MA.html
```

```
running ...
main[1]
```

The debugger should open the applet's frame and start executing it. Because the debugger and the applet are on different threads of execution, you can interact with the debugger and the applet at the same time. The preceding `main[1]` prompt indicates that the debugger is monitoring the applet thread (the main thread) and the `[1]` indicates that we currently are positioned at the topmost stack frame on the method call stack (we'll explain what this means later).

Our applet is supposed to take the number of the button pressed on the left and add it to the number of the button pressed on the right. Try this out—press some of the buttons and check the applet's math.

FIGURE 36.1.

A view of the running applet.

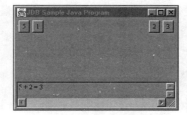

Hmm—unless we learned math differently than the rest of you, there seems to be something wrong with the computation of the applet. Maybe we found another Pentium processor flaw!

Basic Debugger Techniques

To find out what is going on, let's examine the `ComputeSum` method of the `AddNumbers` class. We would like to stop directly in this method without having to move slowly and tediously through the rest of the code.

Setting and Clearing Breakpoints

Fortunately, JDB has a set of commands called *breakpoints* that do exactly that. We'll use breakpoints to stop program execution in the `ComputeSum` method; but first, press the 5 and 3 buttons on the applet to make sure that you see the same things as we do when the program is stopped. After pressing 5 and 3, type the following in the debugger window:

```
main[1] stop in AddNumbers.ComputeSum
Breakpoint set in AddNumbers.ComputeSum
main[1]
```

As you probably can guess, this command tells JDB to stop when the method `ComputeSum` in the class `AddNumbers` is entered. This is convenient to do because the computation part of method that we are interested in is very close to the start of the method. If instead the statement was farther down in the method, it would be tedious to manually move down to the statement of interest every time we hit the breakpoint at the beginning of the method. In this case, we would want to use the `stop at` command in JDB.

The `stop at` command works exactly like the `stop in` command in JDB, except that you specify the line number you want JDB to stop on instead of the method. For instance, look at the `handleEvent` method of `AddNumbers` class. If we wanted to stop at the `if` statement where the program was checking for a push of the number 2 button, we would have entered the following:

```
main[1] stop at AddNumbers:90
Breakpoint set in AddNumbers:90
main[1]
```

However, don't do this, because we want to examine the `ComputeSum` method and not `handleEvent`. We can verify this and see all of the breakpoints currently set by using the `clear` command as follows:

```
AWT-Callback-Win32[1] clear
Current breakpoints set:
      AddNumbers:37
AWT-Callback-Win32[1]
```

As expected, there is only one breakpoint set. Note that it is specified as `AddNumbers:37` instead of as `AddNumbers:ComputeSum`. JDB converts the command `stop in AddNumbers.ComputeSum` to `stop at AddNumbers:37` in order to make its internal bookkeeping easier.

Of course, the real use of the `clear` command is to clear breakpoints when they have outgrown their usefulness. Don't do this, but if you needed to clear the breakpoint we just set, the following would be entered:

```
AWT-Callback-Win32[1] clear AddNumbers.ComputeSum
Breakpoint cleared at AddNumbers.ComputeSum
AWT-Callback-Win32[1]
```

Let's get back to debugging our applet. When we left our applet, it was still running along and there was no prompt in the JDB window. Why hasn't JDB stopped at `ComputeSum`? If you look at the applet code, you notice that the `ComputeSum` method only is called when you press a button in the applet. Press the 2 button to provide this `ComputeSum` method call:

```
main[1]
Breakpoint hit: AddNumbers.ComputeSum (AddNumbers: 37)
AWT-Callback-Win32[1]
```

As you can see in the above output, when you pressed the 2 button the debugger stopped at the `ComputeSum` method as we instructed it to. Note that we are now in a different thread (as shown by the change in prompts from `main[1]` to `AWT-Callback-Win32[1]`) because the AWT windowing manager thread calls the `handleEvent` method in the `AddNumbers` class when a button is pressed in the applet.

We know we are stopped in `ComputeSum` method, but let's get a better sense of our bearings and refresh our memory by looking at where this is in the source code. Fortunately, this line number information is stored in the class when you compile with the `-g` option and we can access this by using the this `list` command of JDB as follows:

```
AWT-Callback-Win32[1] list
33             }
34      35              public void ComputeSum() {
36
37      =>              int Total = LeftNumber - RightNumber;
38
39              String ConvLeft  = String.valueOf(LeftNumber);
40              String ConvRight = String.valueOf(RightNumber);
41              String ConvTotal = String.valueOf(Total);
AWT-Callback-Win32[1]
```

Note that as expected, we are stopped in `ComputeSum` on the first statement, and as luck would have it, right before the computation statement. The observant reader probably already can tell what is wrong, but just pretend that it's a much more complicated computation and that you can't, OK?

Examining Objects

First, let's check our operands for the computation to make sure they are correct. JDB provides three commands to display the contents of objects: `locals`, `print`, and `dump`. `locals` displays the current values of all of the objects defined in the local scope. `print` and `dump` are very similar and are used to display the contents of any object in any scope, including objects defined in the interface for the class. The main difference is that `dump` displays more information about complex objects (objects with inheritance or multiple data members) than `print` does.

Because `LeftNumber` and `RightNumber` are class members, we'll need to use `print` to display them, as follows:

```
AWT-Callback-Win32[1] print LeftNumber
this.LeftNumber = 5
AWT-Callback-Win32[1] print RightNumber
this.RightNumber = 2
AWT-Callback-Win32[1]
```

The operands seem to be exactly as we entered them on the applet. Let's take a look at the local objects to get a feeling for where we are by using the `locals` command as follows:

```
AWT-Callback-Win32[1] locals
  this = AddNumbers[0,0,300x200,layout=java.awt.BorderLayout,
resizable,title=JDB Sample Java Program]
  Total is not in scope.
  ConvLeft is not in scope.
  ConvRight is not in scope.
  ConvTotal is not in scope.
AWT-Callback-Win32[1]
```

As expected, JDB is telling us that none of the local objects have been instantiated yet, so none of the objects are within the local scope yet. Let's move the execution of the method along one statement so that we can see what the value of the computation is. To do this, we need to use the JDB `step` command as follows:

```
AWT-Callback-Win32[1] step
AWT-Callback-Win32[1]
Breakpoint hit: AddNumbers.ComputeSum (AddNumbers:39)
AWT-Callback-Win32[1]
```

JDB moves the execution along one statement and stops. Doing this also triggers another breakpoint, because we are still in `AddNumbers.ComputeSum`. Let's see the following to determine how the computation turned out:

```
AWT-Callback-Win32[1] locals
this = AddNumbers[0,0,300x200,layout=java.awt.BorderLayout,
resizable,title=JDB Sample Java Program]
  Total = 3
  ConvLeft is not in scope.
  ConvRight is not in scope.
  ConvTotal is not in scope.
AWT-Callback-Win32[1]
```

We see that `Total` was instantiated, the addition carried out, and the result put in `Total`. But wait, 5 + 2 doesn't equal 3! Take a look at the following source code:

```
AWT-Callback-Win32[1] list
35          public void ComputeSum() {
36
37              int Total = LeftNumber - RightNumber;
38
39      =>       String ConvLeft  = String.valueOf(LeftNumber);
40          String ConvRight = String.valueOf(RightNumber);
41          String ConvTotal = String.valueOf(Total);
42
43              taResult.setText(ConvLeft + " + " + ConvRight + " = " +
AWT-Callback-Win32[1]
```

Oops—a subtraction sign was used instead of an addition sign! So much for finding another bug in the Pentium processor, but congratulations—you've found your first applet bug in JDB.

Additional JDB Functions

We've found our bug, but don't quit out of AppletViewer yet. We'll use it and the `AddNumbers` class to demonstrate a few more features of JDB that you might find useful in future debugging sessions.

Walking the Method Call Stack with JDB

In the previous section, we used the `locals` JDB command to look at the objects in the current scope. Using the JDB command up, it also is possible to look at the local objects in previous stack frames (which consist of all of the methods that either called `ComputeSum` or called a method that called `ComputeSum`, and so on). For example, let's look at the following to see the state of the `handleEvent` method right before it called the `ComputeSum` method:

```
AWT-Callback-Win32[1] up
AWT-Callback-Win32[2] locals
this = AddNumbers[0,0,300x200,layout=java.awt.BorderLayout,
resizable,title=JDB Sample Java Program]
evt = java.awt.Event[id=1001,x=246,y=28,
target=java.awt.Button[5,5,20x24,label=2],arg=2]
AWT-Callback-Win32[2]
```

As you can see, the `handleEvent` stack frame has two objects in its local frame, the pointer to this `AddNumber` instance and the `Event` object passed to `handleEvent`.

It's possible to use up as many times as your method call stack is deep. To undo the up function and return to a higher method call in the stack, use the JDB `down` command as follows:

```
AWT-Callback-Win32[2] down
AWT-Callback-Win32[1] locals
this = AddNumbers[0,0,300x200,layout=java.awt.BorderLayout,
resizable,title=JDB Sample Java Program]
  Total = 3
  ConvLeft is not in scope.
  ConvRight is not in scope.
  ConvTotal is not in scope.
AWT-Callback-Win32[1]
```

As expected, we are back in the `ComputeSum`'s local stack frame.

Using JDB to Get More Information about Classes

JDB also has two functions for getting more information about classes: `methods` and `classes`. `methods` enables you display all of the methods in a class. For example, examining the `AddNumbers` class with the `methods` command:

```
AWT-Callback-Win32[1] methods
void <init>()
void ComputeSum()
void paint(Graphics)
boolean handleEvent(Event)
AWT-Callback-Win32[1]
```

The `classes` function lists all of the classes that are currently loaded in memory. Here is partial output from the execution of classes on `AddNumbers` (the actual output listed more than 80 classes):

```
AWT-Callback-Win32[1] classes
...
...
0x13a5f70:interface(sun.awt.UpdateClient)
0x13a6160:interface(java.awt.peer.MenuPeer)
0x13a67a0:interface(java.awt.peer.ButtonPeer)
0x13a6880:class(java.lang.ClassNotFoundException)
0x13a6ea8:class(sun.tools.debug.Field)
0x13a7098:class(sun.tools.debug.BreakpointSet)
0x13a7428:class(sun.tools.debug.Stackframe)
0x13a7478:class(sun.tools.debug.LocalVariable)
AWT-Callback-Win32[1]
```

Monitoring Memory Usage and Controlling `finalize`

For some large applets or applications, the amount of free memory might become a concern. JDB's `memory` command enable you to monitor the amount of used and free memory during your debugging session, as follows:

```
AWT-Callback-Win32[1] memory
Free: 2554472, total: 3145720
AWT-Callback-Win32[1]
```

JDB also lets you explicitly demand that the `finalize` method be run on all freed objects through the `gc` (garbage collection) command. This is useful for proving that your applet or application correctly handles deleted objects, which can be difficult to prove normally with small applets and applications because the `finalize` methods are normally called only when the applet or application has run out of free memory.

Controlling Threads of Execution

As you know from Chapter 15, "Threads and Multithreading," Java applets have multiple threads of execution. Using JDB and the threads command, we can view these threads as follows:

```
AWT-Callback-Win32[1] threads
Group sun.applet.AppletViewer.main:
 1.  (java.lang.Thread)0x13a3a00          AWT-Win32                running
 2.  (java.lang.Thread)0x13a2a58          AWT-Callback-Win32    running
 3.  (sun.awt.ScreenUpdater)0x13a2d98    Screen Updater        running
Group group applet-StartApplet.class:
 4.     (java.lang.Thread)0x13a28f0 class running
AWT-Callback-Win32[1]
```

As you can see from the output, there are four threads of simultaneous applet execution. Two correspond to the AWT window management system (threads 1 and 2), one for updating the screen (thread 3), and one for the actual applet itself (thread 4).

JDB provides two commands for controlling the execution of threads: `suspend` and `resume`. Suspending a thread isn't very worthwhile in our simple example, but in multithreaded applications it can be very worthwhile—you can suspend all but one thread and focus on that thread.

But let's try `suspend` and `resume` on our applet to get a feel for their use. To suspend the AWT-Win32 thread, you should note its ID from the threads list and then use this as the argument to suspend, as follows:

```
AWT-Callback-Win32[1] threads
Group sun.applet.AppletViewer.main:
 1.  (java.lang.Thread)0x13a3a00          AWT-Win32                running
...
AWT-Callback-Win32[1] suspend 1
AWT-Callback-Win32[1] threads
Group sun.applet.AppletViewer.main:
```

```
 1.  (java.lang.Thread)0x13a3a00         AWT-Win32                  suspended
 2.  (java.lang.Thread)0x13a2a58         AWT-Callback-Win32      running
 3.  (sun.awt.ScreenUpdater)0x13a2d98 Screen Updater          running
Group group applet-StartApplet.class:
 4.     (java.lang.Thread)0x13a28f0 class                      running
AWT-Callback-Win32[1]
```

As expected, the AWT-Win32 thread is now suspended. Threads are resumed in a completely analogous manner as follows:

```
AWT-Callback-Win32[1] resume 1
AWT-Callback-Win32[1] threads
Group sun.applet.AppletViewer.main:
 1.  (java.lang.Thread)0x13a3a00         AWT-Win32                  running
 2.  (java.lang.Thread)0x13a2a58         AWT-Callback-Win32      running
 3.  (sun.awt.ScreenUpdater)0x13a2d98 Screen Updater          running
Group group applet-StartApplet.class:
 4.     (java.lang.Thread)0x13a28f0 class                      running
AWT-Callback-Win32[1]
```

Using use to Point the Way to Your Java Source Code

In order to execute the list command, JDB takes the line number and grabs the required lines of Java from the source file. To find that source file, JDB reads your CLASSPATH environmental variable and searches all of the paths contained in it. If that path doesn't contain your source file, JDB will be unable to display the source for your program.

This wasn't a problem for us because our search path contained the current directory, but if you set up your applet or application and the source is located in a directory outside of the search path, you'll need to use the use command to add to your path. The use command without any arguments displays the current search path as follows:

```
AWT-Callback-Win32[1] use
\java\classes;.;C:\JAVA\BIN\..\classes;
AWT-Callback-Win32[1]
```

Appending a directory to the search path is unfortunately slightly tedious. You have to retype the entire current path and add the new path. So to add the path \myclasses to the preceding path, we would do the following:

```
AWT-Callback-Win32[1] use \java\classes;.;C:\JAVA\BIN\..\classes;\myclasses
AWT-Callback-Win32[1]
```

Getting More Information About Your Objects with dump

In our debugging section we had an example of how to display an object's value using the print command. In this section, we'll look at JDB's dump command, which is a more useful display command for objects containing multiple data members. The AddNumbers class is a good example (note that this in this case refers to the instantiation of AddNumbers for our applet), as follows:

```
AWT-Callback-Win32[1] dump this
this = (AddNumbers)0x13a3000 {
    ComponentPeer peer = (sun.awt.win32.MFramePeer)0x13a31b0
    Container parent = null
    int x = 0
    int y = 0
    int width = 300
    int height = 200
    Color foreground = (java.awt.Color)0x13a2bb0
    Color background = (java.awt.Color)0x13a2b98
    Font font = (java.awt.Font)0x13a31d0
    boolean visible = true
    boolean enabled = true
    boolean valid = true
    int ncomponents = 3
AWT-Callback-Win32[1] _

    Contrast this with the output from print:

AWT-Callback-Win32[1] print this
this = AddNumbers[0,0,300x200,layout=java.awt.BorderLayout,
resizable,title=JDB Sample Java Program]
AWT-Callback-Win32[1]
```

As you can see, the `dump` command displays the data members for the class, while `print` displays only the key attributes for the class.

Handling Exceptions with `catch` and `ignore`

JDB has two functions for dealing with exceptions: `catch` and `ignore`. `catch`, similar to a breakpoint, enables you to trap exceptions and stop the debugger. This is useful when debugging because it becomes much easier to diagnose an exception when you know the conditions under which it occurred. To catch an exception, simply type `class` and the name of the exception class. In order to trap any exception (the `Exception` exception base class), the following is done:

```
AWT-Callback-Win32[1] catch Exception
AWT-Callback-Win32[1]
```

`ignore` does exactly the opposite of `catch`. It squelches the specified class of exceptions raised by an applet or application. The use of `ignore` is completely analogous to `catch`, as shown by the following:

```
AWT-Callback-Win32[1] ignore ArrayOutOfBoundsException
AWT-Callback-Win32[1]
```

Continuing Program Execution with `cont`

You may be wondering how to restart execution once you reach a breakpoint and execution has stopped. The `cont` command does just that:

```
AWT-Callback-Win32[1] cont
```

As you can see, the program has resumed execution and the JDB prompt will not return until a breakpoint or exception is reached.

Leaving JDB Using the `exit` Command

Although it may be obvious to you already, there is one final command that comes in handy once in any debugging session. The exit command lets you out of the debugger and back into DOS.

Summary

In this chapter, you have learned through hands-on experience about Sun's Java debugger, JDB. Debugging is a learned skill; don't be discouraged if it takes you a long time to debug your first applet or application. As you gain experience doing it, you'll start to recognize the effects of different classes of bugs and be able to solve each bug in shorter amounts of time. Patience is definitely a virtue in software debugging.

Java Documentation

37

by Tony Beveridge

The bane of any software developer's existence is embodied by a seemingly innocuous word: *documentation.* The old coder's war cry, "If it was hard to write, it should be hard to read and use," has no doubt been heard by some readers. Part of this general malaise can be attributed to the sometimes disjointed methods by which software documentation is created—an awkward cycle of creating code, commenting, extracting comments (if any in the first place), formatting in perhaps a word-processing package, preparing, and finally distributing it internally.

However, on some operating systems such as UNIX, editors exist that can be taught to perform such tasks (for example, the ubiquitous Emacs). While useful, such an approach always is parochial. There are no defined standards for commenting C++, C, or even Smalltalk code in a universally understood manner. Code documentation generally remains a weak point of the overall development process, because any code base that requires no maintenance probably is not useful anymore, and any maintenance effort is hampered by poor, incomplete, or missing documentation.

The developers of Java, however, decided to address such issues. It is possible with Java to add code commentary and produce documentation simultaneously and painlessly. Additionally, documentation can be released with Java products, eliminating the time lag between software and its accompanying explanatory text. The Java API documentation is itself generated from the Java class library source code and is copiously hypertext-linked, indexed, and presented attractively. With Java, it might even be possible, in some small way, to actually enjoy this process! We shall explore some of the rationale behind good documentation, the Java tools available for documentation, and metrics that can be used to measure what is finally produced in this chapter.

Documentation: Why Bother?

As mentioned, documentation still is a relatively thorny and unpopular issue. In an attempt to soothe any qualms you might have, we are going to lay out some reasons why you should document your code, and document it well.

Five Reasons to Document

There are more than five reasons to document, but here is a selection of some of the more compelling ones:

- Think of the next person.

  A phrase to consider: staff turnover. You may already have had this happen to you, but imagine the frustration of encountering a large body of code that has no comments. What will be the first task you have to perform on code like this? No doubt it will be to find an obscure bug that has manifested itself after the last developer left. If programmers could be confident that any piece of software they create never will require adjustment, the documentation issue is unimportant. Unfortunately, it would take more years than man has been on the Earth to prove mathematically that a piece of software is correct, so documentation remains important.

■ Your code can be an educational tool.

The value of a well-designed, well-constructed, and well-documented piece of software cannot be underestimated as an educational aid. However, given the complexity of some of the tasks programmers are called on to perform, design and implementation decisions that are made might appear obscure without commentary. Good documentation supports leveraging of intellectual effort.

■ No language is self-documenting.

The phrase, "the language is self-documenting," used to be heard to justify the lack of code comments and explanatory text. If only this were true, but we know differently. Some features of even Java could need to be highlighted for less-experienced developers, including perhaps some in your own organization. An example of this highlighting might be to state in a comment that the implementation of an abstract function is the responsibility of a subclass (that is, a derived class). This fact might seem obvious after a few days, weeks, or months with Java, but it can mean an awful lot to someone just getting started.

■ You can comply with Java coding standards.

Package, class, method, parameter, and variable comments might just form part of a coding standard that you follow, or might wish to follow. This is not to say that draconian measures are called for—just some standards that fall into the general area of "making your life easier." Some suggested standards are described later on.

■ You can automate its production.

With Java, by utilizing the `javadoc` utility it is possible to create slick HTML documentation with hypertext links and inline images by adhering to the defined `javadoc` markup. The markup is the collection of tokens that partially represent the Java API structure. These tokens are optional text tags that allow this generation to be performed. One supposes that it would be possible to integrate such documentation into the language itself. Java is still young—there is time.

Guidelines for Successful Java Documentation

Because you made it this far, we hope that you might also be interested in some guidelines that have proven useful empirically over the course of a number of mostly object-oriented projects. These guidelines, however, are for the most part paradigm- and language-independent. They are offered to augment the basic Java facilities for documentation.

■ Copyright statement

If you are publishing your code on your web server, a public site such as Gamelan, or just allowing people to access it using anonymous FTP, be sure to include a copyright statement. Copyright statements should include items such as the conditions to impose on users of your software and what kind of warranty you do or do not imply. Pro forma text might be, "<*person/organization/*I> hereby release the software into the public domain, and assume or assert no ownership or copyright over said software, permit free and unhindered source code modification and distribution, completely releasing all intellectual and commercial rights," and so on. A more conservative approach would be to allow it to be distributed and reused freely as long as the code derived from your code carries an acknowledgment. This is certainly a more prevalent approach and one hopes that, by and large, it is honored.

■ Modification history

If you are using some form of version control system, you might already have this in place and can easily integrate it with your existing code base. However, if you are not using a tool, it might be germane to include a modification history, in chronological order, for maintenance purposes. Such a history should probably mention the author, date, and a brief but complete description of the changes, additions, and deletions. Because we primarily are interested in javadoc, you also can include some HTML markup tags if desired to spice up the details. Remember not to include items such as line rulers or anchors in your comments, though.

■ javadoc markup

As covered before, because you can simplify the code, comment, and documentation phase with an automatic generator, you should! Java markup is relatively simple and self-consistent, so it presents no barrier to implementation. When writing comments, all you have to do is add a few additional characters and you are there. javadoc itself manages the more complex tasks of rendering a textual representation of the inheritance trees of your classes, the ordering of private, protected, and public members, indexes for constructors and member functions, and many others. Documentation this easy cannot be ignored!

■ Looking ahead

If you are not using a version control tool for your source management, you ought to consider using one of the freely available products such as SCCS (Source Code Control System), RCS (Revision Control System), or CVCS (Concurrent Version Control System). To retrieve these, you can start your search on http://www.yahoo.com and go from there (search for RCS or GNU, perhaps). The details of such packages are beyond the scope of this chapter, but by including their markup as well as javadoc's, you can integrate the two. For example, RCS has keywords such as Id that it will convert to a date, version, time, and so on when you update your source to the RCS *repository* (a holding pen for master copies of source code and history). If you combine this with the `javadoc` `@version` tag covered later, you can have your version control tool fill in the version field for you as a by-product of good source management.

■ Coding standards

We could devote many pages to a consistent and semantically rich coding standards scheme, but will content ourselves with an aspect of coding practice that can increase your code comprehension rate and that of your colleagues: variable naming conventions. These include Hungarian notation, no notation, and various other schemes. The table below shows a simple system that is straightforward, concise, and quick to implement.

Table 37.1. Sample variable naming scheme for Java.

Variable Prefix	Meaning	Example
i	Integer variable	iNumberOfEvents
l	Long integer	lNumberOfEvents
f	Floating-point variable	fNumberOfStars
d	Double variable	dNumberOfNebulae
c	Character	cSmallCharacter
s	String or string buffer	sLabel
t	Thread	tAnimationThread
r	Reference to variable (all variables in Java)	rMemberFunction
x	An exception	xIoException
b	Boolean	bMorePages

The `javadoc` Utility

The thrust of this chapter is to encourage the use of the `javadoc` utility as a useful aid during software development. This section covers the use of HTML as a help system, navigating the generated documentation such as the Java API documents, the tags used to mark up code, and the command-line usage of `javadoc` itself.

HTML as a Help System

Although it seems the obvious choice as a supporting help system for a web programming language, HTML actually offers certain advantages as an API help system. Some are obvious, such as general formatting, graphics inclusion, hypertext linking, and the ability to link to remote sites through the general web structure. Other less obvious advantages include portability, symmetry with one of the intentions of Java (architectural neutrality), and the ability to recite the whole document structure without comprising the links therein (in the case of javadoc-generated documentation). The advantage of portability is sort of obvious, but you can see its value when trying to use an RTF or Windows help file under Solaris.

Navigating the javadoc-Generated Documentation

The HTML documentation that composes the Java API was generated using the javadoc utility with a few exceptions edited by hand that will be discussed later. A discussion of the underlying structure of these documents—a separately obtainable part of the Java Development Kit—and their navigation covers both the online documentation and your own documentation in one fell swoop. In the text that follows, <directory> represents the base directory into which you uncompressed the API documentation. After a little while, you may begin to wonder why there is no applet content in the generated pages—as it would not have been difficult to include it.

API User's Guide Entry Screen

Figure 37.1 shows the first screen that you will see when perusing the Java API User's Guide.

FIGURE 37.1.

The opening screen for the API User's Guide.

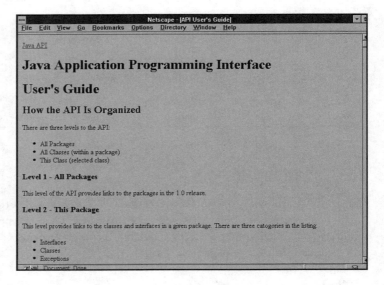

Figure 37.1 is the file <directory>/api/API_users_guide.html, the HTML document that is the entryway to the user's guide. Click the top hypertext link, Java API, to progress to the next page, as shown in Figure 37.2.

FIGURE 37.2.

The package index document, showing the applet packages and others.

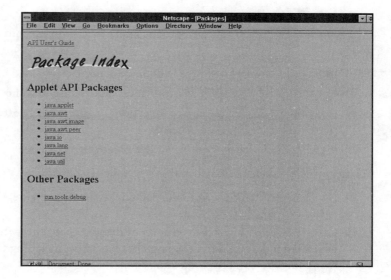

This file, located in `<directory>`/api/Packages.html, has been manually edited post production. Each package as listed corresponds to those present in the java.* and sun.tools.debug packages. Each of these packages is a hypertext link to the classes, interfaces, exceptions, and errors of that package. So, by clicking the java.awt link, you would see Figure 37.3.

FIGURE 37.3.

The java.awt *package API document.*

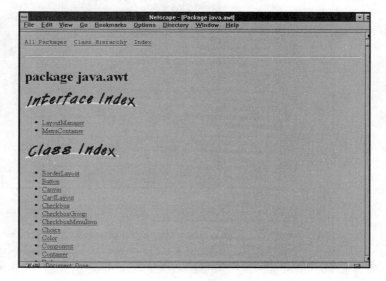

Figure 37.3, `<directory>/api/Package-java.awt.html`), contains a number of interesting navigational features. As you can see, the document is partitioned into a number of indexes, as follows:

■ Interface: All links listed here will jump to interfaces defined in this package.

■ Class: Hypertext jumps to the individual classes are shown here.

■ Exception: The very important exceptions category, where exceptions thrown by classes in this package are detailed.

■ Error: A special category of throwable objects.

At the top of the document, you will see the following links:

■ All Packages: Returns you to the document shown in Figure 37.1, displaying all of the packages available for perusal.

■ Class Hierarchy: Invokes the display of the document `<directory>/api/tree.html`, which is a hypertext list of the Java class hierarchy, including the package that you are examining. You will see something similar to Figure 37.4.

FIGURE 37.4.

Class hierarchy document `tree.html`.

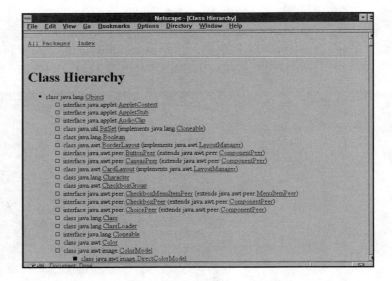

■ Index: Displays the file `<directory>/api/AllNames.html`, which is an alphabetical index allowing searches using the initial character of a variable, method, interface, exception, class, or package. Entries in the list are hypertext-linked to the corresponding explanatory documents. Figure 37.5 shows the top of the index for the Java API documentation.

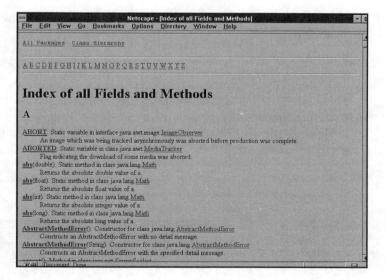

FIGURE 37.5.

Index document
`AllNames.html`.

Class Document

Each class in a package will have its documentation present in a file called `<fully qualified class name>.html`, where `<fully qualified class name>` denotes a full package name specification. Each file has a common structure consisting of the following:

- Class name: Fully qualified class name.

- Class hierarchy: Preformatted inheritance tree for the class. Each superclass is a hypertext link to the corresponding details.

- Class Details: A textual description of the current class, including its immediate superclass and what interfaces it implements, if any.

- Class comment: The descriptive class comment.

- Indexes: The variable, constructor, and method indexes. A one sentence description follows the index entry. For variable indices, types are excluded. For methods, return type is excluded. For both methods and constructors, parameter types only are listed. Each abridged entry in the index is a hypertext link to the expanded description.

- Descriptions: Each particular entity (variable, constructor, method) has a different possible documentation display. For more details on this, see Table 37.2. The method descriptions, apart from any comments or tags that have been defined, also might include a hypertext entry to a method that is being overridden by this method. This could be of assistance in a number of situations, including the determination of the rationale for doing so and checking design decisions.

To also aid in navigation, the top of the document has hypertext links that enable you to jump to the following:

- the All Packages document
- Class Hierarchy
- the contents of the package of this class
- the previous and next class, interface, exception, or error in the package, determined alphabetically within each type of package component
- the Index document

All of these document types have been covered in previous sections. Figure 37.6 shows the top of the java.awt.Panel class page.

FIGURE 37.6.

The AWT Panel class help page,
java.awt.Panel.html.

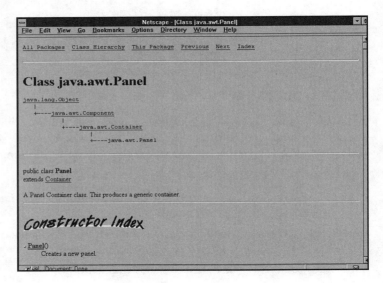

javadoc Markup

We have mentioned already that documentation generation is achieved by executing the javadoc utility. However, we have only briefly touched upon the fact that a tag-marking scheme is required for source code files to be suitable candidates for parsing. This section covers all of the details regarding this text markup, and reiterates some of the ways in which you can enhance the basic javadoc scheme.

> **NOTE**
>
> Even though javadoc will generate linked and attractive documentation, it is not a substitute for well-written comments.

The command-line usage of javadoc is covered later.

What Documentation javadoc Will Generate

Documentation can be generated for the following:

- Packages
- Classes
- Interfaces
- Exceptions
- Methods
- Variables

Note that only text will be generated for public and protected aspects of objects. This is in accordance with the basic object-oriented principle of encapsulation—a human API browser should not be aware necessarily of the internals of class, for example. Do not take this as a method to avoid documenting implementations, though!

Embedding HTML Sequences

Virtually any of the standard HTML tags can be embedded inside source text for eventual inclusion into the generated documents. Common sense dictates (as does Sun Microsystems) that formatting tags, anchors, lists, horizontal rulers, and other tags might interfere with the documents that are produced by javadoc. It is a reasonably good way of adding some extra information in a visually striking way, though—such things are best determined empirically.

Available Tags

The following table defines each currently available tag, its scope, and associated semantics. Note that they are only significant when enclosed by the special comment-opening characters /** and closing characters */ (like a fancy C comment, really). The semantics are expanded later along with some code examples. (Note: The letters *fq* in the following table are an acronym for *fully qualified*.)

Table 37.2. Defined javadoc markup tags.

Tag/string	Scope	Semantics
@see classname	Class	"See also" hypertext link to the class specified
@see fq-classname	Class	Hyperlinked "see also" entry

continues

Table 37.2. continued

Tag/string	*Scope*	*Semantics*
`@see fq-classname#method-name`	Class	Hyperlinked "see also" entry to the method in the given class
`@version version text`	Class	"Version" entry
`@author author`	Class	Creates an "Author" entry
`@see classname`	Variable	"See also" hypertext link to the named class
`@see fq-classname`	Variable	Hyperlinked "see also" entry to the given class
`@see fq-classname#method-name`	Variable	Hyperlinked "see also" entry to the method in the named class
`@param parameter-name description`	Method	Parameter specification for the "Parameters" section
`@return description`	Method	"Returns" section, specifying the return value
`@exception fq-class-name description`	Method	"Throws" entry, which contains the name of the exception that might be thrown by the method

There are some conditions that apply to the use of tags, and they are as follows:

- Class names: javadoc will prepend the name of the current package to a bare class name if the source itself is resident in a package. There capability also exists to fully qualify class names if it's necessary to reference a class in a package other than the current one.

- Tag grouping: Repeated tags must be sequentially ordered. Keep all like tags together or javadoc will become confused.

- Format: All tags are prepended with the @ character and are placed at the beginning of a comment line. Leading white space and asterisks are ignored when the tag is searched for. The examples later show this clearly.

- Length: All comments can be spread over a number of lines. In fact, a one-line comment (certainly for class scope) is too short. Have you anything else to say to enlighten your reader?

Class Comment Example

A class comment is arguably the most important you can make! Be sure to include a general description of the intent, general behavior, version, authors—perhaps including some of the look ahead tokens for version control, date, and any reference to related classes. Listing 37.1 shows a rather short class comment.

Listing 37.1. Example class comment.

```
//===============================================================================
/**
 * This class is part of a subsystem to parse a configurable grammar token stream
 * using various recovery schemes, as detailed in the specification, under section
 * 2.3, Finite State Machine recovery. An internally-mounted Web page
 * <A HREF=http://ow:8080/specifications/parser/fsmrecov2.3>details this</a>.
 * <br>
 * @see org.parser.fsm for the finite state machine details
 * @see java.io.InputStrean for the protocol our token stream adheres to
 * @author T Beveridge
 * @Author Natasha Brown
 * @version 12/10/95, 1.00
 */
//===============================================================================

class StackedTokenStream extends org.tokenStream implements Runnable {
```

Note the placement of comment lines and text. There also are some extra features here, in that we have included our own hypertext reference to a specification document on our internal web server. The use of the <br> tag also inserts an empty line for neatness. Multiple tags have been used to reflect the two authors of the class, and our version details will show as a date followed by our own version number.

Method Comment Example

Remember that only public or protected methods will have documentation created. It is, of course, your decision whether to include comments for private methods, but for all except the most trivial (such as accessors), it is good software engineering practice to include comments.

> **TIP**
>
> javadoc takes the first sentence of a method comment and uses it for the index entry. Therefore, it is a good idea to make this sentence descriptive. For a constructor, rather than having, "Constructor. Taking X arguments…", use, "Constructor taking X arguments, …".

Describing parameters is helpful in Java, because there is no syntactic means of ascribing the C++ concept of ascribing state constancy to a parameter; this even though some parameters might never be modified when used by the method. The description of exceptions also is excellent practice because they will either have to be caught by your client's code, caught and rethrown, or passed on. Listing 37.2 illustrates a helpful method comment.

Listing 37.2. Example method comment.

```
//==============================================================================
/**
 * This method determines if the Finite State Machine is in one of the 2
 * (desirable) states given. The StringBuffer parameter is the only one of the 3
 * that may change during the execution of this call. Note that this method may
 * become private, so it may be a good idea to avoid it ! <br>
 * Has not been modified for some considerable time so could be considered stable
 * (or obsolete).<br> @param rStateOne  An instance of FsmState. The order is
 * irrelevant @param rStateTwo  An instance of FsmState. The order is irrelevant
 * @param rStrBuffer <b>volatile</b> This wil be updated during this call with the
 * state actually encountered if this function returns true
 * @return true if one of the two states has been encountered ; false (!) otherwise
 * @exception java.io.IOException Thrown when the Fsm delegator attempts to fetch a
 * token and fails. Unusual
 * @exception org.exceptions.FsmDead Thrown when the Finite State Machine is in a
 * GC'ablestate.
 */
//==============================================================================

protected boolean duplexState(FsmState rStateOne, FsmState rStateTwo, StringBuffer
➥rStrBuffer) {
          if (bTerminated)
                throw new org.exceptions.FsmDead("FSM: Dead state entered");
```

Again, note the inclusion of <br> tags to introduce blank lines and the use of a boldface "volatile" comment on the rStrBuffer description to indicate its potential value change.

Variable Comment Example

Because only the comments of protected and public variables are candidates for documentation inclusion, you might not see many of these. They seem to appear mainly for FINAL variables, which are really just a Java method for introducing constant values. Remember that variable comments for javadoc can only contain @see directives. Listing 37.3 shows a sample variable comment.

Listing 37.3. Sample variable comment.

```
//=============================================================================
/**
 * This boolean variable holds our live/dead status. It is held to be true through
 * out the useful life of the Finite State Machine, being rendered false only when
 * the associated token stream is in error or throws an exception.
 * @see org.io.streams.StackedTokenStream
 */
//=============================================================================

protected boolean bTerminated;
```

Generating Documentation

Now we cut to the chase. We will discuss how to generate your documentation, where it can reside, platform differences, and errors that can occur.

■ Where do documents go on creation?

Documents go wherever you happen to be, actually. What this means is best explained with an example. If you are in directory X, and you generate documentation for your package org.utilities, javadoc will dump its output in directory X. This is not particularly unfriendly unless you have manually edited Packages.html—if you have, the javadoc process will overwrite your changes! The moral of this example is that javadoc is essentially a batch utility if you don't want to change directories too often. There also is a command-line option you can supply to alter this behavior.

■ Merging your own packages with the Java API documentation

This is entirely possible though not necessarily advisable. All you really have to do is edit the Packages.html file and insert your own hypertext links to your package documents. Note that merging your own documents this way will not include them in either the index or class hierarchy.

■ Platform differences

This depends very much upon your own system setup. For example, suppose you are using Windows NT javadoc to generate documents and these documents are targeted to be stored on a network drive whose native type is UNIX. This will generate documents that can be accessed under NT but not under a UNIX-based browser. Why is this? Case sensitivity. Generating from NT, javadoc seems to ignore case and the result is hypertext-linked documents that show up as errors under UNIX. This is a minor point, but if you are batch-creating documentation for a large package or number of packages, it might save you some time. In this sort of environment, maybe you should just go with UNIX-based generation!

■ Other errors

Watch out for the command-line syntax. You must specify a full package name, and the source must be available and readable. Any other course of action equals frustration. Make sure that you can write in the directory you are currently in or are directing the `javadoc` HTML documents to.

`javadoc`: **Command-Line Usage**

`javadoc` is just about the simplest utility in the JDK. The syntax is as follows:

```
javaDoc [options] {Package Name or File Name}.........
```

Available options are as follows:

`-d <directory>`

This instructs `javadoc` to redirect output to `<directory>`. The default is the current directory.

`-classpath`

This allows the specification of a classpath. It is the same as `javac` and overrides the CLASSPATH environment variable.

`-verbose`

This instructs `javadoc` to print a list of files loaded during execution. From JDK Beta 2, this might include files loaded from a ZIP file.

Measuring Your Documentation Quality

`javadoc` certainly is a tremendous help when it comes to automating the sometimes arduous task of creating software documentation. One aspect it does not cover is that of quality. This section attempts to provide some heuristics that can be applied to determine if the documents you are producing are worthy of a readership. Please note that a subset of this information also is included in the book *Object Oriented Software Metrics* by Mark Lorenz and Jeff Kidd, which is a recommended read for those interested in object-oriented metrics.

The list that follows presents metrics that you might consider adopting:

■ Size/existence of class comment

If the object was important enough to warrant a class, it certainly has a purpose, provides some service, collaborates with others, or acts autonomously. Otherwise you probably would not have bothered, so it therefore deserves a comment—and not just one that mentions the date and version, either! As an API reader, you should be able to read the overall class comment and either discard the class from consideration or investigate further. Without a class comment of some depth, such a task is rendered more difficult. At least 50 words would be required for a small class, such as a support class.

■ Size/existence of method comments

Again, for similar reasons to the above, a method should be commented if it is regarded as central to the public or protected behavior of a class. Implementation methods are arguably more important to comment, but remember—they won't be visible to your readers. Around 20 to 25 words is a good baseline for method comments.

■ Number of methods/classes/interfaces/variables with comments

For public or protected methods, classes and others, a coverage of less than 80 percent should be a cause for concern. Unless you are creating a popular class such as a string, for example, its use might not necessarily jump out at your audience. Comment it and they might just want to use it.

Currently, there is no way in Java to automate this process of documentation-quality measurement. However, if you avail yourself of the Beta 2 source code and adhere to the source license agreement, it would be possible to modify the `javadoc` source code to incorporate such abilities. This will at least give you timely statistics on quality automatically if you require them. The `javadoc` source code itself is in the package `java.tools.javadoc`.

Summary

This summary presents some possible improvements in `javadoc`—though not exhaustively—and a final endorsement of its use.

Potential Improvements

As with all tools, there always are improvements that could be made. Some of the more interesting ones include the following:

■ Package comments

There is no facility currently for package comments.

■ Incremental updates

To allow the documentation for just a particular class to be generated in the target directory without rewriting some of the reference files.

■ Tag granularity

For example, it is possible only to provide authors on a class basis. It sometimes is desirable to note authors of methods, too, in a consistent fashion.

- Object Oriented Analysis/Object Oriented Design concepts tags

  It would be reasonably useful to provide some way of noting design decisions in a way that is separate from the rest of the documentation. An example might be that a particular class is tightly coupled with certain other classes, or that it might be only ever part of an aggregation.

- Metrics

  There is no provision for integration or production of metric information regarding quality.

- Liven up the documents

  Because one of the objectives of Java is to make Web pages come alive, some applets that augment the utility of the API documents would be good!

This chapter has shown that `javadoc` is a simple and reasonably effective tool for generating API documentation quickly and effectively. Used properly, it can create useful documents to aid the users of packages. It is recommended.

Native Methods and Libraries

38

by Charles L. Perkins

In this chapter we'll discuss all the reasons you might (or might not) want to write `native` methods in Java, all of Java's built-in optimizations, and the tricks you can use to make your programs faster. You'll also learn the procedure for creating, making headers and stubs for, and linking `native` methods into a dynamically loadable library.

Let's begin, however, with the reasons that you might want to implement `native` methods in the first place.

There are only two reasons that you might need to declare some of your methods `native`— that is, implemented by a language other than Java.

The first, and by far the best reason to do so, is because you need to utilize a special capability of your computer or operating system that the Java class library does not already provide for you. Such capabilities include interfacing to new peripheral devices or plug-in cards, accessing a different type of networking, or using a unique and valuable feature of your particular operating system. Two more concrete examples are acquiring real-time audio input from a microphone or using 3D "accelerator" hardware in a 3D library. Neither of these is provided to you by the current Java environment, so you must implement them outside Java, in some other language (currently C or any language that can link with C).

The second, and often illusory, reason to implement `native` methods is speed—illusory, because you rarely need the raw speeds gained by this approach. It's even more rare to not be able to gain that speed-up in other ways (as you'll see later in the chapter). Using `native` methods in this case takes advantage of the fact that, at present, the Java release does not perform as well as, for example, an optimized C program on many tasks. For those tasks, you can write the "needs to be fast" part (critical, inner loops, for example) in C, and still use a larger Java shell of classes to hide this "trick" from your users. In fact, the Java class library uses this approach for certain critical system classes to raise the overall level of efficiency in the system. As a user of the Java environment, you don't even know (or see) any side effects of this (except, perhaps, a few classes or methods that are `final` that might not be otherwise).

Disadvantages of `native` Methods

Once you decide you'd like to, or must, use `native` methods in your program, this choice costs you dearly. Although you gain the advantages mentioned earlier, you lose the portability of your Java code.

Before, you had a program (or applet) that could travel to any Java environment in the world, now and forever. Any new architectures created—or new operating systems written—were irrelevant to your code. All it required was that the (tiny) Java Virtual Machine (or a browser that had one inside it) be available, and it could run anywhere, anytime—now and in the future.

Now, however, you've created a library of native code that must be linked with your program to make it work properly. The first thing you lose is the ability to "travel" as an applet; you simply can't be one! No Java-capable browser currently in existence allows native code to be loaded with an applet, for security reasons (and these are good reasons). The Java team has struggled to place as much as possible into the java packages because they are the only environment you can *count* on as an applet. (The sun packages, shipped primarily for use with stand-alone Java programs, are not always available to applets.)

> **NOTE**
>
> Actually, any classes that anyone writes *without* native code should be able to be loaded with an applet, as long as they depend only on the java packages. Unfortunately, many of the sun packages contain classes that *must* use native code to provide crucial, missing functionality from the java packages. All these missing pieces, and some additional multimedia and sound capabilities, will be added to the java packages in the future. (This has been informally promised in discussions I've had with the Java team.)

Losing the ability to travel anywhere across the Net, into any browser written now or in the future, is bad enough. What's worse, now that you can't be an applet, you have further limited yourself to only those machines that have had the Java Virtual Machine ported to their operating system. (Applets automatically benefit from the wide number of machines and operating systems that *any* Java-capable browser is ported to, but now you do not.)

Even worse, you have assumed something about that machine and operating system by the implementation of your native methods. This often means that you have to write different *source* code for some (or all) of the machines and operating systems on which you want to be able to run. You're already forced, by using native methods, to produce a separate binary library for every machine and operating system pair in the world (or at least, wherever you plan to run), and you must continue to do so forever. If changing the source is also necessary, you can see that this is not a pleasant situation for you and your Java program.

The Illusion of Required Efficiency

If, even after the previous discussion, you *must* use native methods anyway, there's help for you later in this chapter—but what if you're still thinking you need to use them for efficiency reasons?

You are in a grand tradition of programmers throughout the (relatively few) ages of computing. It is exciting, and intellectually challenging, to program with constraints. If you believe efficiency is always required, it makes your job a little more interesting—you get to consider all sorts of baroque ways to accomplish tasks, because it is the efficient way to do it. I myself was caught up in this euphoria of creativity when I first began programming, but it is creativity misapplied.

When you design your program, all that energy and creativity should be directed at the design of a tight, concise, minimal set of classes and methods that are maximally general, abstract, and reusable. (If you think that is easy, look around for a few years and see how bad most software is.) If you spend most of your programming time on thinking and rethinking these fundamental goals and how to achieve them, you are preparing for the future. A future where software is assembled as needed from small components swimming in a sea of network facilities, and anyone can write a component seen by millions (and reused in their programs) in minutes. If, instead, you spend your energy worrying about the speed your software will run *right now* on some computer, your work will be irrelevant after the 18 to 36 months it will take hardware to be fast enough to hide that minor inefficiency in your program.

Am I saying that you should ignore efficiency altogether? Of course not! Some of the great algorithms of computer science deal with solving hard or "impossible" problems in reasonable amounts of time—and writing your programs carelessly can lead to remarkably slow results. Carelessness, however, can as easily lead to incorrect, fragile, or nonreusable results. If you correct all these latter problems first, the resulting software will be clean, will naturally reflect the structure of the problem you're trying to solve, and thus will be amenable to "speeding up" later.

> **NOTE**
>
> There are always cases where you *must* be fanatical about efficiency in many parts of a set of classes. The Java class library itself is such a case, as is anything that must run in real-time for some critical real-world application (such as flying a plane). Such applications are rare, however.
>
> When speaking of a new kind of programming that must soon emerge, Bill Joy (one of Sun's founders) likes to invoke the four S's of Java: small, simple, safe, and secure. The "feel" of the Java language itself encourages the pursuit of clarity and the reduction of complexity. The intense pursuit of efficiency, which increases complexity and reduces clarity, is antithetical to these goals.

Once you build a solid foundation and debug your classes, and your program (or applet) works as you'd like it to, *then* it's time to begin optimizing it. If it's just a user interface applet, you may need to do nothing at all. The user is very slow compared to modern computers (and getting relatively slower every 18 months). The odds are that your applet is already fast enough—but suppose it isn't.

Built-In Optimizations

Your next job is to see whether your release supports turning on the "just-in-time" compiler, or using the `java2c` tool.

The first of these is an experimental technology that, while a method's bytecodes are running in the Java Virtual Machine, translates each bytecode into the native binary code equivalent for the local computer, and then keeps this native code around as a cache for the next time that method is run. This trick is completely transparent to the Java code you write. You need know nothing about whether or not it's being done—your code can still "travel" anywhere, anytime. On any system with "just-in-time" technology in place, however, it runs a lot faster. Experience with experimental versions of this technology shows that, after paying a small cost the first time a method is run, this technique can reach the speed of compiled C code.

> **NOTE**
>
> More details on this technique, and the java2c tool, are presented in the next chapter. As of the 1.0 release, neither of these tools are in the Java environment, but both are expected in a later release (perhaps 1.1).

The java2c translator takes a whole .class file full of the bytecodes for a class and translates them (all at once) into a portable C source code version. This version can then be compiled by a traditional C compiler on your computer to produce a native-method-like cached library of fast code. This large cache of native code will be used whenever the class's methods are called, but only on the local computer. Your original Java code can still travel as bytecodes and run on any other computer system. If the virtual machine automatically takes these steps whenever it makes sense for a given class, this can be as transparent as the just-in-time technology. Experience with an experimental version of this tool shows that fully optimized C performance is achievable. (This is the best anyone can hope to do!)

So you see, even without taking any further steps to optimize your program, you may discover that for your release of Java (or for releases elsewhere or coming in the near future), your code is already fast enough. If it is not, remember that the world craves speed. Java will only get faster, and the tools will only get better. Your code is the only permanent thing in this new world—it should be the best you can make it, with no compromises.

Simple Optimization Tricks

Suppose that these technologies aren't available or don't optimize your program far enough for your taste. You can profile your applet or program as it runs, to see in which methods it spends the most time. Once you know this crucial information, you can begin to make *targeted* changes to your classes.

> **TIP**
>
> Use `java -prof ...` to produce this profile information. In an earlier release (and, presumably, some later release) the `javaprof` tool can "pretty-print" this information in a more readable format. (`javaprof` is not in the 1.0 release—but try the latest Java release's documentation for details.)
>
> Before you begin making optimizations, you also may want to save a copy of your "clean" classes. As soon as computer speeds allow it (or a major rewrite necessitates it), you can revert to these classes, which embody the "best" implementation of your program.

First, identify the crucial few methods that take most of the time (there are almost always just a few, and often just one, that take up the majority of your program's time). If they contain loops, examine the inner loops to see whether they: call methods that can be made `final`, call a group of methods that can be collapsed into a single method, or create objects that can be reused rather than created anew each loop.

If you notice that a long chain of, for example, four or more method calls is needed to reach a destination method's code, *and* this execution path is in one of the critical sections of the program, you can "short-circuit" directly to that destination method in the topmost method. This may require adding a new instance variable to reference the object for that method call directly. This quite often violates layering or encapsulation constraints. This violation, and any added complexity, is the price you pay for efficiency.

If, after all these tricks (and the numerous others you should try that have been collected over the years into various programming books), your Java code is still *just too slow*, you will have to use `native` methods after all.

Writing `native` Methods

For whatever reasons, you've decided to add `native` methods to your program. You've already decided which methods need to be `native`, and in which classes, and you're rarin' to go.

First, on the Java side, all you need to do is delete the method bodies (all the code between the brackets—{ and }—and the brackets themselves) of each method you picked and replace them with a single semicolon (;). Then add the modifier `native` to the method's existing modifiers. Finally, add a `static` (class) initializer to each class that now contains `native` methods to load the native code library you're about to build. (You can pick any name you like for this library— details follow.) You're done!

That's all you need to do in Java to specify a `native` method. Subclasses of any class containing your new `native` methods can still override them, and these new Java methods are called for instances of the new subclasses (just as you'd expect).

Unfortunately, what needs to be done in your native language environment is not so simple.

The Example Class

Imagine a version of the Java environment that does not provide file I/O. Any Java program needing to use the file system would first have to write `native` methods to get access to the operating system primitives needed to do file I/O.

This example combines simplified versions of two actual Java library classes, `java.io.File` and `java.io.RandomAccessFile`, into a single new class, `SimpleFile`:

```java
public class  SimpleFile {
    public static final  char     separatorChar = '>';
    private protected     String  path;
    private protected     int     fd;

    public  SimpleFile(String s) {
        path = s;
    }

    public String  getFileName() {
        int  index = path.lastIndexOf(separatorChar);

        return (index < 0) ? path : path.substring(index + 1);
    }

    public String  getPath() {
        return path;
    }

    public native boolean   open();
    public native void      close();
    public native int       read(byte[]  buffer, int  length);
    public native int       write(byte[]  buffer, int  length);

    static {
        System.loadLibrary("simple");  // runs when class first loaded
    }
}
```

> **NOTE**
>
> The unusual `separatorChar` (>) is used simply to demonstrate what an implementation might look like on some strange computer whose file system didn't use any of the more common path separator conventions. Early Xerox computers used > as a separator, and several existing computer systems still use strange separators today, so this is not all that farfetched.

`SimpleFiles` can be created and used in the usual way:

```
SimpleFile  f = new SimpleFile(">some>path>and>fileName");

f.open();
f.read(...);
f.write(...);
f.close();
```

The first thing you notice about `SimpleFile`'s implementation is how unremarkable the first two-thirds of its Java code is! It looks just like any other class, with a class and an instance variable, a constructor, and two normal method implementations. Then there are four `native` method declarations. You'll recognize these, from previous discussions, as being just a normal method declaration with the code block replaced by a semicolon and the modifier `native` added. These are the methods you have to implement in C code later.

Finally, there is a somewhat mysterious code fragment at the very end of the class. You might recognize the general construct here as a `static` initializer. Any code between the brackets—{ and }—is executed exactly once, when the class is first loaded into the system. You take advantage of that fact to run something you *want* to run only once—the loading of the native code library you'll create later in this chapter. This ties together the loading of the class itself with the loading of its native code. If either fails for some reason, the other fails as well, guaranteeing that no "half-set-up" version of the class can ever be created.

Generating Header and Stub Files

In order to get your hands on Java objects and data types, and to be able to manipulate them in your C code, you need to include some special .h files. Most of these will be located in your release directory under the subdirectory called include. (In particular, look at native.h in that directory, and all the headers it points to, if you're a glutton for detail punishment.)

Some of the special forms you need must be tailored to fit your class's methods precisely. That's where the `javah` tool comes in.

Using javah

To generate the headers you need for your native methods, first compile SimpleFile with javac, just as you normally would. This produces a file named SimpleFile.class. This file must be fed to the javah tool, which then generates the header file you need (SimpleFile.h).

> **TIP**
>
> If the class handed to javah is inside a package, it prepends the package name to the header filename (and to the structure names it generates inside that file), after replacing all the dots (.) with underscores (_) in the package's full name. If SimpleFile had been contained in a hypothetical package called acme.widgets.files, javah would have generated a header file named acme_widgets_files_SimpleFile.h, and the various names within it would have been renamed in a similar manner.
>
> When running javah, you should pass it only the class name itself, and not the full filename, which has .class on the end.

The Header File

Here's the output of javah SimpleFile:

```
/* DO NOT EDIT THIS FILE - it is machine generated */
#include <native.h>
/* Header for class SimpleFile */

#ifndef _Included_SimpleFile
#define _Included_SimpleFile
struct Hjava_lang_String;

typedef struct ClassSimpleFile {
#define SimpleFile_separatorChar 62L
struct Hjava_lang_String *path;
long fd;
} ClassSimpleFile;
HandleTo(SimpleFile);

extern /*boolean*/ long SimpleFile_open(struct HSimpleFile *);
extern void SimpleFile_close(struct HSimpleFile *);
extern long SimpleFile_read(struct HSimpleFile *,HArrayOfByte *,long);
extern long SimpleFile_write(struct HSimpleFile *,HArrayOfByte *,long);
#endif
```

> **NOTE**
>
> HandleTo() is a "magic" macro that uses the structures created at runtime by the stubs you'll generate later in this chapter.

The members of the `struct` generated above are in a one-to-one correspondence with the variables of your class.

In order to "massage" an instance of your class gently into the land of C, use the macro `unhand()` (as in "unhand that Object!"). For example, the `this` pseudo-variable in Java appears as a `struct HSimpleFile *` in the land of C, and to use any variables inside this instance (you), you must `unhand()` yourself first. You'll see some examples of this in a later section in this chapter.

Using `javah -stubs`

To "run interference" between the Java world of Objects, arrays, and other high-level constructs and the lower-level world of C, you need stubs. (*Stubs* are pieces of "glue" code that automatically translate arguments and return values back and forth between the worlds of Java and C.)

Stubs can be automatically generated by `javah`, just like the headers. There isn't much you need to know about the stubs file, just that it has to be compiled and linked with the C code you write to allow it to interface with Java properly. A stubs file (`SimpleFile.c`) is created by running `javah` on your class by using the option `-stubs`.

> **NOTE**
>
> One interesting side-effect of stub generation is the creation of *method signatures*, informally called method descriptions elsewhere. These signatures are quite useful— they can be passed to special C functions that allow you to call back into the Java world from C. You can use stub generation to learn what these signatures look like for different method arguments and return values, and then use that knowledge to call arbitrary Java methods from within your C code. (Brief descriptions of these special C functions, along with further details, appear later in this chapter.)

The Stubs File

Here's the result of running `javah -stubs SimpleFile`:

```
/* DO NOT EDIT THIS FILE - it is machine generated */
#include <StubPreamble.h>

/* Stubs for class SimpleFile */
/* SYMBOL: "SimpleFile/open()Z", Java_SimpleFile_open_stub */
stack_item *Java_SimpleFile_open_stub(stack_item *_P_,struct execenv *_EE_) {
    extern long SimpleFile_open(void *);
    _P_[0].i = SimpleFile_open(_P_[0].p);
    return _P_ + 1;
}
/* SYMBOL: "SimpleFile/close()V", Java_SimpleFile_close_stub */
stack_item *Java_SimpleFile_close_stub(stack_item *_P_,struct execenv *_EE_) {
    extern void SimpleFile_close(void *);
```

```
      (void) SimpleFile_close(_P_[0].p);
      return _P_;
}
/* SYMBOL: "SimpleFile/read([BI)I", Java_SimpleFile_read_stub */
stack_item *Java_SimpleFile_read_stub(stack_item *_P_,struct execenv *_EE_) {
      extern long SimpleFile_read(void *,void *,long);
      _P_[0].i = SimpleFile_read(_P_[0].p,((_P_[1].p)),((_P_[2].i)));
      return _P_ + 1;
}
/* SYMBOL: "SimpleFile/write([BI)I", Java_SimpleFile_write_stub */
stack_item *Java_SimpleFile_write_stub(stack_item *_P_,struct execenv *_EE_) {
      extern long SimpleFile_write(void *,void *,long);
      _P_[0].i = SimpleFile_write(_P_[0].p,((_P_[1].p)),((_P_[2].i)));
      return _P_ + 1;
}
```

Each comment line contains the method signature for one of the four `native` methods you're implementing. You can use one of these signatures to call into Java and run, for example, a subclass's overriding implementation of one of your `native` methods. More often, you'd learn and use a different signature to call some useful Java method from within C to get something done in the Java world.

You do this by calling a special C function that is part of the Java run-time called `execute_java_dynamic_method()`. Its arguments include the target object of the method call and the method's signature. The general form of a fully qualified method signature is `any/package/name/ClassName/methodName(...)X`. (You can see several in the stub's output's comments, where `SimpleFile` is the class name and there is no package name.) The `X` is a letter (or string) that represents the return type, and the ... contains a string that represents each of the argument's types in turn. (Here are the letters —and strings—used, and the types they represent, in the example: [`T` is array of type `T`, `B` is byte, `I` is int, `V` is void, and `Z` is boolean.)

The method `close()`, which takes no arguments and returns void, is represented by the string `"SimpleFile/close()V"` and its inverse, `open()`, that returns a boolean instead, is represented by `"SimpleFile/open()Z"`. Finally, `read()`, which takes an array of bytes and an int as its two arguments and returns an int, is `"SimpleFile/read([BI)I"`. (See the "Method Signatures" section in the next chapter for the full details.)

Creating `SimpleFileNative.c`

Now you can, at last, write the C code for your Java `native` methods.

The header file generated by `javah`, `SimpleFile.h`, gives you the prototypes of the four C functions you need to implement to make your native code complete. You then write some C code that provides the native facilities that your Java class needs (in this case, some low-level file I/O routines). Finally, you assemble all the C code into a new file, include a bunch of required (or useful) `.h` files, and name it `SimpleFileNative.c`. Here's the result:

```
#include "SimpleFile.h"      /* for unhand(), among other things */
```

```c
#include <sys/param.h>        /* for MAXPATHLEN */
#include <fcntl.h>            /* for O_RDWR and O_CREAT */

#define LOCAL_PATH_SEPARATOR  '/'     /* UNIX */

static void  fixSeparators(char *p) {
    for (;  *p != '\0';  ++p)
        if (*p == SimpleFile_separatorChar)
            *p = LOCAL_PATH_SEPARATOR;
}

long  SimpleFile_open(struct HSimpleFile  *this) {
    int    fd;
    char   buffer[MAXPATHLEN];

    javaString2CString(unhand(this)->path, buffer, sizeof(buffer));
    fixSeparators(buffer);
    if ((fd = open(buffer, O_RDWR | O_CREAT, 0664)) < 0)      /* UNIX open */
        return(FALSE);  /* or, SignalError() could "throw" an exception */
    unhand(this)->fd = fd;          /* save fd in the Java world */
    return(TRUE);
}

void  SimpleFile_close(struct HSimpleFile  *this) {
    close(unhand(this)->fd);
    unhand(this)->fd = -1;
}

long  SimpleFile_read(struct HSimpleFile  *this, HArrayOfByte  *buffer,
                                                    ➥ long  count) {
    char  *data    = unhand(buffer)->body; /* get array data   */
    int    len     = obj_length(buffer);   /* get array length */
    int    numBytes = (len < count ? len : count);

    if ((numBytes = read(unhand(this)->fd, data, numBytes)) == 0)
        return(-1);
    return(numBytes);         /* the number of bytes actually read */
}

long  SimpleFile_write(struct HSimpleFile  *this, HArrayOfByte  *buffer,
                                                    ➥ long  count) {
    char  *data = unhand(buffer)->body;
    int    len  = obj_length(buffer);

    return(write(unhand(this)->fd, data, (len < count ? len : count)));
}
```

Once you finish writing your .c file, compile it by using your local C compiler (usually called cc or gcc). On some systems, you may need to specify special compilation flags that mean "make it relocatable and dynamically linkable."

NOTE

If you don't have a C compiler on your computer, you can always buy one. You also could get a copy of the GNU C compiler (gcc), one of the best C compilers in the world, which runs on almost every machine and operating system on the planet. The best way to get gcc is to buy the "GNU release" on CD-ROM, the profits of which go to support the Free Software Foundation. You can find both the GNU CD-ROM and the Linux CD-ROM (which includes GNU) in select places that sell software or technical books, or you can contact the F.S.F. directly. The GNU CD-ROM is a bit pricey, and, though the Linux CD-ROM is very inexpensive, if you can't afford either, or want the latest version and already own a CD-ROM, you can download the gzip file `ftp://prep.ai.mit.edu/pub/gnu/gcc-2.7.2.tar.gz`, which contains all 7M of the latest gcc release. (If you'd like to make a donation to, or buy gcc or its manual from, the F.S.F., you can e-mail them at `gnu@prep.ai.mit.edu` or call 617-542-5942.)

Some Useful Functions

When writing the C code for native implementations, a whole set of useful (internal) macros and functions is available for accessing Java run-time structures. (Several of them were used in `SimpleFileNative.c`.)

Let's take a brief digression to understand some of them a little better.

WARNING

Don't rely on the exact form given for any of the following macros and functions. Because they're all internal to the Java run-time, they're subject to change at any moment. Check to see what the latest versions of them look like in your Java release before using them.

NOTE

The following brief descriptions are taken from an alpha release of Java, because descriptions of them for the 1.0 release were not available as of this writing. How Java data types map into C types, and vice versa, will be detailed in future documentation. Refer to it for more details on that or on any of the sparsely documented items below. (Many are listed just to give you a taste of the capabilities of the available functions.)

The following

```
Object   *unhand(Handle *)
int      obj_length(HArray *)
```

returns a pointer to the data portion of an object and returns the length of an array. The actual pointer type returned is not always Object *, but varies, depending on the type of Handle (or HArray).

While the following:

```
ClassClass    *FindClass(struct execenv  *e, char  *name, bool_t  resolve)
HArrayOfChar  *MakeString(char  *string, long  length)
Handle        *ArrayAlloc(int  type, int  length)
```

finds a class (given its name), makes an array of characters of length length, and allocates an array of the length and type.

Use the function:

```
long  execute_java_dynamic_method(ExecEnv *e, HObject *obj, char *method_name,
                                  ➥char *signature, ...);
```

to call a Java method from C. e is NULL to use the current environment. The target of the method call is obj. The method method_name has the given method signature. It can have any number of arguments and returns a 32-bit value (int, Handle *, or any 32-bit C type).

Use the following:

```
HObject  *execute_java_constructor(ExecEnv *e, char *classname, ClassClass *c,
                                   ➥char *signature, ...);

long  execute_java_static_method(ExecEnv *e, ClassClass *c, char *method_name,
                                 ➥char *signature, ...);
```

to call a Java constructor from C and call a class method from C. c is the target class; the rest are as in execute_java_dynamic_method().

Calling this:

```
SignalError(0, JAVAPKG "ExceptionClassName", "message");
```

posts a Java exception that will be thrown when your native method returns. It is somewhat like the Java code:

```
throw new ExceptionClassName("message");
```

Finally, here are some useful string functions:

```
void  javaStringPrint(Hjava_lang_String *s)
int   javaStringLength(Hjava_lang_String *s)

Hjava_lang_String *makeJavaString(char  *string, int  length)

char  *makeCString(Hjava_lang_String *s)
char  *allocCString(Hjava_lang_String *s)

unicode  *javaString2unicode(Hjava_lang_String *s, unicode  *buf, int  len)
char     *javaString2CString(Hjava_lang_String *s, char     *buf, int  len)
```

The first two methods print a Java String (like System.out.print()), and get its length, respectively. The third makes a Java String out of a C string. The fourth and fifth do the reverse, turning a Java String into a C string (allocated from temporary or heap storage, respectively). The final two methods copy Java Strings into preexisting Unicode or ASCII C buffers.

Compiling the Stubs File

The final step you need to take in the C world is to compile the stubs file SimpleFile.c by using the same compilation flags you used for SimpleFileNative.c.

> **NOTE**
>
> If you have several classes with native methods, you can include all their stubs in the same .c file, if you like. Of course you might want to name it something else, such as Stubs.c, in that case.

You're now finished with all the C code that must be written (and compiled) to make your loadable native library.

A Native Library

Now you'll finally be able to tie everything together and create the native library, simple, that was assumed to exist at the beginning of this chapter.

Linking It All

It's time to link everything you've done into a single library file. This looks a little different on each system that Java runs on, but here's the basic idea, in UNIX syntax:

```
cc -G SimpleFile.o SimpleFileNative.o -o simple
```

The -G flag tells the linker that you're creating a dynamically linkable library; the details differ from system to system.

> **NOTE**
>
> By naming the library simple, you're disobeying a UNIX convention that dynamic library names should have the prefix lib and the suffix .so (on your system, these prefixes and suffixes may differ). You can call your library libsimple.so to obey the convention, if you like, but just for the clarity of this example, the simpler name was used.

Using Your Library

Now, when the Java class SimpleFile is first loaded into your program, the System class attempts to load the library named simple, which (luckily) you just created. Look back at the Java code for SimpleFile to remind yourself.

How does it locate it? It calls the dynamic linker, which consults an environment variable named LD_LIBRARY_PATH that tells it which sequence of directories to search when loading new libraries of native code. Because the current directory is in Java's load path by default, you can leave "simple" in the current directory, and it will work just fine.

Summary

This chapter discussed the numerous disadvantages of using native methods, about the many ways that Java (and you) can make your programs run faster, and also about the often illusory need for efficiency.

It detailed the procedure for creating native methods, from both the Java and the C sides, in detail—by generating header files and stubs, and by compiling and linking a full example.

After working your way through this difficult material, you've mastered one of the most complex parts of the Java language. You now know how the Java run-time environment itself was created, and how to extend that powerful environment yourself, at its lowest levels.

Java's Virtual Machine, Bytecodes, and More

39

by Charles L. Perkins

This chapter reveals the inner workings of Java. You'll find out all about Java's vision, Java's virtual machine, those bytecodes you've heard so much about, that mysterious garbage collector, and why you might worry about security but don't have to.

Let's begin, however, with the big picture.

The Big Picture

The Java team is very ambitious. Their ultimate goal is nothing less than to revolutionize the way software is written and distributed. They've started with the Internet, where they believe much of the interesting software of the future will live.

To achieve such an ambitious goal, a large fraction of the Internet programming community itself must be marshaled behind a similar goal and given the tools to help achieve it. The Java language, with its four S's (small, simple, safe, secure), and its flexible, Net-oriented environment, hopes to become the focal point for the rallying of this new legion of programmers.

To this end, Sun Microsystems has done something rather gutsy. What was originally a secret, tens-of-millions-of-dollars research and development project, and 100 percent proprietary, has become a free, open, and relatively unencumbered technology standard upon which anyone can build. They are literally *giving it away* and reserving only the rights they need to maintain and grow the standard.

> **NOTE**
>
> Actually, as Sun's lawyers have had more and more time to think, the original intentions of the Java team get further obscured by legal details. It is still *relatively* unencumbered, but its earlier releases were completely unencumbered. Let's hope that this is not a pattern that will continue.

Any truly open standard must be supported by at least one excellent, freely available "demonstration" implementation. Sun has already shipped the final release of the API. In parallel, several universities, companies, and individuals have already expressed their intention to duplicate the Java environment, based on the open API that Sun has created.

Several other languages are even contemplating compiling down to Java bytecodes, to help support them in becoming a more robust and widespread standard for moving executable content around on the Net.

Why It's a Powerful Vision

One of the reasons this brilliant move on Sun's part has a real chance of success is the pent-up frustration of literally a whole generation of programmers who desperately want to share their code with one another. Right now, the computer science world is balkanized into factions at universities and companies all over the world, with hundreds of languages, dozens of them widely used, dividing and separating us all. It's the worst sort of Tower of Babel. Java hopes to build some bridges and help tear down that tower. Because it is so simple, because it's so useful for programming over the Internet, and because the Internet is so "hot" right now, this confluence of forces should help propel Java onto center stage.

It deserves to be there. It is the natural outgrowth of ideas that, since the early 1970s inside the Smalltalk group at Xerox PARC, have lain relatively dormant in the mainstream. Smalltalk, in fact, invented the first object-oriented bytecode interpreter and pioneered many of the deep ideas that Java builds on today. Those efforts were not embraced over the intervening decades as a solution to the general problems of software, however. Today, with those problems becoming so much more obvious, and with the Net crying out for a new kind of programming, the soil is fertile to grow something stronger from those old roots, something that just might spread like wildfire. (Is it a coincidence that Java's previous internal names were Green and OAK?)

This new vision of software is one in which the Net becomes an ocean of objects, classes, and the open APIs between them. Traditional applications have vanished, replaced by skeletal frameworks like the Eiffel Tower, into which can be fitted any parts from this ocean, on demand, to suit any purpose. User interfaces will be mixed and matched, built in pieces, and constructed to taste—whenever the need arises—*by their own users*. Menus of choices will be filled by dynamic lists of *all* the choices available for that function, at that exact moment, across the entire ocean (of the Net).

In such a world, software distribution is no longer an issue. Software will be *everywhere* and will be paid for through a plethora of new micro-accounting models, which charge tiny fractions of cents for the parts as they are assembled and used. Frameworks will come into existence to support entertainment, business, and the social (cyber-)spaces of the near future.

This is a dream that many of us have waited *all our lives* to be a part of. There are tremendous challenges to making it all come true, but the powerful winds of change we all feel must stir us into action, because, at last, there is a base on which to build that dream—Java.

The Java Virtual Machine

To make visions like this possible, Java must be ubiquitous. It must be able to run on any computer and any operating system—now, and in the future. In order to achieve this level of portability, Java must be very precise not only about the language itself, but about the environment in which the language lives. You can see, from earlier in the book and Appendix B, that the Java environment includes a generally useful set of packages of classes and a freely available implementation of them. This takes care of a part of what is needed, but it is crucial also to specify exactly how the run-time environment of Java behaves.

This final requirement is what has stymied many attempts at ubiquity in the past. If you base your system on any assumptions about what is "beneath" the run-time system, you lose. If you depend in any way on the computer or operating system below, you lose. Java solves this problem by *inventing* an abstract computer of its own and running on that.

This "virtual" machine runs a special set of "instructions" called bytecodes that are simply a stream of formatted bytes, each of which has a precise specification of exactly what each bytecode does to this virtual machine. The virtual machine is also responsible for certain fundamental capabilities of Java, such as object creation and garbage collection.

Finally, in order to be able to move bytecodes safely across the Internet, you need a bulletproof model of security—and how to maintain it—and a precise format for how this stream of bytecodes can be sent from one virtual machine to another. (For more on security issues, see Chapter 40, "Java Security.")

Each of these requirements is addressed in this chapter.

> **NOTE**
>
> This discussion blurs the distinction between the run-time and the virtual machine of Java. This is intentional but a little unconventional. Think of the virtual machine as providing *all* the capabilities, even those that are conventionally assigned to the run-time. This book uses the words "run-time" and "virtual machine" interchangeably. Equating the two highlights the single *environment* that must be created to support Java.
>
> Much of the following description is based closely on the latest "Virtual Machine Specifications" documents (and the 1.0 bytecodes, which had just emerged as of this writing), so if you delve more deeply into the details online, you should cover some familiar ground.

An Overview

It is worth quoting the introduction to the Java virtual machine documentation here, because it is so relevant to the vision outlined earlier:

> The Java virtual machine specification has a purpose that is both like and unlike equivalent documents for other languages and abstract machines. It is intended to present an abstract, logical machine design free from the distraction of inconsequential details of any implementation. It does not anticipate an implementation technology, or an implementation host. At the same time it gives a reader sufficient information to allow implementation of the abstract design in a range of technologies.

However, the intent of the … Java project is to create a language … that will allow the interchange over the Internet of "executable content," which will be embodied by compiled Java code. The project specifically does not want Java to be a proprietary language, and does not want to be the sole purveyor of Java language implementations. Rather, we hope to make documents like this one, and source code for our implementation, freely available for people to use as they choose.

This vision … can be achieved only if the executable content can be reliably shared between different Java implementations. These intentions prohibit the definition of the Java virtual machine from being fully abstract. Rather, relevant logical elements of the design have to be made sufficiently concrete to allow the interchange of compiled Java code. This does not collapse the Java virtual machine specification to a description of a Java implementation; elements of the design that do not play a part in the interchange of executable content remain abstract. But it does force us to specify, in addition to the abstract machine design, a concrete interchange format for compiled Java code.

The Java virtual machine specification consists of the following:

- The bytecode syntax, including opcode and operand sizes, values, and types, and their alignment and endian-ness
- The values of any identifiers (for example, type identifiers) in bytecodes or in supporting structures
- The layout of the supporting structures that appear in compiled Java code (for example, the constant pool)
- The Java `.class` file format

Each of these is covered in this chapter.

Despite this degree of specificity, there are still several elements of the design that remain (purposely) abstract, including the following:

- The layout and management of the run-time data areas
- The particular garbage-collection algorithms, strategies, and constraints used
- The compiler, development environment, and run-time extensions (apart from the need to generate and read valid Java bytecodes)
- Any optimizations performed, once valid bytecodes are received

These places are where the creativity of a virtual machine implementor has full rein.

The Fundamental Parts

The Java virtual machine can be divided into five fundamental pieces:

- A bytecode instruction set
- A set of registers
- A stack
- A garbage-collected heap
- An area for storing methods

Some of these might be implemented by using an interpreter, a native binary code compiler, or even a hardware chip—but all these logical, abstract components of the virtual machine must be supplied in *some* form in every Java system.

> **NOTE**
>
> The memory areas used by the Java virtual machine are not required to be at any particular place in memory, to be in any particular order, or even to use contiguous memory. However, all but the method area must be able to represent align 32-bit values (for example, the Java stack is 32 bits wide).

The virtual machine, and its supporting code, is often referred to as the run-time environment, and when this book refers to something being done at run-time, the virtual machine is what's doing it.

Java Bytecodes

The Java virtual machine instruction set is optimized to be small and compact. It is designed to travel across the Net, and so has traded off speed-of-interpretation for space. (Given that both Net bandwidth and mass storage speeds increase less rapidly than CPU speed, this seems like an appropriate trade-off.)

As mentioned, Java source code is "compiled" into bytecodes and stored in a `.class` file. On Sun's Java system, this is performed using the `javac` tool. It is not exactly a traditional "compiler," because `javac` translates source code into bytecodes, a lower-level format that cannot be run directly, but must be further interpreted by each computer. Of course, it is exactly this level of "indirection" that buys you the power, flexibility, and extreme portability of Java code.

> **NOTE**
>
> Quotation marks are used around the word "compiler" when talking about `javac` because later in this chapter you will also learn about the "just-in-time" compiler,

which acts more like the back end of a traditional compiler. The use of the same word "compiler" for these two different pieces of Java technology is unfortunate, but somewhat reasonable, because each is really one-half (either the front or the back end) of a more traditional compiler.

A bytecode instruction consists of a one-byte opcode that serves to identify the instruction involved and zero or more operands, each of which may be more than one byte long, that encode the parameters the opcode requires.

> **NOTE**
>
> When operands are more than one byte long, they are stored in big-endian order, high-order byte first. These operands must be assembled from the byte stream at run-time. For example, a 16-bit parameter appears in the stream as two bytes so that its value is `first_byte * 256 + second_byte`. The bytecode instruction stream is only byte-aligned, and alignment of any larger quantities is not guaranteed (except for "within" the special bytecodes `lookupswitch` and `tableswitch`, which have special alignment rules of their own).

Bytecodes interpret data in the run-time memory areas as belonging to a fixed set of types: the primitives types you've seen several times before, consisting of several signed integer types (8-bit `byte`, 16-bit `short`, 32-bit `int`, 64-bit `long`), one unsigned integer type (16-bit `char`), and two signed floating-point types (32-bit `float`, 64-bit `double`), plus the type "reference to an object" (a 32-bit pointer-like type). Some special bytecodes (for example, the `dup` instructions), treat run-time memory areas as raw data, without regard to type. This is the exception, however, not the rule.

These primitives types are distinguished and managed by the compiler, `javac`, not by the Java run-time environment. These types are not "tagged" in memory, and thus cannot be distinguished at run-time. Different bytecodes are designed to handle each of the various primitive types uniquely, and the compiler carefully chooses from this palette based on its knowledge of the actual types stored in the various memory areas. For example, when adding two integers, the compiler generates an `iadd` bytecode; for adding two floats, `fadd` is generated. (You'll see all this in gruesome detail later.)

Registers

The registers of the Java virtual machine are just like the registers inside a "real" computer.

> **NOTE**
>
> *Registers* hold the machine's state, affect its operation, and are updated after each byte-code is executed.

The following are the Java registers:

- ■ pc, the program counter, which indicates what bytecode is being executed
- ■ optop, a pointer to the top of the operand stack, which is used to evaluate all arithmetic expressions
- ■ frame, a pointer to the execution environment of the current method, which includes an activation record for this method call and any associated debugging information
- ■ vars, a pointer to the first local variable of the currently executing method

The virtual machine defines these registers to be 32 bits wide.

> **NOTE**
>
> Because the virtual machine is primarily stack-based, it does not use any registers for passing or receiving arguments. This is a conscious choice skewed toward bytecode simplicity and compactness. It also aids efficient implementation on register-poor architectures, which most of today's computers, unfortunately, are. Perhaps when the majority of CPUs out there are a little more sophisticated, this choice will be reexamined, though simplicity and compactness may still be reason enough!
>
> By the way, the pc register is also used when the run-time handles exceptions; catch clauses are (ultimately) associated with ranges of the pc within a method's bytecodes.

The Stack

The Java virtual machine is stack-based. A Java stack frame is similar to the stack frame of a conventional programming language—it holds the state for a single method call. Frames for nested method calls are stacked on top of this frame.

> **NOTE**
>
> The *stack* is used to supply parameters to bytecodes and methods, and to receive results back from them.

Each stack frame contains three (possibly empty) sets of data: the local variables for the method call, its execution environment, and its operand stack. The sizes of these first two are fixed at the start of a method call, but the operand stack varies in size as bytecodes are executed in the method.

Local variables are stored in an array of 32-bit slots, indexed by the register vars. Most types take up one slot in the array, but the long and double types each take up two slots.

> **NOTE**
>
> long and double values, stored or referenced through an index N, take up the (32-bit) slots N and N + 1. These 64-bit values are thus not guaranteed to be 64-bit-aligned. Implementors are free to decide the appropriate way to divide these values among the two slots.

The execution environment in a stack frame helps to maintain the stack itself. It contains a pointer to the previous stack frame, a pointer to the local variables of the method call, and pointers to the stack's current "base" and "top." Additional debugging information can also be placed into the execution environment.

The operand stack, a 32-bit first-in-first-out (FIFO) stack, is used to store the parameters and return values of most bytecode instructions. For example, the iadd bytecode expects two integers to be stored on the top of the stack. It pops them, adds them together, and pushes the resulting sum back onto the stack.

Each primitive data type has unique instructions that know how to extract, operate, and push back operands of that type. For example, long and double operands take two "slots" on the stack, and the special bytecodes that handle these operands take this into account. It is illegal for the types on the stack and the instruction operating on them to be incompatible (javac outputs bytecodes that always obey this rule).

> **NOTE**
>
> The top of the operand stack and the top of the overall Java stack are almost always the same. Thus, "the stack," refers to both stacks, collectively.

The Heap

The heap is that part of memory from which newly created instances (objects) are allocated.

The heap is often assigned a large, fixed size when the Java run-time system is started, but on systems that support virtual memory, it can grow as needed, in a nearly unbounded fashion.

Because objects are automatically garbage-collected in Java, programmers do not have to (and, in fact, *cannot*) manually free the memory allocated to an object when they are finished using it.

Java objects are referenced indirectly in the run-time, via handles, which are a kind of pointer into the heap.

Because objects are never referenced directly, parallel garbage collectors can be written that operate independently of your program, moving around objects in the heap at will. You'll learn more about garbage collection later.

The Method Area

Like the compiled code areas of conventional programming language environments, or the TEXT segment in a UNIX process, the method area stores the Java bytecodes that implement almost every method in the Java system. (Remember that some methods might be `native`, and thus implemented, for example, in C.) The method area also stores the symbol tables needed for dynamic linking, and any other additional information debuggers or development environments might want to associate with each method's implementation.

Because bytecodes are stored as byte streams, the method area is aligned on byte boundaries. (The other areas are all aligned on 32-bit word boundaries.)

The Constant Pool

In the heap, each class has a constant pool "attached" to it. Usually created by `javac`, these constants encode all the names (of variables, methods, and so forth) used by any method in a class. The class contains a count of how many constants there are and an offset that specifies how far into the class description itself the array of constants begins. These constants are typed through specially coded bytes, and have a precisely defined format when they appear in the `.class` file for a class. Later in this chapter, a little of this file format is covered, but everything is fully specified by the virtual machine specifications in your Java release.

Limitations

The virtual machine, as currently defined, places some restrictions on legal Java programs by virtue of the choices it has made (some were previously described, and more will be detailed later in this chapter).

These limitations and their implications are

- 32-bit pointers, which imply that the virtual machine can address only 4GB of memory (this may be relaxed in later releases)

- Unsigned 16-bit indices into the exception, line number, and local variable tables, which limit the size of a method's bytecode implementation to 64K (this limitation may be eliminated in the final release)
- Unsigned 16-bit indices into the constant pool, which limits the number of constants in a class to 64K (a limit on the complexity of a class)

Bytecodes in More Detail

One of the main tasks of the virtual machine is the fast, efficient execution of the Java bytecodes in methods. Unlike in a discussion about generality versus efficiency, this is a case where speed is of the utmost importance. Every Java program suffers from a slow implementation here, so the run-time must use as many "tricks" as possible to make bytecodes run fast. The only other goal (or limitation) is that Java programmers must not be able to see these tricks in the behavior of their programs.

A Java run-time implementer must be extremely clever to satisfy both these goals.

The Bytecode Interpreter

A bytecode interpreter examines each opcode byte (bytecode) in a method's bytecode stream, in turn, and executes a unique action for that bytecode. This might consume further bytes for the operands of the bytecode and might affect which bytecode will be examined next. It operates like the hardware CPU in a computer, which examines memory for instructions to carry out in exactly the same manner. It is the software CPU of the Java virtual machine.

Your first, naive attempt to write such a bytecode interpreter will almost certainly be disastrously slow. The inner loop, which dispatches one bytecode each time through the loop, is notoriously difficult to optimize. In fact, smart people have been thinking about this problem, in one form or another, for more than 20 years. Luckily, they've gotten results, all of which can be applied to Java.

The final result is that the interpreter shipped in the current release of Java has an extremely fast inner loop. In fact, on even a relatively slow computer, this interpreter can perform more than 590,000 bytecodes per second! This is really quite good, because the CPU in that computer does only about 30 times better using *hardware*.

This interpreter is fast enough for most Java programs (and for those *requiring* more speed, they can always use `native` methods), but what if a smart implementor wants to do better?

The "Just-in-Time" Compiler

About a decade ago, a really clever trick was discovered by L. Peter Deutsch while trying to make Smalltalk run faster. He called it "dynamic translation" during interpretation. Sun calls it "just-in-time" compiling.

The trick is to notice that the really fast interpreter you've just written—in C, for example—already has a useful sequence of native binary code for each bytecode that it interprets: *the binary code that the interpreter itself is executing.* Because the interpreter has already been compiled from C into native binary code, for each bytecode that it interprets, it passes through a sequence of native code instructions for the hardware CPU on which it is running. By saving a copy of each binary instruction as it "goes by," the interpreter can keep a running log of the binary code it *itself* has run to interpret a bytecode. It can just as easily keep a log of the set of bytecodes that it ran to interpret an entire method.

You take that log of instructions and "peephole-optimize" it, just as a smart compiler does. This eliminates redundant or unnecessary instructions from the log, and makes it look just like the optimized binary code that a good compiler might have produced.

> **NOTE**
>
> This is where the name compiler comes from, in "just-in-time" compiler, but it's really only the back end of a traditional compiler—the part that does code generation. By the way, the front end here is `javac`.

Here's where the trick comes in. The next time that method is run (in exactly the same way), the interpreter can now simply execute directly the stored log of binary native code. Because this optimizes out the inner-loop overhead of each bytecode, as well as any other redundancies between the bytecodes in a method, it can gain a factor of 10 or more in speed. In fact, an experimental version of this technology at Sun has shown that Java programs using it can run as fast as compiled C programs.

> **NOTE**
>
> The parenthetical in the last paragraph is needed because if anything is different about the input to the method, it takes a different path through the interpreter and must be relogged. (There are sophisticated versions of this technology that solve this, and other, difficulties.) The cache of native code for a method must be invalidated whenever the method has changed, and the interpreter must pay a small cost up front each time a method is run for the first time. However, these small bookkeeping costs are far outweighed by the amazing gains in speed possible.

The `java2c` Translator

Another, simpler, trick, which works well whenever you have a good, portable C compiler on each system that runs your program, is to translate the bytecodes into C and then compile the

C into binary native code. If you wait until the first use of a method or class, and then perform this as an "invisible" optimization, it gains you an additional speedup over the approach outlined previously, without the Java programmer needing to know about it.

Of course, this does limit you to systems with a C compiler, but there are extremely good, freely available C compilers. In theory, your Java code might be able to travel with its own C compiler, or know where to pull one from the Net as needed, for each new computer and operating system it faced. (Because this violates some of the rules of normal Java code movement over the Net, though, it should be used sparingly.)

If you're using Java, for example, to write a server that lives only on *your* computer, it might be appropriate to use Java for its flexibility in writing and maintaining the server (and for its capability of dynamically linking new Java code on the fly), and then to run `java2c` by hand to translate the basic server itself entirely into native code. You'd link the Java run-time environment into that code so that your server remains a fully capable Java program, but it's now an extremely fast one.

In fact, an experimental version of the `java2c` translator inside Sun shows that it can reach the speed of compiled and optimized C code. This is the best that you can hope to do!

> **NOTE**
>
> Unfortunately, as of the 1.0 release, there is still no publicly available `java2c` tool, and Sun's virtual machine does not perform "just-in-time" compilation. Both of these have been promised in a later release (perhaps 1.1).

The Bytecodes Themselves

Let's look at a (progressively less and less) detailed description of each class of bytecodes.

For each bytecode, some brief text describes its function, and a textual "picture" of the stack, both before and after the bytecode has been executed, is shown. This text picture will look like the following:

```
..., value1, value2 => ..., value3
```

This means that the bytecode expects two operands—`value1` and `value2`—to be on the top of the stack, pops them both off the stack, operates on them to produce `value3`, and pushes `value3` back onto the top of the stack. You should read each stack from right to left, with the rightmost value being the top of the stack. The ... is read as "the rest of the stack below," which is irrelevant to the current bytecode. All operands on the stack are 32-bits wide.

Because most bytecodes take their arguments from the stack and place their results back there, the brief text descriptions that follow only say something about the source or destination of values if they are *not* on the stack. For example, the description "`Load integer from local variable.`" means that the integer is loaded onto the stack, and "`Integer add.`" intends its integers to be taken from—and the result returned to—the stack.

Bytecodes that don't affect control flow simply move the pc onto the next bytecode that follows in sequence. Those that do affect the pc say so explicitly. Whenever you see byte1, byte2, and so forth, it refers to the first byte, second byte, and so on, that follow the opcode byte itself. After such a bytecode is executed, the pc automatically advances over these operand bytes to start the next bytecode in sequence.

> **NOTE**
>
> The next few sections are in "reference manual style," presenting each bytecode separately in all its (often redundant) detail. Later sections begin to collapse and coalesce this verbose style into something shorter, and more readable. The verbose form is shown at first because the online reference manuals will look more like it, and because it drives home the point that each bytecode "function" comes in many nearly identical bytecodes, one for each primitive type in Java.

Pushing Constants onto the Stack

```
bipush          ... => ..., value
```

Push one-byte signed integer. byte1 is interpreted as a signed 8-bit value. This value is expanded to an int and pushed onto the operand stack.

```
sipush          ... => ..., value
```

Push two-byte signed integer. byte1 and byte2 are assembled into a signed 16-bit value. This value is expanded to an int and pushed onto the operand stack.

```
ldc1            ... => ..., item
```

Push item from constant pool. byte1 is used as an unsigned 8-bit index into the constant pool of the current class. The item at that index is resolved and pushed onto the stack.

```
ldc2            ... => ..., item
```

Push item from constant pool. byte1 and byte2 are used to construct an unsigned 16-bit index into the constant pool of the current class. The item at that index is resolved and pushed onto the stack.

```
ldc2w           ... => ..., constant-word1, constant-word2
```

Push long or double from constant pool. byte1 and byte2 are used to construct an unsigned 16-bit index into the constant pool of the current class. The two-word constant at that index is resolved and pushed onto the stack.

```
aconst_null    ... => ..., null
```

Push the `null` object reference onto the stack.

```
iconst_m1      ... => ..., -1
```

Push the `int` `-1` onto the stack.

```
iconst_<I>     ... => ..., <I>
```

Push the `int` `<I>` onto the stack. There are six of these bytecodes, one for each of the integers 0-5: `iconst_0`, `iconst_1`, `iconst_2`, `iconst_3`, `iconst_4`, and `iconst_5`.

```
lconst_<L>     ... => ..., <L>-word1, <L>-word2
```

Push the `long` `<L>` onto the stack. There are two of these bytecodes, one for each of the integers 0 and 1: `lconst_0`, and `lconst_1`.

```
fconst_<F>     ... => ..., <F>
```

Push the `float` `<F>` onto the stack. There are three of these bytecodes, one for each of the integers 0-2: `fconst_0`, `fconst_1`, and `fconst_2`.

```
dconst_<D>     ... => ..., <D>-word1, <D>-word2
```

Push the `double` `<D>` onto the stack. There are two of these bytecodes, one for each of the integers 0 and 1: `dconst_0`, and `dconst_1`.

Loading Local Variables onto the Stack

```
iload          ... => ..., value
```

Load `int` from local variable. Local variable `byte1` in the current Java frame must contain an `int`. The value of that variable is pushed onto the operand stack.

```
iload_<I>      ... => ..., value
```

Load `int` from local variable. Local variable `<I>` in the current Java frame must contain an `int`. The `value` of that variable is pushed onto the operand stack. There are four of these bytecodes, one for each of the integers 0-3: `iload_0`, `iload_1`, `iload_2`, and `iload_3`.

```
lload          ... => ..., value-word1, value-word2
```

Load `long` from local variable. Local variables `byte1` and `byte1` + 1 in the current Java frame must together contain a long integer. The values contained in those variables are pushed onto the operand stack.

```
lload_<L>      ... => ..., value-word1, value-word2
```

Load `long` from local variable. Local variables `<L>` and `<L>` + 1 in the current Java frame must together contain a long integer. The value contained in those variables is pushed onto the operand stack. There are four of these bytecodes, one for each of the integers 0-3: `lload_0`, `lload_1`, `lload_2`, and `lload_3`.

```
fload          ... => ..., value
```

Load `float` from local variable. Local variable `byte1` in the current Java frame must contain a single precision floating-point number. The `value` of that variable is pushed onto the operand stack.

```
fload_<F>      ... => ..., value
```

Load `float` from local variable. Local variable `<F>` in the current Java frame must contain a single precision floating-point number. The `value` of that variable is pushed onto the operand stack. There are four of these bytecodes, one for each of the integers 0-3: `fload_0`, `fload_1`, `fload_2`, and `fload_3`.

```
dload          ... => ..., value-word1, value-word2
```

Load `double` from local variable. Local variables `byte1` and `byte1` + 1 in the current Java frame must together contain a double precision floating-point number. The value contained in those variables is pushed onto the operand stack.

```
dload_<D>      ... => ..., value-word1, value-word2
```

Load `double` from local variable. Local variables `<D>` and `<D>` + 1 in the current Java frame must together contain a double precision floating-point number. The value contained in those variables is pushed onto the operand stack. There are four of these bytecodes, one for each of the integers 0-3: `dload_0`, `dload1`, `dload_2`, and `dload_3`.

```
aload          ... => ..., value
```

Load object reference from local variable. Local variable `byte1` in the current Java frame must contain a return address or reference to an object. The `value` of that variable is pushed onto the operand stack.

```
aload_<A>      ... => ..., value
```

Load object reference from local variable. Local variable `<A>` in the current Java frame must contain a return address or reference to an object. The `value` of that variable is pushed onto the operand stack. There are four of these bytecodes, one for each of the integers 0-3: `aload_0`, `aload_1`, `aload_2`, and `aload_3`.

Storing Stack Values into Local Variables

```
istore         ..., value => ...
```

Store `int` into local variable. `value` must be an `int`. Local variable `byte1` in the current Java frame is set to `value`.

```
istore_<I>      ..., value => ...
```

Store int into local variable. value must be an int. Local variable <I> in the current Java frame is set to value. There are four of these bytecodes, one for each of the integers 0-3: istore_0, istore_1, istore_2, and istore_3.

```
lstore          ..., value-word1, value-word2 => ...
```

Store long into local variable. value must be a long integer. Local variables byte1 and byte1 + 1 in the current Java frame are set to value.

```
lstore_<L>      ..., value-word1, value-word2 => ...
```

Store long into local variable. value must be a long integer. Local variables <L> and <L> + 1 in the current Java frame are set to value. There are four of these bytecodes, one for each of the integers 0-3: lstore_0, lstore_1, lstore_2, and lstore_3.

```
fstore          ..., value => ...
```

Store float into local variable. value must be a single precision floating-point number. Local variable byte1 in the current Java frame is set to value.

```
fstore_<F>      ..., value => ...
```

Store float into local variable. value must be a single precision floating-point number. Local variable <F> in the current Java frame is set to value. There are four of these bytecodes, one for each of the integers 0-3: fstore_0, fstore_1, fstore_2, and fstore_3.

```
dstore          ..., value-word1, value-word2 => ...
```

Store double into local variable. value must be a double precision floating-point number. Local variables byte1 and byte1 + 1 in the current Java frame are set to value.

```
dstore_<D>      ..., value-word1, value-word2 => ...
```

Store double into local variable. value must be a double precision floating-point number. Local variables <D> and <D> + 1 in the current Java frame are set to value. There are four of these bytecodes, one for each of the integers 0-3: dstore_0, dstore_1, dstore_2, and dstore_3.

```
astore          ..., handle => ...
```

Store object reference into local variable. handle must be a return address or a reference to an object. Local variable byte1 in the current Java frame is set to value.

```
astore_<A>      ..., handle => ...
```

Store object reference into local variable. handle must be a return address or a reference to an object. Local variable <A> in the current Java frame is set to value. There are four of these bytecodes, one for each of the integers 0-3: astore_0, astore_1, astore_2, and astore_3.

```
iinc            -no change-
```

Increment local variable by constant. Local variable byte1 in the current Java frame must contain an int. Its value is incremented by the value byte2, where byte2 is treated as a signed 8-bit quantity.

```
Wide            -no change-
```

Precedes iload, lload, fload, dload, aload, istore, lstore, fstore, dstore, astore, or iinc. byte1 and byte 2 of the following bytecode form an unsigned 16-bit index that replaces the 8-bit index of the bytecode following.

Managing Arrays

```
newarray        ..., size => result
```

Allocate new array. size must be an int. It represents the number of elements in the new array. byte1 is an internal code that indicates the type of array to allocate. Possible values for byte1 are as follows: T_BOOLEAN (4), T_CHAR (5), T_FLOAT (6), T_DOUBLE (7), T_BYTE (8), T_SHORT (9), T_INT (10), and T_LONG (11).

An attempt is made to allocate a new array of the indicated type, capable of holding size elements. This will be the result. If size is less than zero, a NegativeArraySizeException is thrown. If there is not enough memory to allocate the array, an OutOfMemoryError is thrown. All elements of the array are initialized to their default values.

```
anewarray       ..., size => result
```

Allocate new array of objects. size must be an int. It represents the number of elements in the new array. byte1 and byte2 are used to construct an index into the constant pool of the current class. The item at that index is resolved. The resulting entry must be a class.

An attempt is made to allocate a new array of the indicated class type, capable of holding size elements. This will be the result. If size is less than zero, a NegativeArraySizeException is thrown. If there is not enough memory to allocate the array, an OutOfMemoryError is thrown. All elements of the array are initialized to null.

> **NOTE**
>
> anewarray is used to create a single dimension of an array of objects. For example, the request new Thread[7] generates the following bytecodes:
> ```
> bipush 7
> anewarray <Class "java.lang.Thread">
> ```
> anewarray can also be used to create the outermost dimension of a multidimensional array. For example, the array declaration new int[6][] generates this:

```
bipush 6
anewarray <Class "[I">
```
(See the section "Method Signatures" for more information on strings such as [I.)

`multianewarray` `..., size1 size2...sizeN => result`

Allocate new multidimensional array. Each `size<I>` must be an `int`. Each represents the number of elements in a dimension of the array. `byte1` and `byte2` are used to construct an index into the constant pool of the current class. The item at that index is resolved. The resulting entry must be an array class of one or more dimensions.

`byte3` is a postive integer representing the number of dimensions being created. It must be less than or equal to the number of dimensions of the array class. `byte3` is also the number of elements that are popped off the stack. All must be `int`s greater than or equal to zero. These are used as the sizes of the dimensions. An attempt is made to allocate a new array of the indicated class type, capable of holding `size<1> * size<2> * ... * <sizeN>` elements. This will be the `result`. If any of the `size<I>` arguments on the stack is less than zero, a `NegativeArraySizeException` is thrown. If there is not enough memory to allocate the array, an `OutOfMemoryError` is thrown.

NOTE

`new int[6][3][]` generates these bytecodes:
```
bipush 6
bipush 3
multianewarray <Class "[[[I"> 2
```
It's more efficient to use `newarray` or `anewarray` when creating arrays of single dimension.

`arraylength` `..., array => ..., length`

Get length of array. `array` must be a reference to an array object. The `length` of the array is determined and replaces `array` on the top of the stack. If `array` is null, a `NullPointerException` is thrown.

```
iaload          ..., array, index => ..., value
laload          ..., array, index => ..., value-word1, value-word2
faload          ..., array, index => ..., value
daload          ..., array, index => ..., value-word1, value-word2
aaload          ..., array, index => ..., value
baload          ..., array, index => ..., value
caload          ..., array, index => ..., value
saload          ..., array, index => ..., value
```

Load <*type*> from array. array must be an array of <*type*>s. index must be an int. The <*type*> value at position number index in array is retrieved and pushed onto the top of the stack. If array is null, a NullPointerException is thrown. If index is not within the bounds of array, an ArrayIndexOutOfBoundsException is thrown. <*type*> is, in turn, int, long, float, double, object reference, byte, char, and short. <*type*>s long and double have two word values, as you've seen in previous load bytecodes.

```
iastore          ..., array, index, value => ...
lastore          ..., array, index, value-word1, value-word2 => ...
fastore          ..., array, index, value => ...
dastore          ..., array, index, value-word1, value-word2 => ...
aastore          ..., array, index, value => ...
bastore          ..., array, index, value => ...
castore          ..., array, index, value => ...
sastore          ..., array, index, value => ...
```

Store into <*type*> array. array must be an array of <*type*>s, index must be an int, and value a <*type*>. The <*type*> value is stored at position index in array. If array is null, a NullPointerException is thrown. If index is not within the bounds of array, an ArrayIndexOutOfBoundsException is thrown. <*type*> is, in turn, int, long, float, double, object reference, byte, char, and short. <*type*>s long and double have two word values, as you've seen in previous store bytecodes.

Stack Operations

```
nop          -no change-
```

Do nothing.

```
pop          ..., any => ...
```

Pop the top word from the stack.

```
pop2         ..., any2, any1 => ...
```

Pop the top two words from the stack.

```
dup          ..., any => ..., any, any
```

Duplicate the top word on the stack.

```
dup2         ..., any2, any1 => ..., any2, any1, any2, any1
```

Duplicate the top two words on the stack.

```
dup_x1       ..., any2, any1 => ..., any1, any2, any1
```

Duplicate the top word on the stack and insert the copy two words down in the stack.

```
dup2_x1      ..., any3, any2, any1 => ..., any2, any1, any3, any2, any1
```

Duplicate the top two words on the stack and insert the copies two words down in the stack.

```
dup_x2      ..., any3, any2, any1 => ..., any1, any3,any2,any1
```

Duplicate the top word on the stack and insert the copy three words down in the stack.

```
dup2_x2     ..., any4, any3, any2, any1 => ..., any2, any1, any4,any3,any2,any1
```

Duplicate the top two words on the stack and insert the copies three words down in the stack.

```
swap        ..., any2, any1 => ..., any1, any2
```

Swap the top two elements on the stack.

Arithmetic Operations

```
iadd        ..., v1, v2 => ..., result
ladd        ..., v1-word1, v1-word2, v2-word1, v2-word2 => ..., r-word1, r-word2
fadd        ..., v1, v2 => ..., result
dadd        ..., v1-word1, v1-word2, v2-word1, v2-word2 => ..., r-word1, r-word2
```

v1 and v2 must be *<type>*s. The vs are added and are replaced on the stack by their *<type>* sum. *<type>* is, in turn, `int`, `long`, `float`, and `double`.

```
isub        ..., v1, v2 => ..., result
lsub        ..., v1-word1, v1-word2, v2-word1, v2-word2 => ..., r-word1, r-word2
fsub        ..., v1, v2 => ..., result
dsub        ..., v1-word1, v1-word2, v2-word1, v2-word2 => ..., r-word1, r-word2
```

v1 and v2 must be *<type>*s. v2 is subtracted from v1, and both vs are replaced on the stack by their *<type>* difference. *<type>* is, in turn, `int`, `long`, `float`, and `double`.

```
imul        ..., v1, v2 => ..., result
lmul        ..., v1-word1, v1-word2, v2-word1, v2-word2 => ..., r-word1, r-word2
fmul        ..., v1, v2 => ..., result
dmul        ..., v1-word1, v1-word2, v2-word1, v2-word2 => ..., r-word1, r-word2
```

v1 and v2 must be *<type>*s. Both vs are replaced on the stack by their *<type>* product. *<type>* is, in turn, `int`, `long`, `float`, and `double`.

```
idiv        ..., v1, v2 => ..., result
ldiv        ..., v1-word1, v1-word2, v2-word1, v2-word2 => ..., r-word1, r-word2
fdiv        ..., v1, v2 => ..., result
ddiv        ..., v1-word1, v1-word2, v2-word1, v2-word2 => ..., r-word1, r-word2
```

v1 and v2 must be *<type>*s. v2 is divided by v1, and both vs are replaced on the stack by their *<type>* quotient. An attempt to divide by zero results in an `ArithmeticException` being thrown. *<type>* is, in turn, `int`, `long`, `float`, and `double`.

```
irem        ..., v1, v2 => ..., result
lrem        ..., v1-word1, v1-word2, v2-word1, v2-word2 => ..., r-word1, r-word2
frem        ..., v1, v2 => ..., result
drem        ..., v1-word1, v1-word2, v2-word1, v2-word2 => ..., r-word1, r-word2
```

v1 and v2 must be *<type>*s. v2 is divided by v1, and both vs are replaced on the stack by their *<type>* remainder. An attempt to divide by zero results in an `ArithmeticException` being thrown. *<type>* is, in turn, `int`, `long`, `float`, and `double`.

```
ineg        ..., value => ..., result
lneg        ..., value-word1, value-word2 => ..., result-word1, result-word2
fneg        ..., value => ..., result
dneg        ..., value-word1, value-word2 => ..., result-word1, result-word2
```

value must be a *<type>*. It is replaced on the stack by its arithmetic negation. *<type>* is, in turn, int, long, float, and double.

NOTE

Now that you're familiar with the look of the bytecodes, the summaries that follow will become shorter and shorter (for space reasons). You can always get any desired level of detail from the full virtual machine specification in the latest Java release.

Logical Operations

```
ishl        ..., v1, v2 => ..., result
lshl        ..., v1-word1, v1-word2, v2 => ..., r-word1, r-word2
ishr        ..., v1, v2 => ..., result
lshr        ..., v1-word1, v1-word2, v2 => ..., r-word1, r-word2
iushr       ..., v1, v2 => ..., result
lushr       ..., v1-word1, v1-word2, v2-word1, v2-word2 => ..., r-word1, r-word2
```

For types int and long: arithmetic shift-left, shift-right, and logical shift-right.

```
iand        ..., v1, v2 => ..., result
land        ..., v1-word1, v1-word2, v2-word1, v2-word2 => ..., r-word1, r-word2
ior         ..., v1, v2 => ..., result
lor         ..., v1-word1, v1-word2, v2-word1, v2-word2 => ..., r-word1, r-word2
ixor        ..., v1, v2 => ..., result
lxor        ..., v1-word1, v1-word2, v2-word1, v2-word2 => ..., r-word1, r-word2
```

For types int and long: bitwise AND, OR, and XOR.

Conversion Operations

```
i2l         ..., value => ..., result-word1, result-word2
i2f         ..., value => ..., result
i2d         ..., value => ..., result-word1, result-word2
l2i         ..., value-word1, value-word2 => ..., result
l2f         ..., value-word1, value-word2 => ..., result
l2d         ..., value-word1, value-word2 => ..., result-word1, result-word2
f2i         ..., value => ..., result
f2l         ..., value => ..., result-word1, result-word2
f2d         ..., value => ..., result-word1, result-word2
d2i         ..., value-word1, value-word2 => ..., result
d2l         ..., value-word1, value-word2 => ..., result-word1, result-word2
d2f         ..., value-word1, value-word2 => ..., result

int2byte    ..., value => ..., result
int2char    ..., value => ..., result
int2short   ..., value => ..., result
```

These bytecodes convert from a `value` of type `<lhs>` to a `result` of type `<rhs>`. `<lhs>` and `<rhs>` can be any of `i`, `l`, `f`, and `d`, which represent `int`, `long`, `float`, and `double`, respectively. The final three bytecodes convert types that are self-explanatory.

Transfer of Control

```
ifeq        ..., value => ...
ifne        ..., value => ...
iflt        ..., value => ...
ifgt        ..., value => ...
ifle        ..., value => ...
ifge        ..., value => ...

if_icmpeq   ..., value1, value2 => ...
if_icmpne   ..., value1, value2 => ...
if_icmplt   ..., value1, value2 => ...
if_icmpgt   ..., value1, value2 => ...
if_icmple   ..., value1, value2 => ...
if_icmpge   ..., value1, value2 => ...

ifnull      ..., value => ...
ifnonnull   ..., value => ...
```

When `value` `<rel>` `0` is true in the first set of bytecodes, `value1` `<rel>` `value2` is true in the second set, or `value` is `null` (or not `null`) in the third, `byte1` and `byte2` are used to construct a signed 16-bit offset. Execution proceeds at that offset from the `pc`. Otherwise, execution proceeds at the bytecode following. `<rel>` is one of `eq`, `ne`, `lt`, `gt`, `le`, and `ge`, which represent equal, not equal, less than, greater than, less than or equal, and greater than or equal, respectively.

```
lcmp        ..., v1-word1, v1-word2, v2-word1, v2-word2 => ..., result

fcmpl       ..., v1, v2 => ..., result
dcmpl       ..., v1-word1, v1-word2, v2-word1, v2-word2 => ..., result

fcmpg       ..., v1, v2 => ..., result
dcmpg       ..., v1-word1, v1-word2, v2-word1, v2-word2 => ..., result
```

`v1` and `v2` must be `long`, `float`, or `double`. They are both popped from the stack and compared. If `v1` is greater than `v2`, the `int` value 1 is pushed onto the stack. If `v1` is equal to `v2`, `0` is pushed onto the stack. If `v1` is less than `v2`, `-1` is pushed onto the stack. For floating-point, if either `v1` or `v2` is `NaN`, `-1` is pushed onto the stack for the first pair of bytecodes, `+1` for the second pair.

```
if_acmpeq   ..., value1, value2 => ...
if_acmpne   ..., value1, value2 => ...
```

Branch if object references are equal/not equal. `value1` and `value2` must be references to objects. They are both popped from the stack. If `value1` is equal/not equal to `value2`, `byte1` and `byte2` are used to construct a signed 16-bit offset. Execution proceeds at that offset from the `pc`. Otherwise, execution proceeds at the bytecode following.

```
goto        -no change-
goto_w      -no change-
```

Branch always. byte1 and byte2 (plus byte3 and byte4 for goto_w) are used to construct a signed 16-bit (32-bit) offset. Execution proceeds at that offset from the pc.

```
jsr           ... => ..., return-address
jsr_w         ... => ..., return-address
```

Jump subroutine. The address of the bytecode immediately following the jsr is pushed onto the stack. byte1 and byte2 (plus byte3 and byte4 for goto_w) are used to construct a signed 16-bit (32-bit) offset. Execution proceeds at that offset from the pc.

```
ret           -no change-
ret_w         -no change-
```

Return from subroutine. Local variable byte1 (plus byte2 for ret_w are assembled into a 16-bit index) in the current Java frame must contain a return address. The contents of that local variable are written into the pc.

> **NOTE**
>
> jsr pushes the address onto the stack, and ret gets it out of a local variable. This asymmetry is intentional.
>
> The jsr and ret bytecodes are used in the implementation of Java's finally keyword.

Method Return

```
return        ... => [empty]
```

Return (void) from method. All values on the operand stack are discarded. The interpreter then returns control to its caller.

```
ireturn       ..., value => [empty]
lreturn       ..., value-word1, value-word2 => [empty]
freturn       ..., value => [empty]
dreturn       ..., value-word1, value-word2 => [empty]
areturn       ..., value => [empty]
```

Return <type> from method. value must be a <type>. The value is pushed onto the stack of the previous execution environment. Any other values on the operand stack are discarded. The interpreter then returns control to its caller. <type> is, in turn, int, long, float, double, and object reference.

> **NOTE**
>
> The stack behavior of the "return" bytecodes may be confusing to anyone expecting the Java operand stack to be just like the C stack. Java's operand stack actually consists of a number of discontiguous segments, each corresponding to a method call. A return

bytecode empties the Java operand stack segment corresponding to the frame of the returning call, but does not affect the segment of any parent calls.

Table Jumping

```
tableswitch    ..., index => ...
```

`tableswitch` is a variable-length bytecode. Immediately after the `tableswitch` opcode, zero to three `0` bytes are inserted as padding so that the next byte begins at an address that is a multiple of four. After the padding are a series of signed 4-byte quantities: default-offset, low, high, and then high-low+1 further signed 4-byte offsets. These offsets are treated as a 0-based jump table.

The `index` must be an `int`. If `index` is less than low or index is greater than high, default-offset is added to the `pc`. Otherwise, the index-low'th element of the jump table is extracted and added to the `pc`.

```
lookupswitch ..., key => ...
```

`lookupswitch` is a variable-length bytecode. Immediately after the `lookupswitch` opcode, zero to three 0-bytes are inserted as padding so that the next byte begins at an address that is a multiple of four. Immediately after the padding is a series of pairs of signed 4-byte quantities. The first pair is special; it contains the default-offset and the number of pairs that follow. Each subsequent pair consists of a match and an offset.

The key on the stack must be an `int`. This key is compared to each of the matches. If it is equal to one of them, the corresponding offset is added to the `pc`. If the key does not match any of the matches, the default-offset is added to the `pc`.

Manipulating Object Fields

```
putfield    ..., handle, value => ...
putfield    ..., handle, value-word1,value-word2 => ...
```

Set field in object. `byte1` and `byte2` are used to construct and index into the constant pool of the current class. The constant pool item is a field reference to a class name and a field name. The item is resolved to a field block pointer containing the field's width and offset both in bytes.

The field at that offset from the start of the object referenced by `handle` will be set to the value on the top of the stack. The first stack picture is for 32-bit, and the second for 64-bit wide fields. This bytecode handles both. If `handle` is null, a `NullPointerException` is thrown. If the specified field is a static field, an `IncompatibleClassChangeError` is thrown.

```
getfield    ...,handle => ..., value
getfield    ...,handle => ..., value-word1,value-word2
```

Fetch field from object. byte1 and byte2 are used to construct an index into the constant pool of the current class. The constant pool item will be a field reference to a class name and a field name. The item is resolved to a field block pointer containing the field's width and offset both in bytes.

handle must be a reference to an object.

The value at offset into the object referenced by handle replaces handle on the top of the stack. The first stack picture is for 32-bit, and the second for 64-bit wide fields. This bytecode handles both. If the specified field is a static field, an IncompatibleClassChangeError is thrown.

```
putstatic      ..., value => ...
putstatic      ..., value-word1, value-word2 => ...
```

Set static field in class. byte1 and byte2 are used to construct an index into the constant pool of the current class. The constant pool item will be a field reference to a static field of a class. That field will be set to have the value on the top of the stack. The first stack picture is for 32-bit, and the second for 64-bit wide fields. This bytecode handles both. If the specified field is not a static field, an IncompatibleClassChangeError is thrown.

```
getstatic      ..., => ..., value
getstatic      ..., => ..., value-word1, value-word2
```

Get static field from class. byte1 and byte2 are used to construct an index into the constant pool of the current class. The constant pool item will be a field reference to a static field of a class. The value of that field is placed on the top of the stack. The first stack picture is for 32-bit, and the second for 64-bit wide fields. This bytecode handles both. If the specified field is not a static field, an IncompatibleClassChangeError is thrown.

Method Invocation

```
invokevirtual      ..., handle, [arg1, [arg2 ...]], ... => ...
```

Invoke instance method based on run-time type. The operand stack must contain a reference (handle) to an object and some number of arguments. byte1 and byte2 are used to construct an index into the constant pool of the current class. The item at that index in the constant pool contains the complete method signature. A pointer to the object's method table is retrieved from the object reference. The method signature is looked up in the method table. The method signature is guaranteed to exactly match one of the method signatures in the table exactly.

The result of the lookup is an index into the method table of the named class that is used to look in the method table of the object's run-time type, where a pointer to the method block for the matched method is found. The method block indicates the type of method (native, synchronized, and so on) and the number of arguments (nargs) expected on the operand stack.

If the method is marked synchronized, the monitor associated with handle is entered.

The base of the local variables array for the new Java stack frame is set to point to handle on the stack, making handle and the supplied arguments (arg1, arg2, ...) the first nargs local variables of the new frame. The total number of local variables used by the method is determined, and the execution environment of the new frame is pushed after leaving sufficient room for the locals. The base of the operand stack for this method invocation is set to the first word after the execution environment. Finally, execution continues with the first bytecode of the matched method.

If `handle` is `null`, a `NullPointerException` is thrown. If during the method invocation a stack overflow is detected, a `StackOverflowError` is thrown.

`invokenonvirtual    ..., handle, [arg1, [arg2, ...]], ... => ...`

Invoke instance method based on compile-time type. The operand stack must contain a reference (`handle`) to an object and some number of arguments. `byte1` and `byte2` are used to construct an index into the constant pool of the current class. The item at that index in the constant pool contains the complete method signature and class. The method signature is looked up in the method table of the class indicated. The method signature is guaranteed to exactly match one of the method signatures in the table.

The result of the lookup is a method block. The method block indicates the type of method (`native`, `synchronized`, and so on) and the number of arguments (`nargs`) expected on the operand stack. (The last three paragraphs are identical to the previous bytecode.)

`invokestatic       ..., , [arg1, [arg2, ...]], ... => ...`

Invoke class (static) method. The operand stack must contain some number of arguments. `byte1` and `byte2` are used to construct an index into the constant pool of the current class. The item at that index in the constant pool contains the complete method signature and class. The method signature is looked up in the the method table of the class indicated. The method signature is guaranteed to match one of the method signatures in the class's method table exactly.

The result of the lookup is a method block. The method block indicates the type of method (`native`, `synchronized`, and so on) and the number of arguments (`nargs`) expected on the operand stack.

If the method is marked `synchronized`, the monitor associated with the class is entered. (The last two paragraphs are identical to those in `invokevirtual`, except that no `NullPointerException` can be thrown.)

`invokeinterface    ..., handle, [arg1, [arg2, ...]], ... => ...`

Invoke interface method. The operand stack must contain a reference (`handle`) to an object and some number of arguments. `byte1` and `byte2` are used to construct an index into the constant pool of the current class. The item at that index in the constant pool contains the complete method signature. A pointer to the object's method table is retrieved from the object reference. The method signature is looked up in the method table. The method signature is guaranteed to exactly match one of the method signatures in the table.

The result of the lookup is a method block. The method block indicates the type of method (native, synchronized, and so on) but, unlike the other "invoke" bytecodes, the number of available arguments (nargs) is taken from byte3; byte4 is reserved for future use. (The last three paragraphs are identical to those in invokevirtual.)

Exception Handling

athrow   ..., handle => [undefined]

Throw exception. handle must be a handle to an exception object. That exception, which must be an instance of Throwable (or a subclass) is thrown. The current Java stack frame is searched for the most recent catch clause that handles the exception. If a matching "catch-list" entry is found, the pc is reset to the address indicated by the catch-list pointer, and execution continues there.

If no appropriate catch clause is found in the current stack frame, that frame is popped and the exception is rethrown, starting the process all over again in the parent frame. If handle is null, then a NullPointerException is thrown instead.

Miscellaneous Object Operations

new   ... => ..., handle

Create new object. byte1 and byte2 are used to construct an index into the constant pool of the current class. The item at that index must be a class name that can be resolved to a class pointer, class. A new instance of that class is then created and a reference (handle) for the instance is placed on the top of the stack.

checkcast   ..., handle => ..., [handle ¦ ...]

Make sure object is of given type. handle must be a reference to an object. byte1 and byte2 are used to construct an index into the constant pool of the current class. The string at that index of the constant pool is presumed to be a class name that can be resolved to a class pointer, class.

checkcast determines whether handle can be cast to a reference to an object of that class. (A null handle can be cast to any class.) If handle can be legally cast, execution proceeds at the next bytecode, and the handle remains on the stack. If not, a ClassCastException is thrown and the stack is emptied.

instanceof   ..., handle => ..., result

Determine whether object is of given type. handle must be a reference to an object. byte1 and byte2 are used to construct an index into the constant pool of the current class. The string at that index of the constant pool is presumed to be a class name that can be resolved to a class pointer, class.

If `handle` is `null`, the `result` is `0` (false). Otherwise, `instanceof` determines whether `handle` can be cast to a reference to an object of that class. The `result` is `1` (true) if it can, and `0` (false) otherwise.

Monitors

```
monitorenter        ..., handle => ...
```

Enter monitored region of code. `handle` must be a reference to an object. The interpreter attempts to obtain exclusive access via a lock mechanism to `handle`. If another thread already has `handle` locked, the current thread waits until the `handle` is unlocked. If the current thread already has `handle` locked, execution continues normally. If `handle` has no lock on it, this bytecode obtains an exclusive lock. (A `null` in either bytecode throws `NullPointerException`.)

```
monitorexit         ..., handle => ...
```

Exit monitored region of code. `handle` must be a reference to an object. The lock on `handle` is released. If this is the last lock that this thread has on that `handle` (one thread is allowed to have multiple locks on a single `handle`), other threads that are waiting for `handle` are allowed to proceed. (A `null` in either bytecode throws `NullPointerException`.)

Debugging

```
breakpoint          -no change-
```

Call breakpoint handler. The breakpoint bytecode is used to overwrite a bytecode to force control temporarily back to the debugger prior to the effect of the overwritten bytecode. The original bytecode's operands (if any) are not overwritten, and the original bytecode is restored when the breakpoint bytecode is removed.

The _quick Bytecodes

The following discussion, straight out of the Java virtual machine documentation, shows you an example of the cleverness mentioned earlier that's needed to make a bytecode interpreter fast:

> The following set of pseudo-bytecodes, suffixed by _quick, are all variants of standard Java bytecodes. They are used by the run-time to improve the execution speed of the bytecode interpreter. They aren't officially part of the virtual machine specification and are invisible outside a Java virtual machine implementation. However, inside that implementation they have proven to be an effective optimization.
>
> First, you should know that `javac` still generates only non-_quick bytecodes. Second, all bytecodes that have a _quick variant reference the constant pool. When _quick optimization is turned on, each non-_quick bytecode (that has a _quick variant)

resolves the specified item in the constant pool, signals an error if the item in the constant pool could not be resolved for some reason, turns itself into the _quick variant of itself, and then performs its intended operation.

This is identical to the actions of the non-_quick bytecode, except for the step of overwriting itself with its _quick variant. The _quick variant of a bytecode assumes that the item in the constant pool has already been resolved, and that this resolution did not produce any errors. It simply performs the intended operation on the resolved item.

Thus, as your bytecodes are being interpreted, they are automatically getting faster and faster! Here are all the _quick variants in the current Java run-time:

```
ldc1_quick
ldc2_quick
ldc2w_quick

anewarray_quick
multinewarray_quick

putfield_quick
putfield2_quick
getfield_quick
getfield2_quick
putstatic_quick
putstatic2_quick
getstatic_quick
getstatic2_quick

invokevirtual_quick
invokevirtualobject_quick
invokenonvirtual_quick
invokestatic_quick
invokeinterface_quick

new_quick
checkcast_quick
instanceof_quick
```

If you'd like to go back in this chapter and look at what each of these does, you can find the name of the original bytecode on which a _quick variant is based by simply removing the _quick from its name. The bytecodes putstatic, getstatic, putfield, and getfield have two _quick variants each, one for each stack picture in their original descriptions. invokevirtual has two variants: one for objects and for arrays (to do fast lookups in java.lang.Object).

NOTE

One last note on the _quick optimization, regarding the unusual handling of the constant pool (for detail fanatics only):

When a class is read in, an array `constant_pool[]` of size `nconstants` is created and assigned to a field in the class. `constant_pool[0]` is set to point to a dynamically allocated array that indicates which fields in the `constant_pool` have already been resolved. `constant_pool[1]` through `constant_pool[nconstants - 1]` are set to point at the "type" field that corresponds to this constant item.

When a bytecode is executed that references the constant pool, an index is generated, and `constant_pool[0]` is checked to see whether the index has already been resolved. If so, the value of `constant_pool[index]` is returned. If not, the value of `constant_pool[index]` is resolved to be the actual pointer or data, and overwrites whatever value was already in `constant_pool[index]`.

The `.class` File Format

You won't be given the entire `.class` file format here, only a taste of what it's like. (You can read all about it in the release documentation.) It's mentioned here because it is one of the parts of Java that needs to be specified carefully if all Java implementations are to be compatible with one another, and if Java bytecodes are expected to travel across arbitrary networks—to and from arbitrary computers and operating systems—and yet arrive safely.

The rest of this section paraphrases, and extensively condenses, the latest release of the `.class` documentation.

`.class` files are used to hold the compiled versions of both Java classes and Java interfaces. Compliant Java interpreters must be capable of dealing with all `.class` files that conform to the following specification. (Use `java.io.DataInput` and `java.io.DataOutput` to read and write `.class` files.)

A Java `.class` file consists of a stream of 8-bit bytes. All 16-bit and 32-bit quantities are constructed by reading in two or four 8-bit bytes, respectively. The bytes are joined together in big-endian order.

The class file format is presented below as a series of C-struct-like structures. However, unlike a C `struct`, there is no padding or alignment between pieces of the structure, each field of the structure may be of variable size, and an array may be of variable size (in this case, some field prior to the array gives the array's dimension). The types `u1`, `u2`, and `u4` represent an unsigned one-, two-, or four-byte quantity, respectively.

Attributes are used at several different places in the `.class` format. All attributes have the following format:

```
GenericAttribute_info {
    u2 attribute_name;
    u4 attribute_length;
```

```
      u1  info[attribute_length];
}
```

The `attribute_name` is a 16-bit index into the class's constant pool; the value of `constant_pool[attribute_name]` is a string giving the name of the attribute. The field `attribute_length` gives the length of the subsequent information in bytes. This length does not include the four bytes needed to store `attribute_name` and `attribute_length`. In the following text, whenever an attribute is required, names of all the attributes that are currently understood are listed. In the future, more attributes will be added. Class file readers are expected to skip over and ignore the information in any attributes that they do not understand.

The following pseudo-structure gives a top-level description of the format of a class file:

```
ClassFile {
    u4   magic;
    u2   minor_version;
    u2   major_version;
    u2   constant_pool_count;
    cp_info          constant_pool[constant_pool_count - 1];
    u2   access_flags;
    u2   this_class;
    u2   super_class;
    u2   interfaces_count;
    u2   interfaces[interfaces_count];
    u2   fields_count;
    field_info       fields[fields_count];
    u2   methods_count;
    method_info      methods[methods_count];
    u2   attributes_count;
    attribute_info   attributes[attribute_count];
}
```

Here's one of the smaller structures used:

```
method_info {
    u2   access_flags;
    u2   name_index;
    u2   signature_index;
    u2   attributes_count;
    attribute_info   attributes[attribute_count];
}
```

Finally, here's a sample of one of the later structures in the `.class` file description:

```
Code_attribute {
    u2   attribute_name_index;
    u2   attribute_length;
    u1   max_stack;
    u1   max_locals;
    u2   code_length;
    u1   code[code_length];
    u2   exception_table_length;
    {   u2     start_pc;
        u2     end_pc;
        u2     handler_pc;
        u2     catch_type;
    }   exception_table[exception_table_length];
```

```
    u2  attributes_count;
    attribute_info  attributes[attribute_count];
}
```

None of this is meant to be completely comprehensible (though you might be able to guess at what a lot of the structure members are for), but just suggestive of the sort of structures that live inside .class files. Because the compiler and run-time sources are available, you can always begin with them if you actually have to read or write .class files yourself. Thus, you don't need to have a deep understanding of the details, even in that case.

Method Signatures

Because methods signatures are used in .class files, now is an appropriate time to explore them in detail—but they're probably most useful to you when writing the native methods.

> **NOTE**
>
> A *signature* is a string representing the type of a method, field, or array.

A field signature represents the value of an argument to a method or the value of a variable and is a series of bytes in the following grammar:

```
<field signature> := <field_type>
<field type>      := <base_type> ¦ <object_type> ¦ <array_type>
<base_type>       := B ¦ C ¦ D ¦ F ¦ I ¦ J ¦ S ¦ Z
<object_type>     := L <full.ClassName> ;
<array_type>      := [ <optional_size> <field_type> ]
<optional_size>   := [0-9]*
```

Here are the meanings of the base types: B (byte), C (char), D (double), F (float), I (int), J (long), S (short), and Z (boolean).

A return-type signature represents the return value from a method and is a series of bytes in the following grammar:

```
<return signature>   := <field type> ¦ V
```

The character V (void) indicates that the method returns no value. Otherwise, the signature indicates the type of the return value. An argument signature represents an argument passed to a method:

```
<argument signature>  := <field type>
```

Finally, a method signature represents the arguments that the method expects, and the value that it returns:

```
<method_signature>    := (<arguments signature>) <return signature>
<arguments signature> := <argument signature>*
```

Now, let's try out the new rules: a method called `complexMethod()` in the class `my.package.name.ComplexClass` takes three arguments—a `long`, a `boolean`, and a two-dimensional array of `shorts`—and returns this. Then, `(JZ[[S)Lmy.package.name.ComplexClass;` is its method signature.

A method signature is often prefixed by the name of the method, or by its full package (using an underscore in the place of dots) and its class name followed by a slash (/) and the name of the method, to form a *complete method signature*. Now, at last, you have the full story! Thus, the following

```
my_package_name_ComplexClass/complexMethod(JZ[[S)Lmy.package.name.ComplexClass;
```

is the full, complete method signature of `complexMethod()`. (Phew!)

The Garbage Collector

Decades ago, programmers in both the Lisp and the Smalltalk community realized how extremely valuable it is to be able to ignore memory deallocation. They realized that, although allocation is fundamental, deallocation is forced on the programmer by the laziness of the system—*it* should be able to figure out what is no longer useful, and get rid of it. In relative obscurity, these pioneering programmers developed a whole series of garbage collectors to perform this job, each getting more sophisticated and efficient as the years went by. Finally, now that the mainstream programming community has begun to recognize the value of this automated technique, Java can become the first really widespread application of the technology those pioneers developed.

The Problem

Imagine that you're a programmer in a C-like language (probably not too difficult for you, because these languages are the dominant ones right now). Each time you create something, anything, *dynamically* in such a language, you are completely responsible for tracking the life of this object throughout your program and mentally deciding when it will be safe to deallocate it. This can be quite a difficult (sometimes impossible) task, because any of the other libraries or methods you've called might have "squirreled away" a pointer to the object, unbeknownst to you. When it becomes impossible to know, you simply choose *never* to deallocate the object, or at least to wait until every library and method call involved has completed, which could be nearly as long.

The uneasy feeling you get when writing such code is a natural, healthy response to what is inherently an unsafe and unreliable style of programming. If you have tremendous discipline—and so does everyone who writes every library and method you call—you can, in principle, survive this responsibility without too many mishaps. But aren't you human? Aren't they? There must be some small slips in this perfect discipline due to error. What's worse, such errors are virtually undetectable, as anyone who's tried to hunt down a stray pointer problem in C will tell you. What about the thousands of programmers who don't have that sort of discipline?

Another way to ask this question is: Why should any programmers be forced to have this discipline, when it is entirely possible for the system to remove this heavy burden from their shoulders?

Software engineering estimates have recently shown that for every 55 lines of production C-like code in the world, there is one bug. This means that your electric razor has about 80 bugs, and your TV, 400. Soon they will have even more, because the size of this kind of embedded computer software is growing exponentially. When you begin to think of how much C-like code is in your car's engine, it should give you pause.

Many of these errors are due to the misuse of pointers, by misunderstanding or by accident, and to the early, incorrect freeing of allocated objects in memory. Java addresses both of these—the former, by eliminating explicit pointers from the Java language altogether and the latter, by including, in every Java system, a garbage collector that solves the problem.

The Solution

Imagine a run-time system that tracks each object you create, notices when the last reference to it has vanished, and frees the object for you. How could such a thing actually work?

One brute-force approach, tried early in the days of garbage collecting, is to attach a reference counter to every object. When the object is created, the counter is set to 1. Each time a new reference to the object is made, the counter is incremented, and each time such a reference disappears, the counter is decremented. Because all such references are controlled by the language—as variables and assignments, for example—the compiler can tell whenever an object reference might be created or destroyed, just as it does in handling the scoping of local variables, and thus it can assist with this task. The system itself "holds onto" a set of root objects that are considered too important to be freed. The class `Object` is one example of such a V.I.P. object. (V.I.O.?) Finally, all that's needed is to test, after each decrement, whether the counter has hit `0`. If it has, the object is freed.

If you think carefully about this approach, you will soon convince yourself that it is definitely correct when it decides to free anything. It is so simple that you can immediately tell that it will work. The low-level hacker in you might also feel that if it's *that* simple, it's probably not fast enough to run at the lowest level of the system—and you'd be right.

Think about all the stack frames, local variables, method arguments, return values, and local variables created in the course of even a few hundred milliseconds of a program's life. For each of these tiny, nano-steps in the program, an extra increment—at best—or decrement, test, and deallocation—at worst—will be added to the running time of the program. In fact, the first garbage collectors were slow enough that many predicted they could never be used at all!

Luckily, a whole generation of smart programmers has invented a big bag of tricks to solve these overhead problems. One trick is to introduce special "transient object" areas that don't need to be reference counted. The best of these generational scavenging garbage collectors today can take less than 3 percent of the total time of your program—a remarkable feat if you realize that many other language features, such as loop overheads, can be as large or larger!

There are other problems with garbage collection. If you are constantly freeing and reclaiming space in a program, won't the heap of objects soon become fragmented, with small holes everywhere and no room to create new, large objects? Because the programmer is now free from the chains of manual deallocation, won't they create even more objects than usual?

What's worse, there is another way that this simple reference counting scheme is inefficient, in space rather than time. If a long chain of object references eventually comes full circle, back to the starting object, each object's reference count remains at least 1 *forever*. None of these objects will ever be freed!

Together, these problems imply that a good garbage collector must, every once in a while, step back to compact or to clean up wasted memory.

> **NOTE**
>
> *Compaction* occurs when a garbage collector steps back and reorganizes memory, eliminating the holes created by fragmentation. Compacting memory is simply a matter of repositioning objects one-by-one into a new, compact grouping that places them all in a row, leaving all the free memory in the heap in one big piece.
>
> Cleaning up the circular garbage still lying around after reference counting is called *marking and sweeping*. A mark-and-sweep of memory involves first marking every root object in the system and then following all the object references inside those objects to new objects to mark, and so on, recursively. Then, when you have no more references to follow, you "sweep away" all the unmarked objects, and compact memory as before.

The good news is that this solves the space problems you were having. The bad news is that when the garbage collector "steps back" and does these operations, a nontrivial amount of time passes during which your program is unable to run—all its objects are being marked, swept, rearranged, and so forth, in what seems like an uninterruptible procedure. Your first hint to a solution is the word "seems."

Garbage collecting can actually be done a little at a time, between or in parallel with normal program execution, thus dividing up the large time needed to "step back" into numerous so-small-you-don't-notice-them chunks of time that happen between the cracks. (Of course, years of smart thinking went into the abstruse algorithms that make all this possible!)

One final problem that might worry you a little has to do with these object references. Aren't these "pointers" scattered throughout your program and not just buried in objects? Even if they're only in objects, don't they have to be changed whenever the object they point to is moved by these procedures? The answer to both of these questions is a resounding *yes*, and overcoming them is the final hurdle to making an efficient garbage collector.

There are really only two choices. The first, brute force, assumes that all the memory containing object references needs to be searched on a regular basis, and whenever the object references found by this search match objects that have moved, the old reference is changed. This assumes that there are "hard" pointers in the heap's memory—ones that point directly to other objects. By introducing various kinds of "soft" pointers, including pointers that are like forwarding addresses, the algorithm improves greatly. Although these brute-force approaches sound slow, it turns out that modern computers can do them fast enough to be useful.

> **NOTE**
>
> You might wonder how the brute-force techniques identify object references. In early systems, references were specially tagged with a "pointer bit," so they could be unambiguously located. Now, so-called conservative garbage collectors simply assume that if it looks like an object reference, it is—at least for the purposes of the mark and sweep. Later, when actually trying to update it, they can find out whether it really is an object reference or not.

The final approach to handling object references, and the one Java currently uses, is also one of the very first ones tried. It involves using 100 percent "soft" pointers. An object reference is actually a handle, sometimes called an "OOP," to the real pointer, and a large object table exists to map these handles into the actual object reference. Although this does introduce extra overhead on almost every object reference (some of which can be eliminated by clever tricks, as you might guess), it's not too high a price to pay for this incredibly valuable level of indirection.

This indirection allows the garbage collector, for example, to mark, sweep, move, or examine one object at a time. Each object can be independently moved "out from under" a running Java program by changing only the object table entries. This not only allows the "step back" phase to happen in the tiniest steps, but it makes a garbage collector that runs literally in parallel with your program much easier to write. This is what the Java garbage collector does.

> **WARNING**
>
> You need to be very careful about garbage collection when you're doing critical, real-time programs (such as those mentioned in Chapter 37 that legitimately require `native` methods)—but how often will your Java code be flying a commercial airliner in real-time, anyway?

Java's Parallel Garbage Collector

Java applies almost all these advanced techniques to give you a fast, efficient, parallel garbage collector. Running in a separate thread, it cleans up the Java environment of almost all trash (it is conservative), silently and in the background, is efficient in both space and time, and never steps back for more than a small amount of time. You should never need to know it's there.

By the way, if you want to force a full mark-and-sweep garbage collection to happen soon, you can do so simply by calling the System.gc() method. You might want to do this if you just freed up a majority of the heap's memory in circular garbage, and want it all taken away quickly. You might also call this whenever you're idle, as a hint to the system about when it would be best to come and collect the garbage. This "meta knowledge" is rarely needed by the system, however.

Ideally, you'll never notice the garbage collector, and all those decades of programmers beating their brains out on your behalf will simply let you sleep better at night—and what's wrong with that?

The Security Story

Speaking of sleeping well at night, if you haven't stepped back yet and said, "My Goodness! You mean Java programs will be running rampant on the Internet?" you better do so now, for it is a legitimate concern. In fact, it is one of the major technical stumbling blocks (the others being mostly social and economic) to achieving the dream of ubiquity and code sharing mentioned earlier in this chapter.

Why You Should Worry

Any powerful, flexible technology can be abused. As the Net becomes mainstream and widespread, it, too, will be abused. Already, there have been many blips on the security radar screens of those of us who worry about such things, warning that (at least until today), not enough attention has been paid by the computer industry (or the media) to constructively solving some of the problems that this new world brings with it. One of the benefits of solving security once and for all will be a flowering unseen before in the virtual communities of the Net; whole new economies based on people's attention and creativity will spring to life, rapidly transforming our world in new and positive ways.

The downside to all this new technology, is that we (or someone!) must worry long and hard about how to make the playgrounds of the future safe for our children, and for us. Fortunately, Java is a big part of the answer.

NOTE

For more information about security issues with Java, please see Chapter 40, "Java Security."

Why You Might Not Have To

What gives me any confidence that the Java language and environment will be *safe*, that it will solve the technically daunting and extremely thorny problems inherent in any good form of security, especially for networks?

One simple reason is the history of the people, and the company, that created Java. Many of them are the very smart programmers referred to throughout the book, who helped pioneer many of the ideas that make Java great and who have worked hard over the decades to make techniques such as garbage collection a mainstream reality. They are technically capable of tackling and solving the hard problems that need to be solved. In particular, from discussions with Chuck McManis, one of Java's security gurus, I have confidence that he has thought through these hard problems deeply, and that he knows what needs to be done.

Sun Microsystems, the company, has been pushing networks as the central theme of all its software for more than a decade. Sun has the engineers and the commitment needed to solve these hard problems, because these same problems are at the very center of both its future business and its vision of the future, in which networking is the center of everything—and global networks are nearly useless without good security. Just this year, Sun has advanced the state of the art in easy-to-use Internet security with its new SunScreen products, and it has assigned Whitfield Diffie to oversee them, who is the man who discovered the underlying ideas on which essentially *all* interesting forms of modern encryption are based.

Enough on "deep background." What does the Java environment provide *right now* that helps me feel secure?

Java's Security Model

Java protects you against potential "nasty" Java code via a series of interlocking defenses that, together, form an imposing barrier to any and all such attacks.

CAUTION

Of course, no one can protect you from your own ignorance or carelessness. If you're the kind of person who blindly downloads binary executables from your Internet browser and runs them, you need read no further! You are already in more danger than Java will ever pose.

As a user of this powerful new medium, the Internet, you should educate yourself to the possible threats this new and exciting world entails. In particular, downloading "auto-running macros" or reading e-mail with "executable attachments" is just as much a threat as downloading binaries from the Net and running them.

Java does not introduce any new dangers here, but by being the first mainstream use of executable and mobile code on the Net, it is responsible for making people suddenly aware of the dangers that have always been there. Java is already, as you will soon see, much less dangerous than any of these common activities on the Net, and can be made safer still over time. Most of these other (dangerous) activities can never be made safe. So please, do not do them!

A good rule of thumb on the Net is this: Don't download anything that you plan to execute (or that will be automatically executed for you) except from someone (or some company) you know well and with whom you've had positive, personal experience. If you don't care about losing all the data on your hard drive, or about your privacy, you can do anything you like, but for most of us, this rule should be law.

Fortunately, Java allows you to relax that law. You can run Java applets from anyone, anywhere, in relative safety.

Java's powerful security mechanisms act at four different levels of the system architecture. First, the Java language itself was designed to be safe, and the Java compiler ensures that source code doesn't violate these safety rules. Second, all bytecodes executed by the run-time are screened to be sure that they also obey these rules. (This layer guards against having an altered compiler produce code that violates the safety rules.) Third, the class loader ensures that classes don't violate name space or access restrictions when they are loaded into the system. Finally, API-specific security prevents applets from doing destructive things. This final layer depends on the security and integrity guarantees from the other three layers.

Let's now examine each of these layers in turn.

The Language and the Compiler

The Java language and its compiler are the first line of defense. Java was designed to be a safe language.

Most other C-like languages have facilities to control access to "objects," but also have ways to "forge" access to objects (or to parts of objects), usually by (mis-)using pointers. This introduces two fatal security flaws to any system built on these languages. One is that no object can protect itself from outside modification, duplication, or "spoofing" (others pretending to be that object). Another is that a language with powerful pointers is more likely to have serious bugs that compromise security. These pointer bugs, where a "runaway pointer" starts modifying some other object's memory, were responsible for most of the public (and not-so-public) security problems on the Internet this past decade.

Java eliminates these threats in one stroke by eliminating pointers from the language altogether. There are still pointers of a kind—object references—but these are carefully controlled to be safe: they are unforgeable, and all casts are checked for legality before being allowed. In addition, powerful new array facilities in Java not only help to offset the loss of pointers, but add additional safety by strictly enforcing array bounds, catching more bugs for the programmer (bugs that, in other languages, might lead to unexpected and, thus, bad-guy-exploitable problems).

The language definition, and the compilers that enforce it, create a powerful barrier to any "nasty" Java programmer.

Because an overwhelming majority of the "Net-savvy" software on the Internet may soon be Java, its safe language definition and compilers help to guarantee that most of this software has a solid, secure base. With fewer bugs, Net software will be more predictable—a property that thwarts attacks.

Verifying the Bytecodes

What if that "nasty" programmer gets a little more determined, and rewrites the Java compiler to suit his nefarious purposes? The Java run-time, getting the lion's share of its bytecodes from the Net, can never tell whether those bytecodes were generated by a "trustworthy" compiler. Therefore, it must *verify* that they meet all the safety requirements.

Before running any bytecodes, the run-time subjects them to a rigorous series of tests that vary in complexity from simple format checks all the way to running a theorem prover, to make certain that they are playing by the rules. These tests verify that the bytecodes do not forge pointers, violate access restrictions, access objects as other than what they are (InputStreams are always used as InputStreams, and never as anything else), call methods with inappropriate argument values or types, or overflow the stack.

Consider the following Java code sample:

```java
public class VectorTest {
    public int  array[];

    public int  sum() {
        int[]  localArray = array;
        int    sum        = 0;

        for (int  i = localArray.length;  --i >= 0;  )
            sum += localArray[i];
        return sum;
    }
}
```

The bytecodes generated when this code is compiled look something like the following:

```
        aload_0          Load this
        getfield #10     Load this.array
        astore_1         Store in localArray
        iconst_0         Load 0
        istore_2         Store in sum
        aload_1          Load localArray
        arraylength      Gets its length
        istore_3         Store in i
    A:  iinc 3 -1        Subtract 1 from i
        iload_3          Load i
        iflt B           Exit loop if < 0
        iload_2          Load sum
        aload_1          Load localArray
        iload_3          Load i
        iaload           Load localArray[i]
        iadd             Add sum
        istore_2         Store in sum
        goto A           Do it again
    B:  iload_2          Load sum
        ireturn          Return it
```

> **NOTE**
>
> The excellent examples and descriptions in this section of the book are paraphrased from the tremendously informative security paper in the (alpha) Java release. I'd encourage you to read whatever the latest version of this document is in newer releases, if you want to follow the ongoing Java security story. Also, check out the next chapter for more information.

Extra Type Information and Requirements

Java bytecodes encode more type information than is strictly necessary for the interpreter. Even though, for example, the `aload` and `iload` opcodes do exactly the same thing, `aload` is always used to load an object reference and `iload` used to load an integer. Some bytecodes (such as `getfield`) include a symbol table reference—and that symbol table has *even more* type information. This extra type information allows the run-time system to guarantee that Java objects and data aren't illegally manipulated.

Conceptually, before and after each bytecode is executed, every slot in the stack and every local variable has some type. This collection of type information—all the slots and local variables—is called the *type state* of the execution environment. An important requirement of the Java type state is that it must be determinable statically by induction—that is, before any program code is executed. As a result, as the run-time systems read bytecodes, each is required to have the following inductive property: given only the type state before the execution of the bytecode, the type state afterward must be fully determined.

Given "straight-line" bytecodes (no branches), and starting with a known stack state, the state of each slot in the stack is therefore always known. For example, starting with an empty stack:

iload_1	Load integer variable. Stack type state is I.
iconst 5	Load integer constant. Stack type state is II.
iadd	Add two integers, producing an integer. Stack type state is I.

> **NOTE**
>
> Smalltalk and PostScript bytecodes do not have this restriction. Their more dynamic type behavior does create additional flexibility in those systems, but Java needs to provide a secure execution environment. It must therefore know all types *at all times*, in order to guarantee a certain level of security.

Another requirement made by the Java run-time is that when a set of bytecodes can take more than one path to arrive at the same point, all such paths must arrive there with exactly the same type state. This is a strict requirement, and implies, for example, that compilers cannot generate bytecodes that load all the elements of an array onto the stack. (Because each time through such a loop the stack's type state changes, the start of the loop—"the same point" in multiple paths—would have more than one type state, which is not allowed.)

The Verifier

Bytecodes are checked for compliance with all these requirements, using the extra type information in a .class file, by a part of the run-time called the *verifier*. It examines each bytecode in turn, constructing the full type state as it goes, and verifies that all the types of parameters, arguments, and results are correct. Thus, the verifier acts as a gatekeeper to your run-time environment, letting in only those bytecodes that pass muster.

> **WARNING**
>
> The verifier is *the crucial piece* of Java's security, and it depends on your having a correctly implemented (no bugs, intentional or otherwise) run-time system. As of this writing, only Sun is producing Java run-times, and its are secure. In the future, however, you should be careful when downloading or buying another company's (or individual's) version of the Java run-time environment. Eventually, Sun will implement validation suites for run-times, compilers, and so forth to be sure that they are safe and correct. In the meantime, *caveat emptor*! Your run-time is the base on which all the rest of Java's security is built, so make sure it is a good, solid, secure base.

When bytecodes have passed the verifier, they are guaranteed not to cause any operand stack under- or overflows, use parameter, argument, or return types incorrectly, illegally convert data from one type to another (from an integer to a pointer, for example), nor access any object's fields illegally (that is, the verifier checks that the rules for `public`, `private`, `package`, and `protected` are obeyed).

As an added bonus, because the interpreter can now count on all these facts being true, it can run much faster than before. All the required checks for safety have been done up front, so it can run at full throttle. In addition, object references can now be treated as capabilities, because they are unforgeable—capabilities allow, for example, advanced security models for file I/O and authentication to be safely built on top of Java.

> **NOTE**
>
> Because you can now trust that a `private` variable really is private, and that no bytecode can perform some magic with casts to extract information from it (such as your credit card number), many of the security problems that might arise in other, less safe environments simply vanish! These guarantees also make erecting barriers against destructive applets possible, and easier. Because the Java system doesn't have to worry about "nasty" bytecodes, it can get on with creating the other levels of security it wants to provide to you.

The Class Loader

The class loader is another kind of gatekeeper, albeit a higher-level one. The verifier was the security of last resort. The class loader is the security of first resort.

When a new class is loaded into the system, it is placed into (lives in) one of several different "realms." In the current release, there are three possible realms: your local computer, the firewall-guarded local network on which your computer is located, and the Internet (the global Net). Each of these realms is treated differently by the class loader.

> **NOTE**
>
> Actually, there can be as many realms as your desired level of security (or paranoia) requires. This is because the class loader is under your control. As a programmer, you can make your own class loader that implements your own peculiar brand of security. (This is a radical step: you may have to give the users of your program a whole bunch of classes—and they give you a whole lot of trust—to accomplish this.)
>
> As a user, you can tell your Java-capable browser, or Java system, what realm of security (of the three) you'd like it to implement for you right now, or from now on.
>
> As a system administrator, Java has global security policies that you can set up to help guide your users to not "give away the store" (that is, set all their preferences to be unrestricted, promiscuous, "hurt me please!").

In particular, the class loader never allows a class from a "less protected" realm to replace a class from a more protected realm. The file system's I/O primitives, about which you should be *very* worried (and rightly so), are all defined in a local Java class, which means that they all live in the local-computer realm. Thus, no class from outside your computer (from either the supposedly trustworthy local network or from the Internet) can take the place of these classes and "spoof" Java code into using "nasty" versions of these primitives. In addition, classes in one realm cannot call upon the methods of classes in other realms, unless those classes have explicitly declared those methods `public`. This implies that classes from other than your local computer cannot even *see* the file system I/O methods, much less call them, unless you or the system wants them to.

In addition, every new applet loaded from the network is placed into a separate package-like name space. This means that applets are protected even from each other! No applet can access another's methods (or variables) without its cooperation. Applets from inside the firewall can even be treated differently from those outside the firewall, if you like.

> **NOTE**
>
> Actually, it's all a little more complex than this. In the current release, an applet is in a package "namespace" along with any other applets from that *source*. This source, or origin, is most often a host (domain name) on the Internet. This special "subrealm" is used extensively in the next section. Depending on where the source is located, outside the firewall (or inside), further restrictions may apply (or be removed entirely). This model is likely to be extended in future releases of Java, providing an even finer degree of control over which classes get to do what.

The class loader essentially partitions the world of Java classes into small, protected little groups, about which you can safely make assumptions that will *always* be true. This type of predictability is the key to well-behaved and secure programs.

You've now seen the full lifetime of a method. It starts as source code on some computer, is compiled into bytecodes on some (possibly different) computer, and can then travel (as a `.class` file) into any file system or network anywhere in the world. When you run an applet in a Java-capable browser (or download a class and run it by hand using `java`), the method's bytecodes are extracted from its `.class` file and carefully looked over by the verifier. Once they are declared safe, the interpreter can execute them for you (or a code generator can generate native binary code for them using either the "just-in-time" compiler or `java2c`, and then run that native code directly).

At each stage, more and more security is added. The final level of that security is the Java class library itself, which has several carefully designed classes and APIs that add the final touches to the security of the system.

The Security Manager

`SecurityManager` is an `abstract` class that was recently added to the Java system to collect, in one place, all the security policy decisions that the system has to make as bytecodes run. You learned before that you can create your own class loader. In fact, you may not have to, because you can subclass `SecurityManager` to perform most of the same customizations.

An instance of some subclass of `SecurityManager` is always installed as the current security manager. It has complete control over which of a well-defined set of "dangerous" methods are allowed to be called by any given class. It takes the realms from the last section into account, the source (origin) of the class, and the type of the class (stand-alone, or loaded by an applet). Each of these can be separately configured to have the effect you (the programmer) like on your Java system. For nonprogrammers, the system provides several levels of default security policies from which you can choose.

What is this "well-defined set" of methods that are protected?

File I/O is a part of the set, for obvious reasons. Applets, by default, can open, read, or write files only with the express permission of the user—and even then, only in certain restricted directories. (Of course, users can always be stupid about this, but that's what system administrators are for!)

Also in this protected set are the methods that create and use network connections, both incoming and outgoing.

The final members of the set are those methods that allow one thread to access, control, and manipulate other threads. (Of course, additional methods can be protected as well, by creating a new subclass of `SecurityManager` that handles them.)

For both file and network access, the user of a Java-capable browser can choose between three realms (and one subrealm) of protection:

- *unrestricted* (allows applets to do anything)
- *firewall* (allows applets within the firewall to do anything)
- *source* (allows applets to do things only with their origin Internet host, or with other applets from there)
- *local* (disallows all file and network access)

For file access, the *source* subrealm is not meaningful, so it really has only three realms of protection. (As a programmer, of course, you have full access to the security manager and can set up your own peculiar criteria for granting and revoking privileges to your heart's content.)

For network access, you can imagine wanting many more realms. For example, you might specify different groups of trusted domains (companies), each of which is allowed added privileges when applets from that group are loaded. Some groups can be more trusted than others, and you might even allow groups to grow automatically by allowing existing members to recommend new members for admission. (The Java seal of approval?)

In any case, the possibilities are endless, as long as there is a secure way of recognizing the original creator of an applet.

You might think this problem has already been solved, because classes are tagged with their origin. In fact, the Java run-time goes far out of its way to be sure that that origin information is never lost—any executing method can be dynamically restricted by this information anywhere in the call chain. So why *isn't* this enough?

Because what you'd really like to be able to do is permanently "tag" an applet with its original creator (its true origin), and no matter where it has traveled, a browser could verify the integrity and authenticate the creator of that applet. Just because you don't know the company or individual that operates a particular server machine doesn't mean that you *want* to mistrust every applet stored on that machine. It's just that, currently, to be really safe, you *should* mistrust those applets.

If somehow those applets were irrevocably tagged with a digital signature by their creator, and that signature could also guarantee that the applet had not been tampered with, you'd be golden.

NOTE

Luckily, Sun is planning to do exactly that for Java, as soon as export restrictions can be resolved.

Here's a helpful hint of where the team would like to go, from the security documentation: "...a mechanism exists whereby public keys and cryptographic message digests can be securely attached to code fragments that not only identify who originated the code, but guarantee its integrity as well. This latter mechanism will be implemented in future releases."

Look for these sorts of features in every release of Java; they will be a key part of the future of the Internet!

One final note about security. Despite the best efforts of the Java team, there is always a trade-off between useful functionality and absolute security. For example, Java applets can create windows, an extremely useful capability, but a "nasty" applet could use this to spoof the user into typing private password information, by showing a familiar program (or operating system) window and then asking an expected, legitimate-looking question in it. (The 1.0 release adds a special banner to applet-created windows to solve this problem.)

Flexibility and security can't both be maximized. Thus far on the Net, people have chosen maximum flexibility, and have lived with the minimal security the Net now provides. Let's hope that Java can help tip the scales a bit, enabling much better security, while sacrificing only a minimal amount of the flexibility that has drawn so many to the Net.

Summary

In this chapter we discussed the grand vision that some of us have for Java, and about the exciting future it promises.

Under the hood, the inner workings of the virtual machine, the bytecode interpreter (and all its bytecodes), the garbage collector, the class loader, the verifier, the security manager, and the powerful security features of Java were all revealed.

You now know *almost* enough to write a Java run-time environment of your own—but luckily, you don't have to. You can simply download the latest release of Java—or use a Java-capable browser to enjoy most of the benefits of Java right away.

I hope that Java ends up opening new roads in your mind, as it has in mine.

Java Security

40

*by Dan
Thomsen and
Tim Tiemens*

The reaction to Java varies from person to person. Everyone is excited about the functionality that Java provides, but the security considerations polarize people. Either the reaction is "Oh no! you can't do that" or "What is the big deal? It is just a new language." In this chapter we hope to explain the "Oh No!" reaction by discussing in depth the security risk involved in Java. Then, you can decide if Java security is important for you.

The answer to the first question, "Isn't Java just another computer language?" is yes, but it's how Java is used that opens up the question of security. Java interpreters make it easier than ever before to run new programs on your system; just point and click. (As the warning in Figure 40.1. shows, there are security concerns.)

FIGURE 40.1.

All Java applets in standalone windows come with a warning that shows they are risky.

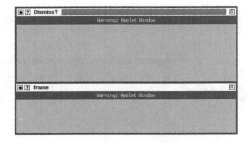

Once we have discussed the security issues we discuss the Java security mechanisms in detail.

Why Is Security an Issue with Java?

There are no known security vulnerabilities in Java. It is too new, and the developers are working hard to make sure none arise. Experts are skeptical about how secure Java can ever be, however, given how it is planned to be used. We hope to explain these issues so that you can understand them and make your own choice.

Consider the rate at which you currently introduce new programs to your system. If you are purchasing programs, you have to take a trip to the corner software market, and unless you are Mr. Gates, you are going to be able to purchase only a couple of titles. Now think of the time it takes to install the program. If you are surfing the net and bringing back non-Java programs, you may have to compile and then install them. Figuring in work and a social life, that is maybe five to ten programs a week.

Compare that with Java. Once the number of Java applets builds up, you could run new programs on your system as fast as you can find them and click on them. Even figuring in a generous social life, that could easily be hundreds of programs a week.

While the sheer numbers add to some of the risk, as we discuss latter, the biggest risk comes from the fact that you are not going to know who wrote all these programs. Not that you need to know the author of every program you run personally, but the easiest attack on your system is to get you to run a piece of hostile code.

If someone with a mischievous and malevolent bent from, say, Dubuque, Iowa can place a program on a general server, thousands of people may download the program before the undesired side effect of wiping out the hard disk is found. If the perpetrator was unfortunate enough to leave his or her name in the source code, he will be thoroughly chastised. While a reprisal over the Internet is only mildly annoying, it won't take too many malicious shareware incidents until the victims jump in their cars and drive to Dubuque with pitchforks and burning torches in hand (see Figure 40.2). When the program is anonymous, however, the real-world consequences are null. There is no place for the angry mob to congregate and vent its frustration.

FIGURE 40.2.

If you write malicious programs, beware of mobs of angry computer users seeking vengeance!

Assuming evolution takes care of the stupid perpetrators of mayhem, that leaves the smart perpetrators who post their programs anonymously. They will be able to post their increasingly sophisticated pranks unhindered. Why? Because people love free software. If you tell me a program balances my check book and whitens my teeth for only $299.95 I will scorn it as cheap marketing. However, if the same program is free, I will download a copy ASAP, because, hey, you never know. Effective anonymity from anonymous re-mailers and by people posting from compromised accounts is going to be a part of the Internet for a long time.

Corporations and other organizations have a reputation to maintain, and as a result, they police themselves and remove any malicious programs from their archives. But in the end you are faced with the decision while your mouse is hovering over some unknown applet, "Is this applet going to sauté my system?"

Creating a hostile applet is not easy. A lot of effort has been placed in making Java as safe as possible. Many will argue that creating a hostile applet is not even possible. However, for those that have seen many a "secure" program fall under the sheer pressure of constant probing over time, the possibility of an application being secure when it is first released is extremely low.

Next, instead of getting lost in the nuts and bolts of Java security right away, we are going to discuss some security concepts. Then we show you how Java security maps into these concepts.

Kinds of Attack

The form of attack that is going to be used the most against a system using Java is the "Trojan horse" attack. The old "Cool, they left us this huge wooden horse with wheels. Let's take it inside" becomes "Cool, here's a Java applet that whitens teeth. Let's run it."

The parallels between the two attacks are astounding. In both cases the attackers found it was too difficult to breach the outer defenses. In the Troy example, it was the city wall. In the computer example it was the connection from your system to the network.

Just what can this applet do once it gets inside? There are three broad classifications of malicious behavior:

- Disclosure of information
- Compromising the information integrity
- Denial of service

We will take a moment to look at each one of these to see just what damage a piece of malicious code running on your system can do.

Denial of Service

One of the easiest attacks to perform and one of the most difficult ones to stop is denial of service. Denial of service, in a nutshell, is that some resource of the system that you were depending on is no longer available to you. This can range from simply crashing the computer (where everything is unavailable) to just eating up all your CPU time and slowing your machine to a crawl.

Say the applet begs you to store some configuration information on your hard disk. (It is true that applets can beg; see the *"Security Manager"* section.) You think, "I will only let it read and write the one file. What harm can that do?" The applet can now write one very large file, however, filling up your disk and preventing you from saving other work. Once you realize it was the rogue applet, it's an easy fix, but tracking the problem down is very annoying.

Consider this: once you click on that button you don't know what that applet is doing. Is the applet really calculating a personal whitening formula based on your tooth enamel density or is it trying to calculate Pi to the last digit? (A classic denial of service attack—one used by countless science fiction heroes against malevolent computers.) Again, all this attack does is annoy you, but there is nothing in Java to prevent it. (Note that you can set the process priority for the applet thread low, but if you really believe the applet is doing useful work, you won't.)

> **NOTE**
>
> Some computer systems are highly important to organizations. Thus, denial of some service would be catastrophic. If, for example, the malicious program could clog up the computer used for the stock exchange, the costs to investors could be staggering.

Crashing the whole computer from Java is going to be extremely difficult because a great deal of care has gone into creating and testing the Java exception handlers that catch faults in Java applets.

Compromising Information Integrity

This is a more insidious attack (assuming you have valuable data on the system). What is it worth to you to make sure that information remains as accurate as it was when you entered it? Consider, for example, your personal budget. What if a hostile program modified the balance of your checking account so you thought you afford that copy of DOOM with smell-o-vision. Most likely the cost to you is some embarrassment and an overdraft checking penalty.

For an organization, however, the costs could be much larger. The malicious code could modify the financial statements for a company's prospectus, which could cause lawsuits for misrepresentation. If the malicious code modifies a patient's record or the software that is used in a pacemaker, the consequences could be death.

In terms of Java, every possible step has been taken to control that a Java applet cannot modify files on the client system.

Disclosure of Information

Another serious attack is disclosure of information. If the information is important to the success of an organization, consider what a competitor can do with that information. Corporate espionage is a real threat, especially from foreign companies where the legal reprisals are much more difficult to enforce.

Assuming the computer is hooked to the Internet, it is as easy as pie for the malicious program to send the information home to the evil-doers. The program could use e-mail or communicate with an Internet server.

In terms of Java, once again every possible precaution has been taken to ensure that an applet cannot read other files on the system. Targeting specific sensitive files is even more problematic, because it's difficult for a malicious program to know what is sensitive and what isn't.

The Information Bucket

Now that you have seen some of the attacks, we describe how those attacks are stopped in traditional secure systems. One of the basic premises of computer security is to contain information so that you know where it came from, who has modified it, and where the information can go. Let's call this concept an "information bucket." The idea is to put all the related information into the same bucket, and then control who can access that bucket. See Figure 40.3 for some examples. The bucket has also been called the *access class, security perimeter,* or in DoD systems, the *security level.*

FIGURE 40.3.

Security starts with clearly labeling and storing information into separate buckets.

For example, most computer systems have the concept of users. Each user gets his or her own little bucket to play in. All the user's files reside in that bucket, and the user controls access to them.

The system needs to control not only who can access a bucket, but which programs can run in that bucket and what those programs can access. Communication between programs must also be controlled. Programs could signal the information to other programs, which then write the information down in another bucket, as illustrated in Figure 40.4. So which programs can talk to each other must be strictly controlled as well. To summarize, a bucket has a set of programs and a set of files the programs can access. If there is no overlap between buckets, the system is very secure. No one could read or modify data, or consume system resources from another bucket.

## Chapter 40

FIGURE 40.4.

Communication between programs running in different buckets must be controlled as well.

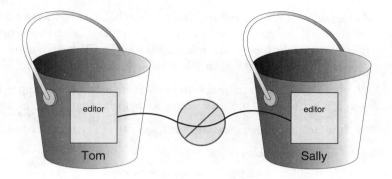

This would be the equivalent of giving everyone their own computer and not letting them talk to each other. This is obviously an overly restrictive way to solve the security problem. People need to share information. As long as everyone knows what resources are in their bucket and carefully share their information with others, the system is still relatively secure.

The problem comes when the bucket boundaries have not been defined, people are not aware of them, or the bucket boundaries overlap. For example, if two different buckets can read and write the same file, information can flow between the two buckets. In other words, the bucket leaks. Leaky buckets are an indication of potential security problems. Combine leaky/overlapping buckets with a complex system where the number of buckets is very large and it becomes difficult to even discuss how secure the system is.

Once you start opening up the system to allow information to flow between buckets, a new problem raises its head: transitive information flow between buckets. Consider if you give Sally information from your bucket. How do you know that Sally is going to keep your information secret? She may give it to Tom, and because Tom doesn't know any better he gives it to Polly, your arch enemy (see Figure 40.5).

FIGURE 40.5.

Once information is allowed to move between buckets it is difficult to know where it is going to stop.

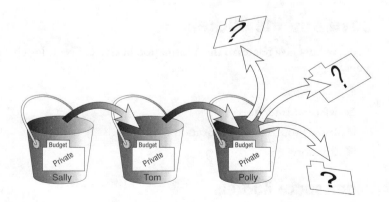

As we said earlier, some information needs to be shared between buckets. That is, some leaks are necessary. Special programs can be set up that monitor data being transferred between buckets to ensure only the proper data is leaving the bucket. These programs are trusted to only let the proper data through. It is their job to make sure the entire bucket is not drained.

Writing a program that comes with a guarantee is a difficult thing to do. The easiest approach is to make the trusted program simple so that the program can be analyzed for correctness.

So, you can get a rough measure of the security of a system by considering these three factors:

1. how many buckets there are
2. how much overlap there is between buckets
3. how trusted the programs are protecting those data channels (if information is allowed to move between buckets)

The more overlap between buckets, the more information can flow through the system, and the more analysis is required to ensure the system is secure.

The mechanism that enforces the separation between buckets must also be scrutinized, because it is one of those trusted programs. If information flows between the buckets in ways that was not intended, the system has a covert channel. If any one of the security components that are discussed in the *"Security Protection"* section has a flaw your system could be compromised. Remember, your Java browser is your friend; it is the only thing protecting you from those potentially hostile applets.

Another consideration for the security of a system is "Are there any exceptions to the bucket policy?" For example, many systems let an administrator play around in any bucket on the system. The problem is not that we don't trust administrators, but rather that it gives attackers an opening. Now, rather than trying to find a covert channel to peek into another bucket, the attackers try to trick the system into thinking they are the administrator.

Java and the Buckets

Let's see how Java relates to the information bucket concept. Java has several different kinds of buckets.

- Namespace
- Method Interfaces
- Inter-Process Communication
- Memory

Namespace Buckets

The first kind of buckets is the namespace buckets. There are two types of namespace buckets: local and network. The rationale for this split is that all applets originating from the local system can be given special privileges because the administrator checked them out before installing them. The network bucket is divided up into smaller buckets: one for each network address. (See Figure 40.6.)

FIGURE 40.6.

The Java namespace is divided into local and network buckets, with network being further subdivided into a names space for each network address.

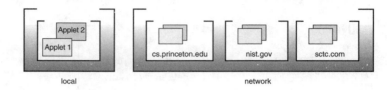

This means that applets that are from different classes but from the same network site are in the same bucket. This raises a red flag because we have different applets sharing the same bucket. Obviously, the applets are coming from the same network site, so you may think they should be compatible. However, if the applets are from a general server such as a university where a number of people can download applets, or a large service provider where you can rent space for a Web page (such as America Online), the applets could be written by different authors with very different intents. (See Figure 40.7.)

FIGURE 40.7.

Applets loaded from the same network location are in the same namespace, even though the applets could be written by a diverse set of authors.

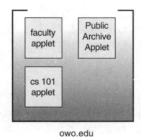
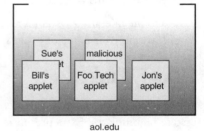

An applet may be able to trick another applet at the same site into using its code rather the code of an applet from a different site. Note that the internal class definitions and library calls are always checked first so they can never be replaced by code from an outsider applet.

Method Interface Buckets

The second kind of bucket in Java is the object-oriented interfaces to the Java applets. Each applet can have a public interface that other applets can call. If an applet declares a method as private, it is the only applet that can access the method (see Figure 40.8). The problem with this approach is the buckets are designed by the applications builders. Not all of them are conscientious or trustworthy.

In fact, many applets and code fragments are going to be written by people not concerned with security. People will also integrate applets and code fragments together as they need them. Who knows what the resulting security of these franken-applets will be. All you know for sure is that the applet is contained into one of the namespace buckets.

FIGURE 40.8.

Java methods can be public or be hidden from other applets by being declared private.

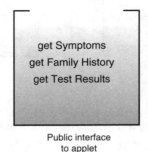
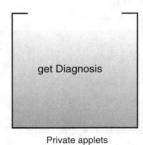

get Symptoms
get Family History
get Test Results

get Diagnosis

Public interface
to applet

Private applets

Interprocess Communication Bucket

Who can the applet talk to? An applet can almost always talk to one server on the Internet. Thus, there is almost always a channel for the applet to disclose information. Access to other applets or programs is strictly controlled.

Access to the operating system is also tightly controlled. This can be used to prevent the applet from learning your name or other system attributes.

Memory Bucket

When it all comes down to it, the only real buckets are the chunks of memory that the Java system manipulates. Extra precautions have been taken to ensure applets cannot poke around in memory that has not been allocated to them.

This is done by strictly controlling access to the pointer type. Pointers cannot be manipulated by the applet. If an applet could modify a pointer directly, they could point the pointer off into the memory of another applet or even a different namespace bucket. This would be a serious covert channel.

One denial-of-service attack that works against Java is to repeatedly create new objects until all the available memory is gone.

This is why people concerned about security are worried about Java. Although Java separates data into different buckets, some buckets overlap. Also, a great deal of trust must be placed in code that controls pointers.

Improving Java Security Outside of Java

Now that you have an idea of what some of the vulnerabilities are, we look at what can be done outside of Java to protect against them. As pointed out, some buckets overlap, but the overlap is difficult to exploit. Thus, the attacks to be concerned about are covert channels and attacks that use the administrator interface.

The covert channels could only be exploited by malicious code. If you can block malicious code you can prevent the covert channels from being exploited. Detecting malicious code is a challenging job, but that is what the Java Verifier does. We discuss the Java Verifier, with its strengths and weaknesses, in the *"Security Protection"* section.

Digital Signatures

Another alternative to avoid malicious code is to only run applets that are written without malicious intent. Obviously you can't quickly and accurately determine the intent of a program. However, if you can be one-hundred percent guaranteed that the applet was written by a person you trust, you know the program was not written with malicious intent. However, you must also guarantee that the code was not modified after your trusted friend finished it.

Crypto-seals or digital signatures allow this by detecting if any changes have been made once your friend signed the applet. Digital signatures even detect if the applet was modified en route to your workstation from the server.

Software Engineering

Simple errors are a common source of security vulnerabilities. You know your trusted friend didn't put in any intentional security violations, but did he or she put one in accidentally?

Consider this scenario. Bobby's friend Peter writes an applet that turns scanned images into electronic postcards. Peter makes the applet publicly available on the local school server.

Greg notices that Peter made the `getImage()` method public. So Greg writes an applet that puts a canceled stamp on the postcard. The idea is that Greg wants people to use his applet at the same time. Greg's applet also copies the image back to Greg's server.

Bobby uses the applet to send his mom a postcard of her with a beehive hairdo. Mom retaliates by scanning in that picture of Bobby when she made him be the dresser dummy for his sister's prom dress: green taffeta, ribbons and all.

Now Greg has just acquired a very interesting, and potentially profitable image. Good software engineering on Peter's part could have prevented this unfortunate incident. Remember if the software is free, you are getting what you paid for in terms of software engineering.

If you think this example is contrived, think again. It is exactly these kinds of vulnerabilities that were found in the early versions of the HotJava web browser system libraries[1]. One of the biggest effects on good software engineering is going to be the near random combination of all the applets as people borrow prewritten code fragments and add them to their applications. In the past, people have focused on making their programs work, not on making them secure. There is no reason to believe that will change because of Java. One can hope that solid standard libraries evolve, but it will take time.

Risk Analysis

We have talked about some of the potential vulnerabilities, but what does it mean to you? Are you at risk when using Java? To figure out your risk you must answer several questions:

- Do I have anything to protect from disclosure or unwanted modification?
- Is my system so critical that a denial of services attack must be avoided?
- Is anyone out there trying to get me or my information?
- What is the cost of a compromise?
- What does it cost not to use Java?

If you do not have anything to protect on your system, running Java browsers are not a problem because you have nothing to lose. If your system is running software for remote pacemakers, don't run Java! All other cases fall somewhere between these two extremes and require you to quantify some values.

First, is anyone out to get you? The answer to this is always yes. The propagation of the myriad of computer viruses clearly indicates that there are always going to be people who want to do mischief. As a rule these people have been annoying and random, so they are not really a high-grade threat.

If, however, you are a corporation or large organization, you have information to protect. Competitors are not always going to play by the rules. Now you must figure how much it is going to cost you if your data is compromised and weigh it against the cost of not running Java.

Most people running personal computers out of their homes will probably decide that Java is worth the risk because it saves them time downloading and running software and saves them money (as long as you remove potentially embarrassing data such as things that might involve green taffeta or powder blue leisure suits). Note, if the system is a home business and a personal system, the home business is at risk.

Organizations are faced with much tougher choices.

---

[1]Drew Dean and Dan S. Wallach, "Security Flaws in the HotJava Web Browser", November 3, 1995, Note: Covers HotJava 1.0 alpha 3. URL: `ftp://ftp.cs.princeton.edu/reports/1995/501.ps.Z`

Security for Organizations

Java is a wonderful tool, but as we have pointed out there are lots of security considerations. These considerations are much more important for organizations.

As organizations become more interconnected, their need to be connected grows. The trend in the past for many organizations has been to introduce the technology without analyzing its effect on the organization. As a result, the ways that information flows through an organization grows. In terms of the bucket model, it's like just having one big bucket.

Going back to less connected systems with fewer functions is almost impossible for these organizations. Nowhere is this more apparent than in Java. Java brings easy-to-use interfaces that run on a wide variety of platforms. What organization isn't going to look to Java to solve some of its problems?

The problem with using Java in an organization is that organizations have something to protect. They could lose face, assets, data integrity, or worse. On a personal level the risks are much smaller.

Organizations have to protect themselves not only from outsiders but also from honest mistakes by their own people. As you will see in the next section, many of the final security decisions reside with the end user. In a large organization you can be guaranteed that some user is going to make a bad decision sometime, no matter how much training he or she has, and no matter what clever warning posters the company puts up.

Organizations can have several alternatives for reducing the risk in how they use Java.

Isolating the Organization's Java Capability

The first alternative is to isolate the corporate network from the Internet (see Figure 40.9). The firewall must stop all requests for Java applets. If someone needs an applet from the Internet, they can request an administrator to go get it. The administrator evaluates the applet, tests it, and then installs it on the internal net. In this approach, the corporate network is treated as one big information bucket. This reduces the risk of getting a malicious applet for the following reasons:

- The number of applets is greatly reduced because only needed applets are brought in
- The administrator only gets applets from a trusted source
- The administrator reviews the applet

The threat is not eliminated, however, because the malicious code inside an applet could be cleverly hidden. The malicious Java applet may still be able to e-mail home. This solution severely limits Java and only reduces the risk, but it may be suitable for some organizations.

FIGURE 40.9.

One solution for improving Java security for organizations is to not allow users to download applets from the Internet. All applets are downloaded and checked by a Java administrator.

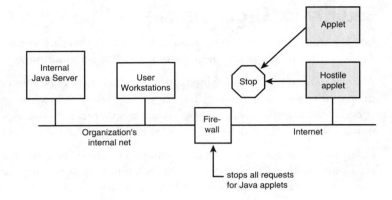

Network Separation

Another approach is completely separating the corporate network from the Internet. Internet workstations would be on a separate net (see Figure 40.10). When Java is needed, employees go to the Internet workstations that have full Java access. This approach is inconvenient, but very secure because there is no sensitive data on the Java net.

FIGURE 40.10.

Another approach to improve security is to keep Java off the internal net entirely. Java is still available, but it is inconvenient.

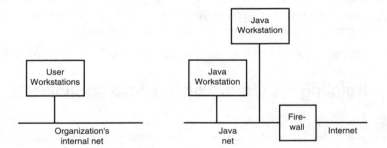

Advanced Firewall Protection

A hot topic on the firewalls mailing list has been about whether in the future Java applets could be checked at the firewall. The check would be to ensure that the applet had been digitally signed by someone the organization trusts. If the applet was not signed, or if the applet was tampered with, the applet is rejected (see Figure 40.11). The advantage of this approach is that the approach is much easier to administer.

> **NOTE**
>
> For those interested in joining the firewall mailing list write a message to `firewalls@greatcircle.com` that contains the line `subscribe firewalls user@host`.

FIGURE 40.11.

In the future, firewalls could be required to ensure that all applets have been digitally signed before being allowed into the internal network.

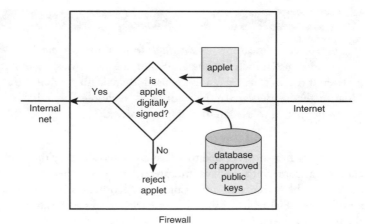

Users may still sneak applets past the firewall, but the Java verify could be modified to require valid digital signatures as well. Then, even local applets must be approved before they can be executed. Hopefully this functionality will be available soon.

So, Is Java Secure?

Java has no inherent design flaws that make it insecure. However, there are several places where security could be improved. Also, a great deal of trust must be placed in the Java browser to ensure that the applet is properly contained. Even one small implementation error could compromise the entire system.

As a result, there is always the potential that the next applet you bring inside is a Trojan horse that exploits a newly-discovered vulnerability in the Java browser.

Every precaution has been taken to make Java as safe as possible, but in the end everyone must weigh the risks and decide for themselves.

In the next section we discuss the mechanics of Java security and provide some important tips for increasing the security of using Java at your site.

Security Protection in Java

What follows is a generic description of the security measures *available* to all implementations of a Java Interpreter (that is, any software capable of executing Java applets). The section discusses which components of the Java interpreter are performing the security checks and what those checks are. Discussions of what security measures are available for your favorite Java Interpreter are given later in the chapter.

The security measures applied to a class are determined by the origin of the class. The built-in classes that come with the Java interpreter have fewer checks applied to them because they are assumed to be correct and non-malicious. All other classes go through a much more stringent set of checks. Figure 40.12 shows the security checks each class must go through depending on the origin of the class.

FIGURE 40.12.

An overview of security checks. The built-in classes are subjected to a small subset of the available security checks (path 1). Classes loaded from the network (path 2) and classes from the local system (path 3) are subjected to more security checks.

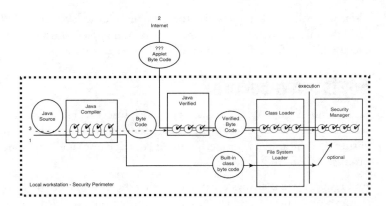

Figure 40.12 also introduces the concept of a security perimeter. For our purposes, we'll consider the security perimeter to be the line that separates those things you can control from those things you can't.

First we discuss the path followed by built-in classes that make up the system.

Security Checks for Built-In Classes

For built-in classes, the assumption is that the code is part of the system and therefore must be trusted. Because the code is trusted, many of the checks that could be applied at load- or runtime are not applied, as shown in Figure 40.12. Note that because these classes really are part of the Java interpreter, many of them must be loaded before any checks could be applied anyway.

The built-in classes are those classes stored on your local file system that are located in any of the directories in your CLASSPATH. Your CLASSPATH is an environment variable that contains a colon separated list of directories. Your exact CLASSPATH is user- and system-dependent, but here is an example:

```
CLASSPATH="/usr/local/java/classes/:/usr/share/java/classes
```

One of those directories contains the built-in class file. Again, the exact name of this file is system-dependent, but some of the names used for this file include moz2_0.zip or lib/classes.zip.

CAUTION

Only install vendor-supplied classes as built-in Java classes. Never, ever, store classes of unknown origins in any directory on your CLASSPATH. Putting an unknown class in this directory turns off many of the security checks that are protecting you from malicious code.

The built-in classes are only checked by the following components:

- Java compiler
- File system loader
- Security Manager (optional)

Java Compiler

The Java compiler is a big step toward making sure that the any Java class does not contain any security violations. As shown in Figure 40.13, the Java compiler turns Java source code file into a bytecode file. The Java compiler ensures that the safety rules of the Java language are obeyed.

FIGURE 40.13.

The Java compiler turns Java source code into byte code if the code meets the Java Languages safety requirements.

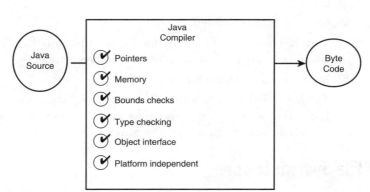

Some of the numerous safety mechanisms in the Java compiler are as follows:

■ Pointers

Java does not have pointers directly to memory. Instead pointers are a special type that must be de-referenced by the Java system to access the data. Java pointers can be thought of as keys that let you access the data associated with the key—without the key you cannot access the data. The Java compiler checks to make sure pointers are not manipulated in any way. Java provides no pointer arithmetic mechanisms and does not allow typecasts into the Java pointer type. This prevents a malicious program from making a key.

■ Memory and garbage collection

Java programmers do not allocate and manage memory. All memory management is handled for them. The Java Interpreter decides where to bind the class fields and class methods to memory, not the Java compiler. The Java Interpreter provides no mechanism to discover the results of this binding.

Garbage collection of unused memory is automatic. This means that programmers do not have to explicitly free up memory they are no longer using. This provides protection against some types of memory object reuse.

■ Array bounds checking

Java classes are not allowed to access beyond the end of an array. Arrays remain the same size from creation to destruction, and the runtime prevents indexing overruns and underruns.

■ Strict type-checking

Type checking is enforced to ensure that the compile time type and the runtime type of variables are compatible. Casts are checked to ensure validity. No casts are allowed to the internal Java pointer type. (See the previous Pointers bullet for more information.)

■ Enforced access modifiers

All access to an object must go through its public interface. This ensures that an object's `private` methods or `private` data stays private.

■ Implementation Independent

The Java language specification does not allow "implementation dependent" results. Everything occurs in a specified order that does not vary between Java Interpreters. Thus code behaves the same on all platforms.

File System Loader

Built-in classes are protected to a degree by the file system loader. As shown in Figure 40.14, the file system loader performs one security relevant function. It has the responsibility of placing the built-in classes in a namespace that is separate from the namespace used by other classes. This provides an extra level of protection from unauthorized manipulation by classes.

FIGURE 40.14.

File system loader checks for built-in classes.

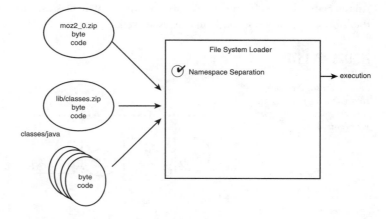

Security Manager for Built-In Classes

Built-in classes need not be subjected to any Security Manager checks. Any use of the security features provided by the Security Manager is completely voluntary. Built-in classes are usually supplied by the vendor and require access to system resources without interference from the Security Manager. One reason for this is because the vendor implements the SecurityManager class and puts it in the built-in class file that is loaded with the Java Interpreter. Thus, the Security Manager checks cannot be applied to loading the SecurityManager class, because there is no Security Manager available yet to apply the checks!

Those classes that you write and compile and store in a directory on your CLASSPATH are not forced to call the Security Manager. Thus, you are turning off an important set of security checks for your classes, something we don't recommended.

For now, it's sufficient to say that built-in classes are allowed to do the following:

- read files
- write files
- load libraries on the client
- run new processes on the client
- delete files (by running processes that in turn delete the file)
- cause the Java Virtual Machine to exit
- connect to port(s) on the client
- connect to port(s) on 3rd party host
- create popup windows without the warning border

Security Checks for Non-Built-In Classes

All the classes that are not built-in go through a series of security checks as seen in Figure 40.15. All the classes loaded from the network are non-built-in classes. Most of the classes loaded from the local system are non-built-in classes as well.

FIGURE 40.15.

Security checks for non-built-in classes. Network classes do not go through a Java compiler that is under your control.

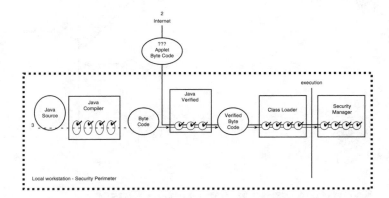

All Java classes are compiled by an approved, trusted Java compiler, or are they? Because you control the Java compiler, you hopefully are using a good compiler that you can trust to safely compile Java byte code. When you get a Java applet from the net you have no control over the compilation process. The individual producing the applet may have used a bad compiler, or the byte code may have been tampered with after it was produced. Because the Java source and Java compiler are outside of your security perimeter, you can rely on none of the security related mechanisms built into the language or the compiler.

As Figure 40.15 shows, classes under your control follow path three through the compiler you control. However, most of the classes you load follow path two from the Internet (where you do not control the compiler). From a security point of view, it is the bytecode that matters, not the Java source. A benign example is when a buggy Java compiler is used and generates "illegal" pointer arithmetic bytecodes. A malicious example is when an attacker specifically modifies either the compiler or the bytecodes to produce a class that no legitimate Java compiler could ever generate.

These are the practical implications from having the Java source and Java compiler outside of your security perimeter: You can't prevent either the buggy compiler nor the malicious compiler from producing bytecodes that could cause your computer system to perform unauthorized actions.

Fortunately, the Java interpreter does elaborate checks before loading and executing a class. Each Java class is checked by the following components:

■ The Java Verifier

■ The Class loader

■ The Security Manager

We discuss each component in turn.

Verifier

The Java Verifier is used to check the bytecode to make sure that the safety features of the Java language are followed. As Figure 40.16 shows, the Java Verifier takes byte code, checks it, and only passes the code through if the checks are passed.

FIGURE 40.16.
Java Verifier analyzes the byte codes to ensure that the safety features of the Java language are followed.

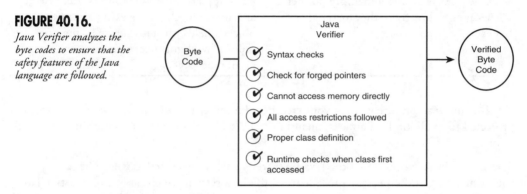

The purpose of the Verifier is to allow the Java Interpreter to retain three important properties. These three properties follow:

1. Applets do not forge pointers, and always use pointers correctly

2. Applets must use pointers (that is, no alternative access mechanisms exist)

3. All access restrictions are properly followed

These three properties combine to enable us to make strong security-relevant statements about the system. For example, consider an Applet `credit` of the type `Credit.class` that stores your credit card number in one of its private fields, called `ccnumber`. The security-relevant assertion we make is this: "No other applet can access `credit.ccnumber`." One way to show this assertion is true is to examine the ways another applet, `attack` of the type `Attack.class`, could attempt to access `credit.ccnumber`. Some sample attacks are given in Table 40.1.

Table 40.1. These potential attack techniques are stopped by the Java Verifier.

Potential Attack Method	*Property that Prevents the Attack*
attack simply accesses `credit.ccnumber`	#3—All access restrictions are properly followed. Because `Credit.class` declared `ccnumber` to be type `private`, access is denied.
attack creates a class `FakeCredit.class`, which also has a field `ccnumber`, but makes `ccnumber` in `FakeCredit.class` public. Then, attack tries something like this: `stolencc = ((FakeCredit)credit).ccnumber;`	#1—Applets cannot forge pointers and must always use pointers correctly. The attempt to recast the pointer `credit` to a pointer of type `FakeCredit` is not allowed.
`attack.class` creates a memory pointer that points directly to the storage that `credit.ccnumber` uses.	#2—Applets must use pointers. Because no alternative mechanisms exist to access an object's fields, the creation of a "memory pointer" will not succeed in accessing `credit.ccnumber`.

The first implication is that when your credit card number is stored in a private location, it is protected from all kinds of attacks: unauthorized disclosure, unauthorized modification, and so on.

The second implication is that the Java Interpreter itself is protected as well. The Java system itself (including and especially those parts of the Java system which perform security related functions, e.g. the Security Manager) are protected from malicious modification because of these three properties.

Other aspects of the Java Interpreter help ensure these three properties remain true. The principle protection mechanism concerns Java's memory-management system. Of primary importance is that bytecodes do not use pointers to a memory location. Instead, the bytecodes use "capabilities" or "handles" to denote access requests. These "capabilities" are resolved to actual memory locations only by the Java Interpreter. Property #2 is a direct consequence of the fact that the Java Interpreter provides instructions of the form "Load this pointer (Capability, for example) into this register." It does not provide instructions of the form "Load the contents of this memory location into this register."

Another memory-management protection mechanism results from the fact that the Java Interpreter decides where in physical memory to place the class (or pieces of the class.) Thus, the declaration of a class need not have any bearing on the physical location of the class in memory.

In terms of the credit card example above, our `attack.class` faces two distinct problems if it is going to "forge a pointer" to `credit.ccnumber`.

First, using the only starting point available to it (the capability we've been referring to as `credit`), it must determine the memory location of `credit.ccnumber`. Remember, though, the Java Interpreter has incredible flexibility in determining memory locations. Gone are the days where a simple "memory location of `credit` plus eight equals the memory location of `credit.ccnumber`."

Second, if `attack.class` does somehow accomplish this feat, and learns that the memory location of `credit.ccnumber` is "0x2BAD," it still hasn't won. The Java Virtual Machine provides no mechanism to perform the function "Load the contents of memory location 0x2BAD." To succeed, `attack.class` must construct a request in the form of a Capability such that the same memory location is accessed, but where the access control mechanisms are bypassed. (The first row in Table 40.1 shows what happens when you take the obvious approach and simply refer to `credit.ccnumber` in a normal manner; the access control mechanism prevents it.) It is becoming difficult to imagine how our `attack.class` might succeed. It still may be possible for `attack.class` to access or modify `credit.ccnumber`; the memory management system just makes it very unlikely that a "forged memory pointer" method is going to succeed.

Details on the Verifier can be found in "Low Level Security in Java."[2] A summary of that paper is presented here. The Verifier performs four separate passes when examining a Java class to be loaded.

The first pass is mainly a syntactic check. It ensures that the class "magic number" is present in the first part of the class file. It also ensures that the class file is neither too short nor too long.

The second pass consists of all the verification that can be accomplished without looking at the class method bytecodes. This pass ensures that every class has a superclass and that the constant pool is constructed and referenced properly.

The third pass consists of checking the bytecodes of each method in the class. A "Data-flow" analysis is performed on each method to ensure various invariants hold true regarding the stack and registers. At the end of this check, it is known that no stack overflows or underflows can occur. Also, each method call is checked to ensure that the correct number and type of arguments are used.

The fourth pass consists of those tests that have been delayed from the third pass due to efficiency reasons. If possible, pass three avoids actually loading the class file. The checks in the fourth pass occur the first time a class is referenced by the Java Interpreter. Further checks occur the first time a field or method within the class is called. These checks ensure that the field or method exists, that all the types match, and that the current execution context has access to the field or method.

---

[2] Frank Yellin, "Low Level Security in Java", Dec 19, 1995
URL: `http://java.sun.com/sfaq/verifier.html`

Class Loader

After incoming code has been checked by the Verifier, the protections in Java class loader are invoked. The primary function of the class loader is to create and maintain separate *namespaces*. As shown in Figure 40.17, the class loader begins with a verified Java class, and performs namespace separation on it in preparation for execution.

FIGURE 40.17.

Class loader security checks for built-in classes.

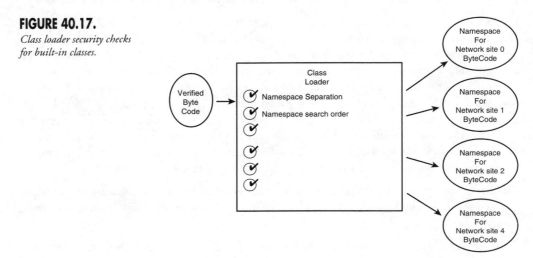

Each network source is given its own namespace and built-in classes are given their own namespace to share.

Additional protections associated with this level are provided by using a safe method to search the namespaces for a class reference. When any class references another class, the file system source namespace is searched first (that is, the built-in classes are searched first). If no match is found, the namespace of the referencing class is searched. If still no match is found, an error is returned. By fixing the order of namespace searches in this manner, it makes it impossible for network source classes to override any filesystem source class. It also makes it impossible for a file system source class to access a network source class by accident.

> **CAUTION**
>
> The surprising implication of namespaces separated by network source creates the strange situation where you should distrust your immediate neighbors more than anyone else! This is because your applet is put into the same namespace as all the other applets loaded from the same server that loaded your applet. This feature supports the applet writer who wants to split the applet into one or more classes: each class is in the same namespace as the others, and thus have access to each other. But this same feature

introduces a security vulnerability. If you fail to take proper precautions in your code (for example, you make `Credit.ccnumber public` instead of `private`), your applet is vulnerable to attack from other applets. For example, if `Attack.class` is loaded from the same server as `Credit.class`, the simple access of `credit.ccnumber` succeeds. This vulnerability is of special concern to those Java class providers who are using some sort of shared host to serve applets. For example, all `aol.com` applets, no matter who writes them, are placed in the same namespace. Programmers beware!

Security Manager Security Checks for Classes

The Security Manager is used to provide a flexible access control mechanism for all classes. Any time a class needs to access a system resource, such as a file, the Security Manager is invoked. For each request the storage manager returns if the access is allowed or denied. As shown in Figure 40.18, the Security Manager acts a guardian for the system resources.

FIGURE 40.18.

Security Manager guards system resources from Java classes. Java classes can only access system resources if the Security Manager approves.

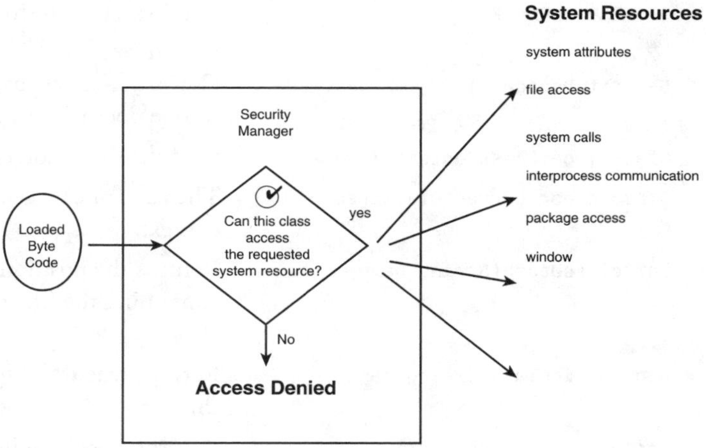

System Resources

system attributes

file access

system calls

interprocess communication

package access

window

Security Manager

Loaded Byte Code

Can this class access the requested system resource?   yes

No

Access Denied

Any time a non-built-in class accesses a system resource it must first ask permission from the Security Manager. Classes are prevented from bypassing the Security Manager because none of the system resources are available to ordinary classes. If a class wants to access a resource it must be defined as a method. Only the built-in classes can access system resources directly. However, each built-in class protects its public methods (those that ordinary classes can use) by having those public methods call the Security Manager.

For example, suppose you have a new system resource (say, access to the CD-ROM) that you want to make available to ordinary classes. To do this, you create a new class, create a public method like `readCDrom()`, and store the new class in the directory for built-ins. Now any class can call readCDrom() to read the CD-ROM. If you want to control access to readCDrom(), you add a call to the Security Manager in the readCDrom() method. Now classes can access the CD-ROM if the Security Manager says it is okay.

All built-in classes which provide access to the system resources are expected to use the Security Manager. The Security Manager provides methods to be called by the built-in classes to check for authorization before performing certain actions. Tables 40.2 and 40.3 provide a list of the protected and public methods, respectively, as well as a short explanation of each the method's purpose[3].

Table 40.2 lists the fields and methods of interest to programmers wishing to extend or modify the behavior of the Security Manager. For the most part, only programmers creating a Java-capable browser need to be concerned with these fields and methods.

Table 40.2. Protected variables and methods (for use by SecurityManager programmers).

Field or Method	Purpose
boolean inCheck	Local variable to store state of a "security check in progress."
SecurityManager()	Constructs a new SecurityManager object (if one doesn't exist already).
Class[] getClassContext()	Gets the execution context of this Class.
ClassLoader currentClassLoader()	The current ClassLoader in the execution context.
int classDepth(String name)	Returns the position of the stack frame containing the first occurrence of the named class.
boolean inClass(String name)	Returns true if the specified String is in this Class.
boolean inClassLoader()	Returns a boolean indicating whether or not the current ClassLoader is equal to null.

Table 40.3 lists the methods of interest to all Java users. These SecurityManager methods determine the set of security-relevant checks that the Java Interpreter can perform. Java users can use this table to gain an understanding for which system resources are protected.

---

[3]Sun Microsystems, Java Development Kit Source Code. *File:* java/src/java/lang/SecurityManager.java. *File:* java/src/java/io/File.java. *Information:* URL: http://java.sun.com/JDK-beta2/index.html *Distribution:* URL: ftp://ftp.javasoft.com/pub/JDK-1_0-solaris2-sparc.tar.Z

Table 40.3. `Public` **variables and methods (for use by** `SecurityManager` **programmers and by Java system programmers.**

Field or method	Purpose
`boolean getInCheck()`	Returns whether there is a security check in progress.
`Object getSecurityContext()`	Returns an implementation-dependent `Object` that encapsulates enough information about the caller's current execution context; this context is used to perform some of the security checks later.
`checkCreateClassLoader()`	Checks to see if the `ClassLoader` has been created. It is used to prevent the installation of additional class loaders.
`checkAccess(Thread g)`	Checks to see if the caller can modify the specified thread. The specified thread is allowed to modify the current thread group.
`checkAccess(ThreadGroup g)`	Checks to see if the specified thread group is allowed to modify the thread group.
`checkExit(int status)`	Checks to see if the caller can exit the Virtual Machine (with an `exit()` call).
`checkExec(String cmd)`	Checks to see if the caller can create a new process (that is, run a program).
`checkLink(String lib)`	Checks to see if the caller can cause the specified dynamic library to be loaded and linked (and thus used as native code).
`checkRead(FileDescriptor fd)`	Checks to see if the caller can read the file descriptor.
`checkRead(String file)`	Checks to see if the caller can read the file with the specified system-dependent filename.
`checkRead(String file, Object context)`	Checks to see if the caller's current execution context and the indicated execution context can both read the file with the specified system-dependent filename.
`checkWrite(FileDescriptor fd)`	Checks to see if the caller can write the file descriptor.

continues

Table 40.3. continued

Field or method	Purpose
checkWrite(String file)	Checks to see if the caller can write the file with the specified system-dependent filename.
checkDelete(String file)	Checks to see if the caller can delete the file with the specified system-dependent file name.
checkConnect(String host, int port)	Checks to see if the caller can create a socket connected to the specified port on the specified host.
checkConnect(String host, int ➡port, Object context)	Checks to see if the caller's current execution context and the indicated execution context can both create a socket connected to the specified port on the specified host.
checkListen(int port)	Checks to see if the caller can create a server socket to listen to the specified local port.
checkAccept(String host, int port)	Checks to see if the caller can accept a connection request to the specified port on the specified host.
checkPropertiesAccess()	Checks to see if the caller has access to the system properties.
checkPropertyAccess(String key)	Checks to see if the caller has access to the system property named by key.
checkPropertyAccess ➡(String key, String def)	Checks to see if the caller has access to the system property named by key and def.
boolean checkTopLevelWindow ➡(Object window)	Checks to see if the caller can create top-level windows. A return of false means that the window creation is allowed, but the window will indicate some sort of visual warning. A return of true means the creation is allowed with no special restrictions. (To disallow the creation entirely, this method throws a SecurityException.)
checkPackageAccess(String pkg)	Checks to see if the caller can access a package.

Field or method	Purpose
`checkPackageDefinition(String pkg)`	Checks to see if the caller can define classes in a package—that is, if the caller can add a new class to the package.
`checkSetFactory()`	Check to see if the caller can set a networking-related object factory.

The `SecurityManager.class` provided in the distribution is not intended to be used directly. Instead, each Java Interpreter is to create its own subclass of the `SecurityManager.class` in order to implement the desired security policy and security policy controls. Indeed, if some forgetful Java Interpreter tries to use the default Security Manager, it will quickly see that the default answer to every "May I do this?" question is "No."

By designing the Security Manager subsystem this way, Java Interpreters are provided great flexibility in controlling system resources. Security Policies as simple as "No" and as complex as "Bring up a dialog box to get the user's permission unless permission has been previously granted, but still always if the request involves deleting a file, but never ask if the execution stack indicates that the request is coming from a built-in class" can both be implemented using the same basic Security Manager mechanism.

The standard pattern for adding Security Manager access checks to system resources is to create an enclosing "guard" function which combines a query to the Security Manager with the actual call to the system resource.

```
public boolean isFile() {
        SecurityManager security = System.getSecurityManager();
        if (security != null) {
            security.checkRead(path);
        }
        return isFile0();
    }
```

In this code fragment, the public method `isFile()` first queries the Security Manager (through the call to the `security.checkRead(path)`).

If the Security Manager won't allow the "read" permission on the file specified by `path`, the call to `security.checkRead(path)` will throw a `SecurityException`. Because this exception is not caught by the `isFile()` function, the exception will propagate to the caller of `isFile()` immediately. Thus, when an exception is thrown, the low-level function `isFile0()` will not be called.

If the Security Manager will allow the "read" permission on the file specified by `path`, the call to `security.checkRead(path)` will return without error, and the next statement, containing the call to `isFile0()` will be executed.

The previous example shows how the set of public functions in the `SecurityManager` class can be used in creative manners. Because the `SecurityManager` class has no direct support for the check <tt>checkIsAFile()</tt>, the check <tt>checkRead()</tt> is used instead.

For the Security Manager to be effective, it must have the cooperation of *all* the built-in classes that control a system resource. If just one built-in class is implemented that does not follow this "guard" pattern, the consequences could be disastrous. For example, an unguarded `write()` could allow an applet to overwrite the Java Interpreter's built-in classes with classes that are all unguarded. When that happens, the security of the system evaporates.

Additionally, the Security Manager relies on the proper functioning of the other security components. These previous levels provide protection against an applet that creates its own version of the Security Manager and protection against unauthorized modification of the built-in Security Manager.

Also, the extent of this cooperation determines the "upper limit" on the kinds of functionality that can be controlled. For example, the built-in classes supporting network functionality (e.g. HTTP, FTP, and so on), currently allow security control to take one of these four forms:

1. disallow all network accesses
2. allow network accesses only to the network source from which the class was loaded
3. disallow network accesses to network sources inside the firewall if the code was loaded from a network source outside the firewall
4. allow all network accesses

Security in Specific Java Interpreters

Now that we've covered the generic mechanisms available to all Java Interpreters, we can now look at some of the available Java Interpreters.

Right now, the generic security concepts in Java are being scrutinized heavily. But it is not the case that each particular Java Interpreter is being subjected to the same level of scrutiny. The danger here lies in assuming that because the concepts are secure, the implementation is secure as well. This need not be the case.

Two things that every implementation of a Java Interpreter depends on are this:

1. that the Java Virtual Machine is implemented properly. Without this, there is no guarantee that the built-in classes are safe from unauthorized modifications.
2. that the built-in libraries are implemented properly (including the Security Manager). Without this, there is no guarantee that the built-in classes as stored on disk (among other things) will remain free of corruption.

In summary:

1. Everyone needs to know Java's weaknesses in theory
2. Everyone needs to know their Java Interpreter's weakness in implementation.

Number 2 is every bit as important as Number 1 if your goal is practical security.

These upcoming sections provide some details on the following Java Interpreters:

- Sun's Appletviewer
- Sun's HotJava
- Netscape Navigator 2.0

AppletViewer

The AppletViewer application is Sun's utility application capable of rendering Java classes. It is included as part of the Java Development Kit, 1.0 version.

The AppletViewer enables you to run applets without using a completely functioning World Wide Web browser. It is mainly intended as an applet developer's tool—it has the ability to understand only the <APPLET> tag.

Figure 40.19 shows the AppletViewer's security control dialog.

FIGURE 40.19.

AppletViewer security control dialog.

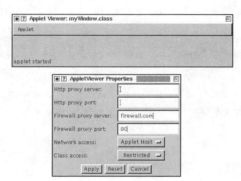

The AppletViewer application allows control over the following security-related items:

- The HTTP proxy server and port
- The Firewall proxy server and port
- Network access. The available settings are

  None

  Applet host

  Unrestricted

■ Class access: The available settings are

restricted

unrestricted

The AppletViewer has additional security behavior. This behavior is controlled by access control lists. One list controls the set of files that can be read, and another controls the set of files that can be written. By default, both of these lists are empty.

Files (and directories) can be added to either list by creating a file called $HOME/.hotjava/properties or C:\.hotjava\properties. The directives acl.read and acl.write enable the user to specify sets of files that are readable and writeable, respectively.

For example, adding this line

```
acl.read=/home/tmp/:/home/pub/somefile
```

to your properties file would let the AppletViewer get a list of files in the directory /home/tmp/ and any of its subdirectories, and would let the AppletViewer read the contents of the file /home/pub/somefile.

Adding this line

```
acl.write=/home/tmp/:/home/pub/pubdata
```

would let the AppletViewer create new files in the directory /home/tmp/ and would let the AppletViewer write the contents of the file /home/pub/pubdata.

> **CAUTION**
>
> Once you give applets the ability to create a file or to write a file, there is no way to restrict the size of file the applet writes. It is free to create a file large enough to consume all available disk space, if it so desires.

HotJava

HotJava, version 1.0 alpha3, is Sun's Java Web browser. Its inclusion in this list, however, is mostly for historic reasons. As of this writing, a new version of HotJava is in development; the version discussed here is not compatible with the new Java API. It is reasonable to assume that this dialog will change in the new HotJava version that is compatible with the new Java API. It is also reasonable to assume that the properties file as used by the AppletViewer application will also be accessed by HotJava.

Figure 40.20 shows HotJava's security control dialog.

FIGURE 40.20.

*HotJava security control
dialog.*

The HotJava application allows control over the following security-related items:

- ▪ `Enter desired security mode`—Grants applets access to information. The available settings are:

  `No access`—Applets are not able to load information from the network

  `Applet Host`—Only allow an applet to load information from its host

  `Firewall`—Outside applets can load information outside the firewall

  `Unrestricted`—Applets can load information from anywhere

- ▪ `Apply security mode to applet loading`—Grants applets access to loading other applets. This item interacts with the `desired security mode`. When this item is selected, the behaviors are as follows:

  `No access`—No applets are loaded. HotJava will not interpret any applets

  `Applet Host`—Only applets specified with a `file:` URL can be loaded

  `Firewall`—Only applets that are inside your firewall can be loaded

  `Unrestricted`—All applets can be loaded

- ▪ `Enter the kind of domain you're using`—Allows the user to choose between

  Sun's Network Information Services (NIS)

  Domain Naming Service (DNS)

- ▪ `Configure firewall...`—This brings up another dialog that enables the user to specify a set of firewall hosts or domains.

The HotJava version 1.0 alpha3 release does not permit applets to write files or modify files in any manner.

Netscape Navigator

Netscape Navigator, beginning with version 2.0, is a Java-capable Web browser.

Figure 40.21 shows Navigator's security control dialog.

FIGURE 40.21.

Netscape Navigator security control dialog.

As the dialog shows, the security preferences in Netscape Navigator concerning Java are straightforward. Java is either enabled (by default) or is disabled.

But, even when Java is enabled, it operates in a very restricted environment. Currently, there is no way for a Netscape Navigator user to remove any of these restrictions:

- Applets cannot read or write files on the local hard drive at all. (In particular, it cannot read or write the `properties` file mentioned earlier.)

- Applets are restricted to reading only nine system properties. These properties allow the Java Applet to access some information about the system that is executing the Java Applet. This information includes the Java Interpreter vendor name and Interpreter version number, the character used to separate components of a filename (e.g. "/"), the character used to separate lines, and so on.

- Applets are permitted to open a network connection to its originating host, but no others.

- Applets specified by a `file:` URL that do not reside in the `CLASSPATH` are loaded by the applet `Class` Loader.

> **CAUTION**
>
> Applets that happen to reside in your `CLASSPATH`, however, are not loaded by the applet `Class` Loader. Instead, they are loaded by the file system loader.
>
> Remember, for security reasons all Java Interpreters check the set of built-in classes before checking elsewhere. This rule applies to class loading as well. By loading a class

from the CLASSPATH before loading from another source, all applets are prevented from installing their own private set of what *should be* built-in classes. For example, if the SecurityManager class had not been loaded when a mischievous applet attempted to load http://www.badguy.com/SecurityManager.class, the Java Interpreter will actually load SecurityManager.class from the local system, not from the external system.

Summary

We have collected the cautions and warnings given throughout the chapter into short practical guides to make your Java experience a safer one:

1. Be aware that the *availability* of security measures does not guarantee the *use* of security measures.

2. Never, ever, place an unknown .class file in any directory that is in your CLASSPATH.

3. Never load a .class from a file: URL (unless you know that your Java Interpreter does not treat file: URLs as built-ins).

4. Be alert that classes being loaded from the same network source can access each other.

5. Be sure you trust the vendor that implements your Java Interpreter.

6. Be aware that giving write access to a file means you cannot control the *size* of the file.

Bringing in programs of unknown origin and running them on your system is a risky business. Java has been designed to take as much risk out of running these unknown programs as possible. Taking the precautions we have outlined in this chapter can further reduce the risks. However, some risks remain. Everyone needs to decide for themselves if the benefits of Java outweigh the risks.

FURTHER JAVA SECURITY INFORMATION ON THE WEB

■ Joseph A. Bank, "Java Security", Dec. 8, 1995

URL: http://swissnet.ai.mit.edu/~jbank/javapaper/javapaper.html

■ James Gosling and Henry McGilton, "The Java Language Environment: A White Paper", October 1995

URL: ftp://ftp.javasoft.com/docs/whitepaper.ps.tar.Z

■ Sun Microsystems, "Frequently Asked Questions—Applet Security", Jan. 9, 1996 version 1.0 Beta 2

URL: http://java.sun.com/sfaq/

- Sun Microsystems, "HotJava: The Security Story", May 19, 1995

  URL: `http://java.sun.com/1.0alpha3/doc/security/security.html`
- Sun Microsystems, "The Java Language Specification", DRAFT—Version 1.0 Beta, October 30, 1995

  URL: `http://java.sun.com/JDK-beta2/psfiles/javaspec.ps`

PART

JavaScript

Introduction to JavaScript

41

by Paul Colton

One of the most intriguing and exciting aspects of the World Wide Web is its capability to offer interactive content to many people. Thousands upon thousands of pages are linked together across the globe, each accessible with a single mouse click. The Web is the largest collection of information available to a single person since the beginning of time. As incredible as these notions may be, the users of the Web demand more. As technology on the Web improves, users want more interaction, more sophistication, more visually appealing content, and above all, these users want to be able to create this content themselves.

Java has turned the promise of interactivity into reality. For the first time, programmers can create small software programs, or applets, that can be distributed and executed easily on the World Wide Web. Netscape Communications (http://www.netscape.com) has single-handedly helped to thrust this new technology into the mainstream by incorporating Java into its popular Navigator software. For the first time, Web sites can finally interact with their users. Sophisticated applications like paint programs, spreadsheets, games, and complex math engines can now run in the browser window, among HTML pages, without the need of specialized hardware or software, other than a Java-enabled browser such as Netscape's Navigator.

Two distinct solutions to interactive content creation have formed on the Web: the simple-to-use Hypertext Markup Language (HTML), and the sophisticated and powerful Java programming language. With these two tools, users can create the visually compelling content and have it merge seamlessly with the interactive applications that Java offers. Nevertheless, what seems to be missing is a system for bringing these two technologies closer together.

Welcome to JavaScript

Netscape Communications saw the need for a bridge between these two technologies. They began working on a new scripting language that could have a place between HTML and Java, yet be powerful enough to link the two technologies together. When Netscape's new scripting language was introduced, it was known as LiveScript. It was immediately incorporated into their Navigator product in an effort to quickly have it adopted by the Internet community. Soon thereafter, seeing the potential of a joint effort, Netscape and Sun teamed to help LiveScript become more mainstream and to establish it as *the* standard in the Internet community for Web-based scripting. Because LiveScript syntax was so similar to Java's syntax, Sun and Netscape decided to rename their new product to make it more recognizable. It would now be called JavaScript.

JavaScript was created as an easy-to-use, open, cross-platform scripting language that could link together objects and resources from both HTML and Java. While Java applets are primarily developed by programmers, JavaScript was intended to be used by HTML page authors to dynamically control the interaction and behavior of their pages. JavaScript is unique in that it has been designed to be complementary to and integrated with both HTML and Java. One of the most important benefits JavaScript offers is its capability to reduce network traffic by keeping simple tasks local. In other words, instead of the server performing tasks and returning the results to the browser, the browser can handle some of the tasks locally, thus giving the user quicker response times.

JavaScript has been endorsed by over 25 industry-leading companies, including America Online, Inc., Apple Computer, Inc., Architext Software, Attachmate Corporation, AT&T, Borland International, Intuit, Inc., and Silicon Graphics, Inc. These companies plan to introduce products adopting the JavaScript language which will help to establish it in the Web community. JavaScript has also been submitted to the appropriate standards bodies for industry review and commenting.

These four chapters on JavaScript provide an introduction into JavaScript and do not cover the entire scope of JavaScript. They are here as a starting point into your exploration of this new and unique scripting language. Because JavaScript is still an evolving language, some of its features and commands may change in the future. Every effort has been made to make the information contained here as timely as possible.

Learning JavaScript

JavaScript is based on the powerful Java language in its syntax and usage, yet is interpreted, not compiled. What this means is that the JavaScript application code is downloaded as text into the browser along with the HTML text. The code is executed within the browser, enabling you to develop simple applications that can interact with and assist your users.

With JavaScript, you can respond to events from the user such as mouse clicks, mouse movement over a link, and form input. You can build dynamic pages that change according to your user's requests, or even play sounds or run applets when a user enters or leaves your page. This type of capability at the client level allows for tremendous interactivity with the users of your Web pages.

The JavaScript language resembles Java, but is simpler and easier to learn. A JavaScript application may be as short as one line or take several pages. The complexity depends on the extent in which your script interacts with the page it is in. One of the first uses of JavaScript for most authors is in form validation. Form validation is the ability for an HTML form to check the input from a user *before* it is submitted, which greatly improves performance on your server as well as decreases user frustration. Listing 41.1 shows a simple example of form validation.

Listing 41.1. A simple form validation example.

```
<HTML>
<BODY>
<FORM NAME="demoform" onSubmit="if(!demoform.name.value)
    { alert('You left the name field blank'); return false; }">
```

continues

Listing 41.1. continued

```
<INPUT NAME="name"">
<INPUT TYPE="submit">
</FORM>
</BODY>
</HTML>
```

The short HTML document in Listing 41.1 is a testament to the power and simplicity of JavaScript. The document displays a form that cannot be submitted until something is entered into the name field. If the field is left blank, a window will open stating You left the name field blank. Once information has been entered, the form may be submitted normally.

Learning JavaScript isn't difficult, but requires considerably more effort than HTML. Despite its simplicity, JavaScript is based on a programming language, making it much more sophisticated than HTML. It requires a time investment and a lot of experimentation. Fortunately, JavaScript applications are easy to develop and easy to test; this ultimately leads to a speedier grasp of the JavaScript language. As an added benefit, by learning JavaScript, you will have begun your journey into Java programming. JavaScript is based on Java, so many of the commands and constructs are similar, if not the same. The next section discusses the similarities and differences in these two languages.

JavaScript and Java

JavaScript was designed to help the nonprogrammer in creating interactive applications for the Web and to facilitate the integration of Java and HTML. Despite these two seemingly different roles, JavaScript and Java are based on the same basic principles. They are both programming languages with similar commands and syntax, they are both object-oriented, and they are both open- and cross-platform. Following is a comparison of the two languages.

Comparing and Contrasting

JavaScript is very similar to Java in its syntax, but many of the similarities stop there. JavaScript is an interpreted language, meaning that JavaScript code runs directly within the browser and requires no compilation, whereas Java requires compilation prior to execution. In addition, JavaScript supports a smaller set of data types compared to Java, and JavaScript methods do not require special declarations like Java methods.

In contrast to Java, JavaScript contains many built-in objects that require minimal effort for their creation. JavaScript has no classes or class inheritance like Java, but rather relies on its built-in set of objects to be extended in order to suit the needs of the programmer. Because JavaScript is interpreted and not compiled, all object references are checked at runtime, whereas

Java requires that all references exist at compile time. Also, a variable's datatype need not be declared in JavaScript like is it required in Java.

Another major difference between Java and JavaScript is in JavaScript's tight integration with HTML. Java applets may be called from within an HTML document by use of the `<APPLET>` tag, but the actual compiled code resides in a separate file. JavaScript enables you to embed the source code directly into the HTML code, resulting in a single file for both HTML code and JavaScript source code.

Security Considerations

Like Java, JavaScript has been designed from the ground up to be a secure language. Neither Java nor JavaScript allows the use of pointers, which is commonly the cause of security violations. Because JavaScript is an interpreted language, there are no compile-time memory allocation concerns, which are another potential cause of security violations. In addition, in order to minimize the effectiveness of malicious programs, disk writes are not allowed in either Java or JavaScript.

In the Java language, the application code is compiled into byte-code on the server. This byte-code file, generally with a `.class` extension, is the actual program that is received and run by the Java-enabled browser. This `.class` file, because it is compiled, does not contain the original source code of the application, thus making your source code unavailable to the user. In contrast, because JavaScript code is embedded in the HTML as plain text, the user may view the source to the HTML file, and in turn, view the source code to your JavaScript application. Currently, it is not possible to protect the source code other than by placing a copyright notice in the source of your JavaScript application.

Integrating JavaScript and Java

One of the much-touted features of JavaScript is its capability to directly interact with Java applications. In the Java code, useful properties can be exposed to allow a JavaScript application to get or set these properties and alter the state or performance of the Java application. This same paradigm also applies to Netscape Navigator plug-ins, meaning a JavaScript could query and alter the performance of a plug-in, as well.

In the first released version of JavaScript, which is included in Netscape Navigator 2.0, this tightly coupled interaction with Java is not yet implemented. The next major release of JavaScript, slated to appear in Netscape Navigator 2.1, will enable you to call Java methods from JavaScript directly and get and set public Java fields. This integration will allow for more dynamic content and interactivity within pages that contain both Java applets and JavaScript code.

Many future applications on the World Wide Web will feature complex and sophisticated interfaces and interactivity. For example, suppose you wanted to create an HTML page that contained the logo of your company on top, a visually integrated three-dimensional image of an automobile in the center, descriptive text about the automobile below, and form controls for rotating the automobile in any direction you desired. This HTML page sounds exciting, but you would face very complex programming issues if you were trying to develop such an application entirely in Java.

By allowing Java to perform the tasks it is best at, perhaps rotating and rendering the 3D car image, JavaScript can handle the interaction between the form controls and the Java application, sending the Java applet messages about what the user has chosen as rotation angles. Finally, HTML can be used to establish the framework, displaying the title logo, and building the actual form elements. By integrating all these technologies together, HTML, JavaScript, and Java, the development and implementation of highly interactive Web pages can become easier and faster to complete.

Halfway to Java with JavaScript

One of the most promising aspects of learning JavaScript is that it will enable you to begin understanding the basic structures of object-oriented programming. Object-oriented programming is rapidly becoming the standard in programming languages of the future. Today, C++ has set the standard for object-oriented programming, and is used widely across the globe. It is no wonder that both JavaScript and Java resemble the syntax of C and C++. Many of the constructs of those languages have been passed on to JavaScript and Java, making it easier for programmers to transition to these new languages.

If you have never programmed before, JavaScript will enable you to begin the process of understanding how these languages work. Because of the similarities between JavaScript and Java, once you have learned and grasped the basic concepts of JavaScript, you will already be well on your way to mastering Java. With the combination of these two languages at your disposal, compelling and interactive content is yours for the making. Spending the time reading these chapters carefully, completing all of the examples, and then, of course, experimenting with your own applications will soon make you a master at these powerful tools.

JavaScript Requirements

JavaScript, unlike Java, requires few resources to use and program. One of the exciting aspects of JavaScript is that nearly anyone can use it and develop their own applications right away. Most users already have all of the tools they need on their computers right now. Because JavaScript is an interpreted language and not compiled, the usual requirements associated with compiled languages, compilers, linkers, debuggers, and so on, are not needed. As a result, JavaScript imposes a very minimal set of requirements in order to begin developing with it immediately.

Required Software and Hardware

Because JavaScript was developed by Netscape, Netscape's Navigator program is the first program to support JavaScript directly. Every version of the Netscape Navigator across all platforms supports JavaScript. These platforms includes Macintosh, Windows, Solaris, SunOS, HP-UX, IRIX, AIX, Digital UNIX, Linux, NetBSD, and FreeBSD. In turn, the hardware requirements for running JavaScript are the same as the requirements for running the Netscape Navigator. In other words, if you are currently using the Netscape Navigator for Web browsing, you already have all of the hardware and software required to run JavaScript applications.

Developing for JavaScript is as simple as running JavaScript applications. Because JavaScript is interpreted, and therefore completely plain-text-based, *any* editor can be used to create JavaScript-enabled Web pages. Whichever editor you use now, whether it be NotePad for Windows, vi or emacs on UNIX, SimpleText on the Mac, or any of the host of HTML editors, they all have the capability to produce JavaScript code. Because JavaScript does not need to be compiled, as soon as you save your JavaScript code, you can immediately test it, right in your browser.

With over 25 companies already dedicated to providing tools and applications based on JavaScript, including Netscape, there will soon be a large collection of tools available to more specifically focus on the development process of JavaScript applications. Netscape's Navigator Gold product contains a full What You See Is What You Get (WYSIWYG) HTML editor built into the browser and allows you to enter JavaScript code directly. By being able to instantly switch back and forth between JavaScript source and the final HTML page, Navigator Gold promises to make it even easier for anyone to create compelling, JavaScript-based Web pages.

Authoring with JavaScript

Creating a JavaScript program is a relatively simple process. Using any text editor, you may begin typing in JavaScript statements to expand the role of your current HTML pages, create entirely new pages using only JavaScript, or mix both HTML and JavaScript. This section will cover some of the issues and syntax in creating a JavaScript application, as well as information on how to embed your JavaScript code into your HTML documents.

Creating Your Script

In order for your browser to recognize that there is JavaScript code in your file, two special tags have been introduced.

```
<SCRIPT>...</SCRIPT>
```

Between these two tags, JavaScript code may be inserted and the browser will recognize the JavaScript code while loading your page. The <SCRIPT> tag also has attributes that can be specified.

```
<SCRIPT LANGUAGE="JavaScript">...</SCRIPT>
```

The LANGUAGE attribute specifies the language to use for the script. Currently, only "LiveScript" and "JavaScript" are used. The "LiveScript" name is a legacy attribute from an older version of JavaScript.

```
<SCRIPT SRC="http://myjavascript.js">...</SCRIPT>
```

The SRC attribute is optional and, if given, specifies an URL that loads the text of a script. A script from a SRC is evaluated before in-page scripts. Also, any SRC URL should use the .js suffix.

```
<SCRIPT LANGUAGE="language" SRC=url>...</SCRIPT>
```

You may also specify both a LANGUAGE and a SRC attribute together.

The JavaScript code is evaluated *after* the entire page loads, and if you are using any JavaScript functions, they will be stored by the browser, but not executed without a specific call to that function.

In order to create a script, simply use your favorite text or HTML editor and begin typing in JavaScript code. Listing 41.2 illustrates a simple JavaScript program.

Listing 41.2. The first JavaScript example.

```
<HTML>
<HEAD>
<SCRIPT>
document.write("<H1>JavaScript is Fun!</H1>")
</SCRIPT>
</HEAD>
<BODY>
<h2>This is normal HTML.</h2>
</BODY>
</HTML>
```

When the script is run, it produces what is shown in Figure 41.1. The JavaScript is Fun! message is produced by the JavaScript code, while the This is normal HTML. is HTML text. Notice how the JavaScript statement document.write() is inserted between the HTML tags <SCRIPT>...</SCRIPT>. This tells the browser that JavaScript code is located between the tags and not standard HTML.

## Chapter 41

FIGURE 41.1.

JavaScript application displaying a message in the Netscape Navigator along with HTML text.

Embedding the Script in Your HTML

Now that you know how to create a simple JavaScript program, there are some issues to address concerning embedding your JavaScript into HTML documents. As we have already seen, the <SCRIPT>...</SCRIPT> tags are used to denote JavaScript code from normal HTML code. Browsers that do not recognize a particular tag generally ignore them, so the <SCRIPT> and </SCRIPT> tags would not show up on a non-JavaScript-enabled browser. Unfortunately, the code within the SCRIPT tags would not be ignored but would display as unwanted output on your web page. Netscape Navigator solves this problem by enabling you to use HTML comment tags to comment out the portion of JavaScript code that other browsers would treat as plain text. In other words, when a browser that cannot support JavaScript comes across the comment tags, it will ignore everything in between them, where Netscape Navigator will not. Listing 41.3 uses the same code from Listing 41.2, but now comments out the portion that non-JavaScript browsers could not understand.

Listing 41.3. A JavaScript example with commented-out code.

```
<HTML>
<HEAD>
<SCRIPT>
<!-- Begin to hide script content from old browsers.
document.write("<H1>JavaScript is Really Fun!</H1>")
// End the hiding here. -->
</SCRIPT>
</HEAD>
<BODY>
<H2>This is normal HTML.</H2>
</BODY>
</HTML>
```

Notice the <!-- and --> tags. These are HTML tags denoting a comment within the document. Netscape Navigator knows to look within these tags for JavaScript code. You may have also noticed two slashes // before the End the hiding here statement. Because we were within the SCRIPT tags, Netscape Navigator would try to execute the line as a statement. The two forward slashes is a JavaScript statement for denoting a comment line. The combination of the HTML comment tags and JavaScript comment tags help to ensure compatibility of your documents across many different types of browsers that fully suppport HTML commenting. Chapters 41 and 42 contain more in-depth examples of creating JavaScript applications, including JavaScript applications with functions.

Running Your Script

Running your JavaScript code is as easy as viewing an HTML page. Once your code is complete, simply load the page into your browser for instant results. This ability to instantly run and check your JavaScript code is another powerful feature of JavaScript. In the development and testing process of a JavaScript application, your computer does not need to be connected to a network. You can edit, test, and execute your JavaScript applications without ever being online. This can be a real advantage when hourly connect charges are a concern. Also, because you are testing your applications locally, load times will be extremely fast, and because JavaScript executes the code immediately, your entire development process will be extremely efficient and rewarding.

Future Enhancements to JavaScript

JavaScript is still in its infancy and as of this writing, the final version of JavaScript has not yet been released. Some of the features of JavaScript may change in the future, and new features will surely be added. Nevertheless, the core technology of JavaScript will not change any time soon. When new versions of JavaScript arrive, minor changes may have to be made to older code, but most code should work unmodified. It is also important to note that JavaScript has already been submitted to appropriate standards committees.

Future versions of JavaScript promises total integration with Java applets as well as integration with Netscape Navigator plug-ins. Other new software systems that use JavaScript extensively are also available. For example, Netscape's LiveWire system uses server-based JavaScript code to integrate together database engines and HTML, as well a host of other capabilities. One of the best ways to stay abreast of the latest changes in this fast-moving industry is to stay tuned to the various resources available to you on the Internet.

JavaScript Resources

As JavaScript expands in popularity and its usage becomes more widespread, more and more resources will become available. Currently, there are many Web sites that contain example JavaScript applications as well as tutorials, documentation, and collections of other resources on JavaScript on the Web. Following are a few web sites of interest; these sites will also point you to other sites containing even more information on Java and JavaScript:

- Netscape Communications, Inc. (`http://www.netscape.com`), the creators of JavaScript, have JavaScript demos online as well as full documentation on the JavaScript language. The latest version of the Netscape Navigator is always available on their site as well. Netscape also offers a secure developer's forum for the exchange of ideas and questions about JavaScript, Java, and other issues (`http://developer.netscape.com`).

- Sun Microsystems, Inc. (`http://www.sun.com`), the creators of Java, hosts a site completely dedicated to Java and JavaScript (`http://java.sun.com`). Here you will find the latest happenings related to Java as well as the latest development tools and examples.

- Live Software (`http://www.livesoftware.com`), a company that provides software solutions for interactive content creation, hosts a JavaScript Resource Center (`http://jrc.livesoftware.com`) that contains links to many Java and JavaScript sites on the Web, as well as all of the source code mentioned in these four chapters on JavaScript and other example JavaScript applications. In addition, there is also a news group available from Live software for the discussion of JavaScript programming and other technical issues (news://news.livesoftware.com/livesoftware.javascript.developer).

- Gamelan (`http://www.gamelan.com`) has grown to become one of the Internet's largest collection of Java applets. It now also includes JavaScript collections on the Internet.

There are also books available on JavaScript that go into more detail than these chapters. They cover expanded issues of JavaScript, as well as providing more examples on how to best utilize JavaScript for your requirements. *Teach Yourself JavaScript in 21 Days* by Sams Publishing is an example of one of these books.

Summary

JavaScript is a powerful, interpreted scripting language that is built-in to the Netscape Navigator software. JavaScript is full-featured and allows for the creation of dynamic pages, interactive content, forms input checking, and much more.

JavaScript's syntax is based on Java's syntax, but otherwise remains as a different language with a different role. JavaScript excels in its ability to add client-side processing of forms, create HTML content on-the-fly, and tightly integrate HTML with Java.

JavaScript requires only a text editor for the creation of applications, and because Netscape's Navigator has a built-in JavaScript interpreter, JavaScript applications may be run immediately after they have been typed in simply by loading them into the browser window.

JavaScript enables you to embed your JavaScript code directly into an HTML document with the use of the <SCRIPT>...</SCRIPT> tags. By hiding the code from other browsers using HTML comment tags and JavaScript comment statements, you can try to ensure that your JavaScript page stays compatible with most browsers that do not support JavaScript.

The next chapter delves into the JavaScript language itself, its syntax, and how you can use the language to create your own JavaScript-enabled Web pages.

The JavaScript Language

42

by Paul Colton

The JavaScript language is not difficult to learn, but it does require knowledge of many of the syntax conventions of Java. An understanding of these conventions is necessary to adequately use JavaScript. It may be helpful to gain a thorough understanding of the Java syntax and conventions by reading some of the earlier chapters in this book before proceeding.

JavaScript Fundamentals

This section covers the basic components of the JavaScript language. These components include variables and values, data types, literals, properties, arrays, and comment statements. As the basic building blocks of JavaScript, an understanding of these fundamentals is the first step toward the mastery of the JavaScript language.

Variables and Values

JavaScript variables are similar to variables in any other programming language; they hold values that you use in your application. JavaScript enables you to name your case-sensitive variables so you may reference them elsewhere in your code. You can name variables anything you wish. You may opt to use descriptive names such as `number_of_times_clicked`, or short, generic names such as `foo`. The only restrictions on variable names is that they must begin with a letter or underscore (_).

JavaScript variables can contain the following different types of values:

- numbers, for example, 14 or 1.25
- logicals (Boolean), can be True or False
- strings, for example, `Hello World`

JavaScript also recognizes the `null` keyword for specifying null values for variables. JavaScript has reduced the confusion in deciding which data type to use for different types of numbers. JavaScript uses a single data type for numbers, which means that a JavaScript *number* can contain the equivalent of integers, reals, and doubles without the need for specialized types. In addition, JavaScript handles Date objects with this same data type, further simplifying code development under JavaScript.

The var statement is used to declare variables in JavaScript. Each variable is given a name and optionally an initial value. Outside of a function, the var statement is optional, but it is highly recommended that you always use var to avoid the possibility of overwriting local variables with global variables. Local variables are generally declared within a function with the intention that only the function will be able to use the variable. Global variables are declared outside of any function, making the variable available to any function. Therefore, to avoid conflict, the var statement will ensure your variables safety in these situations. Following is the syntax for the var statement:

```
var varname [= value] [..., varname [= value] ]
```

Multiple variables may be declared from one var statement. The following example demonstrates this:

```
var num_cans = 10, price_per_can = 2.0;
```

Data Types

JavaScript fully supports variables of different data types, but does so loosely to enable you, the programmer, to more quickly develop applications without the headache of strict type specification prior to execution. JavaScript applications can handle a great number of different types of data, but JavaScript manages to do this with only three distinct data types. In addition, JavaScript can decide for you what data type your variable should be during script execution.

Converting between different types is very easy and straightforward. Data types are converted automatically when your JavaScript application runs. JavaScript follows one simple rule when converting types; it performs the conversion from left to right. In other words, the right-hand operand will be converted to the type of the left-hand operand. No matter how complex the conversion, JavaScript always follows this left-to-right approach.

For example, if you had the following variables:

- ▪ var1 = "10"
- ▪ var2 = 20

Then performed the following statements:

- ▪ x = var1 + var2
- ▪ y = var2 + var1

The first statement would convert var2 to a string, because the operand on the left, var1, is a string. The result would be that x would contain the string "1020". In contrast, the second statement would convert var1 to a number, because the operand to its left, var2, is a number. The two numbers would then be added together to form the result of 30 in y.

As you saw in the previous example, JavaScript can convert strings that contain numeric characters into numbers quite easily. If a string contains non-numeric values, such as "Paul", and you try to set a number variable to contain that value, JavaScript will generate an error because it cannot convert "Paul" into a numeric value.

Literals

Many times when creating new variables, you need to specify an initial value. These types of fixed values are called literals. Literals are not variables, but rather, constant expressions of values for data types. For example, some literal values could include

```
24
```

```
72.745
```

```
"programming is fun"
```

When expressing literal values for integers, you may use three different bases. You may use decimal (base 10), hexadecimal (base 16), or octal (base 8) format. To specify a decimal literal, simply use a series of digits without any leading zeros. For example

`42` (a decimal literal)

To specify an octal literal, precede the number with a leading 0 (zero). Octal literals can only include digits 0-7. For example

`010` (an octal literal)

Finally, when specifying a hexadecimal literal, precede the number with a leading 0x (or 0X). Hexadecimal literals can include all digits (0 - 9) and the letters a-f and A-F. For example:

`0xFF` (a hexadecimal literal)

A floating-point literal is specified by the following parts: a decimal integer, a decimal point, another decimal integer, an exponent, and a type suffix. The exponent is specified by using an e or E followed by an integer that can be signed by proceeding it with a - or a +. A floating-point literal should have at least one digit plus either a decimal point or e or E. For example

`4.25` (floating point literals)

`.4e3`

`2E-8`

`-6.2e9`

A Boolean literal is specified by one of two values: true or false. Finally, string literals are specified by using zero or more characters enclosed in double or single quotes. For example

`"banana"` (string literals)

`'pear'`

`"goodbye \t forever"`

As in the last example, string literals can also contain special characters. Following is a list of the JavaScript special characters for string literals:

\b	(backspace)
\f	(form feed)
\n	(new line character)
\r	(carriage return)
\t	(tab character)

Properties

JavaScript objects, discussed later in this chapter, generally have properties associated with them. Object properties can be either variables or functions. These properties can be accessed in two different ways. The first approach to accessing the properties of objects is as follows:

```
objectName.propertyName
```

Once you have an object, creating properties for that object is as simple as assigning a value to a property name. For example, suppose you had an object named person. To give the person object some properties, you would simply use the following statements:

```
person.name = "John";
person.age = 24;
person.height = 68;
person.weight = 155;
```

These statements would add the four properties name, age, height, and weight to the person object.

Arrays

Because JavaScript uses the same data structure for the storage of properties and arrays, they generally are treated as the same thing. In other words, they are so closely related that you may access properties through arrays and vice versa. For example, you could access the properties mentioned in the prior section as follows:

```
person["name"] = "John";
person["age"] = 24;
person["height"] = 68;
person["weight"] = 155;
```

In addition, you may also use array indices to access your properties; for example, to access the "name" property in the person object, since it is the first property, you can use the following:

```
person[0] = "John"
```

As you can see, JavaScript is very lenient in the use and access of object properties. This simplicity in the JavaScript allows you to spend more time on the development of applications, rather than specifics of the language. Listing 42.1 is an example of a simple JavaScript function that assists in the creation of arrays.

Listing 42.1. A JavaScript function for creating arrays.

```
function MakeArray(n) {
    this.length = n;
    for (var i = 1; i <= n; i++) {
        this[i] = 0 }
        return this
        }
}
```

To use this function, simply use the JavaScript new command, for example

```
myarray = new MakeArray(10);
```

This creates an array called myarray with 10 elements, with all elements initially set to zero.

Comments

Comments in source code are commonly used by the script author to explain what the program is doing. In addition, the comment statement is also useful in helping to make JavaScript code hidden to browsers that do not support JavaScript. The syntax for the comment statement is as follows:

1. // a single line of commented text, do not need to close comment
2. /* one or more lines of commented text, must close comment */

Notice that single-line comments may use either the // or the /* */ pair. Multiple-line comments must use the /* */ pair. Everything after the // on the same line, or within the /* */ pair will be ignored by JavaScript. For example, using the code from Listing 42.1, you could hide the code from non-Netscape browsers as follows:

```
<SCRIPT>
<!-- This line begins the comment, hiding the following code from non-Netscape
➥browsers
function MakeArray(n) {
   this.length = n;
   for (var i = 1; i <= n; i++) {
     this[i] = 0 }
     return this
     }
}
// --> This ends the commenting. Note the // that hide the HTML comment code from
➥JavaScript
</SCRIPT>
```

Reserved Words

JavaScript currently contains 53 reserved words. These words cannot be used for variable, function, method, or object names. Some of the words are not currently being used by JavaScript, but rather are reserved for future use. Table 42.1 contains the list of current reserved words.

Table 42.1. JavaScript reserved words.

abstract	extends	int	super
boolean	false	interface	switch
break	final	long	synchronized
byte	finally	native	this
case	float	new	throw

catch	for	null	throws
char	function	package	transient
class	goto	private	true
const	if	protected	try
continue	implements	public	var
default	import	return	void
do	in	short	while
double	instanceof	static	with
else			

Looping and Conditional Statements

JavaScript looping and conditional statements allow for a great variety of tasks to be performed in your application. Using any of JavaScript's looping statements, you can repeat a series of statements until a certain condition is met. Additionally, with conditional statements, you can limit the execution of JavaScript code based on a certain criteria, or update information based on yet another criteria. Following are the current JavaScript looping statements:

`for`

`while`

There are many uses for these statements. Listing 42.2 illustrates a simple example of looping and conditional statements.

Listing 42.2. Looping and conditional statement example.

```
<HTML>
<BODY>
<SCRIPT>
for(var i=0;i<10;i++) {
    document.write("You are on number " + i + "!<BR>");
    if(i == 5)
        document.write("You are halfway there.<P>");
}
</SCRIPT>
</BODY>
</HTML>
```

This example will loop 10 times using the `for` loop and print the words `You are on number` followed by the current number. When the loop reaches 5, an `if` statement is checking for that value, and when it finds that the loop is on 5, the `if` statement prints the words `You are halfway there`. (See Figure 42.1.)

FIGURE 42.1.

Looping and conditional statement example.

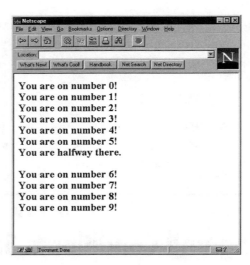

Comparison Operators

When performing looping or conditional statements in JavaScript, you may need to use a comparison of two values to continue or to terminate your loop or condition. In JavaScript, when performing a comparison, you must use a comparison operator between the two values you are comparing. What you get in return is a Boolean value representing the outcome of the comparison. The operators allowed in a JavaScript comparison are shown in Table 42.2.

Table 42.2. Comparison operators.

Operator	Result
Equal (==)	Returns true if the operands are equal
Not equal (!=)	Returns true if the operands are not equal
Greater than (>)	Returns true if the left operand is greater than the right operand
Less than (<)	Returns true if the right operand is greater then the left operand
Less than or equal to (<=)	Returns true if the left operand is less than or equal to the right operand
Greater than or equal to (>=)	Returns true if the left operand is greater than or equal to the right operand

for

The `for` statement enables you to create a loop in JavaScript that can initialize a statement, update an expression, and loop until a condition is met. This statement consists of three optional expressions. These expressions are all enclosed in a single set of parenthesis and are separated by a semicolon (;). Following the `for` loop statement is a block of code to be executed in the loop. The syntax for a `for` loop follows:

```
for ([initial statement]; [condition]; [update expression]) {
    statements
}
```

The initial statement in a `for` loop may also contain a variable declaration, which is accomplished using the `var` keyword. This section is generally used to initialize a variable counter. This section, like the other sections in a `for` loop, is optional. The condition statement in a `for` loop is evaluated each time the loop completes its block of code. If the condition fails, the loop terminates. Otherwise, the update expression is executed. The update expression generally will increment a counter. Following is an example of a `for` statement:

```
for (var i = 0; i < 10; i++) {
    total = total + i;
    display_total(total);
}
```

This example will run through 10 iterations before ending the `for` loop. During each iteration `i` is incremented by 1—using `i++`—until the statement `i < 10` is no longer true. Note that for single-line code blocks, the brace pairs (`{ }`) are not needed.

for...in

The JavaScript `for...in` statement is not to be confused with the `for` statement. The `for...in` statement iterates a variable over all properties of an object. The `for...in` syntax is as follows:

```
for (var in obj) {
    statements
}
```

Notice the `in` keyword between the *var* and the *obj*. This keyword sets *var* to the first property of *obj*. As the statement progresses, it will move through all of the properties of *obj*, until reaching the last one. Upon reaching the last property, the `for` statement will exit.

Here is an example:

```
function display_properties_of_object(obj, obj_name) {
    var result = "";
    i = "";
    for (i in obj)
        result += obj_name + "." + i + " = " + obj[i] + "\n";
    return result;
}
```

This example will run through all of the properties of `obj` and display them as well as the property's value. Notice that for a single statement following the `for...in` statement, braces (`{ }`) are not required.

while

The `while` statement in JavaScript is very similar to the `for` statement, but is more simple to use. The `while` statement will keep executing a block of code it contains until the condition it is testing is false. Following is the syntax for the `while` statement:

```
while (condition) {
     statements
}
```

Following is an example of the `while` statement in use:

```
money = 0.00;
while (money < 100.00) {
     money += 5.00;
 }
```

This example continues to loop until the variable `money` reaches its goal of `100.00`. Note that the second zero after the decimal point is not needed, but is used to make code reading easier and to signify to the code reader that we are using currency. The extra zero has no effect on the final outcome of the program.

break and continue

In a `while` or `for` loop, a `break` statement terminates the loop and continues executing the code following the terminated loop. The syntax of a `break` statement is the statement itself with no other options:

```
break
```

Here's an example of a `break` statement that terminates when a variable reaches a certain limit:

```
function func(x) {
     var i = 0;
     while (i < 5) {
          if (i == 2)
               break;
          i++;
     }
     return i*x;
}
```

In this example, when the variable `i` reaches the value of 2, the `while` loop terminates.

The `continue` statement terminates the execution of the current block in a loop and continues the loop with the next iteration. The syntax of a `continue` statement is the statement itself with no other options:

```
continue
```

Here's an example of a `continue` statement that terminates when a variable reaches a certain limit:

```
function func(x) {
    var i = 0;
    while (i < 5) {
        if (i == 2)
        continue;
        i++;
    }
    return i*x;
}
```

In this example, when the variable `i` reaches the value of 2, the `while` loop skips the `i++` line and continues the loop.

if...else

The `if...else` is JavaScript's conditional testing statement. This statement enables you to test a condition and if it is true, execute a block of code. Optionally you can execute a block of code if the statement evaluates to false. This is done using the `else` statement. The `if...else` statement may be nested. Following is the syntax for the `if...else` statement:

```
if (condition) {
    statements
} [else {
    else statements
}]
```

An example of this statement follows:

```
if ( rate_book(javascript_book) == "*****") {
    good = true;
} else
    good = false;
```

Again, as in other JavaScript statements, if a single statement follows the `if` or `else` statement, the use of the brace pairs (`{ }`) is optional.

Conditional Expression

A conditional expression in JavaScript is a way to test a value whose result can be one of two values. For example

```
old_enough = (age >= 16) ? "Drive Home" : "Walk Home"
```

This statement first tests the condition within the parenthesis. If `age` is indeed greater than or equal to 16, then the first value after the question mark (?) is chosen. Otherwise, if the comparison is false, the second value after the question mark is chosen. If `age` were set to 17, `old_enough` would be set to `Drive Home`.

with

The JavaScript `with` statement enables you to specify an object as the default object when executing statements within its block of code. The syntax for the `with` statement is as follows:

```
with (object) {
    statements
}
```

An example of the `with` statement that uses the `Math` object as the default object follows:

```
with (Math) {
    a = PI * r*r;
    x = r * cos(theta);
    y = r * sin(theta);
}
```

Operators

In JavaScript, as in other languages, operators are used to perform actions between two operands. For example, when assigning values to variables, you would use assignment operators; when adding numbers together, you would use arithmetic operators; and when concatenating two strings together, you would use string operators. This section briefly covers all the different types of operators that are available to you in JavaScript.

Assignment Operators

Assignment operators are used to assign a value from a right operand to its left operand. The most basic and widely used assignment operator is the equal sign (=). It assigns the value of the right operand to the left result. For example: x=100 would assign 100 to the variable x. Like in C and C++, in JavaScript there are some shorthand notations for assignments. For example

x += y is equal to x = x + y

x -= y is equal to x = x - y

x <<= y is equal to x = x << y

This shorthand applies to all the arithmetic and bitwise operators.

String Operators

The JavaScript string operators include the comparison operators mentioned previously as well as the concatenation operator (+) for concatenating two strings together. For example, the following statement

```
"Java" + "Script"
```

would result in the string

```
"JavaScript"
```

You may also use the shorthand notation for string concatenation. For example, if a string `str1` contains the value `"Java"`, the following statement

```
str1 += "Script"
```

would also result in the string `"JavaScript"`.

Arithmetic Operators

JavaScript supports eight basic arithmetic operators. Table 42.3 lists the operators, their function, and an example.

Table 42.3. Arithmetic operators.

Operator	Function Performed	Example
+	Addition	x = a + b
-	Subtraction	y = a - b
*	Multiplication	x = a * b
/	Division	y = a / b
%	Modulus	12 % 5 = 2
++	Increment	x++
- -	Decrement	y - -
-	Unary negation	x = -y

Logical and Bitwise Operators

Logical operators enable you to test two Boolean values and return a Boolean value based on the two tested. There are three logical operators. Table 42.4 shows these operators.

Table 42.4. Logical operators.

Operator	Function Performed	Example
&&	AND, true if both are true	expr1 && expr2
¦¦	OR, true if either is true	expr1 ¦¦ expr2
!	NOT, negates operand	!expr

Bitwise operators perform bitwise operation on their operands. That is, rather than treat their operands as numbers, they are treated as a set of bits (zeros and ones). Bitwise operators perform their operation at the bit level in JavaScript, but return their results as a number. Table 42.5 shows the JavaScript bitwise operators and their functions.

Table 42.5. Bitwise operators.

Operator	Function Performed	Example
&	Bitwise AND. Returns a one if *both* operands are ones.	x = a & b
¦	Bitwise OR. Returns a one if *either* operand is one.	y = a ¦ b
^	Bitwise XOR. Returns a one if *one but not both* operands are one.	x = a ^ b
<<	Shifts bits left specified times.	x = a << 4
>>	Shifts bits right specified times.	y = b >> 5
>>>	Zero-fill right shift.	x = a >>>2

When shifting bits to the left with <<, excess bits on the left are discarded and zero bits are shifted in from the right.

When shifting bits to the right with >>, excess bits on the right are discarded and copies of the leftmost bit are shifted in from the left.

When zero-fill shifting bits to the right with >>>, excess bits on the right are discarded and zero bits are shifted in from the left.

Operator Precedence

When JavaScript is evaluating an expression, a precedence is chosen for the order of evaluation. For example, the statement:

```
a = (b + c) * d;
```

would first perform the operation inside of the parenthesis, the addition of b and c then multiply that result with d, then assign the result to a. The following list shows the precedence of JavaScript operators from lowest to highest:

comma ,

assignment = += -= *= /= %= <<= >>= >>>= &= ^= ¦=

conditional ?:

logical-or ¦¦

logical-and `&&`

bitwise-or `¦`

bitwise-xor `^`

bitwise-and `&`

equality `==` `!=`

relational `<` `<=` `>` `>=`

shift `<<` `>>` `>>>`

addition/subtraction `+` `-`

multiply/divide/modulus `*` `/` `%`

negation/increment `!` `~` `-` `++` `--`

call, member `()` `[]` `.`

Functions and Objects

JavaScript is based on the object-oriented model of Java. It follows then, that JavaScript is also object-oriented. In JavaScript, an object is an entity whose properties are JavaScript variables or other objects. Functions can also be associated with objects. These functions can perform actions specific to that object, such as a `Math` object having a `sin()` function. When JavaScript functions are associated with objects, they are then referred to as methods. This section covers JavaScript functions and objects and how to create them.

Creating Functions

In JavaScript, the `function` statement is used to create new functions. Functions each have their own unique name as well as an optional parameter list. JavaScript functions play an important role in the development of applications. Functions are a set of JavaScript procedures that enable you to perform specific actions and can be called anywhere in your current application. When using Netscape Navigator, for example, any function that has been defined in the current page may be called.

When defining your own functions, the `function` statement is used. For example

```
function center_string(msg) {
    document.write("<CENTER>" + msg + "</CENTER>");
}
```

The preceding function would center any string that was passed to it when called. For example

```
<SCRIPT LANGUAGE="JavaScript">
center_string("Hello World");
</SCRIPT>
```

When using functions in your HTML code, it is generally a good idea to place your functions in the <HEAD>..</HEAD> portion of the page. That way, when the page is loaded, any functions that may be needed for the page will be loaded already.

Functions may also return values upon completion. This is accomplished by using a `return` statement that specifies the return value. Functions cannot be nested; that is, you cannot place functions within other functions or themselves. Following is the syntax of the `function` statement:

```
function name([param] [, param] [..., param]) {
     statements
}
```

The *params* indicate that you may use one or more parameters in a JavaScript function. Following is an example of a `function` statement in use:

```
function rate_book(rating) {
     var i;
     var result = "";
     for (i = 0; i < rating; i++)
          result += "*";
     return result;
}
```

The preceding example declares a function that returns a string of stars ("*") based on the rating number you give it.

The JavaScript `return` statement is used to send back values from a function once it has completed. The syntax for a `return` statement is simply

```
return expressions
```

An example of the `return` statement in use can be seen in the `function` example above, as well as the following example:

```
function cubeit( x ) {
     return x * x * x;
}
```

This example will return the cube (x^3) of the value passed into the `cubeit()` function.

Calling Functions

Once your functions have been created, calling them is a simple process. You may call functions directly, as in

```
doSomething();
```

You may call functions through an object by using an object's methods.

JavaScript methods are functions that have been associated with an object. You can define a function as an object's method in the same way you would define a normal property, but instead of using a literal or variable value, you would use a function name. The next section discusses creating JavaScript objects.

To call a function that has been set as part of an object, you would use the same procedure as if you were accessing a property of the object, for example

```
object.methodname(params);
```

Creating Objects

Creating a new object in JavaScript requires two steps. In the first step, you must create a function for that object. In the second step, you must create an instance of that object with the keyword new. For example, to create the person object referenced in the previous section, you would write the following function:

```
function person(name, age, height, weight) {
    this.name=name;
    this.age=age;
    this.height=height;
    this.weight=weight;
}
```

The this keyword lets the function know to refer to itself when making the property assignments. When defining functions, you may also use other objects as properties in that function.

Now that you have written the function, creating a new object is very straightforward. For example, to create a new person object, you would use the following statement:

```
aperson = new person("Paul", 24, 68, 155);
```

This statement would create an object called aperson whose values would be assigned to those passed in the statement. You are not limited to the number of new objects that you can create.

Adding methods to your objects involves specifying the function to use for your method in the definition of the object. For example, if you wanted to add a method called printstats to the previous object, you would use the following:

```
function person(name, age, height, weight) {
    this.name=name;
    this.age=age;
    this.height=height;
    this.weight=weight;
    this.printstats = printstats;
}
```

The printstats function would have to be defined in order to specify it as a method in an object. Adding a method to an object definition ensures that all newly created objects contain the method. To add a method to a single instance of an object, that is, to only the object you are using and not to the definition itself, you could use the following statement:

```
object.printstats = printstats;
```

This would have the same effect when called as the method in the object definition above, but would not carry across to newly created objects.

Built-In Objects

Whenever you load a page into Netscape's Navigator, whether the page has JavaScript in it or not, Navigator automatically creates a number of objects that correspond to the page. These objects contain all the information that is pertinent to that page including the contents of the page, color information, frame information, and other information.

Navigator objects give the JavaScript programmer great control and flexibility over the page that is being viewed and interacted with by the user. The three most useful of the Navigator objects are the window object, the document object, and the form object.

In addition to these newly created objects, JavaScript contains three objects that are always available to you. These objects are the string object, the Math object, and the Date object, which are discussed at the end of this section.

Object Hierarchy

When any document is loaded into the Netscape Navigator program, a new collection of objects is instantly created to describe the current document and browser window. These objects are created in a hierarchy. Figure 42.2 illustrates the hierarchy of these objects.

FIGURE 42.2.

The hierarchy of Navigator objects.

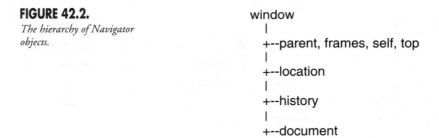

```
window
  |
  +--parent, frames, self, top
  |
  +--location
  |
  +--history
  |
  +--document
```

The window object is the top-level object in the Navigator object hierarchy. It contains properties that apply for the entire window. If you are using frames, there will be a window object for each frame window on your page. The location object contains properties for the current URL for the page. The history object contains properties for any previously visited URLs.

The document object contains properties for the content in the current page. It contains properties for such things as the title of the page, its colors, and its location. The document object also contains other objects such as the forms and forms' elements on a page, links on the page, and anchors on the page. Figure 42.3 illustrates the hierarchy for the document object.

FIGURE 42.3.
The hierarchy for the document object.

```
+---document
  |
  +---forms
  |    |
  |  elements (text fields, textarea,
  |                checkbox, password,
  |                radio, select, button, submit, reset)
  +---links
  |
  +---anchors
```

The Window Object

The window object is the top-level, "parent" object to all other Navigator objects. It enables you to do some very nifty things. For example, you can pop up a dialog window when a user clicks the wrong button, or open a context-sensitive help window when the user requires additional assistance. The window object has properties for all of the frames in your framesets as well. In addition, you can also control the status message at the bottom of the Navigator window using this object. This is a useful feature for providing content-sensitive clues to what the user is pointing to.

Examples of Window Object Properties

Some of the more useful properties of the window object are frames and status. Using the frames property enables you to access the individual documents of the frameset in JavaScript. For example, let's say you had a document with two frames, one called `frame1` and the other called `frame2`. Using the following statement

```
window.frames['frame1'].document.bgColor = "red";
```

would set the background color of `frame1` to red. Because the window object is the top-level object, you may omit the window object when referring to properties or objects of the window. For example, the preceding statement could also be written as this:

```
frames['frame1'].document.bgColor = "red";
```

The status property of the window object enables you to display a message on the status bar of the Navigator window. For example, the following statement

```
window.status = "Programming JavaScript is Fun!";
```

would set the status bar of the Navigator window to `Programming JavaScript is Fun!`

Examples of Window Object Methods

The window object also contains some useful methods for interacting with the user. For example, the `alert()` and `confirm()` methods enable you to display a message to the user in a small pop-up window. For example, the statement

```
window.alert("What are you doing!");
```

would pop up a window with the message What are you doing! in it. The user could then click the OK button to proceed.

If you seek some sort of confirmation from the user, you can use the `confirm()` method. It enables you to receive back a true or false depending on the response of the user. For example, the statement

```
window.confirm("Are you sure you want to leave?");
```

would pop up a window with the message Are you sure you want to leave? in it. The user could then click the OK button, which would return a Boolean true value, or the CANCEL button, which would return a Boolean false value. Your JavaScript code could then perform different tasks based on the user's response.

Another interesting method of the window object is the `open()` method. With this method, your HTML documents can open their own Navigator windows and write content to them on the fly. The `open()` method is called in the following way:

```
windowVar = window.open("URL", "windowName", ["windowFeatures"])
```

An example of all three of these methods in an actual HTML document is given in the next chapter.

The Document Object

The document object is perhaps the most useful and powerful of the Navigator objects. With the document object, your JavaScript code can generate HTML code on the fly, as well as react to a user entering or leaving your page. For example, the following code segment will generate HTML code depending on the time of day:

```
<SCRIPT>
    now = new Date();
    if(now.getMinutes() > 17 || now.getMinutes() < 6)
        document.write("It's dark out here!");
    else
        document.write("All I do is work.");
</SCRIPT>
```

In the preceding example, if the current time is after 5 P.M., the message It's dark out here! gets printed on the page. Otherwise, the message All I do is work. is displayed.

Examples of Document Object Properties

The document object contains many useful properties. Some of these properties include the link colors: `alinkColor`, `linkColor`, and `vlinkColor`; the document colors: `bgColor` and `fgColor`; and general document information like title, referrer, and a collection of all forms in the document.

These properties can be accessed directly, as in any JavaScript property. For example, to set the link colors in the current document, you could use the following statements:

```
document.linkColor = "blue";

document.alinkColor = "red";

document.vlinkColor = "purple";
```

To check the referrer of the current document, you could simply view the value from the following statement:

```
wherefrom = document.referer;
```

Another very powerful property in the document object is the `forms` property. This property allows for full access to all the field values, which enables you to both read and write to them. The forms object is discussed in more detail further in this chapter.

Examples of Document Object Methods

Some of the most useful methods in the JavaScript language come from the document object. The document object only contains a few methods: `clear`, `close`, `open`, `write`, and `writeln`; but these are generally used the most. Specifically, the `write` and `writeln` methods enable you to generate text in your current document. The `writeln` method is identical to the `write` method except that it also appends a newline character to the end of the string. Using these methods is easy, for example

```
document.write("Hello World");

document.writeln("How are you?");
```

The `open` and `close` methods enable you to clear the entire contents of a document so that you may begin writing into them without having any other information in the window prior to your writing.

The Form Object

Another very important Navigator object is the form object. With this object, you can name your forms and check, modify, or create values in the forms. This is a very powerful tool. This object enables you to check the value of form fields before a form is submitted to the server.

The forms property enables you to access all of the form field information from the current forms on the page. For example, say you had a form named `myform` with two text fields called `field1` and `field2`. You could access the values of these fields as such:

```
value1 = document.forms[0].field1.value;

value2 = document.forms[0].field2.value;
```

Notice the zero as the index into the forms property. This specifies the first form in the document. If you had multiple forms, you would use each successive number to access the respective form. You can also access the form by name directly. For example, using the previous example as a reference:

```
value1 = document.myform.field1.value;

value2 = document.myform.field2.value;
```

The form object contains an object for each field in the form to which you are referring. The available objects for each of the fields are: `checkbox`, `hidden`, `radio`, `reset`, `submit`, `text`, and `textarea`.

All these objects contain a `name` and `value` property; that is, you can access the name and value of a particular field with the following statement:

```
document.myform.field.name;

document.myform.field.value;
```

Some of the objects contain extra information. For example, both the `radio` and `checkbox` field types contain a `checked` property to state whether or not the form element has been checked. For example, you could check to see if a checkbox had been checked with the following statements:

```
if(document.myform.mycheckbox.checked == true)
     document.write("Checked");
else
     document.write("Not checked");
```

The form object only has one method, `submit`. Using this method, you can submit the form to the URL that was specified in the `ACTION` property of the `FORM` tag. For example, in the following form

```
<FORM ACTION="doit.cgi"></FORM>
```

the `submit` method of the form object would cause the browser to submit the form to the `doit.cgi` program.

Other Built-In Objects

JavaScript contains other built-in objects and functions so that you do not have to create them. These functions are commonly used and most languages provide some sort of build-in support for them. The JavaScript language currently contains three built-in objects: the string object, the Math object, and the Date object.

The string object is created whenever you create a variable and assign it a string value. For example, the statement

```
astring = "JavaScript is Fun";
```

would create a string object called `astring`. String literals are also string objects. The methods to the string object are located in the object reference section of this chapter.

The Math object contains mathematical functions and methods. Your JavaScript program can call them directly. These methods include `sin`, `tan`, `random`, and `pow`. For example, the following statement sets the variable `sinanswer` to the sine of 1.2456:

```
sinanswer = Math.sin(1.2456);
```

The Date object is used for working with dates and times. Even though JavaScript does not have a date data type, JavaScript still enables you to work quite extensively with date and time elements. To create a new Date object, you would use the following syntax:

```
datevar = new Date(parameters);
```

The parameters for the Date object can be any of the following:

1. Nothing, creates today's date and time.
2. A string representing a date in the following format: "Month day, year hours:minutes:seconds." If you omit hours, minutes, or seconds, they will be set to zero.
3. A set of integer values for year, month, and day. For example, `Xmas96 = new Date(96,11,25)`.
4. A set of integer values for year, month, day, hour, minute, and seconds. For example, `Xmas96 = new Date(96,11,25,10,45,15)`.

Notice that we used 11 instead of 12 for the month. In JavaScript, seconds, minutes, hours, day, and months all begin with 0, not 1.

JavaScript also contains a few built-in functions. Perhaps the most useful is the `eval` function. This function takes as its parameter a string or numeric expression. If the parameter is a numeric expression, it is evaluated and the result returned. If the expression is a string expression, it is first converted into a numeric expression, then evaluated and the result returned. The benefit of this function is in accepting expressions from forms, for example, and being able to evaluate them directly.

Event Handling

Events are actions that occur when a user performs some type of action. For example, when a user clicks on a button, that can trigger an event to occur under JavaScript. When running JavaScript applications under the Netscape Navigator, they generally are largely event-driven. For example, when checking values in a form, the JavaScript application does not check the input until the user types a key, hits return, or some other action is performed. JavaScript contains several events that are triggered when a user performs certain actions. This section covers those events.

JavaScript Events

Creating event handlers under JavaScript is easy. Event handlers are embedded in documents as attributes of HTML tags. In order words, many of the current HTML tags can have event handlers associated with them. For example

```
<INPUT TYPE="button" VALUE="GO" onClick="makeitgo(this.form)">
```

Because of the new JavaScript attribute onClick for the INPUT tag, this statement calls the function makeitgo() when the button is clicked. Browsers that do not support JavaScript will ignore the extra attribute. JavaScript contains a total of nine event handlers. Table 42.6 shows these event handlers and when they occur:

Table 42.6. JavaScript events and event handlers.

Event	*Occurs when...*	*Event Handler*
blur	User removes input focus from form element	onBlur
click	User clicks on form element or link	onClick
change	User changes value of text, textarea, or select element	onChange
focus	User gives form element input focus	onFocus
load	User loads the page in the Navigator	onLoad
mouseover	User moves mouse pointer over a link or anchor	onMouseOver
select	User selects form elements input field	onSelect
submit	User submits a form	onSubmit
unload	User exits the page	onUnload

Besides the actual event handlers, many objects have methods that can simulate an event occurring. For example, the button object has a `click` method that emulates the button being clicked by a user. These emulated clicks, however, will not signal an event handler.

The onClick Event Handler

The `click` event occurs when an object in a form that has the capability to be clicked, such as a button form element or a submit form element, is clicked by the user. The `onClick` event handler can then call a function or execute JavaScript code in place. For example, the following statement

```
<input type="button" name="Click Me" onClick="alert('You have clicked me!');">
```

will cause an alert window to open whenever the user clicks on the button. In addition, a custom function could be called instead, for example

```
<input type="button" name="Click Me" onClick="confirmClick()">
```

This would call the function `confirmClick` when the user clicked on the button. Of course, the function would need to exist in the current document for this to work.

The onSubmit Event Handler

The `submit` event occurs when a user submits a form. The `onSubmit` event handler can then call a function or execute JavaScript code in place. For example, the following statement

```
<form name="myform" action="doit.cgi" onSubmit="confirmSubmission()">
```

calls the function `confirmSubmission` when the user selects the submit button for this form. This enables you to preprocess any information and check the values of any fields prior to calling the URL stated in the `action` attribute, in this case, `doit.cgi`.

Your function or statement in an `onSubmit` event handler must return true to allow the form to be submitted; return false to prevent the form from being submitted.

The onChange Event Handler

The `change` event occurs when a `select`, `text`, or `textarea` field loses focus and its value has been modified. The `onChange` event handler can then call a function or execute JavaScript code in place. For example, the following statement

```
<input name="phone" onChange="checkPhone(this.form)">
```

calls the function `checkPhone` when the user loses focus on the text input field by moving to another field. This enables you to preprocess the information instantly and check the value of the field prior to form submission.

Notice how we passed this.form to the function. As you will see in the next chapter, this allows your function to access the form values directly.

The onLoad Event Handler

The load event occurs when Netscape Navigator finishes loading a window or all frames within a <FRAMESET>. The onLoad event handler can then call a function or execute JavaScript code in place. For example, the following statement

```
<body onLoad="alert('Welcome to my site!')">
```

displays an alert with the message Welcome to my site! as soon as the page finishes loading. This event is very useful for making sure that the entire page has been loaded prior to continuing on to some other action.

Other Event Handlers

The other events, including mouseover and unload, work much the same way as the main events discussed previously. Each event can be handled by an event handler in your document. Using these event handlers can greatly increase the interactivity and flexibility with which you can create dynamic content using JavaScript.

For example, using the unload event, you can tell your users goodbye when they leave your site. A simple example might be

```
<body onUnload="alert('Thank you for visiting!')">
```

which opens an alert window with the message Thank you for visiting! when they leave the current document.

Color Reference

JavaScript contains color string literals that can be used in place of their corresponding RGB color values. These literals can be used in the JavaScript alinkColor, bgColor, fgColor, linkColor, and vlinkColor properties and the fontcolor method. In your HTML code, you may also use these literals to define the COLOR attributes of the BODY and FONT tags. For example, <FONT COLOR="blue">color</FONT>. Table 42.7 is the list of current color string literals with their corresponding RGB values.

Table 42.7. Color string literals.

aliceblue	ghostwhite	navajowhite
antiquewhite	gold	navy
aqua	goldenrod	oldlace

aquamarine	gray	olive
azure	green	olivedrab
beige	greenyellow	orange
bisque	honeydew	orangered
black	hotpink	orchid
blanchedalmond	indianred	palegoldenrod
blue	indigo	palegreen
blueviolet	ivory	paleturquoise
brown	khaki	palevioletred
burlywood	lavender	papayawhip
cadetblue	lavenderblush	peachpuff
chartreuse	lawngreen	peru
chocolate	lemonchiffon	pink
coral	lightblue	plum
cornflowerblue	lightcoral	powderblue
cornsilk	lightcyan	purple
crimson	lightgoldenrodyellow	red
cyan	lightgreen	rosybrown
darkblue	lightgrey	royalblue
darkcyan	lightpink	saddlebrown
darkgoldenrod	lightsalmon	salmon
darkgray	lightseagreen	sandybrown
darkgreen	lightskyblue	seagreen
darkkhaki	lightslategray	seashell
darkmagenta	lightsteelblue	sienna
darkolivegreen	lightyellow	silver
darkorange	lime	skyblue
darkorchid	limegreen	slateblue
darkred	linen	slategray
darksalmon	magenta	snow
darkseagreen	maroon	springgreen
darkslateblue	mediumaquamarine	steelblue
darkslategray	mediumblue	tan

continues

Table 42.7. continued

darkturquoise	mediumorchid	teal
darkviolet	mediumpurple	thistle
deeppink	mediumseagreen	tomato
deepskyblue	mediumslateblue	turquoise
dimgray	mediumspringgreen	violet
dodgerblue	mediumturquoise	wheat
firebrick	mediumvioletred	white
floralwhite	midnightblue	whitesmoke
forestgreen	mintcream	yellow
fuchsia	mistyrose	yellowgreen
gainsboro	moccasin	

Summary

Learning JavaScript requires knowledge of the fundamentals of the language including how to create and use variables and values, the different data types, literals, and properties.

Looping is achieved in JavaScript using the for, for...in, and while statements, while using the continue and break statement to break out of a loop or skip to the next iteration of a loop. JavaScript conditional expressions are achieved using the if...else statement. Lastly, the for...in statement iterates across an object and the with statement is used for specifying the default object in a group of statements.

The JavaScript operators enable you to perform variable assignments, mathematical calculations, string operations, bitwise operations, and logical operations.

JavaScript functions enable you to create a set of statements that can be used as your basic building block for JavaScript applications. These functions can then be used to create objects.

JavaScript contains many built-in objects that are useful for modifying your pages or for retrieving information from forms on those pages. These built-in objects include Date objects, string objects, and Math objects for performing more sophisticated mathematical operations such as sin() and cos().

JavaScript also contains a full set of events that can be caught by your JavaScript application. These events enable you to handle button clicks, page reloads, or even when someone leaves your page.

The next chapter illustrates many of the functions of JavaScript that have been discussed in this chapter.

Building JavaScript Applications

43

by Paul Colton

With JavaScript, there are many types of applications that can be created. JavaScript offers a wide collection of tools for you to create a variety of applications and to add interactive content to your World Wide Web pages. JavaScript also enables you to add greater usability to your forms by providing feedback when something is left blank or entered incorrectly. In addition, JavaScript can increase the amount of direct feedback users receive when visiting your site.

Introducing the Possibilities

Some of the possibilities with JavaScript are instant user feedback when a user moves over an object, enters a new section, or even when a user leaves your site. When using forms, the user can be given much more descriptive warnings and messages about what they have done incorrectly, and because JavaScript runs on the client, the user can keep trying to fill out the form without making a single request to your server.

Another possibility with JavaScript is building a system for automatic language translation. With JavaScript, it is possible to detect who your user is, given that they have previously "signed on," and have your site's output be in a language that is suited to that visitor.

Spell checking is another possibility. With JavaScript, you could set up a form that automatically spell checks all entries before they are submitted. The possible applications are limitless; from context-sensitive help to college financial planners, JavaScript enables you to add a level of interaction that is orders of magnitude greater than HTML, and you can achieve this without any complicated programming.

This section covers four JavaScript examples in detail. Each program is broken into small sections, and each section is discussed. At the end of the section, the source code is reprinted in its entire form for convenience. These examples give a good overview of the possibilities and uses of JavaScript in practical, everyday situations on the Web. All of these examples are available on the CD-ROM as well as on Live Software's JavaScript Resource Center on the World Wide Web at http://jrc.livesoftware.com/.

Your First Example: Messages to the User

This first example demonstrates JavaScript's capability to interact with the user. JavaScript has two built-in objects for directly communicating with the user; they are the alert() object and the confirm() object. In addition, JavaScript allows for the specification of a message that is displayed in the Netscape Navigator status bar. This enables you to display a context-sensitive message to the user without disrupting the display. The following example includes a demonstration of context-sensitive messages.

To begin your JavaScript file, start with the standard HTML header tags:

```
<HTML>
<HEAD>
```

Immediately following the <HEAD> tag, you should specify the beginning of your JavaScript functions by using the <SCRIPT> tag. In this example, we don't use any functions, so the tag is not necessary here. We will include the tags as placeholders for future expansion. There are two commented lines between the tags describing the program. You may use this space for copyright information, author information, or whatever you wish.

```
<SCRIPT>
    // JavaScript Form Validation Demo
    // by Paul Colton
</SCRIPT>
```

Notice that the preceding comments use the single-line comment notation, the double forward slashes (//).

Before closing the <HEAD> tag, you should place the title of the page here. In this example, we use JavaScript User Messages.

```
<TITLE>JavaScript User Messages</TITLE>
</HEAD>
```

Next we open the <BODY> tag. In this example, we set a background color to white and the text color to black. The <BODY> tag is followed by a title and a small picture.

```
<BODY BGCOLOR=FFFFFF TEXT=000000>
<CENTER>
<FONT SIZE=+2>JavaScript's User Messages</FONT><BR>
<IMG WIDTH=108 HEIGHT=26 SRC="../images/previewercredit.gif">
</CENTER>
```

The next section is a short description of what this demo tries to demonstrate. Some of the tags such as <HR> and <SMALL> are purely cosmetic.

```
<HR>
<SMALL>
Following are examples of different ways to send a message to a user.
Click on the links to see what actions they perform. Some links may
perform without clicks!<BR>
</SMALL>
<HR>
<FONT SIZE=+2><UL>
```

This next section begins to add some new tags that you normally would not see in a standard HTML page. These are the event handlers that JavaScript recognizes in order to perform specific actions. For example, the next line uses the onClick() event handler. This event is triggered when the user clicks on the link with their pointer. In this case, the event would call the object alert() and pass it the parameter Thank you!. Notice that the onClick() tag requires its parameters to be in quotes. If any of these parameters needs quotes, such as the alert() function, you must use single quotes in place of double quotes. This ensures that your browser properly recognizes the parameter list.

```
<LI><A HREF="index.html" onClick="alert('Thank you!')">Please click me.</A>
<P><UL>
```

When the link is clicked, a window pops up with the message specified. Figure 43.1 illustrates this.

816

FIGURE 43.1.

JavaScript `alert()` *object.*

The next set of lines contains a little more JavaScript code than the previous set. Notice that in these lines, the `onClick()` event handler contains several statements. As a matter of fact, the `onClick()` handler contains an `if...else` statement right in the `<A HREF>` tag. This example uses the other JavaScript message object, the `confirm()` object. This object is similar to `alert()`, but it gives the user a choice of responses rather than a single OK button. In this example, the user may click OK or Cancel, each delivering its own `alert()` response.

```
<LI><A HREF="index.html" onClick="
    if(confirm('Are you sure about this?'))
        alert('Confidence is a great thing!');
    else
        alert('Maybe next time, hang in there.');">A question for you.</A>
<P><UL>
```

Figure 43.2 illustrates the `confirm()` object as used in the preceding example.

FIGURE 43.2.

The JavaScript
`confirm()` *object.*

This next section demonstrates the use of context-sensitive messages in the Navigator status bar. The first five letters of the alphabet are displayed. When your mouse pointer is moved over them, they trigger the specified `onMouseOver()` event handler, which sets the status bar to a short message describing the letter. The statement for setting the status bar in JavaScript is: `self.status="string"`.

```
<LI>Check the status bar:
<A HREF="index.html" onMouseOver="self.status='A is for Apple';return true">A</A>
<A HREF="index.html" onMouseOver="self.status='B is for Boy';return true">B</A>
<A HREF="index.html" onMouseOver="self.status='C is for Cool';return true">C</A>
<A HREF="index.html" onMouseOver="self.status='D is for Dog';return true">D</A>
<A HREF="index.html" onMouseOver="self.status='E is for Elephant';return true">E</A>
<P><UL>
```

Figure 43.3 illustrates the preceding example.

The final section in this example shows how you can use the `onMouseOver()` event handler for displaying an `alert()` or `confirm()` message. If the mouse pointer is moved over the link, you do not need to click the link; an `alert()` window opens with a short message. This could be used to warn a user of a potential problem associated with selecting the link.

FIGURE 43.3.

Setting the Navigator status bar with onMouseOver().

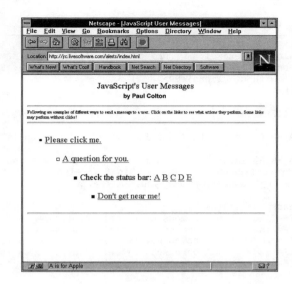

```
<LI><A HREF="index.html" onMouseOver="alert('You're a little too close!')">Don't
➥get near me!</A><P>
</UL></UL></UL></UL>
</FONT><P><HR>
</BODY></HTML>
```

Figure 43.4 illustrates the preceding example.

FIGURE 43.4.

Using onMouseOver() *with an* alert() *object.*

Listing 43.1 is the complete HTML source for the previous example.

Listing 43.1. Complete code listing for User Messages demo.

```
<HTML><HEAD>
<SCRIPT>
// JavaScript Form Validation Demo
// by Paul Colton
</SCRIPT>
<TITLE>JavaScript User Messages</TITLE>
</HEAD>
<BODY BGCOLOR=FFFFFF TEXT=000000>
<CENTER>
<FONT SIZE=+2>JavaScript's User Messages</FONT><BR>
<IMG WIDTH=108 HEIGHT=26 SRC="../images/previewercredit.gif">
</CENTER>
<HR>
```

continues

Listing 43.1. continued

```
<SMALL>
Following are examples of different ways to send a message to a user.
Click on the links to see what actions they perform. Some links may
perform without clicks!<BR>
</SMALL>
<HR>
<FONT SIZE=+2>
<UL>
<LI><A HREF="index.html" onClick="alert('Thank you!')">Please click me.</A><P>
<UL>
<LI><A HREF="index.html" onClick="if(confirm('Are you sure about this?'))
➥alert('Confidence is a great thing!'); else alert('Maybe next time, hang in
➥there.');">A question for you.</A><P>
<UL>
<LI>Check the status bar:
<A HREF="index.html" onMouseOver="self.status='A is for Apple';return true">A</A>
<A HREF="index.html" onMouseOver="self.status='B is for Boy';return true">B</A>
<A HREF="index.html" onMouseOver="self.status='C is for Cool';return true">C</A>
<A HREF="index.html" onMouseOver="self.status='D is for Dog';return true">D</A>
<A HREF="index.html" onMouseOver="self.status='E is for Elephant';return true">E</
A><P>
<UL>
<LI><A HREF="index.html" onMouseOver="alert('You\'re a little too close!')">Don't
➥get near me!</A><P>
</UL></UL></UL></UL>
</FONT><P><HR>
</BODY></HTML>
```

Form Validation: A Correct Form, the First Time

This next example is perhaps one of the most widely-used facilities of JavaScript: the capability to verify and check form input *before* it is submitted to the server. The following example consists of three form fields: a name field, an e-mail field, and a phone number field. Figure 43.5 is a view of the three fields.

The following example performs three specific types of checks on this form. First, it makes sure that all three fields are not left blank. Second, it makes sure that the e-mail field value contains the @ symbol somewhere in the field. Finally, the phone number is checked to make sure it contains only digits and that it is only either 10 or 12 digits. It will also automatically add the dashes for the user after the phone number has been entered. The full source, with all tags, is included at the end of the section.

This form-validation example uses several JavaScript functions in order to perform its validation checks on the form. The first and most important function is the submit_page() function. It is called when the user clicks the submit button to submit all the entered information. This function is responsible for calling the other remaining functions.

FIGURE 43.5.

*A Web form with name,
e-mail, and phone fields.*

```
<SCRIPT>
    // JavaScript Form Validation Demo
    // by Paul Colton
    function submit_page(form) {
```

The following statement creates a variable called `foundError`. Notice how the `var` keyword is used. This variable keeps track of whether the program has found any mistakes with the form submissions.

```
var foundError = false;
```

Here we call the `isFieldBlank()` function. (This function is defined later in the code.) This function returns `true` if the name field is blank. Otherwise it returns `false`. Notice in Figure 43.6 that if the name field is blank, an `alert()` is used to let the user know.

```
// Make sure the name field is not blank
if(isFieldBlank(form.name)) {
    alert("You left the Name field blank.");
    foundError = true;
}
```

FIGURE 43.6.

The `alert()` *window
when a field is left blank.*

Here we call the `isFieldBlank()` function again to check if the e-mail field is blank.

```
// Make sure the email field is not blank
if(!foundError && isFieldBlank(form.email)) {
    alert("You left the Email field blank.");
```

```
        foundError = true;
}
```

We now check our final field with the `isFieldBlank()` function to see if the phone field is blank. Each time, if an error is found, the user is immediately alerted.

```
// Make sure the phone field is not blank
        if(!foundError && isFieldBlank(form.phone)) {
            alert("You left the Phone field blank.");
            foundError = true;
        }
```

If the program makes it this far, we now know that there is something in all of the fields. Another function is now called, the `isValidEmail()` function. This function checks for the presence of the "@" symbol. If it does not exist, the user is alerted. If it is there, the code moves on to the next check, the phone number check.

```
// Now make sure the email is valid
if(!foundError && !isValidEmail(form.email)) {
    alert("You did not enter a valid email address.");
    foundError = true;
}
```

The last check the program makes ensures the phone number is valid. It first checks to see if the correct number of digits are present, and then it makes sure they are all numbers. If there is no error, dashes are automatically added to the phone number (see Figure 43.7), and we proceed.

```
// If we don't aldredy have an error, check the phone number
if(!foundError && !isValidPhoneNumber(form.phone)) {
    alert("You did not enter a valid phone number.");
    foundError = true;
}
```

FIGURE 43.7.

Dashes are automatically added to the phone number.

If by this time there is still no error, no errors have occurred. The program now prints a thank-you message that indicates a successful form submission. (See Figure 43.8.)

```
        if(!foundError) {
            document.open();
            document.write("<HTML><HEAD><TITLE>Form Verification Demo</TITLE><
            ➥HEAD>");
            document.write("<BODY BGCOLOR=FFFFFF TEXT=000000><CENTER>");
            document.write("<H1>Thank you for your submission.</H1>");
            document.write("</CENTER></BODY></HTML>");
            document.close();
        }
}
```

FIGURE 43.8.

A successful form submission after validation.

The other functions used in this form are listed at the end of the section.

Now we proceed to the actual form. Notice that the input fields do not contain any JavaScript tags.

```
<FORM NAME="verifyInputDemo" METHOD="get">
Name : <INPUT TYPE="text" NAME="name" SIZE=50>
Email : <INPUT TYPE="text" NAME="email" SIZE=50>
Phone : <INPUT TYPE="text" NAME="phone" SIZE=50>
```

The submit button, on the other hand, contains the `onClick()` event handler. Notice that the event handler calls the function we reviewed previously, `submit_page()`. It also passes as a parameter `this.form`. This tells the function where to get the information about the form field values.

```
<INPUT TYPE="button" NAME="Submit" VALUE="Submit Form"
onClick="submit_page(this.form)">
```

Following is the complete source listing to the preceding example.

Listing 43.2. Complete code listing for the Form Validation demo.

```
<HTML>
<HEAD>
<TITLE>Form Verification Demo</TITLE>
<SCRIPT>
    // JavaScript Form Validation Demo
    // by Paul Colton

    function submit_page(form) {
        var foundError = false;
```

continues

Listing 43.2. continued

```
        // FIRST CHECK FOR BLANK FIELDS

        // Make sure the name field is not blank
        if(isFieldBlank(form.name)) {
            alert("You left the Name field blank.");
            foundError = true;
        }

        // Make sure the email field is not blank
        if(!foundError && isFieldBlank(form.email)) {
            alert("You left the Email field blank.");
            foundError = true;
        }

        // Make sure the phone field is not blank
        if(!foundError && isFieldBlank(form.phone)) {
            alert("You left the Phone field blank.");
            foundError = true;
        }

        // NOW LET'S CHECK THAT THE FIELDS ARE VALID

        // Now make sure the email is valid
        if(!foundError && !isValidEmail(form.email)) {
            alert("You did not enter a valid email address.");
            foundError = true;
        }

        // If we don't already have an error, check the phone number
        if(!foundError && !isValidPhoneNumber(form.phone)) {
            alert("You did not enter a valid phone number.");
            foundError = true;
        }

        if(!foundError) {
            document.open();
            document.write("<HTML><HEAD><TITLE>Form Verification Demo</TITLE></
            ➥HEAD>");
            document.write("<BODY BGCOLOR=FFFFFF TEXT=000000><CENTER>");
            document.write("<H1>Thank you for your submission.</H1>");
            document.write("</CENTER></BODY></HTML>");
            document.close();
        }
    }

// Check for a blank field
function isFieldBlank(theField) {
    if(theField.value.length == 0)
        return true;
    else
        return false;
}

// Check for a valid email address (Does it contain a "@")
➥function isValidEmail(theField) {
    var foundSymbol = false;
```

```
        for(var i=0; i<theField.value.length; i++) {
            var ch = theField.value.substring(i,i+1)
            if (ch == "@")
                foundSymbol=true;
        }

        return foundSymbol;
}

// Check that a phone number has the correct number of digits
➥function isValidPhoneNumber(theField) {
        var inStr = theField.value;
        var inLen = inStr.length;

        // If this is a ten digit number XXXYYYZZZZ
        if(inLen == 10) {

            for(var i=0; i<inLen; i++) {
                var ch = inStr.substring(i,i+1)
                if (ch < "0" || "9" < ch)
                    return false;
            }

            var  fixedNumber = inStr.substring(0,3)
                        + "-"
                        + inStr.substring(3,6)
                        + "-"
                        + inStr.substring(6,10) ;

            theField.value = fixedNumber;

            alert("Reformatted the Phone field to '" + fixedNumber + "'.");

            return true;
        }

        // Is this is a twelve digit number WWXXXYYYZZZZ
        if (inLen == 12) {

            /* check country code */
            for (var i = 0; i < 2; i++) {
                var ch = inStr.substring(i,i+1)
                if (ch < "0" || "9" < ch)
                    return false;
            }

            /* check area code */
            for (var i = 2; i < 5; i++) {
                var ch = inStr.substring(i,i+1)
                if (ch < "0" || "9" < ch)
                    return false;
            }

            /* check prefix */
            for (var i = 5; i < 8; i++) {
                var ch = inStr.substring(i,i+1)
```

continues

Listing 43.2. continued

```
                if (ch < "0" || "9" < ch)
                    return false;
            }

            /* check body */
            for (var i = 8; i < 12; i++) {
                var ch = inStr.substring(i,i+1)
                if (ch < "0" || "9" < ch)
                    return false;
            }

            var  fixedNumber = inStr.substring(0,2)
                    + "-"
                    + inStr.substring(2,5)
                    + "-"
                    + inStr.substring(5,8)
                    + "-"
                    + inStr.substring(8,12) ;

            theField.value = fixedNumber;

            alert("Reformatted the Phone field to '" + fixedNumber + "'.");

            return true;
        }

        return false;
    }

</SCRIPT>
</HEAD>

<BODY BGCOLOR=FFFFFF TEXT=000000>
<CENTER>
<FONT SIZE=+2>JavaScript Form Verification Demo 3</FONT><BR>
<IMG WIDTH=108 HEIGHT=26 SRC="../images/previewercredit.gif">
</CENTER>

<HR>

<SMALL>
In addition to checking if a form field has been left blank, this example will try
to ensure
that your email address is somewhat valid.<BR>
</SMALL>

<HR>

<FORM NAME="verifyInputDemo" METHOD="get">

<B><PRE>
 Name : <INPUT TYPE="text" NAME="name" SIZE=50>
Email : <INPUT TYPE="text" NAME="email" SIZE=50>
Phone : <INPUT TYPE="text" NAME="phone" SIZE=50>
</PRE></B>
```

```
<CENTER>
<INPUT TYPE="button" NAME="Submit" VALUE="Submit Form"
onClick="submit_page(this.form)">
</CENTER>
</FORM>
<HR>
</BODY></HTML>
```

Interactive Forms: A Loan Planner

This example illustrates some of the more interactive uses for JavaScript. This application, based on a Netscape demonstration application, calculates the principal or monthly payments for a loan when you specify the number of payments and the interest rate. The example uses several of the event handlers to handle user input. In addition, it also uses the Math object to perform its calculations. Figure 43.9 shows the Loan Planner's interface.

FIGURE 43.9.

The Loan Planner interface.

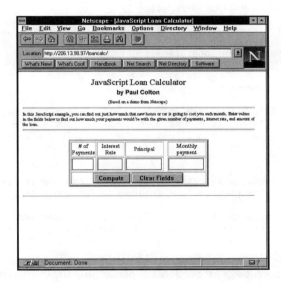

This example also contains several functions, which are responsible for performing the calculations based on the user input. The following function, checkNumber(), checks to see if the input value is made up of entirely digits and gives an alert() if the value does not.

```
function checkNumber(input, min, max, msg) {

    msg = msg + " field has invalid data: " + input.value;

    var str = input.value;
    for (var i = 0; i < str.length; i++) {
        var ch = str.substring(i, i + 1)
```

```
        if ((ch < "0" || "9" < ch) && ch != '.') {
            alert(msg);
            return false;
        }
    }
    var num = 0 + str
```

This next section verifies that the numbers are within range for the given field.

```
if (num < min || max < num) {
    alert(msg + " not in range [" + min + ".." + max + "]");
    return false;
}
input.value = str;
return true;
}
```

The next several functions are responsible for computing the missing field. In other words, if you enter the principal, it computes monthly payments. If you enter the monthly payments, it computes the principal.

```
function computeField(input) {

    if (input.value != null && input.value.length != 0)
        input.value = "" + eval(input.value);
    computeForm(input.form);
}

function computeForm(form) {
    if ((form.payments.value == null || form.payments.value.length == 0) ||
        (form.interest.value == null || form.interest.value.length == 0) ||
        (form.principal.value == null || form.principal.value.length == 0)) {
        return;
    }

    if (!checkNumber(form.payments, 1, 480, "# of payments") ||
        !checkNumber(form.interest, .001, 99, "Interest") ||

        !checkNumber(form.principal, 100, 10000000, "Principal")) {
        form.payment.value = "Invalid";
        return;
    }
```

This section takes care of actually performing the calculations for the Loan Planner.

```
    var i = form.interest.value;

    if (i > 1.0) {
        i = i / 100.0;
        form.interest.value = i;
    }
    i /= 12;

    var pow = 1;
    for (var j = 0; j < form.payments.value; j++)
        pow = pow * (1 + i);
    form.payment.value = (form.principal.value * pow * i) / (pow - 1)
}
```

This function clears all fields on the screen.

```
function clearForm(form) {
    form.payments.value = "";
    form.interest.value = "";
    form.principal.value = "";
}
```

The Loan Planner interface is built around a table. Within that table, the fields exist for the form. Notice that all the fields contain an onChange() event handler that called the computeField() function. When entering values, you can hit the Tab key to proceed to the next field. JavaScript automatically updates the field on which you were just working.

```
<TD><INPUT TYPE=TEXT NAME=payments  SIZE=5 onChange=computeField(this)> </TD>
<TD><INPUT TYPE=TEXT NAME=interest  SIZE=6 onChange=computeField(this)> </TD>
<TD><INPUT TYPE=TEXT NAME=principal SIZE=9 onChange=computeField(this)> </TD>
<TD> </TD>
<TD><INPUT TYPE=TEXT NAME=payment   SIZE=9 onChange=computeField(this)> </TD>
```

When the user is ready to compute, the onClick() event handler calls the computeForm() function to perform all the calculations.

```
<INPUT TYPE="button" VALUE="Compute"      onClick=computeForm(this.form)>
<INPUT TYPE="reset"  VALUE="Clear Fields" onClick=clearForm(this.form)> </TD>
```

Figure 43.10 shows a completed form with actual numbers computed and inserted by JavaScript.

FIGURE 43.10.

A completed Loan Planner form.

Listing 43.3. The complete code for the Loan Planner demo.

```
<HTML>
<HEAD>
<TITLE>JavaScript Loan Calculator</TITLE>

<SCRIPT LANGUAGE="LiveScript">
    // JavaScript Loan Calculator
    // by Paul Colton
    // based on a demo by Netscape Communications, Inc.

function checkNumber(input, min, max, msg) {

        msg = msg + " field has invalid data: " + input.value;

        var str = input.value;
        for (var i = 0; i < str.length; i++) {
            var ch = str.substring(i, i + 1)
            if ((ch < "0" || "9" < ch) && ch != '.') {
                alert(msg);
                return false;
            }
        }
    }
```

continues

Listing 43.3. continued

```
            var num = 0 + str
            if (num < min || max < num) {
                alert(msg + " not in range [" + min + ".." + max + "]");
                return false;
            }
            input.value = str;
            return true;
    }

    function computeField(input) {

        if (input.value != null && input.value.length != 0)
            input.value = "" + eval(input.value);
        computeForm(input.form);
    }

    function computeForm(form) {

        if ((form.payments.value == null || form.payments.value.length == 0) ||
            (form.interest.value == null || form.interest.value.length == 0) ||
            (form.principal.value == null || form.principal.value.length == 0)) {
            return;
        }

        if (!checkNumber(form.payments, 1, 480, "# of payments") ||
            !checkNumber(form.interest, .001, 99, "Interest") ||

            !checkNumber(form.principal, 100, 10000000, "Principal")) {
            form.payment.value = "Invalid";
            return;
        }

        var i = form.interest.value;

        if (i > 1.0) {
            i = i / 100.0;
            form.interest.value = i;
        }
        i /= 12;

        var pow = 1;
        for (var j = 0; j < form.payments.value; j++)
            pow = pow * (1 + i);
        form.payment.value = (form.principal.value * pow * i) / (pow - 1)
    }

    function clearForm(form) {
        form.payments.value = "";
        form.interest.value = "";
        form.principal.value = "";
    }
</SCRIPT>
<TITLE>JavaScript Loan Calculator</TITLE>
</HEAD>
```

```
<BODY BGCOLOR=FFFFFF TEXT=000000>

<CENTER>
<FONT SIZE=+2>JavaScript Loan Calculator</FONT><BR>
<IMG WIDTH=108 HEIGHT=26 SRC="../images/previewercredit.gif"><BR>
<SMALL>(Based on a demo from Netscape)</SMALL>
</CENTER>

<HR>

<SMALL>
In this JavaScript example, you can find out just how much that new
house or car is going to cost you each month. Enter values in the fields below
to find out how much your payments would be with the given
number of payments, interest rate, and amount of the loan.<BR>
</SMALL>

<HR>

<CENTER>
<FORM method=POST>

<TABLE border=4>
<TR>
<TD><DIV ALIGN=CENTER>  # of<br>Payments</DIV></TD>
<TD><DIV ALIGN=CENTER>Interest<br>Rate</DIV></TD>
<TD><DIV ALIGN=CENTER>Principal</DIV></TD>
<TD> </TD>
<TD><DIV ALIGN=CENTER> Monthly<br> payment</DIV></TD>
</TR>

<TR>
<TD><INPUT TYPE=TEXT NAME=payments  SIZE=5 onChange=computeField(this)> </TD>
<TD><INPUT TYPE=TEXT NAME=interest  SIZE=6 onChange=computeField(this)> </TD>
<TD><INPUT TYPE=TEXT NAME=principal SIZE=9 onChange=computeField(this)> </TD>
<TD> </TD>
<TD><INPUT TYPE=TEXT NAME=payment   SIZE=9 onChange=computeField(this)> </TD>
</TR>

<TR>
<TD ALIGN="center" COLSPAN=5>
<INPUT TYPE="button" VALUE="Compute"       onClick=computeForm(this.form)>
<INPUT TYPE="reset"  VALUE="Clear Fields"  onClick=clearForm(this.form)> </TD>
</TR>
</FORM>
</TABLE>
</FORM>
</CENTER>
<P><HR>
</BODY></HTML>
```

Creating New Windows: An Image Previewer

The final example in this chapter demonstrates how to open new windows and build your own custom content in those windows. The example illustrates a simple image previewer that uses JavaScript. Given a selection of images, the user can choose to select the preview button to open a smaller, separate window to view the image. The user can then select other images and browse through them without closing the preview window. Figure 43.11 shows the Image Previewer interface.

FIGURE 43.11.

The Image Previewer interface.

The source code begins with a function named select_item(). This is actually a C++ type constructor for a select_item() object. This object is used to decode the <SELECT> form field.

```
function select_item(name, value) {
      this.name = name;
      this.value = value;
  }
```

This next function is the one actually responsible for decoding the contents of the <SELECT> field. The function runs through all of the SELECT items and checks to see which one was selected by the user. It then returns a select_item() object to the caller.

```
function get_selection(select_object) {
    contents = new select_item();

    for(var i=0;i<select_object.options.length;i++)
        if(select_object.options[i].selected == true) {
            contents.name = select_object.options[i].text;
```

```
        contents.value = select_object.options[i].value;
    }
    return contents;
}
```

This function is responsible for actually building the new page and filling it with the preview image.

```
function display_image(formfield) {
    selection = get_selection(formfield.imagename);
```

Notice the following line; it opens a new window, setting many of the window properties as it opens.

```
myWindow = window.open("", "Preview",
"toolbar=0,location=0,directories=0,status=0,menubar=0,
scrollbars=0,resizable=0,copyhistory=0,width=200,height=255");
```

Note that the third parameter in the `window.open()` statement has been broken into two lines in order to fit on the page. In the final JavaScript code, this line should be one continuous line with no breaks within the quotes.

The current available properties are as follows:

- toolbar = [yes|no] or [0|1]
- location = [yes|no] or [0|1]
- directories = [yes|no] or [0|1]
- status = [yes|no] or [0|1]
- menubar = [yes|no] or [0|1]
- scrollbars = [yes|no] or [0|1]
- resizable = [yes|no] or [0|1]
- copyhistory = [yes|no] or [0|1]
- width = pixel width
- height = pixel height

These properties control which portions of the Navigator window you want visible. In this example, we will turn all the options off. Figure 43.12 shows the Image Previewer alongside the preview window.

Here, using `document.write()`, we will write in the HTML code necessary for creating our preview image. Notice that we must first call `document.open()` before writing to the window:

```
myWindow.document.open();
myWindow.document.write("<HTML><HEAD>");
myWindow.document.write("<TITLE>Preview</TITLE>");
myWindow.document.write("</HEAD><BODY BGCOLOR=FFFFFF TEXT=000000>");
myWindow.document.write("<FORM><CENTER><B><FONT SIZE=+1>" +
    ➥selection.name + "</FONT></B><HR>");
myWindow.document.write("<IMG HSPACE=0 VSPACE=0 HEIGHT=150 WIDTH=150 " +
    ➥SRC='http://jrc.livesoftware.com/ip/" + selection.value + "'>");
```

FIGURE 43.12.

The Image Previewer preview window.

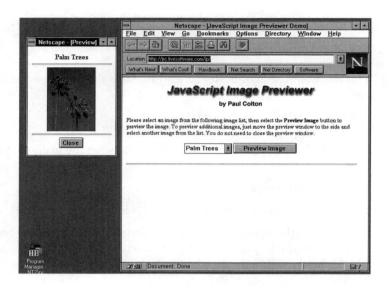

The next line is responsible for creating the close button in the preview window. It uses an onClick() event handler and calls window.close() directly when the button is pushed. This will close the preview window.

```
myWindow.document.write("<HR><FORM><INPUT TYPE='button' VALUE='Close' " +
    ➥"onClick='window.close()'></FORM>");
myWindow.document.write("</CENTER>");
myWindow.document.write("</BODY></HTML>");
myWindow.document.close();
}
```

The following line is the "Preview Image" button. It uses the onClick() event handler to call the display_image() function.

```
<input type=button value="Preview Image" onClick="display_image(this.form)">
```

Listing 43.4. The complete code to the Image Previewer demo.

```
<HTML>
<HEAD>
<SCRIPT>
    // JavaScript Image Preview Demo
    // by Paul Colton

    function select_item(name, value) {
        this.name = name;
        this.value = value;
    }

    function get_selection(select_object) {
        contents = new select_item();

        for(var i=0;i<select_object.options.length;i++)
```

```
            if(select_object.options[i].selected == true) {
                contents.name = select_object.options[i].text;
                contents.value = select_object.options[i].value;
            }

        return contents;
    }

    function display_image(formfield) {

        selection = get_selection(formfield.imagename);

        myWindow = window.open("", "Preview",
"toolbar=0,location=0,directories=0,status=0,menubar=0,scrollbars=0,resizable=0,
➡copyhistory=0,width=200,height=255");

        myWindow.document.open();
        myWindow.document.write("<HTML><HEAD>");
        myWindow.document.write("<TITLE>Preview</TITLE>");
        myWindow.document.write("</HEAD><BODY BGCOLOR=FFFFFF TEXT=000000>");
        myWindow.document.write("<FORM><CENTER><B><FONT SIZE=+1>" +
            selection.name + "</FONT></B><HR>");
        myWindow.document.write("<IMG HSPACE=0 VSPACE=0 HEIGHT=150 WIDTH=150 " +
            "SRC='http://jrc.livesoftware.com/ip/" + selection.value + "'>");
        myWindow.document.write("<HR><FORM><INPUT TYPE='button' VALUE='Close' " +
            "onClick='window.close()'></FORM>");
        myWindow.document.write("</CENTER>");
        myWindow.document.write("</BODY></HTML>");
        myWindow.document.close();
    }
</SCRIPT>
<TITLE>JavaScript Image Previewer Demo</TITLE>
</HEAD>

<BODY BGCOLOR=FFFFFF TEXT=000000>

<CENTER>
<IMG WIDTH=346 HEIGHT=34 SRC="previewertitle.gif"><BR>
<IMG WIDTH=108 HEIGHT=26 SRC="../images/previewercredit.gif">
</CENTER>

<FORM NAME="previewForm">

Please select an image from the following image list, then
select the <B>Preview Image</B> button to preview the image.
To preview additional images, just move the preview window
to the side and select another image from the list. You do
not need to close the preview window.<p>

<CENTER>
<select NAME="imagename">
<option value="image1.gif">Palm Trees
<option value="image2.gif">Sunset
</select>

<input type=button value="Preview Image" onClick="display_image(this.form)">
</CENTER>
</FORM><HR>
</BODY></HTML>
```

Summary

JavaScript creates many new ways to interact with users. Using JavaScript's event handlers, your pages can now respond to users' clicks before they move to the next page. You can provide context-sensitive help in the status bar, or open a window when a user simply moves over an area on your page. These types of dynamic user feedback are crucial to expanding the role of the Internet in new and more interactive ways.

Validating form input now allows your server to work smarter instead of harder. Let the user's client handle the load of verifying that the input is correct, and then it can be sent to your server error-free.

JavaScript allows for sophisticated mathematical applications to run completely on the client side, which again frees up valuable resources on your server and, at the same time, gives your users near instant feedback to their requests.

Using JavaScript, there are many possibilities for the creation of new user interfaces. Opening new windows and creating your own custom interface can greatly increase the value of your site to your users. These features are only the tip of the iceberg when it comes to the potential of JavaScript. Even though a scripting language, JavaScript is full-featured and robust enough for almost any application.

The next chapter covers some advanced issues in using JavaScript, including using JavaScript with frames and using HTTP cookies.

Advanced Techniques
with JavaScript

by Paul Colton

IN THIS CHAPTER

As seemingly complex as the previous chapter's examples were, they only begin to scratch the surface of JavaScript's potential. JavaScript has been designed to be extensible and powerful. With its eventual tight integration with Java and Navigator plug-ins, JavaScript promises to be one of the most useful tools available to the Web programmer.

Many of the newer technologies in Navigator are becoming more tightly integrated into JavaScript. The most important of these new technologies are Netscape Frames and Persistent Client State HTTP Cookies. Frames allow your Navigator to divide its pages into separate sections. Each section may have its own content, fixed or dynamic, but more importantly, each "frame" can have its own JavaScript application running within it. Additionally, the JavaScript applications can communicate and interact between frames.

Persistent Client State HTTP Cookies, or just *cookies*, allow a server to send information to a client for local storage. They are persistent in that the information will be retained across multiple sessions, and will be retrievable by a server in the future. In other words, you may visit a site, enter your preferences for viewing, and the next day it will know who you are. Also, an online catalog can use cookies to track visitors across the site and allow them to use the "shopping cart" model for shopping, checking out only when they have made all of their selections. Cookies allow for greater flexibility in interactive content, and JavaScript makes programming them much easier.

For both the Frames section and Cookies section, there are convenience functions that have been made available by Bill Dortch of hIdaho Design. These routines make programming Frames and Cookies under JavaScript much easier, and take much of the burden off the programmer.

The following sections contain code examples and explanations as well as the toolkits to assist you in your development of these more advanced JavaScript applications. The examples show how to use JavaScript in the context of Frames and Cookies, as well as an example of using timers within JavaScript. Following the three examples is a case study of a real-world product using most of the JavaScript features that have been discussed thus far.

Using Frames with JavaScript

Frames and JavaScript blend together almost seamlessly in the way they interact and interoperate. Many functions that are difficult to accomplish on a single page are relatively easy using frames. For example, having a list of current users in one frame, generated by JavaScript, and a chat session in another frame between all of the users, is something that has already been done using JavaScript and Frames.

Netscape Communications' new Web site makes extensive use of Frames and JavaScript in trying to simplify the process of navigating through their extensive Web site. By using JavaScript, they can dynamically build the content of all of their frames, without having many different versions of HTML pages for each possible outcome. Because of the simplicity of JavaScript over Java, situations like Frames and tables are best suited for JavaScript applications:

Implementing them in Java would require more overhead in time than creating each HTML page individually. Figure 44.1 shows the new Netscape Web site.

FIGURE 44.1.

The Netscape Web site using Frames.

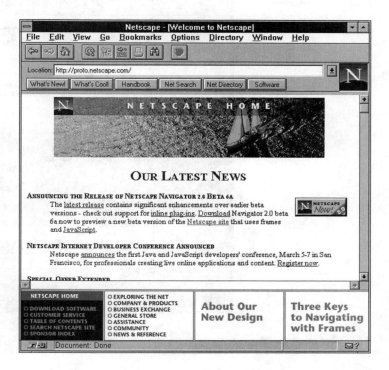

The example provided for this section demonstrates the integration of Frames and JavaScript by creating a system for dynamically selecting background and foreground color attributes and updating the page in real time. The interface contains three frames stacked vertically. The first frame contains sample HTML to view your color options, the second frame contains a form for selecting which color options to change, and the third frame contains a list of JavaScript color names that can be selected to change the currently selected item to that color. Figure 44.2 shows the interface for the Frames sample application.

The example application is not included here due to its length. It is included on the CD-ROM and is available online at `http://jrc.livesoftware.com/`.

To assist in the development of Frames-based JavaScript applications, the hIdaho Frameset has been made available by Bill Dorch of hIdaho Design. This toolkit greatly simplifies the process of communicating between frames with JavaScript applications. The next section details the usage of the Frameset and provides the complete source code to the toolkit.

FIGURE 44.2.

The interface to the JavaScript Frames demo.

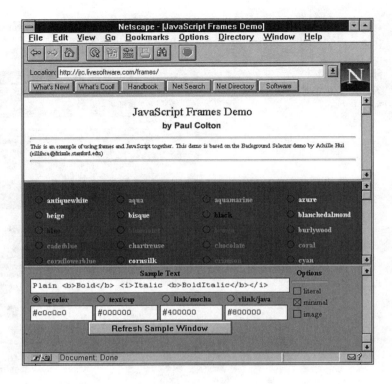

The hIdaho Frameset

When creating multi-frame JavaScript applications, calling functions within other frames can sometimes become tricky and confusing. The problem arises when a function in one frame needs to call a function in another. In this case, the calling function must know the specific location of the function it is calling in the frameset hierarchy. The hIdaho Frameset eliminates this problem by allowing you to register functions and specify in which frame they are located. After registering a function, you can call a function in another frame without specifying the specifics of the location of the function within its frameset hierarchy.

For example, if you had a function in another frame, the following statement could be one hypothetical way on calling the function:

```
frames[AnotherFrameName].functionInAnotherFrame("param1", "param2");
```

Notice in the above statement the necessity of having to know the name of the frame in the frameset for each function that you need to call. Using the hIdaho Frameset, once you have registered the function, you can call the function by name and not be concerned with the name of the frame that the function is located in. The following statement shows a call to a hypothetical function in another frame:

```
parent.Exec ("functionInAnotherFrame", "param1", "param2");
```

The hIdaho Frameset consists of five main functions:

- Register (*frameName*, *functionName*)

  The Register function registers a function's name and its location within the frameset tree.

  The *frameName* parameter specifies the name of the caller's frame. Notably, this does not need to be hard coded, but can be obtained at runtime from the self.name property. The Register function (as with the other Frameset functions) is called in the immediate parent frame [in other words, parent.Register (self.name, "myFunction")]. The call is passed up the frameset tree to the topmost frameset, where the function name is stored. If successful, Register returns true; if not, (because either the function name is already registered, or the name table is full), it returns false.

- UnRegister (*functionName*)

  The UnRegister function unregisters a function's name. The frame name need not be specified, as all registered function names must be unique (since we have, in effect, a global name space).

- UnRegisterFrame (*frameName*)

  The UnRegisterFrame function unregisters all functions registered for the specified frame.

  This is most useful when called from an onUnload event handler.

- IsRegistered (*functionName*)

  The IsRegistered function returns true if the specified function has been registered; otherwise it returns false.

- Exec (*functionName*, *param1*, *param2*, ... , *paramn*)

  The Exec function locates and calls the specified function, passing it any parameters given.

  The Exec function returns the value returned by the specified function. If the function specified is not registered, Exec returns null.

  One incidental benefit of using Exec is that it is not generally harmful to call a function that is not currently registered, or even loaded, so long as a return value of null is checked for. No JavaScript alert will be generated. However, a better practice would be to call IsRegistered before Exec, or at least to call IsRegistered for one function in a frame containing a group of "public" functions, at the start of any block of code that Execs one or more of those functions. In this manner, IsRegistered can be used to synchronize frames during the loading process, especially when used in a timer loop. For example:

```
function initialize () {
  if (!parent.IsRegistered ("functionInAnotherFrame")){
    setTimeout ("initialize()", 250);  // try again in .25 seconds
```

```
      return;
    }
    [...]
    var retval = parent.Exec ("functionInAnotherFrame", "param1", "param2");
    [...]
  }
  [...]
  <body onload="initialize()">
```

More information on the hIdaho Frameset is available on the hIdaho Web site at http://
www.hidaho.com/frameset/. The source code to the hIdado Frameset is shown in Listing 44.1.

Listing 44.1. Complete source code to the hIdaho Frameset.

```
<script language="JavaScript">
<!-- begin script
// ************************************************************************
// The hIdaho Frameset. Copyright (C) 1996 Bill Dortch, hIdaho Design.
// Permission is granted to use and modify the hIdaho Frameset code,
// provided this notice is retained.
// ************************************************************************
var debug = false;
var amTopFrameset = false; // set this to true for the topmost frameset
var thisFrame = (amTopFrameset) ? null : self.name;
var maxFuncs = 32;
function makeArray (size) {
  this.length = size;
  for (var i = 1; i <= size; i++)
    this[i] = null;
  return this;
}
var funcs = new makeArray ((amTopFrameset) ? maxFuncs : 0);
function makeFunc (frame, func) {
  this.frame = frame;
  this.func = func;
  return this;
}
function addFunction (frame, func) {
  for (var i = 1; i <= funcs.length; i++)
    if (funcs[i] == null) {
      funcs[i] = new makeFunc (frame, func);
      return true;
    }
  return false;
}
function findFunction (func) {
  for (var i = 1; i <= funcs.length; i++)
    if (funcs[i] != null)
      if (funcs[i].func == func)
        return funcs[i];
  return null;
}
function Register (frame, func) {
  if (debug) alert (thisFrame + ": Register(" + frame + "," + func + ")");
```

```
    if (Register.arguments.length < 2)
      return false;
    if (!amTopFrameset)
      return parent.Register (thisFrame + "." + frame, func);
    if (findFunction (func) != null)
      return false;
    return addFunction (frame, func);
}
function UnRegister (func) {
    if (debug) alert (thisFrame + ": UnRegister(" + func + ")");
    if (UnRegister.arguments.length == 0)
      return false;
    if (!amTopFrameset)
      return parent.UnRegister (func);
    for (var i = 1; i <= funcs.length; i++)
      if (funcs[i] != null)
        if (funcs[i].func == func) {
          funcs[i] = null;
          return true;
        }
    return false;
}
function UnRegisterFrame (frame) {
    if (debug) alert (thisFrame + ": UnRegisterFrame(" + frame + ")");
    if (UnRegisterFrame.arguments.length == 0)
      return false;
    if (!amTopFrameset)
      return parent.UnRegisterFrame (thisFrame + "." + frame);
    for (var i = 1; i <= funcs.length; i++)
      if (funcs[i] != null)
        if (funcs[i].frame == frame) {
          funcs[i] = null;
        }
    return true;
}
function IsRegistered (func) {
    if (debug) alert (thisFrame + ": IsRegistered(" + func + ")");
    if (IsRegistered.arguments.length == 0)
      return false;
    if (!amTopFrameset)
      return parent.IsRegistered (func);
    if (findFunction (func) == null)
      return false;
    return true;
}
function Exec (func) {
    if (debug) alert (thisFrame + ": Exec(" + func + ")");
    var argv = Exec.arguments;
    if (argv.length == 0)
      return null;
    var arglist = new makeArray(argv.length);
    for (var i = 0; i < argv.length; i++)
      arglist[i+1] = argv[i];
    var argstr = "";
    for (i = ((amTopFrameset) ? 2 : 1); i <= argv.length; i++)
      argstr += "arglist[" + i + "]" + ((i < argv.length) ? "," : "");
    if (!amTopFrameset)
```

continues

Listing 44.1. continued

```
    return eval ("parent.Exec(" + argstr + ")");
  var funcobj = findFunction (func);
  if (funcobj == null)
    return null;
  return eval ("self." + ((funcobj.frame == null) ? "" : (funcobj.frame + "."))+
funcobj.func + "(" + argstr + ")");
}
// *****************************************************************
// End of hIdaho Frameset code.
// *****************************************************************
// end script -->
</script>
```

Persistent Client State HTTP Cookies

As stated earlier, HTTP cookies are a mechanism for the server to send and retrieve information from the client. This simple mechanism enables you to extend the capabilities of your Web sites tremendously. The code in this section gives an example of how to use cookies to store and retrieve information from the client.

With the mechanism of cookies in place, complex sites can be created. For example, developing applications utilizing the code made available here enables you to create systems for tracking all of your users, tracking how long a user is staying on your site, and creating a full online ordering catalog. The provided toolkit also makes it extremely easy to use cookies in your applications and Web sites. A single command can set and retrieve cookies.

Another added advantage in using cookies is their ability to expire after a predetermined amount of time. In the example to follow, the cookie value you enter expires after 24 hours. You can have the values expire right away, in a week, or whatever time interval you desire. It is also possible to request that a cookie only be retrieved securely, which would ensure the privacy of your users if you were using cookies to transfer passwords.

The sample application, as shown in Figure 44.3, uses a very simple form to illustrate the setting and getting of cookies. Notice how the entire code statement that checks for the user's input sets the cookie value and alerts them if the field is blank is all contained within a single <FORM> tag statement.

```
<FORM NAME="demoForm" onSubmit="
    if(demoForm.name.value.length != 0) {
        var expdate = new Date ();
        expdate.setTime(expdate.getTime() + (60 * 60 * 1000));
        SetCookie('DemoName', demoForm.name.value, expdate);
        alert('Cookie has been set to ' + demoForm.name.value + '.');
        return false;
    } else {
        alert('You left the Name field blank.');
        return false;
    }">
```

FIGURE 44.3.

The HTTP cookie demo.

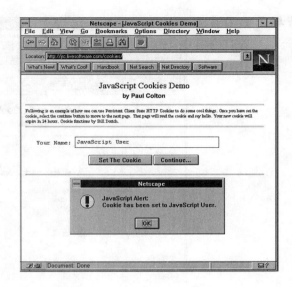

Because we have established the preceding code as the response to a `Submit`, using an ordinary `submit` button will set the cookie:

```
<INPUT TYPE="submit" VALUE="Set The Cookie">
```

To proceed to the next page, we use the `window.open()` function. Before moving to the next page, we perform an extra check to make sure that the cookie was set:

```
<INPUT TYPE="button" VALUE="Continue..."
    onClick="
        if(GetCookie('DemoName') == null)
            alert('Did you set the cookie?')
        else
            window.open('page2.html', '_top')">
```

Once you have submitted the form on the first cookie example page, the second page simply calls the `GetCookie()` function to retrieve the cookie value from the Navigator as this line illustrates:

```
document.write("Welcome back " + GetCookie('DemoName') + ".");
```

Figure 44.4 shows the result of the second page from the cookie example.

Listing 44.2 shows the listing for the first Web page of the cookie demo. Note that the cookie toolkit code (see Listing 44.4) should be inserted at the top of this source code as denoted by the comment `<!-- PLACE COOKIE TOOLKIT HERE -->`.

FIGURE 44.4.

Retrieving a cookie value from the Navigator.

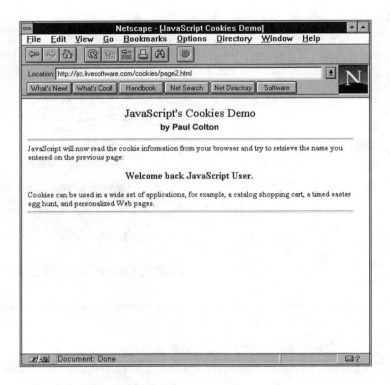

Listing 44.2. Source code for Page 1 of the Cookies Demo.

```
<HTML><HEAD>
<!-- PLACE COOKIE TOOLKIT HERE -->
<TITLE>Cookie Demo</TITLE></HEAD>
<BODY BGCOLOR=FFFFFF TEXT=000000>
<CENTER>
<FONT SIZE=+2>JavaScript Cookies Demo</FONT><BR>
<IMG WIDTH=108 HEIGHT=26 SRC="../images/previewercredit.gif"><BR>
</CENTER>
<HR>
<SMALL>
Following is an example of how one can use Persistent Client State HTTP Cookies
to do some cool things. Once you have set the cookie, select the continue button
to move to the next page. That page will read the cookie and say hello. Your new
cookie will expire in 24 hours. Cookie functions by Bill Dortch.<BR>
</SMALL>
<HR>
<FORM NAME="demoForm" onSubmit="
    if(demoForm.name.value.length != 0) {
        var expdate = new Date ();
        expdate.setTime(expdate.getTime() + (60 * 60 * 1000));
        SetCookie('DemoName', demoForm.name.value, expdate);
        alert('Cookie has been set to ' + demoForm.name.value + '.');
        return false;
    } else {
```

```
            alert('You left the Name field blank.');
            return false;
    }">
<PRE>
   Your Name: <INPUT TYPE="text" NAME="name" SIZE=40>
</PRE>
<P>
<CENTER>
<INPUT TYPE="submit" VALUE="Set The Cookie">
 <INPUT TYPE="button" VALUE="Continue..."
    onClick="
        if(GetCookie('DemoName') == null)
            alert('Did you set the cookie?')
        else
            window.open('page2.html', '_top')">

</FORM>
</CENTER>
<HR>
</BODY>
</HTML>
```

Listing 44.3 shows the code for the second Web page of the Cookies Demo. As in the previous listing, the cookie toolkit code (see Listing 44.4) should be inserted at the top of this source code as denoted by the comment <!-- PLACE COOKIE TOOLKIT HERE -->.

Listing 44.3. Source code for Page 2 of the Cookies Demo.

```
<HTML><HEAD>
<!-- PLACE COOKIE TOOLKIT HERE -->
<TITLE>Cookie Demo</TITLE></HEAD>
<BODY BGCOLOR=FFFFFF TEXT=000000>
<CENTER>
<FONT SIZE=+2>JavaScript's Cookies Demo</FONT><BR>
<IMG WIDTH=108 HEIGHT=26 SRC="../images/previewercredit.gif"><BR>
</CENTER>
<HR>
JavaScript will now read the cookie information from your browser and try to
retrieve the name you entered on the previous page:
<center><h3>
<SCRIPT>
document.write("Welcome back " + GetCookie('DemoName') + ".");
</SCRIPT>
</h3></center>
Cookies can be used in a wide set of applications, for example,
a catalog shopping cart, a timed easter egg hunt, and personalized Web
pages.<BR>
<HR>
</BODY>
</HTML>
```

Cookie Toolkit

The source code in Listing 44.4 contains the latest cookie toolkit from hIdaho Design. The source code contains usage information as well as an example of how to use the toolkit. The latest version is available from `http://www.hidaho.com/cookies/`.

Listing 44.4. Complete source to cookie toolkit.

```
<script language="JavaScript">
<!-- begin script
//
//   Cookie Functions - Second Helping   (21-Jan-96)
//   Written by:  Bill Dortch, hIdaho Design <bdortch@netw.com>
//   The following functions are released to the public domain.
//
//   The Second Helping version of the cookie functions dispenses with
//   my encode and decode functions, in favor of JavaScript's new built-in
//   escape and unescape functions, which do more complete encoding, and
//   which are probably much faster.
//
//   The new version also extends the SetCookie function, though in
//   a backward-compatible manner, so if you used the First Helping of
//   cookie functions as they were written, you will not need to change any
//   code, unless you want to take advantage of the new capabilities.
//
//   The following changes were made to SetCookie:
//
//   1.  The expires parameter is now optional - that is, you can omit
//       it instead of passing it null to expire the cookie at the end
//       of the current session.
//
//   2.  An optional path parameter has been added.
//
//   3.  An optional domain parameter has been added.
//
//   4.  An optional secure parameter has been added.
//
//   For information on the significance of these parameters, and
//   and on cookies in general, please refer to the official cookie
//   spec, at:
//
//       http://www.netscape.com/newsref/std/cookie_spec.html
//
//
//   "Internal" function to return the decoded value of a cookie
//
function getCookieVal (offset) {
  var endstr = document.cookie.indexOf (";", offset);
  if (endstr == -1)
    endstr = document.cookie.length;
  return unescape(document.cookie.substring(offset, endstr));
}


//
//   Function to return the value of the cookie specified by "name".
//      name - String object containing the cookie name.
```

```
//      returns - String object containing the cookie value, or null if
//        the cookie does not exist.
//
function GetCookie (name) {
  var arg = name + "=";
  var alen = arg.length;
  var clen = document.cookie.length;
  var i = 0;
  while (i < clen) {
    var j = i + alen;
    if (document.cookie.substring(i, j) == arg)
      return getCookieVal (j);
    i = document.cookie.indexOf(" ", i) + 1;
    if (i == 0) break;
  }
  return null;
}


//
//  Function to create or update a cookie.
//    name - String object containing the cookie name.
//    value - String object containing the cookie value.  May contain
//      any valid string characters.
//    [expires] - Date object containing the expiration date of the cookie.  If
//       omitted or null, expires the cookie at the end of the current session.
//    [path] - String object indicating the path for which the cookie is valid.
//       If omitted or null, uses the path of the calling document.
//    [domain] - String object indicating the domain for which the cookie is
//       valid.  If omitted or null, uses the domain of the calling document.
//    [secure] - Boolean (true/false) value indicating whether cookie transmission
//       requires a secure channel (HTTPS).
//
//  The first two parameters are required.  The others, if supplied, must
//  be passed in the order listed above.  To omit an unused optional field,
//  use null as a place holder.  For example, to call SetCookie using name,
//  value and path, you would code:
//
//      SetCookie ("myCookieName", "myCookieValue", null, "/");
//
//  Note that trailing omitted parameters do not require a placeholder.
//
//  To set a secure cookie for path "/myPath", that expires after the
//  current session, you might code:
//
//      SetCookie (myCookieVar, cookieValueVar, null, "/myPath", null, true);
//
function SetCookie (name, value) {
  var argv = SetCookie.arguments;
  var argc = SetCookie.arguments.length;
  var expires = (argc > 2) ? argv[2] : null;
  var path = (argc > 3) ? argv[3] : null;
  var domain = (argc > 4) ? argv[4] : null;
  var secure = (argc > 5) ? argv[5] : false;
  document.cookie = name + "=" + escape (value) +
    ((expires == null) ? "" : ("; expires=" + expires.toGMTString())) +
    ((path == null) ? "" : ("; path=" + path)) +
    ((domain == null) ? "" : ("; domain=" + domain)) +
```

continues

Listing 44.4. continued

```
    ((secure == true) ? "; secure" : "");
}

//  Function to delete a cookie. (Sets expiration date to current date/time)
//     name - String object containing the cookie name
//
function DeleteCookie (name) {
  var exp = new Date();
  exp.setTime (exp.getTime() - 1);   // This cookie is history
  var cval = GetCookie (name);
  document.cookie = name + "=" + cval + "; expires=" + exp.toGMTString();
}
// end script -->
</script>
```

A JavaScript Clock

Another very useful tool in JavaScript is its capability to set timers. With the `setTimeout()` method, you can specify a number of milliseconds to wait before calling a function. This can be used for delays, defaulting to certain selections if the user has not chosen, or even building a real-time, JavaScript-based clock.

The following example implements a real-time digital clock under JavaScript. Figure 44.5 shows the clock in action.

FIGURE 44.5.

A real-time JavaScript digital clock.

The function TOfunc(), once started, repeatedly sets a timer to call itself every second and display the current time. This simple approach allows JavaScript to display a fully working digital clock that updates itself every second:

```
function TOfunc() {
      TO = window.setTimeout( "TOfunc()", 1000 );
      var today = new Date();
      document.forms[0].elements[0].value = today.toString();
   }
```

Turning off the clock is accomplished by calling the clearTimeout() function that clears all timeouts:

```
<input type="radio" name="rad" value="OFF" checked
  onClick="
     if( enabled ) {
        clearTimeout( TO );
        enabled = 0;
     }"> OFF
```

Listing 44.5 is the complete listing for the JavaScript clock.

Listing 44.5. Complete source for JavaScript digital clock.

```
<TITLE>JavaScript Clock</TITLE>
</HEAD>
<BODY BGCOLOR=FFFFFF TEXT=000000>
<CENTER>
<FONT SIZE=+2>JavaScript Clock</FONT><BR>
<IMG WIDTH=108 HEIGHT=26 SRC="../images/previewercredit.gif">
</CENTER>
<HR>
<center>
<SMALL>
Click the 'ON' button to start the clock, 'OFF' to stop it.
</SMALL>
</CENTER>
<HR>
<form>
<center>
<input type="text" name="disp" value="" size=25
     onFocus="this.blur()" >
<br>
<input type="radio" name="rad" value="OFF" checked
  onClick="
     if( enabled ) {
        clearTimeout( TO );
        enabled = 0;
     }"> OFF
<input type="radio" name="rad" value="ON"
  onClick="
     if( !enabled ) {
        TO = setTimeout( 'TOfunc()', 1000 );
        enabled = 1;
     }" > ON
```

continues

Listing 44.5. continued

```
<br>
</center>
</form>
<HR>
</BODY>
</HTML>
```

Case Study: LiveSite

LiveSite by Live Software is an example of an application that uses JavaScript to extend its core capabilities. The LiveSite system is an application that interfaces with Web servers through the Windows CGI protocol. LiveSite is a site management system that enables users to create Web sites online using their browser and forms-based templates. Without using any HTML, users can create sophisticated Web sites with almost no limit on size or content. The user's page information is then stored in a relational database for future modifications and updates. Because the user must enter information using forms, the LiveSite system makes extensive use of JavaScript's capability to validate form input before submitting the form.

When a user is building a page using the LiveSite system, there are many choices for background patterns, stock imagery, rule imagery, and bullet imagery. Each of these could present a daunting list to read through in making a decision for which image to use. By utilizing JavaScript, the program can provide an image previewing system whereby the user can preview the images in a smaller JavaScript-created window without interfering with the form they are currently working on. This allows for greater flexibility and ease of use.

A demonstration version of the LiveSite system is provided on the CD-ROM so that you may experiment with the actual application. Updated versions of LiveSite software are available from `http://www.livesite.com/`. Figure 44.6 shows one of LiveSite's page creation forms that utilizes JavaScript.

FIGURE 44.6.

A LiveSite page using form validation through JavaScript.

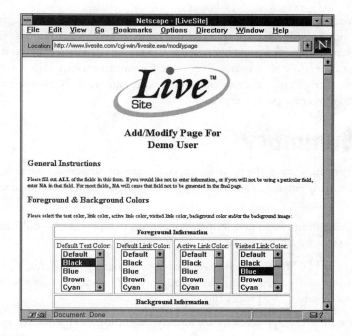

Troubleshooting

Inevitably, code in any language is bound to have some bugs. JavaScript has a fairly robust system for reporting errors to you. Generally, when JavaScript finds an error, it will alert you with a window that specifies the error and the associated line. Many times—as any programmer that has ever debugged code would know—this information is still not enough.

Some of the best steps to take in debugging JavaScript code are to carefully review your logic and make sure you are using correct syntax. Make sure all lines end in a semicolon (;), and make sure all braces are properly closed. When using if...else statements or other statements that allow single lines after the statement without braces, for example:

```
for(var i=0;i<10;i++)
    document.write("The number is: " + I);
```

it may make your code easier to debug by adding the braces even when they are not needed; that is, substitute the above example with

```
for(var i=0;i<10;i++) {
    document.write("The number is: " + I);
}
```

That way, you can more quickly see what the for loop should be containing. There are also many resources available on the Internet for help. Sometimes, some of the best help can come from viewing other people's source code. A good starting point is Live Software's JavaScript Resource Center (`http://jrc.livesoftware.com/`), which contains numerous examples and links to other JavaScript sites. Netscape Communications also maintains a developers site for JavaScript and other technologies. You can reach Netscape's site by contacting `http://developer.netscape.com/`.

Summary

By using some of the more advanced features of Netscape, such as frames and cookies, JavaScript can truly emerge as a uniquely powerful language for Web-based scripting and application development.

Using Frames and JavaScript, applications that previously could only be accomplished with C/C++ or Java can now be fully implemented.

Using HTTP cookies and JavaScript opens many possibilities, including complete online commerce applications using the "shopping cart" model for user tracking and JavaScript for order taking and order processing.

Commercial applications are already beginning to emerge utilizing JavaScript, and with the information you now have at hand, you too can create dynamic and compelling content and applications using JavaScript.

PART

Appendixes and Glossary

Java Language Summary

by I

IN THIS APPENDIX

This appendix contains a summary or quick reference for the Java language, as described in this book.

> **NOTE**
>
> This is not a grammar overview, nor is it a technical overview of the language itself. It's a quick reference to be used after you already know the basics of how the language works. If you need a technical description of the language, your best bet is to visit the Java Web site (`http://java.sun.com`) and download the actual specification, which includes a full BNF grammar.

Language keywords and symbols are shown in a monospace font. Arguments and other parts to be substituted are in italic monospace.

Optional parts are indicated by brackets (except in the array syntax section). If there are several options that are mutually exclusive, they are shown separated by pipes (|) like this:

```
[ public | private | protected ] type varname
```

Reserved Words

The following words are reserved for use by the Java language itself (some of them are reserved but not currently used). You cannot use these terms to refer to classes, methods, or variable names:

abstract	do	import	public	try
boolean	double	instanceof	return	void
break	else	int	short	volatile
byte	extends	interface	static	while
case	final	long	super	
catch	finally	native	switch	
char	float	new	synchronized	
class	for	null	this	
const	goto	package	throw	
continue	if	private	throws	
default	implements	protected	transient	

Comments

```
/* this is the format of a multiline comment */
// this is a single-line comment
/** Javadoc comment */
```

Literals

number	Type int
number[l ¦ L]	Type long
0x*hex*	Hex integer
0X*hex*	Hex integer
0*octal*	Octal integer
[*number*].*number*	Type double
number[f ¦ f]	Type float
number[d ¦ D]	Type double
[+ ¦ -] *number*	Signed
*number*e*number*	Exponent
*number*E*number*	Exponent
'*character*'	Single character
"*characters*"	String
""	Empty string
\b	Backspace
\t	Tab
\n	Line feed
\f	Form feed
\r	Carriage return
\"	Double quote
\'	Single quote
\\	Backslash
\uNNNN	Unicode escape (NNNN is hex)
true	Boolean
false	Boolean

Variable Declaration

[byte ¦ short ¦ int ¦ long] *varname*	Integer (pick one type)
[float ¦ double] *varname*	Floats (pick one type)
char *varname*	Characters
boolean *varname*	Boolean
classname varname	Class types
type *varname*, *varname*, *varname*	Multiple variables

The following options are available only for class and instance variables. Any of these options can be used with a variable declaration:

[static] *variableDeclaration*	Class variable
[final] *variableDeclaration*	Constants
[public ¦ private ¦ protected] *variableDeclaration*	Access control

Variable Assignment

`variable = value`	Assignment
`variable++`	Postfix Increment
`++variable`	Prefix Increment
`variable--`	Postfix Decrement
`--variable`	Prefix Decrement
`variable += value`	Add and assign
`variable -= value`	Subtract and assign
`variable *= value`	Multiply and assign
`variable /= value`	Divide and assign
`variable %= value`	Modulus and assign
`variable &= value`	AND and assign
`variable ¦ = value`	OR and assign
`variable ^= value`	XOR and assign
`variable <<= value`	Left-shift and assign
`variable >>= value`	Right-shift and assign
`variable <<<= value`	Zero-fill right-shift and assign

Operators

`arg + arg`	Addition
`arg - arg`	Subtraction
`arg * arg`	Multiplication
`arg / arg`	Division
`arg % arg`	Modulus
`arg < arg`	Less than
`arg > arg`	Greater than
`arg <= arg`	Less than or equal to
`arg >= arg`	Greater than or equal to
`arg == arg`	Equal
`arg != arg`	Not equal
`arg && arg`	Logical AND
`arg ¦¦ arg`	Logical OR
`! arg`	Logical NOT
`arg & arg`	AND
`arg ¦ arg`	OR
`arg ^ arg`	XOR
`arg << arg`	Left-shift
`arg >> arg`	Right-shift
`arg >>> arg`	Zero-fill right-shift

`~ arg`	Complement
`(type)thing`	Casting
`arg instanceof class`	Instance of
`test ? trueOp : falseOp`	Tenary (`if`) operator

Objects

`new class();`	Create new instance
`new class(arg,arg,arg...)`	New instance with parameters
`object.variable`	Instance variable
`object.classvar`	Class variable
`Class.classvar`	Class variable
`object.method()`	Instance method (no args)
`object.method(arg,arg,arg...)`	Instance method
`object.classmethod()`	Class method (no args)
`object.classmethod(arg,arg,arg...)`	Class method
`Class.classmethod()`	Class method (no args)
`Class.classmethod(arg,arg,arg...)`	Class method

Arrays

NOTE

The brackets in this section are parts of the array creation or access statements. They do not denote optional parts as they do in other parts of this appendix.

`type varname[]`	Array variable
`type[] varname`	Array variable
`new type[numElements]`	New array object
`array[index]`	Element access
`array.length`	Length of array

Loops and Conditionals

`if ( test) block`	Conditional
`if ( test ) block`	
`else block`	Conditional with `else`

```
switch (test) {                       switch (only with integer or char
    case value : statements           types)
    case value : statements
    ...
    default : statement
}


for (initializer; test; change ) block    for loop


while ( test ) block                       while loop


do block                                   do loop
while (test)


break [ label ]                            break from loop or switch
continue [ label ]                         continue loops


label:                                     Labeled loops
```

Class Definitions

```
class classname block                      Simple Class definition
```

Any of the following optional modifiers can be added to the class definition:

```
[ final ] class classname block            No subclasses
[ abstract ] class classname block         Cannot be instantiated
[ public ] class classname block           Accessible outside
                                           package
class classname [ extends Superclass ] block    Define superclass
class classname [ implements interfaces ] block  Implement one or more
                                                 interfaces
```

Method and Constructor Definitions

The basic method looks like this, where *returnType* is a type name, a class name, or void.

```
returnType methodName() block              Basic method
returnType methodName(parameter, parameter, ...) block  Method with
                                                        parameters
```

Method parameters look like this:

```
type parameterName
```

Method variations can include any of the following optional keywords:

[abstract] *returnType methodName*() *block*	Abstract method
[static] *returnType methodName*() *block*	Class method
[native] *returnType methodName*() *block*	Native method
[final] *returnType methodName*() *block*	final method
[synchronized] *returnType methodName*() *block*	Thread lock before executing
[public ¦ private ¦ protected] *returnType methodName*()	Access control

Constructors look like this:

classname() *block*	Basic constructor
classname(*parameter, parameter, parameter...*) *block*	Constructor with parameters
[public ¦ private ¦ protected] *classname*() *block*	Access control

In the method/constructor body you can use these references and methods:

this	Refers to current object
super	Refers to superclass
super.*methodName*()	Calls a superclass's method
this(...)	Calls class's constructor
super(...)	Calls superclass's constructor
return [*value*]	Returns a value

Packages, Interfaces, and Importing

import *package.className*	Imports specific class name
import *package*.*	Imports all classes in package
package *packagename*	Classes in this file belong to this package

```
interface interfaceName [ extends anotherInterface ] block
[ public ] interface interfaceName block
[ abstract ] interface interfaceName block
```

Exceptions and Guarding

```
synchronized ( object ) block
```
Waits for lock on *object*

```
try block
catch ( exception ) block
[ finally block ]
```
Guarded statements
Executed if *exception* is thrown
Always executed

```
try block
[ catch ( exception ) block ]
finally block
```
Same as previous example (can use optional catch or finally, but not both)

Class Hierarchy Diagrams

by Charles L. Perkins

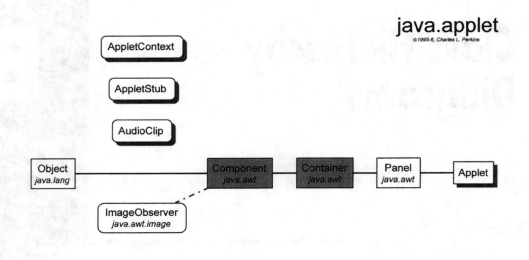

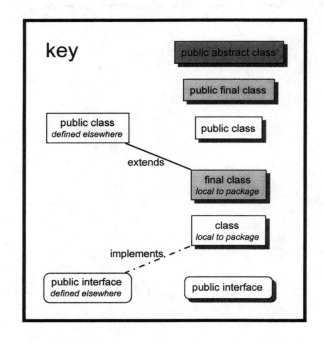

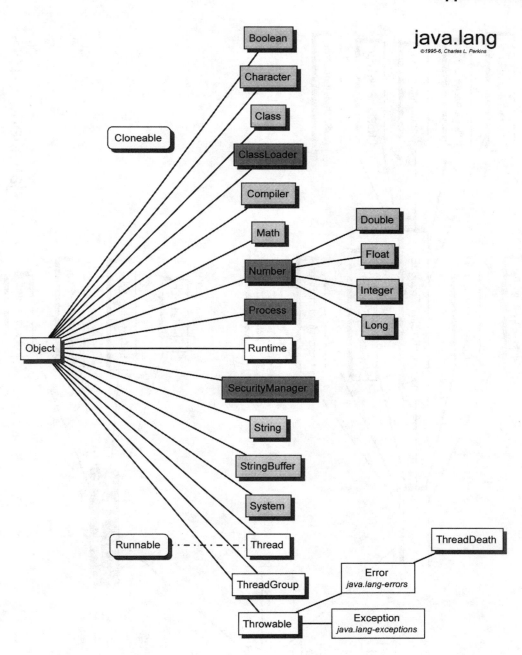

java.lang
©1995-6, Charles L. Perkins

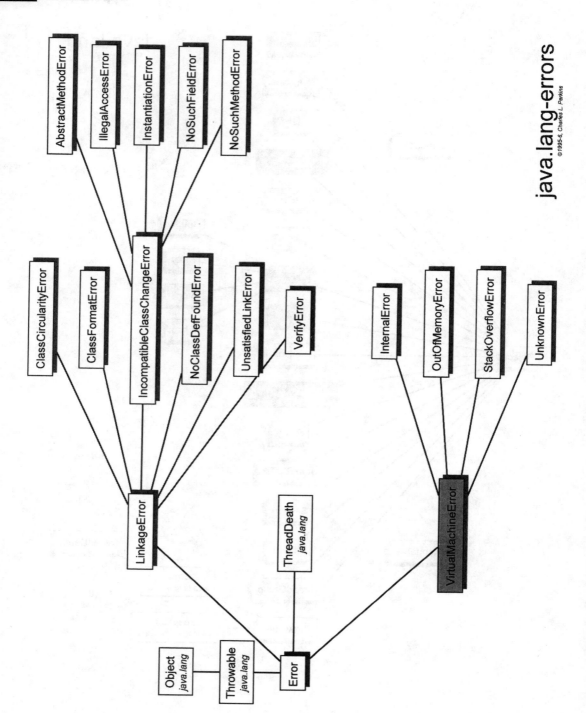

java.lang-errors

©1995-6, Charles L. Perkins

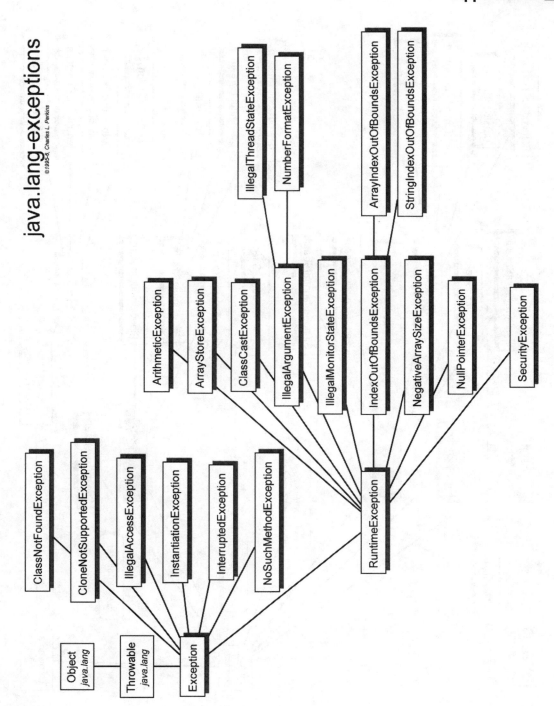

java.lang-exceptions
©1995-6, Charles L. Perkins

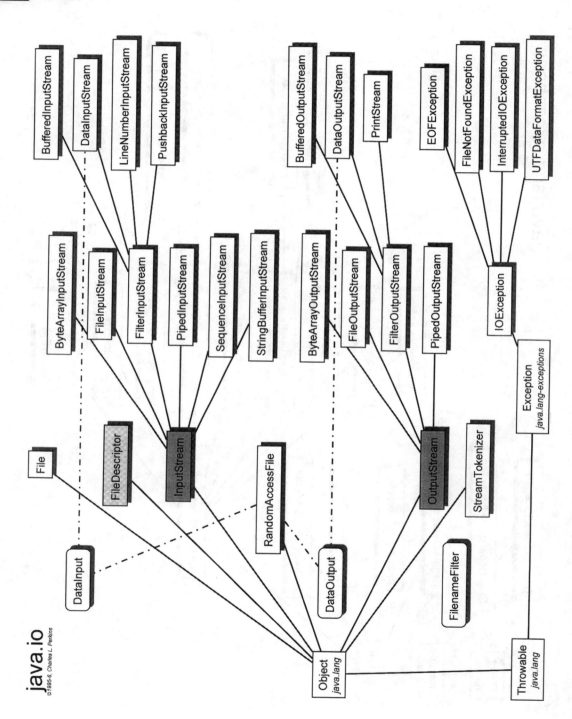

java.io
©1995-6, Charles L. Perkins

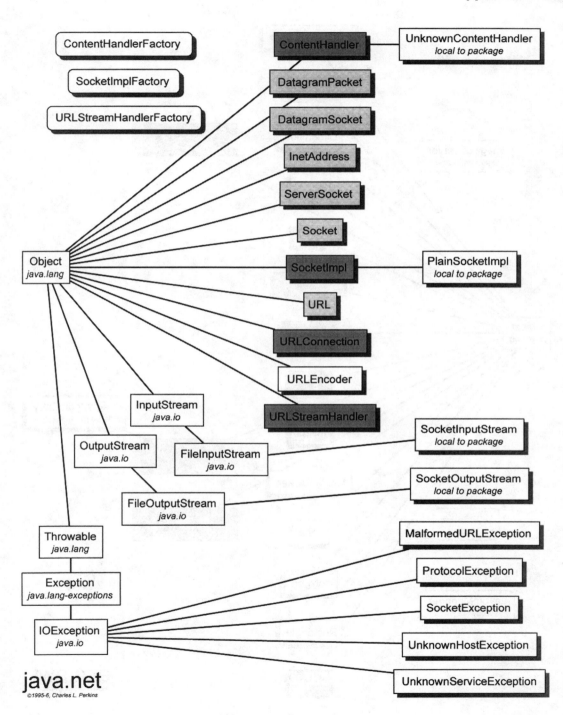

java.net

©1995-6, Charles L. Perkins

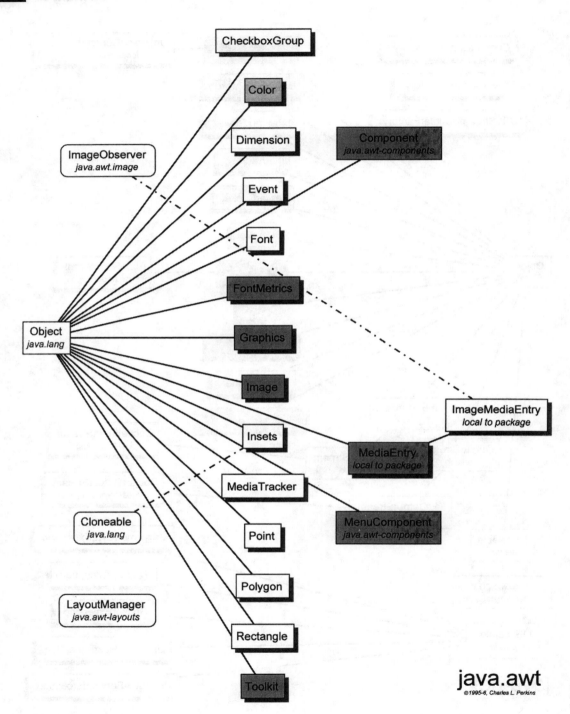

CheckboxGroup

Color

Dimension

ImageObserver
java.awt.image

Component
java.awt-components

Event

Font

FontMetrics

Object
java.lang

Graphics

Image

ImageMediaEntry
local to package

Insets

MediaEntry
local to package

MediaTracker

MenuComponent
java.awt-components

Cloneable
java.lang

Point

LayoutManager
java.awt-layouts

Polygon

Rectangle

java.awt
©1995-6, Charles L. Perkins

Toolkit

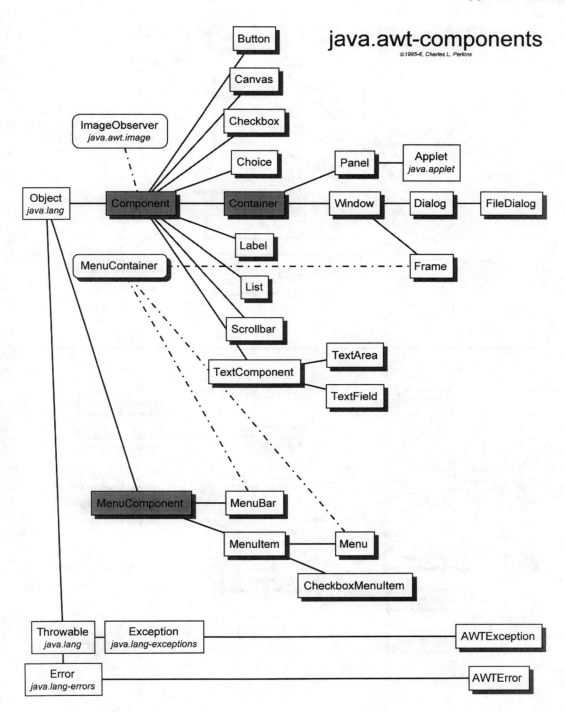

java.awt-components
©1995-6, Charles L. Perkins

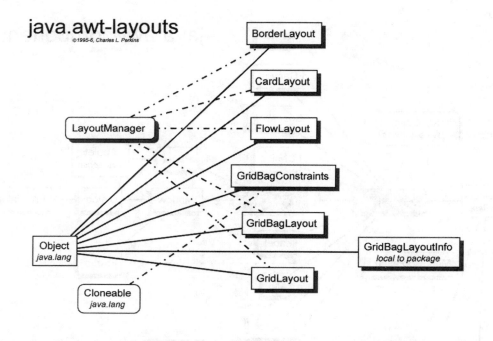

java.awt-layouts
©1995-6, Charles L. Perkins

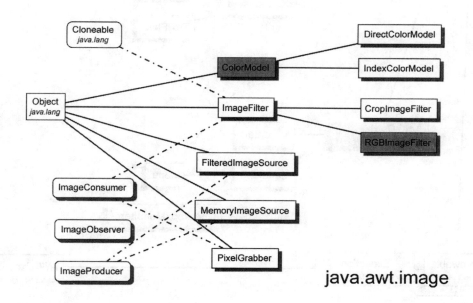

java.awt.image

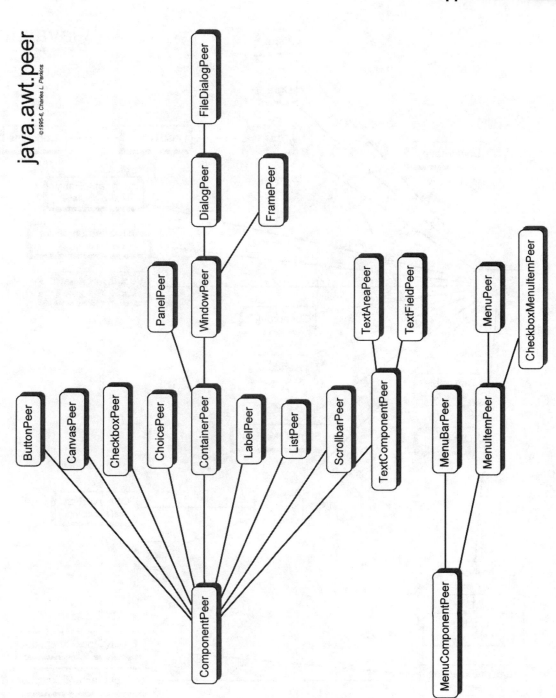

java.awt.peer
©1995-6, Charles L. Perkins

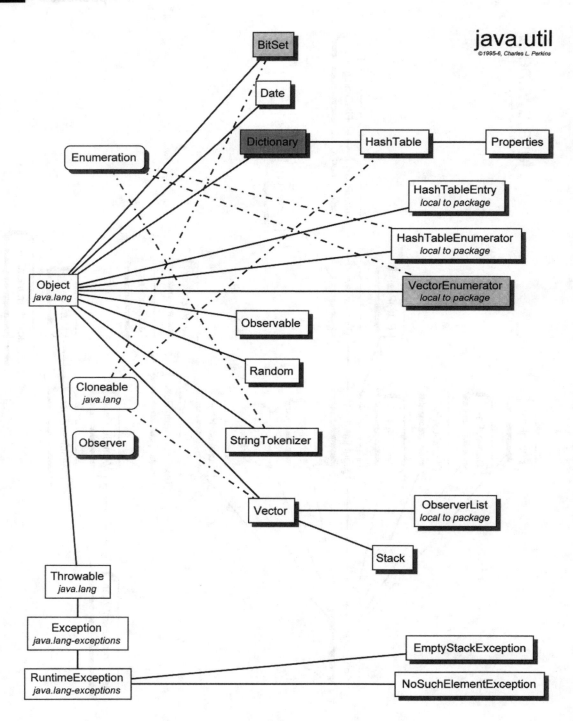

java.util
©1995-6, Charles L. Perkins

About These Diagrams

The diagrams in this appendix are class hierarchy diagrams for the package Java, and for all the subpackages recursively below it in the Java 1.0 binary release.

Each page contains the class hierarchy for one package (or a subtree of a particularly large package) with all its interfaces included, and each class in this tree is shown attached to its superclasses, even if they are on another page. A detailed key is located on the first page of this appendix.

I supplemented the API documentation by looking through all the source files to find all the (missing) package classes and their relationships.

I've heard there are various programs that automatically layout hierarchies for you, but I did these the old-fashioned way. (In other words, I *earned* it, as J.H. used to say). One nice side effect is that these diagrams should be more readable than a computer would produce, though you will have to live with my aesthetic choices. I chose, for example, to attach lines through the center of each class node, something that I think looks and feels better overall but which on occasion can be a little confusing. Follow lines through the center of the classes (not at the corners, nor along any line not passing through the center) to connect the dots mentally.

The Java Class Library

C

by Laura Lemay

This appendix provides a general overview of the classes available in the standard Java packages (that is, the classes that are guaranteed to be available in any Java implementation). This appendix is intended for general reference; for more specific information about each variable (its inheritance, variables, and methods), as well as the various exceptions for each package, see the API documentation from Sun at `http://java.sun.com`. A copy of the 1.0 API documentation is on the CD-ROM included with this book.

java.lang

The `java.lang` package contains the classes and interfaces that are the core of the Java language.

Interfaces

Cloneable	Interface indicating that an object may be copied or cloned
Runnable	Methods for classes that want to run as threads

Classes

Boolean	Object wrapper for `boolean` values
Character	Object wrapper for `char` values
Class	Run-time representations of classes
ClassLoader	Abstract behavior for handling loading of classes
Compiler	System class that gives access to the Java compiler
Double	Object wrapper for `double` values
Float	Object wrapper for `float` values
Integer	Object wrapper for `int` values
Long	Object wrapper for `long` values
Math	Utility class for math operations
Number	Abstract superclass of all number classes (`Integer`, `Float`, and so on)
Object	Generic `Object` class, at top of inheritance hierarchy
Process	Abstract behavior for processes such as those spawned using methods in the `System` class
Runtime	Access to the Java runtime
SecurityManager	Abstract behavior for implementing security policies
String	Character strings
StringBuffer	Mutable strings

System	Access to Java's system-level behavior, provided in a platform-independent way.
Thread	Methods for managing threads and classes that run in threads
ThreadDeath	Class of object thrown when a thread is asynchronously terminated
ThreadGroup	A group of threads
Throwable	Generic exception class; all objects thrown must be a Throwable

java.util

The java.util package contains various utility classes and interfaces, including random numbers, system properties, and other useful classes.

Interfaces

Enumeration	Methods for enumerating sets of values
Observer	Methods for enabling classes to be observe Observable objects

Classes

BitSet	A set of bits
Date	The current system date, as well as methods for generating and parsing dates
Dictionary	An abstract class that maps between keys and values (superclass of HashTable)
Hashtable	A hash table
Observable	An abstract class for observable objects
Properties	A hash table that contains behavior for setting and retrieving persistent properties of the system or a class
Random	Utilities for generating random numbers
Stack	A stack (a last-in-first-out queue)
StringTokenizer	Utilities for splitting strings into individual "tokens"
Vector	A growable array of Objects

java.io

The java.io package provides input and output classes and interfaces for streams and files.

Interfaces

DataInput	Methods for reading machine-independent typed input streams
DataOutput	Methods for writing machine-independent typed output streams
FilenameFilter	Methods for filtering file names

Classes

`BufferedInputStream`	A buffered input stream
`BufferedOutputStream`	A buffered output stream
`ByteArrayInputStream`	An input stream from a byte array
`ByteArrayOutputStream`	An output stream to a byte array
`DataInputStream`	Enables you to read primitive Java types (`ints`, `chars`, `booleans`, and so on) from a stream in a machine-independent way
`DataOutputStream`	Enables you to write primitive Java data types (`ints`, `chars`, `booleans`, and so on) to a stream in a machine-independent way
`File`	Represents a file on the host's file system
`FileDescriptor`	Holds onto the UNIX-like file descriptor of a file or socket
`FileInputStream`	An input stream from a file, constructed using a filename or descriptor
`FileOutputStream`	An output stream to a file, constructed using a filename or descriptor
`FilterInputStream`	Abstract class which provides a filter for input streams (and for adding stream functionality such as buffering)
`FilterOutputStream`	Abstract class which provides a filter for output streams (and for adding stream functionality such as buffering)
`InputStream`	An abstract class representing an input stream of bytes; the parent of all input streams in this package
`LineNumberInputStream`	An input stream that keeps track of line numbers
`OutputStream`	An abstract class representing an output stream of bytes; the parent of all output streams in this package
`PipedInputStream`	A piped input stream, which should be connected to a `PipedOutputStream` to be useful
`PipedOutputStream`	A piped output stream, which should be connected to a `PipedInputStream` to be useful (together they provide safe communication between threads)

PrintStream	An output stream for printing (used by `System.out.println(...)`)
PushbackInputStream	An input stream with a 1-byte push back buffer
RandomAccessFile	Provides random access to a file, constructed from filenames, descriptors, or objects
SequenceInputStream	Converts a sequence of input streams into a single input stream
StreamTokenizer	Converts an input stream into a series of individual tokens
StringBufferInputStream	An input stream from a `String` object

java.net

The `java.net` package contains classes and interfaces for performing network operations, such as sockets and URLs.

Interfaces

ContentHandlerFactory	Methods for creating `ContentHandler` objects
SocketImplFactory	Methods for creating socket implementations (instance of the `SocketImpl` class)
URLStreamHandlerFactory	Methods for creating `URLStreamHandler` objects

Classes

ContentHandler	Abstract behavior for reading data from a URL connection and constructing the appropriate local object, based on MIME types
DatagramPacket	A datagram packet (UDP)
DatagramSocket	A datagram socket
InetAddress	An object representation of an Internet host (host name, IP address)
ServerSocket	A server-side socket
Socket	A socket
SocketImpl	An abstract class for specific socket implementations
URL	An object representation of a URL
URLConnection	Abstract behavior for a socket that can handle various Web-based protocols (`http`, `ftp`, and so on)

| `URLEncoder` | Turns strings into `x-www-form-urlencoded` format |
| `URLStreamHandler` | Abstract class for managing streams to object referenced by URLs |

java.awt

The `java.awt` package contains the classes and interfaces that make up the Abstract Windowing Toolkit.

Interfaces

| `LayoutManager` | Methods for laying out containers |
| `MenuContainer` | Methods for menu-related containers |

Classes

`BorderLayout`	A layout manager for arranging items in border formation
`Button`	A UI pushbutton
`Canvas`	A canvas for drawing and performing other graphics operations
`CardLayout`	A layout manager for HyperCard-like metaphors
`Checkbox`	A checkbox
`CheckboxGroup`	A group of exclusive checkboxes (radio buttons)
`CheckboxMenuItem`	A toggle menu item
`Choice`	A popup menu of choices
`Color`	An abstract representation of a color
`Component`	The abstract generic class for all UI components
`Container`	Abstract behavior for a component that can hold other components or containers
`Dialog`	A window for brief interactions with users
`Dimension`	An object representing width and height
`Event`	An object representing events caused by the system or based on user input
`FileDialog`	A dialog for getting filenames from the local file system
`FlowLayout`	A layout manager that lays out objects from left to right in rows
`Font`	An abstract representation of a font

FontMetrics	Abstract class for holding information about a specific font's character shapes and height and width information
Frame	A top-level window with a title
Graphics	Abstract behavior for representing a graphics context, and for drawing and painting shapes and objects
GridBagConstraints	Constraints for components laid out using GridBagLayout
GridBagLayout	A layout manager that aligns components horizontally and vertically based on their values from GridBagConstraints
GridLayout	A layout manager with rows and columns; elements are added to each cell in the grid
Image	An abstract representation of a bitmap image
Insets	Distances from the outer border of the window; used to lay out components
Label	A text label for UI components
List	A scrolling list
MediaTracker	A way to keep track of the status of media objects being loaded over the Net
Menu	A menu, which can contain menu items and is a container on a menubar
MenuBar	A menubar (container for menus)
MenuComponent	The abstract superclass of all menu elements
MenuItem	An individual menu item
Panel	A container that is displayed
Point	An object representing a point (x and y coordinates)
Polygon	An object representing a set of points
Rectangle	An object representing a rectangle (x and y coordinates for the top corner, plus width and height)
Scrollbar	A UI scrollbar object
TextArea	A multiline, scrollable, editable text field
TextComponent	The superclass of all editable text components
TextField	A fixed-size editable text field
Toolkit	Abstract behavior for binding the abstract AWT classes to a platform-specific toolkit implementation
Window	A top-level window, and the superclass of the Frame and Dialog classes

java.awt.image

The `java.awt.image` package is a subpackage of the AWT that provides classes for managing bitmap images.

Interfaces

ImageConsumer	Methods for receiving image created by an `ImageProducer`
ImageObserver	Methods to track the loading and construction of an image
ImageProducer	Methods for producing image data received by an `ImageConsumer`

Classes

ColorModel	An abstract class for managing color information for images
CropImageFilter	A filter for cropping images to a particular size
DirectColorModel	A specific color model for managing and translating pixel color values
FilteredImageSource	An `ImageProducer` that takes an image and an `ImageFilter` object, and produces an image for an `ImageConsumer`
ImageFilter	A filter that takes image data from an `ImageProducer`, modifies it in some way, and hands it off to an `ImageConsumer`
IndexColorModel	A specific color model for managing and translating color values in a fixed-color map
MemoryImageSource	An image producer that gets its image from memory; used after constructing an image by hand
PixelGrabber	An `ImageConsumer` that retrieves a subset of the pixels in an image
RGBImageFilter	Abstract behavior for a filter that modifies the RGB values of pixels in RGB images

java.awt.peer

The `java.awt.peer` package is a subpackage of AWT that provides the (hidden) platform-specific AWT classes (for example, Motif, Macintosh, Windows 95) with platform-independent interfaces to implement. Thus, callers using these interfaces need not know which platform's window system these hidden AWT classes are currently implementing.

Each class in the AWT that inherits from either `Component` or `MenuComponent` has a corresponding peer class. Each of those classes is the name of the `Component` with `-Peer` added (for example, `ButtonPeer`, `DialogPeer`, and `WindowPeer`). Because each one provides similar behavior, they are not enumerated here.

java.applet

The `java.applet` package provides applet-specific behavior.

Interfaces

`AppletContext`	Methods to refer to the applet's context
`AppletStub`	Methods for implementing applet viewers
`AudioClip`	Methods for playing audio files

Classes

`Applet`	The base applet class

Differences Between Java and C/C++

D

by Michael Morrison

IN THIS APPENDIX

It is no secret that the Java language is highly derived from the C and C++ languages. Because C++ is currently considered the language of choice for professional software developers, it's important to understand what aspects of C++ Java inherits. Of possibly even more importance is what aspects of C++ Java doesn't support. Because Java is an entirely new language, it was possible for the language architects to pick and choose which features from C++ to implement in Java and how.

The focus of this appendix is to point out the differences between Java and C++. If you are a C++ programmer, you will be able to appreciate the differences between Java and C++. Even if you don't have any C++ experience, you can gain some insight into the Java language by understanding what C++ discrepancies it clears up in its implementation. Because C++ backwardly supports C, many of the differences pointed out in this appendix refer to C++, but inherently apply to C as well.

The Preprocessor

All C/C++ compilers implement a stage of compilation known as the preprocessor. The C++ preprocessor basically performs an intelligent search and replace on identifiers that have been declared using the #define or #typedef directives. Although most advocators of C++ discourage use of the preprocessor, which was inherited from C, it is still widely used by most C++ programmers. Most of the processor definitions in C++ are stored in header files, which complement the actual source code files.

The problem with the preprocessor approach is that it provides an easy way for programmers to inadvertently add unnecessary complexity to a program. What happens is that many programmers using the #define and #typedef directives end up inventing their own sublanguage within the confines of a particular project. This results in other programmers having to go through the header files and sort out all the #define and #typedef information to understand a program, which makes code maintenance and reuse almost impossible. An additional problem with the preprocessor approach is that it is weak when it comes to type checking and validation.

Java does not have a preprocessor. It provides similar functionality (#define, #typedef, and so on) to that provided by the C++ preprocessor, but with far more control. Constant data members are used in place of the #define directive, and class definitions are used in lieu of the #typedef directive. The result is that Java source code is much more consistent and easier to read than C++ source code. Additionally, Java programs don't use header files; the Java compiler builds class definitions directly from the source code files, which contain both class definitions and method implementations.

Pointers

Most developers agree that the misuse of pointers causes the majority of bugs in C/C++ programming. Put simply, when you have pointers, you have the ability to trash memory. C++ programmers regularly use complex pointer arithmetic to create and maintain dynamic data structures. In return, C++ programmers spend a lot of time hunting down complex bugs caused by their complex pointer arithmetic.

The Java language does not support pointers. Java provides similar functionality by making heavy use of references. Java passes all arrays and objects by reference. This approach prevents common errors due to pointer mismanagement. It also makes programming easier in a lot of ways simply because the correct usage of pointers is easily misunderstood by all but the most seasoned programmers.

You may be thinking that the lack of pointers in Java will keep you from being able to implement many data structures, such as dynamic arrays. The reality is that any pointer task can be carried out just as easily and more reliably with objects and arrays of objects. You then benefit from the security provided by the Java runtime system; it performs boundary checking on all array indexing operations.

Structures and Unions

There are three types of complex data types in C++: classes, structures, and unions. Java only implements one of these data types: classes. Java forces programmers to use classes when the functionality of structures and unions is desired. Although this sounds like more work for the programmer, it actually ends up being more consistent, because classes can imitate structures and unions with ease. The Java designers really wanted to keep the language simple, so it only made sense to eliminate aspects of the language that overlapped.

Functions

In C, code is organized into functions, which are global subroutines accessible to a program. C++ added classes and in doing so provided class methods, which are functions that are connected to classes. C++ class methods are very similar to Java class methods. However, because C++ still supports C, there is nothing discouraging C++ programmers from using functions. This results in a mixture of function and method use that makes for confusing programs.

Java has no functions. Being a purer object-oriented language than C++, Java forces programmers to bundle all routines into class methods. There is no limitation imposed by forcing programmers to use methods instead of functions. As a matter of fact, implementing routines as methods encourages programmers to organize code better. Keep in mind that strictly speaking there is nothing wrong with the procedural approach of using functions, it just doesn't mix well with the object-oriented paradigm that defines the core of Java.

Multiple Inheritance

Multiple inheritance is a feature of C++ that allows you to derive a class from multiple parent classes. Although multiple inheritance is indeed powerful, it is complicated to use correctly and causes lots of problems otherwise. It is also very complicated to implement from the compiler perspective.

Java takes the high road and provides no direct support for multiple inheritance. You can implement functionality similar to multiple inheritance by using interfaces in Java. Java interfaces provide object method descriptions, but contain no implementations.

Strings

C and C++ have no built-in support for text strings. The standard technique adopted among C and C++ programmers is that of using null-terminated arrays of characters to represent strings.

In Java, strings are implemented as first class objects (`String` and `StringBuffer`), meaning that they are at the core of the Java language. Java's implementation of strings as objects provides several advantages:

■ The manner in which you create strings and access the elements of strings is consistent across all strings on all systems

■ Because the Java string classes are defined as part of the Java language, and not part of some extraneous extension, Java strings function predictably every time

■ The Java string classes perform extensive runtime checking, which helps eliminate troublesome runtime errors

The `goto` Statement

The dreaded `goto` statement is pretty much a relic these days even in C and C++, but it is technically a legal part of the languages. The `goto` statement has historically been cited as the cause for messy, impossible to understand, and sometimes even impossible to predict code known as "spaghetti code." The primary usage of the `goto` statement has merely been as a convenience to substitute not thinking through an alternative, more structured branching technique.

For all these reasons and more, Java does not provide a `goto` statement. The Java language specifies `goto` as a keyword, but its usage is not supported. I suppose the Java designers wanted to eliminate the possibility of even using `goto` as an identifier! Not including `goto` in the Java language simplifies the language and helps eliminate the option of writing messy code.

Operator Overloading

Operator overloading, which is considered a prominent feature in C++, is not supported in Java. Although roughly the same functionality can be implemented by classes in Java, the convenience of operator overloading is still missing. However, in defense of Java, operator overloading can sometimes get very tricky. No doubt the Java developers decided not to support operator overloading to keep the Java language as simple as possible.

Automatic Coercions

Automatic coercion refers to the implicit casting of data types that sometimes occurs in C and C++. For example, in C++ you can assign a `float` value to an `int` variable, which can result in a loss of information. Java does not support C++ style automatic coercions. In Java, if a coercion will result in a loss of data, you must always explicitly cast the data element to the new type.

Variable Arguments

C and C++ let you declare functions, such as `printf`, that take a variable number of arguments. Although this is a convenient feature, it is impossible for the compiler to thoroughly type check the arguments, which means problems can arise at runtime without you knowing. Again Java takes the high road and doesn't support variable arguments at all.

Command-Line Arguments

The command-line arguments passed from the system into a Java program differ in a couple of ways from the command-line arguments passed into a C++ program. First, the number of parameters passed differs between the two languages. In C and C++, the system passes two arguments to a program: `argc` and `argv`. `argc` specifies the number of arguments stored in `argv`. `argv` is a pointer to an array of characters containing the actual arguments. In Java, the system passes a single value to a program: `args`. `args` is an array of `Strings` that contains the command line arguments.

In C and C++, the command-line arguments passed into a program include the name used to invoke the program. This name always appears as the first argument, and is rarely ever used. In Java, you already know the name of the program because it is the same name as the class, so there is no need to pass this information as a command-line argument. Therefore, the Java runtime system only passes the arguments following the name that invoked the program.

Java Resources

by John December

This is a list of online information sources about the Java programming language, the Java-enabled browsers, and related technologies.

> **NOTE**
>
> Much of the information in this appendix changes often. For updates on the Java information sources listed in this appendix, visit
>
> `http://www.december.com/works/java/info.html`

Sun's Java Sites

Sun Microsystems, the developers of Java, offers the best online one-stop, comprehensive source of technical documentation and information about Java on their Web site at `http://java.sun.com/`.

Also, see Sun's Java contest Web site, `http://javacontest.sun.com/`.

Some sites around the world mirror this information, so you can pick a server from the list below that is close to you, or consult Sun's list of Java mirror sites. Here are sites that are known to be updated frequently:

- Dimension X, San Francisco, California, `http://www.dnx.com/java/`
- Javasoft (Sun Microsystems), Aspen, Colorado, USA, `http://www.javasoft.com/`
- Wayne State University, Detroit, Michigan, USA, `http://www.science.wayne.edu/java/`
- SunSITE Singapore, National University of Singapore, `http://sunsite.nus.sg/hotjava/`

Java Information Collection Sites

These are high-level Java information collection sites outside of Sun Microsystems:

- Gamelan: an excellent collection of Java demos and information; includes a large collection of Java applets; well-organized and frequently updated.

  `http://www.gamelan.com/`

- JavaScript information: contains links to information to JavaScript; includes technical information links plus links to example applications.

  `http://www.c2.org/~andreww/javascript/`

- WWW Virtual Library entry for Java: this includes links to events, reference information, resources, and selected applications/examples.

  `http://www.acm.org/~ops/java.html`

- JARS: Java Applet Rating Service; the hope here is to rate the best applets (top 1 percent, 5 percent, and so on). Includes categories of applets.

  `http://www.surinam.net/java/jars/jars.html`

- Applets.com: a collection of applets, including a list of new applets, an evaluated list of "cool" applets, and a library of applets; from Applets Corporation.

  `http://www.applets.com/`

- Java Study Group Homepage: this is a study group of the New York City C++ and C Special Interest Group whose parent organization is the New York City PC Users Group. This web includes group meeting notes, upcoming speakers, Java information resources, and other information.

  `http://www.inch.com/~nyjava/`

- Java Developer: "A public service FAQ devoted to Java Programming," includes resources, a job clearing house, and a large section on "How Do I...".

  `http://www.digitalfocus.com/digitalfocus/faq/`

- comp.lang.java FAQ: Frequently Asked Questions (FAQ) for comp.lang.java; includes basic information about participating in the discussion and reference information.

  `http://www.city-net.com/~krom/java-faq.html`

Java Discussion Forums

These are forums where you can take part in or monitor discussions about Java:

- comp.lang.java: Usenet newsgroup for discussing the Java programming language.

  `news:comp.lang.java`

- Digital Expresso: (the web formerly known as "J*** Notes"), a weekly summary of the traffic in Java newsgroups and mailing lists.

  `http://www.io.org/~mentor/DigitalEspresso.html`

Notable Individual Java Webs

These individual webs focus on some specific aspect of Java development, information, or products:

- Commercial Java Products: a description of a variety of commercial products related to Java, from Internet World.

  `http://www.iworld.com/InternetShopper/1Java_products.html`

- Java Class Hierarchy Diagrams: diagrams that show the class hierarchy for Java packages; very useful for quickly getting an idea of Java class relationships; developed by Charles L. Perkins.

  `http://rendezvous.com/java/hierarchy/index.html`

896

> **NOTE**
>
> These diagrams are also shown in Appendix B. (Charles L. Perkins is also the author of Chapters 15, 16, 38, and 39 in this book.)

■ Programming Active Objects in Java, by Doug Lea: a discussion of object-oriented design issues and features as they relate to Java.

`http://g.oswego.edu/dl/pats/aopintro.html`

■ Java Online Bibliography: a listing of key online articles and press releases about Java and related technology.

`http://www.december.com/works/java/bib.html`

Java Index Sites

These are indexes of Java information:

■ Yahoo Index entry for Java

`http://www.yahoo.com/Computers/Languages/Java/`

■ Yahoo Index entry for HotJava Web browser

`http://www.yahoo.com/Computers_and_Internet/Internet/World_Wide_Web/Browsers/`
`HotJava/`

Object-Oriented Information

Because Java is an object-oriented language, these sites can help you connect to more information about object-oriented terminology, design, and programming:

■ Object-Oriented Information Sources Index: a searchable index to a variety of object-oriented information sources, including research groups, archives, companies, books, and bibliographies.

`http://cuiwww.unige.ch/OSG/OOinfo/`

■ Object-Oriented Design Online Reference Guide: a guide to online information sources about object-oriented design. This guide was created by Howie Michalski, Lead Database Engineer, Infrastructure, CompuServe, Inc.

`http://www.clark.net/pub/howie/OO/oo_home.html`

■ C++ Glossary: this glossary lists terms related to the C++ language. Because C++ is closely related to Java, these terms are also important in Java development.

`http://info.desy.de/pub/uugna/html/cc/text/glossary/index.html`

Java Players and Licensees

These are key press announcements from licensees and developers of Java products:

- Adobe Systems, Inc.: "Adobe To Integrate Java Technology for Web Publishing." Press release, December 7, 1995. [Portable Document Format]

  `http://www.adobe.com/PDFs/PR/9512/951206.java.pdf`

- Borland International: "Borland International to Deliver Tools For Sun's Java Internet Programming Language." Press release, November 8, 1995.

  `http://www.borland.com/Product/java/javapress.html`

- IBM Corporation: "IBM licenses Java technology from Sun Microsystems for use in Internet products." Press release, December 6, 1995.

  `http://www.ibm.com/News/javapr.html`

- Lotus Development Corporation: "Lotus Outlines Plans to Deliver Powerful Integration of Notes And World Wide Web—Announces Lotus Notes Server That Includes Native Notes Support for HTTP, HTML and Java Technology." Press release, December 13, 1995.

  `http://www.Lotus.com/corpcomm/3406.htm`

- Macromedia: "Macromedia & Sun Microsystems To Develop Internet Tools And Technology." Press release, October 30, 1995.

  `http://www.macromedia.com/Industry/Macro/Ucon/News/sun.html`

- Metrowerks, Inc.: "Metrowerks Collaborates with Sun Microsystems to Provide Java Programming Tools in CodeWarrior Product for Macintosh." Press release, November 10, 1995.

  `http://www.metrowerks.com/news/press/java.html`

- Microsoft Corporation: "Internet Strategy Day." Press releases, December 7, 1995.

  `http://www.microsoft.com/internet/press.htm`

- Natural Intelligence, Inc.: "'ROASTER' Announcement." Press release, October 18, 1995.

  `http://www.natural.com/pages/products/roaster/roasterpr.html`

- Netscape Communications Corporation: "Netscape and Sun Announce Javascript, the Open, Cross-Platform Object Scripting Language for Enterprise Networks and the Internet." Press release, December 4, 1995.

  `http://home.netscape.com/newsref/pr/newsrelease67.html`

- Netscape Communications Corporation: "Netscape to License Sun's Java Programming Language." Press release, May 23, 1995.

  `http://home.netscape.com/newsref/pr/newsrelease25.html`

■ Oracle Corporation: "Oracle PowerBrowser to Integrate Java Technology with Oracle's Network Loadable Objects." Press release, October 30, 1995.

`http://www.oracle.com/info/news/java.html.`

■ Silicon Graphics, Inc.: "Silicon Graphics, Sun Microsystems and Netscape join forces to take the Web to the next level." Press release, December 4, 1995.

`http://www.sgi.com/Products/cosmo/sgisun.html`

■ Spyglass, Inc.: "Spyglass Licenses Sun Microsystems' Java for Spyglass Mosaic." Press release, November 8, 1995.

`http://www.spyglass.com/current/nov895.html`

■ Symantec Corporation: "Symantec Releases first Java development environment for Windows 95/NT." Press release, December 13, 1995.

`http://www.Symantec.com/lit/dev/javapress.html`

VRML Resources

F

by Adrian Scott, Ph.D.

900

There are a wealth of VRML resources available on the Internet that contain the latest information. This appendix provides a short introduction to some of these resources.

General VRML Information

The VRML Repositories are a great place to find information on software products. The FAQ contains general information.

VRML Repositories on the Web

The three main repositories for VRML information are as follows:

The VRML Repository at the San Diego Supercomputer Center (`http://www.sdsc.edu/vrml/`) includes information on various VRML tools, software, and example applications. This is the most up-to-date repository:

`http://vrml.wired.com/` includes an archive of the VRML e-list.

`http://www.eit.com/vrml/` features the public domain VRML artwork files.

FAQ (Frequently Asked Questions) Web Pages

The main VRML FAQ is maintained by Jan Hardenbergh and is located at

`http://www.oki.com/vrml/VRML_FAQ.html`

The FAQ includes information on configuring your HTTP server to transmit the MIME types for VRML and compressed VRML.

VRML Specification

The Version 1.0 Specification for Virtual Reality Modeling Language is at

`http://www.hyperreal.com/~mpesce/vrml/vrml.tech/vrml10-3.html`

A VRML-enabled version of the spec is at

`http://www.virtpark.com/theme/vrml/`

A version of the spec is available in Japanese at

`http://tje12.is.s.u-tokyo.ac.jp:10000/~takuya/vrml/vrml.html`

VRML Browsers

WebFX from Paper Software runs on Windows PCs:

`http://www.paperinc.com`

Webspace is a VRML browser available on various machines. SGI version:

`http://webspace.sgi.com`

Others:

`http://www.tgs.com/~template`

InterVista's WorldView VRML browser runs on Windows PCs:

`http://www.intervista.com`

VRScout from Chaco is available on Windows PCs:

`http://www.chaco.com`

WhurlWind is available on PowerMacs running QD3D:

`http:/www.info.apple.com/qd3d/Viewer.HTML`

Virtus Voyager is available for Macintosh and Power Macintosh:

`http://www.virtus.com/voyager.html`

SDSC (the San Diego Supercomputer Center) is developing a VRML browser for SGI/UNIX machines, with source code available free for noncommercial use:

`http://www.sdsc.edu/EnablingTech/Visualization/vrml/webview.html`

VRWeb, along with its source code, is available on UNIX machines:

`http://hyperg.iicm.tu-graz.ac.at/vrweb/`

Newsgroups

Newsgroups for VRML are just starting to be created. They are a good place for beginners to ask questions.

`comp.lang.vrml`

This is being discussed as a potential new VRML newsgroup.

`alt.lang.vrml`

This newsgroup exists, but has low propagation and low traffic. The FAQ for `alt.lang.vrml` is at

`http://www.virtpark.com/theme/vrmlfaq.html`

E-Lists

The main e-list for discussion of VRML is the unmoderated www-vrml list. Expect a minimum of 30 messages a day on this list; it's not for the faint-hearted. Hope springs eternal for a good newsgroup to complement the e-list! For information, e-mail `majordomo@wired.com` with the message `info www-vrml`. A digest version also exists, which concatenates the daily messages into one message. E-mail `majordomo@wired.com` with the message `info www-vrml-digest` for more information. Because of the volume of postings to the www-vrml list, please read the list for several days before posting, so you can get a feel for what's discussed. And if you have questions like "When will such-and-such browser be available?" please try the VRML Repositories mentioned in this section first. If you have problems with a VRML browser, please e-mail the relevant company.

Two other VRML e-lists exist. They are the vrml-modeling and vrml-behaviors lists. The vrml-behaviors list is starting to get busy as people propose ideas for behaviors in VRML 2.0. For information e-mail `listserv@sdsc.edu` with the message `info vrml-modeling` or `info vrml-behaviors`.

An e-list about business applications and models for virtual worlds is `vworlds-biz`. E-mail `listserv@best.com` with the message `info vworlds-biz`.

Software

If you are interested in writing your own VRML browser, you will want to start with QvLib, a parser for the VRML 1.0 specification.

QvLib parser is a program that parses VRML files. An SGI version is at

`ftp://ftp.sgi.com/sgi/inventor/2.0/qv1.0.tar.Z`

Old versions corresponding to Pre-1.0 VRML Specification drafts are available for LINUX, IRIX, Sun, NT and Mac at

`ftp://ftp.vrml.org/pub/parser/`

Authoring Tools

Authoring tools let you create VRML worlds, generally using a 3D user interface. Using them is much easier than trying to write VRML by hand.

Webspace Author is a new authoring package for SGIs from SGI:

`http://webspace.sgi.com`

The nice thing about Webspace Author is that it has good support for VRML-specific features, such as LOD (level of detail) editing, WWWInlines, and optimizing file sizes.

Home Space Builder is a VRML-compatible authoring tool for PCs from Paragraph:

`http://www.us.paragraph.com/whatsnew/homespce.htm`

It works well once you understand the interface, though the file sizes can be large.

Fountain is a VRML authoring tool for PCs from Caligari:

`http://www.caligari.com`

It builds nicely on Caligari's experience developing Truespace, a 3D modeller, and can act like a VRML browser too.

Create your own simple VRML home world out of 3D fonts using Instant VRML Home World at

`http://www.aereal.com/instant`

Aereal Phonts creates very small files (around 4K) because it uses VRML primitives. Aereal Phonts also lets you have your simple home world automatically hosted by Aereal's web server, so that you can instantly have your own VRML URL.

Portal is a tool for building VRML worlds from Inner Action Corporation, running on Microsoft Windows operating systems:

`http://www.well.com/user/jack/`

WRLGRID from the SDSC generates tile or grid geometries in VRML format:

`http://www.sdsc.edu/EnablingTech/Visualization/vrml/`

Radiance software is developing Ez3d-VR, a VRML authoring tool:

`http://www.radiance.com/~radiance`

Ez3d has several modules, has VRML-specific features, and is available on several platforms.

Converters

If you are using 3D models that have been created with CAD or 3D modeling software, you can use conversion software to translate the model into VRML format.

Keith Rule has added VRML output support to his popular freeware converter, `wcvt2pov`:

`http://www.europa.com/~keithr`

DXF2IV converts DXF files to Open Inventor (what VRML is based on). Available at

`ftp://ftp.sgi.com`

You can use iv2vrml to finish the conversion.

INTERCHANGE for Windows from Syndesis Corporation:

`syndesis@beta.inc.net`

is a commercial format translator that supports more than thirty 3D file formats, including VRML.

OBJ2WRL and TRI2WRL convert `Wavefront obj` (object) files and Alias `tri` (triangle) files to VRML, from the SDSC:

`http://www.sdsc.edu/EnablingTech/Visualization/vrml/`

Object File Format (OFF) to VRML:

`http://coney.gsfc.nasa.gov/Mathews/Objects`

Java/VRML Companies

There is a small group of companies doing the initial development in the intersection of Java and VRML.

Aereal (`http://www.aereal.com`) develops Java/VRML/database content sites.

Construct (`http://www.construct.net`) creates high-end VRML Web sites, including Java-enabled VRML.

Dimension X (`http://www.dnx.com`) has developed Liquid Reality, a Java-based VRML browser.

Paper Software (`http://www.paperinc.com`) has developed a Java API for its WebFX VRML browser.

Sun Microsystems (`http://java.sun.com`) is working with SGI and other companies on bringing 3D to Java.

Silicon Graphics (`http://webspace.sgi.com`) is developing a Java API for its 3D software, including its VRML offerings.

WorldMaker (`http://earth.path.net/worldmaker`) is developing software for advanced Java/VRML behaviors and multiuser VRML.

Interesting VRML Web Sites

It can be a challenge finding interesting VRML sites on the web. Here are some URLs to get you started.

Here's the home of the Interactive Media Festival:

`http://vrml.arc.org/`

Proteinman's Top Ten VRML Sites is a top ten list of VRML sites that can be accessed in VRML:

`http://www.virtpark.com/theme/proteinman/home.wrl.gz`

and HTML

`http://www.virtpark.com/theme/proteinman/home.html`

Here are some simple VRML models:

http://www.vrml.org/vrml/

Check here for many VRML-related links:

http://www.lightside.com/3dsite/cgi/VRML-index.html

The CAVE is at

http://www.ncsa.uiuc.edu/EVL/docs/html/CAVE.overview.html

and

http://jaka.eecs.uic.edu/dave/vrml/CAVE/

Build your own cell membrane at

http://bellatrix.pcl.ox.ac.uk

Step-by-Step Origami at

http://www.neuro.sfc.keio.ac.jp/~aly/polygon/vrml/ika

Aereal Serch is a database of VRML links, viewable in VRML

http://www.virtpark.com/theme/serch/home.wrl.gz

and HTML

http://www.virtpark.com/theme/cgi-bin/serch.html

An interactive application that lets you move around objects through the use of HTML forms and CGI at

http://andante.iss.uw.edu.pl/viso/vrml/colab/walk.html

Fractal lovers can check out a page on VRML fractals at

http://kirk.usafa.af.mil/~baird/vrml

The Inter-Galacticum (http://www.virtpark.com/theme/cgi-bin/ig.wrl) is a bunch of worlds created on-line by users of Virtual World Factory (http://www.virtpark.com/theme/factinfo.html).

Kahlua, a Java wrapper for Open Inventor 2.0 (which is similar to VRML 1.0) running on SGI and Solaris platforms, lets you write Inventor programs in Java:

http://www.cs.brown.edu/people/jsw/kahlua

Writings That Have Inspired VRML-ers

There are several science fiction books that pioneers in Java and VRML will refer to as a source of inspiration for their work in VRML.

Snow Crash and *The Diamond Age* by Neal Stephenson

Neuromancer and others by William Gibson

True Names by Vernor Vinge

The Rim by Andrew Besher

Glossary

anchor   A part of a hypertext document that is either the source or destination of a hypertext link. A link might extend from an anchor to another document, or from another document to an anchor. When anchors are the starting points of these links, they are typically highlighted or otherwise identified in the hypertext browser as hotspots.

API (Java) Application Programming Interface   The set of Java packages and classes—included in the Java Developers Kit (JDK)—that programmers use to create applets.

ASCII   American Standard Code for Information Interchange. A 7-bit character code that can represent 128 characters, some of which are control characters used for communications control and are not printable.

applet   A Java program that can be included in an HTML page with the APPLET element and observed in a Java-enabled browser.

application (Java)   A computer program—written in Java—that executes independently of a Java-enabled browser through the Java interpreter included in the Java Development Kit.

attribute   A property of an HTML element, specified in the start tag of the element. The attribute list of the APPLET element is used to identify the location of applet source code (with the Codebase attribute) and the name of the Java class (with the Code attribute).

block (Java)   The code between matching curly braces { and }.

Boolean   A data type that has a value of true or false.

browser   A software program for observing the Web. A synonym for a Web client.

bytecode   The machine-readable code that is created as the result of compiling a Java language source file. This is the code distributed across the network to run an applet. Bytecodes are architecture neutral; the Java-capable browser ported to a particular platform interprets them.

cast (verb)   To change an expression from one data type to another.

child class   A subclass of a class (its parent class). It inherits public (and protected) data and methods from the parent class.

class   A template for creating objects. A class defines data and methods and is a unit of organization in a Java program. It can pass on its public data and methods to its subclasses.

compiler   A software program that translates human-readable source code into machine-readable code.

constructor   A method named after its class. A constructor method is invoked when an object of that class is made.

content handler   A program loaded into the user's HotJava browser that interprets files of a type defined by the Java programmer. The Java programmer provides the necessary code for the user's HotJava browser to display/interpret this special format.

CPU   Central Processing Unit.

CERN (*Centre European pour la Recherche Nucleaire*)   The European laboratory for particle physics, where the World Wide Web originated in 1989. (See `http://www.cern.ch/`.)

CGI (Common Gateway Interface)   A standard for programs to interface with Web servers.

client   A software program that requests information or services from another software application (server) and displays this information in a form required by its hardware platform.

DTD (Document Type Definition)   A specification for a markup language such as HTML.

domain name   The alphanumeric name for a computer host; this name is mapped to the computer's numeric Internet Protocol (IP) address.

element   A unit of structure in an HTML document. Many elements have start and stop tags; some have just a single tag and some can contain other elements.

FTP (File Transfer Protocol)   A means to exchange files across a network.

garbage collection   The process by which memory allocated for objects in a program is reclaimed. Java automatically performs this process.

Gopher   A protocol for disseminating information on the Internet using a system of menus.

hotspot   An area on a hypertext document that a user can click on to retrieve another resource or document.

HTML (HyperText Markup Language)   The mechanism used to create Web pages. Web browsers display these pages according to a browser-defined rendering scheme.

HTTP (HyperText Transfer Protocol)   The native protocol of the Web, used to transfer hypertext documents.

home page   An entry page for access to a local web; a page that a person or company defines as a principal page, often containing links to other pages containing personal or professional information.

HotJava   A Web browser designed to execute applets written in the Java programming language.

hypermedia   Hypertext that includes multimedia: text, graphics, images, sound, and video.

hypertext   Text that is not constrained to a single sequence for observation; Web-based hypertext is not constrained to a single server for creating meaning.

imagemap   A graphic inline image on an HTML page that potentially connects each pixel or region of an image to a Web resource. User retrieves the resources by clicking on the image.

instance   An object.

interface   A set of methods that Java classes can implement.

Internet   The cooperatively run, globally distributed collection of computer networks that exchange information via the TCP/IP protocol suite.

Java   An object-oriented programming language for creating distributed, executable applications.

Java-enabled browser   A World Wide Web browser that can display Java applets.

link   A connection between one hypertext document and another.

method   A function that can perform operations on data.

MIME (Multipurpose Internet Mail Extensions)   A specification for multimedia document formats.

Matrix   The set of all networks that can exchange electronic mail either directly or through gateways. This includes the Internet, BITNET, FidoNet, UUCP, and commercial services such as America Online, CompuServe, Delphi, and Prodigy. This term was coined by John S. Quarterman in his book *The Matrix* (Digital Press, 1990).

Mosaic   A graphical Web browser originally developed by the National Center for Supercomputing Applications (NCSA). It now includes a number of commercially licensed products.

NCSA   National Center for Supercomputing Applications, at the University of Illinois at Champaign-Urbana, developers and distributors of NCSA Mosaic.

native methods   Class methods that are declared in a Java class but implemented in C.

navigating   The act of observing the content of the Web for some purpose.

Net   An informal term for the Internet or a subset (or a superset) of the Matrix in context. For example, a computerized conference via e-mail may take place on a BITNET host that has an Internet gateway, thus making the conference available to anyone on either of these networks. In this case, the developer might say, "Our conference will be available on the Net." One might even consider discussion forums on commercial online services to be "on the Net," although these are not accessible from the Internet.

object   A variable defined as being a particular class type. An object has the data and methods as specified in the class definition.

overload (verb)   To use the same name for several items in the same scope; Java methods can be overloaded.

packet   A set of data handled as a unit in data transmission.

package (Java)   A set of classes with a common high-level function declared with the `package` keyword.

page   A single file of HyperText Markup Language.

parameter (HTML)   A name and value pair identified by the `Name` and `Value` attributes of the `PARAM` element used inside an `APPLET` element.

parameter list (Java)   The set of values passed to a method. The definition of the method describes how these values are manipulated.

parent class   The originating class of a given subclass.

protocol handler   A program that is loaded into the user's HotJava browser and interprets a protocol. These protocols include standard ones such as HTTP or programmer-defined protocols.

robot   A term for software programs that automatically explore the Web for a variety of purposes. Robots that collect resources for later database queries by users are sometimes called *spiders.*

scope   The program segment in which a reference to a variable is valid.

SGML (Standard Generalized Markup Language)   A standard for defining markup languages; HTML is an instance of SGML. (See `http://www.sgmlopen.org/`.)

server   A software application that provides information or services based on requests from client programs.

site   File section of a computer on which Web documents (or other documents served in another protocol) reside—for example, a Web site, a Gopher site, or an FTP site.

Solaris   Sun Microsystem's software platform for networked applications. Solaris includes an operating system, SunOS.

Sparc (Scalable Processor ARChitecture)   A microprocessor architecture based on very efficient handling of a small set of instructions. (See `http://www.sparc.com/`.)

spider   A software program that traverses the Web to collect information about resources for later queries by users seeking to find resources. Major species of active spiders include Lycos and WebCrawler.

surfing   The act of navigating the Web, typically using techniques for rapidly traversing content in order to find subjectively valuable resources.

tag   The code used to make up part of an HTML element. For example, the `TITLE` element has a start tag, `<TITLE>` and an end tag, `</TITLE>`.

Unicode   A character set that supports many world languages.

URL (Uniform Resource Locator)   The scheme for addressing on the Web. A URL identifies a resource on the Web.

Usenet   A system for disseminating asynchronous text discussion among cooperating computer hosts. The Usenet discussion space is divided into newsgroups, each on a particular topic or subtopic.

TCP/IP (Transmission Control Protocol/Internet Protocol)   The set of protocols used for network communication on the Internet.

VRML (Virtual Reality Modeling Language)   A specification for three-dimensional rendering used in conjunction with Web browsers.

web   A set of hypertext pages that is considered a single work. Typically, a single web is created by cooperating authors or an author and is deployed on a single server with links to other servers—a subset of the Web.

Web (World Wide Web)   A hypertext information and communication system popularly used on the Internet computer network with data communications operating according to a client/server model. Web clients (browsers) can access multi-protocol and hypermedia information using an addressing scheme.

Web server   Software that provides the services to Web clients.

WWW   The World Wide Web.

X   X Window System. A windowing system supporting graphical user interfaces to applications.

See also:

- C++ Glossary

  `http://info.desy.de/pub/uu-gna/html/cc/text/glossary/index.html`

  This glossary lists terms related to the C++ language; because C++ is closely related to Java, these terms can also be helpful.

- Sun's Java Glossary

  `http://java.sun.com/1.1alpha3/doc/misc/glossary.html`

INDEX

SYMBOLS

! (negation) operator, 179-180
!= (not equal to) operator, 176, 179-180
(comment delineator) VRML script, 592
% (modulus) operator, 173, 178
%= (modulus) operator, 182
& (bitwise AND) operator, 173-174
& (Evaluation AND) operator, 179
&& (logical AND) operator, 179-180
&= (AND) operator, 182
* (multiplication) operator, 173, 178
*= (multiplication) operator, 182
*7 (Star 7), 8
+ (addition) operator, 173, 178
++ (increment) operator, 177
+= (addition) operator, 182
- (subtraction) operator, 173, 178
-- (decrement) operator, 177
-= (subtraction) operator, 182
/ (division) operator, 173, 178
/= (division) operator, 182
< (less than) operator, 176
<< (left shift) operator, 173, 175
<= (less than or equal to) operator, 176
= (simple) operator, 182
== (equal to) operator, 176, 179-180
> (greater than) operator, 176
>= (greater than or equal to) operator, 176
>> (right shift) operator, 173, 175

Teach Yourself the Internet in a Week, Second Edition

— *Neil Randall*

The combination of a structured, step-by-step approach and the excitement of exploring the world of the Internet make this tutorial and reference perfect for any user wanting to master the Net. Efficiently exploring the basics of the Internet, *Teach Yourself the Internet* takes users to the farthest reaches of the Internet with hands-on exercises and detailed instructions. Completely updated to cover Netscape, Internet-works, and Microsoft's Internet Assistant.

Price: $25.00 USA/$34.99 CDN   User Level: Beginner-Inter
ISBN: 0-672-30735-9   622 pages

Tricks of the Internet Gurus

— *Various Internet Gurus*

Best-selling title that focuses on tips and techniques that allow the reader to more effectively use the resources of the Internet. A must-have for the power Internet user, *Tricks of the Internet Gurus* offers tips, strategies, and techniques for optimizing use of the Internet. Features interviews with various Internet leaders.

Price: $35.00 USA/$47.95 CDN   User Level: Inter-Advanced
ISBN: 0-672-30599-2   809 pages

Teach Yourself More Web Publishing with HTML in a Week

— *Laura Lemay*

Ideal for those people who are ready for more advanced World Wide Web home page design! The sequel to *Teach Yourself Web Publishing with HTML*, *Teach Yourself More* explores the process of creating and maintaining Web presentations, including setting up tools and converters for verifying and testing pages. Teaches advanced HTML techniques and tricks in a clear, step-by-step manner with many practical examples. Highlights the Netscape extensions and HTML 3.0.

Price: $29.99 USA/$39.99 CDN   User Level: Inter-Advanced
ISBN: 1-57521-005-3   480 pages

The Internet Business Guide, Second Edition

— *Rosalind Resnick & Dave Taylor*

Updated and revised, this guide will inform and educate anyone on how they can use the Internet to increase profits, reach a broader market, track down business leads, and access critical information. Updated to cover digital cash, Web cybermalls, secure Web servers, and setting up your business on the Web, *The Internet Business Guide* includes profiles of entrepreneurs' successes (and failures) on the Internet. Improve your business by using the Internet to market products and services, make contacts with colleagues, cut costs, and improve customer service.

Price: $25.00 USA/$34.95 CDN   User Level: All Levels
ISBN: 1-57521-004-5   470 pages

Teach Yourself Netscape Web Publishing in a Week

— Wes Tatters

Teach Yourself Netscape Web Publishing in a Week is the easiest way to learn how to produce attention-getting, well-designed Web pages using the features provided by Netscape Navigator. Intended for both the novice and the expert, this book provides a solid grounding in HTML and Web publishing principles, while providing special focus on the possibilities presented by the Netscape environment. Learn to design and create attention-grabbing Web pages for the Netscape environment while exploring new Netscape development features such as frames, plug-ins, Java applets, and JavaScript!

Price: $39.99 USA/ $47.95 CDN   User Level: Beginner-Inter
ISBN: 1-57521-068-1   450 pages

Teach Yourself CGI Programming with Perl in a Week

— Eric Herrmann

This book is a step-by-step tutorial of how to create, use, and maintain Common Gateway Interfaces (CGI). It describes effective ways of using CGI as an integral part of Web development. Adds interactivity and flexibility to the information that can be provided through your Web site. Includes Perl 4.0 and 5.0, CGI libraries, and other applications to create databases, dynamic interactivity, and other enticing page effects.

Price: $39.99 USA/$53.99 CDN   User Level: Inter-Advanced
ISBN: 1-57521-009-6   500 pages

Teach Yourself Java in 21 Days

— Laura Lemay and Charles Perkins

The complete tutorial guide to the most exciting technology to hit the Internet in years—Java! A detailed guide to developing applications with the hot new Java language from Sun Microsystems, *Teach Yourself Java in 21 Days* shows readers how to program using Java and develop applications (applets) using the Java language. With coverage of Java implementation in Netscape Navigator and HotJava, along with the Java Development Kit, including the compiler and debugger for Java, *Teach Yourself Java* is a must-have!

Price: $39.99 USA/$53.99 CDN   User Level: Inter-Advanced
ISBN: 1-57521-030-4   600 pages

Presenting Java

— John December

Presenting Java gives you a first look at how Java is transforming static Web pages into living, interactive applications. Java opens up a world of possibilities previously unavailable on the Web. You'll find out how Java is being used to create animations, computer simulations, interactive games, teaching tools, spreadsheets, and a variety of other applications. Whether you're a new user, a project planner, or developer, *Presenting Java* provides an efficient, quick introduction to the basic concepts and technical details that make Java the hottest new Web technology of the year!

Price: $25.00 USA/$34.95 CDN   User Level: All Levels
ISBN: 1-57521-039-8   207 pages

Netscape 2 Unleashed

— Dick Oliver, et. al.

This book provides a complete, detailed, and fully fleshed-out overview of the Netscape products. Through case studies and examples of how individuals, businesses, and institutions are using the Netscape products for Web development, *Netscape 2 Unleashed* gives a full description of the evolution of Netscape from its inception to today, and its cutting-edge developments with Netscape Gold, LiveWire, Netscape Navigator 2.0, Java and JavaScript, Macromedia, VRML, Plug-ins, Adobe Acrobat, HTML 3.0 and beyond, security and Intranet systems.

Price: $49.99 USA/$67.99 CDN   User Level: All Levels
ISBN: 1-57521-007-X   Pages: 800 pages

The Internet Unleashed 1996

— Barron, Ellsworth, Savetz, et. al.

The Internet Unleashed 1996 is the complete reference to get new users up and running on the Internet while providing the consummate reference manual for the experienced user. *The Internet Unleashed 1996* provides the reader with an encyclopedia of information on how to take advantage of all the Net has to offer for business, education, research, and government. The companion CD-ROM contains over 100 tools and applications. The only book that includes the experience of over 40 of the world's top Internet experts, this new edition is updated with expanded coverage of Web publishing, Internet business, Internet multimedia and virtual reality, Internet security, Java, and more!

Price: $49.99 USA/$67.99 CDN   User Level: All Levels
ISBN: 1-57521-041-X   1,456 pages

The World Wide Web Unleashed 1996

— December and Randall

The World Wide Web Unleashed 1996 is designed to be the only book a reader will need to experience the wonders and resources of the Web. The companion CD-ROM contains over 100 tools and applications to make the most of your time on the Internet. Shows readers how to explore the Web's amazing world of electronic art museums, online magazines, virtual malls, and video music libraries, while giving readers complete coverage of Web page design, creation, and maintenance, plus coverage of new Web technologies such as Java, VRML, CGI, and multimedia!

Price: $49.99 USA/$67.99 CDN   User Level: All Levels
ISBN: 1-57521-040-1   1,440 pages

Teach Yourself Web Publishing with HTML in 14 Days, Premier Edition

— Laura Lemay

This book teaches everything about publishing on the Web. In addition to its exhaustive coverage of HTML, it also gives readers hands-on practice with more complicated subjects such as CGI, tables, forms, multimedia programming, testing, maintenance, and much more. The companion CD-ROM is Mac- and PC-compatible and includes a variety of applications that help readers create Web pages using graphics and templates.

Price: $39.99 USA/$53.99 CDN   User Level: All Levels
ISBN: 1-57521-014-2   804 pages

Teach Yourself Web Publishing with HTML 3.0 in a Week, Second Edition

— Laura Lemay

Ideal for those people who are interested in the Internet and the World Wide Web—the Internet's hottest topic! This updated and revised edition teaches readers how to use HTML (Hypertext Markup Language) version 3.0 to create Web pages that can be viewed by nearly 30 million users. Explores the process of creating and maintaining Web presentations, including setting up tools and converters for verifying and testing pages. The new edition highlights the new features of HTML, such as tables and Netscape and Microsoft Explorer extensions. Provides the latest information on working with images, sound files, and video, and teaches advanced HTML techniques and tricks in a clear, step-by-step manner with many practical examples of HTML pages.

Price: $29.99 USA/$39.99 CDN   User Level: Beginner-Inter
ISBN: 1-57521-064-9   518 pages

Web Page Construction Kit (Software)

Create your own exciting World Wide Web pages with the software and expert guidance in this kit! Includes HTML Assistant Pro Lite, the acclaimed point-and-click Web page editor. Simply highlight text in HTML Assistant Pro Lite, and click the appropriate button to add headlines, graphics, special formatting, links, etc. No programming skills needed! Using your favorite Web browser, you can test your work quickly and easily without leaving the editor. A unique catalog feature allows you to keep track of interesting Web sites and easily add their HTML links to your pages. Assistant's user-defined toolkit also allows you to add new HTML formatting styles as they are defined. Includes the #1 best-selling Internet book, *Teach Yourself Web Publishing with HTML 3.0 in a Week, Second Edition,* and a library of professionally designed Web page templates, graphics, buttons, bullets, lines, and icons to rev up your new pages!

PC Computing magazine says, "If you're looking for the easiest route to Web publishing, HTML Assistant is your best choice."

Price: $39.95 US/$46.99 CAN   User Level: Beginner-Inter
ISBN: 1-57521-000-2   518 pages

HTML & CGI Unleashed

— John December & Marc Ginsburg

Targeted to professional developers who have a basic understanding of programming and need a detailed guide. Provides a complete, detailed reference to developing Web information systems. Covers the full range of languages—HTML, CGI, Perl C, editing and conversion programs, and more—and how to create commercial-grade Web Applications. Perfect for the developer who will be designing, creating, and maintaining a Web presence for a company or large institution.

Price: $49.99 USA/$61.95 CDN   User Level: Inter-Advanced
ISBN: 0-672-30745-6   830 pages

Web Site Construction Kit for Windows NT

— Christopher Brown and Scott Zimmerman

The Web Site Construction Kit for Windows NT has everything you need to set up, develop, and maintain a Web site with Windows NT—including the server on the CD-ROM! It teaches the ins and outs of planning, installing, configuring, and administering a Windows NT-based Web site for an organization, and it includes detailed instructions on how to use the software on the CD-ROM to develop the Web site's content—HTML pages, CGI scripts, imagemaps, and so forth.

Price: $49.99 USA/$67.99 CDN   User Level: All Levels
ISBN: 1-57521-047-9   430 pages

Add to Your Sams.net Library Today
with the Best Books for Internet Technologies

ISBN	Quantity	Description of Item	Unit Cost	Total Cost
1-57521-007-X		Netscape Unleashed	$45.00	
1-57521-041-X		The Internet Unleashed, 1996	$49.99	
1-57521-040-1		The World Wide Web Unleashed, 1996	$49.99	
0-672-30745-6		HTML and CGI Unleashed	$49.99	
1-57521-039-8		Presenting Java	$25.00	
1-57521-030-4		Teach Yourself Java in 21 Days	$39.99	
1-57521-009-6		Teach Yourself CGI Scripting with Perl in a Week	$39.99	
0-672-30735-9		Teach Yourself the Internet in a Week, Second Edition	$25.00	
1-57521-004-5		The Internet Business Guide, Second Edition	$25.00	
0-672-30595-X		Education on the Internet	$25.00	
0-672-30718-9		Navigating the Internet, Third Edition	$22.50	
1-57521-064-9		Teach Yourself Web Publishing with HTML in a Week, SE	$29.99	
1-57521-005-3		Teach Yourself More Web Publishing with HTML in a Week	$29.99	
1-57521-014-2		Teach Yourself Web Publishing with HTML in 14 Days, Premiere Edition	$39.99	
1-57521-072-X		Web Site Construction Kit for Windows 95	$49.99	
1-57521-047-9		Web Site Construction Kit for Windows NT	$49.99	
		Shipping and Handling: See information below.		
		TOTAL		

Shipping and Handling: $4.00 for the first book, and $1.75 for each additional book. If you need to have it NOW, we can ship product to you in 24 hours for an additional charge of approximately $18.00, and you will receive your item overnight or in two days. Overseas shipping and handling adds $2.00. Prices subject to change. Call between 9:00 a.m. and 5:00 p.m. EST for availability and pricing information on latest editions.

201 W. 103rd Street, Indianapolis, Indiana 46290

1-800-428-5331 — Orders   1-800-835-3202 — FAX   1-800-858-7674 — Customer Service

Book ISBN 1-57521-049-5

Software Licensing Information

Java™ Developer's Kit

Developed by Sun Microsystems, Inc. 2550 Garcia Avenue Mountain View, California 94043. Copyright © 1994, 1995, Sun Microsystems, Inc.

Copyright and License Information

Java™ and HotJava™ Web development products are owned and licensed exclusively by Sun Microsystems, Inc. Copyright © 1992-95 Sun Microsystems, Inc. All rights reserved. Java, HotJava, the Java/ HotJava Logos, Sun, Sun Microsystems, and the Sun Logo are trademarks or registered trademarks of Sun Microsystems, Inc., in the U.S. and other countries. Products bearing authorized "JAVA- Compatible" or "HOTJAVA-Compatible" logos are based upon Sun's Java and HotJava technologies and are compatible with the APIs for such technologies.

Sun grants to you ("Licensee") a non-exclusive, non-transferable license to use the HotJava and Java binary code versions (hereafter, "Binary Software") without fee. Licensee may distribute the Binary Software to third parties provided that the copyright notice and this statement appear on all copies. Licensee agrees that the copyright notice and this statement will appear on all copies of the software, packaging, and documentation or portions thereof.

In the event Licensee creates additional classes or otherwise extends the Applet Application Programming Interface (AAPI), licensee will publish the specifications for such extensions to the AAPI for use by third-party developers of Java-based software, in connection with licensee's commercial distribution of the Binary Software.

RESTRICTED RIGHTS: Use, duplication, or disclosure by the government is subject to the restrictions as set forth in subparagraph (c) (1) (ii) of the Rights in Technical Data and Computer Software Clause as DFARS 252.227-7013 and FAR 52.227-19.

SUN MAKES NO REPRESENTATIONS OR WARRANTIES ABOUT THE SUITABILITY OF THE BINARY SOFTWARE, EITHER EXPRESS OR IMPLIED, INCLUDING BUT NOT LIMITED TO THE IMPLIED WARRANTIES OF MERCHANTABILITY, FITNESS FOR A PARTICULAR PURPOSE, OR NON-INFRINGEMENT. SUN SHALL NOT BE LIABLE FOR ANY DAMAGES SUFFERED BY LICENSEE AS A RESULT OF USING, MODIFYING, OR DISTRIBUTING THE BINARY SOFTWARE OR ITS DERIVATIVES.

By downloading, using, or copying this Binary Software, Licensee agrees to abide by the intellectual property laws, and all other applicable laws of the United States, and the terms of this License. Ownership of the software shall remain solely in Sun Microsystems, Inc.

Sun shall have the right to terminate this license immediately by written notice upon Licensee's breach of, or non-compliance with, any of its terms. Licensee shall be liable for any infringement or damages resulting from Licensee's failure to abide by the terms of this License.

The JDK 1.0 binary release is based in part on the work of the Independent JPEG Group.

Symantec Café Lite End-User License

NOTICE: SYMANTEC LICENSES THE ENCLOSED SOFTWARE TO YOU ONLY UPON THE CONDITION THAT YOU ACCEPT ALL OF THE TERMS CONTAINED IN THIS LICENSE AGREEMENT. PLEASE READ THE TERMS CAREFULLY BEFORE OPENING THIS PACKAGE, AS OPENING THE PACKAGE WILL INDICATE YOUR ASSENT TO THEM. IF YOU DO NOT AGREE TO THESE TERMS, THEN SYMANTEC IS UNWILLING TO LICENSE THE SOFTWARE TO YOU, IN WHICH EVENT YOU SHOULD RETURN THE FULL PRODUCT WITH PROOF OF PUR-CHASE TO THE DEALER FROM WHOM IT WAS ACQUIRED WITHIN SIXTY DAYS OF PURCHASE, AND YOUR MONEY WILL BE REFUNDED.

LICENSE AND WARRANTY

The software which accompanies this license (the "Software") is the property of Symantec or its licensors and is protected by copyright law. While Symantec continues to own the Software, you will have certain rights to use the Software after your acceptance of this license. Except as may be modified by a license addendum which accompanies this license, your rights and obligations with respect to the use of this Software are as follows:

You may:

(i) use one copy of the Software on a single computer;

(ii) make one copy of the Software for archival purposes, or copy the software onto the hard disk of your computer and retain the original for archival purposes;

(iii) use the Software on a network, provided that you have a licensed copy of the Software for each computer that can access the Software over that network;

(iv) after written notice to Symantec, transfer the Software on a permanent basis to another person or entity, provided that you retain no copies of the Software and the transferee agrees to the terms of this agreement; and

(v) if a single person uses the computer on which the Software is installed at least 80% of the time, then after returning the completed product registration card which accompanies the Software, that person may also use the Software on a single home computer.

You may not:

(i) copy the documentation which accompanies the Software;

(ii) sublicense, rent or lease any portion of the Software;

(iii) reverse engineer, decompile, disassemble, modify, translate, make any attempt to discover the source code of the Software or create derivative works from the Software; or

(iv) use a previous version or copy of the Software after you have received a disk replacement set or an upgraded version as a replacement of the prior version, unless you donate a previous version of an upgraded version to a charity of your choice, and such charity agrees in writing that it will be the sole end user of the product, and that it will abide by the terms of this agreement. Unless you so donate a previous version of an upgraded version, upon upgrading the Software, all copies of the prior version must be destroyed.

No Warranty:

The Symantec is being provided AS-IS, without warranty of any kind. Symantec does not warrant that the Software will meet your requirements or that operation of the Software will be uninterrupted or that the Software will be error-free. SYMANTEC EXPRESSLY DISCLAIMS ALL WARRANTIES, WHETHER EXPRESS OR IMPLIED, INCLUDING THE IMPLIED WARRANTIES OF MERCHANTABILITY, FITNESS FOR A PARTICULAR PURPOSE, AND NONINFRINGEMENT.

Disclaimer of Damages:

REGARDLESS OF WHETHER ANY REMEDY SET FORTH HEREIN FAILS OF ITS ESSENTIAL PURPOSE, IN NO EVENT WILL SYMANTEC BE LIABLE TO YOU FOR ANY SPECIAL, CONSEQUENTIAL, INDIRECT OR SIMILAR DAMAGES, INCLUDING ANY LOST PROFITS OR LOST DATA ARISING OUT OF THE USE OR INABILITY TO USE THE SOFTWARE EVEN IF SYMANTEC HAS BEEN ADVISED OF THE POSSIBILITY OF SUCH DAMAGES.

SOME STATES DO NOT ALLOW THE LIMITATION OR EXCLUSION OF LIABILITY FOR INCIDENTAL OR CONSEQUENTIAL DAMAGES SO THE ABOVE LIMITATION OR EXCLUSION MAY NOT APPLY TO YOU.

IN NO CASE SHALL SYMANTEC'S LIABILITY EXCEED THE PURCHASE PRICE FOR THE SOFTWARE. The disclaimers and limitations set forth above will apply regardless of whether you accept the Software.

U.S. Government Restricted Rights:

RESTRICTED RIGHTS LEGEND. Use, duplication, or disclosure by the Government is subject to restrictions as set forth in subparagraph (c) (1) (ii) of the Rights in Technical Data and Computer Software clause at DFARS 252.227-7013 or subparagraphs (c) (1) and (2) of the Commercial Computer Software-Restricted Rights clause at 48 CFR 52.227-19, as applicable, Symantec Corporation, 10201 Torre Avenue, Cupertino, CA 95014.

General:

This Agreement will be governed by the laws of the State of California. This Agreement may only be modified by a license addendum which accompanies this license or by a written document which has been signed by both you and Symantec. Should you have any questions concerning this Agreement, or if you desire to contact Symantec for any reason, please write: Symantec Customer Sales and Service, 10201 Torre Avenue, Cupertino, CA 95014.

Addendum for Development Language Products:

Because the Software is a Symantec development language product, you have a royalty-free right to include object code derived from the libraries in programs that you develop using the Software and you also have the right to use, distribute, and license such programs to third parties without payment of any further license fees, so long as a copyright notice sufficient to protect your copyright in the program is included in the graphic display of your program and on the labels affixed to the media on which your program is distributed.

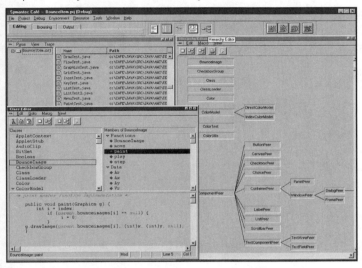

State Sales/Use Tax

In the following states, add sales/use tax: CO–3%; GA, LA, NY—4%; VA–4.5%; KS–4.9%; AZ, IA, IN, MA, MD, OH, SC, WI–5%; CT, FL, ME, MI, NC, NJ, PA, TN–6%; CA, IL, TX–6.25%; MN, WA–6.5%; DC–5.75%.

Please add local tax for: AZ, CA, FL, GA, MO, NY, OH, SC, TN, TX, WA, WI.

Order Information:

- Please allow 2-4 weeks for processing your order.
- Please attach the order form with your payment.
- No P.O. Boxes and no C.O.D.s accepted.
- Order form good in the U.S. only.
- If you are tax-exempt, please include exemption certificate or letter with tax-exempt number.
- Resellers not eligible.
- Offer not valid with any other promotion.
- One copy per product, per order.

What's on the Disc

The companion CD-ROM contains the Java™ Developer's Kit from Sun Microsystems and Symantec's Café™ Lite software. Other shareware programs mentioned in the book, and dozens of useful third-party tools and utilities are also included.

Macintosh Installation Instructions

1. Insert the CD-ROM disc into your CD-ROM drive.
2. When an icon for the CD appears on your desktop, open the disc by double-clicking on its icon.
3. Double-click on the icon named Guide to the CD-ROM, and follow the directions that appear.

Technical Support from Macmillan

We can't help you with Windows or Macintosh problems or software from third parties, but we can assist you if a problem arises with the CD-ROM itself.

E-mail Support: Send e-mail to support@mcp.com.

CompuServe: Type GO SAMS to reach the Macmillan Computer Publishing forum. Leave us a message, addressed to SYSOP. If you want the message to be private, address it to *SYSOP.

Telephone: (317) 581-3833

Fax: (317) 581-4773

Mail: Macmillan Computer Publishing
Attention: Support Department
201 West 103rd Street
Indianapolis, IN 46290-1093

Here's how to reach us on the Internet:

World Wide Web (The Macmillan Information SuperLibrary)
http://www.mcp.com

Internet FTP
ftp.mcp.com (/pub/sams)

Windows NT Installation Instructions

1. Insert the CD-ROM disc into your CD-ROM drive.

2. From File Manager or Program Manager, choose Run from the File menu.

3. Type *drive*:CDSETUP and press Enter, where *drive* corresponds to the drive letter of your CD-ROM. For example, if your CD-ROM is drive D:, type D:CDSETUP and press Enter.

4. Follow the on-screen instructions in the installation program. Files will be installed to a directory named \TYNET, unless you choose a different directory during installation.

CDSETUP creates a Windows Program Manager group called "Java Unleashed." This group contains icons for exploring the CD-ROM.

Windows 95 Installation Instructions

If Windows 95 is installed on your computer and you have the AutoPlay feature enabled, the Guide to the CD-ROM program starts automatically whenever you insert the disc into your CD-ROM drive.

> **NOTE**
>
> The CDSETUP program requires at least 256 colors. For best results, set your monitor to display between 256 and 64,000 colors. A screen resolution of 640 by 480 pixels is also recommended. If necessary, adjust your monitor settings before using the CD-ROM.